Understanding Social Problems

Fourth Canadian Edition

Linda A. Mooney
East Carolina University

M. Morgan Holmes
Wilfrid Laurier University

David Knox
East Carolina University

Caroline Schacht
East Carolina University

NELSON EDUCATION

NELSON / EDUCATION

Understanding Social Problems, Fourth Canadian Edition
by Linda A. Mooney, M. Morgan Holmes, David Knox, and Caroline Schacht

Vice President, Editorial Director:
Anne Williams

Acquisitions Editor:
Maya Castle

Marketing Manager:
Terry Fedorkiw

Developmental Editor:
Liisa Kelly

Photo and Permissions Researcher:
Carrie McGregor

Senior Content Production Manager:
Natalia Denesiuk Harris

Production Service:
Cenveo Publisher Services

Copy Editor:
Kelli Howey

Proofreader:
Ganesan Ramalingam

Indexer:
Diana Witt

Senior Production Coordinator:
Ferial Suleman

Design Director:
Ken Phipps

Managing Designer:
Franca Amore

Interior Design Modifications:
Sharon Lucas

Cover Design:
Martyn Schmoll

Cover Image:
Justin Paget/Corbis

Compositor:
Cenveo Publisher Services

Printer:
RR Donnelley

Library and Archives Canada Cataloguing in Publication Data

Understanding social problems / Linda A. Mooney . . . [et al.]. — 4th Canadian ed.

Includes bibliographical references and indexes.
ISBN 978-0-17-650277-5

1. Social problems—Canada—Textbooks. 2. Canada—Social conditions—1991– —Textbooks. 3. Social problems—Textbooks. 4. Social history—Textbooks. I. Mooney, Linda A

HN103.5.U65 2011
361.1'0971   C2011-904444-7

ISBN-13: 978-0-17-650277-5
ISBN-10: 0-17-650277-7

Brief Contents

Detailed Contents

SECTION 1   Problems of Well-Being   30

Preface

Violence in the home, school, and street; global poverty made even worse in the face of globalization; increasing levels of environmental pollution and depletion of Earth's natural resources; persistent conflict between and within nations; ongoing oppression of minority groups; and the widening gap in health, well-being, and stability between those who hold economic power, prestige, and privilege and those who do not. In *A Guide for the Perplexed*, B. F. Schumacher questions whether a "turning around will be accomplished by enough people quickly enough to save the modern world" (quoted in Safransky 1990: 115). Schumacher notes, "This question is often asked, but whatever the answer given to it will mislead. The answer 'yes' would lead to complacency; the answer 'no' to despair. It is desirable to leave these perplexities behind us and get down to work."

In *Understanding Social Problems*, we "get down to work" by examining how the structure and culture of societies contributes to social problems and their consequences. Understanding the social forces that contribute to social problems is necessary for designing strategies for action—programs, policies, and other interventions intended to ameliorate the social problem.

Academic Features of the New Edition

In response to feedback from teachers, reviewers, and students who have read the second and third Canadian editions of *Understanding Social Problems* (2004, 2007), we have maintained our expanded inclusion of contemporary social theory, and we have added more studies by scholars whose work is focused on issues that affect people in the Canadian context.

Strong Integrative Theoretical Foundations

The three major sociological approaches—structural-functionalism, symbolic interactionism, and conflict theory—are introduced in the first chapter and discussed and applied, where appropriate, to various social problems throughout the text.

To foster the development of a nuanced understanding of contemporary problems, we have added significant discussion of the contributions of perspectives and research developed through feminist, postmodern, and queer theories.

With hundreds of contemporary sources drawn primarily from Canadian research and from the most recent Canadian census data analyses, this edition of *Understanding Social Problems* draws out a timely and thorough approach to problems that students will recognize. The inclusion of global perspectives on social problems will also help students to situate their understandings to contexts broader than the confines of their own local experiences.

Emphasis on the Structure and Culture of Society

As noted, the text emphasizes how the social structure and culture of society contribute to and maintain social problems, as well as provide the basis for alternative solutions.

Review of Basic Sociological Terms

An overview of basic sociological terms and concepts is presented in the first chapter. This overview is essential for students who have not taken an introductory course and is helpful, as a review, for those who have. The first chapter also addresses the relationship of theory to methods to show how specific theories can foster particular methods.

Unique Organization

The order of the 14 chapters reflects a progression from micro to macro levels of analysis, focusing first on problems of health care, drug use, and crime, and then broadening to the widening concerns of population health and welfare, science and technology, large-scale inequality, and environmental problems.

Three chapters merit special mention: "Sexualities" (Chapter 9), "Armed Conflict in Global Perspective" (Chapter 14) and "Environmental Problems" (Chapter 13). Whereas traditional texts approach sexualities through the lens of "deviance," we approach issues related to them as problems only insofar as they reflect dangerous prejudices and social structures and attitudes that have a negative impact on gay, lesbian, bisexual, and transgendered (GLBT) persons. Chapter 14 avoids the pitfalls of examining conflict in simple terms of "legitimate wars" and "illegitimate terrorism" and instead provides a context for understanding how and why armed conflicts occur, and what we might be able to do to reduce both the instance of such conflict and the damage that results when conflict does occur. Chapter 13, on environmental problems, departs from texts that usually pair population concerns with environmental ones to argue that a population explosion threatens world safety; here, we approach environmental problems by looking at how attitudes toward overconsumption of resources and the production of all types of waste threaten global well-being.

Consistent Chapter Format

Each chapter follows a similar format: the social problem is defined, the theoretical explanations are discussed, the consequences of the social problem are explored, and the alternative solutions and policies are examined. A concluding section assesses the current state of knowledge for each social problem.

Standard and Cutting-Edge Topics

In addition to problems that are typically addressed in social problems courses and texts, new and emerging topics are examined. Topics new to the fourth edition include a discussion of how social facts become perceived as social problems (Chapter 1), a critical introduction to controversies in the commercial exploitation of breast cancer in "awareness" campaigns (Chapter 2), and a discussion of the ways that women imprisoned for drug-related offences symbolically construct their own histories as *victims* rather than as *offenders* when seeking parole (Chapter 3). Chapter 5 delivers new coverage of intimate partner violence and abuse in global perspective. In Chapter 9, we pay particular attention to the inclusion of sexuality as a protected identity in Canada's hate crimes law, and we also provide an introduction to the ways in which people think about and treat those who are transgender and transex. The fourth Canadian edition also delivers an entirely new chapter, "Armed Conflict in Global Perspective" (Chapter 14).

In addition to these significant alterations and additions, the fourth edition of *Understanding Social Problems* uses the most recently available updates on Canadian and global statistics and provides updates in the research in each chapter, thus providing an up-to-date *and* long-term view of the social problems we face in Canada and around the globe.

Pedagogical Features of the Fourth Edition

Student-Friendly Presentation

To enhance the book's appeal to students, the fourth edition includes expanded information relevant to this population. In Chapter 1, for example, we present data on the beliefs of Canadian teens about various social problems, and Chapter 3 contains a section on binge drinking and other student alcohol-related problems. Further, Chapter 5 demonstrates the value of discourse analysis in its *Social Problems Research Up Close* feature, and in Chapter 12, "Problems in Education," students may complete a Student Alienation Scale.

Self and Society

The majority of chapters include a social survey designed to help students assess their own attitudes, beliefs, knowledge, or behaviour regarding some aspect of a social problem. Examples include a Criminal Activities Survey (Chapter 4) and an opportunity to compare beliefs against public ideas about poverty (Chapter 10).

The Human Side

To personalize the information being discussed, each chapter includes a feature entitled *The Human Side*. These features describe personal experiences of individuals who have been affected by the social problem under discussion. Examples include the powerful statements of Elijah Harper (Chapter 2) and Celia Haig-Brown (Chapter 12); the tragic experience of Kimberly Rogers (Chapter 10); the pioneering efforts of Craig Kielburger, founder of Free the Children (Chapter 6); and Velma Demerson's fight to have the Ontario government acknowledge that she had been unfairly imprisoned in the 1930s for being pregnant with the child of a Chinese man (Chapter 8). In our chapter on armed conflict in global perspective (Chapter 14), we look at the influence of recruiting propaganda on one young man who volunteered with the Royal Air Force in World War II and who lost his life at age 19; we include some of his drawings as part of the message he delivered home about his place in the war effort.

Social Problems Research Up Close

Now in every chapter, boxes called *Social Problems Research Up Close* present examples of social science research. These boxes demonstrate for students the sociological enterprise from theory and data collection to findings and conclusions. Examples of topics covered include "Moral Constructions of Motherhood in Breastfeeding Discourse" (Chapter 5), "Family, Gender Ideology, and Social Change" (Chapter 7), and "The HPV Vaccine and the Problematization of Women's Bodies" (Chapter 2).

Focus on Technology

Focus on Technology boxes appear in nearly every chapter. These boxes present information on how technology may contribute to social problems and their solutions. For example, in Chapter 4, "Crime and Violence," the *Focus on Technology* feature highlights the use of DNA testing in criminal investigations. In Chapter 13, "Environmental Problems," environmental and health hazards associated with computers are discussed. In Chapter 2, "Illness and Health Care," we examine the hazards of overly aggressive screening for breast and prostate cancers.

Is It True?

Each chapter begins with a series of true/false items to stimulate student interest and thinking. The text provides page references for the discussion so that students can determine for themselves whether statements are factually true, false, or contextual; answers are provided on the last page of each chapter.

Critical Thinking

Every chapter concludes with a section called "Critical Thinking," which includes a selection of discussion topics for developing the ability to work with concepts and data presented in the text.

Ancillaries

About NETA

The **Nelson Education Teaching Advantage (NETA)** program delivers research-based instructor resources that promote student engagement and higher-order thinking to enable the success of Canadian students and educators.

Instructors today face many challenges. Resources are limited, time is scarce, and a new kind of student has emerged: one who is juggling school with work, has gaps in his or her basic knowledge, and is immersed in technology in a way that has led to a completely new style of learning. In response, Nelson Education has gathered a group of dedicated instructors to advise us on the creation of richer and more flexible ancillaries that respond to the needs of today's teaching environments.

The members of our editorial advisory board have experience across a variety of disciplines and are recognized for their commitment to teaching. They include

Norman Althouse, Haskayne School of Business, University of Calgary
Brenda Chant-Smith, Department of Psychology, Trent University
Scott Follows, Manning School of Business Administration, Acadia University
Jon Houseman, Department of Biology, University of Ottawa
Glen Loppnow, Department of Chemistry, University of Alberta
Tanya Noel, Department of Biology, York University
Gary Poole, Director, Centre for Teaching and Academic Growth and School of Population and Public Health, University of British Columbia
Dan Pratt, Department of Educational Studies, University of British Columbia
Mercedes Rowinsky-Geurts, Department of Languages and Literatures, Wilfrid Laurier University
David DiBattista, Department of Psychology, Brock University
Roger Fisher, Ph.D.

In consultation with the editorial advisory board, Nelson Education has completely rethought the structure, approaches, and formats of our key textbook ancillaries. We've also increased our investment in editorial support for our ancillary authors. The result is the Nelson Education Teaching Advantage and its key components: *NETA Engagement, NETA Assessment,* and *NETA Presentation*. Each component includes one or more ancillaries prepared according to our best practices, and a document explaining the theory behind the practices.

NETA Engagement presents materials that help instructors deliver engaging content and activities to their classes. Instead of Instructor's Manuals that regurgitate chapter outlines and key terms from the text, NETA Enriched Instructor's Manuals (EIMs) provide genuine assistance to teachers. The EIMs answer questions like *What should students learn?, Why should students care?,* and *What are some common student misconceptions and stumbling blocks?* EIMs not only identify the topics that cause students the most difficulty, but also describe techniques and resources to help students master these concepts. Dr. Roger Fisher's *Instructor's Guide to Classroom Engagement (IGCE)* accompanies every Enriched Instructor's Manual.

NETA Assessment relates to testing materials: not just Nelson's Test Banks and Computerized Test Banks, but also in-text self-tests, Study Guides and web quizzes, and homework programs like CNOW. Under *NETA Assessment*, Nelson's authors create multiple-choice questions that reflect research-based best practices for constructing effective questions and testing not just recall but also higher-order thinking. Our guidelines were developed by David DiBattista, a 3M National Teaching Fellow whose recent research as a professor of psychology at Brock University has focused on multiple-choice testing. All Test Bank authors receive training at workshops conducted by Prof. DiBattista, as do the copyeditors assigned to each Test Bank. A copy of *Multiple Choice Tests: Getting Beyond Remembering*, Prof. DiBattista's guide to writing effective tests, is included with every Nelson Test Bank/Computerized Test Bank package.

NETA Presentation has been developed to help instructors make the best use of PowerPoint® in their classrooms. With a clean and uncluttered design developed by Maureen Stone of StoneSoup Consulting, *NETA Presentation* features slides with improved readability, more multi-media and graphic materials, activities to use in class, and tips for instructors on the Notes page. A copy of *NETA Guidelines for Classroom Presentations*, by Maureen Stone, is included with each set of PowerPoint slides.

Instructor Ancillaries

Key instructor ancillaries are provided on the *Instructor's Resource CD* (ISBN 978-0-17-660619-0), giving instructors the ultimate tool for customizing lectures and presentations. The IRCD includes

- **NETA Engagement:** The Enriched Instructor's Manual was written by Susan Miller of the University of Manitoba. It is organized according to the textbook chapters and addresses seven key educational concerns, such as typical stumbling blocks student face and how to address them. It also includes elements of a traditional Instructor's Manual, including learning objectives and suggested resources to use in the classroom.
- **NETA Assessment:** The Test Bank was written by Thomas Groulx of St. Clair College. It includes over 800 multiple-choice questions written according to NETA guidelines for effective construction and development of higher-order questions. Also included are approximately 350 true/false questions, 70 short-answer questions, and 70 essay questions. Test Bank files are provided in Word format for easy editing and in PDF format for convenient printing, whatever your system.

  The Computerized Test Bank by ExamView® includes all the questions from the Test Bank. The easy-to-use ExamView software is compatible with Microsoft Windows and Mac. Create tests by selecting questions from the question bank, modifying these questions as desired, and adding new questions you write yourself. You can administer quizzes online and export tests to WebCT, Blackboard, and other formats.
- **NETA Presentation:** Microsoft® PowerPoint® lecture slides for every chapter have been created by Anne Charles of the Conestoga College Institute of Technology and Advanced Learning. There is an average of 30 slides per chapter, many featuring key figures, tables, and photographs from *Understanding Social Problems*, Fourth Canadian Edition. NETA principles of clear design and engaging content have been incorporated throughout.
- **Image Library:** This resource consists of digital copies of figures, short tables, and photographs used in the book. Instructors may use these jpegs to create their own PowerPoint presentations.
- **DayOne:** Day One—Prof InClass is a PowerPoint presentation that you can customize to orient your students to the class and their text at the beginning of the course.

Acknowledgments

This text reflects the contributions of many people. I am especially grateful for the professionalism, patience, and support shown by my colleagues at Nelson Education Canada, especially to Laura Macleod for initially inviting my authorship on the third edition, and to Liisa Kelly and Maya Castle for their support at all stages of the updates to the fourth edition; all have provided encouragement and patience that I have valued greatly. I also gratefully acknowledge the production stage assistance provided by Natalia Denesiuk Harris, Rajachitra, Terry Fedorkiw, and Kelli Howey for her attentive work as copy editor.

My colleagues at Wilfrid Laurier University have been a tremendous support, but some deserve particular recognition. Pat Elliot aided in clearing the intellectual clutter from my own personal research specialization in sexuality, helping to distill it into a format that would be more accessible to students and non-specialist readers. Jeff Stepnisky generously shared his insights and helped with my research questions in areas concerned with mental health. Jasmin Zine and Glenda Wall were generously available to discuss their own current research. My former graduate student Lisa Dias was kind enough to allow her work to be included in the text, and I could not be more proud of her work or grateful for her generosity.

At all stages of writing I have been indebted to my partner, Trevor, whose patience, careful eye, thoughtful ear, and culinary prowess made completion of the work both possible and enjoyable, even when deadlines were tight.

Additionally, we are indebted to those who reviewed this work in draft form and provided valuable insights and suggestions:

Anne Charles, Conestoga College
Shanti Fernando, University of Ontario Institute of Technology
Loretta Gerlach, University of Regina
Lindsay Harris, Algonquin College
Uldis Kundrats, Nipissing University
Karen Moreau-Petti, Niagara College
Joseph O'Shea, Concordia University
Sharon Roberts, University of Western Ontario
Oliver R. Stoetzer, Fanshawe College

Finally, we are always interested in ways to improve the text. We invite your feedback and suggestions for new ideas and material to be included in subsequent editions.

M. Morgan Holmes
Department of Sociology
Wilfrid Laurier University
Waterloo, ON N2L 3C5
E-mail address: mholmes@wlu.ca

Thinking about Social Problems

Is It True?

1. For at least three decades, Canadians have identified the economy, unemployment, and crime as their foremost social concerns.

2. Before the nineteenth century, it was considered a husband's legal right and marital obligation to discipline and control his wife using physical force.

3. Currently, 1.2 billion people live on less than a dollar a day.

4. Questions involving values, religion, and morality can be answered only through scientific research.

5. In a national survey of Canadians 18 and older, about half agreed with the statement, "Anyone who works hard will rise to the top."

Read more here: 1 = p. 2, 2 = p. 5, 3 = p. 2, 4 = p. 19, 5 = p. 4

Answers can be found on p. 29.

Understanding the persistence of such social problems as crime, unemployment, drug abuse, suicide, racism, sexism, and family violence must necessarily temper our optimism for the future. Consider that for the past three decades Canadians have consistently identified the economy, unemployment, and crime as primary areas of social concern (Bibby 1995: 94–95; Bibby 2001: 43). In addition, global political and economic shifts have domestic impacts; thus, "'we' are all some variation of the unsettled, some variation of transient subjectivities, more and more sutured into the 'time' of Global capitalism's networks and contingencies" (Miki 2000: 44). Such instability, argues Miki, feeds problems of racism, even while Canada claims to value cultural pluralism. Canada also faces unique internal stresses: regional economic instability forces migration and creates social upheaval for communities (Marshall and Foster 2002), and in health-care provision "there is concern that local community governance structures may lose some of their community-based authority and not be flexible enough to meet emerging and current needs" (Benoit et al. 2003: 831). These are only two examples of social problems facing Canadian society.

A global perspective on social problems is equally troubling. In 1990, the United Nations published its first annual "Human Development Report." The report focuses on measuring the well-being of world populations according to a "human development index" (HDI) measuring three basic dimensions of human development: longevity, educational attainment, and living standards. The year 2000 report reveals that "globalization is increasing human insecurity by accelerating the spread of crime, disease, and financial volatility" (May 2000: 219). The results—100 million children live and work on the streets, 1.2 billion people live on less than a dollar a day, and 18 million people die every day from communicable diseases.

Problems related to poverty and malnutrition, inadequate education, inadequate health care and the spread of preventable disease, crime, conflict, oppression, environmental destruction, and other social issues are national and international concerns.

This text provides a critical overview of social problems in Canada and around the world. Although the topics covered vary, all chapters share common objectives: to explain how social problems form and persist; to indicate how problems affect individuals, social groups, and societies as a whole; and to examine programs and policies for change. We begin by looking at what characterizes social problems.

1.1 What Is a Social Problem?

There is no universal, constant, or absolute definition of what constitutes a social problem. Rather, we define social problems through a combination of objective and subjective criteria. The criteria vary across societies, among individuals and groups within a society, and across historical periods.

Objective and Subjective Elements of Social Problems

objective element (of a social problem)

Awareness of social conditions through one's own life experience and through reports in the media.

Although social problems take many forms, all share two important elements: an objective social condition and its subjective interpretation. The **objective element** of a social problem refers to the existence of a social condition. Social conditions are objectively real; that is, they exist independently of our perception. Social conditions such as homelessness, financial crises, and joblessness can affect large numbers of people, and often in waves or patterns. Social conditions—such as illness and disease, or the loss of family members to crashes caused by drunk drivers—tend to be experienced at the personal level; however, as you will see, even "personal troubles" connect to larger social phenomena.

The **subjective element** of a social problem refers to beliefs that particular social conditions are harmful to society or to a segment of society, and that we should and can change them. We know, for example, that in addition to the problems mentioned above, crime, drug addiction, poverty, racism, violence, and pollution exist. These social conditions are not considered social problems, however, until a segment of society believes that these conditions diminish the quality of human life.

How a population comes to combine subjective and objective elements to identify some facts as problems is, in itself, an important research question. Spector and Kitsuse (2001) argue that **claims-making activities** are central to the development of the particular view of a social fact as a bona fide social problem. Spector and Kitsuse explain:

> we define social problems as *the activities of individuals or groups making assertions of grievances and claims with respect to some putative conditions*. The emergence of a social problem is contingent upon the organization of activities asserting the need for eradicating, ameliorating, or otherwise changing some condition. (p. 76: emphasis in original)

Moreover, Spector and Kitsuse explain that there is little utility in trying to determine whether a condition actually exists if what we are trying to do is understand what people *perceive* as a social problem. We may see, for example, that hoaxes abound on the internet, forwarded from one person to the next. Such hoaxes often speak to larger social anxieties regarding rapid changes—in gender roles, for example—that many people experience as a threat to existing social structures and deeply held social mores. The hoaxes often warn women to stay in their "proper" social place lest they be robbed or assaulted while out in the public world of politics and commerce. That the warnings claim to be based on recent cases of assault or abductions (that, in fact, never actually happened) is entirely beside the point. Spector and Kitsuse use different examples, but as with the example presented here they "are not concerned whether or not the imputed condition exists" (76). Rather, the point is to understand that defining conditions as problems is a social activity that assumes shared values and shared definitions regarding what counts as a social good: "The emergence of a social problem is contingent upon the organization of activities asserting the need for eradicating, ameliorating, or otherwise changing some condition" (76).

To the extent that sociologists are trained to recognize some conditions as social problems, this textbook begins with the explanation of conditions already recognized as social problems. The book also continues the *claims-making* work of arguing that these are problems precisely because the social conditions described *do* require amelioration, or even eradication. Past (and future) sociological assessments do not necessarily begin from the same shared definitions, and do not apprehend the same objective facts as obvious *problems*.

To sum up: a **social problem** is a social condition that a segment of society demonstrates to be significantly harmful to members of society and in need of remedy. The definition is relative, and is informed by larger social values that shape the way we understand and apprehend social facts. Moreover, as you will see in this chapter's *Self and Society* feature, what we collectively agree are social problems changes over time as our society changes.

subjective element (of a social problem)
The belief that a particular social condition is harmful to society, or to a segment of society, and that it should and can be changed.

claims-making activities
The strategies and actions that individuals or groups undertake to define social conditions as social problems that require remedy.

social problem
A social condition that a segment of society views as harmful to members of society and in need of remedy.

Personal Beliefs about Various Social Problems

Indicate whether you agree or disagree with each of the following statements:

Statement	Agree	Disagree
1. There are some circumstances in which a doctor would be justified in ending a patient's life.	_____	_____
2. It should be possible for a pregnant woman to obtain a *legal* abortion if she wants it for any reason.	_____	_____
3. It should be possible for a pregnant woman to get a *legal* abortion if there is a strong chance of a serious defect in the baby.	_____	_____
4. The death penalty should be exercised in some instances.	_____	_____
5. Immigrants to Canada have an obligation to learn Canadian ways.	_____	_____
6. Marijuana should be legalized.	_____	_____
7. Homosexuality is "always wrong" or "almost always wrong."	_____	_____
8. Homosexuals are entitled to the same rights as other Canadians.	_____	_____
9. Birth control information should be available to teenagers who want it.	_____	_____
10. Natives have too much power in our nation's affairs.	_____	_____
11. There are racial and cultural groups that are discriminated against in my community.	_____	_____
12. Law enforcement is applied evenly to all those who break the law.	_____	_____
13. Anyone who works hard will rise to the top.	_____	_____
14. Corporations have too much power in national life.	_____	_____
15. Bilingualism is a policy worth supporting.	_____	_____
16. In general, values in Canada have been changing for the worse.	_____	_____

Percentage* of Canadians Agreeing with Attitude Statements

	Percentage Agreeing			
Statement Number	1975	1985	1995	2005
1. Doctor-assisted euthanasia	–	–	75	71
2. Abortion "on demand"	–	37	39	43
3. Abortion if "serious defect" in child	85	86	88	84
4. Use of death penalty	79	84	82	66
5. Assimilation expectations	85	–	88	86
6. Legalization of marijuana	27	30	31	45
7. Disapproval of homosexuality	72	71	52	38
8. Extending rights to homosexuals	–	76	67	81
9. Birth control information to teens	94	91	94	93
10. Natives have too much power	7	13	33	26
11. Racial and cultural discrimination	–	54	67	52
12. Law enforcement equitable	37	27	25	31
13. Self-efficacy	45	50	53	50
14. Corporations have too much power	83	73	69	74
15. Endorsement of bilingualism	49	53	55	64
16. Values changing for the worse	–	54	74	58

*Each Project Canada sample consists of a highly representative sample of approximately 1500 Canadian adults 18 years of age and older.
SOURCE: Bibby, Reginald W. Project Canada National Survey Series. Details are available at www.reginaldbibby.com.

Variability in Definitions of Social Problems

Individuals and groups frequently disagree about what constitutes a social problem. For example, the use of physical punishment to discipline children is perceived differently by those who condone its use and those who condemn it. Those who condone it argue that the problem is not the use of corporal punishment, but the intrusion of courts and social agencies into private family matters. Those who condemn it argue that corporal punishment infringes on the right of children to protection of their bodies from harm. They point out that adult acceptance of physical harm as a "normal" part of discipline is a measure of just how damaging it is to the psyche. Such variations in views result from differences in values, beliefs, and life experiences.

Definitions of social problems vary not only within societies, but also across societies and historical periods. For example, prior to the nineteenth century it was a husband's legal right and marital obligation to discipline and control his wife through the use of physical force. Today, the use of physical force is regarded as a social problem and a criminal offence rather than a marital right.

Because social problems can be highly complex, it is helpful to have a framework to assess them. Sociology provides such a framework. Using a sociological perspective to examine social problems requires knowledge of the concepts and methods designed specifically for the purpose of accessing and analyzing social phenomena. In the remainder of this chapter, we discuss some of these concepts and methods.

1.2 Concepts

Social Structure and Culture

Although society surrounds us and permeates our lives, it is difficult to "see" society. A metaphor can help us visualize its two central features to understand it better. Imagine that society is a coin with two sides: on one side, social structure; on the other, culture. Although each "side" is distinct, each is inseparable from the whole. Analysis of the various elements of social structure and culture fosters understanding of the root causes of social problems.

Elements of Social Structure

The *structure* of a society refers to the way society is organized. Society is organized into different parts: institutions, social groups, statuses, and roles.

Those who use structural analysis to assess and understand social regulation and change also understand that structures serve specific functions. For example, Durkheim's research demonstrated that suicide rates were **social facts**—that is, phenomena created by social organization rather than individual acts of desperation. Structural theorists have since argued that a society needs to have cohesion in its different parts, with complementary functions and values. Otherwise, as Durkheim demonstrated, social upheaval and poor institutional cohesion could have catastrophic outcomes.

Institutions An **institution** is an established and enduring organization of social relationships. The five traditional institutions are family, religion, politics,

social facts
Émile Durkheim refers to the phenomena that occur in the world as objectively identifiable facts. If the phenomena arise as a result of structural organization and functional needs, or dysfunctional problems, then those facts are not merely idiosyncratic happenings, but the result of social structures— they are part of the function of the society under consideration. Employment rates, morbidity, and mortality, as well as rates of population growth or decline, are all examples of "social facts."

institution
An established and enduring pattern of social relationships. The five traditional social institutions are family, religion, politics, economics, and education. Institutions are the largest elements of social structure.

economics, and education, but some sociologists argue that other social institutions, such as science and technology, mass media, medicine, sport, and the military, also play important roles in contemporary society.

Many social problems result from inadequacies in institutions or conflicts between institutions. For example, there is concern that unemployment may be influenced by the educational institution's inability to keep up with changing demands and instability in the structure of the economic institution. It is possible, though, that "closer links between education and economy might mean too much business influence over what is taught at all levels of the educational system" (Krahn and Lowe 2002: 46).

Social Groups Institutions are made up of social groups—defined as two or more people who have a common identity, interact, and form a social relationship. For example, the family in which you were reared is a **social group** and part of the family institution. Any specific religion is a social group that forms part of the religious institution.

A social group may be categorized as primary or secondary. A **primary group**, which tends to involve a small number of individuals, is characterized by intimate and informal interaction. Families and friends are examples of primary groups. A **secondary group**, which may involve a small or large number of individuals, is task-oriented and characterized by impersonal and formal interaction. Examples of secondary groups include employers and their employees, and clerks and their customers. Because secondary groups are usually large, primary groups often form inside them, making large structures more manageable on a personal level.

Statuses Just as an institution consists of social groups, a social group consists of statuses. A **status** is a position a person occupies within a social group. The statuses we occupy largely define our social identities. The statuses in a family may consist of mother, father, stepmother, stepfather, wife, husband, child, and so on. Statuses may be either ascribed or achieved. An **ascribed status** is one that society assigns to an individual on the basis of factors over which the individual has no control. For example, we have no control over the sex, race, ethnic background, and socio-economic status into which we are born. Similarly, we are assigned the status of "child," "teenager," "adult," or "senior citizen" on the basis of our age—something we do not choose or control.

An **achieved status** is assigned on the basis of characteristics or behaviour over which an individual has some control. For example, whether or not you achieve the status of university graduate depends partly on personal effort, behaviour, and choices. Critically, however, ascribed statuses may affect the likelihood of achieving other statuses. Canadian research shows that, of those who graduated in 1985, only 35 percent of those from low socio-economic status (SES) families had achieved a university degree by 1999; meanwhile, 62 percent of those from high SES families had achieved a university degree in the same time period (Krahn 2004: 197–98).

Everyone occupies numerous statuses simultaneously. You may simultaneously be a student, parent, tutor, community volunteer, female, and person

social group

Two or more people who have a common identity and who interact and form a social relationship; institutions are made up of social groups.

primary group

A small group characterized by intimate and informal interaction.

secondary group

A group characterized by impersonal and formal interaction.

status

A position a person occupies within a social group.

ascribed status

A status that society assigns to an individual on the basis of factors over which the individual has no control.

achieved status

A status assigned on the basis of some characteristic or behaviour over which the individual has some control.

with a disability. A person's **master status** is the one considered the most significant in a person's social identity. Typically, gender and race cut across all other statuses, though occupation may operate as a master status. Statuses that others perceive to be in conflict, such as "female" and "surgeon," can be difficult to negotiate, and people who occupy such apparently contradictory statuses may face exceptional difficulties.

master status

The status that is considered the most significant in a person's social identity.

Roles Every status is associated with many **roles**—the set of rights, obligations, and expectations associated with a status. Roles guide our behaviour and allow us to predict the behaviour of others. As a student, you are expected to attend class, listen and take notes, study for tests, and complete assignments. Because the status of teacher has recognizable role expectations, you can predict that your teacher will lecture, give exams, and assign grades based on your performance.

A single status involves more than one role. For example, the status of nurse involves different roles for interacting with physicians, with patients, and with their families.

role

A set of rights, obligations, and expectations associated with a status.

Elements of Culture

Whereas *social structure* refers to the organization of society, culture refers to the meanings and ways of life that characterize a society. The elements of culture include beliefs, values, norms, sanctions, and symbols.

Beliefs **Beliefs** refer to definitions and explanations about what is assumed to be true. The beliefs of an individual or group influence whether that individual or group views a particular social condition as a social problem. Does violence in entertainment media lead to increased aggression in children? Is it harmful to preschool-aged children for both parents to work outside the home? Our beliefs regarding these issues influence whether we view the issues as problems. Beliefs influence not only how a social condition is interpreted, but also the existence of the condition. Every day in Canada *The Globe and Mail* publishes its "Globe Poll" of readers' beliefs regarding current events (www.globeandmail.com)—but it is important to remember that beliefs do not constitute sociological knowledge. Sociologists do not accept beliefs as true, but as sources of information about how social relations operate and how they influence the directions that social actors will take. The *Self and Society* feature in this chapter encourages you to assess your own beliefs about various social issues and compare them with national samples of earlier generations of Canadians 18 years of age and older.

beliefs

Definitions and explanations about what is assumed to be true.

Values **Values** are social agreements about what is considered good and bad, right and wrong, desirable and undesirable. Frequently, we apprehend social conditions as social problems when the conditions are incompatible with or contradict closely held values. For example, poverty and homelessness violate the value of human welfare; some types of crimes contradict values of honesty, private property, and nonviolence; racism, sexism, and heterosexism violate values of equality and fairness.

values

Social agreements about what is considered good and bad, right and wrong, desirable and undesirable.

Values can also be central to the development of social problems. Sylvia Ann Hewlett (1992) explains how the values of freedom and individualism are at the root of many of our social problems:

> There are two sides to the coin of freedom. On the one hand, there is enormous potential for prosperity and personal fulfilment; on the other are all the hazards of untrammelled opportunity and unfettered choice. Free markets can produce grinding poverty as well as spectacular wealth; unregulated industry can create dangerous levels of pollution as well as rapid rates of growth; and an unfettered drive for personal fulfilment can have disastrous effects on families and children. Rampant individualism does not bring with it sweet freedom; rather, it explodes in our faces and limits life's potential. (pp. 350–51)

Absent or weak values may also contribute to social problems. For example, many industries do not value protection of the environment and thus contribute to environmental pollution.

norms

Socially defined rules of behaviour, including folkways, mores, and laws.

folkways

The customs and manners of society.

Norms and Folkways Norms are socially defined rules of behaviour. Norms serve as guidelines for personal behaviour and for our expectations of the behaviour of others.

There are three types of norms: folkways, laws, and mores. **Folkways** refer to the customs and manners of society. In many segments of our society, it is customary to shake hands when being introduced to a new acquaintance, to say "excuse me" after sneezing, and to give presents to family and friends on their birthdays. Although no laws require us to do these things, we are expected to do them because they are part of the cultural traditions, or folkways, of the society in which we live.

laws

Norms that are formalized and backed by political authority.

mores

Norms that have a moral basis.

sanctions

Social consequences for conforming to or violating norms. Types of sanctions include positive, negative, formal, and informal.

Laws, Mores, and Sanctions Laws are formalized norms backed by political authority. A person who eats food out of a public garbage container is violating a folkway—no law prohibits this behaviour. However, throwing trash onto a public street is littering and is against the law.

Some norms, called **mores**, have a moral basis. Violations of mores may produce shock, horror, and moral indignation. Both littering and child sexual abuse are violations of law, but child sexual abuse is also a violation of our mores: we view such behaviour as immoral.

All norms are associated with **sanctions**, or social consequences for conforming to or violating norms. When we conform to a social norm, we may be rewarded by a positive sanction. These may range from an approving smile to a public ceremony in our honour. When we violate a social norm, we may be punished by a negative sanction, which may range from a disapproving look to life in prison. Most sanctions are spontaneous expressions of approval or disapproval by groups or individuals—referred to as informal sanctions. Sanctions carried out according to some recognized or formal procedure are formal sanctions. Types of sanctions, then, include positive informal sanctions, positive formal sanctions, negative informal sanctions, and negative formal sanctions (see Table 1.1).

■ **Table 1.1** *Types and Examples of Sanctions*

	Positive	Negative
Informal	Being praised by one's neighbours for organizing a neighbourhood recycling program.	Being criticized by one's neighbours for refusing to participate in the neighbourhood recycling program.
Formal	Being granted a citizen's award for organizing a neighbourhood recycling program.	Being fined by the city for failing to dispose of garbage properly.

Symbols A symbol is something that represents something else. Without symbols, we could not communicate with one another or live as social beings.

The symbols of a culture include language, gestures, and objects whose meaning is commonly understood by the members of a society. In our society, a peace sign communicates the value of nonviolence; a police badge, the authority of law. Sometimes, people attach different meanings to the same symbol. The swastika is an ancient symbol that was supposed to bring good luck. However, its adoption as the official emblem of the Nazi Party and Nazi Germany has encouraged many to view it as a symbol of anti-Semitism, white supremacy, and bigotry.

The elements of social structure and culture just discussed play a central role in the creation, maintenance, and social response to various social problems. Taking a course in social problems helps develop an awareness of how the elements of social structure and culture contribute to social problems. Sociologists refer to this awareness as the "sociological imagination."

symbol
Something that represents something else.

1.3 The Sociological Imagination

The **sociological imagination**, a term developed by C. Wright Mills (1959), refers to the ability to see the connections between our personal lives and the social world in which we live. Use of the sociological imagination enables distinction between "private troubles" and "public issues" and the seeing of connections between the events and conditions of our lives and the social and historical context in which we live.

For example, the fact that one person is unemployed constitutes a private trouble. The fact that thousands of people are unemployed in Canada constitutes a public issue. Once we understand that personal troubles such as HIV infection, criminal victimization, and poverty are shared by other segments of society, we can look for the elements of social structure and culture that contribute to these public issues and private troubles. If the various elements of social structure and culture contribute to private troubles and public issues, then society's social structure and culture must be changed in order to resolve these concerns.

Rather than viewing the private trouble of being unemployed as the result of individual character flaws or lack of skills, we may understand unemployment as a public issue that results from the failure of the economic and political institutions of society to provide job opportunities to all citizens. For example,

sociological imagination
A term coined by C. Wright Mills to refer to the ability to see the connections between our personal lives and the social world in which we live.

structural-functionalism

A sociological perspective that views society as a system of interconnected parts that work together in harmony to maintain a state of balance and social equilibrium for the whole; focuses on how each part of society influences and is influenced by other parts.

conflict theory

The theoretical framework that understands material inequalities to be a driving force behind many social problems. Some sociologists prefer to use "Marxist theory" to name this approach to thinking about social inequalities.

symbolic interactionism

A sociological perspective that emphasizes that human behaviour is influenced by definitions and meanings that are created and maintained through symbolic interaction with others.

feminist theory

A set of diverse perspectives joined by the focus on sex and gender as defining and important categories of oppression.

postmodern theory

A theory that rejects the positivist notion that societies are completely rational and that a single truth about social worlds can be identified. The theory takes account of the competing realities according to and through which people live their lives.

technological innovations in the steel industry threatened job security and altered the way of life for hundreds of Hamilton, Ontario, families in the 1970s (Leach 2005). During the economic recession of the 1980s, employers fired employees so the firms could stay in business or maximize profits, or both. In both cases, social forces rather than individual skills largely determined whether a person was employed or not.

1.4 Theoretical Perspectives

Theories in sociology provide different perspectives from which to view our social world. Sociological theories help us to explain and predict the social world in which we live.

Sociology includes four major theoretical perspectives. A perspective is simply a way of looking at the world. A theory is a set of interrelated propositions or principles designed to explain an observable phenomenon; a theory provides a perspective. **Structural-functionalism** assesses social structures and their functions or dysfunctions; it is often thought of principally as a historical perspective. **Conflict theory** understands differentials in power, well-being, and access to resources. **Symbolic interactionism** asks how people come to agree about the meaning and significance of what occurs between them, and how meanings fit into a society's sensibilities and practical strategies. **Feminist theory** demonstrates that women are marginalized by social structures, in symbolic operations, and in distribution of resources; it also shows that traditional sociological thinking has failed to account for these and other problems facing women. Feminists may use the tools of any combination of other theories, but all agree that the subordinate status of women constitutes a social problem.

In addition to the four central theoretical perspectives, two others—postmodern and "queer" theory—have gained prominence. **Postmodern theory** argues that the progressivist stance of modernism presupposes too easily that subjects and societies are stable and linear, moving toward their best possible manifestation. Postmodernists argue that we need to take account of the fluctuating and fractured aspects of social organization. By doing so we can listen to the shifting voices and needs of those overlooked by positivist assumptions and methods. **Queer theory** has strong ties to feminist work, but also corrects the pervasive assumption that heterosexuality is both natural and ahistorical. Queer theory offers more nuanced accounts of history, social organization, and sexual identity than those offered by the structural-functionalist perspective, for example. Structural-functionalists see the world divided neatly into male and female bodies that fulfill social roles, tasks, and institutional requirements based on heterosexual, prescriptive norms. In addition, queer theory has become a central conceptual model for those who study disability. Scholars who work on disability observe that many of the same prejudices and contestations regarding sexuality and family-based rights—such as the rights of gays, lesbians, and trans-persons to have children, to marry, to have bodily and sexual autonomy, to be seen as desirable and socially valuable—apply to persons with disabilities. Queer theory, thus, extends its utility well beyond the scope of questions focused on sexuality and into more general questions regarding the intersection of embodiment and social regulation.

Every theory offers a variety of explanations about the causes of and possible solutions for social problems, and each is subject to constant revision and refinement of both methods and interests. Sociologists never stop trying to improve on what we can know and to correct what we may have misapprehended before.

Structural-Functionalist Perspective

The structural-functionalist perspective is largely based on the works of Herbert Spencer, Émile Durkheim, Talcott Parsons, and Robert Merton. According to structural-functionalism, society is a system of interconnected parts that work together in harmony to maintain a state of balance and social equilibrium for the whole. For example, each social institution serves important functions for society: family provides a context for reproducing, nurturing, and socializing children; education offers a way to transmit a society's skills, knowledge, and culture to its youth; politics provides a means of governing members of society; economics provides for the production, distribution, and consumption of goods and services; and religion provides moral guidance and an outlet for worship of a higher power.

The structural-functionalist perspective emphasizes the interconnectedness of society by focusing on how each part influences and is influenced by other parts. For example, as a result of changes in technology, colleges and universities are offering more technical programs, and many adults are returning to school to learn new skills that are required in the workplace. The increasing number of women in the workforce has contributed to the formulation of policies against sexual harassment and job discrimination.

Structural-functionalists use the terms "functional" and "dysfunctional" to describe the effects of social elements on society. Elements of society are functional if they contribute to social stability and dysfunctional if they disrupt social stability. Some aspects of society may be both functional and dysfunctional for society. For example, crime is dysfunctional in that it is associated with physical violence, loss of property, and fear. But, according to Durkheim and other functionalists, crime is also functional for society because it leads to heightened awareness of shared moral bonds and increased social cohesion.

Sociologists have identified two types of functions: manifest and latent (Merton 1968). A manifest function is an intended, recognizable consequence or intent. A **latent function** is an unintended, commonly hidden consequence or denied intention. For example, the **manifest function** of education is to transmit knowledge and skills to society's youth. But public elementary schools also serve to stream populations into stratified jobs, and colleges and universities offer a place for young adults to meet potential mates. The job streaming and mate selection functions are not commonly recognized functions of education.

Structural-Functionalist Theories of Social Problems

Two dominant theories of social problems grew out of the structural-functionalist perspective: social pathology and social disorganization.

Social Pathology According to the social pathology model, social problems result from some "sickness" in society. Just as the human body becomes ill when our systems, organs, and cells do not function normally, society becomes "ill"

queer theory

A theory that developed largely out of the late 1980s response to public panics over HIV and to medical system failures to treat with respect and adequate priority the needs of HIV+ persons, especially gay men. Queer theory now asks how sexual identity relates to various problems rooted in oppression and prejudice. It provides an important analytic tool to understand the oppressive treatment of gay, lesbian, bisexual, and transgender persons in societal structures and in cultural representation.

latent function

Consequence that is unintended and often hidden or unrecognized; for example, a latent function of education is to provide schools that function as babysitters for employed parents.

manifest function

A consequence that is intended and commonly recognized; for example, a manifest function of education is to transmit knowledge and skills to youth.

when its parts—elements of the structure and culture—no longer perform properly. For example, problems such as crime, violence, and poverty are often attributed to the breakdown of the family institution, the decline of the religious institution, and inadequacies in our economic, educational, and political institutions.

Social illness also results when members of a society are not adequately socialized to adopt its norms and values. Persons who do not value honesty, for example, are prone to dishonesties of all sorts. Early theorists attributed the failure in socialization to "sick" people who could not be socialized. Later theorists recognized that failure in the socialization process stemmed from "sick" social conditions, not "sick" people. To prevent or solve social problems, members of society must receive proper socialization and moral education, which may be accomplished in the family, schools, churches, and workplace, and through the media.

anomie

A state of normlessness in which norms and values are weak or unclear; results from rapid social change and is linked to many social problems, including crime, drug addiction, and violence.

Social Disorganization According to the social disorganization view of social problems, rapid social change disrupts the norms in a society. When norms become weak or are in conflict with each other society is in a state of **anomie**, or normlessness. Hence, people may steal, physically abuse their partner or children, abuse drugs, commit sexual assault, or engage in other deviant behaviour because the norms regarding these behaviours are weak or conflicting. According to this view, the solution to social problems lies in slowing the pace of social change and strengthening social norms. For example, although the use of alcohol by teenagers is considered a violation of a social norm in our society, this norm is weak. The media portray young people drinking alcohol, teenagers teach one another to drink alcohol and buy fake identification cards to purchase alcohol, and parents model drinking behaviour by having a few drinks after work or at a social event. Solutions to teenage drinking may involve strengthening norms against it through public education, restricting media depictions of youth and alcohol, imposing stronger sanctions against the use of fake IDs to purchase alcohol, and educating parents to model moderate and responsible drinking behaviour.

Conflict Perspective

conflict perspective

A sociological perspective that views society as comprising different groups and interests competing for power and resources.

Whereas the structural-functionalists view society as a cooperation of different parts working together, the **conflict perspective** views society as a struggle among different groups and interests competing for power and resources. This perspective sees conflict and struggle as the central feature of our social world, in which some groups have power and benefit from hierarchical social arrangements.

The conflict perspective originates with the classic works of Karl Marx. Marx argued that all societies go through stages of economic development. As societies evolve from agricultural to industrial, concern over meeting survival needs is replaced by concern over making a profit, the hallmark of a capitalist system. Industrialization leads to the development of two classes of people: the bourgeoisie, or the owners of the means of production (e.g., factories, farms, businesses), and the proletariat, or the workers who earn wages.

The division of society into two broad classes of people—owners with power and workers dependent upon them—benefits the owners of the means of production. The workers, who may earn only subsistence wages, are denied access to the many resources available to the wealthy owners. According to Marx, the bourgeoisie use their power to control the institutions of society to their advantage. For example, Marx suggested that religion serves as an "opiate of the masses" that distracts attention from the suffering in working-class conditions and focuses the workers' attention on spirituality, God, and the afterlife rather than on such worldly concerns as living conditions. In essence, religion diverts workers' attention so that they concentrate on heaven's rewards for living a moral life rather than on challenging exploitation.

Conflict Theories of Social Problems

There are two general types of conflict theories of social problems: Marxist and non-Marxist. Marxist theories focus on social conflict that results from economic inequalities; non-Marxist theories focus on social conflict that results from competing values and interests among social groups.

Marxist Conflict Theories According to contemporary Marxist theorists, social problems result from the class inequality inherent to capitalism. As we shall explore later, many social problems are linked to poverty.

In addition to creating an impoverished class of people, capitalism also encourages "corporate violence." **Corporate violence** may be defined as actual harm or risk of harm inflicted on consumers, workers, and the general public as a result of decisions by corporate executives or managers. Corporate violence can result from corporate negligence, the quest for profits at any cost, and wilful violations of health, safety, and environmental laws (Hills 1987). Our profit-motivated economy may provide encouragement for those who are otherwise good, kind, and law-abiding to participate knowingly in the manufacturing and marketing of defective brakes on jets, faulty fuel tanks on automobiles, and unsafe contraceptive devices such as some intrauterine devices (IUDs). As Eitzen and Baca Zinn (2000: 483) note, the "goal of profit is so central to capitalistic enterprises that many corporate decisions are made without consideration for the consequences."

Marxist conflict theories also focus on the problem of **alienation**, or powerlessness and meaninglessness in people's lives. In industrialized societies, workers often have little power or control over their jobs, which fosters a sense of powerlessness. Furthermore, specialized work requires workers to perform limited, repetitive tasks; as a result, workers may perceive their lives as meaningless.

Alienation is bred not only in the workplace, but also in the classroom. Students have little power over their education and often find their studies lack meaning. Like poverty, alienation is linked to other social problems, such as low educational achievement, violence, and suicide.

Marxist explanations of social problems imply that the solution lies in eliminating inequality among classes of people by creating a classless society, changing work to avoid alienation, and applying stronger controls to corporations to ensure that decisions and practices are based on safety rather than profit considerations.

Non-Marxist Conflict Theories Neo-Marxist conflict theorists are concerned with conflict that arises when groups have opposing values and interests. For

corporate violence

The production of unsafe products and the failure of corporations to provide a safe working environment for their employees.

alienation

The concept used by Karl Marx to describe the condition when workers feel powerlessness and meaninglessness as a result of performing repetitive, isolated work tasks. Alienation involves becoming estranged from one's work, the products one creates, other human beings, or one's self; it also refers to powerlessness and meaninglessness experienced by students in traditional, restrictive educational institutions.

example, anti-abortion activists value the life of embryos and fetuses; pro-choice activists value the right of women to control their own lives, bodies, and reproductive decisions. These different value positions reflect different interpretations of what constitutes a social problem. For anti-abortionists, abortion is the social problem; for pro-choice advocates, restrictions on abortion are the social problem. Value conflicts may occur between diverse categories of people, including non-whites versus whites, heterosexuals versus homosexuals, young versus old, liberals versus conservatives, and environmentalists versus industrialists. Often, these are struggles not simply over meaning but also over recognition, with power differences between the groups informing the stakes of the argument.

Solutions to the problems generated by competing values may involve ensuring that conflicting groups understand each other's views, resolving differences through negotiation or mediation, or agreeing to disagree. Ideally, solutions should be win–win; both conflicting groups should be satisfied with the solution. However, outcomes of value conflicts are often influenced by power: the group with the most power may use its position to influence the outcome of value conflicts.

Both the structural-functionalist and the conflict perspectives address how broad aspects of society, such as institutions and large social groups, influence the social world. This level of sociological analysis is called **macro-sociology**: it looks at the "big picture" of society and suggests how social problems are affected at the institutional level.

macro-sociology

The study of large aspects of society, such as institutions and large social groups.

Symbolic Interactionist Perspective

Another level of sociological analysis, **micro-sociology** focuses on the psychological dynamics of individuals interacting in small groups. Symbolic interactionism reflects the micro-sociological perspective largely developed in the work of early sociologists and philosophers such as Max Weber, Georg Simmel, Charles Horton Cooley, G. H. Mead, W. I. Thomas, Erving Goffman, and Howard Becker. Symbolic interactionism emphasizes that human behaviour is influenced by definitions and meanings that are created and maintained through symbolic interaction with others.

Sociologist W. I. Thomas ([1931] 1966) emphasized the importance of definitions and meanings in social behaviour and in its consequences. He suggested that humans respond to their definition of a situation rather than to the objective situation. Hence, Thomas noted that situations we define as real become real in their consequences.

Symbolic interactionism also suggests that our identity or sense of self is shaped by social interaction. We develop our self-concept by observing how others interact with us and label us. By observing how others view us, we see a reflection of ourselves that Charles Horton Cooley calls the "looking-glass self."

Lastly, the symbolic interaction perspective has important implications for how social scientists conduct research. Max Weber (1864–1920) argued that to understand individual and group behaviour, social scientists must see the world from the eyes of that individual or group. Weber called this approach *Verstehen*, which in German means "empathy." *Verstehen* implies that in conducting research social scientists must try to understand others' views of reality and the subjective aspects of their experiences, including their symbols, values, attitudes, and beliefs.

micro-sociology

The study of the social psychological dynamics of individuals interacting in small groups.

Symbolic Interactionist Theories of Social Problems

A basic premise of symbolic interactionist theories of social problems is that a condition must be defined or recognized as a social problem in order for it to be a social problem.

Based on this premise, Herbert Blumer (1971) suggested that social problems develop in stages:

- First, social problems pass through the stage of societal recognition—the process by which a social problem, for example, drunk driving, is "born."
- Second, social legitimation takes place when the social problem achieves recognition by the larger community, including media, schools, and churches. As the visibility of traffic fatalities associated with alcohol increased, so did the legitimation of drunk driving as a social problem.
- Third, the development of a social problem involves mobilization for action, which occurs when individuals and groups, such as MADD (Mothers Against Drunk Driving), become concerned about how to respond to the social condition. This mobilization leads to the development and implementation of an official plan for dealing with the problem, involving, for example, highway checkpoints, lower legal blood-alcohol levels, and tougher penalties for drunk driving.

Blumer's stage-development view of social problems is helpful in tracing the development of social problems. For example, although sexual harassment and acquaintance rape have occurred throughout the past century (at least!), these issues did not begin to receive recognition as social problems until the 1970s. Social legitimation of these problems was achieved when high schools, colleges and universities, churches, employers, and the media recognized their existence. Organized social groups mobilized to develop and implement plans to deal with these problems. For example, groups successfully lobbied for the enactment of laws against sexual harassment and the enforcement of sanctions against violators of these laws. Groups also mobilized to provide educational seminars on acquaintance rape for students and to offer support services to victims of date rape.

Some disagree with the symbolic interactionist view that social problems exist only if they are recognized. According to this view, individuals who were victims of acquaintance rape in the 1960s may be considered victims of a problem, even though acquaintance rape was not recognized at that time as a social problem.

Labelling theory, a major symbolic interactionist theory of social problems, suggests that a social condition or group is viewed as problematic if it is labelled as such. According to labelling theory, resolving social problems sometimes involves changing the meanings and definitions attributed to people and situations. For example, as long as teenagers define drinking alcohol as "cool" and "fun," they will continue to drink it illegally.

Feminist Perspectives

Feminist theory building is one practice among many in feminist action. Feminist work begins with the observation that the experiences, social relations, and locations of women's lives are missing or discounted in traditional sociology.

labelling theory

A symbolic interactionist theory that is concerned with the effects of labelling on the definition of a social problem (e.g., a social condition or group is viewed as problematic if it is labelled as such) and with the effects of labelling on the self-concept and behaviour of individuals (e.g., the label "juvenile delinquent" may contribute to the development of a self-concept and behaviour consistent with the label).

Harriet Martineau, perhaps the first feminist sociologist, dedicated a chapter of her 1837 study on American society to "The Political Non-Existence of Women." Feminist researchers work to move the specifics of women's lives to the centre of sociological inquiry. Just as multiple sociological perspectives developed from the discipline's earliest inception, so are there multiple forms of feminist theory; however, as Chafetz (1997: 98) explains, in all feminist work "gender comprises a central subject matter of the theory; gender relations are viewed as a problem...Feminist theory seeks to understand how gender is related to social inequities...gender relations are not viewed as...immutable [and] feminist theories can...challenge counteract or change a status quo that disadvantages or devalues women" (ellipses in original). Many contemporary feminist thinkers also use postmodern and queer perspectives; others may be more traditionally inclined, using Marxist theory to account for a political economy of women or to understand how gender operates as a structuring institution that shapes the lives of men and women.

Postmodern Perspectives

Postmodern perspectives in the humanities and social sciences present a turn away from the positivism of earlier perspectives. They instead recognize that subjectivity and interpretation do not move in one unified direction to assess a certain, external reality. As Inglis and Hughson explain it, postmodernism resists simple categorization and rejects as overly restrictive any perspective that seeks to "create fixed categories which claim to be utterly true and objective" (2003: 140).

Among the most prominent postmodernists are Jean-François Lyotard and Jean Baudrillard. Lyotard is most well known for his charge against what he called "metanarratives"—grand stories that aim to explain total phenomena, as Marxism, Freudian psychoanalysis, and liberalism all aim to do. Baudrillard is best known for his work on "simulacra," or the nostalgic attempt to reproduce a past history and society that, in fact, never existed. In Baudrillard's view, the spectacle of Disneyland turns history into a nostalgic commodity to be purchased again and again; reality disappears into an endless repetition of things that never occurred.

Queer Theory Perspectives

Taking up the point of perpetual repetition of something that does not exist, Judith Butler criss-crosses feminism, postmodernism, and queer theory. The queer theory perspective Butler helped create refuses "the commonly assumed distinction between sex and gender, and in dismantling those allegedly causal relations that structure the difference between the two, Butler...foregrounds the 'instability at the very heart of sex'" (Jagose 1996: 90). Rendering clear the instability of "sex" allows sophisticated challenging of social problems that result from accepting the sex/gender model as a "natural" structure. Focusing instead on the manner in which the sex/gender structure functions to support the social problems of sexism, misogyny, and homophobia, queer theory is both an intellectual and a political perspective.

The contributions of Canadian sociologist Aaron Devor are centrally important. His work on gender and sexuality helps people understand the complexities of gender and identity in persons who do not perform gender in "traditional" ways.

Comparing Perspectives

Table 1.2 summarizes and compares the foundational theoretical perspectives, their criticisms, and social policy recommendations as they relate to social problems. Table 1.3 shows the comparative connections of feminist, post-modern, and queer theory. It is important to understand that the contemporary theoretical practices outlined in Table 1.3 often work together in overlapping ways and that each may draw on elements of some, or all, of the foundational theoretical work. In addition, feminist, postmodern, and queer theories are useful in a variety of disciplines outside sociology; as a result, they are very common tools in interdisciplinary discussions of the intersections between science and culture.

■ **Table 1.2** *Comparison of Foundational Theoretical Perspectives*

	Structural-Functionalism	Conflict Theory	Symbolic Interactionism
Representative Theorists	Émile Durkheim Talcott Parsons Robert Merton	Karl Marx C. Wright Mills	George H. Mead Charles Cooley Erving Goffman
Society	Society is a set of inter-related parts; cultural consensus exists and leads to social order; natural state of society—balance and harmony.	Society is marked by power struggles over scarce resources; inequities result in conflict; social change is inevitable; natural state of society—imbalance.	Society is a network of interlocking roles; social order is constructed through interaction as individuals, through shared meaning, make sense out of their social world.
Individuals	Society's institutions socialize individuals; socialization is the process by which social control is exerted; people need society and its institutions.	People are inherently good, but are corrupted by society and its economic structure; groups with power control institutions; "order" is part of the illusion.	Humans are interpretive and interactive; they are constantly changing as their "social beings" emerge and are moulded by changing circumstances.
Cause of Social Problems?	Rapid social change: social disorganization that disrupts the harmony and balance; inadequate socialization, weak institutions, or a combination of these.	Inequality; the dominance of groups of people over other groups of people; oppression and exploitation; competition between groups.	Different interpretations of roles; labelling of individuals, groups, or behaviours as deviant; definition of an objective condition as a social problem.
Social Policy/ Solutions	Repair weak institutions; assure proper socialization; cultivate a strong collective sense of right and wrong.	Minimize competition; create an equitable system for the distribution of resources.	Reduce impact of labelling and associated stigmatization; alter definitions of what is defined as a social problem.
Criticisms	Called "sunshine sociology"; supports the maintenance of the status quo; needs to ask "functional for whom?" Does not deal with issues of power and conflict; incorrectly assumes a consensus.	Utopian model; Marxist states have failed; denies existence of cooperation and equitable exchange. Can't explain cohesion and harmony.	Concentrates on micro issues only; fails to link micro issues to macro-level concerns; too psychological in its approach; assumes label amplifies problem.

■ **Table 1.3** *Comparison of Contemporary Theoretical Perspectives*

	Feminist Theory	Postmodern Theory	Queer Theory
Representative Theorists	Harriet Martineau Dorothy Smith Meg Luxton	Jean Baudrillard Jean-François Lyotard	Judith Butler Michel Foucault Aaron Devor
Society	Society has been measured without accounting for women's contributions or experiences. Women are, however, central actors and agents for change. Feminist work usually combines with other theoretical perspectives.	Rejects the view that societies progress toward their best and most rational potential. Culture is arbitrary. Focuses on internal ruptures, shifts, and perpetual strain/change in any society.	Traditional gender systems benefit a few, powerful groups of elite men and women, but can be dangerous for lesbian, gay, bisexual, and transgendered persons. The devaluation of women is central to homophobia.
Individuals	Challenges the belief in individuals as separate actors; looks at interrelations of persons within and across groups and institutions.	Individuals do not exist as autonomous units. The self is never complete, but always exists only in negotiation with social phenomena around it.	The supposedly private lives of individual persons are actually a very public fixation, governed at multiple, invasive points by law, medicine, and public policy.
Cause of Social Problems?	Separating genders in hierarchized opposition creates potentially dangerous inequalities between men and women with negative consequences across broad social institutions and groups. Women and children are especially vulnerable.	Social problems are not rooted in a single set of causes, but are subject to constantly changing power relations that are especially pervasive and dangerously obscured under globalization. There is no "truth," only claims to truth used to suppress others' agency.	Queer theory developed largely out of the late 1980s response to public panics over HIV and to medical system failures to treat with respect and adequate priority the needs of HIV+ persons, especially gay men. Now asks how sexual identity relates to various problems rooted in oppression and prejudice.
Social Policy/ Solutions	Historical desire for inclusion in liberal institutions of economy, law, and education; challenge policies and institutions that privilege male-centred values and operations.	Reject totalizing objectives; interrogate the use and abuse of knowledge; understand competing knowledge claims by assessing political motivations behind them.	Alter marriage, health, and employment law/policy to include "queer" persons. Remove tacit approval of discriminatory behaviours that threaten the rights of GLBT persons to full citizenship.
Criticisms	Has neglected women from racially, ethnically, and economically marginalized groups. Is not adequately attentive to shared oppressions of women and men in depressed or developing regions.	Is "silly" and jargon-heavy; is a conspiracy to destroy culture; is "against" truth. Even sympathizers may charge it with being overly esoteric and impractical.	Very issues-oriented; subject to internal rifts over authentic and legitimate causes. Poor critique of liberal capitalism; may neglect problems of racism, poverty, and sexism within the groups it seeks to represent.

1.5 Social Problems Research

Research and Methods

The study of social problems is based on research as well as theory. Indeed, research and theory are intricately related. As Wilson (1983) states:

> Most of us think of theorizing as quite divorced from the business of gathering facts. It seems to require an abstractness of thought remote from the practical activity of empirical research. But theory building is not a separate activity within sociology. Without theory, the empirical researcher would find it impossible to decide what to observe, how to observe it, or what to make of the observations. (p. 1)

Most students taking a course in social problems will not become researchers or conduct research on social problems. Nevertheless, we all consume research reported in the media. As consumers of research, we need to understand that our personal experiences and casual observations are less reliable than generalizations based on systematic research. One strength of scientific research is that it is subjected to critical examination by other researchers (see this chapter's *Social Problems Research Up Close* feature). The more you understand how research is done, the better able you will be to critically examine and question research, rather than to passively consume its findings.

The remainder of this section discusses the stages of conducting a research study and the various methods of research used by sociologists. Of critical importance for students and practising sociologists is the need to be aware that the methods we choose can have a strong influence on the conclusions we will generate and the powers our work will serve. Canadian sociologist Dorothy Smith demonstrated, for example, that sociologists' traditional reliance on data produced by other professions—such as medicine, policing, social work, law, and education—produces work that buttresses the powers of those institutions, often to the disadvantage of women and to the detriment of developing knowledge about women's lives.

Stages of Conducting a Research Study

Sociologists progress through various stages in conducting research on a social problem. This section describes the first four stages: formulating a research question, reviewing the literature, defining variables, and formulating a hypothesis.

Formulating a Research Question A research study usually begins with a research question. Where do research questions originate? How does a particular researcher come to ask a particular research question? In some cases, researchers have a personal interest in a specific topic because of their own life experience. Other researchers may ask a particular research question because of their personal values—their concern for humanity and the desire to improve human life. Researchers concerned about the spread of human immunodeficiency virus (HIV) infection may conduct research on such questions as "How does the use of alcohol influence condom use?" and "What

The Sociological Enterprise

Each chapter in this book contains a Social Problems Research Up Close box summarizing a research report or journal article that examines some sociologically significant topic. Some examples of the many journals in sociology are the *Canadian Journal of Sociology, Canadian Review of Sociology and Anthropology, Recherches Sociographiques, Sociologie et Sociétés,* and *Cahiers de Sociologie.* Journal articles are the primary means by which sociologists, as well as other scientists, exchange ideas and information. Most journal articles begin with an *introduction* and *review of the literature*. It is here that the author examines previous research on the topic, identifies specific research areas, and otherwise sets the article up for the reader. It is often in this section that research hypotheses, if applicable, are set forth. A researcher, for example, might hypothesize that the primary social concerns of Canadian adolescents vary on the basis of sex.

The next major section of a standard sociological research article is entitled *sample and methods*. In this section, the author describes the characteristics of the sample, if any, and the details of the type of research conducted. The type of data analysis used is also presented in this section. Using the above research question, a sociologist working on secondary analysis might obtain data from the Project Teen Canada Surveys. Conducted by Canadian sociologist Reginald Bibby, these national surveys of youth aged 15 to 19 have taken place since 1984 at regular intervals.

The final section of a journal article includes the *findings and conclusions*. The findings of a study describe the results—that is, what the researcher found as a result of the investigation. Findings are then discussed within the context of the hypotheses and the conclusions that can be drawn. Other research results are presented in tabular form. Reading tables carefully is an important part of drawing accurate conclusions about the research hypotheses. In reading a table, you should follow the steps below (see the table on the next page):

1. *Read the title of the table and make sure that you understand what the table contains*. The title of the table indicates the unit of analysis (high school students), the dependent variable (social concerns), the independent variable (sex), and what the numbers represent (percentages).

2. *Read the information provided at the bottom of the table, including the source and any other explanatory information*. For example, the information at the bottom of this table indicates that the data are from the Project Teen Canada 2000 survey and that the sample was restricted to Canadians 15 to 19 years old in grades 10 to 12 across Canada, including CEGEP I's in Quebec.

3. *Examine the row and column headings*. This table looks at the social concerns that were identified as "very serious" by male and female teenagers in Canada.

4. *Thoroughly examine the data contained within the table, carefully looking for patterns*. As indicated in the table, there is a general tendency for far more female than male teenagers to see any "person-related" issue as serious. For example, child abuse is seen as "very serious" by 66 percent of females but just 44 percent of males. Similar large differences can be noted in relation to AIDS, violence in schools, teenage suicide, drugs, discrimination, violence against women, poverty, crime, and youth gangs. However, the differences between male and female teenagers are minor in relation to "institutional-related issues," such as the environment, American influence, the economy, the threat of nuclear war, lack of Canadian unity, and Native–white and French–English relations.

educational strategies are effective for increasing safer sex behaviour?" Researchers may also want to test a particular sociological theory, or some aspect of it, to establish its validity or conduct studies to evaluate the effect of a social policy or program. Community groups and social activist organizations may form research questions based on specific concerns in collaboration with academic researchers. Government and industry also hire researchers to answer questions about policy needs and marketing interests.

5. *Use the information you have gathered in step 4 to address the hypotheses.* Clearly, young women are much more likely than young men to express concern about social issues that have a strong person-centred emphasis. When more abstract, structurally related social concerns are raised, however, male teenagers match or exceed female teenagers in their identification of the issue as "very serious."

6. *Draw conclusions consistent with the information presented.* From the table can we conclude that a "compassion gap" exists between male and female teenagers in Canada? Can we conclude, as some have, that "[y]oung females are far more caring, sympathetic, and responsive towards people in general and the disprivileged in particular" (Bibby and Posterski 1992: 141)? Although the data may imply it, it would be premature to reach such a conclusion. More information, from a variety of sources, is needed. The use of multiple methods and approaches to study a social phenomenon is called triangulation.

Primary Social Concerns of Canadian High School Students,* by Gender

	% Viewing as "Very Serious"		
	Nationally	Males	Females
The environment	54%	48%	60%
Child abuse	51	42	59
Teenage suicide	46	36	55
Racial discrimination	45	38	51
Drugs	42	38	47
Violence in schools	42	33	51
Poverty	41	35	46
Violence against women	39	31	46
Crime	38	32	44
AIDS	38	34	42
Bullying	34	26	41
Unequal treatment of women	34	26	40
Youth gangs	33	30	36
Terrorism	31	29	32
American Influence	24	24	24
The Economy	23	24	22
Aboriginal–white relations	21	21	21
Lack of Canadian Unity	19	20	18
French–English relations	16	17	15

*The Project Teen Canada 2008 sample was comprised of Canadians, 15 to 19 years old, in grades 10 to 12 across Canada, including CEGEP I's in Quebec.
SOURCE: Bibby, Reginald W., The Project Teen Canada 2008 National Survey.

Reviewing the Literature After a research question is formulated, the researcher reviews the published material on the topic to find out the state of knowledge on the topic. Reviewing the literature also provides ideas about how to conduct research and helps investigators formulate new research questions. A literature review also serves as an evaluation tool, allowing a comparison of research findings and other sources of information, such as expert opinions, political claims, and journalistic reports.

variable

Any measurable event, characteristic, or property that varies or is subject to change.

operational definition

In research, a definition of a variable that specifies how that variable is to be measured (or was measured) in the research.

hypothesis

A prediction or educated guess about how one variable is related to another variable.

dependent variable

The variable that the researcher wants to explain.

independent variable

The variable that is expected to explain change in the dependent variable.

experiment

A research method that involves manipulating the independent variable to determine how it affects the dependent variable.

control group

A group that is *not exposed* to the influences or variables whose effects we want to measure on a given group.

Defining Variables A **variable** is any measurable event, characteristic, or property that varies or is subject to change. Researchers must operationally define the variables they study. An **operational definition** specifies how to measure a variable. For example, an operational definition of the variable "religiosity" might be the number of times the respondent reports going to church or synagogue. Another operational definition of "religiosity" might be the respondent's answer to the question, "How important is religion in your life? (1 = not important, 2 = somewhat important, 3 = very important)."

Operational definitions are particularly important for defining variables that cannot be directly observed. For example, researchers cannot directly observe concepts such as "mental illness," "sexual harassment," "child neglect," "job satisfaction," and "drug abuse." Nor can researchers directly observe perceptions, values, and attitudes.

Formulating a Hypothesis After defining the research variables, researchers formulate a **hypothesis**, which is a prediction or educated guess about how one variable is related to another variable. The **dependent variable** is the variable that the researcher wants to explain; that is, it is the variable of interest. The independent variable is the variable that is expected to explain change in the dependent variable. In formulating a hypothesis, the researcher predicts how the **independent variable** affects the dependent variable. For example, Mouw and Xie (1999) hypothesized that fluent bilingual children have higher levels of academic achievement than children who are English-only fluent; however, their analysis found "no evidence that fluent bilinguals do better than students who are fluent only in English" (p. 250). In this example, the independent variable is bilingualism and the dependent variable is school achievement. The status of a variable is not eternal. For example, in a study on quality of health in adults, school achievement may be the independent variable and quality of health will be the dependent variable, influenced by levels of education achieved.

Researchers often assess the effects of several independent variables on one or more dependent variables. For example, Jekielek (1998) examined the impact of parental conflict and marital disruption (two independent variables) on the emotional well-being of children (the dependent variable). Jekielek found that both parental conflict and marital disruption (separation or divorce) negatively affect children's emotional well-being. However, children in high-conflict intact families exhibit lower levels of well-being than children who have experienced high levels of parental conflict, but whose parents divorce or separate.

Methods of Data Collection

After identifying a research topic, reviewing the literature, and developing hypotheses, researchers decide which method of data collection to use. Alternatives include experiments, surveys, field research, and secondary data.

Experiments An **experiment** involves manipulating the independent variable to determine how it affects the dependent variable. It requires one or more experimental groups exposed to the experimental treatment(s) and an unexposed **control group**. After the researcher randomly assigns participants to either an experimental or a control group, she or he measures the dependent variable. The experimental groups are exposed to the treatment, and then the researcher measures the dependent variable again. If participants have been randomly assigned to the different groups, it suggests that any difference in the dependent variable among the groups is due to the effect of the independent variable.

Here is an example of a social problems experiment on poverty: providing welfare payments to one group of unemployed single mothers (experimental group) and no such payments to another group of unemployed single mothers (control group). The independent variable is welfare payments; the dependent variable is employment status. The researcher might hypothesize that mothers in the experimental group would be less likely to have a job after 12 months than mothers in the control group. An ethics review board would be needed to determine whether the risks of such a study were justifiable.

The major strength of the experimental method is that it provides evidence for causal relationships—that is, how one variable affects another. A primary weakness is that experiments are often conducted on small samples, usually in artificial laboratory settings; this may mean that the findings may not be generalizable to people in natural settings.

Surveys Survey research involves eliciting information from respondents through questions. An important part of survey research is selecting a sample of those to be questioned. A **sample** is a portion of the population, selected to be representative so that the information from the sample can be generalized to a larger population. For example, instead of asking all abused spouses about their experience, the researcher asks a representative sample of them and assumes that those not questioned would give similar responses. After selecting a representative sample, survey researchers either interview people, ask them to complete written questionnaires, or elicit responses to research questions via computer.

1. *Interviews.* In interview research, trained interviewers ask respondents a series of questions and make written notes about or tape-record the respondents' answers. Interviews may be conducted over the telephone or face to face. One advantage of interview research is that researchers can clarify questions for the respondent and follow up on answers to particular questions. Researchers often conduct face-to-face interviews with groups of individuals who might otherwise be inaccessible. For example, research on women who work as exotic dancers can be difficult to complete because of negative stigma associated with the work. To develop a nuanced theory to explain women's experiences of their work as strippers, Chris Bruckert conducted in-depth interviews with 15 women who had worked for at least a year in the Montreal strip clubs. Her book, *Taking It Off, Putting It On*, provides a Marxist-feminist analysis of the work that she classifies as a unique "insider text" (2002: 10). An insider text does not treat subjects as a means to an end, but seeks to provide a voice for otherwise silenced groups.

   The most serious disadvantages of interview research are cost and the lack of privacy and anonymity. Respondents may feel embarrassed or threatened when asked questions that relate to personal issues such as drug use, domestic violence, and sexual behaviour. As a result, some respondents may choose not to participate in interview research on sensitive topics. Those who do participate may conceal or alter information or give socially desirable answers to the interviewer's questions. A well-trained interviewer will be able to structure interviews to minimize opportunities for successful deception.

2. *Questionnaires.* Instead of conducting personal or phone interviews, researchers may develop questionnaires that they either mail or give to a sample of respondents. Questionnaire research offers the advantages of being less expensive and time consuming than face-to-face or telephone surveys. It also

survey research
A method of research that involves eliciting information from respondents through questions; includes interviews (telephone or face-to-face) and written questionnaires.

sample
In survey research, the portion of the population selected to be questioned.

provides privacy and anonymity to the research participants. This characteristic reduces the likelihood that people will feel threatened or embarrassed when asked personal questions and increases the likelihood that they will provide answers that are not intentionally inaccurate or distorted.

The major disadvantage of mail questionnaires is that it is difficult to obtain an adequate response rate. Many people do not want to take the time or make the effort to complete and mail a questionnaire. Others may be unable to read and understand the questionnaire.

3. *"Talking" computers.* A new method of conducting survey research is to have respondents provide answers to a computer that "talks." Romer and colleagues (1997) found that respondents rated computer interviews about sexual issues more favourably than face-to-face interviews and that the former were more reliable. Such increased reliability may be particularly valuable when conducting research on drug use, stigmatized sexual behaviours, and sexual orientation.

field research

A method of research that involves observing and studying social behaviour in settings in which it naturally occurs; includes participant observation and nonparticipant observation.

Field Research **Field research** involves observing and studying social behaviour in settings in which the behaviour occurs naturally. Two types of field research are participant observation and nonparticipant observation.

In participant observation research, the researcher takes part in the phenomenon being studied to obtain an insider's perspective of the people and/or behaviour being observed. John Stackhouse (1999), a middle-class, white male journalist, spent a week living on the streets of Toronto after having spent eight years living among the poor in India. Stackhouse was criticized as a dilettante, but his method, however briefly employed, allowed him greater access to understanding than simple interviews would have. In nonparticipant observation research, the researcher observes the phenomenon being studied without actively taking part in the group or the activity. For example, Dordick (1997) studied homelessness by observing and talking with homeless individuals in a variety of settings, but she did not live as a homeless person as part of her research.

The main advantage of field research on social problems is that it provides detailed information about the values, rituals, norms, behaviours, symbols, beliefs, and emotions of those being studied. A potential problem with field research is that the researcher's observations may be biased (e.g., the researcher becomes too involved in the group to be objective). In addition, because field research typically relies on small samples, it is less suited to generalization.

Secondary Data Research Sometimes, researchers analyze secondary data: data already collected by other researchers or government agencies, or that exist in forms such as historical documents, police reports, school records, and official records of marriages, births, and deaths. A major advantage of using secondary data is that the data are readily accessible, so researchers avoid the time and expense of collecting their own data. Secondary data are also often based on large representative samples. The disadvantage of secondary data is that the researcher is limited to already available data, often collected for a purpose different from those of the researcher.

1.6 Goals of the Text

This text approaches the study of social problems with several goals in mind:

1. *To provide an integrated theoretical background.* This text reflects an integrative theoretical approach to the study of social problems. More than one

theoretical perspective can be used to explain a social problem because social problems usually have multiple causes.

2. *To develop an understanding that theories and methods can be extremely useful to one research project but not to another.* Many of the contemporary theories discussed in this book developed to meet specific needs not addressed adequately by the foundational perspectives. Nonetheless, contemporary theory may borrow from or develop principles from any of the foundational theories to meet the needs of research task at hand. Knowing your research goals and needs, and developing a theoretical account rather than forcing a problem into a pre-set theory, is an important value and skill for contemporary thinkers.

3. *To encourage development of a sociological imagination.* A major insight of the sociological perspective is that various structural and cultural elements of society have far-reaching effects on individual lives and societal well-being. This insight, known as the sociological imagination, enables us to understand how social forces underlie personal misfortunes and failures, and also contribute to personal successes and achievements. Each chapter emphasizes how structural and cultural factors contribute to social problems, encouraging you to develop your sociological imagination by recognizing how structural and cultural factors influence private troubles and public issues.

4. *To provide global coverage of social problems.* The modern world is often referred to as a "global village." Understanding social problems requires an awareness of how global trends and policies affect social problems. Many social problems call for collective action involving countries around the world; efforts to end poverty, protect the environment, and reduce the spread of HIV are some of the social problems that have been addressed at the global level. Each chapter includes coverage of global aspects of social problems. We hope that this attention to the global aspects of social problems will broaden students' awareness of pressing world issues.

5. *To provide opportunities to assess personal beliefs and attitudes.* Each chapter contains a section called *Self and Society*, which offers an opportunity to assess your attitudes and beliefs regarding some aspect of the social problem discussed. Earlier in this chapter, the *Self and Society* feature allowed you to assess your beliefs about a number of social problems and compare your beliefs with a national sample of Canadians.

6. *To emphasize the human side of social problems.* Each chapter contains a feature called *The Human Side*, which illustrates how social problems have affected individual lives. By conveying the private pain and personal triumphs associated with social problems, we hope to elicit a level of understanding and compassion that may not be attained through the academic study of social problems alone. *The Human Side* in this chapter presents stories about how students, disturbed by various social conditions, have engaged in social activism.

7. *To encourage students to take positive social action.* Individuals who understand the factors that contribute to social problems may be better able to formulate interventions to remedy those problems. Recognizing the personal pain and public costs associated with social problems encourages some to initiate social intervention.

Student Activism

Some people believe that to promote social change one must be in a position of political power, and/or have large financial resources. However, the most important prerequisite for becoming actively involved in improving levels of social well-being may be genuine concern and dedication to a social "cause." The following vignettes provide a sampler of student activism—students making a difference in the world.

- In May 1989, hundreds of Chinese university students protested in Tiananmen Square in Beijing, China, because Chinese government officials would not meet with them to hear their pleas for a democratic government. These students boycotted classes and started a hunger strike. On June 4, 1989, thousands of students and other protesters were massacred or arrested in Tiananmen Square. Their efforts resulted in more transparency in government and greater access to information from outside China.

- In October 1969, less than four months after the "Stonewall Riots" in New York (an event that marked the symbolic beginning of the gay liberation movement) (Goldie 2001), the first meeting of the first gay liberation organization in Canada, the University of Toronto Homophile Association (UTHA), convened. In 1970, a group of eight gay students perceived the need for an organization to assist gays living in a heterosexual-dominated world: they formed Waterloo Universities' Gay Liberation Movement (WUGLM), a group encompassing both the University of Waterloo and Wilfrid Laurier University. In the autumn of 1971 in Saskatoon, the Gay Students Alliance became the first gay group in Saskatchewan. The following year, Gay McGill (originally GAY) became the first anglophone gay organization in Quebec. The costs of student activism at this time and on this issue were often steep. Now, however, organizations for gay, lesbian, bisexual, and transgendered (GLBT) people are common on most campuses.

- On December 6, 1989, the largest mass shooting in Canada occurred when 25-year-old Marc Lepine, armed with a semiautomatic rifle, knives, and bandoliers of ammunition, entered the École Polytechnique in Montreal and killed 14 female students and wounded 13 other students (9 women and 4 men). His rampage, which deliberately targeted women, ended with his suicide. In his suicide note, Lepine wrote: "I have decided to send the feminists, who have always ruined my life, to their maker.... I have decided to put an end to these viragos." The massacre, which occurred in the Polytechnique's engineering building, prompted the Canadian government to proclaim December 6 the National Day of Remembrance and Action on Violence Against Women. Since 1989, students across Canada have held annual commemorative events honouring the women killed and promoting an end to violence in all forms. For example, in Nova Scotia, a Purple Ribbon campaign pays tribute to the murdered women, attempts to raise public awareness of violence against women, and collects donations to benefit transition houses for abused women and their children. The group Men for Change also formed in response to the tragedy. Its purpose is to work toward an end to violence.

- In the early 1970s, U.S. citizen activist Ralph Nader launched PIRGs (Public Interest Research Groups) as a means of harnessing

People can make a difference in society by the choices we make. We may choose to vote for one candidate over another, demand the right to reproductive choice or protest government policies that permit it, drive drunk or stop a friend from driving drunk, repeat a racist or sexist joke or chastise the person who tells it, and practise safe sex or risk the transmission of sexually transmitted diseases. Individuals can also make a difference by addressing social concerns in their occupational role, as well as through volunteer work.

Although individual choices have an important impact, collective social action often has a more pervasive effect. For example, in 1971, engineer Jim

the energy and talent of students in solving social problems. Today, there are more than 200 PIRG chapters in the United States and 19 in Canada (3 in British Columbia, 1 in Nova Scotia, 4 in Quebec, and 11 in Ontario) funded through voluntary student fees. The goals of PIRGs are to motivate civic participation and responsibility by encouraging individuals to become informed, concerned, and active in their communities; to recognize and pursue integrative analyses of societal and environmental issues; to respect and encourage local and global ecosystem integrity; to encourage diversity and social equality for all people by opposing all forms of oppression; to work in a cooperative way, employing a consensual decision-making process; and to work in solidarity with other like-minded environmental and social justice movements. PIRGs in Canada have produced a variety of issue-oriented publications and audio-visual materials on such topics as the food industry, acid rain, nuclear power, tenant rights, Ontario Hydro, freedom of information, and the management of toxic waste. Students Against Sweatshops–Canada (SAS–C), formed after a student net-working conference held at the University of Toronto in 1999, often works through PIRGs (Campuslife 2002).

- In Canada, Britain, and the United States, students have increasingly challenged campus–corporate partnership. "Whether it's bankers on the board of governors, corporate-endowed professorships or the naming of campus buildings after benefactors, all are facing scrutiny from a more economically politicized student body" (Klein 2000: 405).

- The Canadian Federation of Students, founded in 1981, is a cooperative alliance of more than 60 students' unions representing over 450 000 Canadian college and university students. It has declared February 6 a "day of action" to protest the soaring costs of postsecondary education in Canada. On that date in 2002, events were held in more than 70 communities across Canada, including St. John's, Halifax, Charlottetown, Toronto, Windsor, Thunder Bay, Winnipeg, Regina, Vancouver, and Victoria (Canadian Federation of Students Newswire 2002).

Students interested in becoming involved in student activism, or who are already involved, might explore the website for Campusactivism.org—an organization that supports social justice activism and investigative journalism on campuses. These organizations recognize that students and faculty, as part of an "affluent conscience constituency" (Carroll 1997: 11), have long played a critical role in larger social movements for social justice: these include the Civil Rights movement, the anti–Vietnam War movement, the anti-Apartheid movement, the women's rights movement, and the environmental movement (Axelrod 1990, 1995; Eyerman and Jamison 1991).

SOURCES: Axelrod, Paul. 1990. *Making a Middle Class: Student Life in English Canada During the Thirties*. Montreal and Kingston: McGill-Queen's University Press; Axelrod, Paul. 1995. "Spying on the Young in Depression and War: Students, Youth Groups and the RCMP, 1935–1942," *Labour/Le Travail 35*, Spring: 43–63; Canadian Federation of Students Newswire. 2002. "Students Declare February 6 Day of Action." (4 February). http://action.web.ca; Carroll, William K. 1997. "Social Movements and Counterhegemony: Canadian Contexts and Social Theories." In *Organizing Dissent: Contemporary Social Movements in Theory and Practice*, edited by William K. Carroll, pp. 3–38. Toronto: Garamond Press; Eyerman, R., and A. Jamison. 1991. *Social Movements: A Cognitive Approach*, Cambridge: Polity Press; Goldie, Terry. 2001. "Queer Nation?" In *In a Queer Country: Gay & Lesbian Studies in the Canadian Context*, edited by Terry Goldie, pp. 7–26. Vancouver: Arsenal Pulp Press; Klein, Naomi. 2000. *No Logo: Taking Aim at the Brand Bullies*. Toronto: Vintage Canada.

Bohlen, lawyer Irving Stone, and law student Paul Cote formed the Greenpeace Foundation in Vancouver to protest U.S. nuclear tests at Amchitka. In their first direct action, the 11 members of the Greenpeace Foundation set sail in a chartered trawler boat into the bomb testing range. In doing so, they attracted the interest of Canadians living downwind of the test site. The issue subsequently came before the U.S. Supreme Court; four additional tests that had been planned at Amchitka were cancelled. Since that time, Greenpeace has continued in its pursuit of "a moratorium on all those things poisoning us" and become one of the largest environmental groups in the world, with offices in several countries. As Bohlen remarked: "As individuals we are weak. Our strength is created by putting ourselves at risk" (in Nader et al. 1993: 100).

Schwalbe (1998) reminds us that we do not have to join a group or organize a protest to make changes in the world.

> We can change a small part of the social world single-handedly. If we treat others with more respect and compassion, if we refuse to participate in re-creating inequalities even in little ways, if we raise questions about official representation of reality, if we refuse to work in destructive industries, then we are making change (p. 206).

Understanding Social Problems

At the end of each chapter to follow we offer a section entitled *Understanding*, in which we re-emphasize the social origin of the problem being discussed, the consequences, and the alternative social solutions. It is our hope that you will end each chapter with a "sociological imagination" view of the problem and how, as a society, we might approach a solution.

Sociologists have been studying social problems since the Industrial Revolution in the nineteenth century. Industrialization brought about massive social changes: the influence of religion declined; families became smaller and moved from traditional, rural communities to urban settings. These and other changes have been associated with increases in crime, pollution, divorce, and juvenile delinquency. As these social problems became more widespread, the need to understand their origins and possible solutions became more urgent. The field of sociology developed in response to this urgency. Social problems provided the initial impetus for the development of the field of sociology and continue to be a major focus of sociology.

There is no single agreed-upon definition of what constitutes a social problem. Most sociologists agree, however, that all social problems share two important elements: an objective social condition and a subjective interpretation of that condition. Each of the three traditional theoretical perspectives in sociology—structural-functionalist, conflict, and symbolic interactionist—has its own notion of the causes, consequences, and solutions of social problems.

Critical Thinking

1. People increasingly use information technologies as a means of getting their daily news. Research indicates that news on the internet is beginning to replace television news as the primary source of information among computer users (see Chapter 13). What role do the media play in your awareness of social problems? If fewer and fewer corporations control more of our media, how do you think that can shape your understanding of what is and what is not a social problem?

2. Everyone occupies several social statuses, each with its own expectation of role performance—that is, what you should and should not do given the position. List five statuses you occupy, the expectations of their accompanying roles, and any role conflict that may result. What types of social problems are affected by role conflict?

3. Choose a social problem of your own and explain what makes it a problem, not just a neutral fact. Choose two or three from among the foundational and contemporary theories to think about your social problem and note the different kinds of focus you can achieve with each one. See if you can productively combine a foundational with a contemporary theory.

"Is It True?" Quiz: Answers

1 = true; 2 = true; 3 = true; 4 = false; 5 = true

Section 1

Problems of Well-Being

Section 1 deals with problems frequently regarded as private rather than public issues; that is, they are viewed as internally caused or seen as a function of individual free will. People often respond to these problems by assuming that the problem is the fault of the victims—that in some way they have freely chosen their plight. In this set of problems, blame is most often attached to the individuals themselves. Thus, the physically and mentally ill (Chapter 2), the alcoholic and the drug addict (Chapter 3), the criminal and the delinquent (Chapter 4), and the divorced person and the child abuser (Chapter 5) are thought to be bad, weak, immoral, or somehow different from the average person. Consider the following scenarios:

A woman with a limited income decides not to fill an expensive prescription in order to be able to feed her children—she cannot afford both. When her condition worsens, she is blamed for failing to follow her doctor's orders to fill the prescription. A sociological view will observe that the woman did not want to be sick, but rather chose the least of several unfortunate alternatives. In this case, factors that make her condition worse than it might have otherwise been include poverty, the costs of medication not covered by government plans, and a value system that stresses parental responsibility and sacrifice. Had she chosen to fill the prescription, she would risk blame for failures as a parent.

A teenage boy from an urban lower-class neighbourhood begins to sell drugs rather than stay in school or get a regular job. Such a teenager is generally viewed as being "weak" or having "low" morals. Sociologists will instead take account of the class-based context in which an individual with few alternatives seeks to acquire the goods that herald success in a society that places central value on personal wealth. Raised in an environment where the most successful role models are often criminals, legitimate opportunities are few, and peer pressure to use and sell drugs is strong, what are his choices? He can pump gas or serve fast food for minimum wage, or he can sell drugs for thousands of dollars a week.

A student drinks alcohol daily and often cuts classes. Although the public views such behaviour as a personal weakness, sociologists emphasize the role of the individual's socialization and society. For example, a disproportionate number of individuals with drinking problems were reared in homes where one or both parents drank heavily. In the general culture, media portrayals of drinking as desirable, fun, glamorous, and a source of status further promote drinking. Student culture itself often emphasizes bars and drinking parties as primary sources of recreation and affiliation.

A mother comes home from work and finds her children playing and the house in disorder. She decides they need to be beaten with a spoon because of their disobedience. How can we best explain and remedy such behaviour? Repeated research shows that a history of being abused as a child is the strongest independent predictor of who will become a child abuser as an adult. Additionally, myriad socially powerful beliefs contribute to child abuse; these include the acceptance of corporal punishment of children and ambiguity on what constitutes appropriate discipline, the persistence of laws that protect the "right" of parents to use "reasonable force" to physically punish children, and the historical and lingering belief that children are property. To change the behaviour of each individually enraged parent requires that we alter societal beliefs about the punishment of children.

These examples illustrate that many behaviours result more from social factors than from individual choice. To the degree that individuals do make choices, these choices are socially determined—the structure and culture of society limit and influence individual choices. For example, customers in a restaurant cannot choose anything they want to eat; they are limited to what is on the menu. Sociologically, one's social status—male, female, young, old, rich, poor, able-bodied, differently abled—determines one's menu of life choices.

In each of the prior examples, the alternatives present for individuals are limited by the social structure of society and by the cultural and subcultural definitions of appropriate behaviour. While the sociological theories we address throughout this text take different approaches to understanding the problems identified previously, all would agree that problems that at first glance appear to be concerns of individuals are really the result of larger social factors. Society, rather than the individual, is then the primary context in which problems arise and also the primary source of the solutions to those problems. In this and the following sections, we emphasize the importance of the social structure and culture of society as the sources of and the solutions to social problems.

Illness and Health Care

Outline

Is It True?

1. In 2006, the life expectancy at birth of Canadian males exceeded that of females.

2. Worldwide, the predominant mode of HIV transmission is through heterosexual contact.

3. One in five Canadians will be affected by a mental illness at some time in their lives.

4. Lower education levels are associated with higher rates of health problems and mortality.

5. The leading cause of death for youth in Canada is a childhood cancer such as leukemia or osteosarcoma.

Read more here: 1 = p. 35, 2 = p. 39, 3 = p. 45, 4 = p. 55, 5 = p. 36
Answers can be found on p. 69.

© David De Lossy/Getty Images

Over the past 150 years the world has changed in extraordinary ways. Thomas Edison harnessed electricity; Renault built the first motor car; steam engines gave way to high-speed monorail trains and daguerreotype images developed into digital photography; the Wright brothers' first successful flight paved the way for space exploration; and computer memory that had once required whole buildings for storage now fits on microchips the size of fingernail. One of the most profound changes over the last century had been the increase in the average length of life. Since the end of World War II, longevity of life in most developed and developing countries has increased by almost 25 years—the greatest increase seen in the history of humankind (LaPorte 1997). For those in developed nations these life expectancy predictions have remained relatively stable into the twenty-first century.

Despite overall improvements in living conditions and medical care, health problems and health care delivery are major concerns of individuals, families, communities, and nations. In this chapter, we review health concerns in Canada and throughout the world. The World Health Organization (1946) defines **health** as "a state of complete physical, mental, and social well-being" (p. 3). Sociologists are concerned with how social forces affect and are affected by health and illness, why some social groups suffer more illness than others, and how illness affects individuals' sense of identity and relationships with others. Sociologists also examine health-care systems and explore how these systems can be improved.

2.1 The Global Context: Patterns of Health and Disease

The study of patterns of health and disease is called **epidemiology**. The field of epidemiology incorporates several disciplines, including public health, medicine, biology, and sociology. An **epidemiologist** studies the social origins and distribution of health problems in a population and how patterns of health and disease vary among and within societies. In this chapter, we also look at global patterns of morbidity, longevity, mortality, and disease burden.

Patterns of Morbidity

Morbidity refers to acute and chronic illnesses and diseases and the symptoms and impairments they produce. An **acute condition** is short term; by definition, it can last no more than three months. A **chronic condition** is a long-term health problem. The rate of serious morbidity in a population provides one measure of the health of that population. Morbidity may be measured according to the incidence and prevalence of specific illnesses and diseases. **Incidence** refers to the number of new cases of a specific health problem within a given population during a specified period. **Prevalence** refers to the total number of cases of a specific health problem within a population at a given time. For example, in 2007 there were 2.5 million people newly infected with HIV worldwide—of whom 420 000 were children and roughly half were women. In the same year, the worldwide prevalence of HIV was 33.2 million, and there were 2.1 million deaths due to AIDS ("Global Summary of the HIV/AIDS Epidemic"

health
A state of complete physical, mental, and social well-being.

epidemiology
The study of the distribution of disease within a population.

epidemiologist
A scientist who studies the social origins and distribution of health problems in a population and how patterns of illness and disease vary between and within societies.

morbidity
The amount of disease, impairment, and accidents in a population.

acute condition
A health condition that can last no more than three months.

chronic condition
A long-term health problem, such as a disease or impairment.

incidence
The number of new cases of a specific health problem within a given population during a specified period.

prevalence
The total number of cases of a condition within a population that exist at a given time.

2007). Since HIV notification to the Public Health Agency of Canada (PHAC) began in 1985 there have been 62 561 positive cases reported (Health Canada 2007); 19 828 AIDS diagnoses were reported from 1979 to 2004 (Health Canada 2005a: 34). In the same time period, 14 708 deaths were reported (p. 64). The death numbers are higher than reported: social stigma and the pre-2003 absence of policy requiring the reporting of positive HIV test results and AIDS-related deaths reduce the numbers in the PHAC reports. We are also learning that many persons infected with HIV face co-morbidity, with higher rates of both tuberculosis and hepatitis C infections than in the general population. Indeed, in the global population of HIV-positive persons, tuberculosis is the leading cause of death (Health Canada 2007: 133).

If we try to understand the transmission of infection and disease purely as matters of biology, we miss the key social reasons that place particular groups of people at greater risk for infection and death due to infectious disease. As we discuss later in this chapter, patterns of morbidity vary according to material social factors including social class, education, sex, and race. Morbidity patterns also vary according to a society's level of development and the age structure of the population. In developing nations, malnutrition, pneumonia, and parasitic and infectious diseases such as HIV/AIDS, malaria (transmitted by mosquitoes), tetanus, rabies, and measles are major health concerns. In the industrialized world, advances in sanitation, immunizations, and antibiotics have largely controlled infectious and parasitic diseases. However, common overuse of antibiotics in industrialized countries has contributed to a rise in infectious disease, as antibiotics kill the weaker disease-causing germs while allowing variants resistant to the drugs to flourish. Antibiotic resistance, combined with changes in sexual behaviours, is resulting in an increase in Canada of bacterial sexually transmitted infections, including syphilis strains resistant to antibiotic treatment (Health Canada 2002: 22 fn14). Worldwide, the most alarming consequence of the development of drug-resistant germs is the resurgence of tuberculosis, which kills more people yearly than any other infectious disease. Tuberculosis is caused by bacilli that attack and destroy lung tissue; it is spread when infected individuals cough or sneeze. The World Health Organization estimates that one-third of the world's population is infected, although only about 10 percent of infected persons ever develop symptoms (Weitz 2001).

It is not only infectious disease that is influenced by social factors. Noninfectious diseases, such as heart disease, cancer, mental disorders, and respiratory diseases, pose the greatest health threat to the industrialized world.

epidemiological transition

The shift from a society characterized by low life expectancy and parasitic and infectious diseases to one characterized by high life expectancy and chronic and degenerative diseases.

The shift from a society characterized by low life expectancy and parasitic and infectious diseases to one characterized by high life expectancy and chronic and degenerative diseases is called **epidemiological transition**. As societies make the epidemiological transition, diseases that need time to develop, such as cancer, heart disease, Alzheimer's disease, arthritis, and osteoporosis, become more common, and childhood illnesses, typically caused by infectious and parasitic diseases, become less common.

life expectancy

The average number of years that a person born in a given year can expect to live.

Patterns of Longevity

One indicator of the health of a population is the average number of years that individuals born in a given year can expect to live, referred to as **life expectancy**.

■ **Table 2.1** *Countries with the Longest and Shortest Life Expectancies at Birth, 2005–10*

Lowest Life Expectancies		Highest Life Expectancies	
Country	Life Expectancy	Country	Life Expectancy
Afghanistan	43.8	Japan	82.7
Zimbabwe	44.1	China, Hong Kong SAR	82.2
Zambia	45.2	Switzerland	81.8
Lesotho	45.3	Iceland	81.8
Swaziland	45.8	Australia	81.5
Angola	46.8	France	81.2
Central African Republic	46.9	Italy	81.2
Sierra Leone	47.4	Sweden	80.9
Dem. Republic of the Congo	47.5	Spain	80.9
Guinea-Bissau	47.6	Israel	80.7

Note: Only countries or areas with 100 000 persons or more in 2009 are included.

SOURCE: Adapted from United Nations Population Division, 2006. *World Population Prospects: The 2006 Revision, Highlights,* Table A 17, page 80, available at http://www.un.org/esa/population/publications/wpp2006/WPP2006_Highlights_rev.pdf.

Worldwide, life expectancy has increased dramatically over the last 50 years. However, between and within societies, wide disparities exist in life expectancy. "Japan was the first country to attain an average lifespan of over 80 years—more than double that of many less-developed countries" (Ash 2001: 57). In 2000, Japan had the longest life expectancy: 81 years. In the same year, life expectancy was less than 50 in several countries (see Table 2.1). In Canada, a female born in 2002 could expect to live 83.2 years; a man, 76.3 years (Ash 2001: 53).

Patterns of Mortality

Rates of **mortality**, or death—especially those of infants, children, and women—provide sensitive indicators of a population's health. Worldwide, the leading cause of death is infectious and parasitic diseases (World Health Organization 1998). In Canada, the leading causes of death for both women and men are cardiovascular diseases and cancer. In 1999, over one-third of deaths (36 percent) were due to diseases of the circulatory system (e.g., ischaemic heart disease and cerebrovascular diseases) while malignant neoplasms, or cancers, accounted for 28 percent of all deaths (Statistics Canada 2002).

In this chapter, we discuss how patterns of mortality are related to social factors, such as social class, sex, and education. Mortality rates also vary by age. For example, it is only among 15- to 19-year-olds that rates for external causes of death (e.g., suicide, motor vehicle and other types of accidents) are higher than rates for non-external causes of death (deaths arising from physiological processes). Among Canadian youth aged 15 to 19, these external

mortality
Death.

factors account for the two most common causes of death. Motor-vehicle accidents are the leading cause of death for both males and females in this age group (responsible for about 4 in 10 deaths). Suicide remains the second leading cause of death among teenagers 15 to 19 (see Table 2.2). Cancer is the third leading cause of death, while the fourth most common cause of death is homicide. Table 2.2 shows some modest fluctuation in natural causes of death from 2004 to 2005 but the leading four causes of death remain stable, indicating that it is overwhelmingly the case that the greatest threat to young people's health comes from external accidental trauma or deliberate violence. Indeed, the leading causes of death in the top four categories have remained stable over the course of the last decade. That two of the four leading causes of death for youth aged 15 to 19 are the result of violence presents a rather

■ **Table 2.2** *Leading Causes of Death, Total Population, by Age Group and Sex, Canada, Annual*

Place of Residence[1,2]	Age at Time of Death[3]	Sex	Leading Causes of Death (ICD-10)[4,5,6]	Characteristics	2004	2005
Canada	15 to 19 years	Both sexes	Malignant neoplasms [C00-C97]	Rank of leading causes of death[7]	3	3
Canada	15 to 19 years	Both sexes	Diabetes mellitus [E10-E14]	Rank of leading causes of death[7]	10	9
Canada	15 to 19 years	Both sexes	Diseases of heart [I00-I09, I11, I13, I20-I51]	Rank of leading causes of death[7]	5	5
Canada	15 to 19 years	Both sexes	Cerebrovascular diseases [I60-I69]	Rank of leading causes of death[7]	8	7
Canada	15 to 19 years	Both sexes	Influenza and pneumonia [J10-J18]	Rank of leading causes of death[7]	7	8
Canada	15 to 19 years	Both sexes	Congenital malformations, deformations and chromosomal abnormalities [Q00-Q99]	Rank of leading causes of death[7]	6	6
Canada	15 to 19 years	Both sexes	Accidents (unintentional injuries) [V01-X59, Y85-Y86]	Rank of leading causes of death[7]	1	1
Canada	15 to 19 years	Both sexes	Intentional self-harm (suicide) [X60-X84, Y87.0]	Rank of leading causes of death[7]	2	2
Canada	15 to 19 years	Both sexes	Assault (homicide) [X85-Y09, Y87.1]	Rank of leading causes of death[7]	4	4

Notes

1. The geographic distribution of deaths in this table is based on the deceased's usual place of residence.

2. Counts in this table exclude deaths of non-residents of Canada.

3. Age attained at the last birthday preceding death.

4. The cause of death tabulated is the underlying cause of death. This is defined as (a) the disease or injury which initiated the train of events leading directly to death, or (b) the circumstances of the accident or violence which produced the fatal injury. The underlying cause is selected from the conditions listed on the medical certificate of cause of death.

5. World Health Organization (WHO), International Statistical Classification of Diseases and Related Health Problems, 10th Revision (ICD-10).

6. The list for ranking leading causes of death that is used in this table is based on the list that was developed and that is been used by the National Center for Health Statistics of the United States in their annual report on leading causes of death.

7. The ranking of the leading causes of death is based on the number of deaths.

SOURCE: Statistics Canada. Table 102-0561—Leading Causes of Death, Total Population, by Age Group and Sex, Canada, Annual (Table), CANSIM (database). http://cansim2.statcan.gc.ca/cgi-win/cnsmcgi.exe?Lang=E&CNSM-Fi=CII/CII_1-eng.htm (Accessed February 9, 2010).

brutal reality and challenges the assertion that childhood is a carefree time of happiness and security.

Infant and Childhood Mortality Rates The infant mortality rate, the number of deaths of live-born infants under one year of age per 1000 live births (in any given year), provides an important measure of the health of a population. In 2001, 24 countries had infant mortality rates over 100 (UNICEF 2003), a drop from 25 countries in 1999. These data mean that for approximately one-quarter of the world's countries, 1 in every 10 live-born babies died before reaching age one. The African nation of Sierra Leone had the highest infant mortality rate in the world—an alarming 182 infants out of every 1000 live births died before their first birthday. The lowest rates of infant mortality in 1999 were in Sweden and Switzerland, where 3 of every 1000 live-born babies died in their first year of life. In 1999, the Canadian infant mortality rate was 5.3, meaning that fewer than 6 infants per 1000 died before reaching their first birthday. The mortality rate (5.7) of infant boys in that year was slightly higher than the mortality rate (4.8) for infant girls (Statistics Canada 2002).

The **under-five mortality rate**, another useful measure of child health, refers to the rate of deaths of children under age five. Approximately 12 million children younger than five years of age die every year; most of these children live in developing countries. More than half of these deaths are attributed to diarrhea, acute respiratory illness, malaria, or measles, conditions that are either preventable or treatable with low-cost interventions (Rice et al. 2000). Malnutrition is associated with about half of all deaths among children (Rice et al. 2000). Mortality among infants and children declined in most developing countries from the mid-1980s through the 1990s; however, since about 2000, this decline has slowed, stopped, or reversed itself in some countries of sub-Saharan Africa, largely as a result of the rate of HIV infection among infants and children (Rustein 2000).

As much as countries among the most developed in the world enjoy generally low childhood mortality rates, the impact of income inequality inside these highly developed countries on the health and mortality of children can be dramatic. Table 2.3 shows that income distribution disparities between the highest one-fifth of earners and the lowest two-fifths of earners correlated with an increase in Canada's under-5 mortality rank to 6 per 1000 as compared with Sweden's 3 per 1000. The United States, our closest geographic neighbour and a country that many of us find nearly indistinguishable from Canada, holds an even greater income disparity between the highest earners and the lowest, and an under-5 mortality rate that is one-third higher than in Canada.

In Table 2.3, each developed nation with the lowest mortality rate shows the least income inequality across its population. The impact of income on the health of children derives from the material access of parents to medical care, to clean and stable housing, and to a healthful diet and clean water. In Canada, those most at risk are families who live in rural areas that are underserviced in terms of health care and who have the least access to safe housing and clean drinking water. In Manitoba, in 2003, the Kashechewan First Nation community began a boil-water advisory because of *E. coli* contamination in the water supply. Even though 2000 people had been sickened and several had

under-five mortality rate
The rate of deaths among children under age five.

■ **Table 2.3** *Childhood Mortality Rates in Developed Countries: Canada's Ranking*

	Under-5 Mortality Rank	Under-5 Mortality Rate, 2007	Infant Mortality Rate (under 1), 2007	% Share of Household Income 1995–2005*, Lowest 40%	% Share of Household Income 1995–2005*, Highest 20%
Canada	160	6	5	20	40
Denmark	173	4	4	23	36
France	173	4	4	20	40
Netherlands	166	5	4	21	39
Norway	173	4	3	24	37
Sweden	189	3	3	23	37
United States	151	8	7	16	46

SOURCE: Adapted from *The State of the World's Children*, 2009. Available from http://www.unicef.org/sowc09/statistics/statistics.php. Used by permission of UNICEF.

died in the community from contaminated water, by 2005 no help had been offered by either the provincial or federal governments to upgrade the community's water treatment facilities. This neglect contrasts poorly with the attention paid to the community of Walkerton following the water supply crisis that sickened the Ontario town's population and caused several deaths in the spring of 2000.

maternal mortality rate

The numbers of deaths that result from complications associated with pregnancy or childbirth per one thousand pregnant women.

Maternal Mortality Rates The **maternal mortality rate**, a measure of deaths that result from complications associated with pregnancy, childbirth, and unsafe abortion, also provides a sensitive indicator of a population's health status. The three most common causes of maternal death are hemorrhage, infection, and complications arising from unsafe abortions. The maternal mortality rate is a more sensitive indicator than any other social health measure of the disparity between the rich and the poor in a given region. Moreover, of all the health statistics monitored by the World Health Organization, maternal mortality has the largest discrepancy between developed and developing countries. For women in developed countries, the risk of dying from complications of pregnancy or childbirth is very low: of the approximately 530 000 maternal deaths that occur each year, more than 90 percent occur in developing nations (Family Care International 2007). "Safe Motherhood," the exhaustive 2007 report from Family Care International (FCI), argues that "[s]afe motherhood is fundamentally a matter of human rights; all women are entitled to good health and high-quality health services…Maternal deaths are linked to women's low status in society, and their lack of decision-making ability and economic power" (Family Care International 2007: 7). In other words, the dangers of pregnancy and childbirth are not inherent problems of biology but the direct consequence of social injustice. Moreover, even in the face of global economic disparity, providing women in developing nations with access to safe motherhood initiatives has been demonstrated to be highly cost-effective (ibid).

Patterns of Burden of Disease

Although infant and maternal mortality rates are sensitive indicators of population health, there is another means of measuring the health status of a population, one that combines mortality and disability. This alternative approach provides an indicator of the overall **burden of disease** on a population through a single unit of measurement: as a comprehensive unit of measurement, it combines not only the number of deaths, but also the impact of premature death and disability on a population (Murray and Lopez 1996). Called the **disability-adjusted life year (DALY)**, the measurement reflects years of life lost to premature death and years lived with a disability. However, scholars and activists inside the contemporary disability rights movement have criticized the DALY. Disability activists and scholars point out that the DALY views disability through an outmoded medical model of disease. It sees the disability itself, rather than the *social exclusion* of persons with disabilities from opportunities for economic, educational, and social well-being, as the source of the problem (Groce et al. 2000). (See also Chapter 3.)

burden of disease

The number of deaths in a population combined with the impact of premature death and disability on that population.

disability-adjusted life year (DALY)

Years lived with illness or disability. More simply, one DALY equals one year lost of healthy life.

2.2 HIV/AIDS: A Global Health Concern

HIV/AIDS Epi Update 2005

One of the most urgent public health concerns around the globe is the spread of the human immunodeficiency virus (HIV), which causes acquired immunodeficiency syndrome (AIDS). HIV is transmitted through sexual intercourse; through sharing unclean intravenous needles; perinatally (from infected mother to fetus or newborn); through blood transfusions or blood products; and, rarely, through breast milk. Worldwide, the predominant mode of HIV transmission is through heterosexual contact (Inciardi and Harrison 1997). The second most common mode of transmission worldwide is **perinatal transmission**—the transmission of HIV from an infected mother to a fetus or newborn. An estimated 15 percent to 30 percent of babies born to HIV-infected mothers are HIV positive (Ward 1999).

perinatal transmission

The transmission of HIV from an infected mother to a fetus or newborn.

Although homosexual activity accounts for less than 10 percent of new cases worldwide (Stine 1998), men who have sex with other men are the group most at risk for developing HIV/AIDS in Canada. From over 80 percent in 1981–83, the proportion of new infections attributed to this group declined steadily to 30 percent in 1996. By 2002, however, it had increased to about 40 percent; for the same year, intravenous drug use accounted for about 30 percent, and heterosexual contact for about 22 percent (see Figure 2.1) (Statistics Canada 1998b; Health Canada 2005b).

Figure 2.2 shows that the burden of HIV/AIDS is borne mostly in poor countries, which account for 95 percent of all new infections, 80 percent of which are attributed to heterosexual contact (Lamptey 2002: 207–8). The most significant increases in infection rates for global HIV/AIDS are in the heterosexual category.

■ **Figure 2.1** *Estimated Exposure Category Distributions (%) among New HIV Infections in Canada by Time Period*

SOURCE: "HIV/AIDS EPI Updates." Public Health Agency of Canada, May 2005. Catalogue No. 06624042416, p. 3. Reproduced with the permission of the Minister of Public Works and Government Services Canada, 2011.

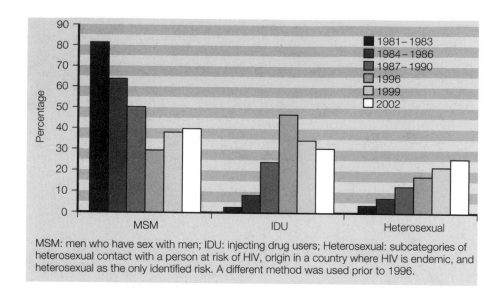

MSM: men who have sex with men; IDU: injecting drug users; Heterosexual: subcategories of heterosexual contact with a person at risk of HIV, origin in a country where HIV is endemic, and heterosexual as the only identified risk. A different method was used prior to 1996.

Since the beginning of the epidemic, AIDS has claimed more than 23 million lives (National AIDS Trust 2005). In 16 countries in sub-Saharan Africa, more than 1 in 10 persons aged 15 to 49 are HIV-infected, and 90 percent of the approximately 2 million children under age 15 who are infected with HIV live in the same sub-Saharan region (United Nations 2008: 9). Although HIV/AIDS originally emerged as an adult health problem, it has become a major killer of children under five years old, especially in developing countries (Adetunji 2000). In seven countries in southern Africa, at least 20 percent of the adult population is living with HIV. In Botswana, where about one in three adults are HIV-infected—the highest prevalence in the world—at least two-thirds of today's 15-year-old boys will die prematurely of AIDS (Joint United Nations Programme on HIV/AIDS 2000a). Since the epidemic began,

■ **Figure 2.2** *Global Distribution of Adults and Children Living with HIV or AIDS at the End of 2001*

SOURCE: "Regular Review Reducing Heterosexual Transmission of HIV in Poor Countries," by Peter R. Lamptey *(British Medical Journal).* 2002. Catalogue No. H1215200SEPDF324. Reproduced with permission from the BMJ Publishing Group.

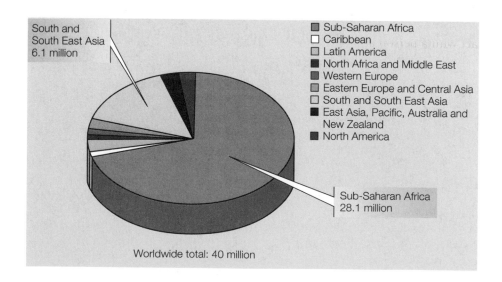

more than 13 million children—95 percent of them in Africa—have lost their mother or both parents to AIDS (Joint United Nations Programme on HIV/AIDS 2000b).

The high rates of HIV in developing countries, particularly sub-Saharan Africa, are having devastating effects on societies. The HIV/AIDS epidemic creates an enormous burden on the limited health-care resources of poor countries. Gains in life expectancy achieved in recent decades have been reversed in some countries. In Botswana, Zambia, and Zimbabwe—countries with high HIV prevalence—life expectancy at birth was lower in 2000 than it was in 1975 (Adetunji 2000). Economic development is threatened by the HIV epidemic, which diverts national funds to health-related needs and reduces the size of a nation's workforce.

HIV/AIDS in Canada

Between 1982, when AIDS was first diagnosed in Canada, and December 31, 2004, 19 824 AIDS cases in adults had been reported to the Centre for Infectious Disease Prevention and Control. The overwhelming majority of these cases involved men (90.9 percent). Health Canada (2005a: 5) reports, "Prior to 1994, only 6.2% of AIDS diagnoses are among adult females [over age 15], this has risen to just over 20% in the past two years...and is most striking in the 15–29 year age group where the proportion of AIDS diagnoses attributed to females increased from 9.9% before 1994 to 45.0% in 2004." Heterosexual contact with a high-risk partner and injection drug use are the two major risk factors for HIV infection in women (Health Canada 2002). While the epidemiological data for Canada indicate that HIV transmission is highest among men who have sex with men, as Figure 2.1 shows, on a global scale, HIV is most prevalent among the heterosexual population.

Young Canadians compose only a small proportion of the total reported cases. Of the cumulative reported AIDS cases in Canadian youth aged 10 to 19, about two of three cases were attributed to the receipt of infected blood and blood products. Among people aged 20 to 24, 51 percent of transmissions were attributed to men who have sex with men and 21 percent to heterosexual contact with a person at risk (Health Canada 2004).

HIV prevalence may be low among Canadian youth, but risk behaviour data on young Canadians suggest cause for concern. Although a national survey of Canadian teens found that 55 percent saw AIDS as a "very serious" issue (Bibby 2001: 43), many Canadian youths are engaging in unsafe sexual practices (see "The Student Sexual Risks Scale" in this chapter's *Self and Society* feature). For example, according to the National Population Health Survey, among sexually active youth aged 15 to 19, 51 percent of females and 29 percent of males reported never or only sometimes using a condom in the past year. Among those 20 to 24 years old, the corresponding figures were 53 percent and 44 percent (Health Canada 2005b; Statistics Canada 1998a). When surveyed regarding their most recent sexual encounters, those in the 20 to 24 age group were twice as likely not to have used a condom during intercourse than those in the 15 to 17 age group (Roterman 2005: 40). Table 2.4 presents some of these data.

The Student Sexual Risks Scale

The following self-assessment allows you to evaluate the degree to which you may be at risk for engaging in behaviour that exposes you to HIV. Safer sex means sexual activity that reduces the risk of transmitting the AIDS virus. Using condoms is an example of safer sex. Unsafe, risky, or unprotected sex refers to sex without a condom or to other sexual activity that might increase the risk of AIDS virus transmission. For each of the following items, check the response that best characterizes your opinion.

A = Agree
U = Undecided
D = Disagree

	A	U	D
1. If my partner wanted me to have unprotected sex, I would probably give in.			
2. The proper use of a condom could enhance sexual pleasure.			
3. I may have had sex with someone who was at risk for HIV/AIDS.			
4. If I were going to have sex, I would take precautions to reduce my risk of HIV/AIDS.			
5. Condoms ruin the natural sex act.			
6. When I think that one of my friends might have sex on a date, I ask him/her if he/she has a condom.			
7. I am at risk for HIV/AIDS.			
8. I would try to use a condom when I had sex.			
9. Condoms interfere with romance.			
10. My friends talk a lot about safer sex.			
11. If my partner wanted me to participate in risky sex and I said we needed to be safer, we would still probably end up having unsafe sex.			
12. Generally, I am in favour of using condoms.			
13. I would avoid using condoms if at all possible.			
14. If a friend knew that I might have sex on a date, he/she would ask me whether I was carrying a condom.			
15. There is a possibility that I have HIV/AIDS.			
16. If I had a date, I would probably not drink alcohol or use drugs.			
17. Safer sex reduces the mental pleasure of sex.			
18. If I thought that one of my friends had sex on a date, I would ask him/her if he/she used a condom.			
19. The idea of using a condom doesn't appeal to me.			
20. Safer sex is a habit for me.			
21. If a friend knew that I had sex on a date, he/she wouldn't care whether I had used a condom or not.			
22. If my partner wanted me to participate in risky sex and I suggested a lower-risk alternative, we would have the safer sex instead.			
23. The sensory aspects (smell, touch, etc.) of condoms make them unpleasant.			
24. I intend to follow "safer sex" guidelines within the next year.			
25. With condoms, you can't really give yourself over to your partner.			
26. I am determined to practise safer sex.			

27. If my partner wanted me to have unprotected sex and I made some excuse to use a condom, we would still end up having unprotected sex. ———— ———— ————

28. If I had sex and I told my friends that I did not use a condom, they would be angry or disappointed. ———— ———— ————

29. I think safer sex would get boring fast. ———— ———— ————

30. My sexual experiences do not put me at risk for HIV/AIDS. ———— ———— ————

31. Condoms are irritating. ———— ———— ————

32. My friends and I encourage each other before dates to practise safer sex. ———— ———— ————

33. When I socialize, I usually drink alcohol or use drugs. ———— ———— ————

34. If I were going to have sex in the next year, I would use condoms. ———— ———— ————

35. If a sexual partner didn't want to use condoms, we would have sex without using condoms. ———— ———— ————

36. People can get the same pleasure from safer sex as from unprotected sex. ———— ———— ————

37. Using condoms interrupts sex play. ———— ———— ————

38. It is a hassle to use condoms. ———— ———— ————

(To be read after completing the scale.)

SCORING: Begin by giving yourself 80 points. Subtract one point for every undecided response. Subtract two points every time that you disagreed with odd-numbered items or with item number 38. Subtract two points every time you agreed with even-numbered items 2 through 36.

INTERPRETING YOUR SCORE: Research shows that students who make higher scores on the SSRS are more likely to engage in risky sexual activities, such as having multiple sex partners and failing to consistently use condoms during sex. In contrast, students who practise safer sex tend to endorse more positive attitudes toward safer sex, and tend to have peer networks that encourage safer sexual practices. These students usually plan on making sexual activity safer, and they feel confident in their ability to negotiate safer sex even when a dating partner may press for riskier sex. Students who practise safer sex often refrain from using alcohol or drugs, which may impede negotiation of safer sex, and often report having engaged in lower-risk activities in the past. How do you measure up?

(BELOW 15) LOWER RISK: (Of 200 students surveyed by DeHart and Birkimer, 16 percent were in this category.) Congratulations! Your score in the SSRS indicates that relative to other students your thoughts and behaviours are more supportive of safer sex. Is there any room for improvement in your score? If so, you may want to examine items for which you lost points and try to build safer sexual strengths in those areas. You can help protect others from HIV by educating your peers about making sexual activity safer.

(15 TO 37) AVERAGE RISK: (Of 200 students surveyed by DeHart and Birkimer, 68 percent were in this category.) Your score on the SSRS is about average in comparison with those of other university students. Although it is good that you don't fall into the higher-risk category, be aware that "average" people can get HIV, too. In fact, a recent survey indicated that the rate of HIV among university students is 10 times that in the general heterosexual population. Thus, you may want to enhance your sexual safety by figuring out where you lost points and work toward safer sexual strengths in those areas.

(38 AND ABOVE) HIGHER RISK: (Of 200 students surveyed by DeHart and Birkimer, 16 percent were in this category.) Relative to other students, your score on the SSRS indicates that your thoughts and behaviours are less supportive of safer sex. Such high scores tend to be associated with greater HIV-risk behaviour. Rather than simply giving in to riskier attitudes and behaviours, you may want to empower yourself and reduce your risk by critically examining areas for improvement. On which items did you lose points? Think about how you can strengthen your sexual safety in these areas. Reading more about safer sex can help, and sometimes student health clinics offer courses or workshops on safer sex.

SOURCE: Reprinted by permission of Dana D. DeHart, Ph.D., Center for Child and Family Studies, University of South Carolina, College of Social Work, Columbia, SC, 29208.

■ **Table 2.4** *Non-Condom Use among Sexually Active 15- to 24-Year-Olds Who Were Single and/or Had Sex with More Than One Partner in Past Year, by Sex and Selected Characteristics, Canada, 2003*

| | Did Not Use Condom the Last Time | | | | | |
| | Total | | Males | | Females | |
	'000	%	'000	%	'000	%
Total	771.8	37.8	350.0	32.7	421.8	43.5
Age group						
15 to 17	65.4	21.5	22.3	14.8	43.1	28.0
18 to 19	146.2	32.5	58.1	25.2	88.0	40.0
20 to 24	560.3	43.6	269.5	39.1	290.7	48.8
Number of partners						
One	533.2	41.0	243.1	38.4	290.1	43.6
More than one	238.6	32.3	106.8	24.6	131.7	43.4
Two	133.4	34.0	49.3	24.2	84.1	44.4
Three	50.4	30.5	26.3	25.7	24.1	38.5
Four or more	54.8	30.3	31.2	24.2	23.5	45.5
Age at first sexual intercourse						
13 or younger	49.4	42.8	22.1	32.1	27.3	58.8
14 to 17	522.2	38.9	235.6	33.0	286.5	45.7
18 or older	200.2	34.4	92.3	32.1	108.0	36.5
Aboriginal						
Yes	41.4	42.4	16.2	41.7	25.1	42.8
No	703.2	37.5	320.9	32.3	382.3	43.5
Marital status						
Single (never married/separated/ divorced/widowed)	754.8	37.5	344.1	32.5	410.7	43.0
Married/Common-law	16.0	63.3		49.2	10.3	75.3
Province/Territories						
Newfoundland and Labrador	11.7	29.6	4.9	23.1	6.9	37.0
Prince Edward Island	2.5	27.5			2.0	43.3
Nova Scotia	18.2	28.6	6.8	22.9	11.4	33.5
New Brunswick	20.1	38.9	7.6	28.2	12.5	50.6
Québec	241.4	44.3	106.6	37.0	134.8	52.4
Ontario	270.5	34.9	130.5	32.0	140.0	38.1
Manitoba	26.5	36.5	12.5	33.3	14.0	39.8
Saskatchewan	19.4	33.9	7.1	24.7	12.3	43.3
Alberta	76.0	40.4	36.4	36.3	39.6	45.1
British Columbia	83.4	36.3	36.2	29.8	47.2	43.5
Territories	2.0	29.9	0.9	28.4	1.2	31.0

SOURCE: Statistics Canada. "Non-Condom Use Among Sexually Active 15- to 24-Year-Olds Who Were Single and/or Had Sex with More Than One Partner in the Past Year, by Sex and Selected Characteristics, Canada, 2003" *(Health Reports)*, Catalogue No. 82-003, Vol. 16, No. 3, May 2005, p. 44.

Understanding HIV transmission and the impact of AIDS is greatly enhanced through the use of two theoretical lenses: these lenses focus attention on the social rather than purely biological issues involved. A **feminist** view of global trends contributes an understanding of how gender interacts with other social factors to make women and youth, especially female youth, particularly vulnerable to HIV infection. We cannot separate out the impact of "unemployment, illiteracy, gender inequalities, lack of information and services, and human rights abuses...factors [that] greatly increase the vulnerability of women, young people, and other marginalized groups" (Lamptey 2002: 209). Poor educational opportunities for girls, the value placed on young girls in the sex trade, and financial instability all combine to coerce young women to have unprotected sex for money. By so doing, they contribute to skyrocketing HIV transmission in the poorest nations.

2.3 Mental Illness: The Invisible Epidemic

The concepts of mental illness and mental health are not easy to define. What it means to be mentally healthy varies across and within cultures. Furthermore, mental health and mental illness may be thought of as points on a continuum. **Mental health** has nevertheless been defined as "the successful performance of mental function, resulting in productive activities, fulfilling relationships with other people, and the ability to adapt to change and to cope with adversity" (U.S. Department of Health and Human Services 1999: ix). **Mental illness** refers collectively to all mental disorders. A **mental disorder** is a health condition that is characterized by alterations in thinking, mood, and behaviour associated with distress, impaired functioning, or both. Although we all experience problems in living, in functioning, and in emotional state, such problems are not necessarily seen as mental illness—they must meet specific criteria (such as level of intensity and duration) specified in the classification manual used to diagnose mental disorders: The Diagnostic and Statistical Manual of Mental Disorders (DSM) (American Psychiatric Association 2000). Although a powerful management tool for use after diagnosis, the DSM, and related medicalization of mental/perceptual difference, has been criticized for its potentially damaging impact on people's day-to-day self-perception (Gergen 1994).

Some examples of mental disorders are presented in Table 2.5.

Extent and Impact of Mental Illness

Canadian data indicate that in Canada, "approximately 20% of individuals will experience a mental illness during their lifetime, and the remaining 80% will be affected by an illness in family members" (Health Canada 2002d: 3). At any given time, three million Canadians are living with some kind of mental illness (Simmie and Nunes 2001). The most common mental disorder, depression, is estimated to affect one in four Canadian women and 1 in 10 Canadian men (Canadian Psychiatric Association 2002). In 2001, major depression was the leading cause of disability in developed nations, including Canada (World Health Organization 2001).

Worldwide, mental disorders accounted for approximately 12 percent of all disability-adjusted life years lost in 2001 (Brundtland 2000; World Health Organization 2001). Five of the leading causes of disability worldwide are mental disorders: major depression, schizophrenia, bipolar disorders, alcohol

feminist

An umbrella term that describes both socio-political activism and academic work. The many sub-categories of feminist thought and action are united by a concern for the well-being of women. Feminists have sought for recognition that women are full human beings entitled to the same personal rights as men. In sociology, feminist work has demonstrated that gender is an important variable to be accounted for in research programs and that the well-being of women is integral to the general welfare of larger society.

mental health

The successful performance of mental function, resulting in productive activities, fulfilling relationships with other people, and the ability to adapt to change and to cope with adversity.

mental illness

A term used to refer collectively to all mental disorders.

mental disorder

A behavioural or psychological syndrome or pattern that occurs in an individual and that is associated with present distress or disability, or with a significantly increased risk of suffering, death, pain, disability, or loss of freedom.

■ **Table 2.5** *Mental Disorders Classified by the American Psychiatric Association*

Classification	Description
Anxiety Disorders	Disorders characterized by anxiety that is manifest in phobias, panic attacks, or obsessive-compulsive disorder
Dissociative Disorders	Problems involving a splitting or dissociation of normal consciousness, such as amnesia and multiple personality
Disorders First Evident in Infancy, Childhood, or Adolescence	Including mental retardation, attention-deficit hyperactivity, and stuttering
Eating or Sleeping Disorders	Including such problems as anorexia and bulimia or insomnia and other problems associated with sleep
Impulse Control Disorders	Including the inability to control undesirable impulses, such as kleptomania, pyromania, and pathological gambling
Mood Disorders	Emotional disorders, such as major depression and bipolar (manic-depressive) disorder
Organic Mental Disorders	Psychological or behavioural disorders associated with dysfunctions of the brain caused by aging, disease, or brain damage (such as Alzheimer's disease)
Personality Disorders	Maladaptive personality traits that are generally resistant to treatment, such as paranoid and antisocial personality types
Schizophrenia and Other Psychotic Disorders	Disorders with symptoms such as delusions or hallucinations
Somatoform Disorders	Psychological problems that present themselves as symptoms of physical disease, such as hypochondria
Substance-Related Disorders	Disorders resulting from abuse of alcohol and/or drugs such as barbiturates, cocaine, or amphetamines

use, and obsessive-compulsive disorders (Brundtland 2000). Contrary to popular belief, children are not immune. Also, those whose parents are experiencing marital breakdown have higher levels of depression and tend to be more antisocial than children in stable homes (Statistics Canada 2005).

Causes of Mental Disorders

Mental illnesses are the result of a number of biological, psychological, and social factors. A broad scope of research has linked many mental disorders with genetic or neurological causes involving some pathology of the brain. However, social and environmental influences, such as poverty, history of abuse, or other severe emotional trauma, also affect individuals' vulnerability to mental illness and mental health problems. The global increase in life expectancy has contributed to mental illnesses that affect the elderly, such as Alzheimer's disease and other forms of cognitive disorder and dementia. War within and between countries may also contribute to mental illness in such forms as combat-related post-traumatic stress disorder. In addition, "many societies and communities that customarily offered support to their needier members through family and social bonds now find it much harder to do so" (Brundtland 2000: 411). Garfinkel and Goldbloom (2000) explain that "the radical shifts in society towards technology, changes in family and societal supports and networks and the commercialization of existence...may account for the current epidemic of depression and other psychiatric disorders" (p. 503). It may be safe to conclude that "the causes of most mental disorders lie in some combination of genetic and environmental factors, which may be biological or psychosocial" (U.S. Department of Health and Human Services 1999: xiv).

2.4 Sociological Theories of Illness and Health Care

The sociological approach to the study of illness, health, and health care differs from medical, biological, and psychological approaches to these topics. Next, we discuss how five sociological theories—structural-functionalism, conflict theory, feminism, symbolic interactionism, and queer theory—contribute to our understanding of illness and health care.

Structural-Functionalist Perspective

The structural-functionalist perspective is concerned with how illness, health, and health care affect and are affected by changes in other aspects of social life. For example, changes in gender-role expectations and norms have led to more women smoking, drinking, and experiencing the negative health effects of these behaviours. Increased modernization and industrialization throughout the world have resulted in environmental pollution—a major health concern. Increasingly, patterns of health and disease are affected by **globalization**—the economic, political, and social interconnectedness among societies throughout the world. For example, increased business travel and tourism has encouraged the globalization of disease, such as the potentially fatal West Nile encephalitis. The virus first appeared in North America in 1999 (Weitz 2001) and the first confirmed case in Canada was discovered in a bird in Windsor, Ontario, in August 2001 (Higgins 2002). In 2003, severe acute respiratory syndrome (SARS) surfaced in 16 countries with a total of 1550 cases and 774 deaths. As of July 2003, Canada had reported 251 cases of SARS and 43 deaths (World Health Organization 2004).

Just as social change affects health, health concerns may lead to social change. The emergence of HIV and AIDS in the gay male population helped unite and mobilize gay rights activists in both Canada and the United States. Concerns over the hazards of using cellular phones while driving led to the 2009 legislation in Canada to outlaw the use of hand-held communication devices while driving.

According to the structural-functionalist perspective, health care is a social institution that functions to maintain the well-being of societal members and, consequently, of the social system as a whole. Illness is dysfunctional in that it interferes with people performing needed social roles. To cope with nonfunctioning individuals and to control the negative effects of illness, society assigns a temporary and unique role to those who are ill—the sick role (Parsons 1951). This role ensures that societal members receive needed care and compassion. At the same time, the role carries with it an expectation that the person who is ill will seek competent medical advice, adhere to the prescribed regimen, and return as soon as possible to normal role obligations.

Structural-functionalists additionally explain the high salaries of physicians by arguing that society must entice people into the medical profession by offering high salaries. Without such an incentive, individuals would not be motivated to endure the rigours of medical training or the stress of being a physician.

globalization

The economic, political, and social interconnectedness among societies throughout the world.

Conflict Perspective

The conflict perspective focuses on how wealth, status, and power, or the lack thereof, influence illness and health care. Worldwide, the have-nots not only experience the adverse health effects of poverty, but also have less access to quality medical care. In societies where women have little status and power, women's life expectancy is lower than in industrialized countries. In such societies, women eat last and eat less, face complications from frequent childbearing and sexually transmitted diseases (because they have no power to demand abstinence or condom use), suffer infections and hemorrhages after genital mutilation (which is practised in 29 countries), and have restricted access to modern health care (World Health Organization 1997). Consider, as well, that while public health measures, improved sanitation systems, proper housing, immunization, and antibiotics have virtually eliminated infectious diseases, such as smallpox, tuberculosis, and cholera, not all Canadians have equally benefited. Largely due to crowded living conditions (i.e., housing densities twice the national average) and poor nutrition, Aboriginal peoples are more vulnerable to TB infection than other Canadian-born persons. They account for 16 percent of all TB cases reported, while non-Aboriginal Canadian-born persons account for only 3 percent of all reported cases (Health Canada 2002: 9).

Medical research agendas are also shaped by wealth, status, and power. Although malaria kills twice as many people annually as does AIDS, malaria research receives less than one-tenth as much public funding as AIDS research (Morse 1998). Similarly, pneumonia and diarrheal diseases constitute 15.4 percent of the total global disease burden, but only 0.2 percent of the total global spending on research (Visschedijk and Simeant 1998). Why? Northern developed countries, which provide most of the funding for world health–related research, do not feel threatened by malaria, pneumonia, and diarrheal diseases. These diseases primarily affect less developed countries in Africa and Asia.

The conflict perspective also focuses on how the profit motive influences health, illness, and health care. The profit motive underlies much of the illness, injury, and death that occur from hazardous working conditions and dangerous consumer products.

socio-economic status (SES)

Status that refers to the combination of economic and social circumstances that shape one's experiences as a member of a given class. SES addresses the likelihood that higher income and a higher place in the social hierarchy are likely to coincide, and that lower status and lower income are also likely to coincide, with attendant privileges for higher SES groups and attendant risks for lower ones.

Feminist Perspectives

Feminist theories take gender to be a central rather than peripheral concern that influences all aspects of social life, including how one experiences health and illness, the unique health risks that women face, and the impact of broad social phenomena on women's health. This chapter has already noted why women face unique risks for HIV transmission and how a lack of control over their own reproductive health brings negative consequences for women's health and well-being. Contemporary studies in women's health demonstrate that quality of life and consequent experiences of health and illness are tied not simply or only to gender, but also to social class, to race and to ethnicity, and to age.

Grann and colleagues found that **socio-economic status (SES)** and race combined, with SES being the strongest predictor for a poor outcome, "contribute to the higher mortality rate of black women" diagnosed with breast cancer (2005: 344). To take breast and reproductive cancers as an example, where a woman lives, what her educational background is, what access she has to medical care—all these things combine to influence her risks for developing

Cancer Screening and the Exploitation of Fear

As a culture, we tend to place great faith in the ability of medicine to provide accurate diagnoses and to heal us of our injuries and diseases. At the same time, our general lack of direct access to and understanding of diagnostic and treatment technologies used in contemporary medicine can make us extremely suspicious about medical practice. As a result, we can have very contradictory attitudes about medical practice, and nowhere is our combination of suspicion and trust more palpable than in the diagnosis and treatment of cancers. In this Focus on Technology feature, we turn our attention to two current areas of controversy in cancer screening and treatment: breast cancer and prostate cancer.

The Hazards of Screening for Cancer

In November 2009, *The New York Times* brought to public attention a recommendation that breast cancer screening for women with no identified predisposition for the development of breast cancer be delayed from age 40 to age 50 in order to avoid overdiagnosis. In Canada, *The Globe and Mail* quickly followed suit with its own commentary on the newly released protocols, originally published in the *Annals of Internal Medicine*. Against the increasing push for blanket screening of women over the age of 40 for breast cancer, the members of the Preventive Task Force (USPSTF) who authored the study recommended against the use of routine mammography in women aged 40 to 49 (USPSTF 2009). The new guidelines followed up on an earlier study from 2002 that had recommended all women over age 40 be screened at least every two years for breast cancer (USPSTF 2002). The new 2009 recommendations build on the conclusions of a long-term study that determined that the risk of false-positive results for the presence of cancer, the potential harms of invasive treatment, and needless exposure to the radiation from diagnostic mammography constituted harms that outweighed any potential benefits of cancer detection in the age group (Nelson et al. 2009).

Over the last two decades, women have embraced their personal responsibility to monitor their health by using regular breast self-exam (BSE) procedures to look for lumps that may signal a cancer developing in the breast. The process of getting women to perform BSE is a form of "responsibilization" that transfers accountability for our health from large environmental hazards and public policy and health-care services to individuals (Gray 2009). Responsibilization is a concept that refers to the movement toward demanding that individuals "become prudent subjects who must 'practice individual responsibility'" (Gray 2009: 327) to look after their own health and safety. In the context of breast cancer screening, responsibilization has required not only that women learn and perform BSE and to go for regularly scheduled clinical breast exams (CBE), even though the long-term data show that BSE has no positive influence to reduce breast cancer deaths and risks exposing women to unnecessary biopsies (Thomas et al. 2002). Furthermore, clinical breast exam carries not only the risks of invasion that we have already mentioned, but also the risk of a false sense of security when we trust clinicians to read radiologic and pathology reports correctly. Yet, recent cases in Canada demonstrate that such trust may be misplaced. In essence, if we trust the screening technology to deliver accurate information, we are missing the human component required for accurate interpretation of test results. In such cases, the problem is our faith in technology and expertise, rather than a failure of the technology itself.

The Hazards of Aggressive Treatment for Non-Aggressive Cancers

In its worst manifestations, the risk of submitting to breast cancer screening has resulted in unnecessary mastectomy when test results were not properly read (CBC News 2010). Explaining the risk-benefit analysis of SBE and CBE, André Picard, MD, medical reporter for *The Globe and Mail*, writes that we have no evidence that SBE is a useful diagnostic technology and that

> Mammography programs would have to screen 1,904 women aged 39–49 for a decade to prevent a single death; in women aged 50–59, they would need to screen 1,339 for 10 years to prevent one death… We cannot ignore, either, that screening not only has benefits, it can cause harm. Younger, premenopausal women have denser breasts and they have far more false-positive results, leading to unnecessary biopsies that are physically painful and psychologically damaging, not to mention the additional exposure to radiation. (Picard 2009)

Just as there has been an increased responsibilization of women for their own health and for identifying cancers specific to women, men have been responsibilized with regard to prostate cancer:

> For health-conscious men, PSA tests are what mammograms are to

(continued)

women—an essential piece of preventive medicine.... But a growing body of evidence shows that the PSA test is a very crude instrument, resulting in a huge number of unnecessary surgeries. (Wente 2010)

However, the value of screening for prostate cancer has come under increased scrutiny in part because there are many reasons that blood PSA levels can be elevated, and in part because even when prostate cancer is diagnosed it is very often a non-aggressive form that will not lead to death even if left untreated. Conversely, the negative effects of treatment can include "erectile dysfunction, urinary incontinence, bowel dysfunction, and death. Additionally, many men who screen positive for prostate cancer face unnecessary anxiety because they may not develop symptoms within their lifetime" (Kuehn 2008).

In other words, the treatment is worse than the disease, and in many cases the disease itself may never become apparent and the men will die at or beyond life expectancy from other causes.

We place our faith in medical technologies as a matter of course, yet long-term data are showing us that increased technological intervention and diagnosis can bring hazards greater than the problems the technologies seek to remedy. Responsibilization of men and women as social agents exploits our fears of death and disease and can make us vulnerable to feelings that we are not acting appropriately as citizens if we resist or

refuse these interventions. Yet it may be the case that at least for certain age groups—men over 75 and women under 50—resistance of these invasive technologies will protect us from a host of potential harms.

SOURCES: *New York Times*, Nov. 2009; *Globe and Mail*, Nov. 17, 2009; USPSTF, 2009; USPSTF, 2002; Nelson 2009; Gray, 2009. CBC NEWS, www.cbc.ca/canada/windsor/story/2010/02/18/windsor-mastectomy-mistake-100218.html accessed Feb. 19, 2010; Wente, Margaret, "Prostate Cancer Dilemma," *Globe and Mail*, Feb. 8, 2010, http://www.theglobeandmail.com/news/opinions/prostate-cancer-dilemma/article1460634/; Picard, André. 2009. http://www.theglobeandmail.com/life/health/base-breast-screening-on-reason-not-passion/article1369247/; Kuehn, Bridget M. 2008. "Prostate Cancer Screening" *JAMA 300*(12):1403.

cancer, how early the cancer will be detected, the kind of treatment she will receive, and ultimately, her chances for survival. (See this chapter's *Focus on Technology* feature for a discussion of the exploitation of our fears about cancer.) Moreover, contemporary research and theory makes clear that trying to treat risk factors as discrete and unrelated is a mistake. Markovic and colleagues (2005) show that societal gender roles, domestic responsibilities, and larger socio-economic and political factors influence national health policy and combine to disadvantage women's health and well-being. For example, though we know that unsafe abortion and a lack of access to contraception are among the leading causes of maternal death in developing nations, the Canadian federal Conservative party has refused to be among the G8 countries to fund access to abortion and contraception in a shared effort to improve maternal health in developing countries (Wente 2010). A lack of knowledge about women's risk factors for conditions such as cervical cancer also works against women. For example, although vaccines to protect against infection caused by strains of human papillomavirus (HPV) promise to prevent the development of gynecological cancers, focus on the role of HPV in the development of over 90 percent of cervical cancers neglects the importance of the other factors—such as diet, smoking, access to proper nutrition, and adequate rest—that also influence the development of those cancers (which, it turns out, occur very rarely even though HPV infection is common). The easy adoption of the vaccine misses the larger health considerations that negatively influence the immune system's ability to fight off HPV infection; the vaccine does nothing to help with these other concerns, and has problematized women's sexuality in particular in order to exploit a market for vaccines whose merits remain unproven (Dias 2009). See this chapter's *Social Problems Research Up Close* feature for a detailed account of the critical research on HPV vaccines.

The HPV Vaccine and the Problematization of Women's Bodies

In a graduate-level major research paper completed at Wilfrid Laurier University, Canadian scholar Lisa Dias examined the manner in which women's bodies are surveilled and exploited, situated as diseased—in contrast to the taken for granted health of men's bodies—and made available to the incursions of both public health agencies and pharmaceutical companies. She argues in her master's research that at least since the production of films intended to educate the public about sexually transmitted infections (STIs), "Perceptions of women's bodies as diseased circulated in public health discourses about STI's...[and] representations of women as 'vectors' of disease circulate" through much of the early twentieth century and its various "social purity" campaigns (Dias 2009: 4). In an extensive study detailing the manner in which campaigns to promote the HPV vaccine have been encoded, Dias demonstrates that now, in the twenty-first century, women's bodies are more aggressively surveilled and problematized than men's bodies are, and that standard cervical screening programs problematize women's sexuality in a manner that men's sexuality is not. In her review of the extant literature on women's healthcare Dias finds that, while women have been a disproportionate focus of reproductive medicine, they have been largely neglected in other areas of health research, such as cardiovascular disease (CVD). Dias's research reminds us that the "common sense" acceptance of women's bodies as particularly "at risk" for reproductive and sexually transmitted diseases leaves us vulnerable to mass acceptance and implementation of vaccination programs whose long-term risks, both in terms of social cost (in the form of stigma) and health cost (in the form of complications or failures of the vaccine) are unknown.

Dias does not argue in any simple manner for rejection or acceptance of the vaccine but urges us instead to beware of the "controversy [of] competing discourses... because these discourses speak to our current state of politics around issues of risk, gender and sexuality," (2009: 6–7). It is the meanings that people attribute to risk, "appropriate femininity," gender, and sexuality that sit at the core of Dias's analysis.

To contextualize current debates about HPV vaccination programs, Dias turns her attention more generally to the historical treatment of TB and cancer as well as AIDS, and finds that there is a long legacy of blaming individuals for their diseases, and holding individuals responsible for the management of their disease as *moral imperatives*. She writes, "It is apparent that the meanings [of cervical cancer] are produced in a sociocultural and historical context, that social understandings of cervical cancer are imbued with moral judgement, and that individuals are held accountable for becoming 'ill' in the first place..." (Dias 2009: 8).

Dias's research provides a symbolic and interpretive analysis of modes of dissemination of information about the HPV vaccine and about cervical cancer and the manner in which the focus on sexual danger and sexual pollution marginalizes young girls and women, setting them up as a target population that will carry the burden of managing the fears that hold sway in the cultural *zeitgeist* regarding sexuality and contagion.

Using qualitative methods, especially discourse analysis, Dias draws out the relationships among forms of power that are brought to bear on the HPV vaccine debate. Dias finds that "through medical and pharmaceutical surveillance women are encouraged to become 'responsible' for their and others' sexual and reproductive health" (p. 22). She draws particular attention to the "Tell Someone" campaign produced by Merck Frosst, the makers of Gardasil, which is the only vaccine currently available in Canada. She finds that the "someone" we are supposed to tell is presented visually and in the language of the pamphlet as exclusively female. Men are not represented as at risk for HPV infection, as carriers of HPV infection, or as persons responsible for having or disseminating knowledge about the risks of HPV infection.

Dias's objective in her research is not to promote the wholesale rejection of vaccination to protect against HPV infection; rather, she argues that "we need to be aware of the type of subject the [health] discourses of HPV and the vaccine are constructing" because the discourses personalize responsibility for health and ignore larger social factors that impede health (p. 64). Lack of access to health care for rural and marginalized women; inadequate nutrition, rest, and exercise; excessive levels of stress; and a constellation of other social hazards all combine to reduce the overall health of women, including their ability to fight off HPV infections on their own. Because many of these women lack access to the health care necessary to get the

(continued)

series of vaccines required to be effective in preventing HPV infection, the vaccines can be expected to have little or no impact in precisely the populations of women they would help most. Simultane- ously, campaigns to "educate" women and girls about HPV unduly problematize and responsibilize women and their bodies, neglecting the role men play in the transmission of HPV.

SOURCE: Dias, Lisa V. 2009. "Burdening Women with Responsibility for Containment: A Discourse Analysis of Public Health Initiatives with Pharmaceutical Advertising for Gardasil, 'the HPV Vaccine'." Major Research Paper, Master of Arts, Wilfrid Laurier University, Waterloo.

Symbolic Interactionist Perspective

Symbolic interactionists focus on (1) how meanings, definitions, and labels influence health, illness, and health care, and (2) how such meanings are learned through interaction with others and through media messages and portrayals. According to the symbolic interactionist perspective of illness, "there are no illnesses or diseases in nature. There are only conditions that society, or groups within it, have come to define as illness or disease" (Goldstein 1999: 31). Psychiatrist Thomas Szasz ([1961] 1970) argues that what we call "mental illness" is no more than a label conferred on those individuals who are different—that is, who don't conform to society's definitions of appropriate behaviour.

Definitions of health and illness vary over time and from society to society. In some countries, being fat is a sign of health and prosperity; in others, it is an indication of mental illness or a lack of self-control. Before medical research documented the health hazards of tobacco, our society defined cigarette smoking as fashionable. Cigarette advertisements still attempt to associate positive meanings—such as youth, sex, and romance— with smoking to entice people to smoke. A study of top-grossing American films from 1985 to 1995 revealed that 98 percent had references that supported tobacco use and 96 percent had references that supported alcohol use (Everett et al. 1998).

A growing number of behaviours and conditions are being defined as medical problems—a trend known as **medicalization**. Hyperactivity, insomnia, anxiety, and learning disabilities are examples of phenomena that some view as medical conditions in need of medical intervention. Increasingly, "normal" aspects of life, such as birth, aging, sexual development, menopause, and death, have come to be seen as medical events (Goldstein 1999).

Symbolic interactionists also focus on the stigmatizing effects of being labelled "ill." A **stigma** refers to any personal characteristic associated with social disgrace, rejection, or discrediting. (Originally, the word "stigma" referred to a mark burned into the skin of a criminal or slave.) Individuals with mental illnesses, drug addictions, physical deformities and impairments, and HIV and AIDS are particularly prone to being stigmatized. Stigmatization may lead to prejudice, discrimination, and even violence against individuals with illnesses or impairments.

Having a stigmatized illness or condition often becomes a master status, obscuring other aspects of a person's social identity. One individual who uses a wheelchair commented: "When I am in my chair I am invisible to some people; they see only the chair" (Ostrof 1998: 36).

medicalization

The tendency to define negatively evaluated behaviours or conditions as medical problems in need of medical intervention.

stigma

Refers to any personal characteristic associated with social disgrace, rejection, or discrediting.

Queer Theory Perspectives

Queer theory developed largely as a response to the management and perception of HIV/AIDS in North America. The theory has drawn attention to the problems that result when HIV transmission risk is seen as something related to sexual identity. High rates of transmission for heterosexual persons proved to be a surprise to epidemiologists: they had assumed that HIV/AIDS would remain inside the gay male community. Careless assumptions about identity and behaviour that failed to note the three central contradictions of identity include these:

1. The identities we declare publicly are not necessarily the identity affiliations we maintain privately.
2. Social imperatives and assumptions about which behaviours are appropriate or unique to certain identity groups have proven to be inaccurate measures of behaviours that people actually follow.
3. The behaviours in which people engage include desires as well as practices. Both are influenced by social location, not by inherent features of biology or simplistic identity categories.

In addition to these observations, gay rights lobbyists, queer theorists, and groups such as the Gay and Lesbian Medical Association (GLMA) successfully contested the classification of homosexuality as a mental health disorder. Simultaneously, they refocused attention on how experiences of homophobia and stigma can have a negative impact on mental health for GLBT persons, or persons who are gay, lesbian, bisexual, or transgender.

2.5 Social Factors Associated with Health and Illness

Public health education campaigns, articles in popular magazines, postsecondary–level health courses, and health professionals emphasize that to be healthy we must adopt a healthy lifestyle. In response, many people have at least tried to quit smoking, follow a healthier diet, and include exercise in their daily or weekly routine. However, health and illness are affected by more than personal lifestyle choices. In the following section, we examine how social factors—such as social class and poverty, education, race, and gender—affect health and illness. Health problems related to environmental problems are discussed in Chapter 14.

Social Class and Poverty

An international group of physicians has identified poverty as the world's leading health problem ("Poverty Threatens Crisis" 1998). Poverty is associated with unsanitary living conditions, hazardous working conditions, lack of access to medical care, and inadequate nutrition (see also Chapter 10).

In Canada, socio-economic status (SES) is related to numerous aspects of health and illness (Health Canada 1999b). For example, self-rated health is strongly linked to income. According to the 1996–97 National Population Health Survey, Canadians who lived in the lowest-income households were four to seven times more likely (depending on race, ethnicity, and sex) to report fair or poor health than those who lived in the highest-income households (Figure 2.3). In

■ **Figure 2.3** *Self-Rated
Health, by Income Level,*
Canadians Aged 12+,
1996–1997*

SOURCE: Adapted from Statistics
Canada. "Self-Rated Health, by
Income Level, Canadians Aged 12+,
1996–1997" *(Statistical Report on
the Health of Canadians),* Catalogue
No. 82-570, 1999.

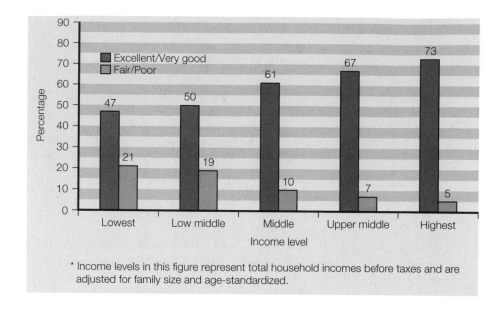

* Income levels in this figure represent total household incomes before taxes and are adjusted for family size and age-standardized.

addition, at each rung up the income ladder, Canadians have less sickness, longer life expectancy, and improved health. "It is estimated that if the death rates of the highest income earners applied to all Canadians, more than one-fifth of all years of life lost before age 65 could be prevented" (Health Canada 1999a: 14). As Figure 2.3 indicates, there is a strong inverse relationship between career earnings and death rates for Canadian men. Compared with those in the lowest quartile of the income distribution, Canadian men in the highest quartile can expect to live 6.3 years longer and have 14.3 more years free of disability. For women, the differences are 3 and 7.6 years, respectively (Health Canada 1999a: 26).

Poor persons are also more likely to report an unmet need for health care. Although in Canada access to universally insured health care remains largely unrelated to income, many low- and moderate-income Canadians have limited or no access to such health services as eye care, dentistry, mental health counselling, and prescription drugs (Health Canada 1999a).

Low socio-economic status is also associated with increased risk of a broad range of psychiatric conditions (Williams and Collins 1999). Rates of depression and substance abuse, for example, are higher in the lower socio-economic classes (Kessler et al. 1994). Why do poor people have higher rates of mental illness? One explanation suggests that individuals from lower socio-economic status groups experience greater stress as a result of their deprived and difficult living conditions. Others argue that members of the lower SES groups are simply more likely to have their behaviours identified and treated as mental illness.

Lower socio-economic groups have higher rates of mortality, in part, because they have higher rates of health risk behaviours, such as smoking, drinking alcohol, being overweight, and being physically inactive. Figure 2.4 shows that despite the widespread belief that executives are prone to stress-related heart attacks, a variety of factors place lower SES groups at higher risk for cardiovascular disease. Even for those who move out of a low SES group in childhood and into a higher SES group in adulthood some significant risks can persist, resulting in increased morbidity for this group. These risks appear to be related to the instability, sense of powerlessness, and persistent stress that a low SES child is more

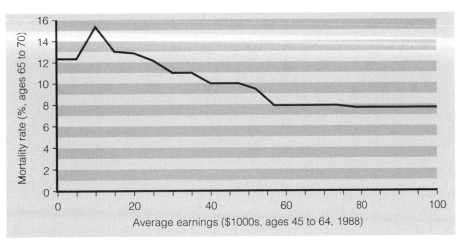

Figure 2.4 *Career Earnings and Death for 500 000 Canadian Men*

SOURCE: Wolfson, M.C. et al. 1993, "Career Earnings and Death: A Longitudinal Analysis of Older Men." *Journal of Gerontology: Social Sciences*, 48 (4) S167–S179. This work is protected by copyright and the making of this copy was with the permission of Access Copyright. Any alteration of its content or further copying in any form whatsoever is strictly prohibited unless otherwise permitted by law.

likely to endure. Such problems may not be remedied by advanced education and have measurable, negative impact on long-term risks for cardiovascular disease (Labonte 1992; Reid 1998). In addition, the lower class tends to experience high levels of stress while having few resources to cope with it (Cockerham 1998). Stress has been linked to a variety of physical and mental health problems, including high blood pressure, cancer, chronic fatigue, and substance abuse.

Education

In general, low levels of education are associated with higher rates of health problems and mortality (Health Canada 1999a). According to the 1996–97 National Population Health Survey, 30 percent of respondents who were university graduates rated their health as "excellent" compared with 19 percent of respondents with less than a high school education (Health Canada 1999a: 42). In addition, less educated women and men have higher rates of suicide. Low birth weight and high infant mortality are also more common among the children of less educated mothers than among children of more educated mothers. Babies of low birth weight (weighing 2500 g or less) are more likely to die in infancy, and those who do survive are more likely to suffer illness, stunted growth, and other health problems into adult life. About 6 percent of babies in Canada are born with low birth weight (Statistics Canada 1998c: 107).

One reason why lower education levels are associated with higher rates of health problems and mortality is that individuals with low levels of education are more likely to engage in health-risk behaviours such as smoking and heavy drinking. The well educated, in contrast, are less likely to smoke and drink heavily, and are more likely to exercise. Women with less education are less likely to seek prenatal care and are more likely to smoke during pregnancy. Research findings suggest that the strong association between education and income best explains differences in health outcomes and mortality rates for high and low SES groups (Lantz et al. 1998).

Gender

Gender issues affect the health of both women and men. Gender discrimination and violence against women produce adverse health effects in girls and women worldwide. Violence against women is a major public health concern: at least one in three women has been beaten, coerced into sex, or abused in some way—most often by someone she knows (United Nations Population Fund 2000). "Although neither health care workers nor the general public typically thinks of battering as a health problem, woman battering is a major cause of injury, disability and death among...women worldwide" (Weitz 2001: 56). In Africa, where the leading cause of death is HIV/AIDS, HIV-positive women outnumber men by 2 million; in part, that is because African women do not have the social power to refuse sexual intercourse or to demand that their male partners use condoms (United Nations Population Fund 2000). As noted earlier, women in developing countries suffer high rates of mortality and morbidity due to the high rates of complications associated with pregnancy and childbirth. The low status of women in many less developed countries results in their being nutritionally deprived and in having less access to medical care than do men. For example, in some countries in Asia and Africa, boys receive more medicine and medical treatment than girls. In Latin America and India, girls are often immunized later than boys or not at all (United Nations Population Fund 2000).

Before the twentieth century, the life expectancy of Canadian women was shorter than that of men. The cause was the high rate of mortality that resulted from complications of pregnancy and childbirth. Currently, however, Canadian women have a higher life expectancy than Canadian men (Statistics Canada 2002).

Although women tend to live longer than men do, they have higher rates of illness and disability than do men (Health Canada 1999a; Verbrugge 1999). Prevalence rates for nonfatal chronic conditions, such as arthritis, thyroid disease, and migraine headache, are typically higher for women. However, men tend to have higher rates of fatal chronic conditions, high blood pressure, heart disease, and diabetes among them. Women also tend to experience a higher incidence of acute conditions, such as colds and influenza, infections, and digestive conditions. "In sum, women live longer than men but experience more illness, whereas men experience relatively little illness but die quickly when illness strikes" (Weitz 2001: 55). As far as mental health goes, men are more likely to abuse drugs and have personality disorders, whereas women are more likely to suffer from mood disorders, such as depression and anxiety (Cockerham 1998).

Men are more prone to chronic and life-threatening diseases, such as coronary disease, because they are more likely than women to smoke, use alcohol and illegal drugs, and work under hazardous conditions. Our culture socializes men to be aggressive and competitive and to engage in risky behaviours (such as playing dangerous sports, driving fast, and being violent), which contributes to their higher risk of death from injuries and accidents. Although women are more likely to attempt suicide, men are more likely to succeed at it because they use deadlier methods. In Canada in 1999, there were 3.8 suicides among men for every suicide among women (Statistics Canada 2002). HIV infections and AIDS deaths in men outnumber those in women on every continent except sub-Saharan Africa (Joint United Nations Programme on HIV/AIDS 2000a). In part, the reason is that the socialization men receive permits and even encourages them to engage in higher-risk sexual behaviour. Men are also less likely than women to seek medical care. Boys who are brought up to believe that "real men don't get sick" often see themselves as invulnerable to illness or risk. The underuse of health services by men reflects this (Joint United Nations Programme on HIV/AIDS 2000a).

Racial and Ethnic Minority Status

In Canada, the risks to health posed by inadequate income, welfare dependency, substandard living conditions, and stresses on mental health and well-being are manifestly apparent in the lives of Aboriginal peoples (Royal Commission on Aboriginal Peoples 1996). The life expectancy of Status Indians (those whose names appear on the Indian Register maintained by the Department of Indian and Northern Affairs pursuant to the *Indian Act*) is seven to eight years shorter than for non-Aboriginal Canadians, and the infant mortality rate double that of the non-Aboriginal population. The rate of accidental death and injury among Aboriginal children is four times that of the non-Aboriginal population; death rates from causes such as birth defects, low birth weight, fetal alcohol syndrome, and respiratory illnesses are consistently and significantly higher among Aboriginal infants and children (Health Canada 1999a; National Council of Welfare 2001). Indigenous Canadians also experience a heightened risk of violent death and elevated rates of injuries, poisonings, and suicide (National Council of Welfare 2001). Among First Nation and Inuit males, the rates of violent death are especially high (Canadian Centre on Substance Abuse 1999).

Indigenous peoples also experience high rates of illicit drug use. First Nation and Métis youth are more likely than non-Indigenous youth to use all types of drugs (*Canadian Aboriginal News* 2001). The use of solvents is significantly higher among Aboriginal youths, and the risk of developing an alcohol problem is two to six times greater than that for other Canadians (Scott 1997). The prevalence of daily smoking among adult Indigenous Canadians occurs at about twice the rate found among the general Canadian population (Canadian Centre on Substance Abuse 1999).

Racial and ethnic prejudice and discrimination may induce psychological distress that adversely affects both physical and mental health status and increases the likelihood of violence and substance abuse. Moreover, **environmental racism**, or the tendency for hazardous waste sites and polluting industries to be located near areas inhabited by those who are poor and socially marginalized, may also contribute to lower levels of health. For example, in the 1980s, the mercury poisoning of the English-Wabigoon river system by local pulp and paper industries led to the virtual destruction of the Grassy Narrows Indians' lifestyle and means of livelihood (Shkilnyk 1985). More recently,

environmental racism
The tendency for hazardous waste sites and polluting industries to be located in areas where the surrounding residential population is an ethnic or racial minority.

patterns of atmospheric cycling have made the North a dumping ground for industrial chemicals that...[are] never used there. The chemicals bioaccumulate, delivering a higher level of toxic concentration to each level up the food chain. As a result, the breast milk of Inuit mothers is 10 times as contaminated as that of southern Canadian women. In both the North and the South, mother's milk is so laden with toxic substances such as PCBs, DDT (and its breakdown product DDE) and lindane, that if it were offered for sale, it would be too contaminated to be approved as human food. (Barlow and May 2000: 184)

This chapter's *The Human Side* feature focuses attention on the health status of Canada's Indigenous peoples.

An Excerpt from Elijah: No Ordinary Hero

Elijah Harper, a Canadian Ojibway-Cree leader, was chief of the Red Sucker Lake Band in Manitoba from 1978 to 1981, served in the Manitoba legislature and as a provincial cabinet minister from 1981 to 1992, and was elected to the House of Commons in 1993. "To some Canadians, especially those of the First Nations, Elijah Harper is a hero...[and] known as the man who, almost singlehandedly, prevented the ratification of the Meech Lake Accord in 1990" (Morton and Weinfeld 1998: 32). Harper acted in the belief that the accord did not adequately address the concerns of First Nations peoples. In this extract, taken from the introduction to Elijah: No Ordinary Hero, *Harper eloquently reminds us why health care is not simply the "private problem" of individuals. Individuals can only do so much; the larger responsibility is society's.*

As a Canadian and an aboriginal person, I could not support an amendment to the supreme law of the country that failed to recognize the place of all the founding cultures of the federation. The suffering of native people is too great.

Aboriginal people in Canada die on average 10 years younger than other Canadians do. Three out of 10 aboriginal families have no furnaces or heat in their homes, yet Canada has one of the highest standards of living in the world. Thirty-four percent have no indoor plumbing; our homes are overcrowded and in poor condition. About 45 percent of aboriginal people are on social assistance. Few of our people are in secondary schools. Only five percent graduate from secondary school. In my province, Manitoba, aboriginal people comprise seven percent of the population, yet they make up 45 percent of the jail population. Family income on reserves is about $10 000, less than half the national average. Alcoholism, drunkenness and solvent abuse are epidemic on some reserves, and we suffer the negative stereotyping that naturally follows from that. Unemployment is about 66 percent; on some reserves, it is as high as 90 percent. Even our languages are in danger. Many have already become extinct. Our religions were forbidden for long enough that much has been forgotten.

But these are only statistics. I cannot bring to you the despair. I bring to you the 15-year-old boy in Winnipeg who will never share a bright future because that child was so depressed by what he saw every day that he took his own belt and hanged himself.... We must attack our problems on two levels. We must attack them as individual problems and we must work to eradicate their origins. We must change personal circumstances and the system. We must build houses for the homeless, but we must also build better communities around them. We must cure the sick, but we must also eliminate the poor water, inadequate sanitation, poor nutrition and poverty that make our people sick. If we don't solve all our problems on those two levels, we will be eternally fighting against a current over which we have no control.

SOURCES: Morton, Desmond, and Morton Weinfeld (eds.). 1998. *Who Speaks for Canada? Words That Shape a Country*. Toronto: McClelland and Stewart Inc. Excerpt from *Elijah: No Ordinary Hero*. Copyright © 1994 by Elijah Harper with Pauline Corneau. Published in Canada by Douglas & McIntyre Ltd.

2.6 Problems in Canadian Health Care

In 2000, the World Health Organization released its report on the first ever analysis of the world's health systems (World Health Organization 2000). The report concluded that France provides the best overall health care among major countries, followed by Italy, Spain, Oman, Austria, and Japan. After presenting a brief overview of Canadian health care, we address some of the major health-care issues in Canada.

Canadian Health Care: An Overview

Canada, like Great Britain, Sweden, Germany, and Italy, has a national health insurance system that is sometimes referred to as socialized medicine. Despite differences in how socialized medicine works in various countries, what is common to all systems of socialized medicine is that the government (1) directly controls the financing and organization of health services, (2) directly pays providers, (3) guarantees equal access to health care, and (4) allows some private care for individuals who are willing to pay for their medical expenses

(Cockerham 1998). However, Canada does not truly have a system of socialized medicine in that the government does not employ Canadian physicians. Rather, the majority of Canada's physicians are independent practitioners in independent or group practices. They are generally paid on a fee-for-service basis and submit their claims directly to the provincial health insurance plan for payment.

The origins of a universal health-care system in Canada can be traced back to 1919. At that time, William Lyon Mackenzie King first raised the idea of national, publicly funded health insurance as part of the Liberal Party platform. However, it took about half a century of intense debate and the persistent efforts of then-Saskatchewan Premier Tommy Douglas, leader of the Co-operative Commonwealth Federation (the precursor to the New Democratic Party), before the Canadian government implemented a universal health-care system. In 1947, Douglas's government pioneered Canada's first universal hospital plan after testing prepaid medical insurance in the Swift Current health district and introducing a public insurance plan for hospital services. Public health-care insurance also began in Saskatchewan with coverage provided for visits to physicians and the services of physicians outside hospitals.

Canada's health-care system, popularly known to Canadians as **medicare**, provides access to universal comprehensive coverage for medically necessary in-patient and outpatient physician services. The role of the federal government in relation to health care is in the setting and administration of national principles for the health-care system, assisting in the financing of provincial health services through fiscal transfers, and fulfilling certain functions for which it is constitutionally responsible. For example, the federal government is responsible for health service delivery to specific groups, including veterans, Indigenous people living on reserves, members of the military, inmates of federal penitentiaries, and the Royal Canadian Mounted Police. However, the management and delivery of health services is the responsibility of each individual province or territory, which plans, finances, and evaluates the provision of hospital care, physician and allied health services, public health, and some aspects of prescription care. As such, our system of health care is perhaps best described as "12 interlocking provincial and territorial plans" (Statistics Canada 1998a).

In 1964, the Hall Royal Commission on Services recommended that the provincial and federal governments introduce a medical program that would eradicate the disparities in Canada's health-care system. The costs of the program were to be borne through taxation. The federal government agreed to share the costs equally with the provinces if each provincial plan satisfied five requirements:

1. Accessibility: reasonable access should be guaranteed to all Canadians.
2. Comprehensiveness: all necessary medical services should be guaranteed, without dollar limit, and should be available solely on the basis of medical need.
3. Universality: all Canadians should be eligible for coverage on uniform terms and conditions.
4. Portability: benefits should be transferable from province to province.
5. Administration by a public, nonprofit agency or commission. (Grant 1993: 401)

In 1972, these recommendations became law.

Evidence suggests that our health-care system is accomplishing what it originally set out to do: to eliminate inequality among Canadians in relation to health-care services. For example, poor women in Toronto have a survival rate

medicare
Canada's health-care system, which provides access to universal comprehensive coverage for medically necessary inpatient and outpatient physician services.

for breast cancer that is 30 percent higher than the rate for poor women in Detroit. For ovarian cancer, the survival rate is 38 percent higher; for cervical cancer, it is 48 percent higher (Armstrong et al. 1998). However, while two-thirds of Canadians in one poll agreed with the statement "Canada's health care system is one of the best in the world," the last decade has seen massive cuts made to that system. As deficit-strapped governments in the 1990s ratcheted back health expenditures, the percentage of Canadians citing health care as a top concern has grown from 5 percent in 1993 to 64 percent in 2000. Between 1991 and 2000, the number of Canadians rating our health-care system as very good or excellent has shrunk from 61 percent to 25 percent; the number of those rating the system as poor or very poor increased threefold over the same time period. Moreover, when forecasting 10 years into the future, 58 percent of Canadians believe that the state of health care in our country will get worse; only 24 percent believe it will get better (Bricker and Greenspon 2001: 189–90). It is evident that the question of how to sustain—if not improve—public health care in Canada will continue to be the subject of intense concern, controversy, and debate.

Unmet Needs

In 2001, of the 30 countries in the Organisation for Economic Co-operation and Development (OECD), only three—the United States, Germany, and Switzerland—spent more than Canada on health care as a proportion of gross domestic product (GDP) (Milne 2002). However, despite spending more than $100 billion on health care in 2001 alone (Kennedy 2001), Canadians confront the closing of emergency room departments and long waits in those that remain; continuing shortages of nurses, physicians, specialists, and costly diagnostic equipment; persistent geographic differences in access to services; a decrease in the number of available hospital beds; and ever-growing waiting lists for scheduled surgeries (Marshall 2001).

Although Canada's universal health insurance system is based on the premise that "all citizens will have access to the care they need within a reasonable time period" (Health Canada 1999b), there are no precise definitions of what constitutes needed care or a reasonable time. One national survey conducted by the Canadian Medical Association (CMA 1999) suggests Canadians perceived a decline in access to health-care services between 1996 and 1998. More recently, their 2001 national survey found that "[w]hen asked to assign a letter grade to the current health care system, Canadians gave it, on average, a B for overall quality." While Canadians assigned a grade of A to "access to family physicians," they awarded a grade of B to "access to community services for youth and seniors" and a grade of C to "access to modern diagnostic equipment, emergency room services, mental health services and medical specialists" (CMA 2001).

In general, Canadians were far more critical of the government's performance in the delivery of health care. While health-care providers, particularly physicians, were given a grade of B, the federal government was given a grade of C. They gave a failing grade (F) to their provincial government's performance on health-care issues. When asked how our current system could be improved, more than 8 in 10 identified the provision of long-term, sustainable funding. A second option, advanced by almost 6 in 10 Canadians, stressed efficient management and the proper allocation of existing funds.

Patients are not the only Canadians complaining of inadequate services. At the 1999 annual meeting of the CMA, physicians asserted that Canada was heading toward a critical shortage of doctors that would threaten patient safety; they also emphasized that there already was a serious shortage of physicians in rural areas and within certain specialties, such as anesthesia, radiology, and obstetrics. It was noted that even in major Canadian cities such as Toronto, patients were being forced to wait for needed surgery because of the shortage (Bricker and Greenspon 2001: 217). It is estimated that by 2021, there will be only one doctor for every 718 patients (compared to one doctor for every 548 patients in 1998) (Kennedy 1999). In addition, physicians have acknowledged that their ability to assist their patients is being jeopardized by the unavailability of the costly equipment they need. For example, while PET (positron emission tomography) scanners are the best way to diagnose and evaluate tumours, there are no publicly funded PET scanners anywhere in British Columbia. In consequence, B.C. physicians must tell patients who require a scan that "they can either pay $2500 for one at a private PET facility in Vancouver, or go out of province or out of country to get it" (Milne 2002: 41).

It is also evident that the aging of the Canadian population (see Chapter 6) will challenge the sustainability of our publicly funded health-care system. Consider that when economist James Frank superimposed the population profile of British Columbia in 2020 on that province's 2000–01 provincial budget, the effect was immense. "The impact of a more aged population immediately added $1.7 billion to health care spending, driving the province's deficit from its projected $1.2 billion that year upwards to nearly $3 billion" (Bricker and Greenspon 2001: 198).

In recent years, the premiers of Ontario and Alberta have both issued challenges to the federal government over health care. In the spring of 2000, for example, the Alberta government passed Bill 11, the *Health Protection Act*, which allowed private, for-profit clinics to perform minor surgical procedures and to keep patients overnight. More recently, the Alberta government seems poised to introduce changes that would allow for greater privatization. In like fashion, in Ontario, the provincial government has threatened that, if Ottawa does not increase transfer payments, it will withdraw pharmacare (a system of subsidizing drug costs) and home care services to senior citizens. Some applaud these developments and argue for privatization: that is, allowing private clinics to play an expanded role in the public system or creating a parallel private system, as in Britain. They argue that privatization will facilitate timely access to quality care and allow provinces to cope with rising health costs. Others, however, suggest that privatization might result in the development of a two-tier system of health care: one for those who can pay for quality care and a second for those who cannot. Among their concerns:

- ability to pay will become more important than need in determining access to quality health care;
- the facilities and doctors available to those with private money will be of a much higher quality than the ones available in the public system;
- the problems in the current system will not necessarily be solved by bringing in private money; and
- private money will only put more cash into the pockets of those in the system who want to increase their incomes; it won't deal with the problems being experienced in facilities or services (Bricker and Greenspon 2001: 196).

The fifth annual Health Care in Canada survey, a nationwide investigation of the attitudes of 800 health professionals and 1200 members of the public, found that when asked what they thought of allowing Canadians to pay to receive speedier services from private clinics, opinion was almost evenly split: while about half (47 percent) of the general public rejected the notion, 49 percent favoured that two-tier approach (Milne 2002: 40). However, many Canadians cherish the ideal of a single-payee, public health system as an important component of our national identity. One study, for example, reported that 25 percent of Canadians identified our health-care system as what makes us unique from other countries (receiving over three times as many mentions as other characteristics such as multiculturalism, freedom, and tolerance [all at 7 percent]). Among those who cited health care as a major symbol of our national identity, almost three-quarters identified public funding and universality as "especially defining features" (Bricker and Greenspon 2001: 196). A 2000 survey reported that while fully three-quarters of Canadians nationwide believe that solving the health-care crisis will cost Canadians more money, 56 percent of Canadians say they are willing to pay more—either out of pocket or through a dedicated health tax—to sustain our system of public health care (Milne 2002: 40).

Access to Dental Care

According to the 1996–97 National Population Health Survey, slightly more than half of all Canadians (55 percent) have dental insurance. Having dental insurance is much more common among children, youths, and working-age adults than among Canadian seniors. Among those 75 years of age and older in Canada, only 25 percent of men and 17 percent of women report having dental insurance. Income differences in relation to dental care are particularly notable: those in the highest income group are about three times as likely to have dental insurance as those in the lowest category. There are also variations in insurance coverage between provinces. Slightly more than 60 percent of residents in Ontario and Alberta have dental insurance versus lows of 40 and 43 percent in Quebec and Newfoundland, respectively. In Canada, dentists work independently of the health-care system except where in-hospital dental surgery is required.

The High Cost of Medications

Except for medication received while in institutional care, the *Canada Health Act* does not cover prescription drugs, nonprescription drugs, and over-the-counter products (e.g., cough and cold remedies, oral hygiene products, and home diagnostic kits). Instead, payers include governments through pharmacare programs, private insurance (including insurance companies, employees, and unions), and patients paying directly. According to the 1996–97 National Population Health Survey, the prescription drug costs of almost two-thirds (61 percent) of Canadians were covered to some extent by government plans or insurance. The greatest percentage was covered under private plans. Seventy-five percent of high-income Canadians had prescription drug plan subsidies in 1996–97, but this benefit was available to only 54 percent of middle-income Canadians and 39 percent of low-income Canadians (Health Canada 1999a).

For those Canadians who lack insurance, the costs of medically necessary drug products may be prohibitively high. A 2001 report by the Canadian Institute for Health Information noted that costs for Canadians paying directly for prescription drugs, over-the-counter remedies, and other non-prescribed products has jumped dramatically—by 125 percent—over the past 12 years. In 2000, the average Canadian spent about $478 on drugs. As health economist Jeremiah Hurley has observed, "[I]f drugs are going to continue to become an important part of medically necessary services, then what does it mean if we have a significant component of financing coming from direct payments by individuals and in what ways might that compromise public access to necessary treatment?" (in Arnold 2001).

At present, only four Canadian provinces provide universal drug plans. British Columbia is the only province that uses a reference-based pricing scheme. Under the scheme, the province pays for only the lowest-cost drug in each of three designated "therapeutic categories" to help reduce costs. In provinces without universal plans, Armstrong and colleagues (1998) note that "not only are many individuals left out, especially among the 'working poor,' but it is very difficult for any particular plan to control costs. At the same time, each of them faces unnecessarily high administrative costs." In consequence, the National Forum on Health has called our current drug plan situation "incompatible with Canada's vision for the health care system." It has recommended the establishment of a single-payer, publicly funded system for medicinal drugs.

Organ Replacement

Organ replacement is not a simple solution to disease; rather, it is a complex intersection of problems with resource allocation, health-care costs, and quality of life concerns. In 1996, surgeons in Canada performed 1578 transplants of kidneys, hearts, lungs, and other organs. Partly because of preventable diseases caused by lifestyle habits, and partly because primary earners have priority when organs are being allocated for transplant, men receive most transplants in general (65 percent), and most heart transplants (84 percent) in particular (Health Canada 1999b; Statistics Canada 1998a).

There is a popular perception that organ transplant "saves or dramatically improves the lives of some 1500 Canadians per year" (Baer 1997: 179). Popular appeals to sign our donor cards reinforce this, and the Canadian Medical Association promotes transplantation as a cost-saving means of treating Canadians (Baer 1997). Where transplantation can reduce suffering, few of us would refuse the right of a patient to receive one. However, studies to support the conclusion that organ transplant improves recipients' quality of life are methodologically haphazard; they also draw attention away from poor survival rates (Joralemon and Fujinaga 1996).

2.7 Strategies for Action: Improving Health and Health Care

Because poverty underlies many of the world's health problems, improving the world's health requires strategies that reduce poverty (see Chapter 10). Other chapters in this text discuss strategies to alleviate problems associated with tobacco and illegal drugs (Chapter 3), hazards in the workplace (Chapter 11), and environmental health problems (Chapter 14). Here, we discuss strategies for improving health, including improvements for maternal and infant health, HIV/AIDS prevention and alleviation, the use of computer technology in health care, and Canada's health-care reform.

Improving Maternal and Infant Health

Several factors contribute to high maternal mortality rates in less developed countries. Poor quality and inaccessible health care, malnutrition, and poor sanitation contribute to adverse health effects of pregnancy and childbirth. In developing countries, only 53 percent of all births are attended to by professionals and nearly 30 percent of women who give birth in developing countries receive no care after the birth (United Nations Population Fund 2000). Also, women in less developed countries experience higher rates of pregnancy and child-bearing and begin child-bearing at earlier ages. Thus, they face the risk of maternal death more often and before their bodies are fully developed (see also Chapter 14). Women in many countries lack access to family planning services, the support of their male partners to use contraceptive methods such as condoms, or both. Consequently, many women resort to abortion to limit their child-bearing, even in countries where abortion is illegal. For more on maternal mortality rates, see Figure 2.5.

Illegal abortions in less developed countries have an estimated mortality risk of 100 to 1000 per 100 000 procedures (Miller and Rosenfield 1996). In contrast, the Canadian mortality risk for therapeutic abortions is very low (Health Canada 1999b). Each year, women worldwide undergo an estimated 50 million abortions, 20 million of which are unsafe, resulting in the deaths of 78 000 women (United Nations Population Fund 2000).

In 1987, the Safe Motherhood Initiative was launched. This global initiative is a partnership of governments, NGOs, agencies, donors, and women's health

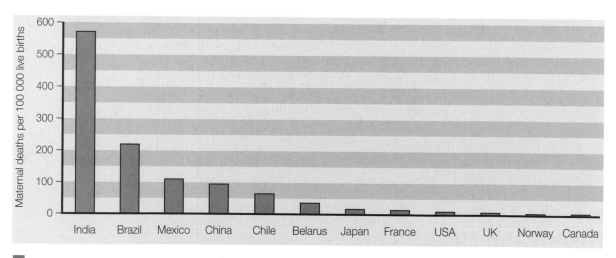

■ **Figure 2.5** *Maternal Mortality Rates in Selected Countries, 1999 Estimates*

SOURCE: "Underreporting of Maternal Mortality in Canada: A Question of Definition," by Turner, Linda A., Margaret Cyr, Robert A. Kinch, Robert Liston, Michael S. Kramer, Martha Fair, and Maureen Heamen. 2002 *(Chronic Diseases in Canada)*, 23(1). Health Canada 2002. Reproduced with the permission of the Minister of Public Works and Government Services Canada, 2011.

advocates working to protect women's health and lives, especially during pregnancy and childbirth. Improving women's health also improves the health of infants: 30 to 40 percent of infant deaths are the result of poor care during labour and delivery (Safe Motherhood Initiative 1998). The cost of ensuring that women in low-income countries get pre- and post- and perinatal health care, family planning services, and newborn care costs about $3 (U.S.) per person per year (Family Care International 1999).

The Safe Motherhood Initiative advocates improving maternal and infant health by first identifying the powerlessness that women face as an injustice countries must remedy. In many countries, men make the decisions about whether or when their wives (or partners) will have sexual relations, use contraception, or bear children. Improving and maintaining the status and power of women involves ensuring that they have the right to make decisions about their health and reproductive lives. Changes must be made in political, health, and legal systems.

The Save the Children Foundation's report "State of the World's Mothers 2004: Children Having Children" found that access to family planning and female education are the two most important determinants of the well-being of mothers and their children. Women must have access to family planning services, affordable methods of contraception, and safe abortion services. The Safe Motherhood Initiative noted that early pregnancy and birth cause the deaths of 70 000 young mothers and 1 million infants each year (2004: 6), and that 2 million unsafe abortions are performed every year on females aged 15 to 19 (2004: 15). The Initiative recommends reforming laws and policies to support women's reproductive health and improve access to family planning services. Doing so would mean removing legal barriers to abortion—a highly controversial issue in many countries. Promoting women's education increases the status and power of women to control their reproductive lives, exposes women to information about health issues, and also delays marriage and child-bearing.

HIV/AIDS Prevention and Alleviation Strategies

One suggested strategy to curb the spread of HIV involves encouraging individuals to get tested for HIV so they can modify their behaviour to avoid transmitting the virus to others, and so they can receive early medical intervention that can slow or prevent the onset of AIDS. Millions of HIV-infected people throughout the world are not aware that they are infected. Many are hesitant to find out if they have HIV because of the stigma associated with HIV/AIDS. HIV testing facilities are also inadequate in many developing countries. However, testing is not enough. Research suggests that individuals who have been diagnosed with HIV often continue to engage in higher-risk behaviours. One study compared behaviours in HIV-infected youth (younger than 25 years) and HIV-infected adults (25 years or older). It found that 66 percent of young women and 46 percent of adult women continued higher-risk behaviours after HIV infection; also, 28 percent of young men with HIV infection and 16 percent of infected adult men engaged in higher-risk behaviour (Diamond and Buskin 2000).

Alleviating HIV/AIDS also requires educating populations about how to protect against HIV and providing access to condoms. However, there continues to be widespread concern that sex education and access to condoms will encourage young people to become sexually active prematurely. Consequently, many sex education programs have focused solely upon abstinence. Several studies have concluded, however, that sex education programs that combine messages about abstinence and safer sex practices (e.g., condom use) may delay the initiation of sexual behaviour as well as increase preventive behaviours among young people who are already sexually active (Joint United Nations Programme on HIV/AIDS 2000c).

Alleviating HIV/AIDS requires making medical interventions accessible and affordable, especially to the poor populations in developing countries. In an effort to combat AIDS in Africa, five of the world's leading pharmaceutical companies have agreed to decrease the price of drugs used to treat HIV. But even at discounted prices, the drugs will be beyond what many Africans can afford.

There is currently no cure for HIV or AIDS. Although various prevention and alleviation strategies may help reduce the spread of HIV and AIDS deaths, the HIV pandemic "will ultimately be controlled only by immunization against HIV using a protective, cheap, simple, and widely available vaccine" (Ward 1999: 199). As of this writing, no such effective vaccine exists, although at least 29 AIDS vaccines have been clinically tested around the world without success (Gottlieb 2000).

Health Promotion

For at least 25 years, federal policy has recognized the importance of individual behaviour as a determinant of health status. In recent years, the focus has shifted from individual behaviour to the socio-economic determinants of behaviour; however, there is no doubt that health education remains an important health promotion strategy at the levels of the individual and of the broader population.

Canadian health education stresses that good nutrition, exercise, and abstention from smoking are important to good health, and it seems that many Canadians are heeding the message. For example, the National Population Health Survey reported that in the 12 months prior to the survey, 47 percent of the respondents had changed a facet of their behaviour to improve their health, while 54 percent recognized that some change was needed. Among the latter group, more than two-thirds (69 percent) indicated that they intended to change their behaviour in the next year. Among those who recognized a need for change, the need most commonly identified was for more exercise followed by reductions in smoking, improved nutrition, and weight loss. An absence of time and personal willpower were identified as the main barriers to making the desired lifestyle changes.

Within this survey, women were more likely than men to report having made changes in their personal behaviours in the year before the survey; women were also more likely to voice their intention to make such changes in the forthcoming year. However, differences based on gender were less notable than differences based on age. With increasing age, "[t]here was a general decline in behaviour change—whether actual, needed, or intended" (Health Canada 1999b). Individuals in Ontario were more likely to report behaviour changes in the previous year and the least likely to report any intended changes in future years. Residents of Quebec (79 percent), British Columbia (73 percent), and Alberta (61 percent) were the most likely to report intentions to change in the next year.

Programs for People with Disabilities

It would be a grave mistake to forget the necessity of ensuring the physical and social health of those who have physical or mental disabilities. People with disabilities in Canada continue to face disadvantage in areas such as work, housing support services, transportation, and income support. Moreover, depending on the specific nature of their disability, they may or may not have access to adequate health-care and education services.

Graham (1999) has noted that "support programs and services available to persons with disabilities, which are so essential to viability within the wider community, vary enormously from one part of the country to another." He points out that in Lloydminster, which straddles the Saskatchewan–Alberta border, a person with a visual disability can obtain certain high-tech equipment on the Alberta side, but not on the Saskatchewan side: "in other words, if you live in Saskatchewan you can get a white cane—but sorry, nothing high tech." Consider as well that only two decades ago, newborns with Down syndrome often died in Canada because of physicians' recommendations that parents not correct a simple stomach blockage (Mitchell 1995: A10).

It has been suggested that a Canadian disability act is necessary to ensure that the rights and needs of people with disabilities in Canada are protected (Kerzner and Baker 1999). In the absence of such an act, organizations such as the Council of Canadians with Disabilities, the Canadian Association for Independent Living Centres, DAWN (the DisAbled Women's Network), and the Coalition of Provincial Organizations of the Handicapped, and institutes such as the Roeher Institute, the Canadian Council on Rehabilitation and Work, the Canadian Centre on Disability Studies, and the National Aboriginal Clearing/Connecting House on Disability Issues, attempt to ensure that both the health and social needs of people with disabilities are not ignored in Canada.

Telemedicine: Computer Technology in Health Care

Computer technology offers numerous ways to reduce costs associated with health-care delivery and to improve patient care. **Telemedicine** involves using information and communication technologies to deliver a wide range of health-care services, including diagnosis, treatment, prevention, health support and information, and education of health-care workers. Telemedicine can involve the transmission of three main types of information: data, audio, and images. A patient's medical records or vital signs (such as heart rate and blood pressure) can be transmitted from one location to another. Many hospitals and clinics store their medical records electronically, allowing doctors to access information about their patients quickly and to update patient data from a distance. Specialized medical databases, such as MEDLINE, can be accessed via the Internet and offer a valuable resource for health-care practitioners and researchers. The public may also use the Internet to gain health information and support. The transmission of radiological images (such as X-ray and ultrasound) from one location to another for the purpose of interpretation or consultation has become one of the most commonly used telemedicine services. Images of tissue samples may also be transmitted to another location, where a pathologist can look at the image on a monitor and offer an interpretation.

telemedicine

Using information and communication technologies to deliver a wide range of health-care services, including diagnosis, treatment, prevention, health support and information, and education of health-care workers.

Benefits of Telemedicine Telemedicine has the potential to improve public health by making health care available in rural and remote areas and by providing health information to health-care workers and to the general population. In addition, "telemedicine allows the scarce resources of specialists and expensive equipment to be shared by a much greater number of patients. Doctors are no longer restricted by geographical boundaries; international specialists are able to spread their skills across continents, without leaving their own hospitals" (LaPorte 1997: 38).

Telemedicine can be used in training and educating health-care professionals and providing health-care workers with up-to-date health information. Telemedicine can also reduce health-care costs by reducing the cost of travel to major health centres or to specialists, and by reducing the length of hospitalization, since patients can be monitored at a distance.

Another benefit of telemedicine is the provision of health information and support services on the Internet. This resource helps empower individuals in managing their health concerns. According to a 2001 survey, over half of Canadians with Internet access visited a health site; 3 in 10 said they had done so at least once in the past week and another 45 percent at least once during the past month. Of those who visited a health site, half judged themselves to be more knowledgeable as a result of their efforts (Bricker and Greenspon 2001: 225). Through e-mail, bulletin boards, and chat rooms, individuals with specific health problems can network with other similarly affected individuals. This social support assists in patient recovery, reduces the number of visits to physicians and clinics, and "provides...individuals [with disabilities] with an opportunity to achieve levels of social integration that were simply not possible before" (LaPorte 1997: 33).

In the twentieth century, advances in public health were largely due to improvements in sanitation and immunization. Advocates of telemedicine have forecast that in the twenty-first century, improvements in public health will result from the increased uses of information technology (LaPorte 1997). Telemedicine holds the promise of improving the health of individuals, families, communities, and nations. But whether or not telemedicine achieves its promise depends, in part, on whether resources are allocated to provide the technology and the training to use it.

Understanding Illness and Health Care

Human health has probably improved more over the past half century than over the previous three millennia (Feachem 2000). Yet the gap in health between rich and poor remains very wide and the very poor suffer appallingly. Health problems are affected not only by economic resources, but also by other social factors, such as aging of the population, gender, education, and race/ethnicity.

Our cultural values and beliefs emphasize the ability of individuals to control their lives through the choices they make. Thus, Westerners view health and illness as results from individual behaviour and lifestyle choices rather than as the result of social, economic, and political forces. Westerners generally agree that an individual's health is affected by the choices that person makes—choices such as whether or not to smoke, exercise, engage in sexual activity, use condoms, and wear a seatbelt. However, if the goal is to improve the health not only of individuals but also of entire populations, then the influence of social, economic, and political forces on the choices that individuals make must be taken into account. Further, by focusing on individual behaviours that affect health and illness, we often overlook both social causes and social solutions of health problems. For example, at an individual level, the public has been advised to rinse and cook meat, poultry, and eggs thoroughly and to carefully wash hands, knives, cutting boards, and so on. The goal is to avoid illness caused by *E. coli* and salmonella bacteria. Whether or not one becomes ill from contaminated meat, eggs, or poultry, though, is affected by more than individual behaviours in the kitchen. Governmental actions can also offer solutions by providing for more food inspectors and stricter regulations on food industries.

Although certain changes in medical practices and policies may help to improve world health, "the health sector should be seen as an important, but not the sole, force in the movement toward global health" (Lerer et al. 1998: 18). Improving the health of a society requires addressing diverse issues, including poverty and economic inequality, gender inequality, population growth, environmental issues, education, housing, energy, water and sanitation, agriculture, and workplace safety. Health promotion is important in the hospital, clinic, or doctor's office—but also in the various settings where people live, work, play, and learn (Antezana et al. 1998).

Perhaps the most critical public health agenda today is reducing the gap between the health of advantaged and disadvantaged populations. Feachem (2000) suggests that "addressing this problem, both between and within countries, constitutes one of the greatest challenges of the new century. Failure to do so properly will have dire consequences for the global economy, for social order and justice, and for civilization as a whole" (p. 1).

Critical Thinking

1. An analysis of 161 countries found that, in general, countries with high levels of literacy have low levels of HIV (World Health Organization and United Nations Joint Programme on HIV/AIDS 1998). However, in the region of the world affected the worst by HIV, sub-Saharan Africa, there is also a relationship between literacy rates and HIV, but the direction of the relationship is reversed. In this region, the countries with the highest levels of HIV infection are also those whose men and women are most literate. What are some possible explanations for this?

2. The Centers for Disease Control and Prevention (CDC) recommends that people aged six and older engage regularly, preferably daily, in light to moderate physical activity for at least 30 minutes. Experts agree that if those "who lead sedentary lives would adopt a more active lifestyle, there would be enormous benefit to the public's health and to individual well-being" (Pate et al. 1995: 406). Yet, in a telephone survey of more than 87 000 adults, only about 22 percent reported being active at the recommended level; 24 percent reported that they led a completely sedentary lifestyle (that is, one without any leisure-time physical activity in the past month). What social and cultural factors contribute to the sedentary lifestyle of many North Americans?

3. Why do you think the American Psychiatric Association (2000) avoids the use of such expressions as "a schizophrenic" or "an alcoholic" and instead uses the expressions "an individual with schizophrenia" or "an individual with alcohol dependence"?

"Is It True?" Quiz: Answers

1 = false; 2 = true; 3 = true; 4 = true; 5 = false

Alcohol and Other Drugs

Outline

Is It True?

1. Alcoholics are seven times more likely to separate or divorce than non-alcoholics.

2. Impaired driving is one of the most common crimes committed by Canadians and a major cause of death in Canada.

3. Of all psychoactive drugs, alcohol is the only one whose consumption has been shown to increase aggression.

4. A greater percentage of Canadians use pot than do the Dutch, although the sale and use of marijuana are not illegal in the Netherlands.

5. The Dutch have decriminalized small quantities of heroin and have one of the lowest addiction rates in Europe.

© David De Lossy/Getty Images

Read more here: 1 = p. 91, 2 = p. 71, 3 = p. 75, 4 = p. 72, 5 = p. 72

Answers can be found on p. 103.

According to data compiled by University of British Columbia researchers on behalf of **MADD** (Mothers Against Drunk Driving), there are more than 1200 impaired driving deaths on Canada's roadways and almost 170 such deaths on Canada's waterways every year. It is estimated that there are 1600 alcohol-related deaths each year. In addition, another 74 000 people are injured each year due to impaired driving. Emotionally, the loss is staggering for families, and financially, the cost to the country each year is high. MADD provides a conservative, minimum cost estimate at $1.9 billion, without any accounting for social costs such as rehabilitation, occupational therapy, and grief counselling. When social costs are factored in, MADD estimates the total annual cost to be closer to $11 billion each year (Mercer and Marshall 2005).

Substance use becomes a social problem, usually defined as *abuse*, when it interferes with the well-being of individuals and the societies in which they live—when it jeopardizes health, safety, work and academic success, family, and friends. Managing the drug problem is a difficult undertaking, though. In dealing with drugs, a society must balance individual rights and civil liberties against the personal and social harm that drugs can exacerbate: fetal exposure, suicide, impaired driving, industrial accidents, mental illness, unemployment, and youth vulnerabilities.

Although the use of alcohol is not always treated as a problem, it can become highly problematic under certain conditions. These conditions usually involve danger to others, especially when driving is involved. Therefore, under the Canadian *Criminal Code*, there are four specific types of driving offences that stem initially from drinking and driving but that extend more broadly to *impairment*:

- The first is "operating or having care or control of a motor vehicle while one's ability to drive is impaired by alcohol or a drug." The term *drug* is broadly defined here to include any substance, legal or illegal, which can cause impairment.
- The second type of offence is "[e]ngaging in impaired driving causing death or bodily harm." The 1985 introduction of this offence was intended to make the penalties for causing serious accidents while impaired harsher than those for "simply" driving while impaired. The maximum penalty for impaired driving causing bodily harm is 10 years' imprisonment and 10 years' driving prohibition; the maximum penalty for impaired driving causing death is 14 years' imprisonment and 10 years' driving prohibition.
- The third type is "[o]perating or having care or control of a motor vehicle with a blood alcohol concentration (BAC) over 0.08 percent." Since May 2009, changes to Ontario laws result in drivers with a BAC level over 0.05 being considered in the "warn" range, because driving ability is significantly impaired enough at this level but below 0.08 to raise the likelihood of an accident more than sevenfold (MTO Fact Sheet: Blood Alcohol Concentration (BAC)). Even if you *could* drive safely, driving with a BAC over 0.08 is a criminal offence in Canada. The specific amount of alcohol that must be consumed to have a BAC over the specified level varies. It depends on such factors as when the individual last ate, what that person's weight and percentage of body fat are, and how quickly the alcohol was consumed. Nevertheless, BAC can be determined through an analysis of a person's blood or urine.
- The final type of offence is "[f]ailing to provide breath or blood samples for analysis without a reasonable excuse." The term *reasonable excuse* refers to an inability to comprehend the demand or to physically comply with it.

MADD

Mothers Against Drunk Driving. A social action group committed to reducing drunk driving.

Larger questions of when to regulate, what to regulate, and who should regulate are complex social issues. Our discussion begins by looking at how drugs are used and regulated in other societies.

3.1 The Global Context: Drug Use and Abuse

drug

Any substance other than food that alters the structure and functioning of a living organism when it enters the bloodstream.

Pharmacologically, a **drug** is any substance other than food that alters the structure or functioning of a living organism when it enters the bloodstream. Using this definition, everything from vitamins to Aspirin constitutes a drug. Sociologically, the term drug refers to any chemical substance that (1) has a direct effect on the user's physical, psychological, and/or intellectual functioning, (2) has the potential to be abused, and (3) has adverse consequences for the individual and/or society. Societies vary in how they define and respond to drug use. Thus, drug use is influenced by the social context of the particular society in which it occurs.

Drug Use around the World

According to United Nations estimates, the prevalence of drug use around the world varies dramatically. The UN World Drug Report (UN-WDR) notes that there are serious methodological problems with attempting to measure drug use for any given region, including the fact that users often comprise a "hidden population," and that asking about use over a specific period of time will yield radically different results than asking about use over the course of a lifetime (UN-WDR 2009: 299). Put more simply, if asked whether they have *ever* used marijuana in their lives, for example, numbers who answer yes will be far higher than if we ask whether people have used marijuana in the last year (ibid). A constructionist approach to understanding social problems will not necessarily see a question about lifetime use providing us with a reliable indication that pot use is a social problem. To determine whether drug use *is* a social problem, we would have to determine that it is factually causative of other social harms. For a constructionist, it is more useful to understand the abuse of alcohol and other drugs as problematic only insofar as it correlates with other social problems (e.g., poverty, marginalization, poor health, negative impact on child welfare, contribution to organized crime, or directly causing harm to non-users—as in the case of impaired driving that causes death or injury). The data in Figure 3.1 deliver a visual understanding of what kinds of substance use have resulted in treatment for users, thus indicating that the level of use for those users had become a significant enough problem to warrant intervention. The graph also shows that the kinds of drugs that become most problematic in a world region vary greatly based on trafficking routes and local laws.

Some differences in international drug use may result in variations in drug policies. Official government policy in the Netherlands, for example, treats the use of such drugs as marijuana, hashish, and heroin as a health issue rather than as a crime issue. Evidence now suggests that marijuana use among Dutch youth is decreasing (Sheldon 2000; UN-WDR 2009).

Although lifetime-use indicators may overstate the degree to which drug use is a problem, data regarding lifetime use can still yield useful information about

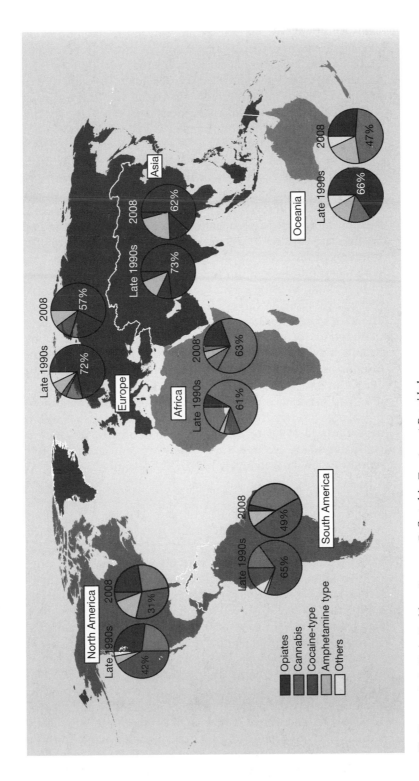

■ **Figure 3.1** *Main Problem Drugs as Reflected in Treatment Provided*

SOURCE: United Nations *World Drug Report 2009* © United Nations Office on Drugs and Crime, http://www.unodc.org/unodc/en/data-and-analysis/WDR-2009.html

what kinds of vulnerabilities correlate with concentrated populations' higher usage rates. In the United Kingdom (Great Britain, Scotland, Wales, and Northern Ireland), for example, one-third of the adult population is estimated to have used drugs at some time—and, of those, 49 percent are under age 30. Statistics also indicate that when compared with non-users, drug users in the United Kingdom are more likely to be male, unemployed, and living in or around London. These numbers do not include the use of alcohol. The data indicate, then, a variety of correlations between vulnerabilities such as urban poverty, geographic location (London is a major port city), educational attainment, and increased drug use.

Great Britain has also adopted a "medical model," particularly in regard to heroin and cocaine. As early as the 1960s, English doctors prescribed opiates and cocaine for patients unlikely to quit using drugs on their own and for the treatment of withdrawal symptoms. By the 1970s, however, British laws had become more restrictive, making it difficult for either physicians or users to obtain drugs legally. Today, British government policy provides for limited distribution of drugs by licensed drug treatment specialists—that is how addicts who might otherwise resort to crime to support their habits get drugs.

In addition to using surveys to measure the prevalence of lifetime drug use, regions will also use surveys that are repeated over extended periods of time. The data so gathered can reveal trends, both upward and downward in particular regions, for specific populations and age groups. Such long-term data from Britain showed that "rave culture" correlated to unprecedented prevalence of drug use in populations not marginalized by class or race (Aldridge 2008: 189–191). However, as these so-called "children of the decade of dance" matured, drug use prevalence dropped (191), and Aldridge's analysis shows that while prevalence has not dropped to its pre-1990 levels, use is well down from levels from the mid-1990s to 2000s (ibid). In short, the UK data demonstrate that population drug-use trends are not always and irretrievably upward, and are not always linked to marginalization or "deviance."

Drug Use in Canada

According to government officials and the media—both institutions with something to gain by promising to pay attention to the problem—there is a drug crisis in Canada. Canadians' concern with drugs, however, has varied over the years. In 1975, almost one in two Canadians (46 percent) identified drugs as a "very serious" problem in our country, but by 1995, this figure had declined to approximately one in three (34 percent). Similarly, while 64 percent of Canadian teens viewed drugs as a "very serious" social concern in 1992, in 2000 only 48 percent did so (Bibby 2001: 181). Currently, groups such as the Canadian Foundation for Drug Policy (CFDP) work to propose "drug laws that are effective and humane." The CFDP was formed in the early 1990s by health-care professionals and academic researchers who were concerned that the laws being enacted by the federal governments (Conservative and Liberal) were unnecessary punitive and were doomed to fail as other prohibition legislation had done. The CFDP continues to publish research and to deliver information aimed at a broad audience, and provide most of it on their website at www.cfdp.ca.

In Canada, the use of alcohol is much more widespread than the use of illicit drugs such as marijuana and cocaine, but our response to drug use is contradictory. On the one hand, we condemn drugs such as heroin; on the other, we encourage and tolerate drugs such as alcohol. At various times in our history, many drugs that are illegal today were legal and readily available. In the 1800s and the early 1900s, opium was routinely used as a pain reliever, and morphine was taken as a treatment for dysentery and fatigue. Amphetamine-based inhalers were legally available until 1949, and cocaine was an active ingredient in Coca-Cola until 1906, when it was replaced with another drug—caffeine (Witters et al. 1992). In the 1950s, anabolic steroids were viewed as "wonder drugs" that could enhance the well-being of sick and malnourished people, promote quick weight gain in cattle, and potentially provide a cure to cancer. Not until 1988, when Canadian athlete Ben Johnson lost his gold medal at the Seoul Olympics for taking a performance-enhancing drug, did many Canadians become aware that the use of anabolic steroids could be problematic.

3.2 Sociological Theories of Drug Use and Abuse

Most theories of drug use and abuse concentrate on what are called psychoactive drugs. These drugs alter the functioning of the brain, affecting the moods, emotions, and perceptions of the user. Such drugs include alcohol, cocaine, heroin, and marijuana. **Drug abuse** occurs when acceptable social standards of drug use are violated, resulting in adverse physiological, psychological, and social consequences, or some combination. For example, when an individual's drug use leads to hospitalization, arrest, or divorce, such use is usually considered abusive. Drug abuse, however, does not always entail drug addiction. **Drug addiction**, or **chemical dependency**, refers to a condition in which drug use is compulsive—users are unable to stop because of their dependency. The dependency may be psychological, in that the individual needs the drug to achieve a feeling of well-being, or physical, in that withdrawal symptoms occur when the individual stops taking the drug.

Various theories provide explanations for why some people use and abuse drugs. Drug use is not simply a matter of individual choice. Theories of drug use explain how structural and cultural forces, as well as biological factors, influence drug use and society's responses to it.

drug abuse

The violation of social standards of acceptable drug use, resulting in adverse physiological, psychological, or social consequences.

drug addiction/chemical dependency

A condition in which drug use is compulsive, and users are unable to stop because of physical or psychological dependency or both.

Structural-Functionalist Perspective

Functionalists argue that drug abuse is a response to the weakening of norms in society. As society becomes more complex and rapid social change occurs, norms and values become unclear and ambiguous, resulting in anomie—a state of normlessness. **Anomie** may exist at the societal level, resulting in social strains and inconsistencies that lead to drug use. For example, research indicates that increased alcohol consumption in the 1830s and the 1960s was a response to rapid social change and the resulting stress (Rorabaugh 1979). Anomie produces inconsistencies in cultural norms regarding drug use. For example, while public health officials and health-care professionals warn of the dangers of alcohol and tobacco use, films still glorify the use of alcohol and tobacco, and the government subsidizes the alcohol industry. Further, such cultural traditions

anomie

A state of normlessness in which norms and values are weak or unclear; results from rapid social change and is linked to many social problems, including crime, drug addiction, and violence.

as giving away cigars to celebrate the birth of a child and celebrating major events with alcohol persist.

Anomie may also exist at the individual level, as when a person suffers feelings of estrangement, isolation, and turmoil over appropriate and inappropriate behaviour. An adolescent whose parents are experiencing a divorce, who is separated from friends and family as a consequence of moving, or who lacks parental supervision and discipline may be more vulnerable to drug use. Thus, from a structural-functionalist perspective, drug use is a response to the absence of a perceived bond between the individual and society, and to the weakening of a consensus on what is considered acceptable. Consistent with this perspective, citing data from a larger U.S. study, Health Canada reports "a strong association between substance use problems and problematic family relationships," with 73 percent of youth with substance dependencies in the U.S. study reporting drug use to cope with dysfunctional, often abusive families (2001: 51).

Feminist Perspectives

Feminist forms of analysis are many, and employ a broad range of methods to understand social problems. No single manner of assessing substance use and dependency applies; feminist work in the area is unified by the drive to illuminate previously neglected assessment of risk factors and substance use problems unique to women. Here, we introduce two unique features of substance use facing women: (1) misuse of prescription drugs and (2) drug use during pregnancy.

In a study using data gathered from 3185 respondents, Simoni-Wastila and colleagues (2004) determined that the women's increased likelihood of being prescribed tranquillizers and other psychoactive drugs significantly increased the probability of using prescription medications for reasons other than, or in excess of, their originally intended medical purpose. The Simoni-Wastila et al. study concludes that being a woman significantly increases vulnerability to misuse of medically prescribed drugs. While theoretical explanations for this increased vulnerability vary, it is clear from other health data that because of their families' dependence on them to be in good health, women tend to pay more attention to their health, aches, and pains than men do. The increased attention puts women in more frequent contact with the health-care system, rendering them more likely recipients of prescription medications for pain, stress, and sleeplessness. In addition, role strain and role conflict may place women at increased risk for stress-related problems; they may try to deal with these by "self-medicating" through the use of alcohol, other controlled substances, and street drugs.

Drug use during pregnancy subjects women to institutional scrutiny and social blaming tactics that men do not face. Negative media attention on pregnant women who use drugs such as cocaine, heroin, and alcohol has been on the rise since the late 1980s; attention geared toward the prevention of fetal alcohol syndrome (FAS) tends to be less sensational. Broad public health campaigns in bars, restaurants, and on television aim to reduce prenatal exposure to alcohol (Figure 3.2, a poster distributed by Health Canada, provides a sample); conversely, the criminal justice system routinely prosecutes marginalized, poor women who use cocaine or heroin during pregnancy (Zivi 2000). Feminists criticize those who blame individual mothers instead of building programs that would prevent circumstances that lead to substance abuse. They argue that criminalization of these mothers "subordinate[s] women's rights and

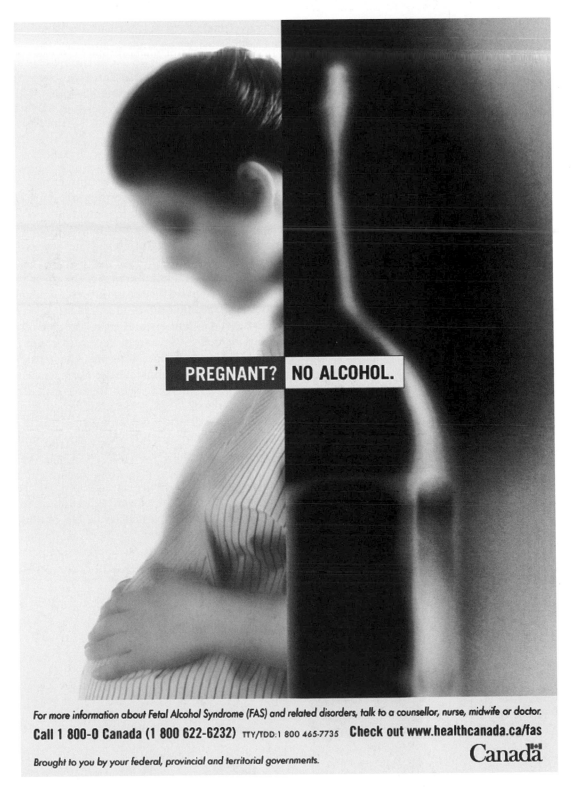

■ **Figure 3.2** *Pregnant? No Alcohol*

SOURCE: Public Health Agency of Canada. Reproduced with the permission of the Minister of Public Works and Government Services Canada, 2011.

needs to those of the fetus" (Zivi 2000: 237). From a feminist perspective, the problem is not a simple act committed by an uncaring mother, but rather, a woman's response to an overwhelmingly negative social situation of poverty, racism, and victimization: it is the social situation that harms both the pregnant woman and the developing fetus. Furthermore, criminalization of this sort treats women as vehicles for breeding purposes, not as persons with the same legal rights to autonomy and agency as men.

Conflict Perspective

Conflict perspectives emphasize the importance of power differentials in influencing drug use behaviour and societal values concerning drug use. From a conflict perspective, drug use occurs as a response to the inequality perpetuated by a capitalist system. Alienated from work, friends, and family, as well as from larger social institutions, people may use drugs to escape the oppression and frustration that correspond to low status.

Conflict theorists highlight the considerable influence of the most powerful members of society to define which drugs are illegal and to set the penalties for their production, sale, and use. Thus, alcohol, the production and sale of which benefits those with power, privilege, and influence, is legal. The sale of alcohol, for example, generates billions of dollars a year in revenues for provincial governments, as well as much federal revenue. Consider the irony: of the $39.8 billion in annual costs from substance abuse to the Canadian economy, the costs of legal drugs were the most significant, with tobacco accounting for $17 billion, alcohol $14.6 billion, and illicit drugs $8.2 billion (Rehm 2006). These numbers are calculated to include the costs of treating illness, of lost productivity, and of law enforcement, with productivity losses accounting for 61 percent of the losses. The CCSA report represents these losses on a per capita basis, as we see in Figure 3.3.

In contrast to the abuse of legal substances, the consumption of "street drugs" such as cocaine and heroin is associated with the powerless and disenfranchised: the poor, minority group members, and, in particular, visible minorities. As Hackler (2000: 213) observes, "the societal demand to punish, stigmatize, and exclude users of certain substances *is not based on pharmacological evidence*" and

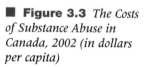
Figure 3.3 *The Costs of Substance Abuse in Canada, 2002 (in dollars per capita)*

SOURCE: Rehm, J. et al. "The Costs of Substance Abuse in Canada 2002." Figure 2. Canadian Centre on Substance Abuse. 2006. www .ccsa.ca. Reproduced with permission of the Canadian Centre on Substance Abuse.

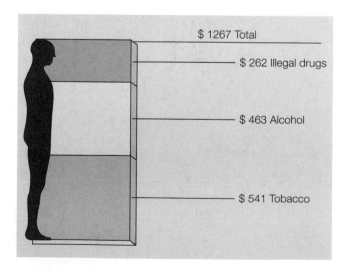

$ 1267 Total

$ 262 Illegal drugs

$ 463 Alcohol

$ 541 Tobacco

evidence of such damage "plays a secondary role in drug policy." The use of opium by Chinese immigrants in the 1800s provides a historical example. The Chinese, who had been brought to Canada to work on the railroads, regularly smoked opium as part of their cultural tradition. However, hostility to opium use emerged in part because of a labour surplus that followed the completion of railway construction and the diminished intensity of the Gold Rush. Green (1986) notes that before this time, in the midst of a labour shortage, "the Chinese were regarded as industrious, sober, economical and law-abiding individuals" (p. 25). As jobs became scarce and the Chinese were viewed as competitors for existing positions, "earlier friendly feelings toward the Chinese changed to hostility.... There was a great demand that Chinese immigration be restricted or discontinued" (p. 24). Simultaneously, opium use, previously viewed as, at worst, "an individual medical misfortune or personal vice, free of severe moral opprobrium" (p. 25), became defined as a significant social "evil." Morgan (1978) observes:

> The first opium laws...were not the result of a moral crusade against the drug itself. Instead, it represented a coercive action directed against a vice that was merely an appendage of the real menace—the Chinese—and not the Chinese per se, but the labouring "Chinamen" who threatened the economic security of the white working class. (p. 59)

Criminalizing drugs such as cocaine, heroin, and marijuana exercises social control over the powerless, political opponents, and minorities. In the 1940s, marijuana was used primarily by minority group members and carried with it severe criminal penalties. However, after white middle-class students began to use marijuana in the 1970s, various lobby groups sought to reduce the penalties associated with its use. Though the nature and pharmacological properties of the drug had not changed, the population of users was now connected to power and influence. Thus, conflict theorists regard the regulation of certain drugs and drug use itself as a reflection of differences in the political, economic, and social power of various interest groups.

Symbolic Interactionist Perspective

Symbolic interactionism, emphasizing the importance of definitions and labelling, concentrates on the social meanings associated with drug use. If the initial drug use experience is defined as pleasurable it is likely to recur, and over time the individual may earn the label of "druggie." If this definition is internalized so that the individual assumes the identity, the behaviour will likely continue and may escalate.

Drug use is also learned through symbolic interaction in small groups. Friends, for example, are the most common source of drugs for teenagers (Leinwand 2000). First-time users learn not only the motivations for drug use and its techniques, but also what to experience. Becker (1966) explains how marijuana users learn to ingest the drug. A novice being coached by a regular user reports this experience:

> I was smoking like I did an ordinary cigarette. He said, "No, don't do it like that." He said, "Suck it, you know, draw in and hold it in your lungs...for a period of time."
> I said, "Is there any limit of time to hold it?" He said, "No, just till you feel that you want to let it out, let it out." So I did that three or four times. (p. 47)

Marijuana users not only learn *how* to smoke, but also learn to label the experience positively. When peers define certain drugs, behaviours, and experiences as not only acceptable but pleasurable, drug use is likely to continue. Interactionists also emphasize that symbols may be manipulated and used for political and economic agendas. "[A]meliorative programs which are imbued with…potent symbolic qualities…are virtually assured wide-spread public acceptance (regardless of actual effectiveness) which in turn advances the interests of political leaders who benefit from being associated with highly visible, popular symbolic programs" (Wysong et al. 1994: 461).

Symbolic interactionist research on how those with drug and alcohol dependencies structure their life histories can explain not only how users take on an identity such as "drug addict" or "alcoholic," but also how they resist such identities. A Canadian study over a period of 12 years concluding in 2004 revealed, for example, that women facing parole hearings in drug trafficking–related offences structured themselves as victims rather than as offenders, and that the members of the parole boards were inclined to facilitate these narratives: "By embracing notions of subordinate and exploited women and dominated and exploiting men, board members accept ideal types of men and women…. According to this perspective, women are caring persons who fall victim to male drug dealers. As a result, female drug traffickers can frequently use gender attributes of frailty and fragility to diminish their responsibility" (Silverstein 2006: 404). Silverstein does not deny that these women are vulnerable to entering drug trafficking because of pre-existing problems such as domestic violence and poverty, but demonstrates how women are made to understand and to narrate themselves only as victims if they are to convince parole boards that they ought to be released from jail. In short, the women learn to understand and portray themselves not principally as drug users, but as victims of a male drug culture.

A study of 54 people in treatment centres and hostels for persons with alcoholism carried out in Copenhagen concluded that while most people in such centres do understand themselves as alcoholics, some actively resist that identity and develop a counter narrative to explain themselves. The research in this group initially sought to understand how people became alcoholics by asking interviewees to answer questions that would illuminate a "drinking career" that had culminated in their residency in programs for people facing health and social problems related to their alcohol use (Järvinen, 2001). One interviewee resisted identification as an alcoholic in a series of narrative maneouvres that sought to establish himself as "in control":

> Whatever reason John may have had to volunteer for the interview, it cannot have been because he felt that he was an "identified alcoholic" prepared to discuss his experiences and need for alcohol treatment. Nevertheless, the line of the study led John—who explicitly declared that he had never been "interested in treatment" or in "ventilating [his] problems with each and everyone"—into a situation wherein he had to negotiate an "alcohol-related life history" for himself. The result was a compromise: John was an alcoholic but an alcoholic in perfect self-command; it was circumstances that had made him an alcoholic, not his alcoholism that had led him into troublesome circumstances… (Järvinen: 279)

Järvinen explains that resistant narratives such as the one above can be thrown into crisis when faced with a direct challenge such as the interview encounter, but that whatever internal inconsistencies appear in these narratives allow the "alcoholic" to save face. Irving Goffman explains the behaviour exhibited by the interviewee in Järvinen's account as a mode of self-protection that maintains an ideal sense of self in social interaction (Järvinen: 277).

Biological and Psychological Theories

Drug use and addiction are likely the result of a complex interplay of social, psychological, and biological forces. Biological research has primarily concentrated on the role of genetics in predisposing an individual to drug use. According to a report by the National Institute on Alcohol Abuse and Alcoholism (NIAAA 2000: xiii), "50 to 60 percent of the risk for developing alcoholism is genetic." Research also indicates that by examining inherited traits, science "can predict [in] childhood with 80 percent accuracy who is going to develop alcoholism later in life" (AAP 1998). Nonetheless, many alcoholics do not have parents who abuse alcohol, and many alcoholic parents have offspring who do not abuse alcohol.

Biological theories of drug use hypothesize that some individuals are physiologically predisposed to experience more pleasure from drugs than others and, consequently, are more likely to be drug users. According to these theories, the central nervous system processes drugs through neurotransmitters in a way that produces an unusually euphoric experience. Individuals not so physiologically inclined report less pleasant experiences and are less likely to continue use (Alcohol Alert 2000; Jarvik 1990).

Psychological explanations focus on the tendency of certain personality types to be more susceptible to drug use. Individuals who are particularly prone to anxiety may be more likely to use drugs as a way to relax, gain self-confidence, or ease tension. For example, research indicates that female adolescents who have been sexually abused or who have poor relationships with their parents are more likely to have severe drug problems (NIDA 2000a). Psychological theories of drug abuse also emphasize that drug use may be maintained by positive and negative reinforcement.

3.3 Frequently Used Legal and Illegal Drugs

Social definitions of which drugs are legal or illegal have varied over time, circumstance, and societal forces. In Canada, two of the most dangerous and widely abused drugs—alcohol and tobacco—are legal. They are also widely available, even to those who are under the legal age to be able to purchase them.

Alcohol

Canadians' attitudes toward alcohol have had a long and varied history (this chapter's *Self and Society* box deals with attitudes toward alcohol). Although alcohol was commonly consumed in early Canada, "the moral climate in Canada after the turn of the century was one in which middle class persons with strong religious convictions were willing to believe the worst of alcohol, tobacco and other drugs.... The typical reaction to these perceived threats was to press for total prohibition" (Giffen et al. 1991: 150). Many have argued that the push for prohibition was a moral crusade (Gusfield 1963) against immigrant groups perceived as more likely to use alcohol. Today, Canada is experiencing a resurgence of concern about alcohol. What has been called a "new temperance" has manifested itself in increased concern about fetal alcohol syndrome and teenage drinking, and calls for strict enforcement of drinking and driving regulations.

Alcohol is the most widely used and abused drug in Canada among both adults and youths (Table 3.1). Although most people who drink alcohol do so moderately and experience few negative effects, alcoholics are psychologically and physically

Alcohol Attitude Test

If you strongly agree with the following statements, write in 1. If you agree, but not strongly, write in 2. If you neither agree nor disagree, write in 3. If you disagree, but not strongly, write in 4. If you strongly disagree, write in 5.

Set 1

_____ 1. If I tried to stop someone from driving after drinking, the person would probably think I was butting in where I shouldn't.

_____ 2. Even if I wanted to, I probably could not stop someone from driving after drinking.

_____ 3. If people want to kill themselves, that's their business.

_____ 4. I wouldn't like someone to try to stop me from driving after drinking.

_____ 5. Usually, if you try to help someone else out of a dangerous situation, you risk getting yourself into one.

_____ Total score for questions 1 through 5

Set 2

_____ 6. My friends would not disapprove of me for driving after drinking.

_____ 7. Getting into trouble with my parents would not keep me from driving after drinking.

_____ 8. The thought that I might get into trouble with the police would not keep me from driving after drinking.

_____ 9. I am not scared by the thought that I might seriously injure myself or someone else by driving after drinking.

_____ 10. The fear of damaging the car would not keep me from driving after drinking.

_____ Total score for questions 6 through 10

Set 3

_____ 11. The speed limit on the open roads spoils the pleasure of driving for most teenagers.

_____ 12. Many teenagers use driving to let off steam.

_____ 13. Being able to drive a car makes teenagers feel more confident in their relations with others their age.

_____ 14. An evening with friends is not much fun unless one of them has a car.

_____ 15. There is something about being behind the wheel of a car that makes one feel more adult.

_____ Total score for questions 11 through 15

Scoring

Set 1. 15–25 points: takes responsibility to keep others from driving when drunk; 5–9 points: wouldn't take steps to stop a drunk friend from driving.

Set 2. 12–25 points: hesitates to drive after drinking; 5–7 points: is not deterred by the consequences of drinking and driving.

Set 3. 19–25 points: perceives auto as means of transportation; 5–14 points: uses car to satisfy psychological needs, not just transportation.

SOURCE: Courtesy of National Highway Traffic Safety Administration. National Center for Statistics and Analysis, from *Drunk Driving Facts*. Washington, D.C.: NHTSA, 1988.

■ **Table 3.1** *Drug Use among Teenagers, Canada, 2008*

"How often do you…"	Weekly or More	One to Three Times a Month	Less Than Once a Month	Never
Smoke cigarettes	12%	4%	7%	77%
Males	11	4	7	78
Females	12	4	7	77
Drink beer, wine, other alcohol	26	29	16	29
Males	31	27	14	28
Females	22	31	17	30
Under 18 total	24	29	16	31
Males	28	28	15	29
Females	20	30	18	32
Smoke marijuana or hashish*	12	9	11	68
Males	16	8	11	65
Females	9	9	11	71
Use other illegal drugs*	4	3	5	88
Males	5	3	5	87
Females	2	3	5	90

SOURCE: Bibby, Reginald W. 2008. The Project Teen Canada 2008 National Survey;
   *Bibby, Reginald W. 2009. *The Emerging Millennials*. Lethbridge: Project Canada Books, p. 75.

addicted to alcohol. Alcoholics, unlike moderate users of alcohol, both suffer from and cause various degrees of physical, economic, psychological, and personal harm as a direct result of their alcohol dependency.

According to the 1996–97 National Population Health Survey (NPHS), more than half (53 percent) of Canadians 12 years of age and older (12.7 million Canadians) reported drinking at least one alcoholic drink per month in the previous year. The largest proportion of regular drinkers (43 percent) consumed, on average, one to six drinks each week. Men were significantly more likely than women to be regular drinkers (63 percent versus 43 percent), especially among those aged 15 to 44, where almost three-quarters of men and half of women drank regularly. Men who drank regularly were also more likely to report a higher average weekly consumption than women were (Health Canada 1999: 171–72). The 2000 Project Canada youth survey found that while one in five Canadian teens drank beer, wine, or other forms of alcohol at least once a week, the weekly level for males was almost twice that of females (Bibby 2001: 97).

Binge drinking, defined as the consumption of five or more alcoholic beverages on at least one occasion, is most common among youth. According to the 1996–97 NPHS, more than one-third (36 percent) of Canadians aged 20 to 24 who were current drinkers drank five or more drinks at least 12 times in the previous year and more than 1 in 10 (13 percent) did so 52 or more times in the previous year. Binge drinking is more prevalent among young Canadian men aged 15 to 19 (52 percent) than among young Canadian women (35 percent). However, the majority of both sexes in the 20- to 24-year-old age group (73 percent of men and 51 percent of women) reported at least one episode of binge drinking (Health Canada 1999: 171).

Not only were binge drinkers more likely to report using other controlled substances, but also the more frequently a student binged, the higher the probability of reporting other drug use. The most commonly reported other drugs used by frequent binge drinkers were, in order, cigarettes, marijuana, hallucinogens, and chewing tobacco (HHS 1998).

According to the NPHS, there is a positive correlation between education and drinking: as education increases, so too does the likelihood that Canadians are regular drinkers. "University graduates were most likely (61 percent) to drink at least once a month, while those with less than high school were least likely (44 percent) to do so." It additionally notes that the relationship between amount consumed and educational attainment "is similar, though less pronounced: with each successive level of education, the likelihood of having had one or more drinks weekly increased. However, university graduates were least likely to have had 14 or more drinks weekly" (Health Canada 1999: 172). This survey also found that the proportion of Canadian men and women who drank at least once per month rose steadily with increases in income, and men and women with higher incomes tended to be heavier drinkers. Among men in the two lower income levels who were drinkers, 24 percent reported at least one episode of heavy or binge drinking, compared with 43 percent of men in the highest income bracket. The rate of heavy drinking among women drinkers in the lowest income level was 13 percent; it dropped to 10 percent at the next income level, then slowly climbed to 19 percent at the highest income level.

Tobacco

Although nicotine is an addictive psychoactive drug and the dangers of second-hand smoke form the basis for Canada's *Non-Smoker's Health Act*, tobacco remains one of the most widely used drugs in Canada. According to the Canadian Tobacco Use Monitoring Survey (CTUMS), in 2001, 5.4 million Canadians (22 percent of the population aged 15 years and older) were smokers. In that

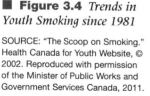

■ **Figure 3.4** *Trends in Youth Smoking since 1981*

SOURCE: "The Scoop on Smoking." Health Canada for Youth Website, © 2002. Reproduced with permission of the Minister of Public Works and Government Services Canada, 2011.

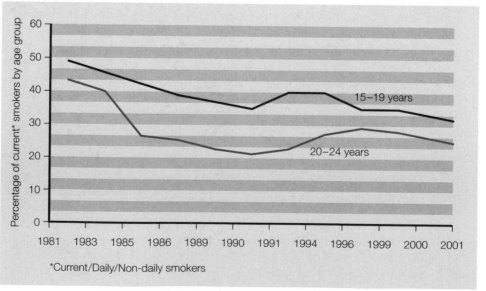

Images of Alcohol and Tobacco Use in Children's Animated Films

The impact of media on drug and alcohol use is likely to be recursive—media images affect drug use while, alternatively, societal drug use helps define media presentations. Previous research has documented the rate of tobacco and alcohol use in print media, advertising, and Hollywood movies. In the present research, Goldstein, Sobel, and Newman (1999) use content analysis to investigate the prevalence of tobacco and alcohol use in children's animated films as one step in assessing the growing concern with media influence on children's smoking and drinking behaviour.

Sample and Methods

The researchers examined all G-rated animated films released between 1937 (*Snow White and the Seven Dwarfs*) and 1997 (*Hercules*, *Anastasia*, *Pippi Longstocking*, and *Cats Don't Dance*). Criteria for sample inclusion included that the film be at least 60 minutes in length and, before video distribution, have been released to theatres. The resulting sample included all of Disney's animated children's films produced during the target years with the exception of three that were unavailable on videocassette. The remaining films included all children's animated films produced by MGM/United Artists, Universal, 20th Century Fox, and Warner Brothers since 1982. Variables coded included the (1) presence of alcohol or tobacco use, (2) length of time of use on screen, (3) number of characters using alcohol or tobacco, (4) value of the character using tobacco or alcohol (i.e., good, neutral, or bad), (5) any implied messages about the drug use, and (6) the type of tobacco or alcohol being used.

Findings and Conclusions

Of the 50 films analyzed, at least one episode of alcohol and/or tobacco use was portrayed in 34 (68 percent) with tobacco use (N = 28) slightly exceeding portrayals of alcohol use (N = 25). Tobacco was used by 76 different characters with an onscreen time of 45 minutes—an average of 1.62 minutes per movie. Characters were most likely to use cigars followed by cigarettes, and pipes. Of the 76 characters using tobacco, 28 (37 percent) were classified as good. Surprisingly, the use of tobacco products by "good" characters has increased rather than decreased over time.

Sixty-two characters, averaging 2.5 per film, were shown using alcohol, with a total duration of 27 minutes across all films. Characters were most likely to consume wine, followed by beer, spirits, and champagne. The number of good characters using alcohol was similar to the number of characters classified as bad. In 19 of the 25 films in which alcohol use was portrayed, tobacco use was also pictured. Although several films portrayed the physical consequences of smoking (N = 10) (e.g., coughing) or drinking (N = 7) (e.g., passing out), no film verbally referred to the health hazards of either drug.

One particularly interesting finding of the research concerned the use of alcohol and tobacco as a visual prop in character development. For example, although cigar smokers were portrayed as tough and powerful (e.g., Sykes in Oliver and Company), pipe smokers were most often older, kindly, and wise (e.g., Geppetto in Pinocchio), and cigarette smokers independent, witty, and intelligent (e.g., the Genie in Aladdin). There was also a tendency for alcohol and tobacco use to be portrayed together. When one, the other, or both are associated with positively defined characters the impact may be detrimental to the lifestyle choices of viewers.

Although this study cannot assess the "impact question," advertising campaigns have been linked to detrimental results. Although in each of these cases the motivation for the use of such appealing characters is clear, the presentation of "good" characters using alcohol and tobacco products in children's animated films remains unexplained. Interpretation of the results is further complicated by the lack of change over time; that is, as our knowledge of the harmful effects of these products increased, their presence in children's films did not, as expected, decrease. In light of these results, the researchers call for an end to the portrayal of alcohol and tobacco use in all children's animated films and associated products (e.g., posters, books, games).

SOURCE: Goldstein, Adam, Rachel Sobel, and Glen Newman. 1999. "Tobacco and Alcohol Use in G-rated Children's Animated Films." *Journal of the American Medical Association* 281: 1121–36.

year, about one in four men and one in five women smoked tobacco. However, compared to two decades ago, fewer Canadians smoke and those that smoke daily are smoking less (down from 20.6 cigarettes in 1985 to 16.2 in 2001). In 2001, more Canadians identified themselves as "former smokers" than as "current smokers" (Health Canada 2001).

Much of the concern about smoking centres on the use of tobacco by young people (see Figure 3.4). In this chapter's *Social Problems Research Up Close* feature, images of tobacco and alcohol use in children's animated films are examined. In 2001, 22.5 percent of Canadian teens aged 15 to 19 reported themselves as current smokers (24 percent of girls and 21 percent of boys). However, at 32 percent, young Canadians aged 20 to 24 have the highest smoking rate of any age group (29 percent of females and 35 percent of males) (Health Canada 2001).

Tobacco was first cultivated by Indigenous people and had a central place in their religious rituals. European settlers believed that tobacco had medicinal properties and its use spread throughout Europe, assuring the economic success of the colonists in North America. Initially, people generally chewed or had tobacco in snuff. In time, smoking gained popularity even though scientific evidence that linked tobacco smoking to lung cancer existed as early as 1859 (Feagin and Feagin 1994).

Today, the health hazards of tobacco use are well documented. Smoking is associated with lung cancer, cardiovascular disease, strokes, emphysema, spontaneous abortion, premature birth, and neonatal death. In Canada, it is estimated that one person dies every 12 minutes of a tobacco-related disease (Health Canada 2001). Tobacco smoke kills more than 45 000 Canadians yearly—more than the combined total of all murders, alcohol-related deaths, car accidents, and suicides (see Figure 3.5). Smoking also reduces the number of years that a person may hope to live without any disability. "Among both men and women, two-thirds of non-smokers will survive without any disability to the age of 65, compared with less than half of smokers. In addition, 25 percent of male non-smokers and 30 percent of female non-smokers who live to the age of 80 will have no disability, compared with less than 10 percent for both men and women who smoke" (Statistics Canada 2001).

By the year 2030, tobacco-related diseases will be the number-one cause of death worldwide, killing one of every six people. Eighty percent of the deaths will

■ **Figure 3.5** *Estimated Deaths in Canada, 1996*

SOURCE: Health Canada for Youth Website, © 2002. Reproduced with the permission of the Minister of Public Works and Government Services Canada, 2011.

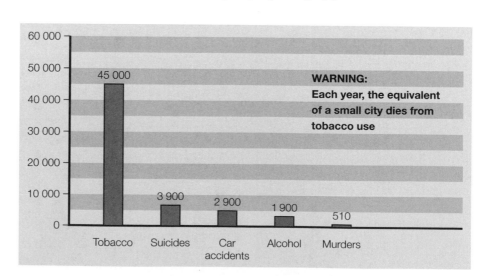

take place in poor nations where many smokers are unaware of the health hazards associated with smoking (Mayell 1999). In an attempt to discourage the use of tobacco by Canadians, governments have introduced various control measures, including media campaigns, public education programs, and legislated restrictions on access to cigarettes, on public smoking, and on sponsorship promotion by the tobacco industry (Health Canada 2002a). In June 2002, the federal government levied a $3.50-per-carton increase in taxes on cigarettes. This increase restored federal tobacco tax rates to their pre-1994 levels. In announcing the increase, Minister of Health Anne McLellan observed: "We know that increasing taxes on tobacco directly reduces the incidence of smoking, which contributes to the overall health of Canadians" (Department of Finance Canada 2002).

Marijuana

Although drug abuse ranks among the top concerns of many Canadians, surveys indicate that illegal drug use of all kinds is far less common than alcohol and tobacco abuse. Marijuana remains the most commonly used and most heavily trafficked illegal drug in the world. It is estimated that more than 40 million Europeans have tried cannabis at least once and that there are 200 to 250 million marijuana users worldwide. According to the Canadian Centre on Substance Abuse, cannabis is the most widely used illicit drug in Canada with nearly 14 percent of Canadians aged 15 and over reporting use in the past year. The CCSA's survey data also showed that slightly more than 39 percent of 15- to 17-year-olds and 69.9 percent of 18- to 19-year-olds reported lifetime use, while roughly one-fifth of those who reported cannabis use in the past year indicated that they use cannabis more regularly on either a weekly (20.1%) or daily (18.1%) basis (CCSA 2009).

Marijuana's active ingredient, THC (delta-9-tetrahydrocannabinol), may act as a sedative or as a hallucinogen, depending on the amount ingested. Marijuana use dates back to 2737 B.C. in China and has a long tradition of use in India, the Middle East, and Europe. In North America, hemp, as it was then called, was used for making rope and as a folk remedy. In the 1920s, Judge Emily Murphy was the first to draw the attention of Canadians to "Marihuana—A New Menace" in her book *The Black Candle*. Although the drug was virtually unknown in Canada at the time, Murphy's book suggested that marijuana had an insidious effect on its users: it drove them insane and caused them to lose all moral sense. However, as Green (1986: 31) has noted, racism appears to have been a "critical component" in Murphy's analysis of the drug problem. According to Murphy, narcotics were part of an international conspiracy "to injure the bright-browed races of the world" and a tactic used by "aliens of colour to bring about the degeneration of the white race." However, "[a]s a result of the considerable media attention devoted to *The Black Candle* and the paucity of challenge or contradictory statements, Murphy's conception of the scourge-like effects of drug use came to dominate Canadian narcotics ideology" (Green 1986: 33).

Among certain groups of young Canadians, cannabis use is even higher. For example, compared with others in the same age cohort, street youth in Canada report higher rates of illicit drug use and heavy drinking. In various studies, the percentage of street youth reporting cannabis use ranges from 66 percent to 88 percent, while between one-quarter and one-half report heavy drinking (Health Canada 1999). In this chapter, *The Human Side* notes the role played by alcohol and other drugs in both the backgrounds and daily lives of Canada's street youths.

An Excerpt from
Mean Streets: Youth Crime and Homelessness

In *Mean Streets: Youth Crime and Homelessness* (1997), Canadian sociologists John Hagan and Bill McCarthy describe the backgrounds and current experiences of homeless youths on the streets of two Canadian cities, Toronto and Vancouver. They report that substance abuse by parents and siblings is common in the backgrounds of these young people and that it is often coupled with poverty, neglect, and physical or sexual abuse.

Sebastian: "My parents threw me out.... They're drug addicts. Hash, weed, coke, crack—everything.... I didn't want to leave but they just threw me out. I had a huge fight with my dad. We'd fight 'cause I'd go, 'quit drugs,' and he would go 'no.'...I'd go, 'quit drinking.' He'd say 'no.' So we just argued about that most of the time. And one day he goes, 'I think it's about time you leave, get on your own.' So I just left." (p. 25)

Robert: "Both my parents were alcoholics, and I had a younger sister and older brother, and, uh, it just got to a point...I mean, we used to get beat up at least four or five times a week. It got to a point where we'd hide and just wait for them to find us...and, um, finally I just couldn't take it anymore." (pp. 25–26)

Jeremy: "When I was 12, I was sent home from school, and my mom said, 'You're out of here' and I said, 'What do you mean?' and she goes, 'You're going to live with your father again.' I said, 'Oh shit.' So I went down to my father's. My dad was an alcoholic, and he always abused me—physically. He'd punch me and stuff like that—throw me up against the walls. And like one night we were going at it, and I turned around, like he punched me a couple of times. I turned around and got a baseball bat out of the bedroom, and I hit him in the head, and then he got back up, and he started

pounding on me big time. Well, the cops came and they took him, and they said, 'You can go live with your mother, right?' My mother had already said, 'We don't want you,' so I said, 'Okay, I'm going to my mother's' and [instead] I went out in the streets." (p. 26)

Gord: "I started smoking dope when I was, like 8, 9 years old, like literally when I was 8 or 9 years old.... Just, sittin' around the pool halls, you know, people giving you joints and stuff.... My family was always poor. Like my mom was always poor. She was, you know, she was always on welfare. So, my older brother sold dope, did whatever he could to make money to help out and to take care of himself. I used to hang out in a pool hall.... And all my brother's friends would get me to hold their dope and stuff, 'cause the cops would come in and I'd be playing video games, you know.... After that it just, you know, I got to know when I was like 10, 10 years old I knew, you know, how to weigh out grams and knew there was sixteen ounces in a pound and twenty-eight grams in an ounce. So when I needed to make my own money, it just seemed totally natural because I knew so many people that would, just, give me dope and say, 'Okay, pay me when you can, right?' It was pretty easy actually. It seemed like the only logical thing to do." (p. 111)

Hagan and McCarthy's research additionally notes that drug use is a common part of the daily lives of homeless youths themselves; more than 80 percent of their respondents acknowledged smoking marijuana, 55 percent used crack or other chemicals, and 43 percent used cocaine. However, they note that drug use is simply one part of the "downward spiral of deviance, danger, and despair" that marks the lives of street youths.

Eva: "Oh, it was fun for a while—we met some really nice people, lots of partying—but down here [Vancouver's East Side] it was different. I found like, people were more violent,

and everybody was into using hard drugs, and everything was just really different, and I ran into things, like I started prostituting and doing illegal stuff [using and selling heroin and armed robbery] and all kinds of crazy stuff down here." (pp. 113–14)

Jordy: "I was selling a bit of drugs here and there, stealing still, doing some shoplifting—videos and records from stores, clothing, everything basically. Just being a hustler, man, just going out and hustling money wherever which way I could. If I could con some old man on the street for five bucks, I'd do it." (p. 115)

Alan: "Like when I walk down the street and I see people panhandling for money, like, I turn around and I look at them, and I go, 'Why are you sittin' here panhandling for money? Why don't you sell some drugs, or go rob someone or something', right? Why do you have to, like, sit there and ask everyone walkin' by for some money?'" (p. 53)

Kathy: "I beat this girl, really, really bad. I was on acid. I was just mad at the whole world. I just wanted anybody to beat up, and she was pouring, bleeding, and I was just hitting her with a steel bar and everything, and everybody's saying, 'What?' and I'm saying to everybody, 'Am I hurting her yet?'" (p. 118)

Simon: "Fifty dollars that you make out there lasts about as long as five dollars does that you make from a paycheck.... With myself I am so ashamed or so mad, and I have really bad feelings about pulling tricks, you know, like I was being used enough sexually in my life, and then I subject myself to it again. So then I need to sedate how I'm feeling, so I usually go and get really drunk. So then 80 percent of that money ends up being drinking money. And, like, you know, you have nothing to do all day and then having fifty bucks, you know, you're looking for a place to spend your money. You're looking for anything to entertain yourself." (p. 222)

SOURCE: Hagan, J., and Bill McCarthy. 1997. *Mean Streets: Youth Crime and Homelessness.* Cambridge, MA: Cambridge University Press. Reprinted with the permission of Cambridge University Press.

Although the effects of alcohol and tobacco are, in large part, indisputable, there is less agreement about the effects of marijuana. The carcinogenic effects of marijuana are as lethal as nicotine's, but other long-term physiological effects are unknown. It appears from emergency room data that cannabis use is a significant factor in injuries and fatalities suffered in car accidents in which the driver has recently used cannabis. The CCSA 2009 paper on cannabis use and driving reports that among "drivers admitted to a regional trauma unit in Toronto, 13.9% tested positive for cannabis, [while 19.7]% of drivers killed in road crashes in Quebec were found to test positive for cannabis. An examination of fatally injured drivers in Canada between 2000 and 2006 revealed that 14.9% of those tested were positive for cannabis" (CCSA 2009: 3).

Cocaine

Cocaine is classified as a stimulant. As such, it produces feelings of excitation, alertness, and euphoria. Although such prescription stimulants as methamphetamine and dextroamphetamine are commonly abused, over the past 10 to 20 years cocaine has become the focus of societal concerns over drug abuse. Its increased use, addictive qualities, physiological effects, and worldwide distribution have fuelled the concerns. More than any other substance, cocaine has led to the present "war on drugs."

Cocaine, made from the coca plant, has been used for thousands of years, and anti-cocaine sentiment did not emerge until the early twentieth century in either the United States or Canada. In the United States, where cocaine was heavily used by urban Blacks, "stereotypes about the effects of cocaine—particularly in producing 'superhuman strength, cunning and efficiency'" coincided "with a wave of repressive measures defined to ensure the subordination of blacks" (Giffen et al. 1991: 14). In Canada, it has been suggested that efforts to suppress the nonmedical use of cocaine stemmed from a highly publicized cocaine scare in Montreal and, in particular, the pioneering efforts of a probation officer of the Montreal Children's Aid Society (Giffen et al. 1991: 37, 85). In 1911, the *Opium and Drug Act* confined the legal use of cocaine and morphine to medical prescriptions; it made any other possession a criminal offence. Cocaine remains an illicit drug under the 1997 *Controlled Drug and Substances Act* (CDSA), but its use and effects are misunderstood. For example, a 1982 *Scientific American* article suggested that cocaine was no more habit forming than potato chips (Van Dyck and Byck 1982). The percentage of Canadians reporting cocaine use is low—less than 1 percent. Its use is higher among Canadian men than among Canadian women, highest among 25- to 34-year-olds (followed by 35- to 44-year-olds and 20- to 25-year-olds), and varies regionally, with British Columbia having the highest rates of use and Newfoundland and Labrador the lowest (CCSA 1999).

Other Drugs

Other drugs abused in Canada include "club drugs" (e.g., LSD, ecstasy), heroin, prescription drugs (e.g., tranquillizers, amphetamines), and inhalants (e.g., glue).

Club Drugs These are illicit, often synthetic drugs commonly used at nightclubs or after-hours clubs, such as rave parties and speakeasies. **Club drugs** include

club drugs
A general term used to refer to illicit, often synthetic drugs commonly used at night clubs or all-night dances called "raves."

MDMA (ecstasy), ketamine ("Special K"), LSD ("acid"), GHB ("liquid ecstasy"), and Rohypnol ("roofies"). Although popular news media have focused attention on a small number of deaths associated with ecstasy use at raves, ecstasy use is small compared with other drug use—less than 1 percent of the population—and its use varies with trends influencing its image and availability. Ecstasy is associated with feelings of euphoria and inner peace, yet critics argue that, as the "new cocaine," it can cause both long-term and short-term negative effects: these include permanent brain damage and hypothermia (Cloud 2000; DEA 2000).

date-rape drugs

Drugs that are used to render victims incapable of resisting sexual assaults.

GHB (gamma hydroxybutyrate) and Rohypnol (flunitrazepam) are often called **date-rape drugs** because of their use in rendering victims incapable of resisting sexual assaults. Rohypnol, currently illegal in both Canada and the United States, is lawfully sold in Europe and Latin America. It belongs to a class of drugs known as benzodiazepines, which also includes such common prescription drugs as Valium, Halcion, and Xanax. Rohypnol is tasteless and odourless; 1 mg of the drug can incapacitate a victim for up to 12 hours (DEA 2000; NIDA 2000b). The first major seizure of Rohypnol occurred in Canada in January 1999; 3500 doses were seized in a raid at a home in North Vancouver, British Columbia. After the raid, an RCMP spokesperson remarked: "[T]he RCMP had been under the impression, up till now, that there wasn't any Rohypnol [problem] in Canada.... Guess what—it's here, so we need to be concerned" (*Vancouver Sun*, January 26, 1999: A1).

Heroin In Canada, the most commonly injected drug is heroin. Injection drug use is most common in Montreal, Toronto, and Vancouver. The precise number of users who inject drugs is not known. In 1999, an estimated 34 percent of all new HIV infections stemmed from injection drug use (Auditor General 2001). Among Native peoples, the percentage of HIV infections attributable to injection drug use is especially high and has risen dramatically over time (from 29.5 percent in 1992–1996 to 52.9 percent during 1997–2001). In Canada, as in other countries, injection drug use is a major cause of the heterosexual transmission of HIV infection, hepatitis, and other infectious diseases (Health Canada 2005).

Prescription Drugs Tranquillizers and antidepressants are often used in the treatment of psychiatric disorders. For example, Prozac, Valium, and Halcion are often prescribed for the treatment of insomnia, anxiety, and depression. In Canada, women are more likely than men are to use these types of drugs: 3.4 percent versus 2.0 for tranquillizers, 4.7 percent versus 2.5 percent for antidepressants, and 4.0 percent versus 2.9 percent for sleeping pills. Their use is also more common among the elderly than among the young. For example, Canadians over the age of 75 have the highest use level of sleeping pills (10.6 percent) and antidepressants (5.3 percent), while those between the ages of 65 and 74 are most likely to use tranquillizers. The divorced, separated, or widowed in Canada are also more likely to use these drugs than those who are single or married. Use of these drugs decreases as income increases (CCSA 1999). Although these drugs are most often obtained through prescription, they are frequently misused. An illegal market for them persists, and prescription misuse is common with other medications, as well.

Amphetamines are stimulants, and are legal when prescribed by a physician. Many common cold remedies contain amphetamines now used to make "crystal meth"—a street drug with skyrocketing abuse levels, especially in rural areas of Canada and the United States. Illegal use of amphetamines, made in clandestine laboratories, has been increasing. Worldwide, the production of amphetamines has increased dramatically in recent decades (*World Drug Report* 1997).

Inhalants Common inhalants include lighter fluid, air fresheners, hair spray, glue, paint, and correction fluid. Beyond those, more than 1000 other household products are currently abused. Canadian surveys suggest that Canadians between the ages of 15 and 17 are the most likely to abuse inhalants (CCSA 1999). Regionally, solvents are used most by people in Quebec (0.2 percent), Ontario (0.1 percent), and Alberta (0.1 percent) (CCSA 1999). Solvent use is also considerably higher among Indigenous and Métis youth than among non-Indigenous populations (Gfellner and Hundelby 1995). Young people often use inhalants mistakenly believing that they are harmless or that any harm caused requires prolonged use. Inhalants are very dangerous because of their toxicity; using them may result in what is called Sudden Sniff Death Syndrome (Join Together 1998).

3.4 Societal Consequences of Drug Use and Abuse

Drugs are a social problem not only because of their adverse effects on individuals, but also as a result of the negative consequences their use has for society as a whole. Everyone is a victim of drug abuse. Drug and alcohol abuse contribute to problems within the family and to crime rates. The economic costs of drug abuse are enormous. Substance abuse and chemical dependencies also have serious consequences for the health of individuals and of populations.

Family Costs

The cost to families of drug use is incalculable. When one or both parents use or abuse drugs, needed family funds may be diverted to purchasing drugs rather than necessities. Children raised in such homes have a higher probability of neglect, behavioural disorders, and absenteeism from school; they also have lower self-concepts and face increased risk of drug abuse (AP 1999; Easley and Epstein 1991; ONDCP 2000; Tubman 1993). Drug abuse is also associated with family disintegration. For example, alcoholics are seven times more likely to separate or divorce than nonalcoholics, and as many as 40 percent of family court problems are alcohol related (Sullivan and Thompson 1994: 347).

Abuse between intimates is also linked to drug use. Research indicates that between 25 and 50 percent of men who are involved in domestic violence have substance abuse problems, and drug use contributes to 7 out of 10 cases of child maltreatment (ONDCP 2000). In a study of 320 men who were married or living with someone, twice as many reported hitting their partner only after they had been drinking, compared with those who reported the same behaviour while sober (Leonard and Blane 1992). According to Statistics Canada's Violence Against Women Survey (VAWS), "women who are married or living with heavy drinkers are five times more likely to be assaulted by their partners than are women who live with nondrinkers" (Johnson 1996: 11). Half of all wife batterers in this survey were reported to have been drinking at the time they assaulted their wives. Women who suffered very serious abuse were approximately twice as likely to report that their spouse had been drinking at the time. The results of the VAWS indicate that "the more a man drinks the greater the likelihood that drinking will be involved in incidents of assault against his wife" (p. 1).

Crime and Drug Use

The relationship between crime and drug use is a complex one, and sociologists disagree as to whether drugs *cause* crime or whether criminal activity leads to drug involvement. Such a simple attribution of a causal relationship between drugs and crime may miss the point altogether; because both crime and drug use are associated with low socio-economic status, poverty may be the more powerful explanatory variable. After extensive study of the assumed drug–crime link, Gentry (1995) concludes, "the assumption that drugs and crime are causally related weakens when more representative or affluent subjects are considered" (p. 491).

In addition to the hypothesized crime–drug use link, some criminal offences are drug defined. For example, driving while intoxicated is one of the most common drug-related crimes. In 2002, Canadian police agencies reported over 82 000 incidents of impaired driving, with a death and injury rate of 7.5 per 100 000 of the population aged 16 and over (Janhevich 2003). Other criminal offences include possession, cultivation, production, and sale of controlled substances, public intoxication, and drunk and disorderly conduct. As Table 3.2 shows, in 1999, cannabis accounted for more than two-thirds of these charges and about half of the charges laid were for possession. In that year, an estimated 19 percent of offenders in the federal correctional system were serving sentences for drug offences (Auditor General 2001). In 2001, almost 92 000 drug offences were recorded by Canadian police agencies. Once again, cannabis offences were the most common, and in 2001 accounted for three out of four drug offences (Statistics Canada 2002b).

■ **Table 3.2** *Number of Persons Charged* for Offences under the Controlled Drugs and Substances Act in Canada during 1999*

Substance	Possession	Trafficking	Importation	Cultivation	Total	Percentage
Heroin	351	800	23	–	1 174	21
Cocaine	3 375	6 990	184	–	10 549	21
Other drugs	1 797	1 561	157	–	3 515	7
Cannabis	21 381	8 112	157	4 697	34 347	70
Total	26 904	17 463	521	4 697	49 585	100
Percentage	54	35	1	10	100	

Note: Data report number of persons charged by most serious offence in a given incident. For example, if a person were charged with armed robbery and possession of a small quantity of drugs at the same time, the drug charge would not show up in the above figures. This policy prevents double counting of the number of persons charged.
*"Number of Persons Charged" means persons charged by police or persons whom the police recommended that charges should be laid against.

SOURCE: *Report of the Auditor General of Canada—2001*, Office of the Auditor General of Canada, 2001. Reproduced with the permission of the Minister of Public Works and Government Services, 2011.

The relationship between drugs, organized crime, and violence has become a major concern in Canada. Citing the conclusions of a 1998 federal government study, the Auditor General (2001: 5) notes,

> the drug trade has a significant impact on Canadians and entails substantial violence.... [W]ith drugs as its primary source of revenue, organized crime has intimidated police officers, judges, juries, and correctional officers. Such intimidation is a direct threat to Canada's philosophy of peace, order, and good government. Of note is that more than 150 deaths since 1994 have been attributed to "biker" wars in Quebec over control of organized crime, including the illicit drug trade.

The Auditor General's report notes that the federal Integrated Proceeds of Crime initiative, developed specifically to investigate organized crime groups, showed that 90 percent of their seizures for proceeds of criminal activity were related to the drug trade. According to the RCMP's Performance Report, the value of assets seized in 1999–2000 was $32 million (Auditor General 2001: 11).

Economic Costs

The economic costs of drug use are high. As Health Canada (1999: 184) has noted, "The 'war on drugs' currently being waged by governments around the world consumes significant government resources in an attempt to deal with drug problems." In 1996, the Canadian Centre on Substance Abuse released a study that estimated that substance abuse cost more than $18.4 billion in Canada a year, or $649 per capita. The largest economic costs of alcohol, which accounted for $7.5 billion, were for lost productivity due to sickness and premature death ($4.14 billion), followed by law enforcement ($1.36 billion) and direct health-care costs ($1.30 billion). The economic costs of tobacco amounted to more than $9.6 billion—including $6.8 billion for lost productivity and $2.68 billion for direct health-care costs. The costs of illicit drug use were estimated to be $1.4 billion, including $823 million for lost productivity due to sickness and disease and $400 million spent on the costs of law enforcement. Since then, the estimated costs have gone up. For example, the 2001 Report of the Auditor General of Canada estimates that the economic costs of illicit drugs alone now exceed $5 billion a year in Canada (Auditor General 2001).

Health Costs

The physical health consequences of drug use to individual users are tremendous: shortened life expectancy; higher morbidity (e.g., cirrhosis of the liver, lung cancer); exposure to HIV infection, hepatitis, and other diseases through shared needles; a weakened immune system; birth defects such as fetal alcohol syndrome; drug addiction in children; and higher death rates. Death rates from drug-induced and alcohol-induced causes are significantly higher for males and First Nations peoples than for females and whites (CCSA 1999; Health Canada 1999). However, the incidence of lung cancer in women has increased dramatically as their smoking rates have increased. In 1998, more Canadian women died from lung cancer (6500) than from breast cancer (5300); lung cancer accounts for almost one in three (32 percent) male cancer deaths and more than one in five female cancer deaths (22 percent) (Health Canada 1999). Keep in mind, though, that drug use—with its attendant health risks—is itself a more likely risk for those who have experienced childhood sexual assault, abuse, and long-term poverty.

Concern that on-the-job drug use may impair performance or cause fatal accidents has led to drug testing. For some employees such tests are routine, both as a

The Question of Drug Testing

The technology available to detect whether a person has taken drugs was used during the 1970s by crime laboratories, drug treatment centres, and the military. Today, employers in private industry have turned to chemical laboratories for help in making decisions on employment and retention, and parents and school officials use commercial testing devices to detect the presence of drugs. An individual's drug use can be assessed through the analysis of hair, blood, or urine. New technologies include portable breath (or saliva) alcohol testers, THC detection strips (for the active ingredient in cannabis), passive alcohol sensors, interlock vehicle ignition systems, and fingerprint screening devices. Counter technologies have even been developed, for example, shampoos that rid hair of toxins and "Urine Luck," a urine additive that is advertised to speed the breakdown of unwanted chemicals.

Canadians are, perhaps, most familiar with drug testing in the context of international sporting events. For example, in August 1999, officials at the 1999 Pan American Games stripped the Canadian roller-hockey team of its gold medal when drug tests showed high levels of an anabolic steroid (Nadrolone) and two stimulants (ephedrine and pseudoephedrine) in the urine samples of the Canadian goaltender, Steve Vézina (Clark 1999: B14). Some argue that testing for drugs should not be limited to athletes, but extended to those in a variety of jobs, including, for example, air traffic controllers, police officers, technicians at nuclear power plants, doctors, nurses, and school bus drivers (McMillan 1991: 30).

While workplace drug and alcohol testing is common in the United States, it is less so in Canada. In 1990, for example, the Toronto-Dominion Bank introduced a mandatory drug-testing policy for both newly hired and returning employees. According to the policy, screening employees for drug use represented an attempt to "maintain a safe, healthy and productive workforce, to safeguard bank and customer funds and information and to protect the bank's policy" (Schmidt 2001). As a result, a complaint was filed with the Canadian Human Rights Tribunal that alleged the policy constituted discrimination on the basis of disability ("any previous or existing mental or physical disability and includes disfigurement and previous or existing dependence on alcohol or a drug"). Although a Canadian Human Rights Tribunal initially issued a finding of non-discrimination, a federal Court of Appeal ruled in 1998 that the policy *did* constitute "adverse-effect discrimination." As defined by then Supreme Court of Canada Justice Bertha Wilson, adverse-effect discrimination refers to "a rule that is neutral on its face but has an adverse discriminatory effect on certain members of the group to whom it applies" (in Dranoff 2001: 38). In consequence, the policy was found to be in violation of the *Canadian Human Rights Act* because it could discriminate against certain employees and was not sufficiently related to job performance.

A similar decision was reached in relation to Imperial Oil's drug and alcohol testing policy for "safety-sensitive" positions within that company. In 1992, four employees of Imperial Oil filed complaints of discrimination with the Ontario Human Rights Commission. One of the complainants maintained that, despite giving up alcohol eight years earlier and participating in a company-sponsored substance abuse program, he had been demoted as a result of the policy. The Ontario Human Rights Commission later ruled that, under the *Ontario Human* condition for employment and as a requirement for keeping their job. This chapter's *Focus on Technology* reviews some of the issues related to drug testing in Canada.

Heavy alcohol and drug use are also associated with negative consequences for an individual's mental health. Longitudinal data on both male and female adults have shown that drug users are more likely to suffer from anxiety disorders, such as phobias; depression; and antisocial personalities (White and Labouvie 1994). Other data confirm that drug users, particularly in adolescence, have a higher incidence of suicide (Bureau of Justice Statistics 1992; Cooper et al. 1992).

Rights Code, alcoholism is a handicap protected from discrimination and that the employer has the duty to accommodate the employee. The Commission ordered Imperial Oil to reinstate the employee in his "safety-sensitive" position and awarded the complainant $21 241 in damages. When Imperial Oil appealed this decision, the Ontario Court of Appeal ruled in July 2000 that Imperial Oil's use of both a pre-employment drug screening test and random drug testing for employees was discriminatory and in violation of the province's human rights code. The court held that a Breathalyzer is permissible for people in high-risk jobs, such as oil refinery workers, pilots, and train engineers, because it determines whether someone is impaired at the moment the test is administered. However, because drug testing measures only past use, not present impairment, future impairment, or likely impairment on the job, the court ruled that Imperial Oil could not justify pre-employment testing or random drug testing for employees.

Under the *Canadian Human Rights Act*, which applies to federal government employees, Crown corporations, and companies in the federal jurisdiction (e.g., banks and airlines), discrimination based on alcohol or drug dependency is prohibited. In 1999, the Canadian Human Rights Commission instituted a policy on drug testing which specified that, unless safety is an issue, drug testing cannot be justified as a bona fide occupational requirement. However, while drug test requirements by employers in the federal jurisdiction are normally considered to be discriminatory, "[n]o law in Canada states that it is illegal for an employer to insist, before or after hiring, that an employee take a test to confirm the absence of drug use.... There is also no constitutional protection against drug testing" (Dranoff 2001: 37). In consequence, a prospective employee who is asked to take a drug test and refuses cannot later complain if not hired. Similarly, if the job applicant consents to take the test and it reveals drug use, the applicant may have no legal remedy if not hired. "It all depends on whether freedom from drug use is a reasonable requirement of the job, and therefore whether human rights protections are infringed" (Dranoff 2001: 37).

Some maintain that if employees in any industry are using drugs, human lives may be in jeopardy because of impaired job performance. An alternative perspective is that drug testing may be harmful.

One concern is accuracy of the tests. Faulty tests may result in either *false positives* (the person who does not use drugs is identified as doing so) or *false negatives* (the person who uses drugs is identified as not doing so). The false-positives problem is serious: an innocent person could lose his or her job because of faulty technology (Brannigan 2000). A second concern is that drug testing may also reveal that a person is pregnant, is being treated for heart disease, or has epilepsy. The person may want these aspects of his or her private life to remain private (Kahn 2000). Third, as we have seen, drug testing may violate basic human rights. The question in a complex and increasingly technologically dependent society is how to balance the rights of an individual with the needs of society as a whole.

SOURCES: Brannigan, Mariha. 2002. "Labs That Test Transportation Workers for Drugs Face Inquiry over Samples." *Wall Street Journal*, October 2: A4; Dranoff, Linda Silver. 2001. *Everyone's Guide to the Law*, 2nd ed. Toronto: HarperCollins Publishers Ltd.; Kahn, Jeffery. 2000. "Criminally Pregnant." CNN. com, October 30; Schmidt, Steve. 2001. "Canadian Courts Restrict Drug Tests." *National Post*, December 19: A1, A8; Clark, Campbell. 1999. "Vézina Says Sorry, But Not for Taking Banned Substances." *National Post*, August 3: B14; McMillan, D. 1991. *Winning the Battle against Drugs*. New York: Franklin Watts.

Marijuana is also linked to short-term memory loss, learning disabilities, motivational deficits, and retarded emotional development.

The societal costs of drug-induced health concerns are also extraordinary. Health costs include the cost of disability insurance, the effects of secondhand smoke, the spread of AIDS, and the medical costs of accident and crime victims, as well as unhealthy infants and children. For example, cocaine use by pregnant women may lead to low-birth-weight babies, increased risk of miscarriage, and abnormal placental functioning (Klutt 2000).

3.5 Treatment Alternatives

Drug treatment reduces drug use by about 40 to 60 percent and is as effective as treating many other chronic diseases, notably diabetes and asthma (NIDA 1999: 15). Helping others to overcome chemical dependency is, however, expensive. For example, Health Canada's National Native Alcohol and Drug Abuse Programs spends about $80 million annually on substance abuse treatment and prevention for on-reserve Aboriginal people, with the majority of these funds used in relation to alcohol abuse (Auditor General 2001). Persons who are interested in overcoming chemical dependency have several treatment alternatives from which to choose. Some options include hospitalization, family therapy, counselling, private and public treatment facilities, behaviour modification, pharmacotherapy (use of treatment medications), community care programs, drug maintenance programs, and employee assistance programs. Two commonly used techniques are inpatient/outpatient programs and supportive communities.

Inpatient/Outpatient Treatment

Inpatient treatment refers "to the treatment of drug dependence in a hospital and includes medical supervision of detoxification" (McCaffrey 1998: 2). Most inpatient programs last between 30 and 90 days and target individuals whose withdrawal symptoms require close monitoring (e.g., alcoholics, cocaine addicts). Some drug-dependent patients, however, can be safety treated as outpatients. Outpatient treatment allows individuals to remain in their home and work environments and is often less expensive. In outpatient treatment, the patient is under the care of a physician who evaluates the patient's progress regularly, prescribes needed medication, and watches for signs of a relapse.

The longer a patient stays in treatment, the greater the likelihood of a successful recovery. Variables that predict success include the user's motivation to change, support of family and friends, criminal justice or employer intervention, a positive relationship with therapeutic staff, and a program of recovery that addresses many of the patient's needs.

Peer Support Groups

Twelve-Step Programs Both Alcoholics Anonymous (AA) and Narcotics Anonymous (NA) are voluntary associations whose only membership requirement is the desire to stop drinking or taking drugs. AA and NA are self-help groups in that they are operated by nonprofessionals, offer "sponsors" to each new member, and proceed along a continuum of 12 steps to recovery. Members are immediately immersed in a fellowship of caring individuals with whom they meet daily or weekly to affirm their commitment. Some have argued that AA and NA members trade their addictions for feelings of interpersonal connectedness; they bond with other group members.

Symbolic interactionists emphasize that AA and NA provide social contexts in which people develop new meanings. Abusers are surrounded by others who convey positive labels, encouragement, and social support for sobriety. Sponsors tell the new members that they can be successful in controlling alcohol and drugs "one day at a time" and provide regular interpersonal reinforcement for doing so. Although thought of as a "crutch" by some, AA members may also take medications to help prevent relapses. In a study of 222 AA members, Rychtarik and colleagues (2000) found that although over half of those surveyed thought the use of relapse-preventing medication was or might be a good idea, 29 percent reported pressures from others to stop taking the medication.

Therapeutic Communities In **therapeutic communities**, which house between 35 and 500 people for up to 15 months, participants abstain from drugs, develop marketable skills, and receive counselling. Synanon, established in 1958, was the first therapeutic community for alcoholics and was later expanded to include other drug users. The longer a person stays at such a facility, the greater the chance of overcoming the dependency. Symbolic interactionists argue that behavioural changes appear to be a consequence of revised self-definition and the positive expectations of others.

In the United States, Stay'N Out, a therapeutic community for the treatment of incarcerated drug offenders, has demonstrated success in reducing recidivism. After participating in the program for at least nine months, only 23 percent of the inmates reoffended, compared with 50 percent of those not receiving treatment. The Cornerstone Program has also been successful with drug abusers in prison. Both programs include a holistic treatment approach that focuses on the social and psychological difficulties of returning to acceptable social roles (Lipton 1994: 336).

Canada, however, lacks therapeutic communities for the treatment of incarcerated drug users outside Quebec, which runs both the ECHO and STOP programs. Instead, two core substance abuse programs are offered by Corrections Canada: the Offender Substance Pre-release Program (which involves about 32 three-hour counselling sessions offered over several months) and Choices (a cognitive-behavioural modification program that calls for about 60 hours of counselling over three to four months).

therapeutic communities

Organizations in which 35 to 100 individuals reside for up to 15 months to abstain from drugs, develop marketable skills, and receive counselling.

3.6 Strategies for Action: Canada Responds

Drug use is a complex social issue exacerbated by the structural and cultural forces of society that contribute to its existence. While the structure of society perpetuates a system of inequality creating in some the need to escape, the culture of society, through the media and normative contradictions, sends mixed messages about the acceptability of drug use. As a result, developing programs, laws, or initiatives that are likely to end drug use may be unrealistic. Nevertheless, since 1987, Canada's Drug Strategy has emphasized the need for a "balanced" approach that combines prevention and education with law enforcement. Among its stated objectives are these: "reducing the demand for drugs; reducing drug-related mortality and morbidity by reducing high-risk behaviours, such as spreading HIV/AIDS through needle sharing; improving the effectiveness of and accessibility to substance abuse information and interventions; restricting the supply of illicit drugs; reducing the profitability of illicit trafficking; and reducing the costs of substance abuse to Canadian society" (Auditor General 2001).

Managing the illicit drug problem in Canada is inherently difficult. It requires the efforts of three levels of government—federal, provincial/territorial, and municipal—and many non-government organizations. Although integrating the efforts of three levels of government is difficult, it is essential.

■ **Table 3.3** *Addressing Illegal Drugs: The Federal Infrastructure*

Federally, 11 departments and agencies are involved in addressing illicit drug use in Canada. The major ones are:

Health Canada	Provides the leadership and coordination for Canada's Drug Strategy. It is involved directly in activities to reduce the demand for and the supply of illicit drugs. Its Office of Controlled Substances is responsible for the legislative control framework to control illicit drugs. The office administers the regulations of the *Controlled Drugs and Substances Act*, which includes processing the licensing and permit requirement for the use of controlled substances for legitimate purposes. The Office of Cannabis Medical Access deals with controls on the medical use of marijuana.
Solicitor General Canada	Plays a leadership and coordinating role in policing, security and corrections under Canada's Drug Strategy. The Department is also engaged in related activities both domestically and internationally.
RCMP	The RCMP's federal drug efforts focus on such activities as seizing drugs, investigating and arresting the upper echelon of criminal organizations involved in the drug trade, and seizing proceeds of crime. The RCMP also undertakes drug enforcement as part of the provincial and municipal policing responsibilities it performs on contract. In addition to participation in many "joint force operations" aimed at combating organized crime, the RCMP also delivers drug prevention programs. It makes some 8000 presentations annually to students, parents, employees, and community groups.
Department of Justice	Prosecutes drug cases and provides expertise to the development of legislation addressing organized crime. It has a pilot initiative, the Toronto Drug Treatment Court Program, that offers alternatives to traditional prosecution.
Canada Border Services Agency	Contributes to reducing the supply of illicit drugs in two ways. Customs intercepts illegal drugs entering Canada at our borders. For instance, it estimates that in 1999 it seized illicit drugs with a street value estimated at $351 million. Taxation audits individuals suspected of selling illicit drugs or engaging in other illegal activities and raises assessments and levies penalties where it finds unreported income. Taxation also investigates suspected tax evasion and recommends prosecution of individuals.
Correctional Services Canada	Is responsible for offenders serving criminal sentences over two years. These include individuals convicted of serious drug offences. CSC provides substance abuse and treatment programs to offenders with drug problems. It also uses security measures, including the use of sniffer dogs and urinalysis testing, to control the supply of illicit drugs in prisons.
Department of Foreign Affairs and International Trade	Collaborates with other federal departments and represents Canada in the international aspects of Canada's Drug Strategy.

SOURCE: *Report of the Auditor General of Canada* (December 2001). Office of the Auditor General of Canada, 2001. Reproduced with the permission of the Minister of Public Works and Government Services, 2011.

Report of the Auditor General of Canada—2001

In recent years, most of the federal government's changes to legislation in relation to illicit drugs have targeted supply rather than demand. These efforts have included the amendment of the Canadian *Criminal Code* to include organized crime offences and the creation of the Financial Transactions and Reports Analysis Centre of Canada. The latter attempts to detect money laundering by monitoring financial transactions (see Table 3.3).

Government Regulations

Drawing upon Solomon (1999), we will review some of the major federal and provincial alcohol and drug laws.

In Canada, the federal government regulates the importation and exportation of alcohol products, alcohol-related excise taxes, and broadcast advertising.

At present, the federal regulations prohibit broadcasting a range of messages, including those that encourage non-drinkers to consume alcohol; that direct their appeal to minors; that suggest that alcohol use is positively associated with social acceptance, personal accomplishment, or success in athletic or business endeavours; or that link the consumption of alcohol with high-risk activities.

In addition, the provinces have some degree of control over the marketing and advertising of alcohol, including such market practices as price discounting, drinking contests, the use of alcohol as prizes, or the dispensing of free drinks. The majority of provincial advertising regulations target lifestyle advertising that might otherwise encourage youths to drink, drink large amounts of alcohol, or drink and drive. Each province in Canada also regulates the control and sale of alcohol within it. Currently, the legal drinking age in all Canadian provinces and territories is 19 except in Quebec, Manitoba, and Alberta where the minimum age is 18.

Harm Reduction

In September 2003, following the election of Mayor Larry Campbell, a former RCMP officer and city coroner (and the inspiration for the CBC drama *DaVinci's Inquest*), the city of Vancouver opened North America's first safe injection site (SIS). The site is popularly perceived as an endorsement and encouragement of drug use, but the reality is that site policies do not allow non-users to access safe injection sites in order to have a new experience. Instead, the goal is to have a positive impact on the reduction of disease and death related to intravenous drug use. In the years from 1992 to 1993, more than 2000 people died from overdose in Vancouver, and the director of the B.C. Centre for Excellence in HIV/AIDS notes that in the absence of such sites, "approximately 30 per cent of addicts are HIV positive and more than 90 per cent have hepatitis C virus" (in Thomson 2003). Vancouver decided to open its first SIS because data from 27 cities in Europe and Australia showed "a profound reduction in overdose deaths and the spread of diseases like HIV and hepatitis C, and a dramatic reduction in the open drug scene" (City of Vancouver 2003). SISs, then, do not promote drug use, but serve as part of a broader public health policy that recognizes the threat of drug use to the health not only of users, but of the broader community as well.

The Vancouver policy and Mayor Campbell were criticized harshly by conservative politicians in both Canada and the United States, with "top anti-drug officials in the United States [saying] Canada is going soft on the war on drugs" (*Economist* 2003). Nonetheless, B.C. Health Officer Dr. Perry Kendall reports that in each of its first two years of operation, the SIS in East Vancouver prevented close to 200 deaths by overdose (Canadian Press Service 2005). The site continues to be controversial, and subject to the vagaries of political funding models. As of 2010, the site is permitted to continue operations following a British Columbia Appeals Court ruling against the Attorney General. The BC decision determined that the operation of Insite is a provincial health matter and that the federal government has no interest in the operations or future structure of the service (Vancouver Coastal Health 2010).

Provincial highway traffic legislation gives police the authority to stop vehicles in a random manner to determine whether the driver has been drinking; the provinces also have the authority to issue, suspend, revoke, and reinstate driving licences. The majority of Canadian provinces have created provisions for automatic provincial licence suspensions so that a person convicted of any federal drinking and driving offence is subject to an automatic mandatory provincial licence suspension. The length of the suspension for a first, second, or subsequent conviction varies in the different provinces and territories. For example, in Manitoba, a 12-month suspension is given for a first offence and a five-year suspension for a second; in Alberta and Saskatchewan, the respective time periods are one and two years; and in Yukon, three months and a year. Moreover, with the exception of Nova Scotia and Quebec, provincial legislation authorizes police to temporarily suspend a driver's licence at roadside if, for example, a driver refuses an officer's demand to provide a breath sample or registers a BAC of 0.05 or higher. In the majority of provinces, the duration of the suspension is 24 hours. Six provinces have enacted additional legislation that authorizes police to impose 90-day administrative licence suspensions (ALS) on those who register a BAC over 0.08 percent or refuse to provide a breath or blood sample.

The provinces have also created several drinking-and-driving countermeasures. These include graduated licence programs for new drivers, which require that they abstain from drinking any alcohol prior to driving; vehicle impoundment programs to deter offenders from driving while prohibited or suspended; alcohol interlock programs, which involve the connection of a small breath-testing instrument to a vehicle that prevents it from being started or driven if the driver's BAC is over a preset limit; and mandatory remedial measures that require offenders, for example, to attend an alcohol awareness program for a first offence or, for a second or subsequent offence, undergo alcohol assessment or participate in a treatment program. The cost of participating in such programs is generally borne by the offender.

In Canada, the *Controlled Drugs and Substances Act* outlines the six federal criminal offences: possession, trafficking, possession for the purpose of trafficking, production, importing or exporting, and "prescription shopping." While the penalties for possession vary depending on the type of drug, the maximum penalties under this act for the majority of offences are severe. For example, for "Schedule 1 Drugs"—cocaine, heroin, opium, phencyclidine, and those drugs that, prior to May 1997, were dealt with under the *Narcotics Control Act*—the maximum penalty for trafficking, possession for the purpose of trafficking, producing, and importing and exporting is life imprisonment. Life imprisonment is also the maximum penalty for importing or exporting any amount of any form of cannabis.

Despite all the attempts to regulate the use of alcohol and drugs, some would argue that the war on drugs has done more harm than good. Duke and Gross (1994) argue that the war on drugs, much like Prohibition, has only intensified other social problems: drug-related gang violence and turf wars, the creation of syndicate-controlled black markets, unemployment, the spread of AIDS, overcrowded prisons, corrupt law enforcement officials, and the diversion of police from other serious crimes. Consistent with conflict theory, still others argue that the "war on drugs" is a war on the poor, while the drug use of the affluent goes largely ignored (Duster 1995). Herbert Gans explained the irony of institutions having vested interests in the continuation of social problems faced by the poor in his famous essay "The Uses of Poverty: The Poor Pay All." In the essay, Gans observes that for all the costs of social problems, they serve a benefit to those in power. Gans's argument rests on exposing the manner in which the poor are used as political scapegoats in order to justify a wide range of social, charity, surveillance, and penal system professions: "penology would be minuscule without the poor, as would the police. Other activities and groups that flourish because of the existence of poverty are the numbers game, the sale of heroin and cheap wines and liquors" (Gans 1971: 21). In the essay, Gans goes on to explain that, furthermore, those in socially powerful positions—including doctors, lawyers, social workers, and judges—depend on the persistence of poverty and its associated "rehabilitation" requirements for their professional and social prestige.

Deregulation or Legalization: The Debate

Deregulation is the reduction of government control over certain drugs. For example, Ontario has opened up the sale of wine to private stores. Since 1999, Canadians who require marijuana for medical purposes have been able to apply for an exemption under Section 56 of the *Controlled Drugs and Substances Act*. In 2002, more than 800 Canadians were permitted by Health Canada to possess marijuana for medical purposes. Moreover, the Marijuana Medical Access Regulations (MMAR) allow people with authorizations to possess and cultivate marijuana for medical purposes (McLellan 2002). Extending this approach, in April 1999, the board of directors of the Association of Canadian Police Chiefs recommended to the federal government that simple possession of marijuana and hashish be decriminalized—that is, that it no longer be an offence under the *Criminal Code*. The board suggested that this strategy would clear a backlog of drug cases in the courts and allow Canadian police services to focus their resources on more serious crimes, such as drug trafficking (Fife 1999); however, the CCSA reports that even in the face of these recommendations, the number of youth charged in 2003 with possession of cannabis had tripled from the number charged in 1993, moving from 1047 to 3294 (CCSA 2007: 24). In part, the increase has to do with the increased production and availability of cannabis, but it has also to do with increased surveillance in schools. The CCSA observes:

> It is relatively common for school principals to collaborate with police forces in an attempt to curb drug use and trafficking within educational institutions. This collaboration takes many forms, but typically it means allowing police to carry out a raid to arrest some small-scale cannabis dealers or users, handing students caught by staff over to the police, or encouraging students to inform on each other. These tough responses aim first of all at sending a no-tolerance message to students and reassuring parents about the principal's attitude toward drug use. While collaboration with police generally succeeds in achieving these goals, very few dealers or users are actually arrested in this way. (2007: 25)

Decriminalization, by contrast, would promote a medical rather than criminal approach to drug use, and would encourage users to seek treatment and adopt preventive practices. Going a step further, proponents for the **legalization** of drugs affirm the right of adults to make an informed choice. They also argue that the tremendous revenues realized from drug taxes could be used to benefit all citizens, that purity and safety controls could be implemented, and that legalization would expand the number of distributors, thereby increasing competition and reducing prices. Drugs would be safer, drug-related crimes would be reduced, and production and distribution of previously controlled substances would be taken out of the hands of the underworld.

deregulation
The reduction of government control of, for example, certain drugs.

decriminalization
The removal of criminal penalties for a behaviour, as in the decriminalization of drug use.

legalization
Making prohibited behaviour legal; for example, legalizing marijuana or prostitution.

Opponents of legalization argue that it would be construed as government approval of drug use and, consequently, drug experimentation and abuse would increase. Further, although the legalization of drugs would result in substantial revenues for the government, drug trafficking and black markets would still flourish due to some drugs, notably crack, remaining illegal. Legalization would also require an extensive and costly bureaucracy to regulate the manufacture, sale, and distribution of drugs. Finally, the position that drug use is an individual's right cannot guarantee that others will not be harmed. It is illogical to assume that a greater availability of drugs will translate into a safer society.

Collective Action

Social action groups such as MADD have successfully lobbied legislators to lower maximum blood alcohol levels for drivers and to introduce zero allowable blood alcohol for young drivers. MADD, with 3.5 million members and 600 chapters in North America, has also put pressure on alcohol establishments to stop "two-for-one" offers and has pushed for laws that hold the bartenders personally liable if a served person is later involved in an alcohol-related accident. Even hosts in private homes can now be held liable if they allow someone who became impaired while drinking at their house to drive. Most important, perhaps, MADD seeks to change the meaning of alcohol use by, for example, redefining drunk driving "accidents" as violent crimes.

Sensitized to the danger of driving while impaired, some high-school principals and school boards have encouraged students to become members of SADD (Students Against Drunk Driving). Members often sign formal pledges and put emblems on their cars to signify a commitment against alcohol. "Dry grads" also encourage students to refrain from drinking alcohol. To reduce the number of teenagers driving while drinking, local groups of parents have also organized parties at bowling alleys or school gyms as alternatives to high-school graduation parties.

Understanding **Alcohol and Other Drugs**

In summarizing what we know about substance abuse, drugs and their use are socially defined. As the structure of society changes, the acceptability of one drug or another changes as well. As conflict theorists assert, the status of a drug as legal or illegal is intricately linked to those who have the power to define acceptable and unacceptable drug use. There is also little doubt that rapid social change, anomie, alienation, and inequality further drug use and abuse. Symbolic interactionism plays a significant role in the process, as well— if people are labelled as "drug users" and expected to behave accordingly, drug use is likely to continue. If there is positive reinforcement of drug use or a biological predisposition to use them, the probability of drug involvement is even higher. Thus, the theories of drug use complement rather than contradict one another.

Drug use must also be conceptualized within the social context in which it occurs. In a study of high-risk youths who had become involved with drugs, Dembo and colleagues (1994) suggest that many youths in their study had been "failed by society":

Many of them were born into economically-strained circumstances, often raised by families who neglected or abused them, or in other ways did not provide for their nurturance and wholesome development... Few youths in our sample received the mental health and substance abuse treatment services they needed. (p. 25)

However, many treatment alternatives, emanating from a clinical model of drug use, assume that the origin of the problem lies within the individual rather than in the structure and culture of society. Although admittedly the problem may lie within the individual at the time treatment occurs, policies that address the social causes of drug abuse provide a better means of dealing with the drug problem in Canada.

Prevention is preferable to intervention, and given the social portrait of hard drug users—young, male, minority—prevention must entail dealing with the social conditions that foster drug use. Some data suggest that marginal youth are particularly vulnerable to drug involvement because of their lack of legitimate alternatives (Van Kammen and Loeber 1994):

Illegal drug use may be a way to escape the strains of the severe urban conditions and dealing illegal drugs may be one of the few, if not the only, ways to provide for material needs. Intervention and treatment programs, therefore, should include efforts to find alternate ways to deal with the limiting circumstances of inner-city life, as well as create opportunities for youngsters to find more conventional ways of earning a living. (p. 22)

However, social policies dealing with drug use have been predominantly punitive rather than preventive.

In Canada and throughout the world, millions of people depend on legal drugs for the treatment of a variety of conditions, including pain, anxiety and nervousness, insomnia, depression, and fatigue. Although drugs used for these purposes are relatively harmless, the cultural message "better living through chemistry" contributes to alcohol and drug use and their consequences. These and other drugs are embedded in a political and economic context that determines who defines what drugs, in what amounts, are licit or illicit, and what programs are developed in reference to them.

Critical Thinking

1. Are alcoholism and other drug addictions a consequence of nature or nurture? If nurture, what environmental factors contribute to such problems? Which of the three sociological theories best explains drug addiction?

2. Measuring alcohol and drug use is often very difficult. The tendency for respondents to acquiesce, or respond in a way they believe is socially desirable, contributes to the problem. Consider this and other problems in doing research on alcohol and other drugs, and how such problems could be remedied.

3. If, as symbolic interactionists argue, social problems are those conditions so defined, how might the manipulation of social definitions virtually eliminate many "drug" problems?

"Is It True?" Quiz: Answers

1 = true; 2 = true; 3 = contextual; 4 = contextual; 5 = true

Crime and Violence

Is It True?

1. In the decade from 1997 to 2007, the rate of *Criminal Code* incidents reported to Canadian police services involving violent crimes rose consistently, reaching their highest level since 1977.

2. Although sociologists have different theories about the causes of crime, they agree that crime is always harmful to society.

3. Approximately half of Canadians believe that capital punishment should be exercised in some circumstances, less than the number that favour capital punishment in either Britain or the United States.

4. Fewer than 1 percent of Canadians regard prostitution as a "very serious" social issue.

5. The majority of Canadian homicide victims had some type of relationship with their murderers.

Read more here: 1 = p. 105, 2 = p. 111, 3 = p. 132, 4 = p. 121, 5 = p. 105
Answers can be found on p. 141.

4.1 A Theory of Justice

For years, popular commentators, religious figures, and politicians have blamed various activities (dancing, listening to popular music, watching WWF wrestling) and public figures (Ludwig van Beethoven, Elvis Presley, Marilyn Manson) for the corruption of youth and dissolution of social values. Olmsted (1988) has noted that, in the past, such diverse pastimes as billiards, parachuting, surfing, pinball, attending the theatre, amateur archaeology, horse racing, butterfly collecting, motorcycling, target shooting, and ballroom dancing have all been identified as morally disreputable and socially problematic activities.

This chapter examines the criminal justice system as well as theories, types, and demographic patterns of criminal behaviour. It also addresses the conceptual problem of understanding why what counts as "crime" changes over time and place. The economic, social, and psychological costs of crime and violence are also examined. The chapter concludes with a discussion of social policies and prevention programs designed to reduce crime and violence in Canada.

Although criminal patterns and justice systems share similar attributes throughout the world, dramatic differences exist in international crime and violence rates. While tiny Gibraltar, with a total area of 6.5 sq. km, has the highest reported crime rate of any country in the world (at 18 316 per 100 000 population) (Ash 2001: 66), in general, industrialized countries have higher rates of reported crime than nonindustrialized countries. There are also variations within industrialized countries. The last year for which we have comparative measures shows that the U.S. homicide rate is three times higher than Canada's, four times higher than Western Europe's, six times higher than Great Britain's, and seven times higher than Japan's (Doyle 2000; Gannon 2001) (see Figure 4.1). It is important to know that although these rates can fluctuate from year to year, the trends in one direction or another are roughly stable. The most recent data on homicide rates in Canada show that "Since 1961, […] there have been two distinct trends. Following a period of stability between 1961 and 1966, the homicide rate more than doubled over the next ten years, reaching a peak of 3.03 homicide victims per 100,000 population in 1975. Since 1975, the rate has gradually declined, with some year-to-year fluctuations. However, the 2006 rate remains higher than rates in the early 1960s" (Li 2007: 2). Moreover, it remains a myth that homicide is a random act with no social determinants at work; Canadian data for 2006 continue to show that in 83 percent of cases homicide victims knew their attackers: a little more than one-third were killed by a family member, while another one-third were killed by an acquaintance and an additional 12 percent were killed by someone known to them through

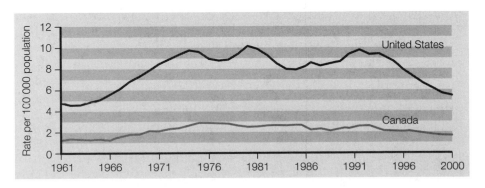

■ **Figure 4.1** *Rates of Homicide, Canada and the United States, 1961–2000*

SOURCE: Statistics Canada, Canadian Centre for Justice Statistics. "Crime Comparison between Canada and the United States (*Juristat*), Catalogue No. 85-002-XPE, 21(11):5, 2001.

criminal activities (Li, 2007: 1). Poverty, isolation, family breakdown, and domestic violence all are distinct factors in these killings, and this chapter discusses the manner in which larger social problems such as these influence crime.

4.2 Sources of Crime Statistics

From the *National Symbol of Canada Act*, which identifies the beaver as symbolic of Canadian sovereignty, to the *Income Tax Act*, whose rules and regulations are bound in an almost 2000-page volume amended yearly, our social life is bound together by laws (Statistics Canada 1998). Although there are 40 000 federal and provincial statutes and a broad range of municipal bylaws that define behaviour in violation of some penal law, "[u]nder the terms of the *Constitution Act*, only those offences defined by federal law can technically be called crimes" (Brantingham et al. 1995). Unlike the United States, which has many state criminal codes, Canada has a single criminal code. Most of the behaviours that we would commonly recognize as crimes (e.g., assault, kidnapping, sexual assault, murder) are contained within the federal *Criminal Code*.

A simple definition of **crime** would be "any act that violates the criminal law." For a violation to be a crime, however, the offender must have acted voluntarily and with intent and have no legally acceptable excuse or justification for the behaviour. Three major types of statistics are used to measure crime: official statistics, victimization surveys, and self-report offender surveys.

crime

The violation of norms that are written into law.

Official Statistics

Since the establishment of the first modern police force, the London Metropolitan Police Force (Scotland Yard) in 1829, police agencies have collected information about crime. Systematic national police statistics have been collected since 1857 in England and Wales, since 1920 in Canada, and since 1930 in the United States (Brantingham et al. 1995). Since 1962, Canada has used a system called the Canadian Uniform Crime Reporting Survey (UCR), developed by Statistics Canada and the Canadian Association of Chiefs of Police "to provide a measure of reliability for crime statistics through providing police agencies with a standardized set of procedures for collecting and reporting crime information" (Evans and Himelfarb 2000).

The UCR system collects information monthly from more than 400 municipal police departments, services, and agencies across Canada on 91 specific categories of crime and offences. This information is compiled and published each year with counts and calculated rates per 100 000 population presented for each province and territory, and for Canada as a whole. Within the UCR, crimes known to the police are grouped into major categories. For example, "Crimes of Violence" groups together such acts as homicide, attempted homicide, assault, abduction, sexual assault, and robbery. "Property Offences" includes such offences as breaking and entering, theft of motor vehicles, possession of stolen goods, and fraud. The UCR additionally provides information on the numbers of persons charged with different types of offences, with separate counts for adults and youths, males and females. The crimes known to police are compiled and published annually in Canada by the Canadian Centre for Justice Statistics (CCJS), the operational arm of the National Justice Statistics Initiative (NJSI).

These statistics have several shortcomings (DiIulio 1999) (see this chapter's *Social Problems Research Up Close* feature). Not only do many incidents of crime

No Crime Epidemic in Canada

Toronto being Toronto, and the national media being mostly located in Toronto, that city's spate of gun violence has become big news.

Front-page coverage. Crime columnists hyperventilating. Politicians rushing to propose quick solutions. America-bashing. The rest of Canada has seen and heard it all. Toronto's problems equal Canada's.

Except that they don't. Step back from the frenzy and look at some numbers.

There were three shooting incidents in Ottawa, for example, before and after Christmas, with two fatalities and several near misses, including a shotgun blast to the rear of a car and the riddling of another with bullets. Amount of coverage in the national media? Zero.

There were two shooting incidents during the same period in Toronto, with two fatalities. Amount of coverage? You saw it.

Toronto is now deemed a violent city. It isn't, no matter what the media report. Canada is said to be becoming a violent country. It isn't, no matter what the media report.

Toronto has a localized violent crime problem in several pockets of the city. It is concentrated, largely but not exclusively, among Jamaican-Canadian youth. To extrapolate widespread violence in the city or the province from this tiny subset of the population grossly distorts reality.

You want violent crime? Consider this: The homicide rate in Western Canada is much higher than that of Ontario. In Manitoba, the rate is 4.3 for every 100,000 people; it's 3.9 in Saskatchewan and 2.7 in Alberta and British Columbia. In Ontario, the rate is 1.5, the same as in Quebec, a province with a much smaller population.

Toronto's deaths—at least the ones the media highlighted—were from shootings. It was therefore taken for granted that Canada had a handgun problem, and politicians rushed to propose remedies.

In Ottawa, by contrast, only two of the 11 homicides in 2005 were gun-related. The others were from beatings and stabbings.

While the media fixate on death by shooting, here's what Statistics Canada reported about homicides in 2004, the last year for which final numbers are available: More murders resulted from stabbings (205) than handguns (172). From 2000 to 2004, more murders were by knives (849) than guns (840).

Throw in murders by strangulation, beating, burning, and what Statscan calls "other methods," and 2.5 times more people were murdered by means other than a gun in 2004.

From 2000 to 2004, homicides in Canada rose by 7 per cent, but the population increased by slightly more than 5 per cent. This is an epidemic of crime? The press coverage suggests yes; the facts say no.

The homicide rate inched up during those years, but the incidence of every other category of serious crime declined, including attempted murder, sexual assault, robbery, break and enter, and theft. And yet, reading and listening to the national media and watching the campaigning politicians with their palliatives, the unsuspecting might believe that Canada is besieged by violent crime.

Predictably, those searching for an explanation to Toronto's murders pointed to the United States, where the homicide rate is eight times that of Canada. Accusers rightly say there are guns aplenty across the border.

But haven't guns always been available in the U.S.? Is there anything new about their availability?

The U.S. supply of guns has been a constant for decades. What's changed is the demand. And where's the demand? Right here in Canada. It's too bad for Americans and for us that guns are so prevalent in the United States. That more of them are showing up in Canada reflects a change in Canadian demand, not U.S. supply.

Crime sells newspapers and drives TV ratings ("if it bleeds, it leads"), which is the most plausible explanation for the media's focus, despite the statistical evidence that serious crime is declining.

An immense amount of pernicious nonsense usually surrounds violent crime reporting and its breathless aftermath. Canada, like all Western societies, has a generalized crime challenge, what with thugs and nasty people around.

Canada's particular problems, however, are inner-city drug- and gang-related: aboriginal gangs in some places, Indo-Canadian ones in B.C.'s Lower Mainland, Jamaican-Canadian ones (and a few others) in Toronto, biker gangs in Quebec and parts of Ontario.

Serious as these problems are, they do not constitute a crime epidemic, media coverage notwithstanding.

SOURCE: "Read My Lips: There Is No Crime Epidemic in Canada," by Jeffrey Simpson *(The Globe and Mail)*, p. A15. Copyright January 4, 2006. Reprinted with permission from *The Globe and Mail*.

go unreported, but police also fail to record all the crime reports they receive. Alternatively, some rates may be exaggerated. Motivation for such distortions may come from the public (e.g., demanding that something be done) or from political or organizational pressures (e.g., budget requests). For example, a police department may "crack down" on drug-related crimes in a given year. The result is an increase in the recorded number of these offences. Such an increase reflects a change in the behaviour of law enforcement personnel, not a change in the number of drug violations. Thus, official crime statistics may be a better indicator of what police are doing than what criminals are doing.

Victimization Surveys

Victimization surveys ask people if they have been victims of crime. Although the first victimization surveys were carried out in the United States in 1966 for the President's Commission on Law Enforcement and Administration of Justice, victimization surveys in Canada have a much shorter history. As Fattah (1991) observes, "[n]o truly national victimization survey was done in Canada until the General Social Survey was carried out by Statistics Canada in 1988." For Statistics Canada's 1999 General Social Survey (GSS), 26 000 people aged 15 and older were interviewed by telephone and asked if they had been victimized by crime and, if so, where and when the crime had occurred and whether or not it had been reported to the police. Respondents were also queried on their perceptions of the level of crime in their neighbourhood, their personal fear of crime, and their views on the criminal justice system (Tufts 2000).

As we have already indicated, youth tend to be vilified in popular consciousness and in the media as increasingly dangerous and violent, even though the data on youth crime do not support this negative view. What is important and often overlooked is that youth are at risk for victimization in crimes, and understanding why requires that we look at the correlations between youth behaviours and their victimization:

> According to police-reported data, in 2003, the risk of violent victimization for children and youth increased as the child ages. Rates of violent victimization for male and female victims remain relatively similar up until the age of 8, after which male rates exceed those of females. The rate of victimization for female victims increases through the teenage years to peak at 2,463 assaults per 100,000 population at age 15. For male victims, rates increase sharply up until age 13 and peak at 2,557 at age 17. Some researchers attribute the increased rate of violent victimization of youth as a direct result of their risk-taking behaviours. (AuCoin 2005: 3)

In other words, AuCoin explains, because youth increase their use of alcohol and other drugs, and are subject to less parental supervision as they get older, they expose themselves to increased victimization risk. Risks outside the home are not the only ones that youth face, of course; youth account for 61 percent of all victims of sexual assault and 60 percent of those assaults occur at the hands of a family member. Moreover, more than half of the abductions of children are carried out not by a stranger—as the media would make it seem—but at the hands of a parent (AuCoin 2005: 1). Clearly, then, there is no simple rationale for the blanket of suspicion tossed over youth who are popularly and perennially depicted as unruly thugs (if they are boys) and hyper-sexed vixens (if they are girls). Figure 4.2 shows the increased victimization of male and female youth as age increases. Furthermore, the same data from Statistics Canada show that youth who are the witnesses to domestic violence face increased risks to their own health, and to becoming abusers themselves in adulthood.

In addition to national surveys, the International Crime Victim Survey (ICVS) collected victimization data using the same questionnaire in many countries, including Canada, in 1989, 1992, 1996–97, and 2000 (Besserer 2002). This survey examines householders' experiences with crime, policing, crime prevention, and sense of safety. According to this survey, on average, only 55 percent of victimization incidents are reported to police, with property crimes more likely to be reported than crimes against persons. In part, this finding reflects the general requirement by insurance companies that individuals

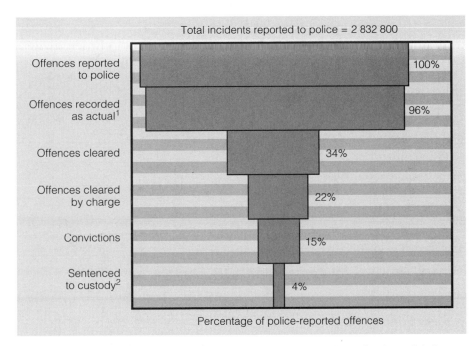

Total incidents reported to police = 2 832 800

Offences reported to police — 100%

Offences recorded as actual[1] — 96%

Offences cleared — 34%

Offences cleared by charge — 22%

Convictions — 15%

Sentenced to custody[2] — 4%

Percentage of police-reported offences

■ **Figure 4.2** *Caseload within the Criminal Justice System*

SOURCE: Adapted from Statistics Canada, Canadian Centre for Justice Statistics, "Uniform Crime Reporting Survey, Adult Court Survey, and Youth Court Survey" *(Juristat)* Catalogue No.85-002-XPE, 21(11):5

[1] An offence is considered "actual" when, following an initial investigation, the police confirm that a criminal offence has occurred. An offence is "cleared" when police are satisfied that they have identified an offender. However, it may not be possible to lay a charge against an offender because he or she is dead, under age 12, has diplomatic immunity, is already in prison, and so on. If, in the view of the police, it is possible to lay a charge against an offender, the offence is cleared by charge.

[2] Includes secure custody only for young offenders and any custodial sentence for adults.

seeking compensation for property stolen or damaged as the result of a criminal act file a police report. Although victimization surveys provide detailed information about crime victims, they provide less reliable data about offenders.

Self-Report Offender Surveys

Self-report surveys ask offenders about their criminal behaviour. The sample may consist of a population with known police records, such as a prison population, or it may include respondents from the general population, such as university students. Self-report data compensate for many of the problems associated with official statistics, but are still subject to exaggerations and concealment. Marcus Felson's research over three decades has repeatedly shown that a wide range of criminal acts never wind up in official crime reporting statistics. Among those activities indicated in self-reports but that rarely get reported to police are cannabis use, underage drinking, shoplifting, private assaults, and many small instances of fraud that add up to billions of dollars (Felson and Boba 2010: 5). The Criminal Activities Survey in this chapter's *Self and Society* feature asks you to indicate whether you have engaged in a variety of illegal activities.

Self-report surveys reveal that virtually every adult has engaged in some type of criminal activity. Why, then, is only a fraction of the population labelled as criminal? Only a small proportion of the total population of law violators is ever convicted of a crime. For example, of 3.4 million household burglaries in the United States in 2005, only 1.9 million were reported to police, with 200 000 arrests following from those resulting in only 4000 convictions (ibid).

Criminal Activities Survey

Read each of the following questions. If, since the age of 18, you have ever engaged in the behaviour described, place a "1" in the space provided. If you have not engaged in the behaviour, put a "0" in the space provided. After completing the survey, read the section on interpretation to see what your answers mean.

Questions	1 (Yes)	0 (No)
1. Have you ever shared a joint with a friend or offered to do so?	_____	
2. Have you ever given a cigarette to a person under 18 in any public place?	_____	
3. Have you ever advertised a reward, "no questions asked," for the return of anything lost or stolen?	_____	
4. Have you ever caused a disturbance in or near a public place by fighting, shouting, swearing, singing, or using insulting or obscene language?	_____	
5. Have you ever begun and/or participated in an office basketball or football pool?	_____	
6. Have you ever used "filthy, obscene, annoying, or offensive" language while on the telephone?	_____	
7. Have you ever punched out for a friend on a time clock so that it appeared that your friend left work later than she or he really did?	_____	
8. Have you ever stolen anything from a dollar store?	_____	
9. Have you ever written a cheque when you knew it was bad?	_____	
10. Have you ever threatened to injure a pet bird or animal?	_____	
11. Have you, at a friend's request, used that friend's bank card to pay bills or withdraw money for your friend?	_____	
12. Have you ever, while driving, damaged a parked car (e.g., in a parking lot) and failed to leave a note for the other driver with your name and address on it?	_____	
13. Have you ever driven your parents' car without their permission?	_____	

Interpretation

Each of the activities described in these questions represents criminal behaviour subject to fines, imprisonment, or both under the *Criminal Code* of Canada in 2002. For each activity, the following table lists the maximum prison sentence and/or fine for a first-time offender. To calculate your "prison time" and any fines, sum the numbers corresponding to each activity you have engaged in.

Maximum Prison Sentence	Maximum Fine	Offence
1. Five years less a day	n.a.	Trafficking (Schedule II drug)
2. Six months	$2000	Furnishing a tobacco product to young person
3. Six months	$2000	Advertising a reward with immunity (e.g., "no questions asked")
4. Six months	$2000	Causing disturbance
5. Six months	$2000	Betting, pool-selling, book-making, etc.
6. Six months	$2000	Indecent telephone calls
7. Six months	$2000	Falsifying employment record

8. Two years	$2000	Theft
9. Ten years	$5000	False pretence or false statement
10. Two years	$1000	Uttering threats
11. Ten years		Unauthorized use of a computer system
12. Five years	$2000	Failing to stop vehicle at scene of accident
13. Six months	$2000	Taking motor vehicle without consent

SOURCES: Rodrigues, Gary P., ed. 1999. *The Police Officer's Manual of Criminal Offences and Criminal Law.* Toronto: Carswell; Solomon, Robert. 1999. "Alcohol and Drug Law." In *Canadian Profile 1999: Alcohol, Tobacco and Other Drugs,* pp. 295–315. Ottawa: Centre on Substance Abuse and Centre for Addiction and Mental Health.

4.3 Sociological Theories of Crime and Violence

Some explanations of crime and violence focus on psychological aspects of offenders, such as psychopathic personalities, unhealthy relationships with parents, and mental illness. Other crime theories focus on potential biological variables, such as central nervous system malfunction, stress, hormones, vitamin or mineral deficiencies, or a presumed genetic predisposition toward aggression. Sociological theories of crime and violence emphasize the role of social factors in criminal behaviour and societal responses to it.

It is important to understand from the outset that not all perspectives approach crime and deviance in purely negative terms. The following discussion of theoretical understandings of crime and deviance shows that sometimes sociologists are interested in the positive features of crime and deviance. Structural-functionalists, for example, understand that criminal activity, such as treason or blasphemy, may encourage change in oppressive social structures and ideas in church and state treatment of persons. Conflict theorists and feminists may agree that the lack of power some individuals and groups have may necessitate breaking the law or deviating from typical behaviours in order to secure increased rights and access to privileges—like property rights or suffrage or personal autonomy. Symbolic interactionists may see in "deviance" the ability for subjects to re-vision their worlds and to make new meanings out of situations. For example, efforts over the last 20 years by various lesbian and gay rights organizations such as EGALE have resulted in recognition that same-sex partners also form families where they care for each other, care for children, and fulfil economic responsibilities. Without the efforts of organizations and persons to publicly demonstrate the place of lesbian and gay families in the larger society, we might still have partners legally unable to provide or to gain access to medical care for their partners or for the children whom they parent every day; we might still have a society that would leave gay and lesbian couples unable to benefit from insurance programs to which they had to contribute by law, and we might still have a society in which violent crimes against gays and lesbians would go unrecognized. From a variety of perspectives, then, we can see how refusing to live by the status quo can extend rights, as well as recognition, to all members of a society instead of only to the powerful.

Structural-Functionalist Perspective

According to Durkheim and other structural-functionalists, crime is functional for society. One of the functions of crime and other deviant behaviour is that it strengthens group cohesion:

> The deviant individual violates rules of conduct [that] the rest of the community holds in high respect; and when these people come together to express their outrage over the offense...they develop a tighter bond of solidarity than existed earlier. (Erikson 1966: 4)

Crime may also lead to social change. For example, an episode of local violence may "achieve broad improvements in city services...[and] be a catalyst for making public agencies more effective and responsive, for strengthening families and social institutions, and for creating public–private partnerships" (National Research Council 1994: 9–10).

While functionalism as a theoretical perspective deals directly with some aspects of crime and violence, it is not a theory of crime per se. Three major theories of crime and violence have developed from functionalism, however. The first, called **strain theory**, was developed by Robert Merton (1957), using Durkheim's concept of anomie, or normlessness. Merton argues that when legitimate means (for example, a job) of acquiring culturally defined goals (for example, money) are limited by the structure of society, the resulting strain may lead to crime.

Individuals, then, must adapt to the inconsistency between means and goals in a society that socializes everyone into wanting the same thing, but provides opportunities for only some (see Table 4.1). Conformity occurs when individuals accept the culturally defined goals and the socially legitimate means of achieving them. Merton suggests that most individuals, even those who lack easy access to the means and the goals, remain conformists. Innovation occurs when an individual accepts the goals of society, but rejects or lacks the socially legitimate means of achieving them. Innovation, the mode of adaptation most associated with criminal behaviour, explains the high rate of crime committed by uneducated and poor individuals who lack access to legitimate means of achieving the social goals of wealth and power.

strain theory

A theory that argues that when legitimate means of acquiring culturally defined goals are limited by the structure of society, the resulting strain may lead to crime or other deviance.

■ **Table 4.1** *Merton's Five Types of Adaptation*

	Culturally Defined Goals	Structurally Defined Means
Conformity	+	+
Innovation	+	−
Ritualism	−	+
Retreatism	−	−
Rebellion	−/+	−/+

Key: (+) = acceptance of/access to; (−) = rejection of/lack of access to; (−/+) = rejection of culturally defined goals and structurally defined means and replacement with new goals and means.

SOURCE: Reprinted with permission of The Free Press, a division of Simon & Schuster Inc. From *Social Theory and Social Structure* by Robert K. Merton. All rights reserved.

There are other ways to adapt to the inconsistency between means and goals. One is ritualism, in which the individual accepts a lifestyle of hard work but rejects the cultural goal of monetary rewards. The ritualist goes through the motions of getting an education and working hard, yet is not committed to the goal of accumulating wealth or power. Retreatism involves rejecting both the cultural goal of success and the socially legitimate means of achieving it. The retreatist withdraws or retreats from society and may become an alcoholic, drug addict, or vagrant. Finally, rebellion occurs when an individual rejects both culturally defined goals and means and substitutes new goals and means. For example, rebels may use social or political activism to replace the goal of personal wealth with the goal of social justice and equality.

While strain theory explains criminal behaviour as a result of blocked opportunities, **subcultural theory** argues that certain groups or subcultures in society have values and attitudes that are conducive to crime and violence. Members of these groups and subcultures, as well as other individuals who interact with them, may adopt the crime-promoting attitudes and values of the group. For example, subcultural norms and values contribute to street crime. Sociologist Elijah Anderson (1994) explains that many inner-city youths live by a survival code on the streets that emphasizes gaining the respect of others through violence—the tougher you are and the more others fear you, the more respect you have in the community.

However, if blocked opportunities and subcultural values are responsible for crime, why don't all members of the affected groups become criminals? **Control theory** may answer that question. Hirschi (1969), consistent with Durkheim's emphasis on social solidarity, suggests that a strong social bond between individuals and the social order constrains some individuals from violating social norms. Hirschi identified four elements of the social bond: attachment to significant others, commitment to conventional goals, involvement in conventional activities, and belief in the moral standards of society. Several empirical tests of Hirschi's theory support the notion that the higher the attachment, commitment, involvement, and belief, the higher the social bond and the lower the probability of criminal behaviour. For example, Laub and colleagues (1998) found that a good marriage contributes to the cessation of a criminal career. Further, Warner and Rountree (1997) report that local community ties, although varying by neighbourhood and offence, decrease the probability of crimes occurring.

Conflict Perspective

Conflict theories of crime suggest that deviance is inevitable whenever two groups have differing degrees of power; in addition, the more inequality in a society, the greater the crime rate in that society. Social inequality may lead individuals to commit crimes such as armed robbery and burglary as a means of economic survival. Other individuals, who are angry and frustrated by their low position in the socio-economic hierarchy, may express their rage and frustration through crimes such as drug use, assault, and homicide. In Argentina, for example, the soaring violent crime rate is hypothesized to be "a product of the enormous imbalance in income distribution...between the rich and the poor" (Pertossi 2000).

subcultural theory

A theory that argues that certain groups or subcultures in society have values and attitudes that are conducive to crime and violence.

control theory

A theory that argues that a strong social bond between a person and society constrains some individuals from violating norms.

According to the conflict perspective, those in power define what is criminal and what is not, and these definitions reflect the interests of the ruling class. Laws against vagrancy, for example, penalize individuals who do not contribute to the capitalist system of work and consumerism. Rather than viewing law as a mechanism that protects all members of society, conflict theorists focus on how laws are created by those in power to protect the ruling class. For example, wealthy corporations contribute money to campaigns to influence politicians to enact tax laws that serve corporate interests (Jacobs 1988), and the "criminal justice system grows increasingly punitive as labour surplus increases"—that is, as greater social control is felt to be needed (Hochstetler and Shover 1997).

Furthermore, conflict theorists argue that law enforcement is applied differentially, penalizing those without power and benefiting those with power. For example, female prostitutes are more likely to be arrested than are the men who seek their services. Unlike street criminals, corporate criminals are often punished by fines rather than by lengthy prison terms. Recent data for Canada show that in 2003–04, 51 percent of adult offenders convicted of break and enter, but just 34 percent of convicted fraud cases, resulted in a prison sentence (Thomas 2004: 12).

Societal beliefs also reflect power differentials. For example, rape myths are perpetuated by the male-dominated culture to foster the belief that women are to blame for their own victimization, thereby, in the minds of many, exonerating the offender. Such myths include the notion that when a woman says "no," she means "yes," that "good girls" don't get raped, that appearance indicates willingness, and that women secretly want to be raped. Not surprisingly, in societies where women and men have greater equality, there are fewer rapes (Sanday 1981).

Symbolic Interactionist Perspective

Two important theories of crime and violence emanate from the symbolic interactionist perspective. The first, **labelling theory**, focuses on two questions: How do crime and deviance come to be defined as such, and what are the effects of being labelled as criminal or deviant? According to Howard Becker (1963):

> Social groups create deviance by making rules whose infractions constitute deviance, and by applying those rules to particular people and labelling them as outsiders. From this point of view, deviance is not a quality of the act a person commits, but rather a consequence of the application by others of rules and sanctions to an "offender." The deviant is one to whom the label has successfully been applied; deviant behaviour is behaviour that people so label. (p. 238)

Labelling theorists make a distinction between **primary deviance**, which is deviant behaviour committed before a person is caught and labelled as an offender, and **secondary deviance**, which is deviance that results from being caught and labelled. After a person violates the law and is apprehended, that person is stigmatized as a criminal. This deviant label often dominates the social identity of the person to whom it is applied. It becomes the person's "master status"; that is, the primary basis on which the person is defined by others.

Being labelled as deviant often leads to further deviant behaviour because (1) the person who is labelled as deviant is often denied opportunities for engaging in non-deviant behaviour, and (2) the labelled person internalizes the deviant label, adopts

labelling theory
A symbolic interactionist theory that is concerned with the effects of labelling on the definition of a social problem (e.g., a social condition or group is viewed as problematic if it is labelled as such) and with the effects of labelling on the self-concept and behaviour of individuals (e.g., the label "juvenile delinquent" may contribute to the development of a self-concept and behaviour consistent with the label).

primary deviance
Deviant behaviour committed before a person is caught and labelled as an offender.

secondary deviance
Deviance that results from being caught and labelled.

a deviant self-concept, and acts accordingly. For example, the teenager who is caught selling drugs at school may be expelled and thus denied opportunities to participate in non-deviant school activities (e.g., sports, clubs) and associate with non-deviant peer groups. The labelled and stigmatized teenager may also adopt the self-concept of a "druggie" or "pusher," and continue to pursue drug-related activities and membership in the drug culture.

The assignment of meaning and definitions learned from others is also central to the second symbolic interactionist theory of crime: **differential association**. Edwin Sutherland (1939) proposed that, through interaction with others, individuals learn the values and attitudes associated with crime as well as the techniques and motivations for criminal behaviour. Individuals who are exposed to more definitions favourable to law violation than unfavourable—for example, "crime pays" versus "do the crime, you'll do the time"—are more likely to engage in criminal behaviour. Children who see their parents benefit from crime or who live in high-crime neighbourhoods where success is associated with illegal behaviour are more likely to engage in criminal behaviour.

differential association

A theory developed by Edwin Sutherland that holds that through interaction with others, individuals learn the values, attitudes, techniques, and motives for criminal behaviour.

Recent work on the influence of labelling and differential association in youth found that already-incarcerated Black youth in Canada had learned early to associate their ascribed racial category with a criminal identity (Manzo and Bailey 2005). The research concludes that incarcerated Black youth "articulate a view of themselves and of Black persons in general that is consistent with certain stereotypes" (p. 298). That is to say, stereotypes about Black persons—for example, that all young Black males are "gangstas"—have a negative impact on these youths; however, because the youths also exhibited some pride in their racial background, Manzo and Bailey believe the youths also have some "resilience" to negative stereotyping. The problem emerges, they argue quite specifically, "when the aspect [the youth] choose to embrace is inherently criminal and, quite possibly criminogenic, such as the gangsta image…these youth have adopted and…extol" (p. 299).

Feminist Theories of Crime

Just as feminist criminology, which has been around for at least three decades, enters a more central position in sociological thinking, it faces a backlash. The backlash targets not only feminist criminology, but also other progressive justice movements, such as those against racism and poverty (Chesney-Lind 2006: 6–9). A central tenet of feminist criminology is that "to truly understand delinquency, the differences between girls' and boys' experiences and 'realities' must be examined…and patriarchy must be central to the study of causes of delinquency" (Belknap and Holsinger 2006: 50). Feminist criminology focuses on how the subordinate position of women in the social structure can influence women's criminal behaviour. For example, Chesney-Lind and Shelden (1992) report that arrest rates for runaway juvenile females are higher than for males, not only because they are more likely to run away as a consequence of sexual abuse in the home, but also because police with paternalistic attitudes are more likely to arrest female runaways than male runaways. By concentrating on gender inequality in society, feminist criminology thus adds insights into understanding crime and violence often neglected by traditional theories.

Noting that criminology has traditionally ignored women's lives and uses the same models to explain women's criminal activity as men's, feminist research explores the very different "pathways" that lead girls and women to criminal activity. Feminist pathway research shows that experiences of abuse, homophobia directed at lesbian youth, and sexual abuse all figure prominently as correlates to delinquency (D'Augelli and Dark 1994; Daly 1992; Faith 1993). The Canadian Mental Health Association (2003) observes that "68% of federally incarcerated women reported childhood physical abuse; 54% reported sexual abuse. Among aboriginal women, 90% reported physical and 61% sexual abuse." In addition to all this, a survey of girls in custody found girls were far more likely to be abandoned by their parents than boys were, even in contemporary North America (Belknap and Holsinger 2006: 58).

Feminist theories of crime also note that what counts as criminal activity for women is frequently bound up with concerns to regulate women's sexuality and reproduction. Racist policy that collides with patriarchal sexism can also be a route to incarceration for delinquency. Velma Demerson's book *Incorrigible* (2004) is an autobiographical account of her year-long incarceration for the "crime" of living with a Chinese man and being pregnant by him. The *Female Refugees Act* of 1897 defined Demerson as incorrigible; the act was not repealed until 1964. Under the act, women between the ages of 16 and 35 could be jailed for anything from "promiscuity" or pregnancy outside marriage to public drunkenness. In Demerson's case, it was her father who alerted the authorities to her cohabitation with her Chinese boyfriend.

Women not only are criminalized in very gendered ways, but also are vulnerable to neglect as victims of crime. As pointed out in our discussion about sexual assault, false beliefs about women significantly reduce the likelihood that they will report a rape; if women do report a rape, these beliefs may mean that they will not receive appropriate and diligent attention and protection through the justice system.

The "common sense" approach to domestic violence as a recognizable social problem has itself presented a problematic and unjust view of abused women. At base, Stephanie Paterson's (2010) research shows, Canadian public policy tends to see domestic violence in patronizing terms, and as a problem best resolved by having abused women exit from their relationships—because it has no viable alternatives for women, it leaves them at risk for further abuse. Paterson explains, citing multiple studies carried out in the 1990s:

> "Protection" from harm requires removal from danger; it requires exit. Women's responses to violence are scrutinized as resistance is narrowly constructed only as exit. Women, then, either leave or stay, falsely dichotomized as either agents or victims and obscured from view are the myriad ways in which women attempt to resist abuse (Mahoney 1991, 1992, 1994). Mahoney's analysis (1992, 1306; cited in Bacchi 1999, 169) led her to characterize this dichotomization as the following: "Either you are on the playing field of liberal competition, in which case you require no protection, or you prove into a category as a victim who is being kept off the field." (2010, 165)

In short, if those who set policy fail to understand the complexity of women's social relationships in terms of their social locations, then we create solutions that are too narrow to be useful, and can actually add to the risk that women face.

4.4 Types of Crime

Criminologists use the terms **conventional crime** or **street crime** to refer to "those traditional illegal behaviours that most people think of as crime" (Koenig 2000). Included here would be offences such as murder, sexual assault, assault, armed robbery, break and enter, and theft. In contrast, the term *nonconventional crime* applies to such crimes as organized crime, white-collar crime, corporate crime, and computer crime.

Most Canadians would be alarmed to hear that violent crimes accounted for 20 percent of all the crimes reported to police in 2008 (Wallace 2009). Because popular news reporting does a poor job of distinguishing between typical offences and the murders it tends to focus on, it is easy to understand why people may tend to assume that the dramatic cases reported on the nightly news are representative of general crimes committed, but this is not the case. In 2008, only 611 of all reported violent crimes were homicides, a rate of only 1.8 homicide deaths per 100 000 population (ibid). Moreover, violent crimes in Canada constitute a minority of the total crimes reported (refer to Figure 4.2).

Street Crime: Violent Offences

Violent crime includes homicide, attempted murder, assault, sexual assault, other sexual offences, abduction, and robbery.

Homicide refers to the wilful killing of one human being by another individual or group of individuals. As mentioned above, although homicide is the most serious of the violent crimes, it is also the least common. When we take a longer historical view, the relative rarity of homicide remains true. Canada's homicide rate, which has been declining since the mid-1970s, remained stable at 1.8 homicides for every 100 000 people (Statistics Canada 2002); the rate declined even further through the first decade of the 2000s and rose only as high as 1.8 homicides for every 100 000 people again in 2008 (Wallace 2009). Furthermore, although homicides tend to be imagined as random crimes committed by strangers, the majority of homicides involve offenders known to their victims. Figure 4.3 shows the longitudinal, generally downward trend of crime rates in Canada.

conventional crime (street crime)

Traditional illegal behaviour that most people think of as crime, including such offences as murder, sexual assault, assault, armed robbery, break and enter, and theft.

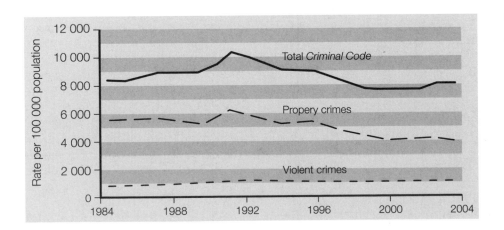

■ **Figure 4.3** *Crime Rate Resumes Its Downward Trend since Peaking in 1991*

SOURCE: Statistics Canada. "Crime Statistics, 2004" *(The Daily)*. Catalogue No. 111-001, www.statscan.ca/Daily/English/ 050721/d050721a.htm.

As these longitudinal analyses show, in 2001, the rate of minor assaults increased by 1 percent over the rate in 2000 and was "the key factor" in the rise in the total violent crime rate in Canada (Statistics Canada 2002). We must, however, remember that rising rates of violent crime may not result from more instances of such acts, but from the frequency of reporting and from the alteration of what counts as a criminal offence (Hackler 2005: 193–208). Hackler advises us to keep this invisible feature of crime analyses in mind: "What has changed is the manner in which we perceive and deal with violence. Many decades ago I carried a pocket knife to school. That is not acceptable today" (2005: 199).

Present trends continue historical data showing that about two-thirds of homicide victims are men, and comprise 90 percent of adults and 86 percent of *all* those accused of homicide (Fedorowycz 1999; Wallace 2004). For both homicide and other violent crimes, the highest risk group for offending is those 16 to 34 years old (Fedorowycz 1999). The majority of homicides committed among marginal groups in North America (e.g., First Nations peoples, African-Americans) are intraracial (Hackler 2000).

Other forms of violent crime are sexual and nonsexual assaults. Both types of assault are distinguished by several categories. In relation to nonsexual assault, these categories are common assault (level 1), assault with a weapon or causing bodily harm (level 2), and aggravated assault (level 3) in which the victim is wounded, maimed, or disfigured. In addition, the *Criminal Code* outlines other types of assaults: these include but are not limited to those committed on a peace officer, an officiating member of the clergy, the Queen, and an internationally protected person.

Sexual assaults are also classified into one of three levels distinguished by the degree of physical harm to the victim: level 1 sexual assault, level 2 sexual assault (sexual assault with a weapon, threats to a third party, or causing bodily harm), and level 3 aggravated sexual assault (in which an offender, in committing a sexual assault, wounds, maims, disfigures, or endangers the life of the victim). In relation to both types of assaults, sexual and nonsexual, the least serious are the most common. Recent data show the total rate to be dropping slightly: in 2003, the rate of sexual assaults in Canada was 74 per 100 000 population; nonetheless, the most serious form of sexual assault spiked dramatically, up 17 percent in 2003 over the previous year (Wallace 2004: 7).

In 2009, Statistics Canada released a new index to measure internal distinctions between violent and non-violent crimes reported in the Uniform Crime Reporting Survey. Figure 4.4 shows that when we create a stable baseline to help us determine whether rates of violent crime are getting generally worse, the picture is not nearly so bad as the popular media would lead us to believe. To help readers understand the index, Statistics Canada notes, "Crime severity is expressed as an index for which 2006 is the base year at 100. In 2007, the index for overall crime was 94.6, down from 119.1 in 1998. This means that crime severity fell by about 20% during the decade" (Statistics Canada 2009a). Figure 4.5 shows the offences most frequently heard in adult court; again, these offences are not the ones that popular news reports focus our attentions on. As we discussed in Chapter 3, the costs of impaired driving in terms of loss of life and injury are far from trivial, yet our collective attitude toward impaired driving is that it is a tragic mistake rather than a criminal behaviour per se, and sentencing for impaired driving remains comparatively lenient compared with other crimes that cause injury or loss of life.

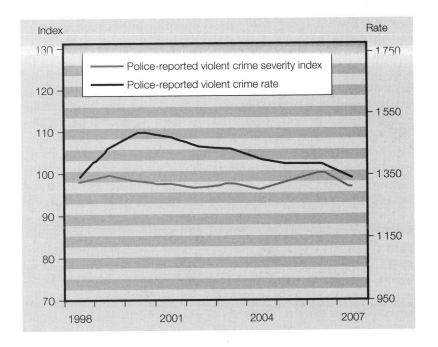

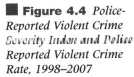 **Figure 4.4** *Police-Reported Violent Crime Severity Index and Police Reported Violent Crime Rate, 1998–2007*

SOURCE: Statistics Canada, 2009. "Police-Reported Crime Severity Index," *The Daily*, April 21, 2009. http://www.statcan.gc.ca/daily-quotidien/090421/dq090421b-eng.htm.

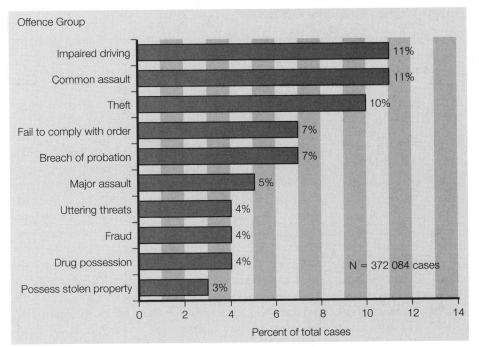

Figure 4.5 *10 Most Frequent Offences Heard in Adult Criminal Court, 10 Provinces and Territories in Canada, 2006–07*

Note: Coverage for Adult Criminal Court Survey data as of 2006/2007 is estimated at 98 percent of national adult criminal court caseload.

SOURCE: Statistics Canada, Canadian Centre for Justice Statistics. "Adult Criminal Court Statistics" *(Juristat)*, Catalogue No. 85-002-XIE, Vol. 28, No. 5, p. 2.

Adult criminal court survey data are not reported in Manitoba, Northwest Territories, and Nunavut. In Quebec, most drug offences are recorded under residual federal statutes, resulting in an undercount of drug possession and drug trafficking cases and an overcount of residual federal statute cases.

Since the 1990s, increasing attention has been directed to **acquaintance rape**—a sexual assault committed by someone the victim knows. The term does

acquaintance rape

Rape that is committed by someone known by the victim.

classic rape

A rape committed by a stranger with the use of a weapon resulting in serious bodily injury.

not appear within the *Criminal Code* of Canada, and the act so described is subsumed within the three levels of sexual assault already noted. Nevertheless, it has been reported that although sexual assaults committed by acquaintances are the most likely to occur, they are the least likely to be reported and the most difficult to prosecute. Unless the sexual assault is what Williams (1984) calls a **classic rape**—that is, the offender was a stranger who used a weapon and the attack resulted in serious bodily harm—victims hesitate to report the crime. They fear not being believed. In addition, the use of "rape drugs," which render their victims unconscious (see Chapter 3), may lower reporting levels even further. It is estimated that only 1 in 10 sexual assaults is reported each year.

Robbery is distinguished from simple theft because it involves force, the threat of force, or making a victim fearful, and is, therefore, considered a violent crime. In 2003, the robbery rate rose for the first time in over a decade, up 5 percent over the previous year, but at levels well below where they had been in 1993 (Wallace 2004: 8). Of all the 28 000 robberies reported in 2003, close to half were committed without a weapon, 14 percent with a firearm, and 38 percent with some other weapon, usually a knife (Wallace 2004: 8). Robberies are generally committed by young people; in the late 1990s, for example, the median age of female robbers in Canada was 16; of male offenders, 21 (Kong 1999).

Street Crime: Property Offences

Property crimes involve acts committed with the intent to gain property without the use or threatened use of violence. Examples of property crime include theft, breaking and entering, motor vehicle theft, fraud, and possession of stolen property. Property crimes have declined since the early 1990s, although as of 2003–04, crimes against property still accounted for 23 percent of all crimes tried in adult court (Thomas 2004: 2). Although youth tend to be perceived as increasingly inclined toward violent assaults, the pattern of crimes committed by youth in 2006–07 continued most often to involve crimes against property (38 percent) (Thomas 2008: 3). Crimes against property include break and enter, theft, vandalism, and mischief.

Reasons why youth are more likely to engage in crimes against property can be explained by taking a variety of theoretical approaches. For example, not having access to property of their own may lead those who feel the stigma of having less to seek illegitimate means of acquiring it. Poor connections to family and to their local communities may encourage youth to seek belonging by joining others to engage in theft, break and enter, and other crimes against property. Those of us who parent youth often find ourselves replacing stolen cellphones and music players and other similar devices, and learn that these kinds of thefts are quotidian occurrences in schools and at neighbourhood parties across the country. In accounting for why these items go missing so easily, youth tend to explain that these thefts are trivial because they do not require confrontation with the victim, and that the devices themselves are toys for the rich who can afford simply to replace them.

While female offenders do commit acts of theft, their thefts are often in conjunction with the far more common offence of prostitution, which accounted for 45 percent of women's offences tried in adult court in 2003–04 while women made up only 15 percent of the total cases in adult court for the same time period (Thomas 2004: 3).

Vice Crimes

A vice crime is an illegal activity that has no complaining party; it is therefore often called a **victimless crime**. Vice crimes include the use of illegal drugs, communicating for the purposes of prostitution, and illegal gambling. Compared with crimes such as murder or robbery, less consensus exists either nationally or internationally that vice crimes should be subject to the criminal law. In the Netherlands, for example, the Prostitution Information Centre in Amsterdam offers a six-day course on "prostitution as a career option," while the Australia Council of Trade Unions recently recognized women in prostitution as a labour sector (CATW 1997). In general, "prostitution is not an issue Canadians have been seeing as particularly pressing" (Bibby 1995). While one in five Canadians identified prostitution as a "very serious" social concern in 1985, a decade later it was mentioned by fewer than 1 percent.

Prostitution is not illegal in Canada; however, it is an offence to publicly communicate with another person for the purpose of buying or selling sexual services. Since 1985, the law has clearly applied to both buyers and sellers, but it has not been evenly applied. Women charged with solicitation are far more likely than their male clients to come from socially disadvantaged positions, to have little recourse to strong legal defence, and to end up incarcerated. Meanwhile, male clients who are charged for securing the services of a prostitute will have the option to pay a fine and/or attend "John school," where for a few hours or a few days they learn in very simple terms that prostitution hurts women.

Organized crime refers to criminal activity conducted by members of a hierarchically arranged structure devoted primarily to making money through illegal means. The *Criminal Code* defines a "criminal organization" as any group, association, or other body consisting of five or more persons, whether formally or informally organized, having as one of its primary activities the commission of an indictable offence for which the maximum punishment is imprisonment for five years or more. Although often discussed under victimless crimes because of its association with prostitution, drugs, and gambling, organized crime tends to use coercive techniques. For example, organized crime groups may force legitimate businesses to pay "protection money" by threatening vandalism or violence.

The traditional notion of organized crime is the Mafia—an international band of interlocked Italian families—but members of many ethnic groups engage in organized crime. Other organized crime groups in Canada include Chinese triads, the Colombian Mafia, outlaw motorcycle gangs, the Russian Mafia, and other ethnic-based drug-trafficking groups. Their activities include drug trafficking, pimping, terrorism, extortion, serious assaults, and homicide (Stamler 2000). In addition, the Organized Crime Impact Study concluded that between $5 billion and $17 billion is laundered annually in Canada. "Money laundering is any act or attempted act to conceal or disguise the identity of illegally obtained proceeds so that they appear to have originated from legitimate sources" (Solicitor General 1999).

Organized crime also occurs at the international level, such as smuggling illegal drugs and arms. In 1999, Canada's *Extradition Act* came into force, expanding Canada's ability to extradite those who are involved in organized crime. In recognition of the borderless nature of organized crime, "Canada is...

victimless crime

An illegal activity, such as prostitution or drug use, that has no complaining party; also called "vice crime."

organized crime

Criminal activity conducted by members of a hierarchically arranged structure devoted primarily to making money through illegal means.

working in the G-8, the United Nations and the Organization of American States to develop and promote international standards to combat transnational crime, and organized crime in particular" (Solicitor General 1999).

Corporate Crime

corporate crime

Both the fraudulent practices that may take place in the course of conducting business—for example, tax evasion and extortion—and also behaviour that is not illegal, but may be immoral and cause significant harm to society. Such business behaviours may be deliberate, as in the Bre-X scandal, or may arise from indifference to the well-being of others, such as not trying much to minimize environmental hazards.

Corporate crime includes both occupational crime, where individuals commit crimes in the course of their employment, and criminal business practices, where corporations violate the law in the interest of maximizing profit. For example, Bre-X, reputedly one of the world's largest stock frauds, cost investors $6 billion. In this case, the Calgary-based company's geologist had sought to make a worthless mining property seem valuable by salting core samples with gold. After his actions became known, the market for Bre-X stock collapsed and the company's shares became worthless (Hagan 2000). Laureen Snider's research on corporate crime in Canada demonstrates how conservative governments and businesses—those that favour "laissez-faire" capitalism—have worked in concert since the 1960s to chip away at legislation designed to protect the general public and employees from corporate abuses, including both financial and social crimes (see Table 4.2).

Occupational crime is motivated by individual gain. Employee thefts of merchandise, or pilferage, is one of the most common types of occupational crime. Other examples include embezzlement, forgery and counterfeiting, and insurance fraud. "Churning" is one example of corporate crime, or crime that benefits the organization. As Sherrill (2000: 304) explains, churning is

a racket in which as many as 10 million customers were sweet-talked into using the case value of their old insurance policies to pay the premiums of new, more expensive policies. They were not warned that the upgrading could be so costly that it would eat up their equity, leaving them with premiums they couldn't afford—and therefore no coverage.

Price-fixing and anti-trust violations are other examples of corporate crime. Snider's research shows that declines in corporate crime rates are not the result

■ **Table 4.2** *Types of Corporate Crime*

Crimes against Consumers/Financial Crimes	Crimes against Employees/Social Crimes	Crimes against the Public/Social Crimes	Crimes against the Employer
Deceptive advertising	Health and safety violations	Toxic waste disposal	Embezzlement
Antitrust violations	Wage and hour violations	Pollution violations	Pilferage
Dangerous products Manufacturer kickbacks	Discriminatory hiring practices Illegal labour practices	Tax fraud Security violations	Misappropriation of government funds
Physician insurance fraud	Unlawful surveillance practices	Police brutality	Counterfeit production of goods
			Business credit fraud

of improved corporate practices; instead, the drops reflect government and business cooperation to approve deregulation and decriminalization agendas previously used more effectively to limit mergers, monopolies, and anti-trust activities (Snider 2000: 173). The results of **neo-liberal** legislation, such as Canada's 1986 *Competition Act*, mean that even if some practices, such as false advertising, remain criminal offences, the ability and will to prosecute them has declined. Furthermore, consumer complaints from 1986 to 1996 show that business practices did not improve, but only that the public's avenues of complaint were curtailed; eventually, government budget cuts resulted in closing all the regional complaint bureaus (Snider 2000: 174).

Corporate violence, another form of corporate crime, refers to the production of unsafe products and the failure of corporations to provide safe working environments for their employees. Corporate violence is the result of negligence, the pursuit of profit at any cost, and intentional violations of health, safety, and environmental regulations. For example, in 1999, General Motors (GM) was ordered to pay $4.9 billion (U.S.) to six people who were severely burned when their car exploded in flames after a rear-end collision. In court, lawyers for the plaintiffs produced an internal GM study that acknowledged that the gas tanks in the Chevrolet Malibu and El Camino, Pontiac Grand Am, and Oldsmobile Cutlass were mounted in unsafe positions—27 cm from the rear bumper. However, the GM study had also pointed out that settling lawsuits that might arise from accidents in which victims were fatally burned (calculated to be $2.40 per car produced) would be cheaper than to change where the tanks were placed (calculated to be $8.59 per car produced). Here, a profit-motivated decision was made and the placement of the gas tanks remained unaltered from 1979 to 1983. Even though the amount awarded was both the biggest product-liability award and the largest personal injury verdict in U.S. history, legal experts opined that the enormous punitive award was unlikely to stand on appeal. "Even with awards in the tens of millions, it is rare for a plaintiff to actually get anything close to the jury's verdict" (White 1999). Ongoing investigation of the April 2010 BP oil-spill disaster has revealed unethical behaviours that may well have been criminal in the neglect of safety standards for deep well drilling in the sea floor. If current questions about BP's practices do reveal deliberate inattention to standards, the company may be found criminally liable not only for the considerable environmental damage to the Gulf of Mexico region but also for the deaths of the 11 rig members who died when the explosion occurred.

In Canada, some have argued that the term **corporate murder** (Swartz 1978) is an appropriate label for deaths resulting from such circumstances. Among the best-known cases are the failures of administrators within the Johns-Manville Corporation to alert workers to the serious health hazards posed by asbestos. Hagan (2000) notes that although these hazards have been recognized "since the turn of the century…people working with it were not informed, and the government bureaucracy and the medical community ignored the hazard." Similarly, he notes that the 1992 explosion at the Westray coal mine in Pictou County, Nova Scotia, "was not an accident, but…the result of conscious decisions by those responsible for the safety of the miners." Twenty-six miners were killed. An official inquiry into the disaster resulted in a report tellingly entitled *The Westray Story: A Predictable Path to Disaster*. In it, Justice Richard concludes that the managers at Westray had "displayed a certain

neo-liberal

The revival of classical liberalism that has occurred since the 1980s. Those who espouse this model for economic and political organization and policy advocate individual rights over group rights, reduction of state powers, and an increased liberalization of free-market capitalism. According to this view, when the market is free to set its own limits, then individual merit will be properly rewarded and everyone will benefit from increased growth in capital and industrial production.

corporate violence

The production of unsafe products and the failure of corporations to provide a safe working environment for their employees.

corporate murder

The label for deaths as a result of unsafe consumer products.

disdain for safety and appeared to regard safety-conscious workers as the wimps in the organization" (in Hagan 2000).

Computer Crime

computer crime

Any violation of the law in which a computer is the target or means of criminal activity.

Computer crime refers to any violation of the law in which a computer is the target or the means of criminal activity. *Hacking*, or unauthorized computer intrusion, is one type of computer crime. In just one month, hackers successfully attacked the computer systems of Walt Disney World, Yahoo, eBay, and Amazon.com through "denial of service" invasions (Kong and Swartz 2000). *Identity theft*—the use of someone else's identification (e.g., social insurance number, birth date) to obtain credit—is another.

Conklin (1998) has identified other examples of computer crime:

- Two individuals were charged with theft of 80 000 cellular phone numbers. Using a device purchased from a catalogue, the thieves picked up radio waves from passing cars, determined private cellular codes, reprogrammed computer chips with the stolen codes, and then, by inserting the new chips into their own cellular phones, charged calls to the original owners.
- A programmer made $300 a week by programming a computer to round off each employee's paycheque down to the nearest 10¢ and then to deposit the extra few pennies in the offender's account.
- An oil company illegally tapped into another oil company's computer to get information that allowed the offending company to underbid the other company for leasing rights.

4.5 Demographic Patterns of Crime

Although virtually everyone violates a law at some time, persons with certain demographic characteristics are disproportionately represented in the crime statistics. Victims, for example, are disproportionately young, lower-class, minority males from urban areas. Similarly, the probability of being an offender varies by gender, age, race, social class, and region.

Gender and Crime

Both official statistics and self-report data indicate that males commit more crimes than females (Figure 4.6). Males are involved in more acts of crime than are females in both adult and youth age groups. The current data in Figure 4.6 repeat a long-established pattern of greater likelihood that males will commit crime. But why are males more likely? One explanation is that society views female lawbreaking as a more serious transgression of gender norms and thus places more constraints on female behaviour: "women may need a higher level of provocation before turning to crime—especially serious crime. Females who choose criminality must traverse a greater moral and psychological distance than males making the same choice" (Steffensmeier and Allan 1995: 88). Further, data suggest that males and females tend to commit different types of crimes. Men, partly because of more aggressive socialization experiences, are more likely than women are to commit violent crimes. The most recent data

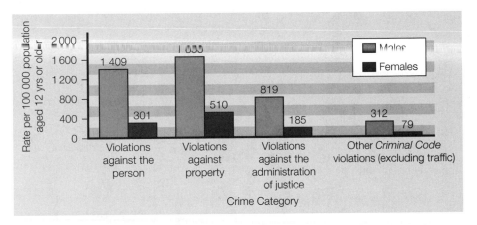

■ **Figure 4.6** *Females Apprehended by Police for Crimes Against the Person at a Rate Five Times Lower Than Males, Selected Police Services, 2005*

Notes: Excludes incidents where the sex and/or age of the accused was unknown. Data are not nationally representative. Based on data from 122 police services representing approximately 71% of the population of Canada in 2005. Rate per 100 000 population for the geographic areas policed by the UCR2 respondents, based on populations provided by Demography Division, Statistics Canada. Populations as of July 1st: preliminary postcensal estimates for 2005.

SOURCE: Statistics Canada, Canadian Centre for Justice Statistics. "Female Offenders in Canada" *(Juristat)*, Catalogue No. 85-002-XIE, Vol. 28, No. 1, Chart 1, p. 3

from Statistics Canada continue to show that women are far less likely to commit crimes than males are, and that crimes committed by women tend to be of a different type, with almost half of their crimes being those against property rather than against persons (Kong and AuCoin 2008, 3). Moreover, when women do commit crimes against persons, it tends to be common assault, rather than the more serious offences of manslaughter, murder, or sexual assault (ibid).

Young Offenders

Popular news media that focus for several weeks on one instance of serious crime may encourage the view that youth are increasingly dangerous and volatile. Consider the coverage of the Boxing Day shootings on Toronto's Yonge Street in 2005 or the murder of an Alberta family in 2006, a crime for which their daughter, who was 13 at the time of the murders, was found guilty. However, the long-term data are far more subtle and do not support the idea that youth are worse or more violent now than ever before.

The popular perception, though, is a powerful political motivator for those who want to prove their commitment to Canadians by getting "tough on crime" (Hogeveen 2005). The political utility of punishment over prevention is clear in the statement of Vic Toews, who, as justice minister, endorsed harsher sentencing policies for all offenders, saying, "When it comes to crime, it is the new government's firm commitment to finally respond to the concerns of police and, most importantly, of ordinary Canadians" (Deveau 2006).

According to police-reported data, the period from age 16 to 17 is the peak age of offending for both violent and property offences (Statistics Canada 2008) and accounts for 55.8 percent of all crimes committed by youth. Incarceration rates for youth remain high, with just over one-fifth to just over one-quarter of all guilty findings resulting in custodial sentences for youth whose cases were resolved in the years between 2002 and 2005 (Thomas 2008: 15). The *Youth Criminal Justice Act* (YCJA) has started to correct the admitted overuse of incarceration that Brian Hogeveen's research shows to have been the herald of the *Young Offenders Act* (YOA) throughout the 1990s, when youth crime rates dropped while incarceration rates increased by 35 percent (2005: 9). Since the YCJA replaced the YOA, incarceration rates have dropped considerably, down from a high of 27 percent in 2002–03 to 17 percent in 2006–07 (Statistics

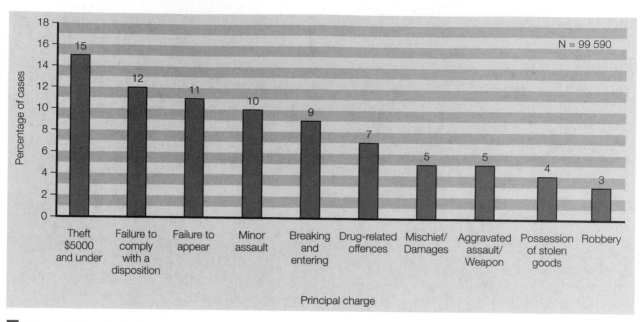

Figure 4.7 *Principal Charge in Youth Courts*

SOURCE: Adapted from Statistics Canada, Canadian Centre for Justice Statistics, "Youth Court Statistics, 2000–2001" *(Juristat)*, Catalogue 85-002, Vol. 22, No. 3, p. 4.

Canada 2008). The chart in Figure 4.7 shows that youth criminal activity serious enough to appear before the courts has been declining in all categories. The implications of this drop are twofold: first, that youth criminal activity is on the decline in general, and second, that the YOA was unnecessarily aggressive in targeting youth both at the charge level and at the trial level.

Age and Crime

People who have not reached middle age commit most crime. Youth are the most crime prone, perhaps because this group has adult desires for goods and opportunities still out of their grasp. Why is criminal activity more prevalent among individuals in their teens and early 20s? Younger individuals are more likely to be unemployed or employed in low-wage jobs. As strain theorists argue, they have less access to legitimate means for acquiring material goods.

Various commentators have linked Canada's decreasing crime over the last decade to the country's aging population structure. Specifically, while those between the ages of 15 and 24 have a high risk of offending, this age group has decreased in size by 6 percent since 1991 (Logan 2001: 3). Unlike the 1960s, when the baby boom generation (those born between 1947 and 1966) came into their years of highest risk, the 1990s saw the products of the baby bust years (1967 to 1979). Simply put, "[t]here has been a smaller pool of people who are at the greatest risk with respect to criminal behaviour" (John Howard Society 1999: 2).

Race, Social Class, and Crime

Race is a factor in who is arrested. The overrepresentation of Aboriginal peoples in the Canadian criminal justice system has been commented on for decades by various commissions and task forces. Although Aboriginal peoples represent 2 percent of the adult population in Canada, for the past two decades they have consistently accounted for 15 to 18 percent of admissions to both provincial/territorial and federal sentenced custody (Lonmo 2001: 8). These numbers hold true in the most recent (2006) data from Correctional Services Canada, which also notes that the situation is especially bad for Aboriginal women, who represent 30 percent of those incarcerated in federal prisons.

The overrepresentation of Aboriginal persons in Canada's prisons is particularly marked in the Prairie provinces. When it comes to punishment for youth crime, those of Aboriginal background are punished far more frequently. Citing data from Statistics Canada and Correctional Services, Bryan Hogeveen (2005: 82) notes, "In the prairie provinces of Manitoba and Saskatchewan, three quarters...of youth sentenced to custody were identified as Aboriginal, while less than 20 percent of Manitoba's youth population is identified as Native."

Possible explanations for the overrepresentation of Aboriginal people in Canada's prisons include

- differential treatment by the criminal justice system—being discriminated against by the police, the courts, etc.;
- differential commission of crime and differential offence patterns—committing crimes that are more detectable—more serious or more visible—than those committed by non-Aboriginal people;
- the socio-structural deprivation of Canada's Aboriginal peoples;
- the decline of informal mechanisms of social control within Aboriginal communities; and
- systemic racism (Hartnagel 2000).

Aboriginal offenders also tend to be younger on average than others, and hence less likely to be able to access their full legal rights, and to acquire good legal representation for their defence.

Although some investigators have claimed that certain races are more or less law abiding than others, such research typically fails to define "race," assumes racial purity as a given, treats crime as a unitary phenomenon, and simply presents correlational data on race and crime (Roberts and Gabor 1990). Demonstrating that a correlation exists does not, of course, prove causation.

There are a number of reasons why it would be inaccurate to conclude that race and crime are causally related. First, official statistics reflect the behaviours and policies of criminal justice actors. The high arrest, conviction, and incarceration rates of Aboriginal people may be due to individual and institutional bias not only against them, but also against the lower classes in general. Second, race and social class are closely related in that Aboriginal peoples are overrepresented in the lower classes. Since lower class members lack legitimate means to acquire material goods, they may turn to instrumental, or economically motivated, crimes. Further, subcultural theorists argue that, while the "haves" typically earn social respect through their socio-economic status, educational achievement, and occupational roles, the "have nots" tend to live in communities where respect is based on physical strength and violence. Thus, what seems to be a relationship between race and crime may be, in part, a consequence of the relationship between these variables and social class.

In recent years, changes made by Parliament to the sentencing provisions of the Canadian *Criminal Code* have attempted to address the overrepresentation of Aboriginal peoples in Canada's inmate population. For example, section 718.2 specifies that "all available sanctions other than imprisonment that are reasonable in the circumstances should be considered for all offenders, *with particular attention to the circumstances of aboriginal offenders*" [emphasis added]. While being Aboriginal does not automatically result in a lesser sentence, the Supreme Court of Canada has urged judges, when sentencing an Aboriginal offender, to recognize the "broad systemic and background factors affecting Aboriginal people" (Lonmo 2001: 8). The Correctional Service of Canada also tries to assist Aboriginal people who are incarcerated by including culturally sensitive substance abuse programs, Native liaison services, and Elders' services. The Okimaw Ohci Healing Lodge for federally sentenced Aboriginal women in Maple Creek, Saskatchewan, was developed with and for the First Nations community. Sixty percent of the staff working at this facility, which places a strong emphasis on Aboriginal culture and spirituality, are of Aboriginal descent (Solicitor General 2002).

Region and Crime

In Canada, the distribution of crime varies by region. Historically, crime rates in Canada have generally increased from east to west, with Nova Scotia and Alberta providing exceptions to this general trend—Nova Scotia's crime rate has generally been higher, and Alberta's crime rate lower, than those of their neighbouring provinces (Logan 2001).

Although folk wisdom might suggest that there is more crime in larger cities than in small cities or towns, this belief would be wrong. Greater numbers of crimes occur in larger than in smaller cities, but this pattern must be set against the greater number of people living in such areas. For example, in 2001, the rate of violent crime in Toronto, Canada's largest metropolitan area, was 876 per 100 000—substantially below that of Regina (1614), Saskatoon (1663), Vancouver (1053), and Winnipeg (1309). The rate of property crime in Toronto (2932) was also lower than the property crime rate in these cities; in Regina, it was 9661 per 100 000 population; in Saskatoon, 6616; in Vancouver, 7347; and in Winnipeg, 5967. Indeed, in 2001, Toronto, along with Chicoutimi-Jonquière, Québec City, and Trois-Rivières, had the lowest crime rate among Canada's 25 census metropolitan areas (Statistics Canada 2002).

The newly developed crime severity index measures allow us to see an even more nuanced picture of crime in Canada. The index measures not simply instances of crime, but the prevalence of violent and non-violent crimes, crimes against the person, and crimes against property. Figure 4.8 shows that for 2007 the information we have just discussed holds generally true, even when we are considering regions in terms of the severity as well as the prevalence of crime. With the exception of cities in the western provinces, it is smaller cities that have higher severity indices, with Winnipeg, Regina, and Saskatoon having the worst results in the country.

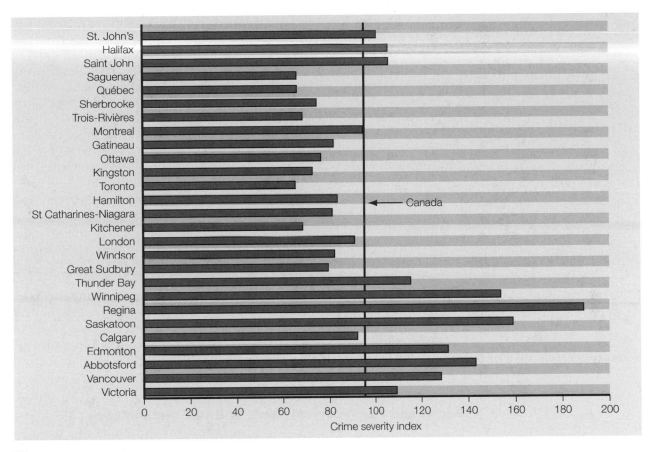

Figure 4.8 *Measuring Crime in Canada*

SOURCE: Statistics Canada, 2009b. "Measuring Crime in Canada: Introducing the Crime Severity Index and Improvements to the Uniform Crime Reporting Survey." Canadian Centre for Justice Statistics. Catalogue No. 85-004-x.

4.6 Costs of Crime and Violence

Crime does not result only or primarily in physical injury and loss of life or property; other, less tangible costs are incurred. Although the immediate victims of criminal acts bear the costs of crime most acutely, a far broader constituency may experience the economic, social, and psychological costs of crime.

Economic Costs of Crime and Violence

Conklin (1998: 71–72) suggests that the financial costs of crime can be classified into at least six categories.

- First are direct losses from crime, such as the destruction of buildings through arson, of private property through vandalism, and of the environment by polluters.
- Second are costs associated with the transferring of property. Bank robbers, car thieves, and embezzlers have all taken property from its rightful owner at

huge expense to the victim and to society. The Organized Crime Impact Study reported that such economic crimes as securities fraud and telemarketing scams cost Canadians at least $5 billion each year (Solicitor General 1999).

- Third are the major costs associated with criminal violence. These include the loss of productivity of injured workers and the medical expenses of victims.
- Fourth are the costs associated with the production and sale of illegal goods and services—in other words, illegal expenditures. When money is spent on drugs, gambling, and prostitution, it diverts funds away from the legitimate economy and enterprises, and lowers property values in high-crime neighbourhoods.
- Fifth are the costs of prevention and protection, the millions of dollars spent on house alarms, security devices, weapons for protection, bars for windows, timers for lights, automobile security systems, and the like.
- Finally, there is the cost of the criminal justice system. According to the Business Network on Crime Prevention (2001), "governments spend almost $12 billion a year on Canada's police services, courts and corrections that make up our criminal justice system." They emphasize that this figure is conservative. It "represents only a small portion of the total costs of crime." According to the 2005 data from Canada's Department of Justice, annual costs of policing, courts, and corrections total closer to $10 billion and the total annual cost of crime is approximately $46 billion; however, such estimates "do not include the cost of white collar crime, tax evasion or stock market manipulation" (Department of Justice 2005).

Social and Psychological Costs of Crime and Violence

Crime and violence entail social and psychological, as well as economic, costs. According to the 2000 International Crime Victimization Survey, more than 8 out of 10 Canadians (83 percent) report feeling very or fairly safe when walking alone in their area after dark. However, Canadians were more pessimistic than people in Finland, Sweden, the United States, or Scotland when asked if they thought they would likely experience a break-in. Only 66 percent of Canadians believed that a break-in was unlikely—compared with 84 percent in Finland, 79 percent in Sweden, 78 percent in the United States, and 71 percent in Scotland. It is perhaps not surprising that 80 percent of Canadians reported the use of at least one type of security measure (e.g., a burglar alarm, special door locks, special window or door grilles, or a high fence) (Besserer 2002).

In various ways, it is evident that the fear of crime and violence affects community life:

> If frightened citizens remain locked in their homes instead of enjoying public spaces, there is a loss of public and community life, as well as a loss of "social capital"—the family and neighbourhood channels that transmit positive social values from one generation to the next. (National Research Council 1994: 5–6)

This is particularly true of women and the elderly who restrict their activities, living "limited lives" as a consequence of fear (Madriz 2000).

White-collar crimes also take a social and psychological toll at both the individual and the societal levels. Moore and Mills (1990) state that the effects of white-collar crime include "(a) diminished faith in a free economy and in business leaders, (b) loss of confidence in political institutions, processes and leaders, and (c) erosion of public morality" (p. 414). Crime also causes personal pain and suffering, the destruction of families, lowered self-esteem, shortened life expectancy, and disease.

4.7 Strategies for Action: Responding to Crime and Violence

In addition to economic policies designed to reduce unemployment and poverty, many social policies and programs have been initiated to alleviate the problem of crime and violence. These policies and programs are directed toward children at risk of being offenders, community crime prevention, criminal justice policies, and legislative action.

Youth Programs

Early intervention programs acknowledge that it is better to prevent crime than to "cure" it once it has occurred. Preschool enrichment programs, such as the Perry Preschool Project, have been successful in reducing rates of aggression in young children. After random assignment of children to either a control or experimental group, experimental group members received academically oriented interventions for one to two years, frequent home visits, and weekly parent–teacher conferences. When control and experimental groups were compared, the experimental group had better grades, higher rates of high-school graduation, lower rates of unemployment, and fewer arrests (Murray et al. 1997).

Recognizing the link between youthful offenders and adult criminality, many anticrime programs are directed toward at-risk youths. These prevention strategies include the federal government's Crime Prevention Initiative, with its focus on proactive programs for high-risk families. Other examples are youth programs such as Boys and Girls Clubs and the national Aboriginal Head Start program. These programs are designed to keep young people "off the streets," provide a safe and supportive environment, and offer activities that promote skill development and self-esteem. According to Gest and Friedman (1994), housing projects with such programs report 13 percent fewer juvenile crimes and a 25 percent decrease in the use of crack.

Community Programs

Programs such as Neighbourhood Watch, Block Parents, Crime Stoppers, and Operation Identification involve local residents in crime-prevention strategies. The objective of such programs is to reduce crime by heightening community efforts to prevent it. Neighbourhood Watch programs, developed with the help of local police departments or services, offer advice to residents on how to best protect their homes and belongings. They encourage neighbourhood members to watch out for and report any suspicious activities they see to the police.

Law Enforcement Agencies

Police policies and practices can also affect crime rates. Seagrave (1997) noted that the mission statement of every Canadian police force in the 1990s contained evidence of formal commitment to the concept of **community policing**.

community policing
When police, community, and local governance structures, including politicians, and religious and educational institutions, work together to prevent crime at local levels. This type of policing is not intended to address large-scale concerns, but to help citizens prevent their neighbourhoods from becoming targets for crimes. Efforts range from Neighbourhood Watch programs to education about the causes of crime. Through informal networks, there can be information sharing between police and community groups.

Community-oriented policing involves collaborative efforts among the police, the citizens of a community, and local leaders. As part of community policing efforts, officers speak to citizens' groups, consult with social agencies, and enlist the aid of corporate and political leaders in the fight against neighbourhood crime (COPS 1998; Lehrur 1999). Officers using community-policing techniques often employ "practical approaches" to crime intervention. Such solutions may include what Felson (1998) calls "situational crime prevention." Felson argues that simply minimizing the opportunity for its occurrence could prevent much crime. For example, cars could be outfitted with unbreakable glass, flush-sill lock buttons, an audible reminder to remove keys, and a high-security lock for steering columns (p. 168).

In addition, programs aimed at crime victims now exist in almost all Canadian police departments. Victim assistance programs are designed to provide crime victims with details on the progress of their case, facilitate the return of property to rightful owners, and act as referral agencies to other support groups in the local community. Often heavily dependent on volunteers, such services may signal the development of a partnership between the police and a local community agency or institution. In Ottawa, the Salvation Army works in collaboration with the Ottawa Police Department to supply victim services. In Montreal, the University of Montreal, in cooperation with the Montreal Urban Community Police, operates the Integrated Victim Assistance program (Seagrave 1997).

Criminal Justice Policy

deterrence

The use of harm or the threat of harm to prevent unwanted behaviours.

The criminal justice system presumes that **deterrence**, or the use of harm or the threat of harm, is an effective way to prevent unwanted behaviours. It assumes that people rationally choose to commit crime, weighing the rewards and consequences of their actions. Thus, the recent emphasis on "get-tough" measures holds that maximizing punishment will increase deterrence and cause crime rates to decrease. Research indicates otherwise. The effectiveness of deterrence is a function not only of the severity of the punishment, but also of the certainty and swiftness of the punishment. Further, "get-tough" policies create other criminal justice problems, including overcrowded prisons, and, consequently, the need for plea-bargaining and early-release programs.

Capital Punishment With capital punishment, the state takes the life of a person as punishment for a crime. Although capital punishment has not been used in Canada since 1962 and was formally abolished in this country in 1976, the federal government retains the right to bring it back. Since the 1970s, Gallup polls have consistently noted that the majority of Canadians believe that the courts are too lenient with offenders: in the fall of 1943, Gallup reported that 80 percent of Canadians were in favour of capital punishment. In 1995, approximately 85 percent of a national random sample of Canadians maintained that the courts did not deal harshly enough with criminals, particularly young offenders, and approximately 82 percent believed that the death penalty should be exercised in some instances (Bibby 1995). Although support for the use of capital punishment has declined in recent years, data from the 2000 Project Canada survey indicate that 74 percent of Canadian adults and 59 percent of Canadian teenagers agree that "the death penalty should sometimes be used to punish criminals" (Bibby 2001: 244).

Those for and against capital punishment take different views on how to convey societal disapproval of murder. Proponents of capital punishment argue that executions of convicted murderers convey public disapproval and intolerance for such heinous crimes. Those against capital punishment believe that no one, including the state, has the right to take another person's life and that putting convicted murderers behind bars for life is a **social death** that conveys the necessary societal disapproval.

Proponents of capital punishment also argue that it deters individuals from committing murder. Critics of capital punishment hold that since most homicides are situational and unplanned, offenders do not consider the consequences of their actions before they commit the offences. Critics also point out that the United States has a much higher murder rate than Canada or Western European nations that do not practise capital punishment—and that death sentences are racially discriminatory. For example, a study on federal capital cases in the United States found that Blacks were less likely than whites to have their sentences reduced through plea-bargaining (Worden 2000).

Capital punishment advocates and opponents use financial arguments, too. Advocates suggest that executing a convicted murderer relieves taxpayers of the costs involved in housing, feeding, guarding, and providing medical care for inmates. Opponents argue that the principles that decide life-and-death issues should not be determined by financial considerations. In addition, due to the lengthy and costly appeal process for capital punishment cases, taking care of convicted murderers for life may actually be less costly than sentencing them to death (Garey 1985).

Advocates and opponents of capital punishment also deal with the issue of protecting society versus the individual. Those who favour capital punishment argue that it prevents convicted individuals from committing other crimes, including the murder of another inmate or prison official. Opponents contend, however, that capital punishment may result in innocent people being sentenced to death. For example, between 1973 and 1999, 76 death-row inmates in the United States were released when new evidence supported their innocence (*Economist* 2000). Further, a report by the (U.S.) Justice Project, entitled "A Broken System," found "serious, reversible error in nearly seven out of ten of the thousands of capital sentences" that were reviewed over the 23-year study period (Liebman et al. 2000). In Russia, it is reported that almost one in three (30 percent) of capital punishment cases may have had judicial errors that resulted in a wrongful execution (MacIntyre 1999). Even though 35 countries abolished the death penalty between 1985 and 1998, as of October 1, 2000, there were 3703 prisoners on death row in the United States (Ash 2001: 69; MacIntyre 1999).

The highly publicized cases of David Milgaard, Guy Paul Morin, and Donald Marshall should remind us that wrongful convictions do occur. David Milgaard served 23 years in various Canadian prisons, including the Oak Ridge institution for dangerous mentally ill offenders in Penetanguishene, Ontario, for the 1970 sex slaying of a Saskatoon nursing aide. He was finally exonerated in 1997 when DNA tests showed that he was not the killer (see this chapter's *Focus on Technology*). Donald Marshall, wrongfully convicted for the 1971 murder of a teenager who was stabbed to death in a Sydney, Nova Scotia park, spent 11 years in prison. Guy Paul Morin was wrongfully convicted in the sex slaying of a young Queensville, Ontario girl, faced two first-degree murder trials, and

social death

The removal of a person from larger society through lifetime imprisonment. By stripping the person of a meaningful position within society, lifetime imprisonment removes from that person an identity and status in the larger world. The prisoner is ejected from the relationship circles necessary for the maintenance of a personal identity.

DNA Evidence

Increasingly, law enforcement officers in Canada, the United States, and Europe are using what is called DNA fingerprinting in the identification of criminal suspects. DNA stands for deoxyribonucleic acid, which is found in the nucleus of every cell and contains an individual's complete and unique genetic makeup. Developed in the mid-1980s, DNA fingerprinting is a general term used to describe the process of analyzing and comparing DNA from different sources to the DNA of a suspect. Evidence that can be used includes evidence found at a crime scene, such as blood, semen, hair, saliva, fibres, and skin tissue.

In the fall of 1998, the FBI (Federal Bureau of Investigation) initiated the Combined DNA Index System. This database contains the DNA fingerprints of 250 000 convicted felons and more than 4600 DNA samples from unsolved crime scenes. Despite the database being in operation less than two years, the "FBI claims that 200 outstanding cases have already been solved" (Kluger 1999: 1). In 1995, Parliament enacted amendments to the Criminal Code of Canada to create the DNA warrant system. A DNA warrant could be issued during criminal investigations for a list of designated offences and DNA samples taken and stored. In that year alone, federal laboratories in Canada handled DNA evidence in the prosecution of 722 murders and 1289 assaults (Statistics Canada 1998: 510). DNA analysis is helpful not just to prosecutors—12 Canadian prisoners were released from custody on the strength of DNA evidence. DNA was used to vindicate Guy Paul Morin and David Milgaard, long after they were wrongfully convicted of murders.

Despite these success stories, there is tremendous concern about the use of DNA evidence and, specifically, questions about how donors would be selected and what methods of data collection would be used.

Libertarians fear possible violations of civil rights, particularly after a court decision by a French judge who ruled that all men in a village would be DNA tested to locate the killer of a 13-year-old girl. In England, police officials legally take samples of blood or skin tissue from every criminal suspect (Gleick 1997: 3). In two murder cases, Canadian police officers conducted mass DNA screenings and asked hundreds of potential suspects to consent to testing. In the first, the 1998 stabbing of a female employee at an adult-video store in Sudbury, Ontario, Sudbury Regional Police officers took DNA from more than 400 possible suspects. In the second, the Port Alberni (British Columbia) RCMP examined DNA from 350 suspects in relation to the 1996 sexual assault and murder of an 11-year-old girl.

While asking possible suspects to consent to testing is legal, some have expressed fear that it may go too far. For example, Toronto lawyer James Lockyer rhetorically asks

spent 17 months in custody. In these cases, and a handful of others, the individuals have fought for their vindication on charges of murder and received, as partial redress, financial settlements from the federal and provincial governments. In the largest settlement to date for a wrongful conviction, Milgaard received $9.25 million in compensation for his legal fees (which totalled $1.5 million), for pain and suffering, for lost income, and for out-of-pocket expenses; his mother received $750 000 for the legal and personal costs she had incurred during her long struggle to prove that her son was innocent (Bourrie 1999). There is, of course, no way of compensating those who have been wrongfully convicted and received, as a penalty, capital punishment.

Rehabilitation versus Incapacitation An important debate focuses on the primary purpose of the criminal justice system: Is it to rehabilitate offenders or to incapacitate them through incarceration? Both **rehabilitation** and **incapacitation** are concerned with recidivism rates, or the extent to which criminals commit another crime. Advocates of rehabilitation believe that changing the criminal can reduce recidivism, whereas proponents of incapacitation think recidivism can best be reduced by placing the offender in prison so that he or she is unable to commit further crimes.

rehabilitation
A criminal justice philosophy that views the primary purpose of the criminal justice system as changing the criminal offender through such programs as education and job training, individual and group therapy, substance abuse counselling, and behaviour modification.

what will happen to those who refuse to provide samples and remarks, "That's where harassment might begin, if police don't take no for an answer." Toronto lawyer and forensic DNA authority Ricardo Federico queries, "Is this what we want, having the science police knocking on everybody's door?" (Maclean's 1999: 13). Concerns have also been expressed in relation to what methods of data collection will be used and potential abuses of analysis results. For example, DNA evidence might be used to simply imply guilt, as in the case of DNA information that indicates "proclivities for aggression" (McCullagh 1999: 1). These concerns explain why, until relatively recently, England had the only nationwide DNA databank in the world (Gleick 1997; Goldberg 1998). Canada's national DNA data bank was established in 1998.

In addition to concern over the potential for DNA fingerprinting to violate the human rights of the broad public, the practice faces a number of challenges at the trial level when it may be brought in as court evidence. Because DNA testing is done mostly by private corporations, Arthur Daemmrich has been able to show that juries are inclined to perceive DNA evidence as unreliable and suspect (1998). The various challenges against DNA evidence include the gathering methods for samples, skills and experience levels of those handling samples, laboratory protocols, means of measuring the degree to which two samples "match," and the statistical arguments about the likelihood that samples matched (Daemmrich 1998: 767). The successful challenging of any or all of these features of DNA sampling has influenced trial outcomes, such as the acquittal of O. J. Simpson.

Nevertheless, the future of DNA fingerprinting is likely to be bright. It's less expensive than ever before, predicted to be as low as $10 a test within a few years, compared to earlier costs of $200 to $300. As technology has become increasingly sophisticated, the time it takes to conduct the analysis has decreased from weeks to days, and portable DNA analysis units are in the making (NIJ 2000a). Further, even if DNA fingerprinting fails to survive the legal scrutiny it's likely to come under, it remains a valuable identification technique used in biology, archaeology, medical diagnosis, paleontology, and forensics.

SOURCES: Daemmrich, Arthur. 1998. "The Evidence Does Not Speak for Itself." *Social Studies of Science* 28(5/6): 741–72; Gleick, Elizabeth. 1997. "The Killer Left a Trace." *Time* (September 1): 150; Goldberg, Carey. 1998. "DNA Databanks Giving Police a Powerful Weapon, and Critics." *New York Times*, February 19: 1; Kluger, Jeffrey. 1999. "DNA Detectives." *Time*, Canadian edition (January 11): 46–47; *Maclean's*. 1999. "Rounding Up Suspects for Their DNA." (December 13): 13; McCullagh, Declan. 1999. "The Debate of DNA Evidence." *Wired News* (July 12): 1. http://www.wirednews.com/news; National Institute of Justice. 2000. "National Commission on the Future of DNA Evidence." Washington, D.C.: U.S. Department of Justice. http://www.ojp.usdoj.gov/hij/dna; Statistics Canada. 1998. *Canada Yearbook 2000*. Ottawa: Ministry of Industry.

Societal fear of crime has led to a public emphasis on incapacitation, a demand for tougher mandatory sentences, and a reduction in the use of probation and parole (DiIulio 1999; Human Rights Watch 2000). Canada is, indeed, locking people up. The International Center for Prison Studies' survey data on Canada's prison population in three-year increments from 1991 to 2001 show that our incarceration rate hit a high of 131 per 100 000 population in 1994–95, and a low of 116 per 100 000 in 2001. Although we imprison fewer members of our population than the United States (724 per 100 000 population) or Russia (564) (see Figure 4.9), our incarceration rate already exceeds those of many other Western democracies. In addition, the *Youth Criminal Justice Act* of 2002–03, with its "get-tough" approach to youth, promises not only to follow a standard of high incarceration rates, but also to increase them, locking up those youth who are from the poorest and most poorly served communities in the country (Hogeveen 2005). As we discussed earlier in the chapter, our rates for youth incarceration are only marginally lower under the YCJA than under the previous YOA in Canada.

Public opinion on how to deal with youth crime is especially divided on the point of punishment. Opinion is influenced in large part by media attention and

incapacitation

A criminal justice philosophy that views the primary purpose of the criminal justice system as preventing criminal offenders from committing further crimes against the public by putting them in prison.

■ **Figure 4.9** *Nations with Highest Rates of Incarceration, 2004*

SOURCE: "Ten Leading Nations in Incarceration Rates," which appeared in *New Incarceration Figures: Growth in Population Continues* (The Sentencing Project). Copyright 2005. Used with permission.

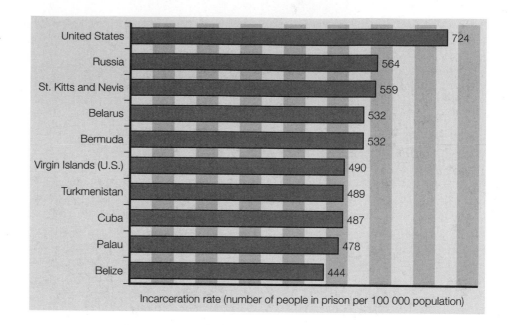

Incarceration rate (number of people in prison per 100 000 population)

political opportunism that makes violent crime appear common rather than atypical. As a result, legislative acts must be relayed to a vacillating public with care. The message to the public has to be that no life will be ruined for the sake of punishing petty offences; however, the jailing of youth through the 1990s shows a judicial reality very different from that message to the public. While rates of incarceration for young offenders were slowly creeping toward American numbers, rates of deviance were slowly declining (Hogeveen 2005: 81). Even in the population most likely to commit crime and commonly perceived to be the most dangerous, criminal activity has been decreasing.

According to the Solicitor General of Canada (2002), approximately $2 billion is spent on Canada's adult federal and provincial correctional systems each year. The annual cost of incarceration for federal prisoners varies by gender; male prisoners cost an average of $79 555 a year and female prisoners cost an average of $169 399, for a combined annual average of $81 206 (Correctional Services Canada 2005). The CSC report on costs of incarceration explains the reason for the nearly doubled annual average for incarcerating women: there are far fewer incarcerated women, yet because they still require the same material and personnel resources for their housing and rehabilitation as men do, the costs of their incarceration are higher per capita. Unfortunately, the Office of the Solicitor General was abolished in 2005 and replaced by the Office for Public Safety, a ministerial portfolio at the federal level that has not, thus far, produced a report on the costs of incarceration, choosing instead to focus on risk assessment. We do know, however, that as of 2007 Correctional Services was still holding 13 171 inmates in prisons across the country, with an annual budget of $1.8 billion (Public Safety Canada 2010: 1).

While incapacitation is clearly enhanced by longer prison sentences, rehabilitation may not be. Rehabilitation assumes that criminal behaviour is caused by sociological, psychological, biological, or a combination of these forces rather than being solely a product of free will. If such forces can be identified, the necessary change can be instituted. Rehabilitation programs include education and job training, individual and group therapy, substance abuse counselling, and behaviour modification. While the evaluation of rehabilitation programs is difficult and results are mixed, incapacitation must of necessity be a temporary measure. Unless all criminals are sentenced to life, at some point approximately 98 percent will be returned to society.

Alternatives to Incarceration In addition to incarceration, there are other strategies that are being pursued. Offenders may be ordered by judges to provide restitution and financially compensate their victims for property loss and personal injury. Electronic monitoring requires a convicted offender to wear an electronic bracelet that is generally placed around an ankle or wrist. "If they stray too far from a receiver unit attached to a telephone, when they are supposed to be home, an alarm sounds at the monitoring centre" (Solicitor General 2002). In cases where an offender does not pose a danger to the community and where the usual jail term would be less than two years, a conditional sentence may be used, requiring the offender to seek treatment, for example. Other community-based alternatives to incarceration include a community service order requiring an offender to work a certain number of hours within the community.

Mediation services, which work in cooperation with the Crown Attorney's office, bring victimizers and their victims together in the belief that both will benefit. For example, committing a crime may require that an offender discount the consequences of his or her act on the victim or blame the victim (e.g., "she's got insurance to cover the loss," "he was asking for it"); it is thought that face-to-face meetings will encourage a sense of personal culpability and compassion for the victim. Similarly, if the *hindsight effect* encourages victims to overestimate the extent to which they could have avoided victimization (Janoff-Bulman et al. 1985), confronting one's victimizer may result in a lessened amount of self-blame. Moreover, insofar as those who have experienced criminal victimization are likely to demonstrate a heightened fear of crime, it may prove personally empowering to see their victimizers as simply other human beings.

Victim and offender mediation represents one of many programs that may flow from a framework of **restorative justice**. Restorative justice "is an approach to justice that focuses on dealing with the harmful effects of crime by engaging victims, offenders and the community in a process of reparation and healing" (Solicitor General 2002). Many Aboriginal communities have traditionally emphasized this model of justice in which

restorative justice
A philosophy primarily concerned with reconciling conflict between the offender, the community, and the victim.

- the focus is on problem solving and restoration of harmony;
- restitution and reconciliation are used as a means of restoration;
- the community acts as a facilitator in the restorative process;
- the offender is impressed with the impact of his action on the total community;
- the holistic context of an offence is taken into account including moral, social, economic, political, and religious and cosmic considerations;
- stigma of offences is removable through conformity;
- repentance and forgiveness are important factors;
- offenders take an active role in the restorative process (Bryant 1999: 21).

Unlike the traditional criminal justice process, restorative justice emphasizes individual and social healing, forgiveness, communication, and joint problem solving rather than punishment. Although the behaviour of the offender is condemned, the value of the offender as an individual is affirmed.

Legislative Action The federal government has taken various steps to combat crime. In relation to organized crime, for example, these steps include the 1994 Anti-Smuggling Initiative, which targets smuggling and distribution networks at the border, in Canada's ports, and across the country; and the 1996 establishment of the *Witness Protection Program Act*, which established a formal, national program to protect those who assist police investigations. Legislative amendments to the *Criminal Code* in 1997 included anti-gang measures that made participation in a criminal organization an indictable offence, punishable by up to 14 years in prison. In 1998, amendments made to the *Corrections and Conditional Release Act* sought to ensure that those convicted of offences related to organized crime were ineligible for accelerated parole review. In 2002, legislative changes included the introduction of three new offences that targeted those involved with criminal organizations; broader powers for law enforcement officers to seize the profits of crime and property used in a crime; and increased protection of law enforcement officers from criminal liability when they commit certain acts that would otherwise be considered illegal when investigating and infiltrating criminal organizations (Department of Justice 2002c).

Legislative efforts have also sought to curtail child sexual exploitation. For example, in 1997, amendments to the *Criminal Code* provided for the prosecution of persons who engage in child sex tourism in other countries and facilitated the apprehension and prosecution of persons who seek out the services of child victims of sexual exploitation in Canada. Bill C-15A, which came into effect on July 23, 2002, makes it illegal to use the internet to communicate with a child for the purpose of committing a sexual offence against that child, as well as to transmit, make available, export, or access child pornography. It also allows the courts to order the deletion of child pornography posted on Canadian computer systems, makes child pornography and the new internet luring offence "triggering offences" for making an application to designate a person as a dangerous offender, allows for the seizure of materials or equipment used to commit a related offence, and simplifies the process of prosecuting Canadians who sexually exploit children in other countries (Department of Justice 2002a).

In 2001, in response to the September 11, 2001, terrorist attacks in New York City and Washington, D.C., Canada's highly controversial *Anti-Terrorism Act* (Bill C-36) passed through the Senate with a vote of 45 to 21 and became law. The *Anti-Terrorism Act*, like its counterpart in the United Kingdom, defines terrorist activity as encompassing acts of violence or destruction that are intended to influence government or intimidate the public. Both definitions require proof that an offence was committed out of religious, ideological, or political motivation. Among its provisions, Canada's *Anti-Terrorism Act* allows police to exercise "preventative arrest" powers and to detain, without judicial warrant, suspected terrorists for up to 48 hours. It also extends the valid period of a wiretap and lowers the standard required to obtain a wiretap. Unlike the United States, Canada does not seek to try suspected foreign terrorists in secret military tribunals. Unlike Britain, where the law provides for a 10-year maximum penalty for simply belonging to a terrorist organization, Canada has not banned membership.

Supporters of the act have argued that, after the September 11 attacks, Canadian security had to be tightened in order to comply with Resolution 1373 of the United Nations Security Council. The resolution "called on all member countries to adopt the necessary measures to prevent any one country from

Racial Profiling after the Terrorist Attacks of 9/11

The following article, written by journalist Stephen Thorne, reminds us of the dangers of stereotyping certain groups within society as "criminals" in general and, in particular, of the human costs of racial profiling. The original, unabridged article can be found on the World Wide Web at http://www.1121_rights-cp.html.

He's lived in the same Toronto house for 32 years, and the thing about Canada that Ahmed Valiallah always loved most was that the people were friendly and helpful. But all that has changed since September 28, when the former schoolteacher was told insurance on his retirement investment, a building in downtown Toronto, was cancelled. The reason? Nabil Al-Marabh, a Kuwaiti with suspected links to the Sept. 11 hijackers, worked in his uncle's copy store in the building Valiallah owns.

It's the latest in a string of cases some say are changing the face of Canada as a fair and tolerant society following the hijackings and subsequent attacks by Islamic extremists. Incidents of ethnic or religious profiling are "quite prevalent and very under-reported," says Riad Saloojee, executive director of the Council on American-Islamic Relations Canada. Some contend that in the rush to fight terrorism, Canadians are losing the very values they're trying to defend. The council has documented 115 cases of threats, harassment, and profiling since the attacks on New York and Washington. Among them:

The former head of the Canadian-Arab Foundation and once-esteemed member of the immigration review board is jailed for six days after she's caught up in a scam perpetrated by two men who came to her for immigration advice; her bail was set at $10,000.

A nuclear engineer is questioned by RCMP and CCIS on everything from his religion to his friendships, then fired from his job at Chalk River. He's rehired after it apparently turns out to be a case of mistaken identity.

A Muslim is asked at the border if he has a rocket launcher in his van.

There have been numerous incidents where Muslims, and Sikhs as well, have inexplicably been ordered off airplanes. It happened to Saloojee. Nobody told him why, except that it was "security-related." "There is this climate where Muslims have been collectively blamed for the actions of those terrorists," says Saloojee. "There is an increased wariness of people who look Arab or look Muslim. I think that's something that's come to light in a lot of these profiling incidents where terrorism is linked to ethnicity or religion."

Valiallah, whose grandfather immigrated to South Africa from India in the 1880s, thought he'd left that kind of persecution behind with South African apartheid in 1969. He has filed suit against the insurance company in Toronto small-claims court claiming that Al-Marabh's guilt or innocence should have no bearing on his property's risk assessment. The insurance company was "high-handed, wanton, abusive, and offensive," the suit says. "Such conduct was based on racial and religious profiling and stereotyping."

Profiling. Stereotyping. Racial discrimination. The words have come up time and time again since Sept. 11. Valiallah's counsel, Harry Kopyto, who successfully represented fired nuclear engineer Mohamed Attiah, says the incidents are driven by fear and mistrust. "As a general rule, persons who are in positions of power, including the police, are jumping the gun," says Kopyto. "They're assuming the worst based on perceived qualities. They see somebody's Arabic or Islamic, the assumption is almost that he must be guilty of something."...

But the RCMP and the Canadian Security Intelligence Service claim they've conducted business as usual. "The RCMP does not profile by race or religion," said Cpl. Benoit Desjardins, an Ottawa-based spokesman. "We do investigate, as in any other case apart from September 11, based on information or complaints we've received. We haven't changed policy about our investigations, except that we've concentrated efforts on that major file."

The Mounties' September 11 tip line had received 8500 calls by the first week of December. Some have been less justified than others, but that didn't necessarily stop the police. In one case, a neighbour's suspicions were aroused when visitors started showing up at the Muslim house next door. Police questioned the owners for several hours. It turned out there had been a death in the family. Retired general Lewis MacKenzie, new security adviser to the Ontario government, says authorities would be nuts not to exercise some degree of profiling based on country of origin—but not on religion or ethnicity.

"People coming from states that sponsor terrorism have to be checked over a little more carefully when they arrive in the country," says MacKenzie. "It seems like common sense to me. It's not ethnic profiling." A bunch of "blond-haired, blue-eyed, six-foot-two Swedes" coming from Kabul, Afghanistan, would warrant just as much attention as anyone else on the plane, he said. MacKenzie says he doesn't believe there are many incidents like the Attiah and Valiallah cases because, if there were, Canadians would be hearing about them. "This type of offensive behaviour wouldn't be tolerated and it wouldn't be kept secret."...

For Valiallah, a proud Canadian, it has been a bitter disappointment. "From my experience, whenever I had difficulties or other people had difficulties and they went to different institutions, there was always a helping hand," he said. "And here, [the insurance company] was pushing me away. I wasn't a Canadian any more."

SOURCE: Thorne, Stephen. 2001. "Victims of Racial Profiling Say Canadians' Attitudes Changing for the Worse." December 21. The Canadian Press.

becoming a haven for terrorists" (Chwialkowska 2001). Critics, however, maintain that the act's definition of terrorism is too broad, that the act contains measures that are open for abuse, and that there are only limited provisions for oversight. Moreover, some have expressed concern that **racial profiling**—the practice of targeting suspects based upon their race—will become a prominent feature of investigations conducted under this act (see this chapter's *The Human Side* feature).

racial profiling
The law enforcement practice of targeting suspects based upon race.

Canada's *Youth Criminal Justice Act* (YCJA), which replaces the *Young Offenders Act* (1984), also represents an attempt to respond to the social problem of crime. The core principles of the YCJA are that

- protection of society is the paramount objective of the youth justice system, which is best achieved through prevention, meaningful consequences for youth crime, and rehabilitation;
- young people should be treated separately from adults under criminal law and in a separate youth justice system that emphasizes fair and proportionate accountability, keeping in mind the dependency and level of development and maturity of youth;
- measures to address youth crime must hold the offender accountable; address the offending behaviour of the youth; reinforce respect for social values; encourage repair of the harm done to victims and the community; respect gender, ethnic, cultural, and linguistic differences; involve the family, community, and other agencies; and be responsive to the circumstances of youth with special requirements; and
- parents and victims have a constructive role to play in the youth justice system, and should be kept informed and encouraged to participate (Department of Justice 2002b).

Understanding **Crime and Violence**

What can we conclude from the information presented in this chapter? Research on crime and violence supports the contentions of both functionalists and conflict theorists. The inequality in society, along with the emphasis on material well-being and corporate profit, produces societal strains and individual frustrations. Poverty, unemployment, urban decay, and substandard schools—the symptoms of social inequality—lead, in turn, to the development of criminal subcultures and definitions favourable to law violation. Further, the continued weakening of social bonds between members of society and society as a whole, the labelling of some acts and actors as "deviant," and the differential treatment of minority groups by the criminal justice system encourage criminal behaviour.

While crime and violence constitute major social problems in society, they are also symptoms of other social problems, such as poverty and economic inequality, racial discrimination, drug addiction, an overburdened educational system, and troubled families. The criminal justice system still struggles to find effective and just measures to deal with crime and criminal offenders. Many citizens and politicians have embraced the idea that society should "get tough" on crime. Get-tough measures include building more prisons and imposing lengthier mandatory prison sentences on criminal offenders. Advocates of harsher prison sentences argue that such measures make society safer. They keep criminals off the streets and deter potential criminals from committing crime. Yet, for example, an analysis of over 200 studies comparing institutionalized and non-institutionalized serious young offenders found that community-based treatment worked better than incarceration in lowering recidivism rates (Lipsey and Wilson 1998). Prison sentences may not only be ineffective in preventing crime, they may even promote it: they create an environment in which prisoners learn criminal behaviour, values, and attitudes from one another.

Rather than getting tough on crime after the fact, some advocate getting serious about prevention. Re-emphasizing the values of honesty, responsibility, and civic virtue is a basic line of prevention with which most agree. The recent move toward restorative justice, a philosophy focused on repairing the victim–offender–community relationship, is in direct response to concerns about an adversarial criminal justice system—one that encourages offenders to deny, justify, or otherwise avoid taking responsibility for their actions. As noted earlier, restorative justice holds that the justice system should be a "healing process rather than a distributor of retribution and revenge" (Siegel 2000: 278). Key components of restorative justice include restitution to the victim, remedy of the harm to the community, and mediation. At a meeting of the United Nations' Congress in Crime Prevention and Treatment of Offenders, a summary resolution, called the *Vienna Declaration*, was approved. The resolution calls for the worldwide use of restorative justice intervention.

Critical Thinking

1. Crime statistics are sensitive to demographic changes. Suggest how the aging of the Canadian population may affect Canadian crime rates as we move into the second decade of the twenty-first century.

2. One of the criticisms of crime theories is that they do not explain all crime, all of the time. Identify the theories of crime that are most useful in explaining categories of crime, for example white-collar crimes, violent crimes, and sex crimes. Explain your choices.

3. The use of technology in crime-related matters is likely to increase dramatically over the next several decades. DNA testing, the use of heat sensors, blood-detecting chemicals, and computer surveillance are just some of the ways that science will help fight crime. As with all technological innovations, however, there is the question "Who benefits?" Do these new technologies have gender, race, and class implications?

"Is It True?" Quiz: Answers

1 = false; 2 = false; 3 = false; 4 = true; 5 = true

Family Problems

5

Is It True?

1. Since the 1970s, most Canadian women have been delaying their first childbirth until their late 20s and early 30s.

2. Inadequate public health resources for dealing with a long-term health-care problem or a physical limitation contribute significantly to problems of elder abuse.

3. Stable divorce rates indicate that Canadians place weak value on marriage.

4. In Canada, a husband who forces his wife to have sex is committing a criminal offence.

Read more here: 1 = p. 146, 2 = p. 161, 3 = p. 147, 4 = p. 156

Answers can be found on p. 181.

© David De Lossy/Getty Images

Though family is generally sentimentalized and spoken about in terms that praise family above all other institutions, a sociological approach to family as a concept, structure, and institution reveals for our consideration those problems that we all know are there but tend to push aside, or to see through the lense of a "common sense" attitude: violence and abuse in intimate and family relationships, problems of divorce, and problems associated with nonmarital and teenage child-bearing. Other problems facing families are discussed in other chapters in this text. For example, families are affected by health problems (Chapter 2), substance abuse (Chapter 3), problems of youth and the elderly (Chapter 6), and problems with employment and poverty (Chapters 10 and 11). Before discussing these problems, we look briefly at the history and diversity of families worldwide, and we provide an overview of the changing patterns and structures of households and families in Canada.

5.1 The Global Context: Families of the World

Family is a central aspect of every society throughout the world, but family forms are diverse. Though we commonly think of family as something that issues forth from the bringing together of separate kinship groups through marriage, family is, in fact, a varying, historically and culturally specific organization of social relationships. It is not always or necessarily the nuclear and reproductively oriented unit so frequently conjured through the term "family." Sometimes marriage is, indeed, required as the formal sanctioning of bonds that will shape property ownership rights, inheritance and lineage laws, and—more recently—will include definitions of responsibilities of family members in the event of marital breakdown. In Canada, we also have formal legal boundaries to recognize the rights and responsibilities of persons to each other in common-law relationships. But families do not have to be defined by marriage. Because same-sex couples are still denied marriage rights throughout most of the United States, and yet clearly take on the usual relationship aspects of families (such as joint property ownership, cohabitation, business cooperation, and—increasingly often—child rearing), this text finds a compelling case to treat these and other unmarried couples, such as those in common-law relationships, as *de facto* families regardless of their legal status.

In Canada, only couples in **heterosexual monogamy** had marriage rights until 2003, when some municipalities began to grant marriage licences to same-sex couples. After years of debate that began long before the first licences were granted, on July 19, 2005 the federal Liberal government passed Bill C-38 through a Senate vote of 47 to 21 in favour (EGALE 2005) to grant equal marriage rights to same-sex couples. In 2001, the Netherlands became the first country in the world to legalize same-sex marriage. Cambodia (Kampuchea) has also extended full and equal marriage rights to homosexuals. Eight other countries, specifically Denmark (along with its dependency, Greenland), Hungary, Norway, Sweden, France, Iceland, Spain, and Germany, have enacted *registered partnership* legislation. To varying degrees, it allows same-sex couples to receive some of the legal benefits of marriage. In contrast, the United States has shown significant opposition to same-sex marriages, with 32 states passing laws forbidding it (Reidmann et al. 2003).

heterosexual monogamy
Exclusive pair-bonding between two opposite-sex persons.

polygamy

A form of marriage in which one person may have two or more spouses.

polygyny

The concurrent marriage of one man to two or more women.

polyandry

The concurrent marriage of one woman to two or more men.

At the global level, a pair-bond base for reproductive families is not the only model for family structures. **Polygamy**—a form of marriage in which one person may have two or more spouses—is practised in some societies. The most common form of polygamy is **polygyny**—the concurrent marriage of one man with two or more women. The second form of polygamy is **polyandry**—the concurrent marriage of one woman with two or more men. Polyandry is rare, but does occur in some groups, including Tibetans and various African groups. Polgyny is relatively common in sub-Saharan Africa, but is not unheard of in more developed regions, including in locations where all forms of polygamy are illegal. For example, while it has been illegal in Canada since 1878, polygyny is practised by a fundamentalist Mormon group in Bountiful, British Columbia; the group has affiliates in Colorado and Arizona in the United States. Another historical polygynous group is the "Perfectionist" Christian sect known as the "Oneida Community." In the mid-nineteenth century, the group set up a polygynous commune in Oneida, New York, as well as the Oneida company. Though the sect dispersed at the end of the nineteenth century, the Oneida company continues to make the flatware that many typical families use to set their tables on a daily basis across North America (Edgerton 1992; Kephart 1963).

The roles and norms that structure families are highly variable across societies. For example, in Asian countries, some parents arrange marriages, selecting mates for their children. Another traditional Asian practice is for the eldest son and his wife to move in with the son's parents, where the wife takes care of her husband's parents. In some societies, it is normative for married couples to view each other as equal partners in the marriage, whereas in other societies, social values dictate that wives be subservient to husbands. The role of children also varies across societies. Some societies expect children as young as five years old to work full time to help support the family. Social acceptance of unmarried couples having children also varies widely throughout the world. Acceptance of this lifestyle ranges from 90 percent or more in parts of Western Europe to fewer than 15 percent in Singapore and India (Global Study of Family Values 1998). Finally, the ease of obtaining a divorce varies by country. Ireland did not allow divorce under any conditions until 1995, when voters took part in a public referendum, for the first time narrowly approving divorce (Thompson and Wyatt 1999). After the referendum, Irish legislation approved the *Family Law (Divorce) Act* in 1996 to permit divorces and remarriages in Ireland. In 2000, the Egyptian Parliament voted to allow women to file for divorce on grounds of incompatibility (Eltahawy 2000). Prior to this law, Egyptian women could file for divorce only in cases of proven physical or psychological abuse. By contrast, a man could get a divorce by simply saying "I divorce you" three times or by filing a paper with the marriage registrar—he did not even have to notify his wife. Under the new law, a woman who wants a divorce must return her husband's dowry and relinquish all financial claims, including alimony.

It is clear, then, that families take shape within specific social and cultural contexts. Neither their strengths nor their weaknesses exist in a vacuum. As we discuss the putative family problems addressed in this chapter—violence and abuse, divorce, and nonmarital and teenage child-bearing—we refer to social and cultural forces that contribute to these problematic events. Next, we look at changing patterns and structures of Canadian families and households.

Changing Patterns and Structures in Canadian Families and Households

The evolving Canadian census alerts us to some of the changes that have occurred in relation to thinking about the family. For example, census data show us that since the first inclusion of common-law arrangements in 1981, those including children have risen from 34 percent of all common-law families to 46 percent (Turcotte 2003: 11). The 2001 Canadian Census was first to include questions recognizing same-sex partners (see Figure 5.1). Question 6 from that census also explicitly recognizes children being raised in same-sex households. To get an accurate sense of how Canada's people live, Statistics Canada alters its questions about families. To meet the changing ways that people define family for themselves, it changes its operational definition of a **census family**. On the 2006 census, a family was defined as a set of people who live together as "married, common-law, or lone-parent—generally as either a spouse, partner, parent, or child" (Milan et al. 2007), and accounted for almost 85 percent of the total population in Canada. By the time the 2006

census family

A now-married couple (with or without never-married sons and/or daughters of one or other spouses), a couple living common-law (again, with or without never-married sons and/or daughters of either or both parents), or a lone parent of any marital status, with at least one never-married son or daughter living in the same dwelling.

■ **Figure 5.1** *Questions 5 and 6 from the 2001 Canadian Census*

SOURCE: Adapted from Statistics Canada. "2001 Canadian Census Questionnaire," Questions 5 and 6, http://www.12.statscan.ca/english/census01/home/questionnaire.cfm.

---

5. Is this person living with a common-law partner? Common law refers to two people of the opposite sex or of the same sex who live together as a couple but who are not legally married to each other.

☐ Yes

☐ No

6. Relationship to Person 1

For each person usually living here, describe his/her relationship to Person 1.

Mark "X" or specify one response only.

Stepchildren, adopted children and children of a common-law partner should be considered sons and daughters.

If none of the choices apply, use the "Other" box to indicate this person's relationship to Person 1. Examples of "Other" relationships to Person 1:

☐ grandparent

☐ cousin

☐ niece or nephew

☐ lodger's husband or wife

☐ room-mate's daughter or son

☐ employee

☐ husband or wife of Person 1

☐ common-law partner (opposite-sex) of Person 1

☐ common-law partner (same-sex) of Person 1

☐ son or daughter of Person 1

☐ son-in-law or daughter-in-law of Person 1

☐ grandchild of Person 1

☐ father or mother of Person 1

☐ father-in-law or mother-in-law of Person 1

☐ brother or sister of Person 1

☐ brother-in-law or sister-in-law of Person 1

☐ lodger or boarder

☐ room-mate

☐ other—Specify

_____

census was carried out, the survey included a question to enumerate the number of married same-sex couples in Canada. Of the 45 300 same-sex couples enumerated in the census, about 7500 (16.5 percent) were married and 37 900 (83.5 percent) were in common-law relationships (ibid). Moreover, the 2006 count of same-sex couples had increased five times as quickly as the number of opposite-sex couples enumerated in the 2001 to 2006 census data (ibid). If the appearance of the so-called "traditional" family is changing, then, it is simultaneously clear that the majority of same-sex couples identifying themselves in the census are adopting more-or-less typical arrangements that include marriage, joint cohabitation, shared property ownership, and raising children. Raising children is remarkable, however, in that it is the one area that has declined since the previous census was carried out, with only 41.4 percent of couples with children. The decline does not necessarily mean that people no longer want to raise children, but that they are delaying child-bearing to significantly later ages:

> A growing proportion of young children aged 4 and under had a mother in her forties as more and more women delayed childbearing. In 2001, 7.8% of children aged 4 and under had a mother who was between the ages of 40 and 49. By 2006, this proportion had increased to 9.4%. (Milan et al. 2007)

Growth in lone-parent families has changed the face of Canadian families and, in 2001, lone-parent families accounted for 15.7 percent of families, the vast majority of which were headed by women (Arnold 2002). In the 1950s and 1960s, the death of a spouse was the major cause of lone parenthood in Canada (with over 60 percent of all lone-parent widows or widowers); now, divorce, separation, and births outside of marriage have become the primary factors involved in the creation of lone-parent families. Although proportional increases in non-traditional families may be quite marked, same-sex couples accounted for fewer than 1 percent of all Canadian couples and 3 percent of common-law couples in 2001.

Divorce, remarriage, and stepfamilies have also become more common in the last several decades. Projections about marital dissolution must take into account that prior to the federal divorce law of 1968 obtaining a divorce was far more difficult. Spikes in the divorce rate following the 1968 act and the 1985 amendments on improving ease of access to divorce are, then, not surprising; they cannot serve as reliable predictors of the future of marriage breakdown in Canada. Indeed, Statistics Canada observes that the annual rate for both marriage and divorce has been declining since the 1990s (Statistics Canada 2004).

For those who do divorce, remarriage remains the most common result (about 75 percent of divorced men and 65 percent of divorced women remarry); however, remarriage is on the decline. There is an increasing tendency to cohabit, particularly among younger divorced persons and among divorced men. Estimates suggest that divorced women in their 30s and 40s are now twice as likely to live common-law as to remarry (Le Bourdais et al. 2001).

Some view the trend toward diversification of family forms as a sign that marriage and family are in serious crisis. Although traditionalists may view cohabitation (both heterosexual and homosexual), divorce, and single parenthood as threats to the institution of marriage, it is unlikely that marriage will disappear. Most Canadians who cohabit eventually marry, although not necessarily to the person with whom they cohabited. Most Canadians still wish to marry, with average ages for marriage being 28 for women and 30 for men. Few adult Canadians expect to remain unmarried; only half of those who delayed marriage past age 30 expect to remain unmarried (Crompton 2005: 2).

Stable divorce rates may suggest a weakening of marriage, but we can also interpret divorce as a sign that marriage retains a very high value, such that a less-than-satisfactory marriage is unacceptable. The rate of out-of-wedlock childbirth and single parenting is also not necessarily indicative of a decline in the value of marriage; it may mean that finding a partner is more difficult. Because women who have children outside of marriage are more likely to live in poverty, they are "less attractive partners to the type of man they would consider marrying" (Crompton 2005: 3). The persistent value placed on family is also evident in a national survey of Canadian teens. The survey found that almost 9 out of 10 (88 percent) expected to get married and also to stay with the same partner for life (87 percent of males and 89 percent of females) (Bibby 2001: 136).

5.2 Sociological Theories of the Family

Beyond the three major sociological theories of the family—structural-functionalism, the conflict perspective, and symbolic interactionism—in this section we see what light feminist and queer perspectives shed on various family problems.

Structural-Functionalist Perspective

The structural-functionalist perspective views the family as a social institution that performs important functions for society, including reproducing new members, regulating sexual activity and procreation, socializing the young, and providing physical and emotional care for family members. According to the structural-functionalist perspective, traditional gender roles contribute to family functioning. Thus, heterosexual two-parent families in which women perform the "expressive" role of managing household tasks and providing emotional care and nurturing to family members and men perform the "instrumental" role of earning income and making major family decisions are viewed as "normal" or "functional." Other family forms, such as single-parent families and same-sex unions, are viewed as abnormal or dysfunctional.

According to the structural-functionalist perspective, increases in divorce and lone-parent families signal a breakdown of the family. This breakdown is the result of rapid social change and social disorganization. The functionalist perspective views the breakdown of the family as one of the primary social problems in the world today—a problem of such magnitude that it leads to such secondary social problems as crime, poverty, and substance abuse.

Functionalist explanations of family problems examine how changes in other social institutions contribute to these problems. For example, a structural-functionalist view of divorce examines how changes in the economy (more dual-earner marriages) and in the legal system (such as the adoption of no-fault divorce) contribute to rising divorce rates. Changes in the economic institution, specifically falling wages among unskilled and semi-skilled men, also contribute to both intimate partner abuse and the rise in female-headed, lone-parent households (Edin 2000).

Conflict Perspective

Conflict theory focuses on how social class and power influence marriages and families. Within families, the unequal distribution of power among women and men may contribute to domestic violence. The traditional male domination of families—a system known as **patriarchy**—includes the attitude that married women are essentially the property of husbands. When wives violate or challenge the male head-of-household's authority, the male may react by "disciplining" his wife or by using anger and violence to reassert his position of power in the family. The unequal distribution of wealth between men and women, with men traditionally earning more money than women, contributes to inequities in power and fosters economic dependence of wives on husbands.

Conflict theorists also emphasize that social programs and policies that affect families are largely shaped by powerful and wealthy segments of society. The interests of corporations and businesses are often in conflict with the needs of families. Hewlett and West (1998) note that corporate interests undermine family life "by exerting enormous downward pressure on wage levels for young, child-raising adults" (p. 32). Government, influenced by corporate interests through lobbying and political financial contributions, enacts policies and laws that serve the interests of for-profit corporations, rather than families.

Symbolic Interactionist Perspective

Symbolic interactionism emphasizes that human behaviour is largely dependent on the meanings and definitions that emerge from small-group interaction. Divorce, for example, was once highly stigmatized and informally sanctioned through the criticism and rejection of divorced friends and relatives. As societal definitions of divorce became less negative, however, the divorce rate increased. The social meanings of single parenthood, cohabitation, and delayed child-bearing and marriage have changed in similar ways. As the definitions of each of these family variations became less negative, the behaviours became more common.

Symbolic interactionists also point to the effects of labelling on one's self-concept and the way the self-fulfilling prophecy can affect family members' behaviour toward one another. The **self-fulfilling prophecy** implies that we behave according to the expectations of others. For example, when a non-custodial divorced parent (usually a father) is awarded visitation rights, he may view himself as a visitor in his children's lives. The meaning attached to the visitor status can be an obstacle to the father's involvement, as the label minimizes the importance of the non-custodial parent's role and results in conflict and emotional turmoil for fathers (Pasley and Minton 2001). Fathers' rights advocates suggest replacing the term *visitation* with such terms as *parenting plan* or *time-sharing arrangement*. These latter terms do not minimize either parent's role.

The symbolic interactionist perspective is useful in understanding the dynamics of domestic violence and abuse. For example, some abusers and their victims learn to define intimate partner violence as an expression of love (Lloyd 2000). **Emotional abuse** often involves using negative labels (e.g., "stupid," "whore," "bad") to define a partner or family member. Such labels negatively affect the self-concepts of abuse victims, often convincing them that they deserve the abuse.

patriarchy

A tradition in which families and societies are male dominated.

self-fulfilling prophecy

A concept referring to the tendency for people to act in a manner consistent with the expectations of others.

emotional abuse

Often involves using negative labels (e.g., "stupid," "whore," "bad") to define a partner or family member. Such labels negatively affect the self-concept of abuse victims, often convincing them that they deserve the abuse.

Feminist Perspectives

Feminist theories of family and kinship structures critique the central presupposition that family is natural and biological. Feminist thinkers find that the three foundational theories all continue to privilege a patriarchal organization of power. Feminist perspectives help us to rethink common assumptions about the basis of family to show that traditional views are based on a male model of economy and politics that "does not work for most women, who typically have childcare and other domestic responsibilities to juggle as well [as paid labour outside the home]" (Luxton 1996: 51).

Regardless of the particular differences in feminist approaches to the idea of family, all focus on sexism against women and problems with the subordination and consequent vulnerability of women and children in the family and marriage. Such problems include economic dependency, the structure of a work world at odds with child-rearing and domestic responsibilities, and sexual assault and other forms of violence within families.

Feminist work on families may also try to reimagine what families can be, what they can accomplish, and how our roles in families might change for the better. For example, just because fathers have traditionally been cast as the powerful sources of (potentially violent) discipline does not mean that they must always fulfill that role; instead, families might become sites for the exercise of gender equality wherein "the raising of children [can] emphasize the qualities needed in building a culture of peace" (Gearing et al. 2001: 57). According to this view, it is not only women and children who are vulnerable in traditional family structures, but also that men lack opportunities to seek change, to pursue peaceful ways of living, and to achieve equality for themselves, their children, and their world (Gearing et al. 2001: 69). This chapter's *Social Problems Research Up Close* feature takes a feminist perspective on the demands of breastfeeding discourse and the challenges that mothers face.

Queer Theory Perspectives

Large segments of the gay and lesbian population have sought marriage rights for same-sex couples, with the group EGALE providing the legal and political muscle to help secure those rights in Canada. Queer theory perspectives, however, are not equal or identical to the political movement in favour of same-sex marriage rights. Rather, the theory seeks to understand what one gains, what one loses, and what one compromises on in the search for the kind of legitimacy that the state confers when it grants people the right to marry. For example, while securing same-sex marriage rights may benefit some gay and lesbian couples with inclusion in state-sanctioned kinship arrangements, those whose personal and kinship arrangements depart more obviously from the nuclear family model will be even further marginalized and isolated (Butler 2004: 104–8).

Regardless of its position on same-sex marriage rights, queer theory and activist groups have emphasized for nearly two decades that gay, lesbian, bisexual, and transgendered (GLBT) persons are all "family." Right-wing condemnations of gay and lesbian couples as examples of moral corruption and threats to traditional families has prompted this. GLBT people are brothers, sisters, aunts, uncles, sons and daughters, and more and more frequently, parents as well. Discrimination may prevent these families from being able to gain access to or provide care in emergency situations to their partners and to the

Moral Constructions of Motherhood in Breastfeeding Discourse

Health Canada and the public health agencies in the provinces have focused their interest in maternal and child well-being with heavy promotion of breastfeeding. Breastfeeding is an advantageous strategy for public services because it is a private rather than a public initiative, and therefore a cost-effective way of downloading responsibility for population health onto individual mothers. Breastfeeding does have many advantages, but Canadian sociologist Glenda Wall (2001) demonstrates the very real problems that confront mothers in a political atmosphere that includes the "re-moralization" of pregnancy, fixation on maternal–infant bonding practices, and child-centred parenting. At the centre of the conflict that Wall's research assesses is the claim that breastfeeding is natural, and, therefore, morally preferable to bottle feeding. She argues that the need to spend enormous effort convincing people that breastfeeding is, indeed, natural and not inappropriately sexual belies that position.

Sample and Methods

The study focused on 20 widely distributed public health pamphlets from Health Canada and the province of Alberta, made available in maternity wards, doctors' offices, through public advertising, or by request to Health Canada.

The public health material was analyzed for the following features: how issues were framed, implicit assumptions, and the resulting understandings of motherhood, breastfeeding, and sexuality.

Findings and Conclusions

Wall determined that there were six specific sites of articulation in which morality, nature, and motherhood were structured in ways that overlooked serious structural and symbolic problems facing mothers on a day-to-day basis, with potentially harmful outcomes for mothers and their children.

1. *Morality and nature.* The most common feature Wall found was the moral overlap of natural mothering and claims to the naturalness of breastfeeding in which the presumed naturalness of an activity is made to be the guarantee of its morality:

   > ...nature in the 1980s and 1990s, has become more commonly understood as a sacred entity, one that is pure, unsullied, ancient, wise, and deserving of respect, and that this has occurred along with increasing popular reverence for nature and natural experiences.
   > The overlap between the breastfeeding discourse and cultural constructions of nature is evident, for example, in the characterization of breast milk as nature's perfect food. (p. 596)

   Wall's analysis of the complete series of publications revealed, however, that the moral purity of the milk "is only as pure as the mother who produces it" (p. 597). It is not simply that nature guarantees purity, but that mothers must adhere to the ideal standards of natural motherhood.

2. *Breastfeeding as the ultimate convenience. For whom?* Wall's research found repeated insistences that breastfeeding is far easier and more convenient than bottle feeding or formula feeding alternatives.

   > Listed in almost all my sources under "benefits to breastfeeding" are the convenience of having the baby's food with you wherever you go and ready at a moment's notice and having time to relax and enjoy your baby. (p. 597)

   One of the obvious problems that this perspective misses is that if the baby's food is always with the mother, then the mother can never be separated from the baby. For however long a baby is being fed exclusively by breast, the mother has no freedom to go anywhere on her own. Wall's research showed that Health Canada publications indicate no concern for mothers as women who might want to do things as *people*, but focus instead on a notion of universal convenience in which "there is no need to sterilize or warm bottles, nor are there any bottles to take with you when you leave home with your child. The process is simple, natural, free" (Health Canada pamphlet from 1991, quoted in Wall 2001: 597).

   Wall's analysis reveals that there is no recognition in the focus on convenience that mothers out in public with hungry infants may experience real limitations. The focus on convenience makes other concerns seem trivial. The inability to move freely in public because of general hostility, demands for "modesty," the physical exhaustion that breastfeeding mothers experience, and problems getting babies to nurse are all neglected, as are the problems of loss of privacy and personal identity, and of dealing with perpetually cranky babies (pp. 597–98).

3. *Contradictory views regarding the character and function of breasts.* Wall's research concludes that for all the public health insistence that breastfeeding is perfectly appropriate in any public space—surely a welcome message at a time when breastfeeding mothers were being escorted by security guards out of shopping malls or into toilets for their babies to have a midday meal in a stall—the reality is that even the public health posters and pamphlets reveal social unease about breasts, keeping the images of breastfeeding mothers "respectable and modest" with their breasts always obscured or covered. Furthermore, as Wall points out, maintaining such modest coverage in public is not easy. Fussing or distractible babies may turn away from the breast, leaving mothers suddenly and repeatedly exposed, and vulnerable to charges of immodesty. Difficulty may be especially great for new mothers trying to negotiate the public's sense of modesty, potential hostility, and their own sense of personal privacy. Yet public health advice, which only implicitly addresses public hostility, makes it all seem so simple:

> A two-piece outfit with a loose top works well for breastfeeding. The top is lifted from the bottom and will keep your breasts covered. A small blanket or shawl over your shoulder can cover your breasts and your feeding baby. If you feel comfortable and confident nursing your baby, others will be at ease. (Health Canada pamphlet from 1996, quoted in Wall 2001: 598)

The real difficulties that breastfeeding mothers face when in public, Wall reports, contribute to the reasons why breastfeeding mothers end up in solitary confinement in their homes—it is not simple to nurse in public (p. 598).

4. *Moral policing of mothering.* Although the various studies on infant–mother bonding, traceable back to the mid-twentieth century work of Bowlby on infant monkeys, suggest that there is a critical and brief period in which mothers and new infants can effectively attach, Wall explains that most have been discredited within social science research. Their discrediting did not, however, result in changes to popular perception. Wall found that the 1970s conclusions on the supposedly fixed critical period for bonding were still being marshalled as evidence in late 1990s Health Canada publications. It was as though a whole world of other research had never occurred. Citing the work of Eyer, Wall explains the continuing popularity of bonding theory:

> Eyer suggests that the zeal with which bonding was accepted is partly explained by the fact that it fit within a "deeply embedded ideology regarding the proper role of women" and notes that the concept has since been broadened beyond its narrow scientific definition to become deeply embedded in popular construction of motherhood. (p. 600)

The result of popular commitments to bonding theory, Wall points out, is that the lives and realities of mothers cease to be important; mothers recede and infants/children take centre stage in the discourse. Moreover, mothers who report problems with breastfeeding are cast in an especially negative light by medical discourses as being very selfish: "Disadvantages to breastfeeding are those factors perceived by the mother to be an inconvenience since there are no known disadvantages to the infant" (Lawrence, quoted in Wall 2001: 601).

5. *The self-regulating mother.* In a world in which mothers, expectant or those with infants, are romanticized "ecosystems" (p. 602), Wall argues that the women disappear as subjects with rights of their own. To be considered proper mothers, women must subordinate their needs and desires to those of the developing fetus or infant. A central feature of what is at stake is a form of quality control:

> The mother here is the ecosystem within which the child's optimum food source is produced. The techniques of the self that characterize the management of pregnancy (eating well; avoiding smoking, alcohol and drugs) also apply here. Food guides for healthy eating and warnings that maternal consumption of alcohol, tobacco, and drugs can harm nursing babies were common in the examined material aimed at mothers. The instructions on the back of the food guide for pregnant and nursing mothers, "How to Build a Better Baby," sum up the understanding being conveyed. Here, both pregnant and breastfeeding mothers are advised to keep the chart in a prominent spot in their kitchen so that "whenever [they] think about a meal or snack, [they] can think about [their] baby too." (p. 603)

(continued)

6. *The neo-liberal self-police state.* Wall finds that at the centre of breastfeeding discourse is a joining of economic and moral imperatives unique to the contemporary social and fiscal conservative movement known as neo-liberalism. Wall explains that neo-liberalism is a backlash movement that rejects the community model of social welfare and emphasizes the individual's need for "choice, self-management, and self-responsibility" (p. 603). Under neo-liberalism, it is every person to him or herself, and it's just too bad for those who can't make it on their own. For mothers, their obligation in a neo-liberal context is to produce better quality children, and to do so with maximum individual efficiency:

> A healthy lifestyle has become a civic moral obligation, and breastfeeding—it is asserted—not only makes for healthier babies, but

also is suggested to have lifelong health benefits. Media presentations of breastfeeding increasingly frame discussion in terms of the costs to the health care system of breastfed versus bottle-fed babies. This is true in the material examined here as well. In a fact sheet developed by Health Canada's (1998a) Canadian Perinatal Surveillance System, we find a typical reference to the fact that "the lower incidence of illness in breastfed babies reduces health care costs." In Health Canada's (1995a) poster "Breast Milk, Accept No Substitutes," it is the health benefits alone that are emphasized and the moral imperative is clear, "Your baby needs your breast milk." (p. 604)

Conclusion

The real reasons why women stop breastfeeding are completely neglected, and so the problems of social isolation, physical exhaustion, lack of child care support, demands

of other children, and public hostility go unresolved.

Poor and young mothers remain most vulnerable to state intrusion into their lives and yet, because they suffer most from the structural, symbolic, and material problems listed above, they also have the lowest rates of breastfeeding in Canada.

Wall proposes, then, that what mothers need is not more social policing or trivializing and unrealistic advice, especially for poor or single mothers—to go to bed with the baby for 24 hours to rest, for example. What is needed is more attention to the feminist recommendations for better support for public child care, restructuring of work, and increased support for parenting.

SOURCE: Wall, Glenda. 2001. "Moral Constructions of Motherhood in Breastfeeding Discourse." *Gender and Society* 15(4): 592–610. © 1992 by SAGE Publications. Reprinted with permission of SAGE Publications.

children they are parenting. Prejudice against GLBT persons may dissuade them from taking part in school activities, and many have found that once they were "out," their families' religious places of worship had no place for them. Isolation and full access to community obligations are central features that we leave out of the equation if we insist that families are defined only in reference to the nuclear, reproductive, heterosexual family.

5.3 Violence and Abuse in Intimate and Family Relationships

Although intimate and family relationships can provide stability and a sense of well-being, they can also involve physical violence, verbal and emotional abuse, sexual abuse, and neglect. In Canada, people are more likely to be physically assaulted, abused and neglected, sexually assaulted and molested, and killed in their own homes and by other family members than anywhere else or by anyone else (Statistics Canada 2001). Before reading further, you may want to take the Abusive Behaviour Inventory in this chapter's *Self and Society* feature.

Abusive Behaviour Inventory

Circle the number that best represents your closest estimate of how often each of the behaviours happened in your relationship with your partner or former partner during the previous six months.

1. Never   2. Rarely   3. Occasionally   4. Frequently   5. Very frequently

		1	2	3	4	5
1.	Called you a name and/or criticized you.	1	2	3	4	5
2.	Tried to keep you from doing something you wanted to do (e.g., going out with friends, going to meetings).	1	2	3	4	5
3.	Gave you angry stares or looks.	1	2	3	4	5
4.	Prevented you from having money for your own use.	1	2	3	4	5
5.	Ended a discussion with you and made the decision himself/herself.	1	2	3	4	5
6.	Threatened to hit or throw something at you.	1	2	3	4	5
7.	Pushed, grabbed, or shoved you.	1	2	3	4	5
8.	Put down your family and friends.	1	2	3	4	5
9.	Accused you of paying too much attention to someone or something else.	1	2	3	4	5
10.	Put you on an allowance.	1	2	3	4	5
11.	Used your children to threaten you (e.g., told you that you would lose custody, said he/she would leave town with the children).	1	2	3	4	5
12.	Became very upset with you because dinner, housework, or laundry was not done when he/she wanted it done or done the way he/she thought it should be.	1	2	3	4	5
13.	Said things to scare you (e.g., told you something "bad" would happen, threatened to commit suicide).	1	2	3	4	5
14.	Slapped, hit, or punched you.	1	2	3	4	5
15.	Made you do something humiliating or degrading (e.g., begging for forgiveness, having to ask his/her permission to use the car or to do something).	1	2	3	4	5
16.	Checked up on you (e.g., listened to your phone calls, checked the mileage on your car, called you repeatedly at work).	1	2	3	4	5
17.	Drove recklessly when you were in the car.	1	2	3	4	5
18.	Pressured you to have sex in a way you didn't like or want.	1	2	3	4	5
19.	Refused to do housework or child care.	1	2	3	4	5
20.	Threatened you with a knife, gun, or other weapon.	1	2	3	4	5
21.	Spanked you.	1	2	3	4	5
22.	Told you that you were a bad parent.	1	2	3	4	5
23.	Stopped you or tried to stop you from going to work or school.	1	2	3	4	5
24.	Threw, hit, kicked, or smashed something.	1	2	3	4	5
25.	Kicked you.	1	2	3	4	5
26.	Physically forced you to have sex.	1	2	3	4	5
27.	Threw you around.	1	2	3	4	5
28.	Physically attacked the sexual parts of your body.	1	2	3	4	5
29.	Choked or strangled you.	1	2	3	4	5
30.	Used a knife, gun, or other weapon against you.	1	2	3	4	5

Scoring: Add the numbers you circled and divide the total by 30 points to find your score. The higher your score, the more abusive your relationship.

The inventory was given to 100 men and 78 women equally divided into groups of abusers/abused and nonabusers/nonabused. The men were members of a chemical dependency treatment program in a hospital and the women were partners of these men. Abusing or abused men earned an average score of 1.8; abusing or abused women earned an average score of 2.3. Nonabusing/abused men and women earned scores of 1.3 and 1.6, respectively.

SOURCE: Shepard, Melanie F., and James A. Campbell. 1992. "The Abusive Behaviour Inventory: A Measure of Psychological and Physical Abuse." *Journal of Interpersonal Violence* 7(3), September: 291–305. Inventory is on pages 303–4. Reprinted with permission of SAGE Publications.

Intimate Partner Violence and Abuse

intimate partner violence

Actual or threatened violent crimes committed against persons by their current or former spouses, boyfriends, or girlfriends.

Globally, one woman in every three has been subjected to violence in an intimate relationship (United Nations Development Programme 2000). **Intimate partner violence** refers to actual or threatened violent crimes committed against persons by their current or former spouses, boyfriends, or girlfriends. The 1999 General Social Survey (GSS) found that rates of violence reported by Canadian men and women were relatively similar (7 percent and 8 percent, respectively). According to the findings of the 2004 General Social Survey, rates of violence in spousal relationships were unchanged in the years from 1999 to 2004, with more than 650 000 women and 540 000 men experiencing some form of violence from a spouse (Statistics Canada 2005a). Those most at risk for spousal abuse are between the ages of 15 and 24, those in common-law relationships, and those whose unions were of less than three years' duration; moreover, the forms of violence directed at women are frequently far more serious, causing greater harm (Statistics Canada 2005a). (See Figure 5.2.) Aboriginal peoples were more likely than other Canadians to report being assaulted by a spouse (about 20 percent of Aboriginal peoples compared with 7 percent of the non-Aboriginal population). "Aboriginal women in particular stand out as being at higher risk of spousal violence" (Johnson and Hotton 2001: 29).

Data from the 1999 GSS also indicate that women are three times more likely to be injured, five times more likely to receive medical attention, and also five times more likely than men to report that they feared for their lives due to the violence they had experienced. Women were also more likely than men to report multiple incidents of spousal violence. Sixty-five percent of women who experienced spousal violence reported being assaulted on more than one occasion; for men, it was 54 percent. Twenty-six percent of women said it happened more than 10 times; for men, it was 13 percent (Bunge 2000: 14).

The 2004 GSS data show that family violence cuts across income and education levels, but also that separate factors, including youth, heavy drinking, common-law relationships of less than three years, and Aboriginal status, increase one's vulnerability. In addition, the survey found that, in general, younger people face the greatest risk of experiencing spousal violence, with the highest rates reported by young women under 25 (5 percent). Men aged 25 to 34 also reported higher rates

■ **Figure 5.2** *More Women Experience Serious Violence Than Men*

SOURCE: Adapted from Statistics Canada. "Family Violence in Canada: A Statistical Profile 2005." (*The Daily*), Catalogue No. 11-001, July 14, 2005, p. 4, www.statscan.ca/Daily/English/050714/d050714a.htm.

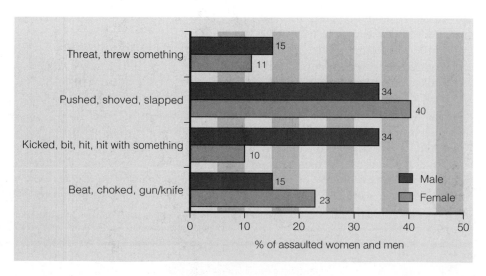

of violence than those who were older (4 percent versus 1 percent). Furthermore, the 2004 GSS reported that the elevated risk of being a victim of spousal violence remained unchanged from the 1999 GSS at four times higher for both men and women living in common-law unions than those in marriages. Finally, "Aboriginal people were three times more likely to be victims of spousal violence. Overall, 21% of Aboriginal people, or 24% of Aboriginal women and 18% of Aboriginal men…had suffered violence from a current or previous spouse or common-law partner in the five-year period up to 2004" (Statistics Canada 2005a).

The World Health Organization has collected international data that put the prevalence of intimate partner abuse into a larger global perspective and has found that, in addition to general assault, a 10-country survey of 24 000 women revealed sexual violence against women at the hands of a partner to be common: "Between 15% and 71% of women reported physical or sexual violence by a husband or partner. Many women said that their first sexual experience was not consensual (24% in rural Peru, 28% in Tanzania, 30% in rural Bangladesh, and 40% in South Africa)" (WHO 2009). Moreover, these assaults take place overwhelmingly at the hands of intimate partners, not strangers as is so commonly imagined to be the case. A brief commentary on the study in the medical journal *The Lancet* highlights some further disturbing results of the study: in short, while men are the most frequent perpetrators of violence, women often hold attitudes that support or even endorse it:

> In several of the study sites, most women thought wife beating was justifiable under some circumstances, including refusal to have sex. These attitudes are symbolic of a general pattern of acceptance of victimisation as part of being female.[6] A culture of silence also prevails. In all countries, the interviewer was the first person many of the abused women had ever talked to about their partner's physical violence.
>
> Even in countries where resources for abused women are available, barriers such as fear, stigma, and the threat of losing their children stopped many women from seeking help. (Fathalla 2005)

In other countries, not only are resources to help women more limited, but also it can be the case that women participate in the abuse of other women. In India, for example, dowry killings involve "a woman being killed by her husband or in-laws because her family is unable to meet their demands for her dowry—a payment made to a woman's in-laws upon her engagement or marriage as a gift to her new family" (UNIFEM 2007: 1). Bride burning, acid attacks, and many deaths ruled as suicides or accidents are linked to dowry disputes. Furthermore, many of these deaths take place in the kitchens of the groom's home, where the wives work closely with their mothers-in-law. The kitchen serves as a convenient location for the deaths because it is specifically the women's domain (that is: the wife is expected to be there), and because it is considered an inherently unsafe location that blends volatile cooking fuels with fire. Sometimes the mother-in-law will participate directly in setting the fire, sometimes she will agree to be called away from the kitchen so that the burning can take place. In India, courts have ruled that "customary payments" to a groom's family are not illegal (Mahapatra 2008), but in 2009 the India Supreme Court expressed outrage at such "barbaric practices" (Venkatesan 2009).

Although research on intimate violence in same-sex relationships is sparse, the few studies conducted on this issue suggest that it is quite common. More than one-third of all previous same-sex relationships and 9 percent of all current same-sex relationships include some experience of violence (Turell 2000).

Many of the dynamics reported to characterize abusive heterosexual relationships, such as alcohol and drug abuse, are also found in same-sex abusive partnerships (Halpern et al. 2004). An additional challenge for those who experience violence in same-sex relationships is that negative stigma and isolation may prevent them from seeking help and exacerbate domestic aggression (Halpern et al. 2004; Turell 2000).

common couple violence

Occasional acts of violence that result from conflict that gets out of hand between persons in a relationship.

intimate terrorism

Almost entirely perpetrated by men, a form of violence that is motivated by a wish to control one's partner and involves the systemic use of not only violence, but economic subordination, threats, isolation, verbal and emotional abuse, and other control tactics. This form of violence is more likely to escalate over time and to involve serious injury.

violent resistance

Acts of violence by a partner that are committed in self-defence. Violent resistance is almost exclusively perpetrated by women against a male partner.

mutual violent control

A rare pattern of abuse when two intimate terrorists battle for control.

sexual aggression

Sexual interaction that occurs against one's will through the use of physical force, pressure, use of alcohol/drugs, or use of position of authority.

Four patterns of partner violence have been identified: common couple violence, intimate terrorism, violent resistance, and mutual violent control (Johnson and Ferraro 2001). **Common couple violence** refers to occasional acts of violence arising from arguments that get out of hand. It usually does not escalate into serious or life-threatening violence. **Intimate terrorism**, violence motivated by a wish to control one's partner, involves the systematic use of not only violence, but also economic subordination, threats, isolation, verbal and emotional abuse, and other control tactics. Intimate terrorism is almost entirely perpetrated by men and is more likely to escalate over time and to involve serious injury. **Violent resistance** refers to acts of violence that are committed in self-defence. Violent resistance is almost exclusively perpetrated by women against a male partner. **Mutual violent control** is a rare pattern of abuse "that could be viewed as two intimate terrorists battling for control" (Johnson and Ferraro 2001: 169).

As we noted briefly above, intimate partner abuse also takes the form of sexual aggression, including forced sexual intercourse. **Sexual aggression** refers to sexual interaction that occurs against one's will through use of physical force, threat of force, pressure, use of alcohol or drugs, or use of position of authority. An estimated 7 to 14 percent of married women have been raped by their husbands (Monson et al. 1996). However, prior to 1983 and the introduction of Canada's sexual assault laws, it was legally impossible for a man in Canada to rape his wife because the rape law contained a marital exemption. A man could be found guilty of rape on his own wife only if he were party to someone else raping her.

Intimate violence can have devastating consequences. Many battered women are abused during pregnancy, resulting in a high rate of miscarriage and birth defects. Psychological consequences for victims of intimate partner violence can include depression, suicidal thoughts and attempts, lowered self-esteem, alcohol and other drug abuse, and post-traumatic stress disorder (National Center for Injury Prevention and Control 2000).

Battering also interferes with employment opportunities. Some abusers prohibit their partners from working. Other abusers will deliberately undermine the possibility of their partners working by "depriving them of transportation, harassing them at work, turning off alarm clocks, beating them before job interviews, and disappearing when they promise to provide child care" (Johnson and Ferraro 2001: 177). Battering also undermines employment by causing repeated absences, impairing ability to concentrate, and lowering self-esteem and aspirations.

Abuse, whether physical or emotional, is a factor in many divorces and is also a primary cause of homelessness. One study of homeless parents found that 22 percent were fleeing from abuse (National Coalition for the Homeless 1999). A second reported that half of homeless women and children were fleeing from abuse ("Domestic Violence and Homelessness" 1998). More recent "snapshots" from Statistics Canada show that the situation for women and children remains dire, with increased percentages of those in shelters fleeing from abuse: "Nearly one-third of all women who had sought temporary accommodation in a shelter for abused women on April 14, 2004 had stayed there at some time during the past.... On this date, there were 3,274 women and 2,835 children in such shelters, 82% of them were escaping abuse. The remaining women and children were there for other reasons such as housing, addictions and mental health issues. Of all women who had stayed in shelters previously, 40% had been there once in the previous year, 38% had been there two to four times, and about 1 in 10 had been to the facility five times or more during the previous year" (Statistics Canada 2005a).

According to Novac and colleagues (1996), housing status and violence are inextricably linked for women who find themselves fleeing from their homes. They observe that "homeless women with histories of family disruption and abuse distinguish being housed from being safe, so that homelessness is a problem for women, but is also a strategy for escaping violence. The relationship between violence and homelessness among women is complex, since there is also a great risk of violence when women are homeless."

The breakup of a relationship may not stop its violence. Recognition that the most dangerous time for victims was after leaving their violent relationships compelled the 1993 enactment of a law against criminal harassment, an offence for which the maximum penalty is 10 years' imprisonment. This law is directed against "stalking" behaviours that may stem from a variety of motives, including the adamant refusal of one partner to believe that the relationship has ended (Kong 1997). Criminal harassment includes repeatedly following, trying to communicate (via cards, letters, e-mails, and so on), or uttering direct or indirect threats or promises of violence or forcible intimacy. Women were the victims of over three-quarters (77 percent) of all incidents of criminal harassment reported to police in Canada in 1999. Although ex-husbands were the accused in more than one-third (36 percent) of incidents reported by women, men were more likely to report being stalked by casual acquaintances than intimate partners. In that year, ex-wives accounted for 11 percent of the perpetrators of criminal harassment incidents reported by men (Johnson and Hotton 2001: 33). The 2004 General Social Survey found that 49 percent of all restraining orders were violated, and for female victims, 52 percent of all orders were violated (AuCoin 2005). Although criminal harassment does not generally culminate in homicide, between 1994 and 2003 it remained a stable precipitating factor in 12 percent of homicides committed by male ex-partners (Beattie 2005: 50). Moreover, when criminal harassment led to homicide, it did so exclusively for female victims; stalking of men did not end in murder of male victims (Beattie 2005: 50).

Although rates for spousal homicide in Canada have been steadily declining since the mid-1990s, spousal homicides accounted for 17 percent of all solved homicides in Canada and for 46 percent of all family homicides between 1996 and 2005 (Ogrodnick, 2007: 9). Further, in an analysis of data for the same time period, the rate of women killed by their spouses was five times higher than the rate for men (Dauvergne 2005a: 10). Aboriginal peoples in Canada continue to suffer disproportionately from spousal homicide; at only 3 percent of the total population in Canada, Aboriginal victims of homicide accounted for 17 percent of all victims in 2004 and 22 percent of all those accused (Dauvergne 2005b: 13).

Table 5.1 shows that domestic violence in Canada accounts for almost 18 percent, or nearly one-fifth, of all solved murders between 1998 and 2007. In other words, although we often imagine murders to be random occurrences, a significant portion of murders take place in the context of intimate, familial relationships. Of the murders solved that we see enumerated in Table 5.1, it is also clear that with 45 of the murders being carried out by men, the general

■ **Table 5.1** *Spousal Homicide in Canada, 1998–2008*

Relationship type[1] (Victims killed by)	2008 number of victims	2008 percent	2007[1] number of victims	2007[1] percent	Average 1998 to 2007 number of victims	Average 1998 to 2007 percent
Family relationship						
Spousal relationship						
Husband (legal)	22	5.2	17	4.1	23	5.1
Husband (Common-law)	10	2.4	21	5.0	21	4.5
Husband (legal, separated and divorced)[2]	9	2.1	6	1.4	15	3.3
Husband (Common-law, separated)[3]	4	0.9	5	1.2	6	1.3
Wife (legal)	6	1.4	4	1.0	3	0.7
Wife (Common-law)	10	2.4	8	1.9	10	2.1
Wife (legal, separated and divorced)[2]	0	0.0	0	0.0	2	0.3
Wife (Common-law, separated)[3]	1	0.2	0	0.0	1	0.1
Same-sex spouse (current or former)[4]	0	0.0	1	0.2	1	0.2
Total spousal	**62**	**14.7**	**62**	**14.9**	**80**	**17.7**

1. Includes only those homicides in which there were known accused. If there were more than one accused, only the closest relationship to the victim was recorded.

2. Includes separated common-law prior to 2005.

3. Separated common-law husband and separated common-law wife were not introduced to the survey until 2005, therefore the average number and percentage are calculated from 2005–07.

4. Separate variables for same-sex spouse and ex-same-sex spouse were created in 2005.

SOURCE: Adapted from Statistics Canada, Canadian Centre for Justice Statistics. "Homicide in Canada." *(Juristat)*, Catalogue No. 85-002-XIE2009004, Vol. 29, no. 4, p. 24.

cycle of abuse

Involves a violent or abusive episode, followed by a makeup period where the abuser expresses sorrow and asks for forgiveness and "one more chance." The calm period may last for days, weeks, or even months; then, the next outburst of violence occurs.

pattern is that women are more than 2.5 times as likely to be killed by a male spouse than men are to be killed by a female spouse; this observation in no way minimizes the murders of men, but speaks purely to the frequency and level of violence that women are likely to face.

In cases of domestic violence, even if they themselves are not being directly abused, children remain vulnerable. According to the 2004 GSS, children are too frequently the observers of violence between spouses. Aboriginal children are especially vulnerable: 46 percent of non-Aboriginal women and 57 percent of Aboriginal women reported that their child(ren) had witnessed domestic violence against their mothers (Johnson and Hotton 2001: 29). Children who witness intimate violence may experience emotional, behavioural, and academic problems, and may commit violence in their own relationships later (Parker et al. 2000). Children may also commit violent acts against a parent's abusing partner.

Why do abused adults stay in abusive relationships? Reasons include love, emotional dependency, commitment to the relationship, hope that things will get better, the view that they "deserve" the violence, guilt, fear, economic dependency, and feeling stuck because of financial dependence and the need to provide food and shelter for children in the relationship. Abuse in relationships is usually not ongoing and constant, but rather occurs in cycles. The **cycle of abuse** involves a violent or abusive episode, followed by a makeup period where the abuser expresses sorrow and asks for forgiveness and "one more chance." This period may last for days, weeks, or even months; then, the next outburst of violence occurs.

Child Abuse

Child abuse refers to the "physical or mental injury, sexual abuse, negligent treatment, or maltreatment of a child under the age of 18 by a person who is responsible for the child's welfare" (Willis et al. 1992: 2). The Canadian Incidence Study of Reported Child Abuse and Neglect (CIS) was the first national study of child maltreatment investigations by child welfare services in Canada. According to the study, the most common reason for investigations was suspected neglect (Figure 5.3). Investigations by child welfare organizations substantiated 34 percent of cases involving suspected physical abuse, 38 percent of suspected sexual abuse cases, 43 percent of suspected neglect cases, and 54 percent of cases involving suspected emotional maltreatment (Trocmé and Wolfe 2001: 5). The majority (69 percent) of substantiated cases of child physical abuse involved inappropriate punishment—hitting a child with either a hand or object that led to physical harm or put the child at substantial risk of harm. The most common form of sexual abuse within substantiated cases involved touching and fondling of the genitals (68 percent); attempted or completed sexual intercourse accounted for about a third (35 percent) of all substantiated cases. The most common form of emotional maltreatment within substantiated cases was a child's exposure to family violence followed by emotional abuse (overtly hostile, punitive treatment, or habitual or extreme verbal abuse) (Trocmé and Wolfe 2001).

Figure 5.4 shows that for all reported forms of abuse except sexual abuse, the most dangerous place for children is at home. In the home—except for sexual abuse, which occurs three times as often at the hands of biological fathers, and neglect, which occurs more than twice as often at the hands of mothers—children face similar risk at the hands of either biological parent. Sexual abuse was more likely to be perpetrated by other relatives, but is far more common among biological parents than one might expect. Although we teach children to fear strangers, Trocmé's data on child abuse show that "Other than parents, relatives [a]re the most frequently identified perpetrators" (Trocmé et al. 2001: 108).

When compared to adults, children and youth are especially likely to be killed by family members (Locke et al. 2001: 15). Of the 1990 solved homicides of children and youths recorded by Canadian police agencies between 1974 and 1999, more than 6 out of 10 (63 percent) were committed by family members. As far as the frequencies for any given year, the data on homicides against children vary and show no obvious pattern (Ogrodnick 2007: 25); all we know is that parents—and especially young parents—are the most likely perpetrators, with over 70 percent of these murders being committed by parents (Dauvergne, 2005b; Ogrodnick, 2007). Moreover, because these killings frequently end in

child abuse

The physical or mental injury, sexual abuse, negligent treatment, or maltreatment of a child under the age of 18 by a person who is responsible for the child's welfare.

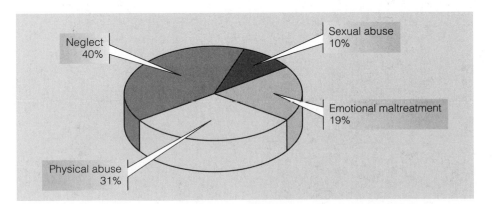

■ **Figure 5.3** *Child Neglect Most Common Reason for Child Maltreatment Investigation*

SOURCE: "The Canadian Incidence Study of Reported Child Abuse and Neglect," National Clearinghouse on Family Violence, Public Health Agency of Canada (1998). Reproduced with the permission of the Minister of Public Works and Government Services Canada, 2011.

■ **Figure 5.4** *Abuse Most Common in the Home*

SOURCE: "The Canadian Incidence Study of Reported Child Abuse and Neglect," National Clearinghouse on Family Violence, Public Health Agency of Canada, Catalogue no. H49151200E, Table 4, 2001. Reproduced with the permission of the Minister of Public Works and Government Services Canada, 2011.

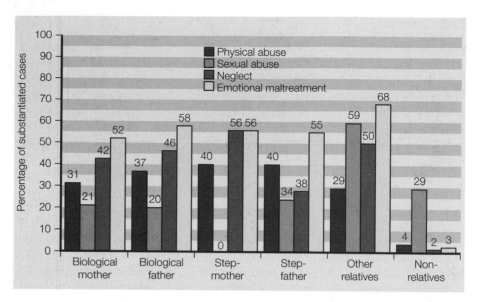

the suicide of the perpetrator (Ogrodnick 2007: 26), efforts to explain the motivation must encompass marital dissolution and depression as causative factors (Dauvergne 2000b: 11). (See Figure 5.5.)

Reviews of research on the effects of child abuse suggest that abused children are at higher risk for aggressive behaviour, low self-esteem, depression, and low academic achievement (Gelles and Conte 1991; Lloyd and Emery 1993). The Canadian Incidence Study (CIS) reports that in more than one-half (56 percent) of cases of substantiated physical abuse, the child was described as having some type of difficulty, with behaviour problems, negative peer involvement, depression or anxiety, violence toward others, and developmental delay the most often indicated difficulties. Among child victims of substantiated sexual abuse, the five most frequently reported difficulties were depression or anxiety, age-inappropriate sexual behaviour, behaviour problems, negative peer involvement, and irregular

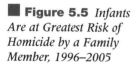

■ **Figure 5.5** *Infants Are at Greatest Risk of Homicide by a Family Member, 1996–2005*

SOURCE: Statistics Canada,"Family Violence in Canada: A Statistical Profile," Catalogue no. 85-224-XIE2008000, October 2008; http://www.statcan.gc.ca/bsolc/olc-cel/olc-cel?lang=eng&catno=85-224-X.

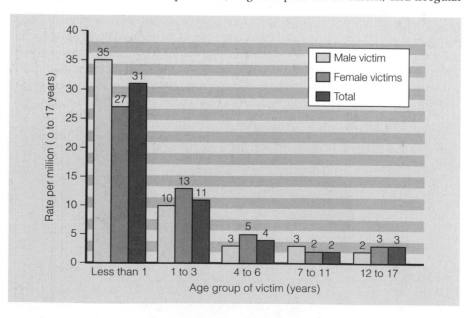

school attendance (Trocmé and Wolfe 2001). Adolescents and adults who were abused as children are more vulnerable to low self-esteem, depression, unhappiness, anxiety, increased risk of substance abuse, criminal activity, and suicide.

Repeated studies have established strong correlations between the early abuse that children suffer and long-term negative health consequences. Like other forms of abuse, the consequences of sexual abuse of male and female children are devastating and long-term. Among females, early forced sex is associated with lower self-esteem, higher levels of depression, running away from home, alcohol and drug use, and more sexual partners (Jasinski et al. 2000; Lanz 1995; Whiffen et al. 2000). Sexually abused girls are also more likely to become pregnant as teens, have more sexual partners in adulthood, acquire sexually transmitted infections, and experience forced sex (Browning and Laumann 1997; Stock et al. 1997). Women who were sexually abused as children also report a higher frequency of post-traumatic stress disorder (Spiegel 2000) and suicide ideation (Thakkar et al. 2000). Spouses who were physically and sexually abused as children report lower marital satisfaction, higher stress, and lower family cohesion than spouses with no abuse history (Nelson and Wampler 2000). Adult males who were sexually abused as children tend to exhibit depression, substance abuse, and difficulty establishing intimate relationships (Krug 1989). Sexually abused males also have a higher risk of anxiety disorders, sleep and eating disorders, and sexual dysfunctions (Elliott and Briere 1992).

Effects of child sexual abuse are likely to be severe when the abuse is forceful, is prolonged, involves intercourse, and was perpetrated by a father or stepfather (Beitchman et al. 1992). The child not only has been violated physically, but also has lost an important social support.

Abused or neglected children may be removed from the home. Provincial child welfare laws permit abused or neglected children to be placed in out-of-home care, such as foster care; however, a preferred approach is to prevent family breakup if it can be done without jeopardizing the welfare of children in the home. **Family preservation programs** are in-home interventions for families who are at risk of having a child removed from the home due to abuse or neglect.

Elder Abuse

Elder abuse includes physical abuse, psychological abuse, financial abuse (such as improper use of the elder's financial resources), and neglect. Elder neglect includes failure to provide basic health and hygiene needs, such as clean clothes, doctor visits, medication, and adequate nutrition. Neglect also involves unreasonable confinement, isolation of elderly family members, lack of supervision, and abandonment. (See Figure 5.6.)

The 1999 GSS asked Canadians 65 years of age or over a series of questions in relation to emotional and financial abuse by children, caregivers (individuals paid or unpaid who provide assistance or health care in the respondent's home), and spouses (including current and former spouses as well as common-law partners). It also asked questions about possible physical or sexual abuse by children, caregivers, or spouses. This survey reports very little physical or sexual violence perpetrated against older Canadians residing in a private household. "[O]nly one percent of this population of seniors indicated that they had been physically or sexually assaulted by a spouse, adult child or caregiver in the five years prior to this survey" (Bunge 2000: 27). Seven percent reported experiencing some type of

family preservation program

An in-home intervention for a family who is at risk of having a child removed from the home because of abuse or neglect.

elder abuse

The physical or psychological abuse, financial exploitation, or medical abuse or neglect of the elderly.

ELDER ABUSE

IT'S TIME TO FACE THE REALITY   www.seniors.gc.ca

FACTS ON THE ABUSE OF SENIORS

Abuse of seniors may involve mistreatment or violence, or even neglect. Abuse can be at the hands of a spouse, an adult child or other family member. Abuse can be inflicted by a caregiver, a service provider, or other person in a situation of power or trust. Abuse can happen when a senior is living in an institution or a private residence.

Abuse can happen when the aggressor wants to intimidate, isolate, dominate or control another human being. Abuse can happen to anyone, in any family or relationship. It can happen to people of all backgrounds, ages, religions, races, cultures and ethnic origins.

An older adult may experience one or more kinds of abuse, including:

- physical or sexual
- psychological and emotional
- financial
- neglect

All these kinds of abuse can happen as single incident or can be a patten or behaviour. An older adult may be perceived by some as vulnerable and a target. In families, caregivers may take out their frustration on seniors who may not want to admit that abuse is happening.

If you know a senior whos is being abused, or a caregiver who is stretched byond the limit, they may need support. Let them know they are not alone. Encourage anyone who is suffering from abuse or who is acting in a violent way, to get help.

Abuse happens when one person hurts or mistreats another. Remember:

- Seniors are entitled to respect.
- Seniors have every right to live in safety and security.
- There is no excuse for abuse.

For more information, call 1 800 O-Canada (1-800-622-6232) or visit www.seniors.gc.ca.

 Government   Gouvernement
of Canada   du Canada

Canadä

■ **Figure 5.6** *Elder Abuse: It's Time to Face the Reality*

SOURCE: Facts on the Abuse of Seniors, published in *Elder Abuse: It's Time to Face the Reality,* URL: http://www.seniors. gc.ca/c.4nt@.jsp?geo=106&cid=155. Human Resources and Skills Development Canada, 2010. Reproduced with the permission of the Minister of Public Works and Government Services Canada, 2011.

emotional or financial abuse, with spouses identified as the perpetrator in the vast majority of cases. The most common form of emotional abuse reported was being verbally put down or called names (5 percent), followed by limiting contact with family or friends (2 percent). Men were more likely than women (9 percent versus 6 percent) to report being victims of emotional or financial abuse by an adult child, caregiver, or spouse. The highest rates of emotional or financial abuse were reported by older adults whose household incomes were between $30 000 and $39 000, who were divorced or separated, who lived in rural areas, and who had some postsecondary education. However, this survey did not include respondents living in institutions (e.g., retirement homes, hospitals), and so cannot provide us with information on the experiences of older Canadians who live in such settings.

According to police-reported statistics, there were 802 cases of violence committed against older adults by family members in 1999, with the most frequent assailant an adult child (43 percent), followed by a spouse (28 percent). The most common offence committed against an older adult by a family member was common assault (54 percent), followed by uttering threats (22 percent).

Factors Contributing to Intimate Partner and Family Violence and Abuse

Research suggests that cultural, community, and individual and family factors contribute to domestic violence and abuse (Willis et al. 1992).

Cultural Factors Violence in the family stems from our society's acceptance of violence as a legitimate means of enforcing compliance and solving conflicts at personal, national, and international levels (Viano 1992). Violence and abuse in the family may be linked to cultural factors, such as violence in the media (see Chapter 4), acceptance of corporal punishment, gender inequality, and the view of women and children as property.

1. *Acceptance of corporal punishment.* **Corporal punishment** involves the use of physical force with the intention of causing a child to experience pain, but not injury, for the purpose of correction or control of a child's behaviour (Straus 2000). Many mental health professionals and child development specialists argue that it is ineffective and damaging to children. Children who experience corporal punishment display more antisocial behaviour and are more violent; as adults, they have an increased incidence of depression (Straus 2000). Yet, many parents accept the cultural tradition of spanking as an appropriate form of child discipline. Moreover, Canadian law specifically allows for the corporal punishment of children. Section 43 of the *Criminal Code* of Canada specifies that "[e]very schoolteacher, parent, or person standing in the place of a parent is justified in using force by way of correction toward a pupil or child, as the case may be, who is under his care, if the force does not exceed what is reasonable under the circumstances." In effect, this section allows children to be assaulted by their parents and teachers, provided that the force used in the assault is "reasonable" and for the child's "correction." Conversely, in such countries as Austria, Cyprus, Denmark, Finland, Italy, Norway, and Sweden, the use of corporal punishment in the home or school is against the law.

2. *Gender role socialization.* Traditional male gender roles have taught men to be aggressive in general and to be dominant in male–female relationships. Male abusers are likely to hold traditional attitudes toward women and

corporal punishment
The use of physical force with the intention of causing a child to experience pain, but not injury, for the purpose of correction or control of a child's behaviour.

male–female roles (Lloyd and Emery 2000). Anderson (1997) found that men who earn less money than their partners are more likely to be violent toward them. "Disenfranchised men then must rely on other social practices to construct a masculine image. Because it is so clearly associated with masculinity in...[our] culture, violence is a social practice that enables men to express a masculine identity" (p. 667). Traditional female gender roles have also taught women to be submissive to their male partner's control.

3. *View of women and children as property.* Before the 1978 *Family Law Reform Act* established that married women remained independent persons, wives were considered "chattel" or property of their husbands in Canada. A husband had a legal right and marital obligation to discipline and control his wife, even through the use of physical force. The historical weight of this view of women as property may contribute to men continuing to treat their wives as they wish. The view of women and children as property also explains marital rape and father–daughter incest. Historically, the penalties for rape were based on property-rights laws designed to protect a man's property—his wife or daughter—from rape by other men; a husband or father "taking" his own property was not considered rape (Russell 1990).

Community Factors Community factors that contribute to violence and abuse in the family include social isolation and inaccessible or unaffordable health care, day care, elder care, and respite care facilities.

1. *Social isolation.* Living in social isolation from extended family and community members increases a family's risk for abuse. Isolated families are removed from material benefits, care-giving assistance, and emotional support from extended family and community members.

2. *Inaccessible or unaffordable community services.* Failure to provide medical care to children and elderly family members (a form of neglect) is sometimes due to the lack of accessible or affordable health-care services in the community. Failure to provide supervision for children and adults may result from inaccessible day care and elder care services. Without elder care and respite care facilities, socially isolated families may not have any help with the stresses of caring for elderly family members and children with special needs.

Individual and Family Factors Individual and family factors associated with intimate partner and family violence and abuse include a family history of violence, drug and alcohol abuse, poverty, and fatherless homes.

1. *Family history of abuse.* Mothers who were sexually abused as children are more likely to physically abuse their own children (DiLillo et al. 2000). Although a history of abuse is associated with an *increased likelihood* of being abusive as an adult, *most* adults who were abused as children do not continue the pattern of abuse in their own relationships (Gelles 2000).

2. *Drug and alcohol abuse.* Alcohol use is reported as a factor in 50 to 70 percent of incidents of physical and sexual aggression in intimate relationships (Lloyd and Emery 2000). Alcohol and other drugs increase aggression in some individuals and enable the offender to avoid responsibility by blaming his or her violent behaviour on the drugs or alcohol.

3. *Poverty.* Abuse in adult relationships occurs among all socio-economic groups. However, Kaufman and Zigler (1992: 284) point to a relationship between poverty and child abuse:

Although most poor people do not maltreat their children, and poverty, per se, does not cause abuse and neglect, the correlates of poverty, including stress, drug abuse, and inadequate resources for food and medical care, increase the likelihood of maltreatment.

5.4 Strategies for Action: Preventing and Responding to Violence and Abuse in Intimate and Family Relationships

Strategies to prevent family violence and abuse include **primary prevention** strategies that target the general population, **secondary prevention** strategies that target groups at high risk for family violence and abuse, and **tertiary prevention** strategies that target families who have experienced abuse (Gelles 1993; Harrington and Dubowitz 1993).

Primary Prevention Strategies

Preventing violence and abuse may require broad, sweeping social changes, such as eliminating the norms that legitimize and glorify violence in society and changing society's sexist character (Gelles 2000). Specific abuse prevention strategies include public education and media campaigns that may help reduce domestic violence by conveying the criminal nature of domestic assault and offering ways to prevent abuse ("When you are angry at your child, count to 10 and call a friend..."). Other prevention efforts focus on parent education to teach parents realistic expectations about child behaviour and methods of child discipline that do not involve corporal punishment.

Another strategy involves reducing violence-provoking stress by reducing poverty and unemployment and providing adequate housing, child-care programs and facilities, nutrition, medical care, and educational opportunities. This chapter's *The Human Side* also points to the need to broaden our understanding of what a family is and to challenge misleading stereotypes about people with disabilities—their intelligence, their credibility, and their sexuality. By doing so, we can be effective in both preventing violence within families and responding to it when it occurs.

Secondary Prevention Strategies

Families at risk of experiencing violence and abuse include low-income families, parents with a history of depression or psychiatric care, single parents, teenage mothers, parents with few social and family contacts, individuals who experienced abuse in their own childhood, and parents or spouses who abuse drugs or alcohol. Secondary prevention strategies, designed to prevent abuse from occurring in high-risk families, include parent education programs, parent support groups, individual counselling, substance abuse treatment, and home visiting programs.

In response to studies that noted family violence is more prevalent in Aboriginal communities, the federal government allotted $7 million to the funding of short-term community-based projects related to family violence in Indian and Inuit communities. These projects were part of the Family Violence and Child Sexual Abuse Initiatives. More than 180 of them, focusing on public awareness, training, community workshops, and research and program development, were funded in Native communities across Canada in the 1990s.

primary prevention (strategies)

Family violence prevention strategies that target the general population.

secondary prevention (strategies)

Prevention strategies that target groups that are thought to be at high risk for family violence.

tertiary prevention (strategies)

Prevention strategies that target families who have experienced family violence.

Family Violence against Women with Disabilities

Probably the single biggest factor affecting the incidence of family violence against women with disabilities is the extent of these women's "families." Women with disabilities must often depend on a variety of people to provide them with assistance in carrying out their everyday lives. For this reason, their "family" is understood to include not only parents, husbands, boyfriends, and other relatives, but also friends, neighbours, and caregivers. Caregivers can include attendants, interpreters, homemakers, drivers, doctors, nurses, teachers, social workers, psychiatrists, therapists, counsellors, and workers in hospitals and other institutions. This large number of people and the intimate physical and emotional contact involved in the care they provide greatly increase the risk of abuse to persons with disabilities.

Women who live in institutional settings, and women who are multiply or profoundly disabled, are most vulnerable to abuse because they are more dependent upon even larger numbers of people and less able to get away. It is estimated that women with disabilities are 1.5 to 10 times as likely to be abused as women without disabilities are, depending on whether they live in the community or in institutions.

While a disability can make it more difficult for a woman to escape or report abuse, social attitudes toward persons with disabilities are probably a bigger factor in her increased vulnerability to violence. The way in which society views persons with disabilities handicaps these women in many ways:

- They tend to be viewed and treated as children, as lacking intelligence.
- They may be trained to be compliant; sometimes, they are punished for assertiveness or for challenging authority figures—in direct contrast to the street-proofing taught to many children in schools.
- Women with disabilities are considered to be non-sexual and are often not given sex education, which can result in an inability to distinguish between abusive behaviour and normal or necessary forms of touching.
- They may be considered incompetent witnesses by police and the courts, particularly if they have difficulty or require assistance in communicating.
- When they do report abuse, they may not be believed.

Prevalence of Abuse

- Research has only just begun in this area, but indications are that women and children with disabilities are one of the most highly victimized groups in our society.
- The degree of risk of sexual abuse of persons with disabilities appears to be at least 150 percent of that for individuals of the same sex and similar age without disabilities.
- It is estimated that only 20 percent of the cases of sexual abuse involving disabled people are ever reported to the police, community service agencies, or authorities.

Barriers to Obtaining Help

It is extremely difficult for any abused woman to leave a situation of abuse.... Battering undermines self-esteem and can make a woman feel she is somehow responsible for her own abuse. For a woman with a disability, this situation is even more difficult. She may be dependent on her abuser for affection, communication, and financial, physical, and medical support. If she reports the abuse, she may risk poverty and loss of housing. She may fear she will not be heard or believed if she speaks out. She may face further violence, institutionalization, or loss of her children if she seeks help. She may not have access to information about existing support services for victims of violence. Even if she has this information, many sources of support may not be accessible. She may not be able to contact the police or women's shelters because they do not have communication devices such as Telecommunication Devices for the Deaf (TDDs). She may not be able to leave her situation because of a lack of accessible transportation. Her lack of options may leave her feeling so powerless and despairing that suicide seems the only viable choice. And if she seeks help in dealing with suicidal thoughts or attempts, she is unlikely to find counselling that takes account of her own reality....

SOURCE: Abridged from *Family Violence against Women with Disabilities*, National Clearinghouse on Family Violence, Health Canada, © 1993. Reproduced with the permission of the Minister of Public Works and Government Services Canada, 2011.

Care was taken to respect the strategies of intervention preferred within Aboriginal communities. Often, Aboriginal peoples view the problem of family violence as a symptom of community dysfunction. In consequence, solutions to the problem are viewed in terms of a holistic, community-wide healing process planned, developed, and implemented by Aboriginal peoples. For example, workshops dealing with issues of abuse may begin with a prayer and a sharing circle or a smudge ceremony using the local root. Communities may also use naming ceremonies and feasts to celebrate different points of healing or encourage survivors to take part in sweat lodges to ask for help for themselves and others. The Medicine Wheel, too, is favoured as a healing tool. The Wheel explains that healthy persons must use all four parts of themselves—physical, mental, emotional, and spiritual. Many versions of the Wheel are used in counselling programs.

Tertiary Prevention Strategies

What social interventions are available to families that are experiencing abuse or neglect? Abused women and children may seek relief at one of Canada's 508 shelters for abused women and their children, or "safe houses." Although shelters differ (see Table 5.2), there are residential facilities in every Canadian province and

■ **Table 5.2** *Types of Shelters*

The term "shelter" is used broadly to refer to all residential facilities for abused women and their dependent children. The types of shelters are defined by the Transition Home Survey as:

Transition Home	Short- or moderate-term (1 day to 11 weeks) first stage emergency housing.
Second Stage Housing	Long-term (3–12 months) secure housing with support and referral services designed to assist women while they search for permanent housing.
Safe Home Network	A network of private homes in rural or remote areas where there is no full-fledged operating shelter. It offers subsidiary very short-term (1–3 days) emergency housing.
Women's Emergency Centre/Shelter	Short-term (1–21 days) respite (temporary relief) for women and their dependent children.
Emergency Shelter	Short-term (1–3 days) respite for a wide population range, not exclusively abused women. Some facilities may provide accommodation for men as well as women. This type of facility may accommodate residents who are not associated with family abuse but are without a home due to an emergency situation (e.g., eviction for non-payment of rent). Other than residential (room and board) services, these shelters offer few additional client services.
Family Resource Centre	An Ontario government initiative that serves a wide range of clients and provides clients with an extensive array of information and referrals as well as residential services.
Other	All other facilities/shelters not otherwise classified. This category may include Rural Family Violence Prevention Centres in Alberta, Interim Housing in Manitoba, and other types of emergency shelters. These services may not be exclusive to abused women.

SOURCE: Statistics Canada, "Children in shelters for abused women," *Family Violence in Canada: A Statistical Profile*, Catalogue no. 85-224-XIE2001000, June 2001; http://www.statcan.gc.ca/bsolc/olc-cel/olc-cel?catno=85-224-XIE&lang=eng#formatdisp.

territory that provide abused women and their children with housing, food, and counselling services. *Safe houses* are private homes of individuals who volunteer to provide temporary housing to abused women who decide to leave their violent homes. Battered men are not allowed to stay at women's shelters, but many shelters help abused men by providing money for a motel room, counselling, and support services. Some communities have abuse shelters for victims of elder abuse. In August 2002, www.shelternet.ca, a website providing point-and-click access to information about shelters for women and children across Canada, was launched in Toronto. A similar website, www.hotpeachpages.net, also provides abused women with helpful information on shelters (Wherry 2002). Recognizing that men also suffer from abuse, in 2008 the government of Canada produced the *Directory of Services and Programs for Abused Men in Canada*, an exhaustive 60-page booklet that contains lists organized by province and territory and printed in both official languages. The booklet is available from the Public Health Agency of Canada (PHAC). The greater number of shelters specifically designed for women and children fleeing from an abusive partner, however, reflects the fact that of those experiencing assault in the home, 83 percent of victims are women (Statistics Canada 2009).

Although efforts are made to keep families together, in cases where the abuser continues to be abusive and/or neglectful a court may order an abusing spouse or parent to leave the home. Abused spouses or cohabiting partners may obtain a restraining order prohibiting perpetrators. However, legal action does not always protect victims of family violence. One Canadian study that tracked 133 cases of domestic violence through the courts for an eight-month period found that almost half of the men charged with assaulting their wives broke bail conditions by harassing, stalking, or moving back in with their wives. While the return of abusive partners into the home may seem shocking, the financial dependence of women and children on male earners for family stability can compel some of the women to take back an abusive partner. The women may sincerely want their partners to change their behaviour, but not to disappear from their lives. Canadian courts have also been notably reluctant to curtail the access of abusive spouses to their children; the courts have held that a husband's commission of an assault upon his wife does not invalidate his application for child custody or the claim that he is a "good father." In situations in which a restraining order prohibits the abusive partner from establishing contact with a current or former spouse, the order itself may be unknowingly breached when the abused spouse voluntarily allows the abusive partner into the home to pick up or deliver their children.

Treatment for abusers may be voluntary or mandated by the court. It typically involves group or individual counselling or both, substance abuse counselling, and training in communication, conflict resolution, and anger management. Those who stop abusing their partners learn to take responsibility for their abusive behaviour, develop empathy for their partners' victimization by learning to see them as human beings instead of as property, reduce their dependency on their partners, and improve their communication skills (Scott and Wolfe 2000).

5.5 Divorce

Between 1968 and 1987, Canada experienced a sevenfold increase in divorce (Ambert 1998: 4). However, divorce rates in Canada peaked in 1987 and have generally declined since then (see Figure 5.7). In 1987, the crude divorce rate

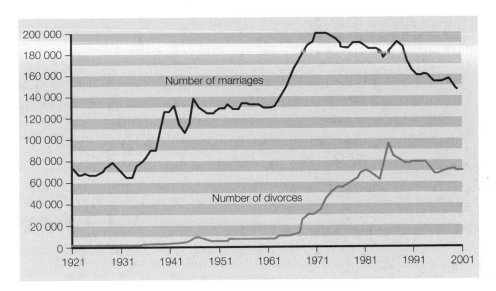

Figure 5.7 *Numbers of Marriages and Divorces in Canada, 1921–2002*

SOURCE: Statistics Canada. "Number of Marriages and Divorces in Canada, 1921–2002." *(The Daily)*, Catalogue No. 11-001, Tuesday, May 4, 2004, www.statscan.ca/Daily/English/040504/d040504a.htm.

(the number of divorces per 100 000 population) was 362.3; in 2000, it was 231.2, and by 2003, the rate had fallen to 223.7 (Statistics Canada 2005b). Individual and relationship factors that contribute to divorce include incompatibility in values or goals, poor communication, lack of conflict resolution skills, sexual incompatibility, extramarital relationships, substance abuse, emotional or physical abuse, neglect, boredom, jealousy, and difficulty coping with change or stress related to parenting, employment, finances, in-laws, and illness. Other demographic and life course factors that are predictive of divorce include marriage order (second and subsequent marriages are more prone to divorce than first marriages), cohabitation (couples who live together before marriage are more prone to divorce), teenage marriage, premarital pregnancy, and low socioeconomic status. A prime feature of divorce is that it appears to be most common in the fifth year of marriage, following the fourth anniversary. From there it declines, with 60 percent of all divorces taking place before the end of 15 years of marriage (Statistics Canada 2004).

Various social factors also contribute to the increased rate of divorce over the past three decades. These include the following structural and cultural forces:

1. *Changing family functions.* Before the Industrial Revolution, the family constituted a unit of economic production and consumption, provided care and protection to its members, and was responsible for socializing and educating children. During industrialization, other institutions took over these functions. For example, the educational institution has virtually taken over the systematic teaching and socialization of children. Today, the primary function of marriage and the family is the provision of emotional support, intimacy, affection, and love. When marital partners no longer derive these emotional benefits from their marriage, they may consider divorce with the hope of finding a new marriage partner to fulfill these needs.

2. *Increased economic autonomy of women.* Before 1940, most wives were not employed outside the home and they depended on their husbands' incomes. However, by the end of the twentieth century, husbands were the

sole earner in merely 14 percent of all husband–wife families (Vanier Institute of the Family 2000: 96). The last women to move into employment outside the home, mothers of young children, have also been entering the labour force in increasing numbers. By 1999, 61 percent of Canadian women with children less than three years of age were employed—more than double the figure in 1976 (Statistics Canada 2000). A wife who is unhappy in her marriage is more likely to leave the marriage if she has the economic means to support herself; an unhappy husband may also be more likely to leave a marriage if his wife is self-sufficient and can contribute to the support of the children.

3. *Increased work demands and dissatisfaction with marital division of labour.* Another factor influencing divorce is increased work demands and the stresses of balancing work and family roles. Workers are putting in longer hours, often working overtime or taking second jobs. Many employed parents—particularly mothers—come home to work a "**second shift**"—the work involved in caring for children and doing household chores (Hochschild 1989). Wives are more likely than husbands to perceive the marital division of labour—household chores and child care—as unfair (Nock 1995). This perception can lead to marital tension and resentment, as reflected in the following excerpt:

> My husband's a great help watching our baby. But as far as doing housework or even taking the baby when I'm at home, no. He figures he works five days a week; he's not going to come home and clean. But he doesn't stop to think that I work seven days a week. Why should I have to come home and do the housework without help from anybody else? My husband and I have been through this over and over again. Even if he would just pick up things from the kitchen table and stack the dishes for me, that would make a big difference. He does nothing. On his weekends off, I have to provide a sitter for the baby so he can go fishing. When I have a day off, I have the baby all day long without a break. He'll help out if I'm not here, but the minute I am, all the work at home is mine. (quoted in Hochschild 1997: 37–38)

4. *Liberalized divorce laws.* Before 1968, adultery was the only ground for divorce in Canada, except in Nova Scotia, where cruelty was sufficient grounds even before Confederation (Morrison 1987). The 1968 *Divorce Act* expanded the "fault grounds" under which a divorce could be granted. In addition to adultery, proof that one's partner had engaged in prohibited activities, such as mental or physical cruelty, gross addiction to alcohol or other drugs, sodomy, bestiality, and homosexual acts, entitled the petitioner to an immediate divorce. The 1968 *Divorce Act* also introduced what are termed **no-fault divorce** grounds that allowed couples to divorce without requiring them to stipulate their specific reason for doing so. In these cases of marital breakdown, couples were required to live apart for a three-year period before applying for a divorce and jointly consent to being divorced. In the event that one party did not wish to be divorced, the court required that five years pass from the time of separation before applying for divorce. In addition, Morton (1990: 213) notes that "[a]s an added protection for the economically dependent spouse in cases of unilateral separation, courts were given the discretion to refuse a divorce if a 'granting of the decree would be unduly harsh or unjust or would affect the making of reasonable arrangements for the maintenance [financial support] of the spouse.'"

second shift

The household work and childcare that employed parents (usually women) do when they return from their jobs.

no-fault divorce

A divorce that is granted based on the claim that there are irreconcilable differences within a marriage (as opposed to one spouse being legally at fault for the marital breakup).

In 1985, a new divorce act became law. Under the current act, only one ground is available for divorce—marital breakdown—but this is defined in three ways: (1) the spouses have lived apart for one year; (2) one of the spouses has committed an act of adultery; (3) one spouse has treated the other with mental or physical cruelty. While proof of fault entitles couples to an immediate divorce, those opting for a one-year separation "may apply for a divorce any time after separation to ensure that their case is heard soon after the year is up" (Morton 1990: 214).

5. *Changing cultural values.* Our society is increasingly characterized by **individualism**—the tendency to focus on one's individual self-interests rather than on the interests of one's family and community. The rising divorce rate has been linked to the continued rise of individualism. "For many, concerns with self-fulfillment and careerism diminished their commitment to family, rendering marriage and other intimate relationships vulnerable" (Demo et al. 2000: 281). **Familism**, in contrast, refers to the view that the family unit is more important than individual interests.

   The value of marriage has also changed. The increased social acceptance of nonmarital sexuality, nonmarital child-bearing, cohabitation, and singlehood reflect the view that marriage is an option rather than an inevitability. The view of marriage as an option, rather than as an imperative, is mirrored by the view that divorce is also an acceptable option. Divorce today has less social stigma than in previous generations. "Marital dissolution, once considered to be a rare, unfortunate, and somewhat shameful deviation from normal family life" (Thompson and Amato 1999: xi), has become part of mainstream society.

6. *Increased life expectancy.* Finally, more marriages today end in divorce, in part, because people live longer than they did in previous generations. Because people live longer today than in previous generations, "'til death do us part" involves a longer commitment than it once did. Indeed, one can argue that "marriage once was as unstable as it is today, but it was cut short by death not divorce" (Emery 1999: 7).

individualism
A value system that stresses the importance of individual happiness.

familism
A value system that encourages family members to put their family's well-being above their individual and personal needs.

Consequences of Divorce

When parents have bitter conflict that cannot be resolved or one parent is abusing the child or the other parent, divorce may offer a solution to family problems; however, it often has negative effects for ex-spouses and their children and contributes to problems that affect society as a whole.

Health Consequences A large number of studies have found that divorced individuals, compared to married individuals, experience lower levels of psychological well-being, including more unhappiness, depression, anxiety, and poorer self-concepts. Divorced individuals also have more health problems and a higher risk of mortality (Amato 2001). Both divorced and never-married individuals are, on average, more distressed than married people because unmarried people are more likely than married people to have low social attachment, low emotional support, and increased economic hardship (Walker 2001).

Economic Consequences In families at the lowest income levels, divorce can improve women's income because men who earn little income can be a drain on the family's finances. However, "there is a clear pattern that the economic well-being of divorced women and their children plunges in comparison to pre-divorce levels" (Demo et al. 2000: 281). The economic costs of divorce are greater for women and children because women tend to earn less than men (see Chapter 8) and mothers devote substantially more time to household and child-care tasks than fathers do. The time that women invest in this unpaid labour restricts their educational and job opportunities as well as their income.

Men are less likely than women to be economically disadvantaged after divorce. Many men enjoy a better financial situation after divorce (Peterson 1996) as they continue to profit from earlier investments in education and career. However, men with low and unstable earnings often experience financial strain following divorce, which often underlies failure to pay child support. When custodial mothers who did not receive child support were asked why they did not receive it, 66 percent gave the reason as "father unable to pay" (Henry 1999).

Effects on Children Although divorce, following high conflict, may improve the emotional well-being of children relative to staying in a conflicted home environment (Jekielek 1998), for many children, parental divorce has detrimental effects. With only one parent in the home, children of divorce, as well as children of never-married mothers, tend to have less adult supervision compared with children in two-parent homes. Lack of adult supervision is related to higher rates of criminality by youths, school failure, and teenage pregnancy (Popenoe 1993). A survey of 90 000 teenagers found that the mere presence of a parent in the home after school, at dinner, and at bedtime significantly reduces the risk of teenage suicide, violence, and drug use (Resnick et al. 1997). Many of the negative effects of divorce on children are related to economic hardship. Economic hardship is associated with less effective and less supportive parenting, inconsistent and harsh discipline, and emotional distress in children (Demo et al. 2000).

In a review of the literature on the effects of parental divorce on university-age students, Nielsen (1999) found that when their parents divorce and their mother remarries within a few years, most children do not suffer serious long-term consequences in terms of self-confidence, mental health, or academic achievements. However, in those cases where the mother does not remarry (about 15 percent), the consequences are more likely to be negative. Children of divorced women who do not remarry tend to experience a reduced standard of living and a lack of parental discipline. These children "fail to develop as much self-control, self-motivation, self-reliance, and self-direction as people their own age whose mothers have remarried" (Nielsen 1999: 547).

Children who live with their mothers may suffer from a damaged relationship with their nonresidential father, especially if he becomes disengaged from their lives. On the other hand, children may benefit from having more quality time with their fathers after parental divorce. Some fathers report that they became more active in the role of father after divorce. One father commented:

> In the last four and a half years, I have developed an incredibly strong and loving bond with my two sons. I am actively involved in all aspects of their lives. I have even coached their soccer and basketball teams.... The time I spend with them is very quality time—if anything, the divorce has made me a better and more caring father...not to say this would not have happened if my marriage had worked out. (quoted in Pasley and Minton 2001: 248)

However, according to Canada's National Child Survey, following parental separation, about one-third of children have little contact with their fathers—irregular visits or none at all. Children born of common-law unions are even less likely to see their fathers than are children born to married parents. "Since fathers who have low levels of contact with their children are least likely to pay child support, many Canadian children are at a high risk of losing both the personal and financial support of their fathers when their parents separate" (National Council of Welfare 1999: 51).

On occasion, custodial parents may actively try to alienate children from the noncustodial parent. Some of these children may develop **parental alienation syndrome (PAS)**, an emotional and psychological disturbance in which children engage in exaggerated and unjustified denigration and criticism of a parent (Gardner 1998). PAS has also been described as a form of child abuse in which one parent encourages the child to hate the other parent (Schacht 2000). Long-term effects of PAS on children can include long-term depression, inability to function, guilt, hostility, alcoholism and other drug abuse, and other symptoms of internal distress (Family Court Reform Council of America 2000).

Some noncustodial divorced fathers discontinue contact with their children as a coping strategy for managing emotional pain (Pasley and Minton 2001). Many divorced fathers are overwhelmed with feelings of failure, guilt, anger, and sadness over the separation from their children (Knox 1998). Hewlett and West (1998: 69) explain that "visiting their children only serves to remind these men of their painful loss, and they respond to this feeling by withdrawing completely."

In conclusion, we note that "while some children emerge from divorce with a strong sense of loss and feelings of anger or despair, others are capable of acknowledging that divorce has pain but also benefits for themselves and other family members" (Thompson and Amato 1999: xix). Factors that determine whether a child is scathed or strengthened by parental divorce include the quality of the child's relationship with both parents, the extent of ongoing conflict versus cooperation between the parents, and the economic circumstances of the child's household. In most circumstances, children adapt to divorce, "showing resiliency, not dysfunction" (Thompson and Amato 1999: xix).

parental alienation syndrome (PAS)

An emotional and psychological disturbance in which children engage in exaggerated and unjustified denigration and criticism of a parent.

5.6 Strategies for Action: Strengthening Postdivorce Families

Negative consequences of divorce for children may be minimized if both parents spend time with their children on a regular and consistent basis and communicate to their children that they love them and are interested in their lives. Parental conflict, in either intact families or divorced families, negatively influences the psychological well-being of children (Demo 1992). Ongoing conflict between divorced parents also tends to result in decreased involvement of non-residential parents with their children (Leite and McKenry 2000). By maintaining a civil co-parenting relationship during a separation and after divorce, parents can minimize the negative effects of divorce on their children.

What can society do to promote cooperative parenting by ex-spouses? One answer is to encourage, or even mandate, divorcing couples to participate in

divorce mediation

A process in which divorcing couples meet with a neutral third party (mediator) who assists the individuals in resolving such issues as property division, child custody, child support, and spousal support in a way that minimizes conflict and encourages cooperation.

divorce mediation. In divorce mediation, divorcing couples meet with a neutral third party, a mediator, who helps them resolve issues of property division, child custody, child support, and spousal support in a way that minimizes conflict and encourages cooperation. Children of mediated divorces adjust better to the divorce than children of litigated divorces (Marlow and Sauber 1990). However, Canadian family lawyer Linda Silver Dranoff has cautioned that mediation is not always feasible and that "[s]pouses who have been bullied or dominated during the marriage may not be capable of holding their own in mediation, while rigid or abusive spouses may not be capable of the necessary flexibility and compromise" (2001: 254).

Another trend aimed at strengthening postdivorce families is the establishment of parenting programs for divorcing parents (Shapiro and Schrof 1995). For example, the B.C. Ministry of the Attorney-General began a pilot program, "Parenting after Separation," which became mandatory in 2001 for all separated couples with custody disputes over their children. Such programs emphasize the importance of cooperative co-parenting for the well-being of children. Parents are taught about children's reactions to divorce, nonconflictual co-parenting skills, and ways to avoid negative behaviour toward their ex-spouses. In some programs, children participate. Taught that they are not the cause of the divorce, children learn how to deal with grief reactions to divorce and how to talk to parents about their concerns.

5.7 Nonmarital and Teenage Child-Bearing

In 1975, there were approximately 31 000 Canadian children born to not-married women (9 percent of all births). In 1996, there were about 103 500 births to not-married women and their babies accounted for just under a third (31 percent) of all births (Vanier Institute of the Family 2000: 55) (see Figure 5.8). To understand the rise in the number of children born to not-married women, we must consider several social factors. What happens when we assess these factors is that we see that nonmarital and early childbearing are not necessarily *problems*, though certain challenges can still arise for these families, especially where policy lags behind cultural change.

Having a baby outside of marriage no longer carries the stigma it once did. For example, by the end of the twentieth century all Canadian provinces and territories (except Alberta and Nova Scotia) had enacted legislation to dispense with the distinction that used to exist in law between "legitimate" and "illegitimate" children. As a result, in terms of financial support and inheritance rights, the legal distinction between children born within marriage and those born outside of it was eliminated (Dranoff 2001).

Singlehood has also become more acceptable and more common. The dictionary once defined a *spinster* as an unmarried woman above age 30. In previous generations, being a spinster meant the fear of isolation, living alone, and being somewhat of a social outcast. Today, women are "more confident, more self-sufficient, and...no longer see marriage as a matter of survival and acceptance" (Edwards 2000: 48). The women's movement created both new opportunities for women and expectations of egalitarian relationships with

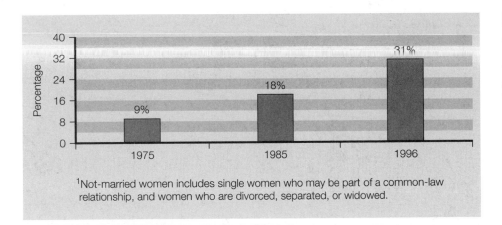

Figure 5.8 *Births to Not-married Women[1] as a Percentage of Total Births (1975, 1985, and 1996)*

SOURCE: Profiling Canada's Families II (The Vanier Institute of Family). Copyright 2000. Used with permission.

[1]Not-married women includes single women who may be part of a common-law relationship, and women who are divorced, separated, or widowed.

men. Increasingly, university-educated women in their 30s and 40s are making "the conscious decision to have a child on their own because they haven't found Mr. Adequate, let alone Mr. Right" (Drummond 2000: 54).

Increased acceptance of cohabitation and same-sex relationships has also contributed to the rising rate of nonmarital births. The term *nonmarital* includes births to the never-marrieds as well as the separated/divorced, widowed, and cohabiting. In 1996, three-quarters of all Canadian children born to not-married women were born into common-law partnerships. In that year, the highest number of births to women who were not married (50 percent) occurred in Quebec—the province with the highest proportion of couples living common-law (24 percent) (Vanier Institute of the Family 2000: 54). As such, "[t]he large majority of children born to mothers who are not married at the time of the child's birth nonetheless begin life in a family with both their biological parents present" (ibid). In other words, though these women were not married, many were in stable common-law relationships.

A recent comparative study of teenage pregnancy in developed countries placed Canada in the "moderate" rate category (45.4 pregnancies/1000 females 15 to 19 years old) (Singh and Darroch 2000). Canada's teen pregnancy rate was about half of the high U.S. rate (83.6), but higher than the low or very low rates found in most developed European countries, such as Belgium (14.1), Denmark (22.7), Sweden (24.9), and Norway (32.3) (Singh and Darroch 2000). Nevertheless, while the pregnancy rate among every other age group of fertile women is decreasing, the teenage pregnancy rate is increasing. Although well below their all-time highs, rates of teen pregnancies have increased from 41.1 per 1000 women aged 15 to 19 in 1987 to 47.1 per 1000 in 1995 to 59.2 in 1997 (Crawford 1997; Health Canada 1999). The number of live births is not as high as these figures suggest, however, because about 40 percent of teenage pregnancies end in abortion (Figure 5.9).

Teenage pregnancy has been related to a variety of factors, including low self-esteem and hopelessness, low parental supervision, and perceived lack of future occupational opportunities. Although lack of information about and access to contraceptives contributes to unintended teenage pregnancy, a U.S. study found that 30 to 40 percent of adolescent pregnancies are intended (Jorgensen 2000). Teenage females who do poorly in school may have little hope of success and achievement in pursuing educational and occupational goals. They may think

■ **Figure 5.9** *Percentage Distribution of Outcomes of Teenage Pregnancy, Women Aged 15 to 19, Canada, 1974 to 1997*

SOURCE: Dryburgh, Heather. 2007. "Teenage Pregnancy." *Health Reports*, Vol. 12, No. 1 Statistics Canada, Catalogue 82-003 http://www.statcan.gc.ca/kits-trousses/preg-gross/preg-gross-eng.htm.

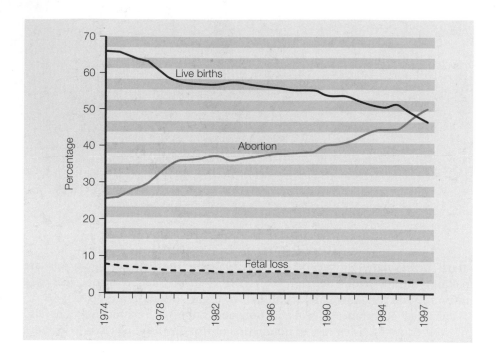

that their only option for a meaningful role in life is to become a parent. In addition, some teenagers feel lonely and unloved and have a baby to create a sense of feeling needed and wanted.

Social Problems Related to Nonmarital and Teenage Child-Bearing

Many sociologists and the general public perceive teenage and unmarried childbirth to be social problems because of the adverse consequences for women and children that are associated with such births. This section outlines reasons for that perception and then presents a feminist view grounded in public health data that challenge this common perception.

1. *Poverty for single mothers and children.* Many unmarried mothers, especially teenagers, have no means of economic support or have limited earning capacity. Single mothers and their children often live in substandard housing and have inadequate nutrition and incomes. Even with public assistance, many unwed parents struggle to survive economically. The public bears some of the economic burden of supporting unmarried mothers and their children, but even with public assistance, many unwed and teenage parents often struggle to survive economically. While child poverty in Canada is not restricted to single-parent families, a far higher proportion of children living with single parents, especially lone-parent mothers, live in low-income circumstances (Reidmann et al. 2003).

2. *Poor health outcomes.* Compared with older pregnant women, pregnant teenagers are less likely to receive timely prenatal care and to gain adequate weight; they are also more likely to smoke and use alcohol and drugs during pregnancy (Jorgensen 2000; Ventura et al. 2000). As a consequence of these and other factors, infants born to teenagers are at

higher risk of low birth weight, of premature birth, and of dying in the first year of life.

3. *Low academic achievement.* Low academic achievement is both a contributing factor and a potential outcome of teenage parenthood. Teens whose parents have not graduated from high school are at higher risk for becoming pregnant (Hogan et al. 2000). Three-fifths of teenage mothers drop out of school; as a consequence, they have a much higher probability of being poor throughout their lives. Because poverty is linked to unmarried parenthood, a cycle of successive generations of teenage pregnancy may develop.

   Some research has found that children of single mothers are more prone to academic problems. However, recent findings indicate that the mother's educational level and ability, rather than the absence of a father, have the most influence on a child's school readiness (Drummond 2000).

4. *Children without fathers.* Shapiro and Schrof (1995) report that children who grow up without fathers are more likely to drop out of school, be unemployed, abuse drugs, experience mental illness, and be a target of child sexual abuse. They also note that "a missing father is a better predictor of criminal activity than race or poverty" (p. 39).

   Others argue that the absence of a father is not, in and of itself, damaging to children. Rather, other conditions associated with female-headed, single-parent families may bring negative outcomes for children. These include low educational attainment of the mother, poverty, and lack of child supervision.

Challenging the Mainstream View of Teenage Child-Bearing

Arline Geronimus is a U.S.-based public health researcher. Her work on teenage mothers shows that the conclusions discussed above with regard to early child-bearing use a white, middle-class population as the benchmark against which all other lives should be assessed. Geronimus argues that delaying child-bearing at least to one's mid-20s is best understood as an adaptive strategy tied to the need to maximize the potential benefits of industrial capitalism, even while surrendering to the mechanisms of a system that render young families especially vulnerable. For those who have something to gain in a system that privileges the middle class, especially those of Euro-American background, delayed child-bearing makes sense; however, for those who have little hope of accessing those limited freedoms, an alternate adaptive strategy may be more useful: early child-bearing (2003: 882). Insofar as there is a crisis in early child-bearing, Geronimus demonstrates, it comes in the general vilification of young black mothers, who form a minority of teen mothers. However, the teen birth rate is higher for young black women than it is for young white women (p. 888).

Geronimus explains that recent welfare reform in the United States punishes young black mothers in particular because the requirement that all adult family members be working "deplete[s] the reserve of kin members available to offer childcare to the others" (p. 890). Similar changes in Canada do the same. As policy, such reforms are based on an inaccurate notion that the mothers would not have been working before. The presupposition is wrong, Geronimus concludes, because it assumes that early child-bearing will interrupt the many years of schooling required for career advancement—a future not open to the young black mothers she studies.

Moreover, Geronimus uses multivariate analyses to show that, if these same young mothers were to delay their child-bearing until their mid-20s, their risk for having babies of low birth weight would double, as would the infant mortality rate; if they delayed child-bearing until their 30s, the risk would be three times higher than for those who have their first children between the ages of 15 and 18 (1997). Current social reform to punish young women in the vulnerable groups Geronimus studies may cause further harm by removing from the mothers the extended kin and social networks available for economic, housing, and child-care support when the mothers are younger:

> Postponing childbearing increases the chance that her young children [will] compete with ailing elders for her energies and decreases the chance that their father will survive through much of their childhood. Her greatest chance of long-term labour force attachment will be if her children's pre-school years coincide with her years of peak access to social and practical support provided by relatively healthy kin. Her best chance of achieving her stated goals is by becoming a mother at a young age. (Geronimus 1997: 425)

Strategies for Action: Interventions in Teenage and Nonmarital Child-Bearing

Some interventions in teenage child-bearing aim at prevention, while other interventions attempt to minimize its negative effects. One intervention is to provide sex education and family planning programs before unwanted or unintended pregnancy occurs. However, sex education programs that emphasize abstinence and do not provide students with access to contraception are unlikely to be highly successful in preventing teenage pregnancy (Jacobs and Wolf 1995).

Other programs aim at both preventing teenage and unmarried child-bearing and minimizing its negative effects by increasing the life options of teenagers and unmarried mothers. Such programs encompass educational programs, job training, and skill building. Other programs designed to help teenage and unwed mothers and their children include public welfare prenatal programs, which help ensure the health of the mother and baby, and parenting classes for both teenage fathers and unmarried mothers.

Strategies to increase and support fathers' involvement with their children are relevant to both children of unwed mothers and children of divorce. These include promoting responsible fatherhood by improving work opportunities for low-income fathers, increasing child support collections, providing parent education training for men, and supporting access and visitation by noncustodial parents. Programs also focus on involving boys and young men in preventing teenage pregnancy and early parenting.

Because teenage parents are less likely than older parents to use positive and effective child-rearing techniques, parent education programs for teen mothers and fathers are an important component of improving the lives of young parents and their children. One such program that utilizes interactive computer technology is presented in this chapter's *Focus on Technology* feature. Geronimus's work, however, shows that conclusions about negative parenting are not as

Parenting Wisely: An Interactive Computer Parenting Education Program

Parenting Wisely (FamilyWorks, Inc. 2000) is an interactive computer parenting education program that teaches communication skills (such as active listening), assertive discipline (such as using praise and setting consequences), and child supervision techniques (such as how to monitor homework and friends). The program contains nine case studies depicting nine problems common in families. After a video of a family problem is shown, three possible responses are presented. Some responses result in a worsening of the situation; others improve the situation. Parents choose a response, see a video of how their choice would work, and get feedback on the pros and cons of their choice. Parents who have difficulty reading can choose to have the computer text read aloud. It usually takes two to three hours to work through the nine case studies.

The nine scenarios include two-parent, single-parent, and stepfamilies from diverse racial and ethnic backgrounds. Preteens and teenagers appear in the scenarios, but Parenting Wisely has been shown to be equally successful with parents of younger children.

Parents who are unfamiliar with computers, as well as those with computer experience, can use the program. It is designed to be entirely self-administered, eliminating the need for an instructor to guide parents through the program. Poorly educated parents without computer experience can easily use the program and commonly report that the program is fun and highly engaging to use (FamilyWorks, Inc. 2000).

How effective is the Parenting Wisely program? A summary of research evaluating the program reveals that parents with preteens and teens showing significant behaviour problems demonstrated increased knowledge in parenting principles and skills, increased use of the parenting skills taught in the program, and reductions in problem behaviours of their children ("Parenting Wisely Evaluation Results" 2000). In one study (Lagges and Gordon 1999), 62 pregnant or parenting teens were randomly assigned to either the Parenting Wisely program or to a control group. Both groups attended a teen parenting class in their high schools. Compared with the control group, the intervention group scored significantly higher at two months' follow-up in parenting knowledge, belief in the effectiveness of positive parenting practices over coercive practices (yelling and spanking), and application of positive parenting skills to hypothetical problem situations. In two studies, children's problem behaviour showed at least a 50 percent reduction one month after parents used the program ("Parenting Wisely Evaluation Results" 2000). A matched control group showed no improvement. In a study with teen mothers, use of the Parenting Wisely program resulted in improved knowledge of parenting principles and skills and problem-solving for toddler misbehaviour.

accurate as many assume them to be. Geronimus explains, citing the work of Carol Massat:

> several studies that employ more detailed multivariate analyses...fail to show teen mothers to be at increased risk of abusing or neglecting their children. No researcher of this topic has applied a research design to account for unmeasured factors...[but] the prevailing wisdom "that adolescent parents are more likely to maltreat their children than are older parents appears to be a myth entrenched in the popular culture." (1997: 413)

The harms that may come to children with young mothers are likely to be secondary to the social harms that compel young motherhood in the first place: increasingly poor health as one's population ages, poverty, lack of access to education and upwardly mobile work, and so forth. It is a research error to treat early child-bearing as the independent variable that influences all outcomes (Geronimus 1997, 2003).

Understanding **Family Problems**

Family problems can best be understood within the context of the society and culture in which they occur. Although domestic violence, divorce, teenage pregnancy, and unmarried parenthood may appear to result from individual decisions, these decisions are influenced by myriad social and cultural forces.

The impact of family problems, including divorce, abuse, and nonmarital child-bearing, is felt not only by family members, but by the larger society as well. Family members experience such life difficulties as poverty, school failure, low self-esteem, and mental and physical health problems. Each of these difficulties contributes to a cycle of family problems in the next generation. The impact on society includes public expenditures to assist single-parent families and victims of domestic violence and neglect, and to combat youth crime and lower worker productivity.

For some, the solution to family problems is rooted in encouraging marriage and discouraging other family forms, such as single parenting, cohabitation, and same-sex unions. But many family scholars argue that the fundamental issue is making sure that children are well cared for, whether or not their parents are married. Some even suggest that marriage is part of the problem, not part of the solution. According to Martha Fineman, "This obsession with marriage prevents us from looking at our social problems and addressing them.... Marriage is nothing more than a piece of paper, and yet we rely on marriage to do a lot of work in this society: It becomes our family policy, our police in regard to welfare and children, the cure for poverty" (quoted in Lewin 2000: 2).

Strengthening marriage is a worthy goal because strong marriages offer many benefits to individuals and their children. However, "strengthening marriage does not have to mean a return to the patriarchal family of an earlier era.... Indeed, greater marital stability will only come about when men are willing to share power, as well as housework and childcare, equally with women" (Amato 2001: 184).

Strengthening marriage does not mean that other family forms should be derided. The reality is that the family comes in many forms, each with its strengths, needs, and challenges. Given the diversity of families today, social historian Stephanie Coontz (2000: 15) suggests, "The only way forward at this point in history is to find better ways to make both marriage and its alternatives work."

Critical Thinking

1. Some scholars and politicians argue that stable families are the bedrock of stable communities. Others argue that stable communities and economies are the bedrock of stable families. Which of these two positions would you take and why?

2. Lloyd and Emery (2000: 25–26) note that "one of the primary ways that power disguises itself in courtship and marriage is through the 'myth of equality between the sexes'.... The widespread discourse on 'marriage between equals' serves as a cover for the presence of male domination in intimate relationships...and allows couples to create an illusion of equality that masks the inequities in their relationships." Do you agree that the modern view of marriage between equal partners is an illusion? Why or why not?

3. Assumptions about what makes a "good family" have influenced research programs. In some cases, conclusions are drawn first and the research is used to justify already existing prejudices. How would you suggest designing a research program on enhancing child welfare for the most vulnerable populations in Canada? What biases would you need to avoid reproducing from traditional research?

"Is It True?" Quiz: Answers

1 = true; 2 = true; 3 = false; 4 = true

Section 2

Problems of Human Diversity

People are diverse. They vary on many dimensions, including age, gender, sexual orientation, and race and ethnicity. In most societies, including Canada, these characteristics are imbued with social significance and are used to make judgments about an individual's worth, intelligence, skills, and personality. Such labelling creates categories of people who are perceived as "different" by others as well as by themselves and, as a result, are often treated differently.

A **minority** is defined as a category of people who have unequal access to positions of power, prestige, and wealth in a society. In effect, minorities have unequal opportunities and are disadvantaged in their attempt to gain societal resources. Even though they may be a majority in terms of numbers, they may still be a minority sociologically. Because the recognition of groups or of individual people is supposed to follow principles of human rights and social justice, regardless of *how many* members of a group there are, many contemporary sociologists prefer to speak of the manner in which some groups are forced or coerced into marginal social positions; we speak, therefore, not of a minority, but of a **marginalized** group. This section of your text recognizes the persistence of the common perception of groups as "minorities," and places that perception in relation to the problems of social inequality that result from marginalization.

Because the process of marginalization involves creating and maintaining *stereotypes*, *prejudices*, and *discriminatory practices*, we consider these processes throughout each of the chapters in this section. Stereotypes are built on sets of assumptions or generalizations about the characteristics of a group of persons. Prejudices are attitudes, often negative, that prejudge individuals and groups. In the sense that we use it here, discrimination refers to the differential treatment of marginalized groups by members of the dominant group and to the harmful effect on marginalized groups and persons. The groups we discuss in this section are all victims of stereotyping, prejudice, and discrimination.

Marginalized groups usually have certain characteristics in common. In general, members are aware of their marginal position, stay within their own group, have relatively low levels of self-esteem, are disproportionately represented in the lower socio-economic strata, and are viewed as having negative traits.

In the following chapters, we discuss categories based on age (Chapter 6), gender (Chapter 7), race and ethnicity (Chapter 8), and sexualities (Chapter 9). Although other categories of minorities exist (e.g., people with disabilities, religious minorities), we have chosen to concentrate on these four groups because each is surrounded by issues and policies that have far-reaching social, political, and economic implications.

The cost for victims of stereotyping, prejudice, and discrimination, as well as the negative consequences for a society such as Canada, which imagines itself as a multicultural, pluralist democracy, are considered. We also consider strategies for change and encourage students to recognize problems from the perspective of those who experience them rather than from the perspective of socially dominant groups.

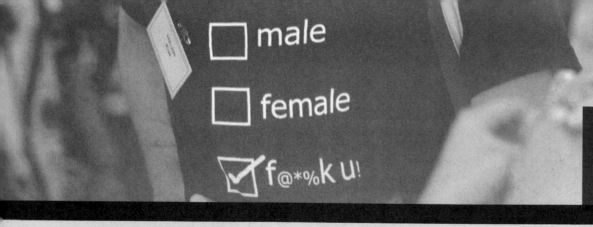

Youth and Aging

Is It True?

1. The concepts of middle age and adolescence have always existed.

2. Every society assigns different social roles to different age groups.

3. Poverty in childhood corresponds with school failure, anxiety and depression, and other health problems later in life.

4. In Canada, there has been a steady increase in the percentage of seniors with low income.

5. By 2011, almost one-quarter of the Canadian population will be aged 65 or older, nearly double the proportion in 1995.

Read more here: 1 = p. 186, 2 = p. 186, 3 = p. 194, 4 = p. 204, 5 = p. 199
Answers can be found on p. 216.

The young and the old are subject to different treatment in societies around the world. These differences in treatment have traditionally been associated with whether the country is more or less industrially developed. Although proportionately more elderly live in developed countries than in less developed ones, these societies have fewer statuses for the elderly to occupy. Their positions as caretakers, homeowners, employees, and producers are often assumed by those 18 to 65. Paradoxically, the less industrially developed the society, the more likely that society is to practise **senilicide**—the killing of the elderly. In some agrarian societies, the elderly are considered a burden: they are left to die or, in some cases, actively killed.

senilicide
The killing of the elderly.

6.1 The Global Context: The Young and the Old around the World

Not all societies treat the elderly as a burden. Scandinavian countries provide government support for in-home care workers for elderly who can no longer perform such tasks as cooking and cleaning. Eastern cultures, such as that of Japan, revere their elderly, in part because of their presumed proximity to honoured ancestors.

Societies also differ in the way they treat children. In less developed societies, children work as adults, marry at a young age, and pass from childhood directly to adulthood without a recognized period of adolescence. In contrast, in industrialized nations, children generally attend school for 12 to 16 years and thus remain financially and emotionally dependent on their families for an extended period.

Because of this extended dependency, Canada treats minors differently from adults. Juveniles have a separate justice system and minimum ages for driving, drinking alcohol, joining the military, entering into a contract, marrying, dropping out of school, and voting. These limitations would not be tolerated if placed on individuals on the basis of sex or race. Hence, **ageism**—the belief that age is associated with certain psychological, behavioural, or intellectual traits, at least in reference to children—is much more tolerated than sexism or racism in Canada.

ageism
The belief that age is associated with certain psychological, behavioural, or intellectual traits.

Despite this differential treatment, people in our country are fascinated with youth and being young. Not always was this the case. The elderly were once highly valued, and younger men even powdered their hair, wore wigs, and dressed in a way that made them look older. It should be remembered, however, that in 1901, only 5.05 percent of the population was 65 or older, and almost half the population (45 percent) was 19 years of age or under (Novak 1997). Being old was rare and respected; to some it signalled that God looked favourably on that individual.

Modernization theory argues that as a society becomes more technologically advanced, the position of the elderly declines (Cowgill and Holmes 1972). As land, often owned by elders, became less important, elders' knowledge and skills about land-based economies lost value. With industrialization, technological skills, training, and education became more important than land ownership.

modernization theory
A theory claiming that as society becomes more technologically advanced, the position of the elderly declines.

6.2 Youth and Aging

Age is largely socially defined. Cultural definitions of what it means to be "old" and "young" vary from society to society, from time to time, and from person to person. Where average life expectancies are very low, the old may be under age 30.

Age is also a variable with dramatic impact on a person's life. Matras (1990) identified the first four of the five points below:

1. Age determines life experiences, since the date of birth determines the historical period in which a person lives.
2. Different ages are associated with different developmental stages (physiological, psychological, and social), as well as abilities; they influence how one perceives and accesses the time period of one's age.
3. Age defines roles and expectations of behaviour. The expression "act your age" implies that some behaviours are inappropriate for people of certain ages.
4. Age influences the social groups to which one belongs. Whether one is part of a sixth grade class, a labour union, or a seniors' bridge club depends on one's age.
5. Age defines legal status. It defines when you can get a driver's licence, vote, get married without your parents' permission, and become eligible for social security benefits.

Childhood, Adulthood, and Elderhood

age grading

The assignment of social roles to given chronological ages.

Every society assigns different social roles to different age groups. **Age grading** is the assignment of social roles to given chronological ages (Matras 1990). Although the number of age grades varies by society, most societies make at least three distinctions: childhood, adulthood, and elderhood.

Childhood The period of childhood in our society is from birth through age 17 and is often subdivided into infancy, childhood, and adolescence. Infancy has always been recognized as a stage of life, but the social category of childhood developed only after industrialization, urbanization, and modernization took place. Before industrialization, infant mortality was high due to the lack of adequate health care and proper nutrition. Once infants could be expected to survive infancy, the concept of childhood emerged, and society began to develop norms in reference to children. In Canada, child labour laws prohibit children from being used as inexpensive labour, educational mandates require that children begin school by the age of six or seven, and the sexual exploitation of children is a serious crime.

sandwich generation

The generation that has the responsibility of simultaneously caring for their children and their aging parents.

Adulthood The period from age 18 through 64 is generally subdivided into young adulthood, adulthood, and middle age. Each status involves dramatic role changes related to entering the workforce, getting married, and having children. The concept of "middle age" developed only recently, as life expectancy has been extended. Some people in this phase belong to the **sandwich generation**, since they are often emotionally and economically responsible for both their young children and their aging parents.

Elderhood At age 65, a person is likely to be considered elderly, a category often subdivided into the young-old, old, and old-old. Membership in one of these categories does not necessarily depend on chronological age. The healthy, active, independent elderly, growing in numbers, is often considered the young-old; the old-old are less healthy, less active, and more dependent. (See Table 6.1.)

6.3 Sociological Theories of Age Inequality

Five sociological theories help explain age inequality and the continued existence of ageism in Canada. These theories—structural-functionalism, conflict theory, symbolic interactionism, feminist theory, and queer theory—are discussed in the following sections.

Table 6.1 *Myths and Facts about the Elderly*

Health

Myth The elderly are always sick; most are in nursing homes.
Fact Almost three out of four seniors aged 65 and older and living at home rate their health as good to excellent. Among seniors aged 85 and older, more than three in four rated their health as good or very good. The likelihood that an individual will live in a special-care home, such as a nursing home or hospital, increases with age; however, the 2001 census found that relatively few seniors live in such a setting (9.2 percent of senior women and 4.9 percent of senior men). Both of these proportions had declined from the time of the 1981 census (Dube 2002).

Mental Status

Myth The elderly are senile.
Fact Although some of the elderly learn more slowly and forget more quickly, most remain oriented and mentally intact. Only 20 to 25 percent develop Alzheimer's disease or some other incurable form of brain disease. Senility is not inevitable as people age.

Crime

Myth The elderly are more likely to be victims of crime than the young are.
Fact Although older people express more fear of crime than younger people do, "studies in Britain, the United States, and Canada show that older people run less risk of victimization than any other group" (Novak 1997).

Sexuality

Myth Sexual satisfaction disappears with age.
Fact Many elderly persons report sexual satisfaction. For example, in a sample of over 1300 respondents comprised of couples 75 years of age and older, over 25 percent reported having sexual intercourse once a week (Toner 1999).

Adaptability

Myth The elderly cannot adapt to new working conditions.
Fact A high proportion of the elderly are flexible in accepting change in their occupations and earnings. Adaptability depends on the individual: many young are set in their ways, and many older people adapt to change readily.

SOURCES: Binstock, Robert H. 1986. "Public Policy and the Elderly." *Journal of Geriatric Psychiatry* 19: 115–43; Canadian Press. 1999; Dube, Francine. 2002. "25% of Households Have Only One Person." *National Post* (October 23): A9; Mulligan, T., and R. F. Pagluta Jr. 1991. "Sexual Interest, Activity and Satisfaction among Male Nursing Home Residents." *Archives of Sexual Behaviour* 20: 199–204; Novak, Mark. 1997. *Aging and Society: A Canadian Perspective*, 3rd ed. Scarborough, ON: Nelson; Toner, Robin. 1999. "A Majority over 45 Say Sex Lives Are Just Fine." *New York Times* (August 4): A10.

Structural-Functionalist Perspective

Structural-functionalism emphasizes the interdependence of society. From a functionalist perspective, the elderly must gradually relinquish their roles to younger members of society. This transition is viewed as natural and necessary to maintain the integrity of the social system. As this process continues, each new group moves up and replaces another, benefiting society and all of its members.

According to **disengagement theory**, the elderly gradually withdraw as they prepare for death, and society also withdraws from the elderly (Cummings and Henry 1961). Meanwhile, the young have learned through the educational institution how to function in the roles surrendered by the elderly. In essence, a balance in society is achieved as social actors fulfil the roles and functions of their respective age groups: the young go to school, adults fill occupational roles, and the elderly, with obsolete skills and knowledge, disengage.

However, given the increasing number of elderly who remain active and socially integrated throughout life, many sociologists now reject disengagement theory. **Activity theory** emphasizes that the elderly disengage in part because they are structurally segregated and isolated, not because of a natural tendency to do so. For those elderly who remain active, role loss may be minimal. In studying 1720 respondents who reported using a senior centre in the previous year, Miner and colleagues (1993) found that those who used the centre were less disengaged and more socially active than those who did not use it.

Conflict Perspective

The conflict perspective focuses on age grading as another form of inequality—both the young and the old occupy subordinate statuses. Some conflict theorists emphasize that individuals at both ends of the age continuum are superfluous to a capitalist economy. Children are untrained, inexperienced, and neither actively producing nor consuming in an economy that requires both. Similarly, the elderly, although once working, are no longer productive and often lack required skills and levels of education. Hence, children are required to go to school in preparation for entry into a capitalist economy, and the elderly are forced to retire.

Other conflict theorists focus on how different age strata represent different interest groups that compete with one another for scarce resources. Debates about funding for public schools, child health programs, and social security largely represent the conflicting interests of the young versus the old.

In spite of popular beliefs that children have easy and secure lives, the Canadian Red Cross has identified these serious problems for Canadian children:

- 25 percent of all children experience abuse before age 16
- boys aged 4 to 7 experience three times greater incidence of sexual abuse than boys in any other age group
- 75 percent of Aboriginal girls under age 18 have been abused
- 8 percent of students experience bullying at school at least once a week
- bullying occurs every seven minutes in schools, but teachers are aware of only 4 percent of all incidents

Symbolic Interactionist Perspective

The symbolic interactionist perspective emphasizes the importance of examining the social meaning and definitions associated with age. Teenagers are often portrayed as

disengagement theory

A theory claiming that the elderly disengage from productive social roles to relinquish these roles to younger members of society. As this process continues, each new group moves up and replaces another, which, according to disengagement theory, benefits society and all of its members.

activity theory

A theory that emphasizes that the elderly disengage, in part, because they are structurally segregated and isolated with few opportunities to take active roles.

lazy, aimless, and awkward. The elderly are also defined in stereotypical ways, contributing to a host of myths about the inevitability of physical and mental decline.

Media portrayals contribute to the negative image of the elderly. The young are typically portrayed in active, vital roles and are often overrepresented in commercials. In contrast, the elderly are portrayed as difficult, complaining, and burdensome; they are often underrepresented in commercials. A study of the elderly in popular films from the 1940s through the 1980s concluded that "older individuals of both genders were portrayed as less friendly, having less romantic activity, and enjoying fewer positive outcomes than younger characters at a movie's conclusion" (Brazzini et al. 1997: 541).

The elderly are also portrayed as childlike in terms of clothes, facial expressions, temperament, and activities—a phenomenon known as **infantilizing elders** (Arluke and Levin 1990). For example, young and old are often paired together. When Grandpa Simpson babysits Bart and his siblings, he invariably falls asleep before Bart's baby sister, Maggie. In popular film the elderly are frequently portrayed as cranky curmudgeons who can't navigate the contemporary world. Finally, the elderly are often depicted in role reversal, cared for by their adult children as in the situation comedies *Golden Girls* and *Frasier*.

Negative stereotypes and media images of the elderly engender **gerontophobia**—a shared fear or dread of the elderly. This feeling may create a self-fulfilling prophecy. In one study, seniors received one of two types of subliminal messages—those negatively stereotyping the elderly (e.g., senile) and those positively stereotyping the elderly (e.g., wise). Compared with those who received negative messages, subjects who received the positive messages scored better on memory tests and were more likely to respond that they would accept life-prolonging health interventions (Begley 2000).

infantilizing elders

The portrayal of the elderly in the media as childlike in terms of clothes, facial expression, temperament, and activities.

gerontophobia

Fear or dread of the elderly.

Feminist Perspectives

Feminist views on aging have developed partly out of interest in gender-based power differences that can be exaggerated as women grow old, and out of interest in experiences that young girls face as they cope with mixed messages about their bodies and sexuality. One such mixed message is that a pubertal body is a sexual one, yet children must be sexually innocent. Recent work has examined how such contradictory expectations can be especially damaging to girls who experience puberty at very early ages (Liao et al. 2005). Popular, persistent messages that a young girl has somehow caused her own pubertal changes by having sexual thoughts form the backdrop for this kind of feminist analysis.

Contemporary feminist work builds on its established demonstration that women face problems of social devaluing as they move beyond their reproductive years. It goes on to examine how gender stereotyping can also have a negative impact on men—as with the insistence that "successful aging" is tied to the ability to maintain sexual virility (Calasanti and King 2005).

Feminist gerontologists challenge us to analyze how we perceive and structure what it means to be old and to examine the vulnerabilities of youth as each stage intersects with the demands of gender expectations. Scholarship in the area has been transformed by feminist insights that question the popular meanings and perceptions of the old, and recognize that for men and women, both, there is not just one way of experiencing being old (Calasanti 2004: 305). Feminist approaches combine an understanding of both structural and symbolic operations in order to understand the vulnerabilities and value of the young and the old (Biggs 2003: 45).

Queer Theory Perspectives

While popular culture promotes a youthful image of gay and lesbian people in TV programs, such as *The L Word, Queer as Folk, Will & Grace*, and *Modern Family*, and queer culture itself can be very youth-oriented in its advertising and targeted publications (e.g., *Xtra Magazine* in Canada), some theorists point out that GLBT people also grow old. (*GLBT* means gay, lesbian, bisexual, and transgendered.) Recent critical work recognizes that growing old can present serious personal and spiritual challenges for men in gay communities and that they must rethink what it means to be a man while aging in the broader gay culture (Long 2001). Studies on gay, lesbian, and bisexual persons as they age suggest that, because they have had to learn to live with negative stigmas anyway, these seniors have **crisis competence**: the ability to cope more easily with adverse social situations (Kehoe 1989); as a result, the self-reports of older gays and lesbians suggest that they do not see themselves as old until past age 70. Conversely, heterosexuals tend to see themselves as old once past age 50 (Heaphy et al. 2004: 884).

For queer youth, their experiences of neglect and of abuse are often linked to homophobia that makes them vulnerable, not only on the streets where they may be gay-bashed, but also in the home, where they may face familial hostility over their sexuality. The very use of the term *queer* as a means of self-identifying is largely a phenomenon of GLBT persons who came of age during the 1990s expansion of rights movements for GLBT persons. The phenomenon of expropriating words from their negative context and deploying them as a positive self-identification is a symbolic, linguistic strategy that Mollie Blackburn (2005) refers to as "**gaybonics**," a crisscrossing of antiracist and anti-homophobic empowerment strategies.

crisis competence

The ability of those who live facing persistent stigma to cope more easily with adverse social situations than those who have not previously encountered much prejudice.

gaybonics

The expropriation of words from their negative context and their redeployment as positive self-identifications to combat racist and homophobic views and behaviours.

6.4 Problems of Youth in Canada

In spite of the presumed benefits of being young, numerous problems are associated with childhood. Indeed, some of our most pressing social problems can be traced to early childhood experiences and adolescent behavioural problems (Weissberg and Kuster 1997). What happens to children is increasingly defined as a social problem.

Children and the Law

Historically, children have had little control over their lives. They are forced to depend both on their parents and on the state. Beginning in the 1950s, however, increases to children's autonomy became popular and were codified in several legal decisions. In 1959, the United Nations General Assembly approved the *Declaration on the Rights of the Child*, maintaining that health care, housing, and education, and freedom from abuse, neglect, and exploitation are fundamental children's rights. Canada is a signatory to the *Convention on the Rights of the Child*, a treaty that has been described as "the most comprehensive human rights document ever adopted by the international community," and ratified by all but two countries (the United States and Somalia).

As required under Article 44 of the Convention, in 1999 the Canadian Coalition for the Rights of Children issued its first five-year nongovernmental progress report to the United Nations. Entitled *The UN Convention on the Rights of the*

Child: How Does Canada Measure Up?, the report concluded that Canada meets most of its obligations under the UN Convention. It notes, for example, that children's right to education is assured in Canadian legislation, which provides for primary and secondary schooling and requires all children to attend school. It acknowledges that the *Canada Health Act* provides free universal health care for all Canadians; that refugee children are eligible for health care, education, and settlement services in Canada; and that our provincial and territorial governments have a duty to intervene to protect a child at risk from abuse or neglect. At the same time, however, the report concludes that Canada had some way to go before achieving full compliance with the Convention:

- Canadian legislation rarely recognizes children specifically and few redress mechanisms are available to them. Thus, children's fundamental freedoms depend on the goodwill of adults. Rights education is not part of core curricula and children's convention rights have not been widely promoted in Canada. In child welfare cases, the child's best interests are weighed against parental rights. In other areas, children's best interests are ignored or interpreted without considering children's views. The general principle of maximum survival and development is not assured for our most vulnerable children: children with disabilities, Aboriginal children, and children in the care of the state.

- Where children live often determines the degree to which their rights are met. Significant differences characterize children's programs and services in different parts of the country. Home care services for families of children with disabilities vary widely, and an effort to create standards or even to define basic services is lacking. Child welfare services are often fragmented and uncoordinated within jurisdictions, and resources are unevenly allocated. For Aboriginal children living on reserves, delivery of services is further complicated by jurisdictional disputes.

- Resources for children's programs and services are often stretched or unstable. Cutbacks to education and the closing of schools undermine access to and the quality of education, especially in special education, citizenship, social studies, and the arts. Child welfare services have been subject to budget cuts in some provinces, despite growing caseloads, chronic waiting lists, and worker burnout. Even with the high number of Aboriginal children affected by disabilities, delivery of services in Aboriginal communities is generally poor or nonexistent.

- Aboriginal children have a disability rate more than twice the national average. They are at greater risk of school failure than other Canadian children. A disproportionate number are victims of abuse and neglect compared to non-Aboriginal children. The suicide rate among Aboriginal youth is about five times the national average.

- An estimated 535 000 children and youth under age 20 have some form of disability. Children with disabilities have varying opportunities to live "full and decent lives," yet the supports and services they need are considered only a privilege. Many families of children with disabilities lack adequate assistance. Early identification and intervention services are not universally available, and the right to appropriate education in the most enabling environment is not guaranteed.

- Our child welfare system continues to fail abused and neglected children. Inquests and inquiries into the deaths of children who were killed by their parents speak of inadequate risk assessments, insufficient training for social workers, a lack of service coordination and information sharing, a shortage of placement facilities, failed foster placements, a crisis orientation, and a lack of long-term planning for children in the care of the state.

- The refugee determination system is slow, and the long wait unduly prolongs uncertainty for children and their families. Family reunification is rarely dealt with in a positive and expeditious manner. The interests of children are ignored in decisions to deport parents. Children, even if born in Canada, do not have to be considered in deportation hearings of their parents.
- Federal and provincial legislation prohibits discrimination against people with disabilities, but people with disabilities, especially children, still experience prejudice. Young people with disabilities experience more abuse and violence than those without disabilities. In addition, dominant adult perspectives on disability issues continue to overlook children's unique needs. For example, provincial building codes include accessibility standards, but these were not designed with children in mind.
- The few complaint mechanisms that are available to children and youth tend to be difficult to access.

These issues remain salient concerns within the Canadian Coalition for the Rights of Children 2001 Report (Covell 2001). The 2001 Report emphasizes that despite unanimous support in Parliament for an all-party resolution to eliminate child poverty by 2000, "a substantial gap remained between promise and reality"—child poverty increased through the 1990s (p. 11) and remained roughly stable, with 15–16% of children living in poverty through the first decade of the 21st century (see Table 6.2). Among other identified shortcomings, the 2001 Report notes Canada's failure to repeal Section 43 of the *Criminal Code* (which provides a defence in law for those who use corporal punishment as a form of discipline) and to ensure that quality child care is both affordable and available (p. 31).

In 2007, the United Nations International Children's Emergency Fund (UNICEF) reported that Canada ranked 12th of 22 of the world's wealthiest

■ **Table 6.2** *Child Poverty in Canada 2000–2008*

Survey or program details:
Survey of Consumer Finances - 3502
Survey of Labour and Income Dynamics - 3889

Geography	Low Income Lines	Statistic	YEAR:	2000	2001	2002	2003	2004	2005	2006	2007	2008
Canada	Low income measure after tax[1]	Percentage of persons in low income under age 18 years		15.7	15.4	15.4	16.1	16.7	15.7	15.1	15.0	15.3

[1]Low income measures (LIMs), are relative measures of low income, set at 50% of adjusted median household income. These measures are categorized according to the number of persons present in the household, reflecting the economies of scale inherent in household size and composition.

SOURCE: Adapted from the Statistics Canada CANSIM database http://cansim2.statcan.gc.ca, table 202-0802 (Persons in Low Income), July 28, 2010.

nations with regard to child welfare. A similar UNICEF report criticized our failure to fulfill the mandate of the 1989 resolution to eliminate child poverty by the year 2000. It noted, "Amid definitional uncertainties [over the term *poverty*], Canada's target year 2000 came and went without agreement on what the target means, or how progress towards it is to be measured, or what policies might be necessary to achieve it" (UNICEF 2005: 19). Figure 6.1 shows the

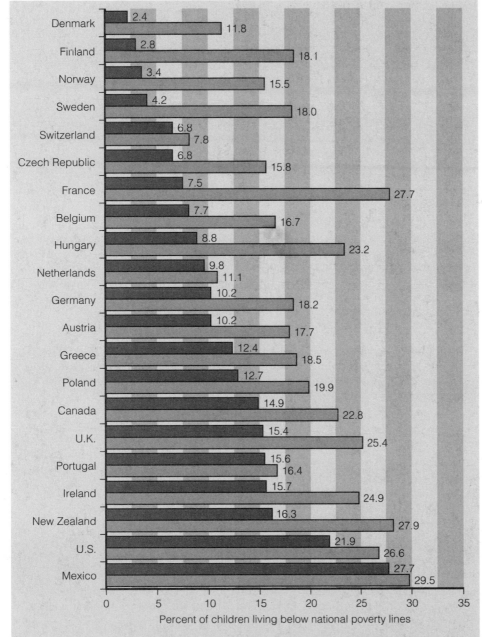

■ Figure 6.1 *The Impact of Taxes and Transfers*

SOURCE: Adapted from Figure 9 in "Child Poverty in Rich Countries—2005," *Innocenti Report Card No. 6*, 2005, UNICEF Innocenti Research Centre, Florence.

The light bars show child poverty rates based on household incomes before government taxes and transfers, while the dark bars show the rates after taxes and transfers. The poverty line in both cases is 50 percent of median post-tax and transfer income.

Table 6.3 *Who Is Likely to Be Poor? Percentage of Canadians Who Are Poor, By Age Group and Select Variables*

	Under Age 15		Aged 15 to 24		All Canadians	
	1996	2001	1996	2001	1996	2001
Total population	23	19	24	20	20	16
With activity limitation	37	28	38	31	31	23
Without activity limitation	23	18	23	19	18	15
Immigrant population	51	42	41	33	28	22
Non-immigrant population	22	17	21	17	18	15
Aboriginal population	52	41	45	37	43	34
Non-Aboriginal population	23	18	24	19	19	16
Visible minority group	43	34	39	32	36	28
Non-visible minority group	20	16	22	17	18	14

SOURCE: "Economic Security, Who Is Likely to Be Poor?," Calculations by the Canadian Council on Social Development using special tabulations from Statistics Canada's Census, 1996 and 2001. Used with permission of the Canadian Council on Social Development.

effect of increasingly conservative tax and welfare policy, demonstrating that when it comes to child population welfare, Canada is among the worst of Western industrial nations. The light bars show child poverty rates based on household incomes before government taxes and transfers, while the dark bars show the rates after taxes and transfers. The poverty line in both cases is 50 percent of median post-tax and transfer income. Table 6.3 shows that in spite of governmental promises and policies, we have made no real progress in eliminating poverty for those under age 18 in Canada.

Poverty and Economic Discrimination

Childhood poverty is related to school failure (Fields and Smith 1998; NIH 2000), negative involvement with parents (Harris and Marmer 1996), serious threats to health and limited emotional development (Brooks-Gunn and Duncan 1997), and a higher likelihood of dropping out of school (Duncan et al. 1998). Even research contesting traditional assumptions about a culture of poverty concludes that children who experience poverty also experience higher levels of anxiety and fear with regard to their own sense of safety: "relative levels of privation dictates that children and youth live within a context of relatively high levels of fear and victimization and that such jeopardy may produce lifelong disadvantage" (Eisler and Schissel 2004: 371). According to the National Longitudinal Survey of Children and Youth (NLSCY), one-quarter of children aged four and five from low-income households (less than $30 000 a year) scored poorly on verbal tests that indicate readiness to learn.

Children also face discrimination in terms of employment, age restrictions, wages, and training programs. Traditionally, children worked on farms and in factories, but were displaced by the Industrial Revolution. In the 1880s, the *Factory Acts* "curbed the employment of both women and children on the grounds of protecting their health" (Krahn and Lowe 1993); by 1929, children under age 14 were legally excluded from factory and mine employment in most provinces. Designed to protect children, the law was also discriminatory in that it prohibited minors from having free access to jobs and economic independence. No such law exists for any other age group.

Without access to their own earnings, those under age 18 are principally reliant upon their families for their stability and well-being. The Canadian Council on Social Development (CCSD) has analyzed primary data from Statistics Canada's survey of Labour and Income Dynamics, and notes that while average family income in the late 1990s and early 2000s rose by 19 percent to keep pace with inflation rates in the same time period, many families remained vulnerable: "[Income] gains were greatest among the wealthiest 10% of families with children: their average pre-tax income rose by 35%...to $208,300 [while] the poorest 10% of families'...average incomes had risen by 7%, to $16,100" (CCSD 2006a: 16–17). In Table 6.4, we see the differences in pre-tax income across the income deciles in Canada, from the poorest to the wealthiest in the years from 1993 to 2003. What the table renders obvious is that children, who have no choice about the conditions in which they live, experience wildly disparate levels of wealth and poverty in Canada. Although we cannot expect to have income data for the current recession, which began after the 2006 census was completed, we can logically assume that nothing about the vulnerabilities that children face would have improved in an era of high job losses, wage freezes, and property devaluations. It is not just income disparity and poverty that we need to be concerned about: a further concern is **depth of poverty**, or how far below and for how long people live below the low income cut-offs (LICOs).

Research from the CCSD underscores the well-known correlations between depth of poverty and general well-being: "deep and persistent poverty has a critical effect on both the short- and long-term development and well-being of children. For example, children who live in persistent poverty are less likely to be academically prepared to start school.... They are more likely to have emotional problems, to exhibit anxiety and aggressive behaviours, and hyperactivity" (CCSD 2006a: 18).

depth of poverty

How far below and for how long people live below the low income cut-offs (LICOs).

■ **Table 6.4** *Average Annual Family Incomes, 1993–2003*

YEAR	LOWEST	2	3	4	5	6	7	8	9	Highest	Canadian Average	Ratio of Highest to Lowest Decile
1993	$15 000	$25 600	$35 900	$44 700	$53 500	$61 800	$71 100	$82 300	$98 900	$154 100	$64 300	10.3
1995	$13 500	$24 700	$35 400	$45 000	$53 800	$64 500	$73 600	$85 000	$102 100	$159 200	$65 600	11.8
1997	$13 500	$24 000	$34 400	$43 500	$53 500	$63 400	$73 700	$85 600	$103 300	$169 500	$66 500	12.6
1999	$14 700	$27 400	$37 500	$47 400	$57 000	$66 600	$77 500	$90 900	$109 300	$186 400	$71 500	12.7
2001	$16 000	$29 200	$39 600	$49 200	$59 600	$69 600	$80 500	$93 800	$114 700	$204 300	$75 700	12.8
2003	$16 100	$29 500	$39 300	$49 100	$59 800	$70 200	$81 200	$95 400	$115 500	$208 300	$76 400	12.9
% increase 1993 to 2003	7.3	15.2	9.5	9.8	11.8	13.6	14.2	15.9	16.8	35.2	18.8	
$ increase 1993 to 2003	$1 100	$3 900	$3 400	$4 400	$6 300	$8 400	$10 100	$13 100	$16 600	$54 200	$12 100	

SOURCE: Calculations by the Canadian Council on Social Development using Statistics Canada's *Survey of Labour and Income Dynamics.* Used with permission of the Canadian Council on Social Development.

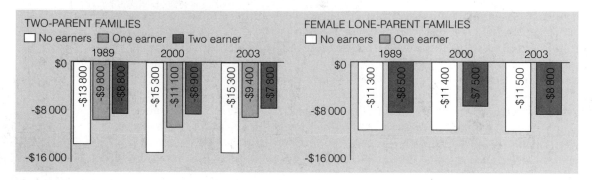

■ Figure 6.2 *The Depth of Child Poverty, By Family Type*

SOURCE: Calculations by the Canadian Council on Social Development using data from Statistics Canada's *Income Trends in Canada*, 2003. Used with permission of the Canadian Council on Social Development.

Figure 6.2 shows that in spite of Canada's declared goal to eradicate child poverty, the depth of poverty that children under the poverty line experience remains profound.

Young people in Canada often find it difficult to obtain any employment. In the years from 1994 to 2004, the unemployment rate for those aged 15 to 19 ranged from 18 percent in 1994 to 13 percent in 2004 (CCSD 2006b). The high of 18 percent may be attributable to the recession of the early 1990s. The CCSD points out that those who do find work tend to hold precarious, low-skill, low-wage jobs with few benefits; such jobs serve neither to build long-term pension security nor to provide effective "ports of entry" (CCSD 2006b). In addition, those who do manage to find work "are typically employed in low paid, tedious positions, often working long hours which interfere with school attendance and academic performance" (Covell 2001: 16). Contemporary changes in the international organization of economy and work "principally affect new hires. In other words, much of the impact falls on young workers entering the job market" (CCSD 2006b: 81). Such problems may contribute to conflicts between the young and the old over resources and benefits.

Kids in Crisis

Childhood is a life stage structured by socio-cultural forces of the past and present. The old roles for children as labourers and farm helpers are disappearing, yet new, clearly defined roles have yet to emerge. While being bombarded by the media, children must face the challenges of an uncertain economic future, peer culture, popular culture, divorce, incidents of abuse, poverty, and crime. Some parents and public commentators who are worried over children's involvement in sex, drug and alcohol use, and violence even argue that childhood as a stage of life is disappearing (Adler 1994). Other theories, such as David Elkind's concept of the "hurried child," had popular appeal in the 1980s. However, Elkind's premise, which includes increased divorce rates and open emotional displays in the home undermining childhood innocence, has been called into question. Some suggest that such worries are ideologically biased accounts that fixate on negatives in a small sector of the population:

Free the Children: Children Helping Children

Free the Children, an international children's organization with more than one million members in more than 45 countries, was founded in 1995 by Canadian Craig Kielburger, then 12 years old. Kielburger first became an advocate for children's rights when he read about the murder of a child from Pakistan who had been sold into bondage as a carpet weaver. Free the Children is a registered nonprofit charitable organization whose mission statement identifies two main goals: (1) to free children from poverty, exploitation, and abuse, and (2) to give children a voice, leadership training, and opportunities to take action on issues that affect them on a local or an international level.

Free the Children has flourished. Members have raised funds for the construction of more than 650 schools in rural areas of developing nations, providing education every day to more than 55 000 children. They have distributed more than 100 000 school kits and over $16 million worth of medical supplies to needy families. They also support potable water projects, health clinics, alternative income cooperatives, and schools in more than 20 developing nations. Their advocacy campaigns have encouraged Canada, Mexico, and Italy to pass legislation that better protects sexually abused children. They have lobbied corporations to adopt labels for child labour–free products. In 2001, Free the Children was selected by the United Nations and the Office of the Special Representative for Children in Armed Conflict to be the lead nongovernmental organization coordinating youth outreach for the decade of peace and nonviolence toward children.

Kielburger has received many awards for his work. These include the Nuclear Age Peace Foundation Award for Leadership in Peace Building (2000), the Roosevelt Freedom Medal (1998), the Governor General's Medal of Meritorious Service (1998), and the State of the World Forum Award (1997). In 2006, Kielburger was listed by The Globe and Mail as one of Canada's "Top 40 Under 40." At age 23, he was the youngest person on the list.

SOURCE: Adapted and abridged from freethechildren.org. Used with permission.

Despite some perceptive insights...their argument falls short on several grounds. First, in their tendency to romanticize families of the past, the authors gloss over the many hardships that children endured throughout history, as well as the fact that in every historical era the way children are raised has been deemed problematic. (Lynott and Logue 1993: 486)

Although past generations of children faced hardship, contemporary threats to children's well-being should not be ignored. This chapter's *The Human Side* describes the growth of an organization devoted to improving the lives of children worldwide. Launched by a Canadian youth, Craig Kielburger, the organization is run by children on behalf of children. Table 6.5 indicates the aspirations of Canada's teens.

6.5 Demographics: The "Greying" of Canada

The population of Canada, as in many other countries around the world, is "greying," or getting older (defined here as age 65 or beyond). In 2001, the median age—the point where precisely one-half of the population is older and the other half younger—reached an all-time high of 37.6 years (see Figure 6.3) (Statistics Canada 2002). The increase in median age is one indicator of Canada's changing population structure.

The number of elderly is increasing for three reasons. First, the 10 million baby boomers born between 1947 and 1966 are aging. Second, life expectancy has increased as a result of better medical care; sanitation, nutrition, and housing improvements; and a general trend toward modernization. Finally, lowered birth

■ **Table 6.5** *Expectations of Teenagers*

"Do you expect to . . ."	% indicating "Yes"		
	Nationally	Males	Females
Pursue a career	95%	94	97
Get the job you want when you graduate	87	86	87
Get married	91	89	91
Stay with the same partner for life	88	85	90
Eventually stay home and raise your children	43	40	45
Own your own home	97	96	98
Be more financially comfortable than your parents	81	82	80
Have to work overtime in order to get ahead	43	48	40
Travel extensively outside of Canada	79	74	83
Be involved in your community	68	67	70
Some day get to where you want to be in life	95	94	96

SOURCES: Bibby, Reginald W. 2009, *The Emerging Millennials*. Lethbridge: Project Canada Books, pp. 105–203; Bibby, Reginald W., The Project Teen Canada 2008 National Survey.

rates mean fewer children and a higher percentage of the elderly. While those aged 65 or over accounted for 13 percent of the population in 2001, projections are that, if fertility rates remain low, their proportion will continue to increase in the years to come (Statistics Canada 2002).

Age Pyramids

age pyramids

Graphlike presentations that show the percentage of a population in various age groups.

Age pyramids are a way of showing in graph form the percentage of a population in various age groups. In 1901, the Canadian age pyramid looked very much like a true pyramid: the base of the pyramid was large, indicating that most people were in their younger years, and the top of the pyramid was much smaller, showing that only a small percentage of the population was elderly. However, by 2001 Canada's age pyramid scarcely resembles a pyramid at all, and reflects the aging of the Canadian population. By the time of the 2006 census, the percentage of the population over age 65 hovered just below 14 percent at 13.7 percent, while the under-15 population had fallen to a record low at 17.7 percent of the population (compare Figure 6.4 and Figure 6.5).

The number of people at various ages in a society is important because the demand for housing, education, health care, and jobs varies as different age groups, particularly baby boomers, move through the pyramid. For example, as Canada "greys," colleges and universities will recruit older students, advertisements will be directed toward older consumers, and housing and medical care needs for the elderly will increase.

Age and Region

Canada ages from west to east with one notable exception—British Columbia, a popular destination for many older Canadians. According to the 2001 census,

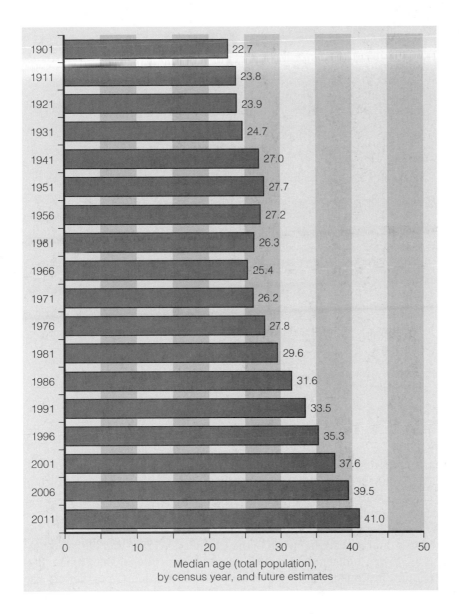

■ **Figure 6.3** *Canada's Aging Population, 1901–2011*

SOURCE: "Canada Facing Age Crunch," by Jennifer Lewington (*The Globe and Mail*), article dated July 17, 2002. Reprinted with permission from The Globe and Mail.

Median age (total population), by census year, and future estimates

Year	Median age
1901	22.7
1911	23.8
1921	23.9
1931	24.7
1941	27.0
1951	27.7
1956	27.2
1961	26.3
1966	25.4
1971	26.2
1976	27.8
1981	29.6
1986	31.6
1991	33.5
1996	35.3
2001	37.6
2006	39.5
2011	41.0

Canada's Prairie provinces (Alberta, Saskatchewan, and Manitoba), Ontario, and the territories have relatively younger residents, while Atlantic Canada and Quebec have populations that are older than the Canadian average. Nunavut and the Northwest Territories have the lowest median ages (22.1 years and 30.1 years, respectively), with the highest proportion of their populations below age 20. Reflecting the high fertility of both Nunavut and the Northwest Territories, approximately half (47 percent) of Nunavut's population, and over one-third (35 percent) of those in the Northwest Territories, are aged 19 and under; these figures compare to the national average of 26 percent. In 2005, the last year for which population data are available, the median age for Nunavut was just shy of 23 years, and is notable for being the only region in Canada with a median age under 30 (Statistics Canada 2005: 8). In general, by 2006 Canada's urban areas

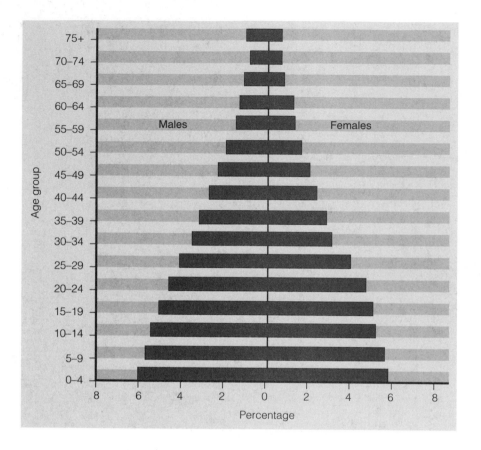

■ **Figure 6.4** *Canadian Population Pyramid, Age and Sex, 1901*

SOURCE: From Mooney/Knox/Schacht/Nelson. *Understanding Social Problems.* © 2005 Nelson Education Ltd. Reproduced by permission. www.cengage.com/permissions.

had a larger working-age population between the ages of 20 and 44; this concentration of a younger workforce has primarily to do with migration out of rural areas (leaving more older people behind) and into larger urban centres (thus reducing the concentration of older people in those areas) where there are more employment opportunities (Statistics Canada 2007).

With birth rates that are higher than the Canadian average and life expectancies that are lower, Indigenous peoples as a group are younger than non-Indigenous peoples in Canada. The high fertility of the Aboriginal population also affects the age profiles of Manitoba and Saskatchewan. The older population of Canada's Atlantic region reflects two factors: low fertility in recent years and the exodus of the young to other areas of Canada. The aging of Quebec's population is largely the result of the low fertility rate in that province.

Age and Gender

sex ratio

The ratio of men to women in a given society or subgroup of society.

The **sex ratio**—the ratio of men to women in a given society or subgroup of society—is expressed in one number: the number of males to every 100 females. The sex ratio reported for the last Canadian census was 96 males to every 100 females. In 2006, out of a total population of 31 612 895, about 51 percent were female, and their median age was 40.4. The median age of males in Canada was a little younger, at 38.6. These differences in median age grow more disparate as men and women get older. In 2006, there were only 71 percent as many men in the 75- to 84-year-old group, and roughly 45 percent as many men over age 85 as there were women.

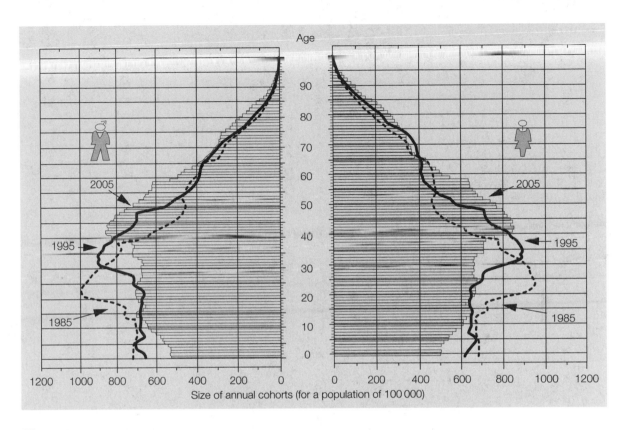

Figure 6.5 *Age Pyramid of the Population for July 1, 1985, 1995, and 2005, Canada.*

SOURCE: Statistics Canada, "Annual Demographic Statistics 2005," 91-213-XIB2005000, April 2006; http://www.statcan.gc.ca/bsolc/olc-cel/olc-cel?lang=eng&catno=91-213-X#olcinfopanel.

The imbalance in the sex ratio is particularly notable at older ages. In 2006, out of the total population there were 2 448 155 women over age 65 but only 1 887 100 males. These differences in the population of elderly people have sociological significance. Men die at an earlier age than women do for both biological and sociological reasons—heart disease, stress, and occupational risk (see Chapter 2). Because of differences in death rates and a greater likelihood of widowed men remarrying, older women are more likely to be widowed and to remain widows, while men are more likely to be married up until the point of death. From an income perspective, these patterns make it more likely that elderly women will be poor (Reidmann et al. 2003: 523).

Age and Social Class

Social class influences how long a person lives. In general, the higher the social class, the longer the person lives, the fewer the debilitating illnesses, the greater the number of social contacts and friends, the less likely the individual is to view him- or herself as "old," and the greater the likelihood of success in adapting to retirement. Higher social class is also related to fewer residential moves, higher life satisfaction, more leisure time, and more positively self-rated health. Functional limitations, such as problems with walking, dressing, and bathing, are also

Facts on Aging Quiz

Answer the following questions about the elderly and assess your knowledge of the world's fastest-growing age group.

	True	False
1. Lung capacity tends to decline in old age.	_____	_____
2. The majority of old people say they are seldom bored.	_____	_____
3. Old people tend to become more religious as they age.	_____	_____
4. A person's height tends to decline in old age.	_____	_____
5. The aged are more fearful of crime than are younger persons.	_____	_____
6. The majority of old people live alone.	_____	_____
7. The five senses all tend to weaken in old age.	_____	_____
8. Older persons who reduce their activity tend to be happier than those who do not.	_____	_____
9. Older persons have more injuries in the home than younger persons.	_____	_____
10. Physical strength tends to decline with age.	_____	_____
11. The aged are the most law abiding of all adult age groups.	_____	_____
12. Older persons have more acute illnesses than do younger persons	_____	_____

Answers: 1, 2, 4, 5, 7, 10, and 11 are true. The others are false.

SOURCE: Palmore, Erdman B. 1999. *Ageism: Negative and Positive.* © Springer Publishing Company, Inc.

---

lower among higher income groups (Seeman and Adler 1998). In short, the higher one's socio-economic status, the greater the likelihood that one will enjoy a longer, happier, and healthier life.

6.6 Problems of the Elderly

dependency ratio

The number of societal members who are under 18 or 65 and over compared to the number of people who are between 18 and 64.

The increase in the number of the elderly worldwide presents a number of institutional problems. The **dependency ratio**—the number of societal members that are under 18 or 65 and over compared with the number of people who are between 18 and 64—is increasing. By 2000, there were 62 dependents for every 100 persons between 18 and 64. Demographic statistics for Canada indicate a dependency ratio that ranges from 68 to 70 per 100 persons of working age in 2056 (Statistics Canada 2008). Some demographers propose that increases of this magnitude in the dependency ratios may lead to a shortage of workers, floundering pension plans, and declining consumer markets. It may also lead to increased taxation as governments struggle to finance elder care programs and services, and heightened intergenerational tensions as societal members compete for scarce resources (Goldberg 2000; Peterson 2000; Schieber 2000). In addition to these macro-level concerns, the elderly face challenges of their own. This chapter's *Self and Society* feature tests your knowledge of the aged and some of these concerns.

Work and Retirement

Retirement is a relatively recent phenomenon. Before social security, individuals continued to work into old age. Today, the proportion of retirees under age 60 is double the rate it was in the late 1970s, and one-quarter of all new retirees are between the ages of 55 and 59. In 1984, the Quebec Pension Plan reduced its minimum age requirements for retirement benefits to age 60 and, in 1987, the Canada Pension Plan followed suit. However, the desire to remain financially independent coupled with a lack of confidence in the social security system may encourage many workers to remain in the labour force past the minimum age requirements (Simon-Rusinowitz et al. 1996).

What one does (occupation), for how long (work history), and for how much (wages) are important determinants of retirement income. Employment provides the foundation for economic resources later in life. Depending upon where one lives in Canada, there are legal protections against being forced to retire. For example, on December 12, 2005, royal assent was granted to the Ontario legislature to repeal mandatory retirement; the new law allowing people to decide their own time for retirement came into effect on December 12, 2006. Some professions may still be subject to mandatory retirement, though; for example, the Supreme Court of Canada ruled in 1995 that mandatory retirement for police officers at age 60 was not discriminatory but a "bona fide occupational requirement" (Dranoff 2001: 71).

Reasons to get rid of mandatory retirement include acknowledgements that some careers cannot begin until over a decade of postsecondary education has been completed, that the task of mothering coupled with mandatory retirement means significantly reduced lifetime earnings for women, and that it makes fiscal sense for governments trying to reduce social welfare program costs to extend years in the labour force.

For the elderly who want to work, entering and remaining in the labour force may be difficult because of negative stereotypes, lower education levels, reduced geographical mobility, fewer employable skills, and discrimination. Moreover, Novak (1997: 197) notes that at least three economic forces may encourage Canadian workers to retire at age 65:

- Some workers with good pension plans may earn more money in retirement than if they keep on working. Taxes, the cost of commuting, clothes, lunches, and other work-related expenses can make working expensive.
- Most private pension plans begin to pay full benefits at age 65...[and] many occupational pension plans penalize a person for staying on past retirement age....
- OAS/GIS payments start at age 65, as do the Canada and Quebec Pension Plan payments. A person who works past age 65 will still get these benefits, but will lose a large portion of them through higher taxes.

Those who wish to enter the workforce at an older age or who, because of financial necessity, find it necessary to re-enter the labour force may be stymied in their attempts. The most common reason that workers over age 45 give for ending their job search is that no work is available. Evidence for the lack of work appears in the fact that, from 1976 to 1994, the average time that unemployed 45- to 64-year-olds were out of work doubled from 17 weeks to 33 weeks. From 1999 to 2001 approximately half of older workers—twice as many as those aged 25 to 34—were in jobs with irregular hours, lower levels of income, and poor benefits; moreover, workers between ages 49 and 65 were more likely than younger workers to be in these more precarious forms of employment for longer durations (Statistics Canada 2004). Although employers cannot advertise a position by age, they can state that the position is an entry level one, or that "two to three years' experience" is required (Knoke and Kalleberg 1994).

Those who do retire may find it difficult to cope with the symbolic message that equates work with worth. A job structures one's life and provides an identity; the end of a job culturally signifies the end of one's productivity. Retirement may also involve a dramatic decrease in personal income. While 60 percent of Canadian men retire between age 55 and 64, 27 percent are living in poverty on less than $10 000 a year, and only 5 percent have an income of over $45 000 a year (Dranoff 2001: 70).

Retirement Income and Poverty

Although the elderly and children are the groups most likely to be classified as low income, this pattern is not true for elderly people living in families. In 1996, the elderly in families were the *least* likely to be low income (8 percent), while children under the age of 18 were the most likely. In the last four decades, seniors in Canada have benefited from rising incomes. In 1951, the average senior earned slightly more than half the income of Canadians of working age; in 1995, the average senior earned $20 300, or almost $84 for every $100 earned by working-aged Canadians (Statistics Canada 1998). As we noted earlier, however, for women the risk of poverty in old age is greater than it is for men:

> In 2003, the low-income rate for women aged 65 and over was 8.7% compared with 4.4% for senior men. For the past decade, however, the poverty rate of older women on their own has varied between 27% and 19% with no significant downward trend over that period. In 2003, 19% of senior women on their own compared with 15% of unattached older men were considered low income. Average incomes of women aged 65 plus who were on their own and living in poverty in 2003 were $2,300 below the poverty line. (Townson 2005)

The Public Health Agency of Canada's 2005 report "Aging and Poverty in Canada" demonstrated that for seniors living below the LICO—the level of annual income determined by Statistics Canada to be necessary to meet minimum needs—the proportions broke down such that

- 18% of women over 80 years of age;
- 38% of women who were separated; 25% of divorced women;
- 17% of widows; 16% of single women
- 22% of tenants
- approximately 10% of disabled seniors
- 13% of immigrants and 225 of seniors from visible minorities

make up the 9 percent population of seniors living below Canada's low-income cutoff (PHAC 2005: 10). We see here a list of vulnerabilities that correlate with poverty, but the vulnerabilities of older women stand out in particular. Why are older women so vulnerable to poverty (ibid)?

When compared to Canadian men, Canadian women are far less likely to have access to private-sector pensions, such as those provided by employers to employees. In 1997, among Canadians 65 to 68 years of age, for example, about one in two men—but only one in four women—received some income from a private pension (Lindsay 2000: 142). "Certain groups, such as First Nations women and women with disabilities, are particularly unlikely to be covered by private pension plans, and the likelihood of poverty is particularly pronounced among elderly women with disabilities" (Nelson and Robinson 2002: 483).

The federal government encouraged Canadians to prepare for their retirement by increasing the maximum annual tax-deductible RRSP contributions to $22 000 in 2010. Even so, it is evident that not all Canadians can afford to pursue such options. Although about half of Canadians report that they are putting away money for retirement, in general, the more individuals earn, the more likely they are to save. The economic crisis that erupted in 2007 had a negative impact both on people's ability to save and on the value of their savings. Statistics Canada reported that by the end of 2008, 75 percent of private-sector employees were without a registered pension plan (RPP), and those who did have RPPs had seen the value of their plans drop in the economic crisis. Meanwhile, though our population's contributions to private pension plans had risen to 54 percent by the late 1990s, in 2008 that level had dropped back down to 50 percent. In other words, this represented a drop of 7.4 percent in those making contributions (Massoulay 2010). Perhaps showing considerable lack of faith in markets, the numbers of those contributing to RRSPs in the same time period had declined from a high of 41 percent to 34 percent by the end of 2008 (ibid). Though it may be decades before we see the impact of the declining ability of Canadians to save for their retirements, we can expect that future poverty rates for the aged will be exacerbated by the trials of the current economy.

At present, Canada's retirement income system comprises three tiers. First, governmental benefits—such as Old Age Security (OAS) and the Guaranteed Income Supplement (GIS)—are designed to forestall the likelihood of poverty by furnishing all seniors with a taxable, flat-rate benefit (adjusted every three months as the Consumer Price Index increases); these benefits are paid monthly regardless of work histories or life circumstances. Second, the government-sponsored Canada Pension Plan (CPP) and the Quebec Pension Plan (QPP) are designed to provide workers with a retirement income based on their pre-retirement earnings from ages 18 to 65. Third, there are private savings, which include employer-sponsored private pension plans, private investments, and RRSPs (Townson 1995).

OAS pension benefits are based on age and residency. A person qualifies for a full OAS pension after having resided in Canada for 40 years after age 18. Those who are ineligible for a full pension may receive a prorated, partial pension after a minimum of 10 years' residency in Canada. For the July–September 2002 period (amounts are adjusted quarterly), the maximum monthly OAS pension was $443.99. While OAS pension is payable at age 65, some exemptions exist. For example, in 2002, those Canadian seniors whose net incomes exceeded $56 968 yearly were required to repay some or all of their OAS benefits. The full OAS pension was clawed back when an individual's net income exceeded $92 381.

The GIS was introduced in 1966 to assist those seniors with little or no income other than their OAS pension. The amount given depends on the pensioner's income, conjugal relationship status, and whether the recipient's partner also receives an OAS pension or Old Age Allowance income. For example, the July–September 2006 rate for the maximum monthly GIS payment to a single pensioner, or to a married person whose spouse or partner did not receive such benefits, was $602.91. In addition, married or common-law spouses of pensioners (opposite-sex or same-sex), as well as the conjugal survivors of deceased pensioners, may also qualify for an Old Age Allowance provided that they are between the ages of 60 and 64 and qualify under an income test.

Although GIS and OAS benefits are unrelated to an individual's prior income history, CPP/QPP benefits are directly based on income earned between age 18 and the time someone claims retirement (between the ages of 60 and 70); the benefits proportionately reflect prior income patterns. Although full benefits do not begin until age 65, partial CPP/QPP payments can be received by retired persons, under certain circumstances, as early as age 60. In September 2002, the maximum pension payable at age 65 under the CPP was $788.75. Nevertheless, by the 1990s, "[t]he federal government was issuing dire warnings about the Canada Pension Plan's ability to meet its obligations" and forecasting that the CPP would be severely strained—if not depleted—by the retirements of Canada's baby boomers (Dranoff 2001: 314). One measure taken to avert this problem has been to significantly increase the contributions paid by workers and their employers.

Health Issues

senescence
The biology of aging.

The biology of aging is called **senescence**. It follows a universal pattern, but does not have universal consequences. "Massive research evidence demonstrates that the aging process is neither fixed nor immutable. Biologists are now showing that many symptoms that were formerly attributed to aging—for example, certain disturbances in cardiac function or in glucose metabolism in the brain—are instead produced by disease" (Riley and Riley 1992: 221). Biological functioning is also intricately related to social variables. Altering lifestyles, activities, and social contacts affects mortality and morbidity. For example, a longitudinal study of men and women between 70 and 79 found that regular physical activity, higher numbers of ongoing positive social relationships, and a sense of self-efficacy enhanced physical and cognitive functioning (Seeman and Adler 1998).

primary aging
Biological changes associated with aging that are due to physiological variables, such as cellular and molecular variation (e.g., grey hair).

secondary aging
Biological changes associated with aging that can be attributed to poor diet, lack of exercise, and increased stress.

Biological changes are consequences of either **primary aging**, caused by physiological variables such as cellular and molecular variation (e.g., grey hair), or secondary aging. **Secondary aging** entails changes attributable to poor diet, lack of exercise, increased stress, and the like. Secondary aging exacerbates and accelerates primary aging.

Although chronic ailments become more common with increased age, the most recently released Statistics Canada research on the lives of older Canadians reveals that a significant proportion—37 percent—of our elderly rate their own health as "excellent" or "very good." For those seniors who live at home, the self-reported health picture is even better, with three out of four rating their health as good to excellent (Statistics Canada 2006). The ability to remain in

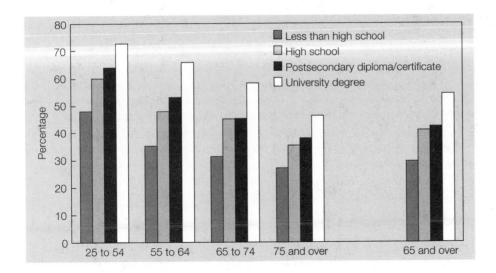

■ **Figure 6.6** *Percentage of Persons Reporting Excellent or Very Good Health by Age Group and Level of Education, 2003*

SOURCE: Statistics Canada, 2006. "A Portrait of Seniors in Canada." Catalogue No. 89-519-XIE, page 46.

one's home is influenced by wealth, which also has a strong correlation with overall health, so these results are not surprising. We can expect that persons with greater wealth will more frequently have better health, and retain their independence longer into old age. A second social determinant that corresponds with the health of seniors is education. Figure 6.6 shows the correspondence of education and health with those who hold higher levels of education showing greater levels of health throughout life.

Some disturbing evidence suggests that health care may be rationed on the basis of age in Canada. For example, in what is believed to be the first large-scale Canadian study to examine treatment for heart attacks among the elderly, the research concluded that "[t]he older you are, the less likely you are to be treated." The research, conducted by Paula Rochon, of the Baycrest Centre for Geriatric Care in Toronto and the Institute for Clinical Evaluative Science, was published in the November 1999 issue of the *Canadian Medical Association Journal*. It tracked more than 15 500 heart-attack patients aged 66 and older in Ontario between April 1993 and March 1995. The findings indicated that almost half (48 percent) of Canadian seniors were not getting the life-saving drugs that greatly improve the chances of survival after a heart attack. Among the 5453 heart-attack patients deemed to be the best candidates for beta-blocker therapy, 30 percent were not provided with these drugs. Women were significantly less likely than men to receive drugs, and seniors who lived in long-term care facilities were twice as likely not to be treated with them. The study also reported that when compared to those seniors aged 66 to 74, older, frailer patients were three times as likely not to be treated with beta-blocker therapy. Moreover, older seniors who received the beta-blockers were often prescribed doses that were lower than what is considered medically acceptable (Arnold 1999).

Living Arrangements

The elderly live in a variety of contexts, depending on their marital status, health, and financial status. In 2001, the elderly comprised over a third of Canada's one-person households, with women more likely than men to be

Children and Grandchildren as Primary Caregivers

The single most significant demographic change of the next several decades will be the dramatic increase in the number of elderly worldwide. The increase in the elderly is associated with a variety of concerns, including who will care for the growing number of the old. A study by Dellman-Jenkins, Blankemeyer, and Pinkard (2000) examines a recent trend in caregiving—young adult children and grandchildren as primary caregivers.

Sample and Methods

The present research focuses on three areas: (1) characteristics of young caregivers and the assistance they provide, (2) the consequences of being a primary caregiver for the individual, and (3) caregivers' social support. Specifically, the researchers "compared the caregiving motivations, experiences and support needs of young adult grandchildren providing assistance to grandparents with those of young adult children caring for their older parents" (p. 178). Participants were recruited from a variety of sources including social service agencies, hospitals, and assisted living facilities. An open-ended interview was used in conjunction with a 65-item questionnaire. The final sample was composed of 43 caregivers—20 daughters, 2 sons, 19 granddaughters, and 2 grandsons (N543). Eighty-one percent of the sample was white, 53 percent married, and 54 percent lived with the care-recipient; the remainder lived in a separate residence.

Findings and Conclusions

Caregiver Role and Assistance Given. Children, compared with grandchildren, were significantly more likely to respond that they were caring for their parents because no one else would. Grandchildren were most likely to respond that they were caring for their grandparent(s) out of a sense of duty and the desire to avoid nursing home care. Grandchildren also reported volunteering to care for grandparent(s) to help their parents.

> When Alzheimer's became apparent, my parents weren't coping well with it and were mean to her (not physically). I couldn't stand it ... I told them I would take her to my house. My dad told me it would be the biggest mistake I ever made. Three years later ... I still disagree.

The modal category for length of caregiving for both grandchildren and children was one to five years, with approximately equal proportions of both providing around-the-clock (47 percent) versus daily assistance (53 percent). Both sets of caregivers provided transportation,

---

divorced or widowed and living on their own. For example, for women between 75 and 84, 42.8 percent live on their own while 38.5 percent of women aged 85 and older live in one-person households (Dube 2002). In contrast, the majority of Canadian men between the ages of 50 and 89 are legally married and living with a spouse. Only among men aged 90 and over are fewer than 60 percent married and living with a partner (Reidmann et al. 2003: 483). The death of a spouse and encroaching poverty often mean that women must sell their family home and move to rental or institutional settings (National Council of Welfare 1998).

Most elderly do not want to be institutionalized, but prefer to remain in their own homes or in the homes of others, such as families and relatives. Some require elder care or assistance with daily living activities (see this chapter's *Social Problems Research Up Close* feature). However, they represent only a small proportion of the elderly population. According to the 2001 census, although the population aged 80 and older has increased 41 percent since 1996, the proportion of the population aged 15 and over which devoted some time to providing unpaid care for a senior was relatively small, at 18.2 percent. In 2001, approximately 20 percent of women and 15 percent of men reported

companionship and emotional support, personal care, and household support (e.g., cleaning house, paying bills, making appointments).

Consequences of Role. Caretakers in general, and single caretakers in particular, reported that caretaking activities interfered with their social life. All caretakers reported spending at least three hours a day in the caretaker role. One 20-year-old granddaughter commented that, "I sometimes get mad because I think I'm doing too much for my grandpa and I don't have a life of my own¼then I feel selfish for having such thoughts" (p. 184). Caretakers also reported strained family relations, particularly with spouse and children.

> I would like to go camping with my husband once in a while, but I can't just get up and go away, because of taking care of my grandparents. Even though they have the medical alert, I'm afraid they won't use it if something goes wrong.

Further, careers were negatively affected as relocating, job performance, and achievement of long-term goals became difficult because of the demands of caregiving. Both groups also reported increases in stress, although this was significantly higher for grandchildren (81 percent) than children (59 percent). Positive outcomes were also expressed, with over 97 percent of respondents identifying some benefit or reward. Grandchildren were most likely to note maintaining a strong relationship with the care-recipient, whereas children more often listed prevention of nursing home placement as the primary benefit.

Sources of Support. All respondents reported seeking informal assistance from some source. Children most often turned to their siblings for help, whereas grandchildren most often turned to their spouse or dating partner. Formal support, although seldom sought, most often came from nursing/home health-care providers or community support groups.

The two generations of care-givers, children and grandchildren, differ little in their caregiving activities, behaviours, and strains. They do, however, differ in their motivation to assist, with grandchildren more often noting attachment rather than need or obligation as the primary reason for becoming a care-giver. Further, the authors conclude, grandchildren are "more likely to report personal rewards (e.g., greater closeness, positive memories), while children were more apt to report instrumental rewards (e.g., providing quality home-care and avoiding nursing home placement)" (p. 185).

SOURCE: Dellman-Jenkins, Mary, Maureen Blankemeyer, and Odessa Pinkard. 2000. "Young Adult Children and Grandchildren in Primary Caregiver Roles to Older Relatives and Their Service Needs." *Family Relations* 49: 177–87.

providing care or assistance to a senior. However, less than 4 percent of women and 2 percent of men reported devoting more than 10 hours of such care in the week preceding census day (Statistics Canada 2002: 35). While well-to-do seniors may opt to live in retirement communities that offer various amenities and activities, there are many other living arrangements that span shared housing, modified independent living arrangements, and nursing homes. With shared housing, people of different ages live together in the same house or apartment; they have separate bedrooms, but share a common kitchen and dining area. In modified living arrangements, the elderly live in their own house, apartment, or condominium within a planned community where special services such as meals, transportation, and home repairs are provided. Skilled or semiskilled health-care professionals are available on the premises, and call buttons are installed so help can be summoned in case of an emergency.

In 2001, 287 480 seniors lived in health-care institutions, including 9.2 percent of senior women and 4.9 percent of senior men (Dube 2002). Nursing home residents are not typical of the elderly—they are more likely to be widowed or quite ill or over 80, or without family to take care of them (Kinsella and Taeuber 1993). An estimated 7 percent of Canada's 3 800 000 seniors require institutional care, and 10.3 percent require some form of home care. In Canada, seniors are the "largest consumers of publicly funded home-care services"; in 1996–97, 5 percent of seniors aged 65 to 75 and 17 percent of those aged 75 and over used home-care services (Health Canada 1999: 166). However, the demand for both publicly funded long-term care beds and home care exceeds their supply.

Victimization and Abuse

Although abuse may take place in private homes by family members, the elderly, like children, are particularly vulnerable to abuse when they are institutionalized. Pillemer and Hudson (1993) conducted interviews with a random sample of nursing home staff and found that 40 percent admitted that during the previous year, they had abused patients psychologically and 10 percent admitted to abusing them physically.

The emerging profile of the abused or neglected elderly person is of a female, 70 years or older, who has physical, mental, and/or emotional impairments and is dependent on the abuser-caregiver for both companionship and help with daily activities. Studies have found that the neglected elderly are older than elder abuse victims are, and have more physical and mental difficulties (Wittaker 1996). Most often, the abuser tends to be an adult child or spouse of the victim who misuses alcohol (Anetzberger et al. 1994). Some research suggests that the perpetrator of the abuse is more often an adult child who is financially dependent on the elderly victim (Boudreau 1993). Whether the abuser is an adult child or a spouse may simply depend on whom the elder victim lives with.

Many of the problems of the elderly are compounded by their lack of interaction with others, loneliness, and inactivity. This reality is particularly true for the old-old. The elderly are also segregated in nursing homes and retirement communities, separated from family and friends, and isolated from the flow of work and school. A cycle is perpetuated—being poor and old results in being isolated and engaging in fewer activities. Such withdrawal affects health, which makes the individual less able to establish relationships or participate in activities.

For older women who are abused, the most common place for them to receive protection is through shelter services; however, qualitative research on shelter services shows that elder abuse victims are not well served by traditional shelter services, which lack understanding of the unique needs of elderly clients:

- Shelters may have higher noise and activity levels than is comfortable for older women.
- Some older women have difficulty fulfilling their work assignments because of their physical or mental conditions.
- The time limit on occupancy can be inadequate in terms of the complexity of some older women's problems.
- Shelter staff are usually unfamiliar with aging and the special needs of older people.
- Problems with health and mobility can hinder the use of shelters, with many lacking wheelchair accessibility.

- Most shelters are not equipped to provide the care needed by some women with health problems (e.g., assistance with bathing, eating, or other activities of daily living or dispensing medications).
- Older women may find it difficult to go to medical appointments and services, and most shelters are not set up to provide this kind of transportation and accompaniment. (Straka and Montminy 2006: 257)

While the common perception of elder abuse is that women are the most likely victims, research shows that when it comes specifically to the problem of abandonment, men are far more likely to be the victims. While only about half as many elderly men as women face physical abuse, a significant number report victimization annually (Mouton et al. 2001). What is remarkable about the problem of neglect faced by so many men is that much of the problem rests on "their refusal to allow for non-family caregiving" (Mouton et al. 2001: 20) when their families are either no longer living or are unable to provide care.

Quality of Life

Although some elderly do suffer from declining mental and physical functioning, many others do not. Consider that nearly half a million Canadians aged 65 or over regularly provide temporary or ongoing child care to their grandchildren, 7 percent spend at least five hours a week helping other seniors (with some providing over 15 hours a week), about 1 in 4 works as a formal volunteer, and 6 in 10 participate in informal volunteer activities (Vanier Institute of the Family 2000: 172).

It should be evident that being old does not mean being depressed, poor, and sick. Some research indicates that the elderly may be less depressed than the young are, with several studies concluding that the elderly may have the lowest depression rates of all age groups (Health Canada 1999). Other research suggests that depression is curvilinear with age, that is, highest at the extremes of the age continuum (DeAngelis 1997). One study suggests that depression of the elderly is better treated by exercise than medication alone, or by medication and exercise combined (Livni 2000).

Among the elderly who are depressed, two social factors tend to be in operation. One is society's negative attitude toward the elderly. Words and phrases such as "old," "useless," and "a has-been" reflect cultural connotations of the aged that influence feelings of self-worth. The roles of the elderly also lose their clarity. How is a retiree supposed to feel or act? What does a retiree do? As a result, the elderly become dependent on external validation that may be weak or absent.

The second factor contributing to depression among the elderly is the process of growing old. This process carries with it a barrage of stressful life events all converging in a relatively short period. These events include health concerns, retirement, economic instability, loss of significant other(s), physical isolation, job displacement, and increased salience of the inevitability of death due to physiological decline. All of these events converge on the elderly and increase the incidence of depression and anxiety; they may also increase the decision not to prolong life (see the *Focus on Technology* feature in this chapter).

Physician-Assisted Suicide and Social Policy

Given the dramatic increase in the number of elderly and the technological ability to extend life, the debate over physician-assisted suicide (PAS) is likely to continue. When 2000 doctors of terminally ill patients were surveyed, 6 percent said they had assisted in patient suicides and 33 percent said they would prescribe lethal amounts of drugs if permitted to by law (Finsterbusch 2001). Further, in a study of pharmacists in Great Britain, 70 percent agreed that it was the patient's right to choose to die, and 57 percent responded that it was also the patient's right to involve the physician in the decision-making process (Hanlon et al. 2000). However, while the "Canadian Medical Association's ethical guidelines state that physicians need not take heroic measures to keep incurable patients alive in the final stages of a disease, a physician might still want court direction in some cases" (Dranoff 2001: 323).

It is a fundamental principle of Canadian law that every adult who is capable of decision-making has the right to consent to or refuse medical treatment, even if the result of the decision is life threatening. For example, the courts have held that adult Jehovah's Witnesses can refuse blood transfusions even if doing so means certain death

(Dranoff 2001: 322). Refusing treatment or discontinuing treatment once in progress is an option as long as individuals are mentally competent. Nevertheless, the 1992 case of Nancy B. in Quebec alerted Canadians to the dilemma faced by some mentally aware patients with incurable diseases who are kept alive by modern technologies.

Nancy B., a young woman in her early 20s, was stricken with Guillain-Barre syndrome, which, in her case, proved unusually debilitating. After two years of being bedridden, unable to breathe without a respirator and paralyzed from the neck down, Nancy B. petitioned the Quebec Superior Court to direct her physician to discontinue treatment. A judge was called to her bedside to hear her submission, and ultimately granted her request. The respirator was turned off and she died under mild sedation. The action of her doctor was considered palliative in nature and, as such, the court concluded that no contravention of the Criminal Code had occurred. However, despite the court's ruling, it remains a criminal offence in Canada to "counsel, aid, or abet" suicide, punishable by a maximum penalty of 14 years' imprisonment. On the other hand, suicide and attempted suicide are not criminal offences. Had Nancy been able to disconnect her own respirator, she would have committed no offence; however, to avoid another being charged, she was forced to appeal to the court.

Even though prosecution is rare against those who have assisted terminally ill patients who expressed the wish to die, anyone who assists another to commit suicide has committed a criminal offence. In cases where a person—whether a doctor, spouse, family member, or friend—has assisted another who is not on the verge of death to commit suicide, the potential penalties are additionally severe. Under Canadian law, the helper "could face murder or manslaughter charges and be liable to life imprisonment, even if the help was requested and the helper acted out of compassion" (Dranoff 2001: 323).

The issue of physician-assisted suicide was also raised in the case of Sue Rodriguez, a 42-year-old Vancouver woman suffering with amyotrophic lateral sclerosis. ALS is a degenerative nerve disease also known as "Lou Gehrig's disease." Rodriguez sought a court declaration that she was entitled to receive assistance in committing suicide when her condition made it physically impossible for her to commit suicide on her own. Both the trial court as well as the B.C. Court of Appeal dismissed her application. In November 1992, in a videotaped presentation to a House of Commons justice subcommittee, Rodriguez urged amendments to the section of the Criminal Code that makes it a crime for one person to assist another's suicide. In 1993, when the case reached the Supreme Court of Canada, her life

6.7 Strategies for Action: Growing Up and Growing Old

Activism by or on behalf of children or the elderly has been increasing in recent years and, as the number of children and elderly grow, such activism is likely to

expectancy was between 2 and 14 months. Her request for physician-assisted suicide was denied in a decision split almost down the middle; five judges held that her appeal should be dismissed while four judges dissented for various reasons. Despite their ruling, Rodriquez committed suicide, aided by an unknown doctor, in February 1994.

The controversy surrounding patient-assisted suicide continues. In 1996, Nancy Morrison, a Halifax respirologist, was charged with homicide after she administered drugs to hasten the death of one of her terminally ill patients. Although "thousands of people signed a petition urging the province to drop the case …[and] a provincial court judge threw the case out in February 1998, saying no jury would convict Morrison, the Crown did not give up until … after its appeal to the Nova Scotia Supreme Court was dismissed" (Dranoff 2001: 324). Morrison was, however, reprimanded for her actions by the Nova Scotia College of Physicians and Surgeons after she admitted acting outside of the accepted standards of medical care.

Until Parliament decides to address this issue, the Canadian courts will have to decide each case on its own. Elsewhere, however, legislatures have already acted. For example, the state of Oregon recognizes the right of PAS with its Death with Dignity Act (DWDA). Two physicians must agree that the patient is terminally ill and is expected to die within six months, the patient must ask three times for death both orally and in writing, and the patient must swallow the barbiturates rather than be injected with a drug by the physician (Annual Report 2000). As of 2005, 246 people had died using the DWDA, or about 1 for every 800 deaths in Oregon in those years; however, not everyone who makes use of the DWDA dies by suicide. According to the annual report for the year 2005, 64 people had received prescriptions to end their lives under the DWDA, but by December 31, only half had used their prescriptions while 15 had died from their ailments and another 17 were still living. In 2000, the Netherlands passed a law that legalized PAS. The law requires that three conditions be met: that there be unbearable suffering, that the case be clinically hopeless, and that a voluntary request for assistance be made (Weber 2000).

One argument against PAS is that the practice is subject to abuses—an overburdened family pressuring a vulnerable loved one, a depressed patient making a hasty decision. Concern also exists that legalizing PAS may disproportionately end the lives of minority, ethnic, or psychiatrically disturbed individuals (Allen 1998). The disability rights organization Not Dead Yet points out that The Oregon Reports already demonstrate that the "safeguards" against abuse are not enforced or even documented…. "The lapse of up to 466 days from initial request for assisted suicide to death shows that people with non-terminal disabilities are receiving lethal prescriptions in violation of the Oregon law," says Diane Coleman, President of Not Dead Yet and co-author of the brief, "and the Reports demonstrate that ill and disabled people are requesting suicide for psychological and social reasons that could be addressed without killing the individual, but no one seems to care." Ellie Jenny, an organizer for Oregon's Not Dead Yet chapter, agrees. "When someone asks for assisted suicide because they feel like a burden, that means they're not getting the right support services, and that's not choice." (Not Dead Yet, Press Releases)

SOURCES: Allen, F. C. L. 1998. "Euthanasia: Why Torture Dying People When We Have Sick Animals Put Down?" *Australian Psychologist* 33: 12–15; Annual Report. 2000. "Oregon's Death with Dignity Act: The Second Year Experience." *Oregon's Death with Dignity Act Annual Report, 1999. Oregon's Death with Dignity Act Annual Report, 2005.* Center for Health Statistics. Oregon Health Division; Dranoff, Linda Silver. 2001. *Everyone's Guide to the Law.* Toronto: HarperCollins Publishers Ltd.; Finsterbusch, Kurt. 2001. *Clashing Views on Controversial Social Issues.* Guilford, CT: Dushkin Publishing; Hanlon, Timothy, Marjorie Weiss, and Judith Rees. 2000. "British Community Pharmacists' View of Physician-Assisted Suicide." *Journal of Medical Ethics* 26: 363–70; Leichtentritt, R. D., and K. D. Rettig. 2000. "Conflicting Value Considerations for End-of-Life Decisions." *Not Dead Yet.* 2005. http://www.notdeadyet.org/docs/press9.html. Poster session at 62nd Annual Meeting of National Council on Family Relations. Minneapolis, MN, November 12; Weber, Kim. 2000. "Dutch Euthanasia Law Passed by Parliament." *Lancet* 356: 1911; Weber, Kim. 2000. "Netherlands Proposal for Comprehensive Euthanasia Legislation." *Lancet* 356: 1666.

escalate and to be increasingly successful. For example, global attention to the elderly led to 1999 being declared the "International Year of Older Persons" (DHHS 1998), while "the first nearly universally ratified human rights treaty in history" deals with children's rights (UNICEF 1998). Activism takes several forms, including collective action through established organizations and the exercise of political and economic power.

Collective Action

Countless organizations work on behalf of children, some of which we have already noted. Others include Aboriginal Family Services, Adoption Council of Canada, Alateen, Boys and Girls Club of Canada, Canadian Child Care Federation, Defence for Children International, Global Alliance on the Sexual Exploitation of Youth, Save the Children–Canada, and UNICEF. Many successes take place at the local level where parents, teachers, corporate officials, politicians, and citizens join together in the interests of children.

Similarly, more than a thousand organizations work toward realizing political power, economic security, and better living conditions for the elderly. These organizations include the Seniors Computer Information Project (Manitoba), Saskatchewan Seniors Mechanism, Alberta Senior Citizens Sport and Recreation Association, Council on Aging of Ottawa-Carleton, Alberta Council on Aging, Assemblée des aînés francophones du Canada, National Advisory Council on Aging, Golden Age Association (Montreal), Society for the Retired and Semi-Retired (Edmonton), and the Canadian Association of Retired Persons (CARP).

One of the earliest and most radical groups in North America was the Gray Panthers, founded in 1970 by Margaret Kuhn. The Gray Panthers in the United States were responsible for revealing the unscrupulous practices of the hearing aid industry, persuading the National Association of Broadcasters to add age to sex and race in the Television Code of Ethics statement on media images, and eliminating the mandatory retirement age. In view of these successes, it is interesting to note that the Gray Panthers, with only 50 000 to 70 000 members, is relatively small when compared with the Canadian Association of Retired Persons (CARP).

CARP is Canada's largest 50-plus lobby group, with more than 400 000 members. A nonprofit association that does not accept funding from any government body, CARP speaks out on a wide range of issues important to those over 50. Its mandate is "to protect what we have and improve our lifestyle." Services of CARP include discounted mail-order drugs, investment opportunities, travel information, volunteer opportunities, a *Spamhunter's Resource Guide* offering practical advice for dealing with unwanted advertising offers, and news updates on issues of concern to those 50 and older. One of their most recent projects, in collaboration with the PRIME television channel, is a one-hour documentary about ageism, "What's Age Got to Do with It" (CARP 2002). There is also the Gay and Lesbian Association of Retiring Persons (GLARP), whose goal is to raise money to develop gay and lesbian retirement communities and retirement resorts (GLARP 2000).

Political and Economic Power

Children rely on others to advance their interests, while the elderly may be able to translate economic power into political. Children are unable to hold office or to vote, but child advocates have wielded much political influence in such areas as child care, education, health-care reform, and crime prevention. At the same time, because of their numbers, aging baby boomers may be particularly well situated to advance their concerns. One economist, noting that the elderly's economic power is considerable, has referred to the elderly as a "revolutionary class" (Thurow 1996). By 2030, almost half of all adults in developed countries and two-thirds of all voters will be near or at retirement age. The growing political power of the aged is already becoming evident: the Netherlands has a new political party called the Pension Party.

Understanding Youth and Aging

What can we conclude about youth and aging in Canadian society? Age is an ascribed status and, as such, is culturally defined by role expectations and implied personality traits. Society regards both the young and the old as dependent and in need of the care and protection of others. Society also defines the young and the old as physically, emotionally, and intellectually inferior. Because of these and other attributions, both age groups are sociologically a minority with limited opportunity to obtain some or all of society's resources.

Although both the young and the old are treated as minority groups, different meanings are assigned to each group. In general, the young are more highly valued than the old are. Functionalists argue that this priority on youth reflects the fact that the young are preparing to take over important statuses while the elderly are relinquishing them. Conflict theorists emphasize that in a capitalist society, both the young and the old are less valued than more productive members of society are. Conflict theorists also point out the importance of propagation, or the reproduction of workers, which may account for the greater value placed on the young than the old. Finally, symbolic interactionists describe the way that images of the young and the old intersect and are socially constructed.

The collective concern for the elderly and the significance of defining ageism as a social problem have resulted in improved economic conditions for the elderly. Currently, they are one of society's more powerful minorities. Research indicates, however, that despite their increased economic status, the elderly are still subject to discrimination in such areas as housing, employment, and medical care. They are victimized by systematic patterns of stereotyping, abuse, and prejudice.

In contrast, the position of children, while improving in some ways, remains tragic in others. Wherever there are poor families, there are poor children (see Chapters 10 and 11). Further, age-based restrictions limit their entry into certain roles, such as employee, and demand others, such as student. While most of society's members would agree that children require special protections, quality-of-life issues and rights of self-determination are only recently being debated.

Age-based decisions are potentially harmful. If budget allocations were based on indigence rather than age, more resources would be available for those truly in need. Further, age-based decisions may encourage intergenerational conflict. Government assistance should not be thought of as a zero-sum relationship—the more resources one group gets, the fewer resources another group receives. Nevertheless, some predict the emergence of a new generation gap in the next decade: one between aging boomers concerned with their pensions and personal security and their younger cohorts who will be forced to bear some of the burden for the boomers' support. This burden must be considered of especial concern within Canada due to the relatively large size of our baby boom generation and the boomers' approaching departure from the labour force. "Retiring baby boomers will have a significant impact on the size of the labour market, especially as relatively small cohorts of young people will be entering it. Boomers, those aged 37 to 55 in 2001, made up 47 percent of the labour force. Ten years later, almost half of the Boomers are 55 or over, and 18 percent are over the age of 60" (Statistics Canada 2002: 10).

Social policies that allocate resources based on need rather than on age would shift the attention of policymakers to remedying social problems rather than serving the needs of special interest groups. Age should not be used to negatively affect an individual's life any more than race, ethnicity, gender, or sexual orientation. While eliminating all age barriers or requirements is unrealistic, a movement toward assessing the needs of individuals and their abilities would be more consistent with the ideal of equal opportunity for all.

Critical Thinking

1. In many ways, society discriminates against children. Children are segregated in schools, in a separate justice system, and in the workplace. Identify everyday examples of the ways in which children are treated like second-class citizens in Canada.

2. Age pyramids pictorially display the distribution of people by age. How do different age pyramids influence the treatment of the elderly?

3. Regarding children and the elderly, what public policies or programs from other countries might be beneficial to incorporate in Canada? Do you think policies from other countries would necessarily be successful here?

4. The meanings and experiences of the aging process are interwoven with social interpretations. Some maintain that our society is characterized by a double standard of aging wherein women grow old and contravene standards of physical attractiveness at an earlier chronological age than do men. What examples can you think of to support or contradict this position?

"Is It True?" Quiz: Answers

1 = false; 2 = true; 3 = true; 4 = false; 5 = true

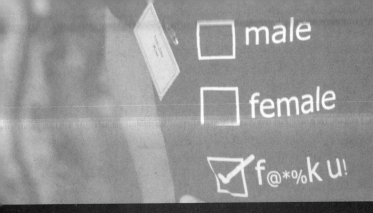

Gender Inequality

7

Is It True?

1. Worldwide, men are less likely to be able to read and write than women.

2. In general, women are socialized into expressive roles and men into instrumental roles.

3. In spite of pay equity legislation in Canada, by 2008 half of all employed women were not receiving equal wages for work of equal value to that performed by men.

4. In Canada, 9 out of 10 persons diagnosed as suffering from eating disorders are women.

5. Women in Canada occupy a greater percentage of legislative positions than do women in any other country in the world.

Read more here: 1 = p. 219, 2 = p. 222, 3 = p. 230, 4 = p. 242, 5 = p. 233

Answers can be found on p. 249.

© AFP/Getty Images

sexism

The belief that there are innate psychological, behavioural, or intellectual differences between females and males and that these differences connote the superiority of one group and the inferiority of another.

multiple jeopardy (also double jeopardy or triple jeopardy)

The disadvantages associated with being a member of two or more minority groups.

gender

The social definitions and expectations associated with being male or female.

sex

A person's biological classification as male or female.

In the previous chapter, we discussed the social consequences of youth and aging. This chapter looks at **sexism**—the belief that innate psychological, behavioural, and/or intellectual differences exist between women and men and that these differences connote the superiority of one group and the inferiority of the other. As with age, such attitudes often result in prejudice and discrimination at both the individual and the institutional levels. Physicians who will not hire male nurses because they believe that women are more nurturing and empathetic and are, therefore, better nurses, reflect individual discrimination. Institutional discrimination, or discrimination built into the fabric of society, is exemplified by the difficulty some women experience in finding employment; they may have no work history and few job skills as a consequence of living in traditionally defined marriage roles.

Discerning the basis for discrimination is often difficult because gender, age, sexual orientation, and race intersect. For example, First Nations people, members of visible minorities, and men and women with disabilities generally earn yearly incomes that are well below the Canadian average (Nelson and Robinson 2002). Women's earnings remain well below those of men. As of 2003, women in full-time employment still earned on average only 70.5 percent of what men did (Statistics Canada 2006: 152). Just getting to the point of having earnings can be a challenge compounded by one's race or ethnicity. Figure 7.1 shows how visible minority status can compound gender inequality in employment status. Such **double** or **triple** (or **multiple**) **jeopardy** occurs when a person is a member of two or more minority groups. In this chapter, however, we emphasize the impact of gender inequality. **Gender** refers to the social definitions and expectations associated with being female or male and should be distinguished from **sex**, which refers to one's biological identity.

7.1 The Global Context: The Status of Women and Men

The 2005 United Nations *Human Development Report* observes that from a global perspective, "Gender disparities are among the deepest and most pervasive of

■ **Figure 7.1** *In Spite of Higher Educational Attainments, Visible Minority Women Face Higher Unemployment*

SOURCE: Statistics Canada. 2006. *Women in Canada, 5th Edition: Women, a Gender Based Statistical Report.* Catalogue no. 89-503-XIE.

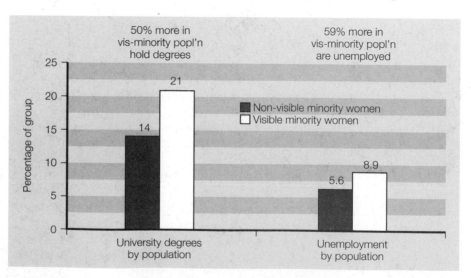

inequalities [and that disparity in developing nations results in] higher mortality rates among girls and women from birth to age 30 inverts the normal demographic gender balance" (2005a: 61). The report notes that inequality is not simply conceptual, but a concrete structural denial of health care, food, and social status.

A recent United Nations report finds that, despite some progress, millions of women around the world remain victims of violence, discrimination, and abuse (Austin 2000; Leeman 2000). For example, worldwide

- over 60 million young girls, predominantly in Asia, are listed as "missing" and are likely the victims of infanticide or neglect;
- two million girls between the ages of 5 and 15 are forced into the sex trade each year;
- half a million women die of complications from childbirth each year—20 times more are seriously injured or disabled in childbirth;
- two-thirds of the world's 876 million illiterates are women;
- one in three women has been abused, beaten, or coerced into sex.

An update on similar data indicates that these problems remain throughout the developing world, especially in sub-Saharan Africa and Asia where barriers to progress include the lack of representation of women's interests in workers' organizations and low representation in basic schooling. As a result,

women migrate to precarious and risky work situations where they are largely engaged in low-skilled occupations such as domestic work and entertainment, or worse, are trafficked in the commercial sex industry. (UN 2005b: 8)

One specific type of violence suffered by millions of women is female genital mutilation (FGM), also referred to as female genital cutting (FGC). Clitorectomy and infibulation are two forms of FGM. In a clitorectomy, the entire glans and shaft of the clitoris are amputated; the labia minora may also be excised. With infibulation, the two sides of the vulva are stitched together in infancy, leaving only a small opening for the passage of urine and menstrual blood. After marriage, the sealed opening is reopened to permit intercourse and delivery; however, the woman is often infibulated again afterward.

A World Bank report explains that FGM/C correlates with other practices. These include the refusal of condoms in some Roman Catholic communities and the prevalence of males who have sex outside of their marriages in other communities. Such practices may increase the risk for contracting infections such as HIV. The report is careful to explain, though, that practices vary widely, so FGM/C is not a reliable predictor for risk; rather, it is one of many markers for *potential* risks in behaviours specific to given communities (de Walque 2006).

Societies that practise clitorectomy and infibulation do so for a variety of economic, social, and religious reasons. Attempts to classify them in simple terms that see the roots simply as "male dominance" or as a form of cultural imprisonment do an injustice to the cultures and the women. Instead of providing reductive explanations, and targeting genital cutting practices for eradication, current wisdom argues that dealing with women's health and well-being in a holistic manner is more important. Ways of doing so include fostering "literacy, leadership skills, and social development, allowing women themselves to decide when is the right time to begin to address change in female genital cutting practices" (Gruenbaum 2005: 431). In short, women's oppression takes place in culturally complex circumstances; consequently, women require complex means of challenging and reducing those inequalities.

While it is easy to view "other" cultures in negative terms because of media fascination with practices such as female genital cutting, such a view neglects the problem of genital surgeries performed on children in North America. Across Canada, in highly specialized hospitals, children's genitals are altered to meet social gender norms regarding appearance, size, and "appropriate" masculinity or femininity. We will deal with this problem in more depth in Chapter 9.

Inequality in Canada

Although attitudes toward gender equality are increasingly liberal, Canada has a long history of gender inequality. Women have had to fight for equality: the right to vote, equal pay for comparable work, quality education, entrance into male-dominated occupations, and legal equality. Even today, most Canadians would agree that our society does not treat women and men equally. As discussed later, many national statistics support this belief: women have lower incomes; hold fewer prestigious jobs; remain concentrated in traditionally female-dominated fields of study at universities, community colleges, and trade apprenticeship programs; and are more likely than men are to live in poverty.

How much do you know about gender inequality's relationship to broad social inequality?

7.2 Sociological Theories of Gender Inequality

Both structural-functionalism and conflict theory concentrate on how the structure of society and, specifically, its institutions contribute to gender inequality. However, these two theoretical perspectives offer opposing views of the development and maintenance of gender inequality. Symbolic interactionism, on the other hand, focuses on the culture of society and how gender roles are learned through the socialization process.

Structural-Functionalist Perspective

Structural-functionalists argue that pre-industrial society required a division of labour based on gender. Women, out of biological necessity, remained in the home performing such functions as bearing, nursing, and caring for children. Men, who were physically stronger and could be away from home for long periods, were responsible for providing food, clothing, and shelter for their families. This division of labour was functional for society and, over time, became defined as both normal and natural. This perspective has been criticized by feminists, as we shall see, for taking a male-centred view of what is presumed to be beneficial for a society.

Industrialization rendered the traditional division of labour less functional, although remnants of the supporting belief system persist. Today, because of day-care facilities, lower fertility rates, and the less physically demanding and dangerous nature of jobs, the traditional division of labour is less functional.

Modern conceptions of the family, to some extent, have replaced traditional ones—families have evolved from extended to nuclear, authority is more egalitarian, more women work outside the home, and there is greater role variation in the division of labour. Functionalists argue, therefore, that as the needs of society change, the associated institutional arrangements also change.

Conflict Perspective

Many conflict theorists hold that the relationship men and women have to the production process shapes male dominance and female subordination. As society evolved to agricultural and industrial modes of production, private property developed, and men gained control of the modes of production while women remained in the home to bear and care for children. Inheritance laws ensured that ownership would remain in men's hands, furthering male domination. Laws that regarded women as property ensured that women would remain confined to the home.

As industrialization continued and the production of goods and services moved away from the home, the male–female gap continued to grow—women had less education, lower incomes, fewer occupational skills, and rarely owned property. World War II necessitated the entry of large numbers of women into the labour force, but in contrast to previous periods, many did not return home at war's end. They had established their own place in the workforce and, facilitated by the changing nature of work and technological advances, now competed directly with men for jobs and wages (Figure 7.2). Recent data on women's employment in Canada shows that, although more women are entering into what have been male-dominated fields—professional, management, and agricultural areas—their wages remain lower on the whole; they are also more likely to work in part-time positions (Statistics Canada 2006: 26).

Conflict theorists also argue that continued male dominance requires a belief system supporting gender inequality. Two such beliefs are that (1) women are inferior outside the home (e.g., they are less intelligent, less reliable, and less rational), and (2) women are more valuable in the home (e.g., they have maternal instincts and are naturally nurturing). Thus, unlike functionalists, conflict theorists hold that the subordinate position of women in society is a

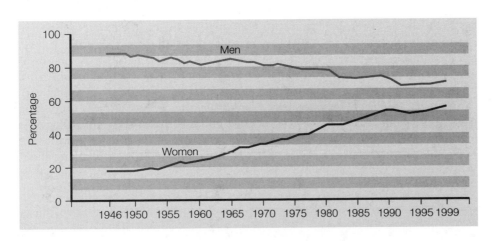

Figure 7.2 *Percentage of Employed Adults Aged 25 and Older, Canada: 1946–1999*

SOURCE: Crompton, Susan, and Michael Vickers. 2000. "One Hundred Years of Labour Force." *Canadian Social Trends*, Summer: 2–6.

consequence of social inducement rather than biological differences that led to the traditional division of labour.

Symbolic Interactionist Perspective

Although some scientists argue that gender differences are innate, symbolic interactionists emphasize that through the socialization process, both females and males are taught the meanings associated with being feminine and masculine. Gender assignment begins at birth, when a child is classified as either female or male. The learning of gender roles is a lifelong process, though, whereby individuals acquire society's definitions of appropriate and inappropriate gender behaviour.

We learn gender roles through family, school, and peer groups, and through popular presentations of girls and boys, and women and men. Most important, however, we learn gender roles through symbolic interaction as the messages others send us reaffirm or challenge our gender performances.

Feminist Perspectives

Feminist contributions to the study of gender have a complex history that many trace to the early contributions of Mary Wollstonecraft, who, in 1792, argued that Rousseau was wrong to have characterized girls as unworthy of education and unsuited to the demands of full citizenship. Feminist thinking is not, then, new, but developed out of and alongside the principles of Enlightenment thought: autonomy and rights for all citizens, the triumph of reason over superstition and prejudice, and the inherent value of human persons. Like other Enlightenment positions still important to contemporary social life, feminism "has an emancipatory goal. [It] is one of the social movements that—alongside the anti-war, youth, civil rights, anti-racism, and green movements—have in the last three decades reshaped modern politics" (Tepperman and Curtis 2004: 189).

What is unique about feminist thinking on gender is that, while classical structural-functionalists tended to see women's subordinate place in social structures as necessary and beneficial, and as a reflection of natural order, feminists showed that the benefits of women's subordination accrue principally to men. "Feminist scholars challenged the idea, embedded in functionalism, that **expressive** and **instrumental roles** in the family were necessarily divided along lines of gender, [and thus] disputed the idea that some family forms were more natural than others..." (Anderson 2005: 440 [boldfacing added]).

Feminism recognizes that the roles we are expected to perform as men or as women result from learning the social expectations of the worlds into which we are born. The idea that gender operates as a manifestation of social norms that vary from region to region has since been extended by the observation that everything we think about "sex" may also be an effect more of culture than of biology. As biologist Anne Fausto-Sterling (2000) has explained, as soon as we begin to talk about what the female sex or the male sex is *supposed* to do, we are talking about social imperatives; that is, we are discussing not biological truth, but social ideas. As Lorber (1998: 213) notes, building on Butler's idea of gender performance:

> Gender is so pervasive that in our society we assume it is bred into our genes. Most people find it hard to believe that gender is constantly created and re-created out of

expressive roles

The nurturing and emotionally supportive roles that women are generally socialized into.

instrumental roles

Task-oriented roles that males are generally socialized into.

human interaction, out of social life, and is the texture and order of social life. Yet gender, like culture, is a human production that depends on everyone constantly "doing gender."

Queer Theory Perspectives

At least since the French lesbian feminist Monique Wittig argued that lesbians were not women (1992) because the term *woman* signals a gender defined by its heterosexual attachment to men, queer scholars have been contesting approaches to gender that take as obvious two genders and that the two must be defined in opposition to each other.

One of the most famous contributors to the contemporary, complex understanding of how gender operates is Judith Butler (1990, 1993). Butler famously argued that gender is a form of performance, something that people have to work at in order to sustain socially meaningful positions as subjects; not something that we *have* but something that we *learn to do*, gender is a status under constant threat of dissolution because it is based in nothing concrete, but only in social mandates grounded in changeable ideological views. Butler's work set the benchmark for understanding gender as contingent, fluid, and unstable, not as a given and easy behaviour but one that has to be learned and constantly repeated if one is to maintain an identity.

Other scholars who have influenced sociological thinking about gender include Suzanne Kessler and Wendy McKenna (1978), who showed that our notions about gender can and should be "confronted with the possibility of other realities" (p. 164) evident in societies that actively recognize more than two, oppositional ways of being gendered.

7.3 Gender Stratification: Structural Sexism

Structural sexism, also known as "institutional sexism," refers to the ways in which the organization of society, and specifically its institutions, subordinates individuals and groups based on their sex classification. Structural sexism has resulted in gender differences in educational attainment, income levels, and occupational and political involvement.

Education and Structural Sexism

In the world's least developed countries, only 70 percent as many women as men are literate and rates for specific countries may be much lower. For example, only 31 percent as many women as men in Chad are literate; in Mali, Burkina Faso, and Yemen, only 41 percent; and in Mozambique, only 50 percent (UN 2005a). (See Table 7.1.) The United Nations observes that "Gender inequality is one of the most powerful brakes on human development. Women's education matters in its own right, but it is also closely associated with child mortality. The under-five mortality rate is more than twice as high for children of illiterate mothers" (UN 2005a: 31).

In Canada, the proportionate number of women with earned university education has increased noticeably over the past decades: "In 2001, 15% of women aged 15 and over had a university degree, up from just 3% in 1971" (Statistics Canada

structural sexism
The ways in which the organization of society, and specifically its institutions, subordinate individuals and groups based on their sex classification.

Table 7.1 *Gender Inequality in Education: Least Developed Nations*

Human Development Rank	Adult Literacy		Youth Literacy		Net Primary Enrolment		Net Secondary Enrolment		Gross Tertiary Enrolment	
	Female rate (% ages 15 and above) 2003	Female rate as % of male rate 2003	Female rate (% ages 15–24) 2003	Female rate as % of male rate 2003	Female ratio (%) 2002–03	Ratio of female to male 2002–03	Female ratio (%) 2002–03	Ratio of female to male 2002–03	Female ratio (%) 2002–03	Ratio of female to male 2002–03
146 Madagascar	65.2	85	68.1	94	—	—	—	—	2	0.83
147 Swaziland	78.1	97	89.4	103	79	1.00	12	1.03	5	1.16
148 Cameroon	59.8	78	—	—	75	1.00	36	1.21	4	0.63
149 Lesotho	90.3	123	—	—	89	1.07	27	1.53	4	1.48
150 Djibouti	—	—	—	—	32	0.80	17	0.69	2	0.81
151 Yemen	28.5	41	50.9	60	59	0.71	21	0.46	5	0.28
152 Mauritania	43.4	73	55.5	82	67	0.97	14	0.77	2	0.27
153 Haiti	50.0	93	66.5	101	—	—	—	—	—	—
154 Kenya	70.2	90	80.7	101	66	1.00	24	0.98	2	0.53
155 Gambia	—	—	—	—	78	0.99	27	0.68	1	0.29
156 Guinea	—	—	—	—	58	0.80	13	0.48	—	—
157 Senegal	29.2	57	41.0	70	54	0.89	—	—	—	—
158 Nigeria	59.4	80	86.5	95	60	0.82	26	0.80	7	0.69
159 Rwanda	58.8	84	75.9	98	88	1.04	—	—	2	0.46
160 Angola	53.8	66	62.6	76	57	0.86	—	—	1	0.65
161 Eritrea	—	—	—	—	42	0.86	18	0.74	(.)	0.15
162 Benin	22.6	49	32.5	56	47	0.69	13	0.48	1	0.24
163 Côte d'Ivoire	38.2	64	51.5	74	54	0.81	15	0.57	4	0.36
164 Tanzania, U. Rep. of	62.2	80	76.2	94	81	0.98	—	—	1	0.44
165 Malawi	54.0	72	70.7	86	—	—	26	0.81	(.)	0.41
166 Zambia	59.7	78	66.1	91	68	0.98	21	0.83	2	0.46
167 Congo, Dem. Rep. of the	51.9	65	61.1	80	—	—	—	—	—	—
168 Mozambique	31.4	50	49.2	64	53	0.91	10	0.70	(.)	0.73
169 Burundi	51.9	78	69.5	92	52	0.84	8	0.78	1	0.45
170 Ethiopia	33.8	69	51.8	82	47	0.85	13	0.57	1	0.33
171 Central African Republic	33.5	52	46.8	67	—	—	—	—	1	0.19
172 Guinea-Bissau	—	—	—	—	38	0.71	6	0.55	(.)	0.18
173 Chad	12.7	31	23.1	42	51	0.68	4	0.31	(.)	0.17
174 Mali	11.9	44	16.9	52	39	0.77	—	—	(.)	—
175 Burkina Faso	8.1	44	14.0	55	31	0.73	7	0.67	1	0.34
176 Sierra Leone	20.5	52	29.9	64	—	—	—	—	(.)	0.40
177 Niger	9.4	48	14.2	54	31	0.69	5	0.67	1	0.34

SOURCE: "Gender Inequality in Education," *United Nations Human Development Report*, 2005, Table 27, pages 147–177.

2006: 15); however, women's representation in advanced graduate degrees remains extremely low with only 27 percent of all completed doctorates going to women in 2001 (Statistics Canada 2006: 15) and 44 percent going to women by 2008 (Statistics Canada 2011: Table 1). Considering that women have been earning more undergraduate degrees than men in Canada for over a decade now, the drop-off in the rate of completion of advanced degrees for women should give us some pause. Additionally, while some traditionally male-dominated fields are no longer male dominated, women's participation levels in mathematics, engineering, and the physical and applied sciences remain relatively low (Table 7.2).

■ **Table 7.2** *University Degrees, Diplomas, and Certificates Awarded by Field of Study and Gender*

	2005/2006[r]	2006/2007[r]	2007/2008[r]	2008/2009	2007/2008 to 2008/2009
		number			% change
Total[1]	**1 050 225**	**1 066 905**	**1 072 488**	**1 112 370**	**3.7**
Male	**443 136**	**449 697**	**455 235**	**471 408**	**3.6**
Female	**606 720**	**616 953**	**617 022**	**640 674**	**3.8**
Personal improvement and leisure[1]	306	213	222	2 892	1 202.7
Male	105	93	102	1 167	1 044.1
Female	201	120	120	1 722	1 335.0
Education[1]	74 052	75 222	75 129	75 492	0.5
Male	17 694	18 018	18 105	18 051	−0.3
Female	56 325	57 171	57 000	57 405	0.7
Visual and performing arts, and communications technologies[1]	37 443	37 830	37 800	41 859	10.7
Male	12 645	12 978	12 993	14 397	10.8
Female	24 798	24 852	24 807	27 462	10.7
Humanities[1]	170 355	170 916	167 664	176 817	5.5
Male	65 910	66 000	65 307	68 436	4.8
Female	104 409	104 892	102 327	108 336	5.9
Social and behavioural sciences, and law[1]	182 010	187 770	189 996	191 016	0.5
Male	63 555	65 316	66 441	66 918	0.7
Female	118 449	122 448	123 549	124 074	0.4
Business, management and public administrations[1]	168 678	175 428	177 537	189 201	6.6
Male	79 248	82 992	84 333	89 547	6.2
Female	89 391	92 394	93 129	99 612	7.0
Physical and life sciences, and technologies[1]	90 441	92 328	93 372	94 113	0.8
Male	40 245	41 439	42 543	43 191	1.5
Female	50 190	50 880	50 820	50 916	0.2
Mathematics, computer and information sciences[1]	36 636	34 242	32 724	33 219	1.5
Male	26 682	24 912	23 844	24 135	1.2
Female	9 954	9 324	8 874	9 075	2.3

(continued)

■ **Table 7.2** *University Degrees, Diplomas, and Certificates Awarded by Field of Study and Gender (Continued)*

	2005/2006r	2006/2007r	2007/2008r	2008/2009	2007/2008 to 2008/2009
Architecture, engineering and related technologies[1]	85 533	86 313	88 470	91 890	3.9
Male	67 551	68 025	69 912	72 504	3.7
Female	17 979	18 273	18 549	19 383	4.5
Agriculture, natural resources and conservation[1]	15 252	15 708	16 032	17 091	6.6
Male	6 768	6 900	7 029	7 434	5.8
Female	8 481	8 808	9 000	9 654	7.3
Health, parks, recreation and fitness[1]	104 748	109 176	113 157	118 941	5.1
Male	29 469	30 795	32 535	34 113	4.9
Female	75 237	78 336	80 601	84 804	5.2
Personal, protective and transportation services	1 761	2 244	2 217	2 823	27.3
Male	1 038	1 287	1 299	1 554	19.6
Female	720	954	915	1 269	38.7
Other[1]	83 007				

r Revised
[1] Includes sex unknown

SOURCE: Statistics Canada, "University enrolment, 2008/2009," *The Daily*, 11-001-XIE, July 14, 2010; http://www.statcan.gc.ca/daily-quotidien/100714/tdq100714-eng.htm.

One explanation for why women earn fewer doctoral degrees than men do is that women are socialized to choose marriage and motherhood over long-term career preparation (Olson et al. 1990). From an early age, women are exposed to images and models of femininity that stress the importance of domestic family life. When 821 undergraduate women were asked to identify their lifestyle preference, fewer than 1 percent selected being unmarried and working full time. In contrast, 53 percent selected "graduation, full-time work, marriage, children, stop working at least until youngest child is in school, then pursue a full-time job" as their preferred lifestyle sequence (Schroeder et al. 1993: 243). Only 6 percent of 535 undergraduate men selected this same pattern. Men do not see a conflict between having children and having a demanding career because they are not expected to be the primary caregivers in the family; if they have promising professional futures, then women are still expected to step aside to provide "support" for their male partners' career development. Additionally, because many professions traditionally coded as "male" will pay more highly to those men who pursue them, individual families will decide that it makes economic sense for the woman to give up her career aspirations to care for children. Whether or not it is accurate to characterize these to be choices freely made or choices constrained by larger socio-economic forces is important for you to assess.

Structural limitations also discourage women from advancing in the educational profession. In 1996, women outnumbered men in elementary and kindergarten teaching positions by approximately four to one and were about equal in number to male teachers at the postsecondary level; however, men as university professors outnumbered them by about two to one (Statistics Canada 1998). Women seeking academic careers may also find that promotion in higher education is more difficult than it is for men. Long and colleagues (1993) examined the promotions of 556 men and 450 women with Ph.D.s in biochemistry. They found that women were less likely to be promoted to associate or full professor, were held to a higher standard than men, and were particularly disadvantaged in more prestigious departments. Throughout Canada, women remain less likely than men are to be full professors (the highest rank), and when employed as full professors women earn less on average than men who are full professors (CAUT Bulletin 2006).

Income and Structural Sexism

When data were first collected in 1967 in Canada on female-to-male earnings, the ratio stood at 58.4 percent. Since that time, it has increased notably. "Earnings have...evolved very differently by gender over the last two decades. They have been stagnant for men, increasing in 2000 for the first time since 1980. In contrast, earnings have increased steadily in each decade for women" (Statistics Canada 2003b). More women are working, and more women are working longer hours. In addition, they are more qualified; since 1980, the proportion of women workers with a university degree has almost tripled, and the proportion of women earners with a university degree now exceeds that of men. However, "[d]espite substantial gains in earnings during the past two decades, women still earn less than men" (Statistics Canada 2003b).

In general, the higher one's education level, the higher one's income. Yet, even when men and women have identical levels of educational achievement and both work full time, women, on the average, earn less than men (Table 7.3). Although women with a university degree earn substantially more than women with lower levels of education, women university graduates who were employed full time all year earned only 74 percent as much as their male counterparts in 1997. Moreover, while gender differences are less pronounced for younger than

■ Table 7.3 *Female to Male Average Earnings Ratio*

	Medial Earnings		
	Males	**Females**	
Age Groups	**(2005 constant dollars)**		**Female-Male Earnings Ratio**
25 to 29 years	37 680	32 104	0.85
30 to 34 years	46 710	36 893	0.79
35 to 39 years	51 586	38 818	0.75
40 to 44 years	53 941	39 540	0.73

Note: Median earnings, in 2005 constant dollars, of full-time full-year employees by age groups and sex, Canada 2005.

SOURCE: Statistics Canada, "Income and Earnings, 2006 Census," 97-563-XIE, May 2008; http://www.statcan.gc.ca/bsolc/olc-cel/olc-cel?catno=97-563-XIE&lang=eng#formatdisp.

■ **Table 7.4** *Annual Average Earnings of Persons Employed Full Time, Full Year, by Educational Attainment, 1997*

Educational Attainment	Women	Men	Women's Earnings as a % of Men's
Less than Grade 9	$21 403	$30 731	69.6
Some secondary school	22 846	35 367	64.6
Secondary school graduate	27 525	37 705	73.0
Some postsecondary	28 360	37 812	75.0
Postsecondary certificate/diploma	29 539	41 868	70.6
University degree	42 661	57 930	73.6
Total average	$30 915	$42 626	72.5

SOURCE: Adapted from Statistics Canada, "Earnings of Men and Women," 13-217-XIB1997000, May 1999; http://www.statcan.gc.ca/bsolc/olc-cel/olc-cel?catno=13-217-XIB&lang=eng.

older women, university-educated women aged 25 to 29 who worked full time all year in 2000 earned 81 cents for every dollar earned by their male counterparts. Among those with only a high school education, women earned 77 cents to the dollar. The persistent earnings gap among these young men and women is partially explained by their different occupational choices, rooted in different fields of study (see Table 7.4).

Earnings are not the same as wages. Earnings can be increased or decreased in a given time period by working more hours or fewer. Often when we look at earnings gaps between men and women, we find that women's reduced earnings are related to women's reduced working hours. Wage gaps exist where there are actual differences in pay for men and women.

In general, the most common occupations held by young women pay less than those that men most commonly pursue, and while the wage gap narrows when women pursue occupations that are most commonly chosen by men, a gap still exists. For example, in 2000, university-educated women aged 25 to 29 who worked in the 10 most common occupations chosen by men of the same age group and qualifications earned about 89 cents for every dollar their male counterparts made (Statistics Canada 2003b). These wage ratios have remained relatively constant throughout the last decade.

The wage gap is widespread and exists in all occupational categories (Table 7.5). For example, even though women in professional and related occupations enjoy considerably higher income than women in other occupational groups, the 2000 earnings ratio for young women and men employed full time all year ranged from just over 80 percent in the sales and marketing category to near parity in elementary teaching, where women earn 98 percent of what men do. The only occupation in which women earn more than men is in social work. Moreover, it is important to keep in mind that what the table shows is that even when men work in fields dominated by women, with the exception of social work, they earn more than the women do.

Tomaskovic-Devey (1993) examined the income differences between males and females and found that the percentage of females in an occupation was the best predictor of an income gender gap—the higher the percentage of females, the lower the pay. Supporting this observation, a team of researchers

■ **Table 7.5** *Average Earnings in the 10 Occupations Most Commonly Held by Those Aged 25 to 29 with a University Degree Working Full-Year, Full Time[1] by Sex, Canada 2000*

	Number		Average Earnings		Women's Earnings as a % of Men's Earnings
	Men	Women	Men	Women	
Ten occupations most commonly held by young men					
Computer and information systems	17 710	6 450	$54 052	$45 915	84.9
Financial auditors and accountants	4 155	5 280	$42 913	$39 990	93.2
Sales marketing and advertising managers	3 125	3 320	$56 440	$46 047	81.6
Retail trade managers	2 645	2 380	$38 122	$31 596	82.9
Secondary school teachers	2 425	4 120	$36 201	$35 546	98.2
Financial and investment analysts	2 400	1 715	$52 208	$44 864	85.9
Retail salespersons and salesclerks	2 175	1 780	$33 167	$26 211	79.0
Mechanical engineers	2 155	260	$51 341	$50 668	98.7
Sales representatives, wholesale trade (non-technical)	2 000	1 425	$44 528	$41 055	92.2
Electrical and electronics engineers	1 925	325	$59 469	$53 196	89.5
Ten occupations most commonly held by young women					
Elementary school and kindergarten teachers	1 625	9 255	$36 243	$35 535	98.0
Computer and information systems	17 710	6 450	$54 052	$45 915	84.9
Financial auditors and accountants	4 155	5 280	$42 913	$39 990	93.2
Registered nurses	360	4 820	$44 688	$41 088	91.9
Secondary school teachers	2 425	4 120	$36 201	$35 546	98.2
Sales, marketing, and advertising managers	3 125	3 320	$56 440	$46 047	81.6
General office clerks	405	2 525	$30 339	$28 348	93.4
Retail trade managers	2 645	2 380	$38 122	$31 596	82.9
Social workers	430	2 285	$35 011	$36 555	104.4
Customer service information and related clerks	1 015	2 260	$32 664	$31 226	95.6

[1]Earners who worked 49 to 52 weeks during the year for 30 or more hours per week.

SOURCE: Statistics Canada, "Earnings of Canadians: Making a Living in the New Economy, 2001 Census," Analysis Series, 2001 Census, 96F0030XIE2001013, March 2003; http://www.statcan.gc.ca/bsolc/olc-cel/olc-cel?lang=eng&catno=96F0030X2001013.

(Kilbourne et al. 1994) analyzed data from the National Longitudinal Survey that included more than 5000 women and more than 5000 men. They concluded that occupational pay is gendered and that "occupations lose pay if they have a higher percentage of female workers or require nurturant skills" (p. 708).

The literature frequently cites two hypotheses to explain why the income gender gap still exists. One is called the **devaluation hypothesis**. It argues that women are paid less because the work they perform is socially defined as less valuable than the work performed by men. Guy and Newman (2004) argued that these jobs are undervalued in part because they include a significant

devaluation hypothesis

The hypothesis that argues that women are paid less because the work they perform is socially defined as less valuable than the work performed by men.

emotional labour

Work traditionally performed by women in the role of providing care and concern for others, either professionally or in the home.

human capital hypothesis

The hypothesis that female–male pay differences are a function of differences in women's and men's levels of education, skills, training, and work experience.

comparable worth

Tasks and jobs that are distinct but have equal value and utility in the workplace and economy.

amount of **emotional labour**: work that involves caring, negotiating, and empathizing with people, all tasks that are rarely specified in job descriptions or performance evaluations. The other hypothesis, the **human capital hypothesis**, argues that female–male pay differences are a function of differences in women's and men's levels of education, skills, training, and work experience. Although these explanations are difficult to test, most researchers agree that there is more support for the devaluation hypothesis than for the human capital hypothesis (England and Li 2006; Padavic and Reskin 2002). One way that researchers test these hypotheses is to compare the earnings of individuals in occupations with comparable worth but different gender compositions. **Comparable worth** refers to the belief that individuals in occupations, even in different occupations, should be paid equally if the job requires "comparable" levels of education, training, and responsibility. In Canada, Ontario's Pay Equity Act was first passed in 1988, yet by 2008 the act had still failed to address persistent failures to compensate individuals equally for work of equal value. Mary Cornish notes that "Ontario's persistent wage gap shows that many women never received the benefit of the province's legislation and others lost the gains they made initially for various reasons, including employer non-compliance, economic restructuring and inadequate government funding of pay equity adjustments and of the Pay Equity Commission and Hearings Tribunal" (2008: 22).

As further explanation for the persistent wage gap, a study based on data obtained from the Survey of Labour and Income Dynamics also finds that women's lower amount of work experience appears to have a significant bearing on the persistent wage gap between men and women (Statistics Canada 1998). This research reports that about 18 percent, or almost one-fifth, of the wage gap reflected the fact that women generally have less experience than their male counterparts, supervise other employees less often, and are involved in administrative decisions less frequently. Several other factors were also associated with the wage gap. These included differences in job tenure and the fact that men are more likely to graduate from programs leading to higher paying jobs and earnings. Marini and Fan (1997) also found support for the human capital hypothesis, although their research supports a third category of variables as well. They found that organizational variables (characteristics of the business, corporation, or industry) explain, in part, the gender income gap. For example, on career entry, employers channel women and men into sex-specific jobs that carry different wage rates.

Work and Structural Sexism

Women now make up one-third of the world's labour force. Worldwide, women tend to work in jobs that have little prestige and low or no pay, where they are the facilitators for others, and where no product is produced. Women are also more likely to hold positions of little or no authority within the work environment and to have more frequent and longer periods of unemployment (United Nations 2000c).

No matter what the job, if a woman does it the work is likely to be valued less than if a man does it. For example, in the early nineteenth century, 90 percent of all clerks were men, and being a clerk was a prestigious profession. As the job became routine, in part because of the advent of the typewriter, the pay and prestige of the job declined and the number of female clerks increased. Today, female clerks predominate, and the position is one of relatively low pay and low prestige.

The concentration of women in certain occupations and men in other occupations is referred to as **occupational sex segregation**. In Canada, as in other countries with sex-typed work, women tend to be more highly concentrated within fewer occupations while men are more evenly distributed across a larger range of occupations (Table 7.6).

In some occupations, sex segregation has decreased in recent years. Data from the 2001 census indicates that women are "making inroads in many 'non-traditional' areas, particularly in highly skilled occupations" (Statistics Canada 2003a: 8). In the 1991–2001 period, women accounted for over one-half of the growth in high-skilled occupations (occupations that normally require a university education). Their numbers doubled in information technology occupations and more than doubled in professional occupations in business and finance. Over the last decade, the number of women managers has increased by more than 40 percent. Despite these and other changes, however, women are still heavily represented in low-prestige, low-wage, **pink-collar jobs** that offer few benefits. A **glass ceiling**—an invisible barrier that prevents women and other minorities from moving into top corporate positions—often victimizes even those women in higher paying jobs. A study of Fortune 500 companies found that women held less than 11 percent of all seats on the Fortune 500 company boards (Klein 1998). Interestingly, Cianni and Romberger's investigation (1997) of visible minority women and men in Fortune 500 companies indicates that gender has more of a role in "organizational treatment" than race.

Sex segregation in occupations continues for several reasons. First, cultural beliefs about what is an appropriate job for a man or a woman still exist. Cejka and Eagley (1999) report that the more undergraduate students believed that an occupation was male or female dominated, the more they attributed success in that occupation to masculine or feminine characteristics. Further, in an examination of gender-role orientations and attitudes toward women as managers, Burke (1994) reports that the men exhibited significantly more negative attitudes toward women as managers than did the women. (He sampled 194 Canadian undergraduate and graduate business students, 71 female and 123 male.) Burke suggests that this finding "augurs badly" for women in at least three ways. As colleagues, these men would be unlikely to endorse initiatives to develop women's careers, or they might actively endorse "backlash" strategies. They are unlikely to provide women with mentorship or sponsorship, and may act as poor role models for other men. Finally, they are unlikely to support the career aspirations of spouses or female partners.

In addition, because of gender socialization, men and women learn different skills and acquire different aspirations. Opportunity structures and expectations for men and women also vary. For example, male employers may exclude women, as may employees who fear the prestige of their profession will be lessened with the entrance of women, or who simply believe that "the ideal worker is normatively masculine" (Martin 1992: 220). Finally, since family responsibilities remain primarily with women, working mothers may feel pressure to choose professions that permit flexible hours and career paths, sometimes

occupational sex segregation

The concentration of women in certain occupations and of men in other occupations.

pink-collar jobs

Jobs that offer few benefits, often have low prestige, and are disproportionately held by women.

glass ceiling

An invisible, socially created barrier that prevents women and other minorities from being promoted into top corporate positions.

Table 7.6 *Distribution of Employment, by Occupation, 1987, 1994, and 2003*

	1987			1994			2003		
	Women	Men	Women as a % of Total Employed in Occupation	Women	Men	Women as a % of Total Employed in Occupation	Women	Men	Women as a % of Total Employed in Occupation
Managerial									
Senior management	0.4	1.6	16.9	0.4	1.5	19.8	0.3	0.7	24.2
Other management	5.8	10.0	30.6	7.4	10.4	36.9	6.4	9.9	36.1
Total management	6.2	11.6	28.9	7.9	12.0	35.1	6.7	10.6	35.4
Professional									
Business and finance	1.9	2.1	40.7	2.4	2.4	44.6	3.0	2.8	48.4
Natural sciences/ Engineering/Mathematics	1.8	6.6	16.7	1.8	7.4	17.0	3.1	9.6	22.0
Social sciences/Religion	2.3	1.9	47.8	3.5	2.2	56.5	4.2	2.1	63.8
Teaching	5.0	2.8	57.3	5.6	3.2	59.4	5.2	2.7	62.9
Doctors/Dentists/ Other health	0.9	0.9	44.1	1.3	1.1	48.7	1.2	1.0	52.1
Nursing/Therapy/ Other health-related	8.0	0.9	87.3	8.1	1.0	87.1	8.4	1.0	87.7
Artistic/Literary/Recreational	2.8	2.0	50.4	3.2	2.3	53.6	3.3	2.5	53.4
Total professional	22.8	17.3	49.8	25.8	19.6	52.2	28.5	21.7	53.4
Clerical and administrative	29.6	7.7	74.4	26.4	7.3	74.9	24.1	7.0	75.1
Sales and service	30.9	18.5	55.7	31.2	19.9	56.4	32.2	19.8	58.7
Primary	2.4	7.3	20.0	2.2	6.7	21.3	1.5	5.3	19.7
Trades, transport, and construction	2.0	27.1	5.3	1.7	25.0	5.4	2.0	25.0	6.6
Processing, manufacturing, and utilities	6.0	10.4	30.2	4.7	9.5	29.2	5.0	10.6	28.9
Total[1]	100.0	100.0	43.0	100.0	100.0	45.3	100.0	100.0	46.6
Total employed (000s)	5 299.3	7 021.4	—	5 934.2	7 177.5	—	7 339.3	8 406.7	—

[1]Includes occupations that are not classified.

SOURCE: Adapted from Statistics Canada, "Women in Canada," 89F0133XIE2003000, March 2004; http://www.statcan.gc.ca/bsolc/olc-cel/olc-cel?catno=89F0133XIE&lang=eng#form atdisp

known as "mommy tracks." Thus, for example, women dominate the field of elementary education, which permits them to be home when their children are not in school.

Politics and Structural Sexism

In 1868, when the first federal general election was held, only men who owned a specified amount of property were allowed to vote; in 1885, the *Electoral Franchise Act* defined a "person" who was eligible to vote as a male who was of other than Mongolian or Chinese origin. While the 1917 *Wartime Election Act* granted wives, sisters, and mothers of servicemen the right to vote, it was not until 1918 that Canadian women won the right to vote in federal elections (Frank 1994). Women over the age of 21 were granted the right to vote in provincial elections in 1916 in Manitoba, Saskatchewan, and Alberta; in 1917 in British Columbia and Ontario; in 1918 in Nova Scotia; in 1919 in New Brunswick; in 1922 in Prince Edward Island; in 1925 in Newfoundland (where initially this right was limited to women over the age of 25); and in 1940 in Quebec (Whitla 1995: 320–22). These rights were first granted to white women; women from certain other ethnic groups did not receive the franchise until later. For example, Mossman (1998: 181) observes that "prior to 1960, aboriginal women (and men) in Canada were entitled to vote only if they gave up their Indian status, a status defined by the federal *Indian Act*." While an Aboriginal woman became automatically "enfranchised" if she married a white man, "it was only in the 1970s that aboriginal women's claims to equality under the *Indian Act* were tested in the Supreme Court of Canada."

Worldwide, the percentage of legislative seats held by women ranges from 30 to 40 percent in Scandinavian countries to less than 1 percent in several Middle Eastern and African countries (Kenworthy and Malami 1999). Further, women hold no more than 8 percent of ministerial positions in any developing country (World Bank 2001: 5). In response to the underrepresentation of women in the political arena, some countries have institutionalized quotas. In India, a 1993 amendment held one-third of all seats in local contests for women. The result? Eight hundred thousand women were elected. A 1996 law in Britain requires a minimum of 20 percent of each party's candidates to be women. Countries with similar policies include Finland, Germany, Mexico, South Africa, and Spain (Sheehan 2000).

There are some signs that Canada is on the road to achieving gender equality in politics. For example, in June 1993, Kim Campbell was elected Progressive Conservative Party leader and, by ascension shortly after, became Canada's first female prime minister (for an admittedly limited term of less than six months). Some years earlier, in December 1989, the election of Audrey McLaughlin as leader of the New Democratic Party (NDP) signalled the first time a Canadian woman had been elected as the leader of a national political party.

Nevertheless, in general, the more important the political office, the lower the probability a woman will hold it. Running for office requires large sums of money, the political backing of powerful individuals and interest groups, and a willingness of the voting public to elect women. Hunter and Denton (1984) note that Canadian political parties have shown a marked tendency to nominate women only after they have suffered losses at the polls or to nominate women in "lost cause" ridings where another party enjoys overwhelming voter support. It is then political party elites that hamper women "in securing nominations in the first place, and beyond this, in gaining nominations which carry a reasonable prospect of victory" (Stark 1992: 454). Minority women have even greater structural barriers to election and, not surprisingly, represent an even smaller percentage of elected officials.

Consider, for example, that while Mary Ellen Smith became, in 1918, the first woman to be elected to the Legislative Assembly in British Columbia and the first woman in the British Empire to serve as a cabinet minister, it was not until 1972 that a Black woman, Rosemary Brown, won a seat in that province. Brown was the first Black woman elected to any Canadian legislature. In 1991, Zanana Akande was the first Black woman to be elected to the Ontario legislature. She was also the first Black woman to become a cabinet minister in that province (Mandell 1995: 347).

Human Rights and Structural Sexism

The status of women in Canada was addressed by the 1970 Report of the Royal Commission on the Status of Women. The Report directed many of its recommendations to legislative reforms in the areas of the criminal law, tax and child care allowances, social assistance, immigration, and family law. The principle guiding the recommendations was that, as citizens, men and women ought to share the same rights and freedoms, have equal opportunities to exercise those rights, and be equally able to fulfill their duties as citizens. However, while advocating that men and women should be treated identically, the Report acknowledged that, on occasion, equality might demand or necessitate "special" or "different treatment" of women. For example, because women can become pregnant, the "special needs" created by pregnancy might demand acknowledgment of difference (e.g., maternity leave), or a shift from "equality of treatment" (formal equality) to "equality of outcome" (substantive equality).

In various ways, Canadian laws have not always benefited men and women in equal fashion. Consider, for example, that until 1983, most women were unable to claim pregnancy benefits under the old *Unemployment Insurance Act* (Atcheson et al. 1984: 20–21); that until 1983, husbands who raped their wives were exempt from criminal proceedings; and that before 1989, women could be fired from their jobs simply for being pregnant. Consider as well that while courts have permitted "businessmen to deduct club fees because men like to conduct business with each other over golf," have held the purchase of a Rolls Royce "to be an incident of a professional expense" (because it enhances professional image), and have sustained claims that "making charitable contributions to enhance one's reputation in a community inheres in the business of manufacturing boxes" (Macklin 1992), Canada's *Income Tax Act* does not regard the cost of child care as a legitimate business deduction.

Attempts to "de-gender" the law have not always proven fully effective. For example, in the case of *Murdoch v. Murdoch*, Irene Murdoch claimed that, based on her contribution of money and labour during 25 years of marriage, she was entitled to half of the property owned by her husband when they divorced.

Her tasks while married had included "haying, raking, swathing, mowing, driving trucks and tractors and teams, quieting horses, taking cattle back and forth to the reserve, dehorning, vaccinating, branding, anything that was to be done...just as a man would" (Dranoff in Mossman 1998: 187). The Supreme Court of Canada's denial of Mrs. Murdoch's claim generated activism by groups concerned with women's rights. By 1980, every Canadian province, with the exception of Quebec, had enacted legislation amending the arrangements for the distribution of property between spouses at the time of separation or divorce.

Although the notion of "equal treatment" sounds fair, does treating those who are unalike the same result in equality? Mossman (1998: 187) observes, "With the benefit of hindsight, many feminists now recognize that the reform legislation in common law provinces was fundamentally flawed, since it assumed that men and women had equal access to economic self-sufficiency." In most cases, women become the custodial parents of dependent children when marriage breaks down. The constraints on full-time employment posed by the parental role, coupled with the wage gap, may continue to create substantive hardship for women upon divorce.

7.4 The Social Construction of Gender Roles: Cultural Sexism

Structural sexism is supported by a system of **cultural sexism** that perpetuates beliefs about the differences between women and men. Cultural sexism refers to the ways in which the culture of society—its norms, values, beliefs, and symbols—perpetuates the subordination of an individual or group because of the sex classification of that individual or group.

cultural sexism

The ways in which the culture of society perpetuates the subordination of individuals based on their sex classification.

For example, the *belief* that females are less valuable than males has serious consequences. One study in Bombay, India, found that of 8000 abortions performed after amniocentesis, 7900 were of female fetuses (Anderson and Moore 1998). Cultural sexism takes place in a variety of settings, including the family, the school, and the media, as well as in everyday interactions.

Family Relations and Cultural Sexism

From birth, males and females are treated differently. For example, the toys male and female children receive convey different messages about appropriate gender roles. Toy manufacturer Mattel had to recall the Barbie doll who spoke, only to say "Math is hard!" and "Let's go shopping!" The company also faced opposition after producing a pink, flowered Barbie computer for girls and a blue Hot Wheels computer for boys. The social significance of the gender-specific computers and the public criticism arose after it was revealed that the accompanying software packages were different—the boys' package had more educational titles (Bannon 2000). This chapter's *Focus on Technology* feature documents the negative consequences of such seemingly harmless differences.

Women, Men, and Computers

Technology has changed the world in which we live. The technological revolution has brought the possibility of greater gender equality because, unlike tasks dominating industrialization, sex differences in size, weight, and strength are less relevant. Although feminists have long decried the gendering of technology, feminist concerns about computer use have largely been met with the assertion that computer technology is gender-neutral. If we understand that technologies are used in and as part of the larger surrounding culture, then it should come as no surprise that computer and communications technologies are used differently, with distinct impacts and with differing outcomes regarding opportunities and hazards for men and women.

Girls spend less time playing video games (to wit, "Game Boy"); consequently, software that appeals to girls is less likely to be manufactured (O'Neal 1998; Children Now 2001). For any generation of young people entering adulthood, the images and information about women's value in society are informed by popular games, by social attitudes, and by conditions of work and play; it is, therefore, important to consider what the current generation has grown up with in the form of major entertainment/games and what they say about gender status. In a study of the 10 top-selling video games for three major systems (Sony PlayStation, Sega Dreamcast, and Nintendo 64), 54 percent of the games contained female characters, whereas 92 percent contained male characters. Of the female characters displayed, over one-third had significantly exposed breasts, thighs, stomachs, midriffs, or bottoms, and 46 percent had "unusually small" waists. Further, despite evidence that girls, contrary to boys, prefer video games that are nonviolent, over half of the female characters were portrayed engaging in violent behaviour (Children Now 2000). A more recent study (Padilla-Walker et al. 2010) demonstrates that in addition to increased risks for both males and females to drink to excess, use drugs, and have lower quality in their interpersonal relationships, for women "video game use was associated with lower self-worth, and both video games and violent video games were associated with lower perceived social acceptance" (p. 109).

Although younger Canadian women are slightly more likely than their male counterparts to report using a computer, in other age categories, men are more likely to do so (Normand 2000: 91). The reasons for the shift have to do with the gendered character of work that men and women take on later. Some research finds that girls are not as interested in computers as boys are, and that when they are interested they define computers as a tool to accomplish a task, a kind of homework helper (in contrast to boys, who define it as a toy to explore). Says Jane Margolis, a researcher at Carnegie Mellon (quoted in Breidenbach 1997: 69):

> Girls want to do something constructive with computers, while boys get into hacking and using computers for their own sake...Computers are just

Household Division of Labour Girls and boys work in the home in about equal amounts until the age of 18, when the female to male ratio begins to change (Robinson and Bianchi 1997: 4). In a study of household labour in 10 Western countries, Bittman and Wajcman (2000) report that "women continue to be responsible for the majority of hours of unpaid labour" ranging from a low of 70 percent in Sweden to a high of 88 percent in Italy (p. 173). The fact that women, even when working full time, contribute significantly more hours to home care than men is known as the "second shift" (Hochschild 1989). The 2001 census, the second census to include questions on unpaid work, found that women "still had the lion's share of the number of hours devoted to unpaid household work" (Statistics Canada 2003a: 17). Approximately 21 percent of women—but only 8 percent of men—devoted 30 hours or more to unpaid household work during the week prior to the census. While 13.3 percent of men reported that they did not do any hours of unpaid household work, only 7.5 percent of women reported likewise (see Table 7.7 on page 238).

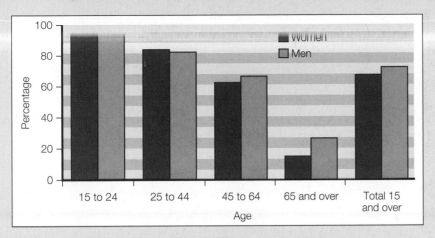

Figure 7.3 *Percentage of Women and Men Who Reported Using the Internet in the Previous 12 Months, 2003*

SOURCE: Statistics Canada, "Women in Canada, 5th edition, A Gender-based statistical report," 89-503-XIE2005001, March 2006; http://www.statcan.gc.ca/bsolc/olc-cel/olc-cel?lang=eng&catno=89-503-X.

one interest of many for girls, while they become an object of love and fascination for boys.

Figure 7.3 shows the access patterns of men and women to the internet over the course of a year, but asking whether we use these technologies is only part of the issue; we must also consider how these tools are being used. Are we using computers and accessing the internet to fulfil fairly low-level administrative functions that are, generally speaking, poorly rewarded as work? Or are we using computers for work that tends to be highly rewarded, such as for solving higher-order problems, or writing algorithms for international trading purposes? For significant changes to take place in reference to women, men, and computers, we must recognize that computers specifically, and technology in general, are not gender-neutral and, in fact, have emerged and flourished within the context of a male-dominated industry. However, if women do not pursue computer-based information technologies, they will have an "intellectual and workplace handicap that can only get worse as technology grows more prevalent" (Currid 1996: 114). How much access we have to technology, and the quality of the technology, must be considered before we can accept any assertion that computers are gender-neutral.

SOURCES: Breidenbach, Susan. 1997. "Where Are All the Women?" *Network World* 14(41): 68–69; Currid, Cheryl. 1996. "Bridging the Gender Gap: Women Will Lose Out Unless They Catch Up with Men in Technology Use." *Informationweek* April 1: 114; Children Now. 2001. "Girls and Gaming: Gender and Video Game Marketing." *Media Now* (Winter). http://www.childrennow.org/media/medianow; Children Now. 2000. "Top Selling Video Games 'Unhealthy' for Girls, Research Shows." News Release, December 12. http://www.childrennow.org/newsroom; Normand, Josee. 2000. "Women and Education." *Women in Canada 2000: A Gender-Based Statistical Report*, pp. 85–96. Ottawa: Statistics Canada Catalogue no. 89-503-XPE; O'Neal, Glenn. 1998. "Girls Often Dropped from Computer Equation." *USA Today*, March 10: D4; Padilla-Walker, Laura et al. 2010. "More Than Just a Game: Video Game and Internet Use During Emerging Adulthood." *Journal of Youth and Adolescence*, Vol. 39:103–113.

Three explanations for the continued traditional division of labour emerge from the literature. The first explanation is the "time-availability approach." Consistent with the structural-functionalist perspective, this position emphasizes that role performance is a function of who has the time to accomplish certain tasks. Because women are more likely to be at home, they are more likely to perform domestic chores.

A second explanation is the "relative resources approach." This explanation, consistent with a conflict perspective, suggests that the spouse with the least power is left the most unrewarding tasks. Since men often have more education, higher incomes, and more prestigious occupations, they are less responsible for domestic labour.

"Gender role ideology," the final explanation, is consistent with a symbolic interactionist perspective. It argues that the division of labour is a consequence of traditional socialization and the accompanying attitudes and beliefs. Females and males have been socialized to perform various roles and to expect their

Table 7.7 *Percentage of Persons Aged 15 and Over, by Number of Unpaid Hours Doing Housework, Canada, 2001**

Women	
No hours	7.5
Fewer than 5 hours	17.4
5 to 14 hours	29.7
15 to 29 hours	23.9
30 or more hours	21.4
Men	
No hours	13.3
Fewer than 5 hours	30.0
5 to 14 hours	33.5
15 to 29 hours	15.4
30 or more hours	7.8

*Refers to the week preceding Census day.

SOURCE: Adapted from Statistics Canada. 2003. 2001 Census: Analysis Series. "The Changing Profile of Canada's Labour Force." Catalogue no. 96F0030XIE2001009 (released February 11, 2003), p. 36.

partners to perform other complementary roles. Women typically take care of the house, men the yard. This division of labour is learned in the socialization process through the media, schools, books, and toys. A recent test of the three positions found that although all three had some support, gender role ideology was the weakest of the three in predicting work allocation (Bianchi et al. 2000). This chapter's *Social Problems Research Up Close* feature examines the influence of gender ideology on the valuation of work performed by adult family members.

The School Experience and Cultural Sexism

Sexism is also evident in the schools. It can be found in the books students read, the curricula and tests they are exposed to, and the different ways teachers interact with students.

Textbooks The bulk of research on gender images in textbooks and other instructional materials documents the way males and females are portrayed stereotypically. For example, Purcell and Stewart (1990) analyzed 1883 storybooks used in schools and found that they tended to depict males as clever, brave, adventurous, and income producing, and females as passive and victimized. Females were more likely to be in need of rescue and were also depicted in fewer occupational roles than males. Witt (1996), in a study of third-grade textbooks from six publishers, reports that little girls were more likely to be portrayed as having both traditionally masculine and feminine traits whereas little boys were more likely pictured as having the masculine characteristics only. These results are consistent with research that suggests that boys are much less free to explore gender differences than females, and with Purcell and Stewart's conclusion that boys are often depicted as having "to deny their feelings to show their manhood" (1990: 184). Although some evidence suggests that male and female textbook characters are increasingly portrayed as equal, portrayals largely remain stereotypical (Evans and Davies 2000).

Teacher–Student Interactions   Sexism is also reflected in the way teachers treat their students. After interviewing 800 adolescents, parents, and teachers in three school districts in Kenya, Mensch and Lloyd (1997) report that teachers were more likely to describe girls as lazy and unintelligent. "And when the girls do badly," the researchers remark, "it undoubtedly reinforces teachers' prejudices, becoming a vicious cycle." Similarly, in the United States, Sadker and Sadker (1990) observed that elementary-school and secondary-school teachers pay more attention to boys than to girls. Teachers talk to boys more, ask them more questions, listen to them more, counsel them more, give them more extended directions, and criticize and reward them more frequently. However, in *The War against Boys*, philosopher Christina Sommers (2000) argues that boys, not girls, are "on the weak side of the educational gender gap" (p. 14). Noting that boys are at a higher risk for learning disabilities and lag behind in reading and writing scores, Sommers argues that the belief about females being educationally shortchanged is untrue (see Chapter 12).

Do the differing expectations and levels of encouragement that females and males receive relate to their varying abilities, as measured by standardized tests, in such disciplines as math and science? In an experiment at the University of Waterloo, male and female university students, all of whom said they were good in math, were shown either a gender-stereotyped or a gender-neutral advertisement. When female students who had seen the female-stereotyped advertisement took a math test, they performed not only lower than women who had seen the gender-neutral advertisements, but lower than their male counterparts (Begley 2000). Research also indicates that standardized tests themselves are biased: they are almost exclusively timed, multiple-choice tests—a format that, some argue, favours males (Smolken 2000).

Media, Language, and Cultural Sexism

One concern voiced by social scientists in reference to cultural sexism is the extent to which the media portrays females and males in a limited and stereotypical fashion, and the impact of such portrayals.

Signorielli (1998) analyzed gender images presented in six media: television, movies, magazines, music videos, TV commercials, and print media advertisements. The specific items selected from each medium were those most often consumed by 12- to 17-year-old girls, for example, the 25 most-watched television shows. The results indicate the following:

- In general, media content stresses the importance of appearance and relationships for girls/women and of careers and work for boys/men.
- Across the six media, 26 to 46 percent of women are portrayed as "thin or very thin" in contrast to 4 to 16 percent of men; 70 percent of girls wanted to look like, fix their hair like, or dress like a character on television, compared with 40 percent of boys.

- In a survey of boys and girls, both agreed that "worrying about weight, crying or whining, weakness, and flirting" are characteristics associated more with girls than with boys and that "playing sports, being a leader, and wanting to kiss or have sex" are more often characteristic of male characters.

Like media images, the words we use and the ways we use them reflect gender inequality. The term *nurse* carries the meaning of "a woman who..." and the term *engineer* suggests "a man who...." The words "broad," "old maid," and "spinster" have no male counterpart. Language is so gender stereotyped that the placement of the word "male" or "female" before titles is sometimes necessary, as in the case of "female police officer" or "male prostitute." Further, as symbolic interactionists note, the embedded meanings of words carry expectations of behaviour.

Virginia Sapiro (1994) has shown how male–female differences in communication style reflect the structure of power and authority relations between men and women. For example, women are more likely to use disclaimers ("I could be wrong but...") and self-qualifying tags ("That was a good movie, wasn't it?"). They reflect less certainty about their opinions. Communication differences between women and men also reflect different socialization experiences. Women are more often passive and polite in conversation; men are less polite, interrupting more often and talking more (Tannen 1990).

7.5 Social Problems and Traditional Gender Role Socialization

Cultural sexism, transmitted through the family, school, media, and language, perpetuates traditional gender role socialization. Gender roles, however slowly, are changing. As one commentator observed (Fitzpatrick 2000: 1), "the hard lines that once helped to define masculine [and feminine] identity are blurring. Women serve in the military, play pro basketball, run corporations, and govern. Men diet, undergo cosmetic surgery, bare their souls in support groups and cook."

gender tourism
The recent tendency for definitions of masculinity and femininity to become less clear, resulting in individual exploration of the gender continuum.

Despite this **"gender tourism"** (Fitzpatrick 2000), most research indicates that traditional gender roles remain dominant, particularly for males who, in general, have less freedom to explore the gender continuum. Social problems that result from traditional gender socialization include the feminization of poverty, social-psychological and health costs, and conflict in relationships.

The Feminization of Poverty

Globally, the percentage of female households is increasing dramatically, with approximately 25 percent of all households in Africa, North America, the Caribbean, and parts of Europe headed by women (Population Reference Bureau 1999). Often living in poverty, many of these households are headed by young women with dependent children and older women who have outlived their spouses. More than 900 million women, worldwide, live on less than $1 a day (United Nations 2000b).

In addition to individual and institutional discrimination, traditional gender-role socialization contributes to poverty among women. Women learn to put family ahead of their education and careers. Women are expected to take primary responsibility for child care, which contributes to the alarming rate of female-headed, lone-parent families in Canada. In 1997, when compared to children in two-parent families, children in female-headed, lone-parent families were almost five times more likely to be in a low-income situation. In that year, more than half of non-elderly females (56 percent) lived below the poverty line. That means they spent more than 54.7 percent of their income on food, shelter, and clothing (Statistics Canada 1999).

Social-Psychological Costs

How shall we best understand gender differences in morbidity and mortality? Although both biological and social factors play a role, social factors may be dominant. As part of masculine gender performance, men tend to engage in more risky behaviours—heavy drinking and smoking, poor diet, lack of exercise, stress-related activities, higher drug use, and a refusal to ask for help. Men are also more likely to work in hazardous occupations than women. For example, men are more likely to be miners than women—an occupation with one of the highest mortality rates in Canada. Women's higher rates of depression are also likely to be rooted in traditional gender roles. The heavy burden of child care and household responsibilities, the gender gap and the occupation gap, and fewer socially acceptable reactions to stress—for example, it is more acceptable for males to drink alcohol than for females—contribute to gender differences in depression (Klein 1997).

Many of the costs of traditional gender socialization are social-psychological in character. Reid and Comas-Diaz (1990) noted that the cultural subordination of women results in women having low self-esteem and being dissatisfied with their roles as spouses, homemakers or workers, mothers, and friends. In a study of self-esteem among more than 1160 students in grades 6 through 10, girls were significantly more likely to have "steadily decreasing self-esteem," whereas boys were more likely to fall into the "moderate and rising" self-esteem group (Zimmerman et al. 1997).

Not all research concludes that women have more negative self-concepts than men do. Summarizing their cross-cultural research on women and men, Williams and Best (1990) found "no evidence of an appreciable difference" in self-concepts (p. 153). They also found no consistency in the self-concepts of women and men in 14 countries: "[I]n some of the countries the men's perceived self was noticeably more favourable than the women's, whereas in others the reverse was found" (p. 152). Research shows that women are becoming more assertive and desirous of controlling their own lives rather than merely responding to the wishes of others or the limitations of the social structure (Burger and Solano 1994).

Men also suffer from traditional gender socialization. Men experience enormous cultural pressure to succeed in their work and earn high incomes. Research indicates that men with higher incomes feel more "masculine" (Rubenstein 1990). Traditional male socialization also discourages males from expressing emotion—part of what Pollock (2000a) calls the "boy code." This chapter's *The Human Side* feature describes the problems and pressures of being male in our society.

The *Human Side*

Real Boys' Voices: The "Boy Code"

Brad, 14

Guys aren't supposed to be weak or vulnerable. Guys aren't supposed to be sweet. A friend of mine died in the hospital...I knew that, as a guy, I was supposed to be strong and I wasn't supposed to show any emotion...I was supposed to be tough...when I went home, I just sat by myself and let myself cry. (p. 17)

Sam, 16

I think most of the macho stuff guys do is stupid...like the kids who do wrestling moves in the hall. At the same time, there are things that I wouldn't do because I'm a guy. I've never gone to a guy friend, for example, and said, "I'm feeling hurt right now and let's talk about it." (p. 31)

Gordon, 18

All the men in my family...have been the epitome of negativity. Some have become wrapped up in infidelity, some abuse, some alcoholism. I don't want to become a man, because I don't want to become this. (p. 53)

Jeff, 16

Your virginity is what determines whether you're a man or a boy in the eyes of every teenage male. Teenage men see sex as a race: the first one to the finish line wins. (p. 69)

Brett, 17

I think most guys are kind of isolated because it's thought of as weird if you have any really close guy friends. To get around it, guys will go fishing or hunting or bowling or something else "masculine," and then talk about personal or serious things while they're doing that activity. (p. 116)

Jesse, 17

From the girls I've spoken to about relationships, one of their biggest complaints is that they're doing all the giving and the guy is doing all the taking. Girls also tend to be better able to understand social situations. Girls can look at someone and tell what they're feeling. They have more social intuitiveness, more than we clueless guys do. I think that makes them more aware of what's happening in a relationship than we are. (p. 253)

Graham, 17

We would live in a better society if guys could share their feelings more easily. But guys still hear mixed messages from our society. On the one hand they hear that it's OK now to talk about their feelings, but on the other hand they still hear that they have to be tough and that only girls get emotional. My friend who talked to me and cried about his girlfriend was on the football team. His teammates would laugh at him if he tried to talk to them about that sort of stuff. (p. 272)

Jake, 16

Ever since I've played Little League the word "win" has been forced into my mind. When I was eight years old, the coach would tell us at the beginning of the season that we were just out there for fun, but I knew that it wasn't true. Every day that there was a game, my day would be ruined. (pp. 280–81)

Dylan, 17

If I get in shape, if I develop a more attractive body, I'd be more popular. It's like the way life is around here, what society shows you. It's a problem to be naturally skinny like me. You're not as athletic or muscular or attractive; you're not as good as the other kids are. (p. 302)

Kirk, 18

I think it's hard growing up in the year 2000. It's definitely hard for a guy. Going through high school is tough. I have pressures in sports, school, life all rolled into one. My parents pressure me to do well in school, do well in sports, and I pressure myself to do well in life...I worry about life a lot. I feel that everything is going to work out for everybody except me, that I'll be left in the dust. (p. 341)

On the average, men in Canada die earlier than women, although gender differences in life expectancy have been shrinking (Statistics Canada 2001). Traditional male gender socialization is linked to males' higher rates of heart disease, cirrhosis of the liver, most cancers, AIDS, homicide, drug- and alcohol-induced deaths, suicide, and firearm and motor vehicle accidents (Wilkins 1996). Females, however, after the age of 15, are twice as likely to suffer from depression as males (Kalb 2000) and much more likely to suffer from anorexia or bulimia. Seven million women and girls suffer from eating disorders (Wilmot 1999).

Conflict in Relationships

Gender inequality also has an impact on relationships. For example, negotiating work and home life can be a source of relationship problems. While men in traditional versus dual-income relationships are more likely to report being satisfied with household task arrangements, women in dual-income families are the most likely to be dissatisfied with household task arrangements (Baker et al. 1996). Further, the belief that one's partner is not doing a fair amount of the housework is associated with a perception of lower spousal social support (Van Willigen and Drentea 1997).

We must consider the practical difficulties of raising families, having careers, and maintaining a happy and healthy relationship with a partner. Successfully balancing work, marriage, and children may require a number of strategies, including a mutually satisfying distribution of household labour, rejection of such stereotypical roles as "supermom" and "breadwinner dad," seeking outside help from others (e.g., child care givers, domestic workers), and a strong commitment to the family unit.

Finally, violence in intimate relationships is gendered (see Chapters 4 and 5). Although men are more likely to be victims of violent crime, women are more likely to be victims of sexual assault and domestic violence that results in physical harm. Violence against women reflects male socialization that emphasizes aggression and dominance over women. Male violence is a consequence of gender socialization and a definition of masculinity which holds that "as long as nobody is seriously hurt, no lethal weapons are employed, and especially within the framework of sports and games—football, soccer, boxing, wrestling— aggression and violence are widely accepted and even encouraged in boys" (Pollock 2000b: 40).

7.6 Strategies for Action: Toward Gender Equality

Efforts to achieve gender equality have been largely fuelled by the feminist movement. Despite a conservative backlash, feminists, and to a lesser extent men's activist groups, have made some gains in reducing structural and cultural sexism in the workplace and in the political arena.

Grassroots Developments

Feminism Feminism is the belief that women and men should have equal rights and responsibilities. However, in its early incarnation, the suffrage movement in Canada, or the "first wave" of feminism, "was less a 'woman's movement' than an attempt on the part of particular men and women, predominantly urban professionals and entrepreneurs, to supervise [the moral development of] society" (Bacchi 1983: 13). First at the local level, and later at the national and provincial levels, thousands of upper- and middle-class women sought to ameliorate a host of social ills. They became active in the temperance movement; in campaigns for religious instruction, better workplace conditions, improvements in public health and child welfare; and in the development of living facilities for single women. Women's early activism in these areas was often linked to "women's auxiliaries, institutes and missionary societies to spread the word of God" (Errington 1993: 73). Established by Christian churches, these groups advanced as the philanthropic extension of women's "natural" expertise as wives, mothers, and "guardians" of moral virtue.

Family, Gender Ideology, and Social Change

One of the most important questions concerning gender is the extent to which gender ideologies affect family roles. An investigation by Zuo and Tang (2000) addresses this issue by focusing on two research questions: (1) Are men less likely than women to believe in the equality of roles? and (2) Is the male "breadwinner" status predictive of beliefs about gender ideology?

Sample and Methods

Data for this investigation came from a randomly selected national U.S. sample of married persons collected by the Bureau of Sociological Research at the University of Nebraska. As part of a larger longitudinal study, respondents (N = 400 married men and 640 married women) were interviewed in 1980, 1983, and 1992. All were between the ages of 18 and 55, 95 percent were white, and 67 percent had 1992 annual incomes between $25 000 and $45 000. The proportion of a husband's income to the total family income measured the independent variable, breadwinner status. For example, a husband who provided 90 percent of the total family income received a higher score than a husband who provided 50 percent of the total family income. The higher a respondent's score, the higher the breadwinner status and the lower the breadwinner status of their spouse. Gender ideology, the dependent variable, was measured by the extent to which a respondent agreed or disagreed with statements concerning (1) the wife's economic role (e.g., "a woman should not be employed if jobs are scarce"), (2) the provider role (e.g., "a husband should be the main breadwinner even if his wife works"), and (3) the woman's maternal role (e.g., "a woman's most important task in life is being a mother"). In combination, these three variables indicated the extent to which respondents adhered to a traditional or an egalitarian (equal partners) gender ideology.

Findings and Conclusions

The results signify that over the years studied, both men and women have shifted toward a more egalitarian gender role ideology. The shift, however, is greater for women than for men. One notable exception is in reference to beliefs about a woman's maternal role. Here, men held more egalitarian beliefs than women. The authors caution, however, that this result does not necessarily indicate that women hold more traditional beliefs about motherhood than men. It may be, for example, that women's stress over the lack of child-care facilities outside of the home is responsible for gender differences on this indicator.

Results also indicate that the higher a husband's breadwinner status, that is, the more he contributes to household finances, the more likely he is to hold traditional gender beliefs. Conversely, the lower a husband's breadwinner status, the more likely he is to hold egalitarian gender beliefs. Similarly, the higher a wife's breadwinner status, that is, the more she contributes to household finances, the more likely she is to hold egalitarian beliefs; the lower her breadwinner status, the more likely she is to hold traditional beliefs.

The authors conclude that the results of their study support what is called the benefits hypothesis. The benefits hypothesis holds that men whose wives earn high wages, that is, men who have lower breadwinner statuses, are likely to embrace rather than be threatened by role equality. Given the empirical support for this hypothesis, the authors predict a continued narrowing in male–female differences in gender role ideology:

> The present trend is that men's breadwinner status continues to decline; more and more individuals perform non-gendered family roles. Based on these facts, it may be predicted that the movement toward egalitarianism for both men and women will continue and a further decrease in the gender gap in gender ideology is down the road. (2000: 36)

SOURCE: Zuo, Jiping, and Shengming Tang. 2000. "Breadwinner Status and Gender Ideologies of Men and Women Regarding Family Roles." *Sociological Perspectives* 43: 29–44.

In 1876, Dr. Emily Howard Stowe founded the Toronto Women's Literary Club, an organization that "in 1883 ... took a name more revealing of its politics: the Toronto Women's Suffrage Association" (Adamson et al. 1988: 33). Stowe's organization launched a campaign to demand the franchise for women at every political level and for women's rights to education and entrance into the prestigious occupations. However, when compared to their counterparts in the United States and England, early Canadian feminists were more likely to engage in a war of words than in firebrand tactics.

In the decades between the first and second waves of the feminist movement, the position of women did improve in Canadian society. Moreover, as Wine and Ristock (1991: 1) have suggested, "[p]erhaps the most impressive impact of the [women's] movement is the massive shift in the consciousness of the Canadian public in terms of affirmation of women's right to equality, including reproductive freedom, equal treatment in the workplace, and freedom from violence." However, it has been acknowledged that the second wave of the women's movement did not always or consistently recognize, include, or champion the needs of all Canadian women equally. For example, women with disabilities often found their needs excluded or marginalized (Driedger 1993). Similarly, Wine and Ristock (1991: 13) have observed that "though women's organizations provided some support,...[t]he activist work of Native women to change section 12(b) of the *Indian Act*, and its denial of treaty rights to Native women who married non-Native men...[was a] battle fought almost entirely by Native women." As Cassidy and colleagues (1998: 26) acknowledge in their discussion of "silenced and forgotten women"—First Nations women, Black women, immigrant women, women with disabilities, and poor women—only recently has the second wave of the women's movement "begun to address criticisms that white, middle-class feminists have denied, dismissed, and denigrated the experiences of differently raced, abled, and classed women."

The Men's Movement As a consequence of the women's rights movement, men began to re-evaluate their own gender status. In *Unlocking the Iron Cage*, Michael Schwalbe (1996) examines the men's movement as both participant and researcher. For three years, he attended meetings and interviewed active members. His research indicates that participants, in general, are white middle-class men who feel they have little emotional support, who question relationships with their fathers and sons, and who are overburdened by responsibilities, unsatisfactory careers, and what is perceived as an overly competitive society.

As with any grassroots movement, several factions co-exist in the men's movement. Some men's organizations advocate gender equality; others developed to oppose "feminism" and what was perceived as male bashing. For example, the Promise Keepers are part of a Christian men's movement that has often been criticized as racially intolerant, patriarchal, and antifeminist. However, one female researcher and author who attended meetings incognito as a man reports: "I'm struck with how close it all sounds like feminism" (Leo 1997).

Today, issues of custody and fathers' rights headline the men's rights movement and have led to increased visibility (Goldberg 1997). Many members of such groups argue that society portrays men as disposable, and that as fathers and husbands, workers and soldiers, they feel that they can be replaced by other men willing to do what they do. They also hold that there is nothing male affirming in society and that the social reforms of the last 30 years have "been the deliberate degradation and disempowerment of men economically, legally and socially" (NCFM 1998: 7). Still other men's advocates focus less on men's rights and more on personal growth, advocating "the restoration of earlier versions of masculinity" (Cohen 2001: 393).

Public Policy

The introduction of policy changes and programs designed to eliminate gender inequality has not been without controversy. Here, we direct attention to sexual harassment and employment equity and note some of the debates these issues have inspired in recent years.

Sexual Harassment Canadian case law has recognized that sexual harassment is a multifaceted phenomenon that may include sexual assault; unwanted touching or patting; leering and sexually suggestive gestures; demands for sexual favours; derogatory or degrading remarks; repeated and unwelcome sexual flirtations, advances, or propositions; the use of sexually degrading words to describe a person; sexist jokes that cause embarrassment; and displaying sexually offensive material. The Law Society of Canada notes that "[w]hether a particular type of conduct constitutes sexual harassment is sometimes difficult to determine" and that although "the severity of the conduct may be the most conclusive factor...what is determinative is a combination of frequency, severity and persistence" (in Mossman 1997: 244). In 1998, complaints of sexual harassment accounted for one-fifth of new complaints brought to the Canadian Human Rights Commission (Dranoff 2001: 73).

There are two types of **sexual harassment**: (1) *quid pro quo*, in which an employer requires sexual favours in exchange for a promotion, salary increase, or any other employee benefit, and (2) the existence of a hostile environment that unreasonably interferes with job performance, as in the case of sexually explicit comments or insults being made to an employee. Sexual harassment occurs at all occupational levels, and some research suggests that the number of incidents of sexual harassment is inversely proportional to the number of women in an occupational category (Fitzgerald and Shullman 1993). Female doctors (Schneider and Phillips 1997) and lawyers (Rosenberg et al. 1997) report high rates of sexual harassment, in the first case by male patients and in the second by male colleagues. Sexual harassment is also a worldwide phenomenon. For example, 70 percent of female government employees in Japan report being sexually harassed at work (Yamaguchi 2000). Finally, sexual harassment is not exclusively a "women's problem." Research suggests that approximately 15 percent of men are subject to it (Henslin and Nelson 1997).

Employment Equity The passage of the *Canadian Human Rights Act* in 1977 provided the legal foundation for **employment equity**. Section 16(1) of the *Canadian Human Rights Act* asserts that it is not a discriminatory practice to adopt or carry out a special program, plan, or arrangement designed to prevent, eliminate, or reduce disadvantages suffered by persons or groups because of race, national or ethnic origin, skin colour, religion, age, sex, family status, marital

sexual harassment
When an employer requires sexual favours in exchange for a promotion, salary increase, or any other employee benefit, or the existence of a hostile environment that unreasonably interferes with job performance, as in the case of sexually explicit remarks or insults being made to an employee.

employment equity
An attempt to ensure that there is a proportional number of designated target groups (e.g., women, visible minorities, Aboriginal peoples, and people with disabilities) throughout all income and occupational levels at ratios that are consistent with the proportion of these groups within the local or regional workforce.

status, or disability by improving their opportunities in respect to goods, services, facilities, accommodations, or employment. Thus, the act implicitly asserts that employment equity does not constitute reverse discrimination. Rather, under the terms of reference of the Canadian Human Rights Commission, charged with administering the act, an employment equity program may be required as part of the settlement of a complaint of discrimination, as a strategic attempt to forestall the future recurrence of discriminatory practices.

The federal *Employment Equity Act* (1985) required the federal public service, federally regulated companies (e.g., banks and Crown corporations), and all private-sector employers with 100 or more employees that did over $200 000 worth of business with the federal government to have employment equity plans and to ensure that their procedures for hiring, firing, promotion, and training were equitable to all groups. The goal was to redress discrimination against women, visible minorities, people with disabilities, and First Nations people. However, the only penalties that could be imposed were for the organization's failure to file yearly progress reports. In 1996, legislative changes to the act made it practically potent. For example, the disadvantaged groups to be protected under this legislation were more precisely defined. Employers were required to identify and eliminate barriers to employment, implement positive policies and practices, prepare a plan defining short-term (under three years) and long-term goals, and establish a timetable for the implementation of these plans. The act is now enforced by the Canadian Human Rights Commission. The Commission has the authority to conduct compliance audits to ensure that "numerical goals (not quotas) are met, to hold tribunals and to levy fines of up to $50 000 for noncompliance with the law" (Dranoff 2001: 57).

Opponents of employment equity argue that, despite the good intentions of its creators, employment equity will not quell discrimination, may well lead us back to the degrading colour/racial/gender consciousness of the past, and may latently function to create resentment of and hostility toward those groups that it seeks to help. Consider, for example, that in August 1999, academics from across Canada wrote letters to officials at Wilfrid Laurier University to protest a job posting for a psychology professor: the posting specified that only women would be considered. "Obviously, at Laurier the commitment to...fairness and the pursuit of academic excellence takes a back seat to social goals like achieving a gender balance in departments. This bodes...ill for your institution, which has gone down in my estimation, as I'm sure it has in that of many academics," read one letter received by the institution. The gender-specific job posting was described by the chairperson of the psychology department at Laurier as an attempt to "address a gender imbalance" in the psychology department at that university; at the time of the posting, in the department 18 professors were men and only 4 were women.

Academics protesting the job posting also submitted numerous queries to the Ontario Human Rights Commission, questioning the university's use of section 14 of the *Ontario Human Rights Code*. The Code stipulates that a special program may be implemented as long as it does not infringe on other rights—such as freedom from discrimination—and "is designed to relieve hardship or economic disadvantage." Although they conceded that women have suffered job discrimination at universities in the past, critics of the gender-specific posting argued that women academics were "hardly a disadvantaged group" (*National Post* 1999: A4).

International Efforts

The Convention to Eliminate All Forms of Discrimination Against Women (CEDAW), also known as the International Women's Bill of Rights, was adopted by the United Nations in 1979. CEDAW establishes rights for women not previously recognized internationally in a variety of areas, including education, politics, work, law, and family life. Over 166 countries have ratified the treaty, including every country in the Western Hemisphere and every industrialized nation in the world but for Switzerland and the United States (Rabin 2000; United Nations 2000a).

In addition to many other global efforts, individual countries have instituted programs or policies designed to combat sexism and gender inequality. For example, Japan has implemented the Basic Law for a Gender-Equal Society, a "blueprint for gender equality in the home and workplace" (Yumiko 2000: 41). The South African Bill of Rights prohibits discrimination on the basis of, among other things, gender, pregnancy, and marital status (IWRP 2000), and China has established a Programme for the Development of Chinese Women, which focuses on empowering women in the areas of education, human rights, health, child care, employment, and political power (*WIN News* 2000).

Understanding Gender Inequality

Gender roles and the social inequality they create are ingrained in our social and cultural ideologies and institutions, and are, therefore, difficult to alter. For example, in almost all societies, women are primarily responsible for child care and men for military service and national defence (World Bank 2001). Nevertheless, as we have seen in this chapter, growing attention to gender issues in social life has spurred some change. Women, traditionally expected to give domestic life first priority, are now finding it acceptable to be more ambitious in seeking a career outside the home. Men, traditionally expected to be aggressive and task oriented, are now expected to be more caring and nurturing. Women seem to value gender equality more than men do, however, perhaps because women have more to gain. For instance, 84 percent of 600 adult women said that the ideal man is caring and nurturing; only 52 percent of 601 adult men said that the ideal woman is ambitious (Rubenstein 1990: 160).

Men also have much to gain by gender equality, though. Eliminating gender stereotypes and redefining gender in terms of equality does not mean liberating only women, but liberating men and our society as well. "What we have been talking about is allowing people to be more fully human and creating a society that will reflect that humanity. Surely that is a goal worth striving for" (Basow 1992: 359). Regardless of whether traditional gender roles emerged out of biological necessity, as the functionalists argue, or out of economic oppression, as the conflict theorists hold, or both, it is clear today that gender inequality carries a high price: poverty, loss of human capital, feelings of worthlessness, violence, physical and mental illness, and death. Surely, the costs are too high to keep paying.

Critical Thinking

1. To some degree, we can observe that gender stands fairly independently as a category for measuring inequality, subordination, health hazards, and so on, with women being those most frequently at risk. However, gender-based oppression may also coincide with larger problems of inequality, especially on the global stage. Explain why this is so, and what hazards result.

2. The chapter indicates that there is a "gender gap" in the number of men and women obtaining doctoral degrees. Why might this be?

3. What have been the interpersonal costs, if any, of sensitizing Canadian society to the "political correctness" of female–male interactions?

4. Why are women more likely to work in traditionally male occupations than men are to work in traditionally female occupations? Are the barriers that prevent men from doing "women's work" cultural, structural, or both? Explain.

"Is It True?" Quiz: Answers

1 = false; 2 = true; 3 = contextual; 4 = false; 5 = false

Critical Studies in Race and Ethnicity

Is It True?

1. Many anthropologists and other scientists have concluded that "races" do not really exist.

2. In Canada, both Islamic and Jewish groups reported a surge in hate crimes directed toward them after the September 11, 2001 attacks.

3. Only in Australia is the proportion of the population born outside the country higher than it is in Canada.

4. Canadian policymakers struggle to promote the view that "diversity" is a social good rather than a social problem.

5. In Sweden, it is against the law to give the Nazi salute.

Read more here: 1 = p. 252, 2 = p. 283, 3 = p. 268, 4 = p. 257, 5 = p. 288

Answers can be found on p. 288.

Canada is becoming increasingly diversified in the racial and ethnic composition of its population. Consider that whereas in 1901 there were only 25 different ethnic groups of ancestry record, Canadians identified more than 200 ethnic groups in answering the 2006 census question on ethnic ancestry (Statistics Canada 2008a). In that year, more than five million individuals, or 16.2 percent of the population, identified themselves as visible minorities (ibid). Many Canadians might be startled to realize that, amid such diversity, some individuals in Canada would kill another human being simply because of skin colour or ethnicity; many others would not be surprised.

In this chapter, we discuss the character and foundations of prejudice to uncover the operations of discrimination and its consequences for both racial and ethnic minorities. We also discuss strategies designed to reduce prejudice and discrimination. We begin by examining racial and ethnic diversity world-wide and in Canada, emphasizing first that the concept of race is based on social rather than biological definitions.

8.1 The Global Context: Diversity Worldwide

From a perspective focused on how human societies and relationships are structured—largely organized into groups with unequal access to power and resources—"race" refers not to biological differences, but to categories people occupy based on ascribed characteristics, such as skin colour. No biological basis for categorizing persons according to race exists; however, sociologists recognize that such categories create important distinctions in how people experience the social world and their place in it. Whatever our internal similarities may be, the process of organizing people into racialized categories focuses people into groups defined by difference and inequality. Since those differences have been largely defined by conflict, they have important social implications for outcomes related to health and well-being. As well meaning as it may be to insist that people are all the same "on the inside," such a stance risks ignoring the specific differences that people experience because of their racialized statuses in societies defined by inequality.

This chapter explores the problems and privileges that arise in social relations structured through race and ethnicity.

The Social Construction of Race

The concept of **race** refers to a category of people believed to share distinct physical characteristics deemed socially significant. Racial groups are some-times distinguished based on such physical characteristics as skin colour, hair texture, facial features, and body shape and size. Some physical variations among people are the result of living for thousands of years in different geo-graphical regions (Molnar 1983). For example, humans living in regions with hotter climates developed darker skin from a natural skin pigment, melanin, which protects the skin from the sun's rays. In regions with moderate or colder climates, people had little need for protection from the sun and developed lighter skin.

race

A category of people who are believed to share distinct physical characteristics that are deemed socially significant.

Cultural definitions of race have taught us to view race as a scientific categorization of people based on biological differences between groups of individuals. Yet, racial categories are based more on social definitions than on biological differences. Anthropologist Mark Cohen (1998) explains that distinctions among human populations are graded, not abrupt. Skin colour is not black or white, but rather ranges from dark to light with many gradations of shades. Noses are not either broad or narrow, but come in a range of shapes. Physical traits such as these, as well as hair colour and other both visible and invisible characteristics, come in an infinite number of combinations. For example, a person with dark skin can have any blood type and can have a broad nose (a common combination in West Africa), a narrow nose (a common trait in East Africa), or even blond hair (a combination found in Australia and Papua New Guinea).

The science of genetics also challenges the notion of race. Geneticists have discovered that "the genes of black and white...[North Americans] probably are 99.9 percent alike" (Cohen 1998: B4). Furthermore, genetic studies indicate that genetic variation is greater within racially classified populations than between racial groups (Keita and Kittles 1997). Classifying people into different races fails to recognize that over the course of human history migration and intermarriage have resulted in the blending of genetically transmitted traits. For example, if you traced your ancestry back as far as the Norman Conquest of 1066, you would find yourself claiming 41 million ancestors (Fitzhugh 1991: 290). With the passage of time, fewer if any individuals can claim that their racial or ethnic ancestry is "pure." Thus, there are no "pure" races; people in virtually all societies have genetically mixed backgrounds. Even analyses that have developed out of the human genome project, which have been able to use genetic markers to determine the locations from which an individual's ancestors originated, are clear to point out that "the connection [between race and biology] is generally quite blurry because of multiple other nongenetic connotation of race, the lack of defined boundaries between populations and the fact that many individuals have ancestors from multiple regions of the world" (Collins 2004: S13). It is for these kinds of reasons that the American Anthropological Association has passed a resolution stating that "differentiating species into biologically defined 'race' has proven meaningless and unscientific" (Etzioni 1997: 39). Scientists who reject the race concept now speak of **populations** when referring to groups that most people would call races (Zack 1998).

populations

The word that scientists who reject the race concept now use when referring to groups that most people would call races.

Clear evidence that race is a social concept is that different societies construct different systems of racial classification and these systems change over time (Niemonen 1999). Leggon (1999) explains, "The major significance of race is not biological but social and political, insofar as race is used as the primary line of demarcation separating 'we' from 'they' and, consequently, becomes a basis for distinctive treatment of a group by another" (p. 382). However, the social significance of "race" remains evident throughout the world.

Patterns of Racial and Ethnic Group Interaction

When two or more racial or ethnic groups come into contact, one of several patterns of interaction may occur, including genocide, expulsion or population transfer, slavery, colonialism, segregation, acculturation, assimilation, pluralism, and amalgamation. These patterns of interaction may occur when two or more groups exist in the same society or when different groups from different societies come into contact. Although not all patterns of interaction between racial and ethnic groups are destructive, author and Mayan shaman Martin Prechtel reminds us that "Every human on this earth, whether from Africa, Asia, Europe, or the Americas, has ancestors whose stories, rituals, ingenuity, language, and life ways were taken away, enslaved, banned, exploited, twisted, or destroyed" (quoted in Jensen 2001: 13).

- **Genocide** refers to the deliberate, systematic annihilation of an entire nation or people. The European invasion of the Americas, beginning in the sixteenth century, resulted in the decimation of most of the original inhabitants of North and South America. For example, labelling Aboriginal peoples as "savages" allowed early settlers and visiting fishermen to commit "atrocities of a most barbaric kind" upon the Beothuk of Newfoundland (Rowe 1977: 146). Indeed, some scholars have claimed that the eventual extinction of the Beothuk resulted from the "sport of Indian hunting": murder committed "for fun" (Horwood 1969) and for the payment of a bounty for each Beothuk killed (Such 1978: 62). Although some Native groups were intentionally killed, others fell victim to diseases brought by the Europeans. In the twentieth century, Adolf Hitler led the Nazi extermination of more than 12 million people, including more than 6 million Jews. More recently, ethnic Serbs have attempted to eliminate Muslims from parts of Bosnia—a process they call "ethnic cleansing."

- **Expulsion** or **population transfer** occurs when a dominant group forces a subordinate group to leave the country or to live only in designated areas of the country. During World War II, about 22 000 Japanese-Canadians lost their rights, had their homes, property, and businesses confiscated, and were confined to internment camps. In addition, the "Deemed Suspect"—refugees from Germany and Austria—were deported from England to Canada and interned here as "enemy aliens." Between 1940 and 1943, 2300 individuals "deemed suspect" were interned in Canada within eight camps (Columbo 1986).

- **Slavery** exists when one group treats another group as property to exploit for financial gain. The dominant group forces the enslaved group to live a life of servitude, without the basic rights and privileges enjoyed by the dominant group. In early American history, slavery was tolerated and legal for three centuries. In what is now Canada, slavery was practised by several Indian tribes on the Northwest Coast, and by Europeans beginning in 1500 in Newfoundland. By 1608, the French brought Black slaves to Canada and the first slave transported directly from Africa sold in 1629. In New France, there were 3604 recorded slaves by 1759, 1132 of whom were Black, the remainder of whom were "panis" (Indians). The "right" of Canadians to own and sell Native people as slaves was declared on May 29, 1733. Canada prohibited the importation of slaves in 1793; that same year, an act of the Upper Canada legislature ruled that all children in its jurisdiction born to slaves after that year were to be free upon reaching age 25 and proposed the gradual emancipation of slaves. Although the last slave auction in Canada was held in 1797 in Montreal, slavery remained technically legal in

genocide
The systematic annihilation of one racial or ethnic group by another.

expulsion (population transfer)
When a dominant group forces a subordinate group to leave the country or to live only in designated areas of the country.

slavery
A condition in which one social group treats another group as property to exploit for financial gain.

colonialism

When a racial or ethnic group from one society takes over and dominates the racial or ethnic group(s) of another society.

segregation

The physical and social separation of categories of individuals, such as racial or ethnic groups.

de jure segregation

Segregation that is required by law.

de facto segregation

Segregation that is not required by law, but exists "in fact," often as a result of housing and socio-economic patterns.

acculturation

Learning the culture of a group different from the one in which a person was originally raised.

assimilation

The process by which minority groups gradually adopt the cultural patterns of the dominant majority group.

secondary assimilation

The integration of different groups in public areas and in social institutions, such as in government, neighbourhoods, schools, and the workplace.

primary assimilation

The integration of different groups in personal, intimate associations such as friends, family, and spouses.

most of Canada until 1834 when it was abolished for the entire British Empire (Winks 1999).

- **Colonialism** occurs when a racial or ethnic group from one society takes over and dominates the racial or ethnic group(s) of another society. The European invasion of North America, the British occupation of India, and the Dutch presence in South Africa before the end of apartheid are examples of outsiders taking over a country and controlling the native population. As a territory of the United States, Puerto Rico is essentially a colony whose residents are U.S. citizens, but who cannot vote in presidential elections unless they move to the mainland.

- **Segregation** refers to the physical separation of two groups in residence, workplace, and social functions. Segregation may be **de jure** (Latin meaning "by law") or **de facto** ("in fact"). For example, Blacks across Canada were treated as inferior from the time they began to settle here. They were prohibited from entering restaurants, hotels, and recreational facilities, and barred from most professions. In Nova Scotia and Ontario, where Blacks were most concentrated, Blacks were often forced into segregated schools. The last segregated school in southwestern Ontario closed in 1956; however, Windsor, Ontario, did not desegregate its public facilities until 1975—it was the last municipality to do so (Henry and Tator 1985: 321–22). In like fashion, because of a range of discriminatory legislation in British Columbia, "where anti-Asian sentiment was endemic from the 1850s to the 1950s…Chinese, Japanese and South Asians could not vote, practise law or pharmacy, be elected to public office, serve on juries or work in public works, education or the civil service" (Dreidger 1999: 1889). Consider as well that in the 1920s and 1930s, Jews were automatically excluded from employment in major institutions, such as banks and the police, and were barred from elite social clubs, beaches, and holiday resorts in Montreal, Toronto, and Winnipeg. Universities set limits on Jewish enrolment (Henry et al. 1995).

- **Acculturation** refers to the loss of the culture in which a person was originally raised to a culture imposed either by immigration or colonization. Acculturation may involve learning the dominant language, adopting new values and behaviours, and changing the spelling of the family name. In some instances, acculturation may be forced. For example, the 1977 passage of the French Language Charter (Bill 101) established French as the official language of Quebec and made French the legal language of work and the public sector. It also resulted in a situation in which educational instruction takes place almost exclusively in French, with English granted "secondary language status." Similarly, the Canadian government's policy of "aggressive civilization" was designed to destroy all aspects of Aboriginal culture. It was imposed throughout the Native residential schools.

- **Assimilation** is the process by which formerly distinct and separate groups merge and become integrated as one. There are two types of assimilation: secondary and primary. **Secondary assimilation** occurs when different groups become integrated in public areas and in social institutions, such as neighbourhoods, schools, the workplace, and in government. **Primary assimilation** occurs when members of different groups are integrated in personal, intimate associations, such as friends, family, and spouses. The degree of acculturation and assimilation that occurs between majority and minority groups depends in part on (1) whether minority group members have voluntary or involuntary contact with the majority group and (2) whether majority group members accept or reject newcomers or minority group members. Groups that voluntarily immigrate and that are accepted by "host" society members will experience an easier time acculturating and assimilating than those that are forced through slavery, frontier expansion, or military conquest into contact with the majority group and are rejected by them.

- **Amalgamation**, also known as **marital assimilation**, occurs when members of different ethnic or racial groups form families and produce children. Although in most societies the norm of **endogamy** influences individuals to marry within their social group, interracial marriages have become more acceptable in Canada in the past few decades. This higher level of acceptance is markedly different from a relatively recent past in which women could be criminalized for marrying "outside" their race; this chapter's *The Human Side* feature looks at the case of Velma Demerson, a woman who was imprisoned in 1939 for her relationship with a Chinese man. The Project Canada national surveys of adults, which have examined attitudes in this country since 1975, report increases in the percentages of those expressing approval toward racial intermarriage (Bibby 2001: 216) (Table 8.1). In 2001, there were 217 500 mixed unions (marriages and common-law unions) involving either persons from two different visible minority groups or one person from a visible minority group and one who is not. Table 8.2 lays out patterns of marriage between persons in mixed unions. Drawn from the 2006 census, Table 8.2 belongs to a larger report that explains that those who are in mixed unions are likely to have been born in Canada, noting that "56% had a partner or spouse who was either a non-visible minority or was a member of a different visible minority group compared to 12% for those who were foreign-born" (Milan et al. 2010: 71). The report explains the increased likelihood of marrying someone with different ancestry for those visible minorities born in Canada by reminding us that those who immigrate usually do so as adults, and have already married in their countries of origin (ibid).

amalgamation

The physical blending of different racial or ethnic groups, resulting in a new and distinct genetic and cultural population; results from the intermarriage of racial and ethnic groups over generations.

marital assimilation

Assimilation that occurs when different ethnic or racial groups become married or pair-bonded and produce children.

endogamy

The social norm that influences people to marry within their social group and discourages interracial and interethnic marriages.

■ **Table 8.1** *Approval of Intergroup Marriage, 1975–2005*

	1975	1990	2005
Whites and Aboriginals	73%	84	93
Whites and Asians	64	82	93
Whites and East Indians/Pakistanis	56	76	91
Whites and Blacks	55	78	92

SOURCE: Bibby, Reginald W. (2006). *The Boomer Factor*: Toronto: Bastian Books, p. 9.

A Dark Passage in Ontario's Past

On the morning of May 3, 1939, 18-year-old Velma Demerson, three months pregnant and wearing her pyjamas, was sitting down for breakfast with the man she planned to marry when there was a loud banging at the door.

In came two Toronto police officers, followed by her father. "Is this her?" one of the officers asked. "That's her," her father said.

In the hour that followed, Ms. Demerson was arrested, driven to a courthouse lockup, placed in a barred cage, questioned about how many times she had had sex and with whom and taken before a magistrate who remanded her in custody in what she thinks was Toronto's Don Jail.

A week later, the magistrate ordered her incarcerated for "incorrigibility" for one year in Belmont House, formally known as the Toronto Industrial Refuge (and now an elegant retirement residence). She subsequently was transferred to the grim Mercer Reformatory for Women.

Her crime: living with a Chinese man, Harry Yip.

Ms. Demerson, now 81, has worked for years to unearth the records of her incarceration. She recently found an internal government memo warning the attorney-general of the time that incarcerating women under the act was possibly an illegal constitutional intrusion into federal criminal justice jurisdiction.

She is now suing the Ontario government for unauthorized imprisonment.

Last night, the Ontario New Democratic Party gave her its annual J. S. Woodsworth Award for making a significant contribution to ending racial discrimination.

Ms. Demerson recalled in an interview the events of that year—a chronicle of official social control of women's lives that a historian who has studied her case and others calls "a horror story."

Hundreds of Ontario women were imprisoned, like Ms. Demerson, under the provincial Female Refuges Act, which stated that "any parent or guardian may bring before a judge any female under the age of 21 years who proves unmanageable or incorrigible."

■ **Table 8.2** *Out-Group Pairing by Visible Minority Group, 2006*

		Couples	
	Total number	Mixed union	Same visible minority group
		percentage	
Visible minority group			
All visible minority groups[1]	1 214 400	23.8	76.2
Japanese	29 700	74.7	25.3
Latin American	85 200	47.0	53.0
Black	136 000	40.6	59.4
Filipino	107 400	33.1	66.9
Southeast Asian	58 100	31.1	68.9
Arab/West Asian	105 700	25.0	74.9
Korean	34 800	19.5	80.5
Chinese	321 700	17.4	82.6
South Asian	327 200	12.7	87.3
Multiple groups or n.i.e.[2]	50 400	58.4	41.6

1. The number of couples by specific visible minority group does not sum to the total because if the two persons in a couple belong to two different visible minority groups, these couples are counted in each group.

2. Belonging to multiple visible minority groups means that respondents reported more than one visible minority group by checking two or more mark-in circles, e.g., Black and South Asian. Less common visible minority groups are reported in the visible minority n.i.e. (not included elsewhere) category. This category includes respondents who reported a write-in response such as Guyanese, West Indian, Kurd, Tibetan, Polynesian and Pacific Islander.

SOURCE: Statistics Canada, "A portrait of couples in mixed unions," *Canadian Social Trends*, 11-008-XIE2010001, No. 89, April 2010; http://www.statcan.gc.ca/bsolc/olc-cel/olc-cel?lang=eng&catno=11-008-X.

The act was not repealed until 1958.

So-called houses of refuge were church-run institutions for women and youths deemed incorrigible. Belmont House's annual report described it as a refuge for feeble-minded women.

The institution was unexpectedly closed six weeks after Ms. Demerson arrived, and she and other inmates secretly were transferred to the Mercer Reformatory, now the site of the Allan Lamport soccer stadium on King Street West.

For the next seven months she operated a sewing machine, worked in the dining hall and slept in a windowless, one-by-two-metre cell. She had to submit to an internal examination in a room with other women.

She was sexually abused by a staff member. She was allowed to speak only half an hour a day. She was not allowed writing materials, a clock or newspapers.

Because of the sexual assaults, when she was sent to Toronto General Hospital to give birth she escaped, wearing only a sheet. Her mother talked her into going back, and Ms. Demerson returned to the reformatory with her infant son.

She told of heading as usual for the jail nursery one morning only to be told by a matron that her child had been taken to hospital. She was given no explanation. She didn't see him for several weeks.

Ms. Demerson was let out after nine months—released early because the King and Queen were visiting Toronto.

Historian Joan Sangster of Trent University says the legislation targeted young working-class women who had sexual liaisons with non-white men.

Lawyer Jill Copeland, who studied the act, says the provision requiring judges to "make reasonable enquiry" into the truth of allegations of incorrigibility was seldom observed.

Ms. Demerson married Mr. Yip, but the marriage ended in divorce three years later. She said that her son was subjected to constant racist insults. He drowned at the age of 26.

SOURCE: "A Dark Passage in Ontario's Past," by Michael Valpy (*The Globe and Mail*), article dated March 22, 2002. Reprinted with permission from The Globe and Mail.

8.2 Multiculturalism in Canada

Pluralism refers to a state in which racial and ethnic groups maintain their distinctness, but respect each other and have equal access to social resources. In Switzerland, for example, four ethnic groups—French, Italian, German, and Romansch—maintain their distinct cultural heritages and group identities in an atmosphere of mutual respect and social equality. Similarly, a policy of cultural pluralism, or **multiculturalism**, is evidenced in the description of Canada as a "mosaic" of peoples, which dates back at the very least to the 1926 publication of Ken Foster's *Our Canadian Mosaic*. Government documents such as *Multiculturalism …Being Canadian* (1987) have—straining their credibility—extended the claim for multiculturalism all the way back to the sixteenth-century "joining" of Europeans with the Aboriginal peoples already in Canada (Day 1998: 42). Richard Day argues that it is an ongoing and deliberate effort of those who build Canadian social policy to deal with the *problem* of diversity by reframing it as a "national jewel" in which "Diversity is present, but only in the context of a perfectly structured (integrated) whole. And, if this unity is to be maintained, the individual elements of the mosaic must be preserved, prevented from exceeding their boundaries" (p. 60). In other words, the perceived threat of multiple racial and ethnic differences must be defused by creating a regularized order out of what would otherwise explode the unity of Canadian culture. Unlike the United States, which, since 1908, has been described by some as a unicultural "**melting pot**," Canada encourages the expression of ethnic and other differences. However, Canada's official policy advocating multiculturalism, not in effect until 1971, was born out of a rather more complex political

pluralism

A state in which racial or ethnic groups maintain their distinctness, but respect each other and have equal access to social resources.

multiculturalism

A philosophy that argues that the culture of a society should represent and embrace all racial and ethnic groups in that society.

melting pot

The product of different groups coming together and contributing equally to a new common culture.

context than many remember or realize. In his speech to the House of Commons on October 8, 1971, Prime Minister Pierre Trudeau committed his government to "a policy of multiculturalism within a bilingual framework…as the most suitable means of assuring the cultural freedom of Canadians" (in Columbo 1986: 353). When launching its policy in 1971, the Canadian government confirmed its commitment to an ideal acknowledging that Canada, while officially bilingual, had no "official" culture—that is, that none of the distinguishable cultures took precedence over the others.

The development of the policy was neither a gesture of beneficence nor a measure intended to right previous wrongs; it was a response to tensions that arose in communities, especially among Ukrainians, not recognized by Trudeau's effort to settle French and English as Canada's official languages. The Royal Commission on Bilingualism and Biculturalism, struck in 1969, revealed that for the bilingual policy to have a hope of succeeding, other official measures would have to be taken to recognize the substantial contributions of non-English and non-French cultures to the creation of Canada as a nation. Wood and Gilbert (2005) found that the popular perception of multiculturalism as a policy rooted in social justice concerns arises from the policy's transmission through schools to those who came of age in the Trudeau years 1969–1982; however, this perception does not accurately reflect "the view of Trudeau and his government that language and culture were to be regarded as separable" (p. 681). In effect, multicultural policy was the most effective way to sell official bilingualism without insisting on official biculturalism.

Since its institutionalization in 1971 Liberal policy, and its revision under the Progressive Conservative government in 1988, multiculturalism has come to mean that as a society Canadians value diversity and plurality. In July 1988, the Progressive Conservative government passed a bill to introduce the *Canadian Multiculturalism Act*, setting forth the multiculturalism policy: to wit, "to recognize all Canadians as full and equal participants in Canadian society." Since 1972, there has been a minister responsible for multiculturalism and, since 1973, a Canadian Multiculturalism Council and a Multiculturalism Directorate within the Department of the Secretary of State. In 1991, a Department of Multiculturalism and Citizenship was established to emphasize that multiculturalism empowers minorities to pursue the dual goals of ethnicity and equality.

Canada's multicultural program, based on the goals of the multicultural policy and the *Canadian Multicultural Act*, has three fundamental goals: (1) identity—fostering a society that recognizes, respects, and reflects a diversity of cultures such that people of all backgrounds feel a sense of belonging and attachment to Canada; (2) civic participation—developing active citizens with both the opportunity and the capacity to help shape the future of Canada and its communities; and (3) social justice—building a society that ensures fair and equitable treatment and that respects the dignity of peoples of all origins and accommodates them. Contemporary critical assessments of official multiculturalism point out, however, that multicultural policy has done little to alleviate the negative influence of racism and ethnocentrism on the life chances of ethnically and racially marked groups in Canada. Some argue that multiculturalism has created only a shallow tolerance of "diversity," attractive only insofar as "this 'food and festivals' brand of aestheticized difference—premised largely on the exotic pleasure of 'visible' and 'edible' ethnicity—emerges from enterprises of more recent vintage: more or less neoliberal schemes engineered to 'sell diversity' and consolidate 'competitive city' status [on cities seeking 'world class' status]" (Goonewardena and Kipfer 2005: 672).

In the following sections, we critically assess the promise and the limitations of official multiculturalism when it comes to meeting its mandate to value and recognize equally all the groups who contribute to the national identity and society that is Canada.

Visible Minorities in Canada

Before 1996, the Canadian census derived indirect information on the numbers and characteristics of persons who were visible minorities from responses to questions on ethnic or cultural origin. However, as of 1996, the Canadian census introduced a new question that asked respondents directly if they were members of one of the population groups defined by the *Employment Equity Act* as "visible minorities," or "persons, other than Aboriginal peoples, who are non-Caucasian in race or non-White in colour." Included under this definition are Chinese, South Asians, Blacks, Arabs and West Asians, Filipinos, Southeast Asians, Latin Americans, Japanese, Koreans, and Pacific Islanders. Census respondents were asked to indicate their population group by checking one or more of 10 mark-in categories.

According to Statistics Canada (2003a), in 2001, 13.4 percent of Canada's total population identified themselves as members of a visible minority. Since 1981, there has been a threefold increase in Canada's visible minority population and, based on current trends, it is expected that by 2016 visible minorities will account for one-fifth of Canada's population (Statistics Canada 2003a). According to Statistics Canada information from the 2006 census, "Between 2001 and 2006, the visible minority population increased at a much faster pace than the total population. Its rate of growth was 27.2%, five times faster than the 5.4% increase for the population as a whole" (Statistics Canada 2008a).

To maintain population growth Canada relies on immigration for about two-thirds of our current growth (Chui et al. 2007: 6), and the highly skilled immigrants that Canada encourages to immigrate are no longer likely to be of European descent (Table 8.3). Those who do emigrate from Europe tend to arrive from Eastern Europe and account for 16.1 percent of all immigrants who arrived in Canada between 2001 and 2006 (Chui et al. 2007: 10). The changes in immigration patterns over the past 25 years have to do with political shifts both in and outside Canada. Chui et al. explain that "changes in Canada's immigration programs to build on social, humanitarian and economic goals, and international events affecting the movements of migrants and refugees" (p. 9) are at the heart of shifts in immigration patterns.

Considerable variation exists in the proportion of visible minorities within Canada's provinces and territories. Ontario and British Columbia, which contain half the country's total population, account for almost three-quarters of the visible minority population. In 2006, visible minorities accounted for 24.8 percent of the population in British Columbia, 22.8 percent in Ontario, and 13.9 percent in Alberta, but just 1.1 percent in Newfoundland and Labrador, while Prince Edward Island has a visible minority population of 1.4 percent, and Nova Scotia

■ Table 8.3 *Top 10 Countries of Birth of Recent Immigrant, 1981–2006*

Order	2006 Census	2001 Census	1996 Census	1991 Census	1981 Census
1	People's Republic of China	People's Republic of China	Hong Kong	Hong Kong	United Kingdom
2	India	India	People's Republic of China	Poland	Viet Nam
3	Philippines	Philippines	India	People's Republic of China	United States of America
4	Pakistan	Pakistan	Philippines	India	India
5	United States of America	Hong Kong	Sri Lanka	Philippines	Philippines
6	South Korea	Iran	Poland	United Kingdom	Jamaica
7	Romania	Taiwan	Taiwan	Viet Nam	Hong Kong
8	Iran	United States of America	Viet Nam	United States of America	Portugal
9	United Kingdom	South Korea	United States of America	Lebanon	Taiwan
10	Colombia	Sri Lanka	United Kingdom	Portugal	People's Republic of China

Note: 'Recent immigrants' refers to landed immigrants who arrived in Canada within five years prior to a given census.

SOURCE: Statistics Canada, "Immigration in Canada: A Portrait of the Foreign-born Populations, 2006 Census," Census Year 2006, Catalogue no. 97-557-XIE, December 2007, p. 10.

has a visible minority population of 4.2 percent. Because many of those in the visible minority population have arrived as well-trained, highly educated immigrants, it is not surprising that the majority of visible minorities live in one of Canada's 25 census metropolitan areas (CMAs). A CMA is an urban area whose principal or central city has a population of at least 100 000. Furthermore, CMAs offer established communities for visible minority immigrants to settle in, making larger urban areas more attractive than rural communities.

Aboriginality

The *Constitution Act, 1982*, defines "aboriginal peoples of Canada" as belonging to four major groups:

1. *Status Indians.* Persons whose names appear on the Indian Register maintained by the Department of Indian and Northern Affairs Canada under the *Indian Act* and who are registered as Indians for the purpose of special entitlements.
2. *Nonstatus Indians.* Those whose Indian status has been extinguished for a variety of reasons and whose names do not appear on the Indian Register. Previously, Indians gave up their official status when they wanted to vote, to drink alcohol off the reserve, or (if they were women) to marry a non-Indian. In 1985, the federal government introduced Bill C-31, which enabled Indian women to regain their legal status if they had lost it by marrying men who did not possess Indian status. The bill also allowed all first-generation children of such marriages and any Indian who had been disenfranchised to regain their legal status as Indian. In consequence, the number of nonstatus Indians has dwindled.

3. *Métis.* The descendants of Indian and non-Indian unions (principally between Indians and Europeans and, prior to Confederation, between Indians and the French). Previously regarded as "half-breeds," the Métis have sought to establish their status within Canadian society, past and present. For example, they have suggested that Louis Riel be regarded as the "Father of Confederation" for the Métis and argued that Riel "intuitively sensed the future for Canada and wanted to guarantee a place for Métis people in that future" (Kilgour 1988: 48).

4. *The Inuit.* This term, meaning "the people," replaced "Eskimos," an Algonquian word meaning "eaters of raw flesh" that is now considered derogatory. The Inuit became the first Aboriginal group in Canada to achieve at least partial self-determination with the creation of Nunavut (Inuktitut for "our land"). First proposed in 1976 as an Inuit homeland by the Inuit Tapirisat (an association of Inuit leaders) and established by the *Nunavut Act* of June 1993, Nunavut became a constitutional entity on April 1, 1999. About 80 percent of Nunavut's total population (about 27 000) is Inuit (Crauford-Lewis 1999: 1686).

In 1996, a question about ancestry and identity of Native persons appeared on the census for the first time: "Is this person an Aboriginal person, that is, North American Indian, Métis, or Inuit (Eskimo)?" The 2001 and 2006 census questionnaires have continued to include this question. In the following section we summarize information from the 2001 and 2006 census reports on Canada's Aboriginal peoples.

By 2001, 976 300 individuals said they were members of at least one of three Aboriginal groups: North American Indian, Métis, or Inuit (Figure 8.1). By 2006, over 1.1 million identified as belonging to one of the three Aboriginal groups in Canada. The increase in the Aboriginal population stems from a high birth rate, an increased tendency of people to identify themselves as Aboriginal, and fewer incompletely enumerated reserves. In 2006, almost one-half (48 percent) of the Aboriginal population was under age 25, and the median age for

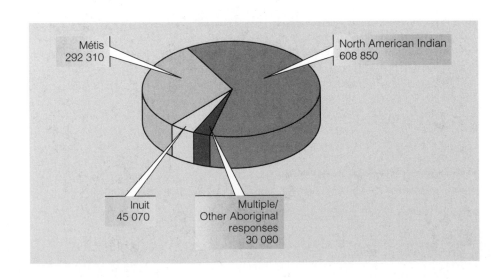

Métis
292 310

North American Indian
608 850

Inuit
45 070

Multiple/
Other Aboriginal
responses
30 080

■ **Figure 8.1** *Aboriginal Makeup, 2001*

SOURCE: Adapted from Statistics Canada. 2003. "Census of Population: Immigration, Birthplace and Birthplace of Parents, Citizenship, Ethnic Origin, Visible Minorities and Aboriginal Peoples." *The Daily*, January 21.

the total population was 22; for the Métis fully one-quarter of the population is aged 14 and under. Compared to these high percentages of young people, seniors account for only 5 percent of the Aboriginal population. To some extent these percentages reflect a high birth rate for the three Aboriginal groups, but the percentages also reflect the reduced life expectancy for North American Indian, Métis, and Inuit people.

The status of Canada's Native peoples reflects the strains of almost 400 years of cultural domination, exploitation, and exclusion. The consequences are not surprising. Native people suffer the lowest levels of education, income, health, and employment in Canada. Social conditions on many Native reserves—the lands set aside for the exclusive use of status Indians—reflect the historical and political neglect that Canada has shown toward its Indigenous peoples. On many reserves, housing fails to meet the most basic structural standards. Less than half of on-reserve homes have sewer or water hook-ups and half can best be described as overcrowded (Frideres 1993). Native men on reserves die, on average, seven years sooner than other Canadians, and the life expectancy for Native women remains six years lower than the national norm (Health Canada 1999). It has been estimated that the suicide rate among the Aboriginal population averages two to seven times that of the Canadian population as a whole (Health Canada 1999).

Table 8.4 gives us a demographic view of Aboriginal groups in Canada, and Table 8.5 provides us with information about Native peoples who self-identify on census reports. Native people do not view themselves as simply part of multicultural Canada; rather, they seek recognition of their sovereign status as the ancestral occupants of Canada. In support of this position, the main conclusion of the 1996 Royal Commission on Aboriginal Peoples "was the need for a complete restructuring of the relationship between aboriginal and non-aboriginal peoples in Canada." Doerr (1999: 3) notes that the recommendations included

Table 8.4 *Size and Growth of the Population by Aboriginal Identity, Canada 1996 and 2006*

Aboriginal Identity	2006	Percentage Change from 1996 to 2006[3]
Total population	31 241 030	9
Aboriginal identity population	1 172 790	45
First Nations people[1]	698 025	29
Metis[1]	389 785	91
Inuit[1]	50 485	26
Multiple and other Aboriginal responses[2]	34 500	34
Non-Aboriginal population	30 068 240	8

Notes:

1. Includes persons who reported a North American Indian, Métis or Inuit identity only.

2. Includes persons who reported more than one Aboriginal identity group (North American Indian, Métis or Inuit) and those who reported being a Registered Indian and/or Band member without reporting an Aboriginal identity.

3. Data have been adjusted to account for incompletely enumerated reserves in 1996 and 2006.

SOURCE: Adapted from Statistics Canada, "Aboriginal Peoples in Canada in 2006, 2006 Census," 97-558-XIE2006001, January 2008; http://www.statcan.gc.ca/bsolc/olc-cel/olc-cel?lang=eng&catno=97-558-X2006001.

Governmental commitment to a new set of ethical principles...acknowledg[ing] and respect[ing] aboriginal cultures and values, the origins of aboriginal nationhood and the inherent right to aboriginal self-determination.

That the further development of aboriginal governments should focus on aboriginal nations rather than single communities...[and] the establishment of an aboriginal parliament which would comprise aboriginal representatives and advise Parliament on matters affecting aboriginal peoples.

The need to significantly increase land holdings for First Nations in southern Canada...[and] a recommendation for an independent lands and treaties tribunal to oversee negotiations among federal, provincial and aboriginal governments on land issues.

Adoption of aboriginal health and healing strategies, an aboriginal peoples international university, educational programs to support aboriginal self-government and public education initiatives to promote cultural sensitivity and understanding among non-aboriginals.

However, in its response to the Report, the federal government limited itself to pursuing four objectives: "renewing partnerships; strengthening aboriginal governance; developing a new fiscal relationship; and supporting strong communities, people and economies" (Doerr 1999: 4). The federal government also issued a Statement of Reconciliation, which expressed regret for past errors and a determination to learn from these errors. It committed $350 million to support community-based healing.

Ethnic Diversity in Canada

Ethnicity refers to a shared cultural heritage or nationality. Ethnic groups may be distinguished based on language, forms of family structures and roles of family members, religious beliefs and practices, dietary customs, forms of artistic expression such as music and dance, and national origin.

ethnicity

A shared cultural heritage or national origin.

■ **Table 8.5** *Number and Percentage of Population Reporting Aboriginal Identity, Canada, Provinces and Territories, 2006*

Provinces and Territories	Number	Percentage
Canada	1 172 790	100
Newfoundland and Labrador	23 450	2
Prince Edward Island	1 730	0.1
Nova Scotia	24 175	2
New Brunswick	17 655	2
Quebec	108 430	9
Ontario	242 495	21
Manitoba	175 395	15
Saskatchewan	141 890	12
Alberta	188 365	16
British Columbia	196 075	17
Yukon Territory	7 580	0.6
Northwest Territories	20 635	2
Nunavut	24 920	2

SOURCE: Statistics Canada, "Aboriginal Peoples in Canada in 2006: Inuit, Métis, and First Nations, 2006 Census," Census Year 2006, Catalogue no. 97-558-XIE, January 2008, p. 11.

Canadians come from a variety of ethnic backgrounds, though "racial" backgrounds may be shared. "Ethnic origin," as defined in the 2001 Canadian census, refers to ethnic or cultural ancestry; it should not be confused with place of birth, citizenship, or nationality. Before 1996, the census question "To which ethnic or cultural group(s) did this person's ancestors belong?" was accompanied by a list of the 15 most frequent ethnic origins. Respondents were asked to mark as many from this list as applicable and were provided with two blank spaces in which they could indicate ethnic origins not included on the list. However, as of the 1996 census, the format of the ethnic origin question was modified. Rather than providing respondents with a list of answer categories, respondents are given four blank spaces to indicate single or multiple ethnic origins. "Canadian" was the fifth most frequently reported ethnic origin in the 1991 census. In recognition of that fact, for the first time in 1996 "Canadian" was included among the examples given of how this question might be answered.

The inclusion of this example "resulted in a major change in the way ethnic origins were reported" (Statistics Canada 1998). In 2001, 6.7 million people (23 percent of Canada's total population) reported their ethnic origin as "Canadian." By 2006, the number reporting "Canadian" as their ethnic origin has risen to just over 10 million, or nearly one-third of the total population. The census allowed respondents to choose more than one origin, as did 4.3 million of those who chose "Canadian" as one of their origins. Statistics Canada accounts for the enormous changes in the reporting of ancestry noting that it is more common now to have mixed unions, and to see individuals with far greater awareness about their family histories and heritage. They do note a distinction between those respondents born in Canada and those born elsewhere: 47.6 percent of Canadian-born respondents listed multiple ancestry, while only 17.2 percent of the foreign-born population noted more than one ethnic ancestry (Statistics Canada 2008c: 10).

Table 8.6 provides us with a generational view of how Canada's population identifies its ethnic background(s). Statistics Canada's decision to include the ethnic category of "Canadian" has not been without controversy. According to Jack Jedwab, the head of the Association for Canadian Studies, injecting nationalism into the census only frustrates the work of researchers. "The sheer number of people who identify themselves as Canadians makes it difficult to determine how many people are not indicating their ethnic background" (*National Post* 1999a: A1). More recently, there has been considerable debate over whether the ethnicity question ought to be deleted from the Canadian census. However, questions regarding ethnicity can help census researchers to assess correlations between health measures, employment, housing, and ethnicity. In refusing to ask the question, we would risk not having the data we need to identify and serve better those populations that are vulnerable to the effects of socio-political prejudice.

charter groups

A term that has been traditionally used in Canada to refer to the English and French and that reflects the historical importance of these groups in Canada's history.

The Québécois

In Canada, we have traditionally spoken of the English and French as "**charter groups**," to reflect the historical importance of these groups in Canada. Although the *British North America Act* of 1867 acknowledged and enshrined the rights and privileges of the French and the British as the founding or charter groups of Canadian society, "the history of English–French relations in Canada

■ Table 8.6 *Top 10 Ethnic Origins by Generational Status for People Aged 15 Years and Over, Canada, 2006*

First Generation			Second Generation			Third Generation or More		
Ethnic origin	Number	%	Ethnic origin	Number	%	Ethnic origin	Number	%
Total population	6 124 560	100.0	Total population	4 006 420	100.0	Total population	15 533 240	100.0
Chinese	916 845	15.0	English	1 035 145	25.8	Canadian	7 236 370	46.6
East Indian	612 460	10.0	Scottish	635 600	15.9	English	3 794 250	24.4
English	547 865	8.9	Canadian	613 445	15.3	French	3 530 505	22.7
Italian	366 205	6.0	German	524 645	13.1	Scottish	2 865 800	18.4
German	352 805	5.8	Irish	496 990	12.4	Irish	2 755 420	17.7
Filipino	288 515	4.7	Italian	439 275	11.0	German	1 604 225	10.3
Scottish	271 545	4.4	French	284 900	7.1	North American Indian	813 405	5.2
Irish	230 975	3.8	Dutch (Netherlands)	253 325	6.3	Ukrainian	642 955	4.1
Polish	213 715	3.5	Ukrainian	212 860	5.3	Dutch (Netherlands)	376 555	2.4
Portuguese	195 480	3.2	Polish	203 725	5.1	Polish	364 980	2.3

Note:

1. Table shows total responses. Because some respondents reported more than one ethnic origin, the sum of the total

SOURCE: Statistics Canada, "Canada's Ethnocultural Mosaic, 2006 Census," 97-562-XWE2006001, April 2008; http://www.statcan.gc.ca/bsolc/olc-cel/olc-cel?catno=97-562-XWE&lang=eng.

is one of competition between two collectivities engaged in constructing and maintaining a society" (Breton 1988: 557). Indeed, Lord Durham's 1839 description of this relationship as "two nations warring in the bosom of a single state" may still strike some as apt. As Behiels (1999: 909) has commented, views similar to Durham's constitute a gross simplification of the character of francophone–anglophone relations, which have "ebbed and flowed in response to changing socioeconomic, political and ideological factors as well as to the commitment of Canada's majority and minority francophone communities to survival and equality."

During the period between Confederation and World War II, the building of institutions in Canada largely favoured the English. The development of the Canadian collective identity, Breton (1988) has argued, was not modelled on something uniquely Canadian, but rather on something decidedly "British" and "Protestant." Although in the English collectivity immigration was pursued as the central means for ensuring the growth of the English-speaking population, in Quebec the concern that French Roman Catholics would be drowned in a British Protestant sea found expression in a policy that encouraged childbearing. Nevertheless, with the influx of English-speaking merchants and settlers into Quebec, the English, although a statistical minority, gradually assumed power. Over time, the English in Quebec became an elite that dominated in the areas of finance, transportation, and staples. English-speaking groups came to dominate the Quebec economy and the politico-bureaucratic groups that strongly influenced the federal government.

Urban migration, a postwar industrial expansion, and reforms made during the 1960s in Quebec encouraged a strong rise in Quebec nationalism. Under the leadership of Jean Lesage, the provincial government initiated a broad range of structural and ideological reforms that increased the role of the state and reduced the power and primacy of the Roman Catholic Church. Francophones in Quebec responded to a steeply declining birth rate and an increase in the number of non-francophone immigrants (many of whom chose to use English at work and for the schooling of their children). Many of them believed that for Quebec to survive as a French-speaking society, the French language would have to be aggressively promoted. More and more, francophones tended to equate their collective identity with the empowerment of Quebec itself. Those who had formerly referred to themselves as "canadien" or "canadien-français" increasingly began to use the term "Québécois" and to assert their belief that Quebec was capable of directing and controlling its own future.

The victory of the Parti Québécois, a political party dedicated to Quebec's achievement of independent nationhood, in the 1976 Quebec election notified Canadians of both the strength of French nationalism within that province and the depth of Québécois dissatisfaction. Neither the 1969 passage of Canada's *Official Languages Act*, nor the passage in 1977 of the French Language Charter (Bill 101) in Quebec, extinguished the perceived threat of assimilation. (Bill 101 established French as the only official language of education, work, and the public sector in that province.)

Since then, "French Canada's attempt to redefine its role within Canada has produced vigorous public debate and considerable political turmoil" (Behiels 1999: 911). The desire to create a French homeland that is predominantly French in character is not, strictly speaking, a "new" idea, but one that has circulated since at least the time of Confederation. However, it gained a sense of immediacy in the early 1990s when Lucien Bouchard's secessionist Bloc Québécois won 54 of the province's 75 federal seats. In 1994, then Parti Québécois leader Jacques Parizeau announced a referendum on the concept of sovereignty-partnership for 1995. The Parti Québécois maintained that should Canada refuse "to negotiate an economic association with an independent Quebec following a majority vote...Quebec would unilaterally declare its independence from Canada" (p. 912).

With polls leading up to the referendum suggesting that the decision would be based on a very close vote, Prime Minister Jean Chrétien promised the Québécois a veto over all major constitutional changes and recognition of Quebec as a distinct society (Balthazar 1997: 8). When the referendum vote was held, 51 percent voted "No" to sovereignty and 49 percent voted "Yes"—a wafer-thin rejection of sovereignty that Parizeau blamed on "money and the ethnic vote." A poll conducted in 1995 reported that one in three Canadians and one in two Quebecers believed that "the country...[would] cease to exist by the end of the decade" (*Maclean's* 1999: 28).

In the aftermath of the referendum, on December 11, 1995, the federal government passed a resolution supporting the concept of Quebec as a distinct society, and on February 2, 1996, Bill C-110—which granted all five regions of Canada, including Quebec, a veto over future constitutional changes—received royal assent and passed into law.

The federal government referred the question of whether or not Quebec had the right to secede unilaterally from Canada to the Supreme Court of Canada. The Supreme Court of Canada later issued the unanimous ruling that Quebec did not have this right either under Canadian constitutional law or under international law. However, the Supreme Court also held the view that

> if Quebec voters demonstrated a clear, and not just a simple, majority on a straightforward question on outright secession, then Ottawa and the other provinces would have an obligation to enter into negotiations with the government of Quebec. They also pointed out that there was no guarantee that such negotiations would succeed or that the territory of the province of Quebec would remain intact if the negotiations succeeded since the rights of the majority had to respect those of the various minorities. (Behiels 1999: 912)

However, the Supreme Court failed to define what it meant by "clear" or "substantial." In November 1999, Prime Minister Jean Chrétien announced that his cabinet had agreed that the federal government would have to act to ensure that these terms were clearly defined. The government tabled the Clarity Bill, which set out the conditions under which Ottawa would negotiate the separation of a province following a referendum win by Yes forces. Although the draft bill declared that a simple majority of 50 percent plus one would not be enough to trigger separation, it did not specify what percentage would.

In response to this move by the federal government, Joseph Facal, Quebec's intergovernmental affairs minister, announced that only Quebec's National Assembly could decide the wording of the referendum and the terms for leaving Canada. According to Facal, "Ottawa, inspired by a Soviet-style law, is trying to impose a real straitjacket on Quebec's political future. It's an assault without precedent on the democratic rights of the people of Quebec to choose the political future it wants to choose" (*National Post* 1999b: A11). For their part, the Bloc Québécois labelled the move "a crime against history," and Quebec premier Lucien Bouchard called Ottawa's move "a strain on Canada's democratic reputation in the eyes of the international community" (*Maclean's* 1999: 83).

An Angus Reid survey of Quebec residents, released on December 14, 1999, found that 80 percent of those polled agreed that a clear referendum question was needed and 59 percent said that a clear majority—more than 50 percent plus one—was needed before Quebec could negotiate separation.

A second poll, conducted by Ekos Research Associates in December 1999, found that only 30 percent of Quebecers would vote for outright independence in a referendum; 64 percent favoured the status quo. Only 17 percent of Quebecers stated that they expected that Quebec would be a country in five years' time—the lowest level ever reported in a survey (*National Post* 1999c: A7).

8.3 Canadian Immigration

Immigration is, arguably, the area of public policy that has had the greatest impact on Canada's history, economy, multicultural identity, and regional diversity. The growing racial and ethnic diversity of Canada is largely attributable to immigration.

The history of Canada's immigration policies is far from exemplary, though. In the 1870s and 1880s, the active effort to recruit immigrants to Canada for labour-intensive industries was accompanied by regulations that sought to pre-serve Canada's "English stock" by restricting or denying entry to certain groups. These regulations reflected the sentiment that, while useful as labourers, certain groups were "undesirable" as permanent residents of Canada. For example, hostility toward Asians and a fear of the "yellow peril" is clear in the statement by Sir John A. Macdonald, Canada's first prime minister, that "a Mongolian or Chinese population in our country…would not be a wholesome element" (in Sher 1983: 33). Canada's 1910 *Immigration Act* gave the government the formal power to "prohibit for a stated period, or permanently, the landing in Canada…of immigrants belonging to any race unsuited to the climate or requirements of Canada." Laws to prohibit anyone who did not come directly to Canada from their country of origin from landing effectively eliminated the entry of people from India, "who had no choice but to book passages on ships through a third country because no direct routes existed to Vancouver" (Bricker and Greenspon 2001: 287). In 1919, regulations explicitly prohibited Doukhobors, Mennonites, and Hutterites.

In 1923, Canada's *Chinese Immigration Act* barred the Chinese entry, and Chinese persons already in Canada were not allowed to sponsor family or rela-tives. In the same year, the federal government listed Poland, Yugoslavia, Hungary, and Romania as "non-preferred" countries for the purposes of immi-gration. Abella and Troper (1998: 108) emphasize that Canada's refusal to accept Jewish refugees from Hitler's Europe reflected the pervasive anti-Semitism of pre-war Canada. They note that when a senior Canadian official was asked by journalists how many Jewish refugees would be admitted after the war, the official responded, "None is too many." "It is perhaps no surprise therefore that Canada had by far the worst record of any Western country for providing sanctuary to the Jews of Europe in the 1930s and 1940s" (Abella 1999: 90).

In 1947, Prime Minister William Lyon Mackenzie King pledged to remove "objectionable discrimination" from the *Immigration Act*. Certain blatantly dis-criminatory features of the Act were removed, but Canada's immigration policy still included "selective restriction." Preferred candidates were British, Irish, French, or American. The Ministry of Citizenship and Immigration was to deter-mine the suitability of other would-be immigrants in light of "the climate, edu-cational, social, industrial, labour, and other requirements in Canada." A person applying to immigrate to Canada could be declared "undesirable" because of "his peculiar customs, habits, modes of life, methods of holding property or his general inability to assimilate."

In the 1950s, the Canadian government, under pressure from other countries of the Commonwealth, began to relax its immigration policies. However, not until the White Paper of 1966 and the Regulations of 1967 was there a call for the abolishment of discrimination based on race, colour, religion, national origin, or gender (not until 1978 was homosexuality officially removed as a prohibited category). Immigration was to respond to Canada's need for workers, and cultural enrichment was added as part of Canada's immigration objectives.

"As of May 15, 2001, 5.4 million people, or 18.4 percent of the total popula-tion, were born outside of Canada" (Statistics Canada 2003b). Only in Australia is the proportion of the population born outside of the country higher than it is in Canada (Statistics Canada 2003a: 5). Of those immigrating to Canada in the

1990s, 58 percent were born in Asia (including the Middle East), 20 percent in Europe, 11 percent in the Caribbean and Central and South America, 8 percent in Africa, and 3 percent in the United States. Among those who immigrated to Canada during the 1990s, the leading country of birth was the People's Republic of China (Statistics Canada 2003a).

Quebec is also being transformed by immigration. "Immigrants make up about 10 percent of the population of Quebec, less than many other provinces, but the fastest growing segment of the population nonetheless" (Bricker and Greenspon 2001: 294).

Canada currently divides its immigration intake into three categories: (1) economic immigrants, who accounted for about 153 000 of those who arrived in 2001; (2) family-status immigrants (a parent, child, spouse, and so on of a Canadian resident), who comprised 66 000 new immigrants; and (3) refugees, who numbered 27 800. Recent changes to our immigration law emphasize the desirability of attracting skilled workers with the selection system placing considerable weight on an applicant's education or trade skills, language proficiency, and "adaptability" (which includes the education of an applicant's spouse) (Janigan 2002). (See this chapter's *Self and Society* feature.)

Canada is a signatory to the 1951 United Nations Convention Relating to the Status of Refugees. The *Immigration Act, 1976*, and the 1992 amendments introduced by Bill C-86 additionally provide for the admission of "designated classes" on humanitarian grounds. A UN Convention refugee is defined as a person who "owing to a well-founded fear of being prosecuted for reasons of race, religion, nationality, membership in a particular social group or political opinion, is outside the country of his nationality and is unable, or owing to such fear, is unwilling to avail himself of the protection of that country." The term *designated classes* is used to refer to "a variety of refugee-like situations including mass outflows...disproportionate punishment for violation of strict exit controls (self-exiles) and, for specific countries, the internally displaced (political prisoners and oppressed people)" (Boyd 2000: 84).

Some notable differences are apparent between the immigrant population and the Canadian-born population. While 44 percent of those who arrived in 2001 spoke neither English nor French, almost 60 percent of those who were adults had a postsecondary degree (compared with 43 percent of the existing population) (Janigan 2002). Compared to those who are Canadian born, recent immigrants, regardless of their country of birth, tend to be in better health—a tendency that reflects the demands of our immigration requirements (Health Canada 1999).

In other ways, however, recent immigrants are less fortunate than Canadian-born residents. For example, although the 2006 census found that males who had immigrated to Canada within the last five years were better educated than their Canadian counterparts (58.2 percent of immigrants held a university degree, while only 19.9 percent of Canadian-born men had achieved a university degree), the immigrant males earned only 63 cents on the dollar compared to the Canadian-born (Statistics Canada, 2009: 21). The situation for women was similar, with average earnings of 56 cents for every dollar earned by their Canadian-born counterparts (ibid). In both cases, these low earnings and higher levels of education represent significant deterioration in opportunity and earning power for recent immigrants, who had earned significantly *more* in 1980

Becoming a Canadian Citizen: Could You Pass the Test?

Canadian citizenship is a relatively new concept. It was not until after World War II that an independent Canadian citizenship was introduced. Before then, Canadians were considered British subjects residing in Canada, rather than Canadian citizens. Generally, people who are born in Canada automatically become Canadian citizens. Also, those born in another country after February 15, 1977, but who have at least one parent who was a Canadian citizen at the time of their birth, are Canadian citizens. Others may apply to become Canadian citizens.

To apply for Canadian citizenship as a "permanent resident," you must be 18 years of age or older and in Canada legally as a permanent resident. You must have lived in Canada for at least three out of the four years right before the day you apply (this three-year residency requirement is waived in the case of children who are under the age of 18). Any time spent in Canada before becoming a resident is counted as half time if it falls within this four-year period; all the time spent in Canada since becoming a permanent resident counts as full time.

Some conditions disqualify individuals from becoming Canadian citizens. Any individual who is or was in prison, on parole, or on probation in the past four years cannot become a Canadian citizen. Similarly, anyone convicted of an indictable offence in the past three years; charged with an indictable offence; or under a deportation order and not currently allowed to be in Canada cannot become a Canadian citizen. Also, anyone facing charges under the Citizenship Act or under investigation for a war crime or a crime against humanity, or who has had his or her Canadian citizenship revoked in the past five years, is not eligible.

To become a Canadian citizen, you must be proficient enough in either of Canada's official languages, English or French, to understand others and have them understand you. This condition means that you need the ability to speak and understand spoken English or French or to read and write in simple English or French. You must pass a written test that asks general questions about Canada's system of governance, its geography, history, and people, and the rights and responsibilities of citizenship. This citizenship test includes specific questions about the economy, geography, and history of the region in which the applicant resides. For those who are visually impaired, oral examinations are available. To pass the citizenship test, applicants must answer at least 12 out of 20 questions correctly.

Those who apply for and meet all the requirements for Canadian citizenship are sent a Notice to Appear to Take the Oath of Citizenship, which tells them when and where their citizenship ceremony will take place. At the ceremony, individuals take the Oath of Citizenship; those who wish to swear the oath of citizenship on their holy book are invited to bring it to the ceremony. At the citizenship ceremony, new Canadians receive certificates of citizenship and commemorative documents that show the date on which they became Canadian citizens.

The following questions, taken from a larger list of sample questions that appear on the website of Citizenship and Immigration Canada, www.cic.gc.ca, are typical of those appearing on the written examination. Could you pass the test?

Sample Questions

1. Who are the Aboriginal peoples of Canada?
2. From whom are the Métis descended?
3. Who were the United Empire Loyalists?
4. When did the *British North America Act* come into effect?
5. Which four provinces first formed Confederation?
6. List each province and territory and when each joined Confederation.
7. When is Canada Day and what does it celebrate?
8. Name two fundamental freedoms protected by the *Canadian Charter of Rights and Freedoms*.
9. List four rights Canadian citizens have.
10. Which legal document recognizes the cultural diversity of Canadians?

than recent immigrants to Canada were earning in the first decade of the 2000s. Using constant dollars, the Statistics Canada data show that average earnings for the recently immigrated have fallen 21.1 percent since 1980 (Statistics Canada 2009: 40). In addition, "[t]he earnings gain associated with immigrant skills, among them language and university education, has fallen" (Statistics Canada 2003c).

Reactions toward immigration are mixed. For example, while data from a 1999 survey indicates that 6 out of 10 Canadians feel that cultural diversity enhances Canadian identity, "[o]nly 14 percent...[said] they would like to see more immigration in future versus 43 percent who like the current levels and 41 percent who would like us to scale down" (Bricker and Greenspon 2001: 297). A poll conducted in the wake of the terrorist attacks on the United States on September 11, 2001, suggests a hardening of attitudes toward both immigrants and refugees (Figure 8.2). For example, this survey found that almost one in two Canadians (49 percent) supported restricting immigration from Muslim countries (*Maclean's* 2001/2002). A second survey, conducted shortly before the first anniversary of the tragedy of 9/11, found that over a third of respondents (35 percent) wanted our immigration laws and quotas tightened greatly, while 34 percent wanted them tightened somewhat; only 3 percent wanted immigration rules relaxed (Granastein 2002). An explanation for the shift in attitudes cannot be attributed only to the events of 9/11; we must also

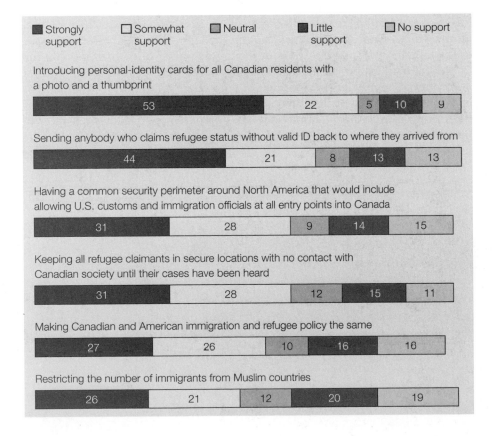

■ Strongly support □ Somewhat support ■ Neutral ■ Little support □ No support

Introducing personal-identity cards for all Canadian residents with a photo and a thumbprint

| 53 | 22 | 5 | 10 | 9 |

Sending anybody who claims refugee status without valid ID back to where they arrived from

| 44 | 21 | 8 | 13 | 13 |

Having a common security perimeter around North America that would include allowing U.S. customs and immigration officials at all entry points into Canada

| 31 | 28 | 9 | 14 | 15 |

Keeping all refugee claimants in secure locations with no contact with Canadian society until their cases have been heard

| 31 | 28 | 12 | 15 | 11 |

Making Canadian and American immigration and refugee policy the same

| 27 | 26 | 10 | 16 | 18 |

Restricting the number of immigrants from Muslim countries

| 26 | 21 | 12 | 20 | 19 |

■ **Figure 8.2** *A Hardening of Attitudes toward Immigrants and Refugees*

SOURCE: *Maclean's.* "Since Sept. 11: The Responses Show How Terrorism and War Have Left Their Mark." (December 31–January 7): 39.

account for people's emotional and psychological responses to the *multiple* uncertainties that 9/11 signals:

> attitudes toward immigration that have become increasingly favorable in recent years are likely to become substantially more negative as a result of the September 11, 2001 "Attack on America." This prediction is based on psychological theorizing and research on the consequences of the direct realistic and symbolic threats that the Attack has engendered, as well as on the impact of the more indirect consequences of the Attack, which include economic and social uncertainty. As a result of this confluence of effects, it is likely that in the next few years, policy makers in the United States and Canada will be faced with a difficult task. (Esses et al. 2002: 79–80)

An Environics poll in August 2002 showed, however, that increased hostility toward immigrants, especially those from Arab countries, correlated strongly with the level of knowledge respondents had about international affairs; in short, the greater the knowledge, the less hostile respondents were. (See Table 8.7 and Table 8.8.) Nonetheless, in both groups, many of the survey's respondents felt there were "too many" immigrants from Asian, Latin American, and African countries. In other words, the events of 9/11 appear to have disturbed what may have been a tenuous form of tolerance among non-immigrant Canadians, a population whose attitudes toward immigrants hardly appear to be positive, based on their responses in the Environics data.

Managing Canada's increasing diversity has also become a challenge for the federal government and municipal governments, for school boards, and for businesses. According to research conducted by the Privy Council Office, federal efforts will be required to fill an expanding gap in providing English training for the young and to match the skills of new immigrants to job openings. At the municipal level, there will be a challenge to deliver services to a multilingual population. The problem of figuring out who needs what is also essential. For example, while 47 percent of new immigrants fall into a low-income bracket, those from Mexico and Central America suffer from unusually high rates of unemployment, and those from Vietnam have marked difficulty with the school system.

■ **Table 8.7** *Immigration Views of Those Very Well Informed about International Affairs, Post 9/11*

	Arab Countries Very Well Informed	Latin American Countries Very Well Informed	Asian Countries Very Well Informed	African Countries Very Well Informed	European Countries Very Well Informed
Too many	39	19	35	27	10
Too few	11	24	14	26	43
Right number	40	45	45	35	40
DK/NA	9	12	6	12	7

SOURCE: "The Impact of September 11th on Immigration," by Jack Jedwab, 2002. *(Association for Canadian Studies)*. Table 6. http//www.acs-aec.ca/Polls/Poll12.pdf. Reprinted with permission.

■ **Table 8.8** *Immigration Views of Those Very Uninformed about International Affairs, Post 9/11*

	Arab Countries Very Uninformed	Latin American Countries Very Uninformed	Asian Countries Very Uninformed	African Countries Very Uninformed	European Countries Very Uninformed
Too many	52	35	53	31	31
Too few	6	14	8	16	17
Right number	29	35	27	38	38
DK/NA	13	17	13	15	13

Those who consider themselves very uninformed on international affairs possess considerably greater degrees in the view that there are too many immigrants from Arab and Asian countries and for that matter from other countries as well.

SOURCE: "The Impact of September 11th on Immigration," by Jack Jedwab, 2002. *(Association for Canadian Studies)*. Table 7. http//www.acs-aec.ca/Polls/Poll12.pdf. Reprinted with permission.

8.4 Sociological Theories of Race and Ethnicity

Some theories of race and ethnicity suggest that individuals with certain personality types are more likely to be prejudiced against or to direct hostility toward minority group members. Sociologists, however, concentrate on the impact of the structure and culture of society on race and ethnicity. The major sociological theories lend insight into the continued subordination of minorities.

Structural-Functionalist Perspective

Functionalists emphasize that each component of society contributes to the stability of the whole. In the past, inequality between majority and minority groups was functional for some groups in society. For example, in the United States, the belief in the superiority of one group over another provided moral justification for slavery, supplying the South with the means to develop an agricultural economy based on cotton. Further, southern whites perpetuated the belief that emancipation would be detrimental for Blacks, who were highly dependent upon their "white masters" for survival (Nash 1962).

Functionalists recognize, however, that racial and ethnic inequality is also dysfunctional for society (Schaefer 1998; Williams and Morris 1993). A society that practises discrimination fails to develop and utilize the resources of minority members. Prejudice and discrimination aggravate social problems, such as crime and violence, war, poverty, health problems, unemployment, and drug use—problems that cause human suffering and financial burdens for individuals and society.

Conflict Perspective

Conflict theorists emphasize the role of economic competition in creating and maintaining racial and ethnic group tensions. Majority group subordination of racial and ethnic minorities reflects perceived or real economic threats by the minority. For example, although 15 000 Chinese were allowed to enter Canada as a pool of inexpensive labour for the building of the transcontinental railway, on its completion, they were treated as unwelcome guests. In 1885, the infamous "head tax" was imposed on every Chinese immigrant to Canada. Initially set at $50, the head tax was increased to $100 in 1900, and three years later to $500—an astronomical amount at that time—in an obvious attempt to restrict the entrance of Chinese and other Asians to Canada.

Further, conflict theorists suggest that capitalists profit by maintaining a surplus labour force; that is, having more workers than are needed. A surplus labour force ensures that wages remain low, because someone is always available to take a disgruntled worker's place. Minorities who are disproportionately unemployed serve the interests of the business owners by providing surplus labour, keeping wages low, and, consequently, enabling the owners to maximize profits.

Conflict theorists also argue that the wealthy and powerful elites foster negative attitudes toward minorities to maintain racial and ethnic tensions among workers. As long as workers are divided along racial and ethnic lines, they are less likely to join forces to advance their own interests at the expense of the capitalists. In addition, the "haves" perpetuate racial and ethnic tensions among the "have nots" to deflect attention away from their own greed and exploitation of workers.

Struggles over political power also affect interactions between groups organized by race and ethnicity. When the first free elections were held in South Africa, the Black African National Congress (ANC), led by Nelson Mandela, campaigned on a platform that promised several plans of affirmative action—these would reverse the four decades of apartheid that barred Black South Africans from political participation and denied them many basic human rights. The White Nation Party, trying to maintain the position of political power it had held during apartheid, also promised affirmative action in the 1994 election campaign, but it did not announce this change in platform until two months before the election, when polls began to predict a landslide victory for the African National Congress (Guillebeau 1999).

Symbolic Interactionist Perspective

The symbolic interactionist perspective focuses on how meanings and definitions contribute to the subordinate position of certain racial and ethnic groups. The different connotations of the colours white and black are a case in point. The white knight is good, and the black knight is evil; angel food cake is white, devil's food cake is black. Other negative terms associated with black include black sheep, black plague, black magic, black mass, blackballed, and blacklisted. The continued use of such derogatory labels as Jap, Gook, Spic, Frog, Kraut, Coon, Chink, Wop, and Mick also confirms the power of language in perpetuating negative attitudes toward minority group members.

For example, research by Donakowski and Esses (1996) concludes that the labels used to refer to minority groups play a role in the attitudes that are expressed toward them. In their research, 108 Canadian university students responded to a questionnaire that assessed attitudes toward Native peoples, as well as three components of attitudes: stereotypes (characteristics attributed to the group), symbolic beliefs (beliefs that the group promotes or threatens cherished values, customs, and traditions), and emotions. Five different labels were used for the group: Aboriginal peoples, First Nations people, Native Canadians, Native Indians, and Native peoples. Among non-Native students, the term *Aboriginal peoples* was associated with the most positive attitude, followed by Native peoples, Native Indians, First Nations people, and Native Canadians.

Noting that attitudes toward Native peoples were less favourable when the labels Native Canadians and First Nations were used, the researchers conclude that this stemmed, in part, from the symbolic beliefs that came to mind in response to these labels. When labelled Native Canadians or First Nations people, Native peoples were viewed as more likely to threaten national unity than when the three other labels were used. The researchers conclude, "it is possible that when the label First Nations People is used, individuals may be more likely to base their attitudes toward the group on beliefs about the political role of Natives in Canada. A Native activist organization in Canada goes by a similar name: 'Assembly of First Nations'...[and the label may] remind people that Natives are now working within Canadian society toward more autonomy and political power" (p. 90).

The labelling perspective directs us to consider the role that negative stereotypes play in race and ethnicity. **Stereotypes** are exaggerations or generalizations about the characteristics and behaviour of a particular group. Negative stereotyping of minorities leads to a self-fulfilling prophecy. As Schaefer (1998: 17) explains:

> Self-fulfilling prophecies can be devastating for minority groups. Such groups often find that they are allowed to hold only low-paying jobs with little prestige or opportunity for advancement. The rationale of the dominant society is that these minority individuals lack the ability to perform in more important and lucrative positions. Training to become scientists, executives, or physicians is denied to many subordinate group individuals, who are then locked into society's inferior jobs. As a result, the false definition becomes real. The subordinate group has become inferior because it was defined at the start as inferior and was therefore prevented from achieving the levels attained by the majority.

stereotypes

Oversimplified or exaggerated generalizations about a category of individuals. Stereotypes are either untrue or are gross distortions of reality.

Feminist Perspectives

Students are often surprised to find that feminists and women from racially and ethnically marginalized groups do not necessarily share an easy alliance. The reason for tensions between women seeking social justice *as women* and women seeking social justice from social locations also marked by race and ethnicity is that "general" feminist approaches to social justice have taken whiteness for granted and have assumed that being a woman was both an essential and universal trait. Feminist historical roots in Eurocentric, bourgeois values from Mary Wollstonecraft to Betty Friedan have tended to neglect the specific concerns of women from non-dominant groups.

In Canada, for example, the National Action Committee on the Status of Women (NAC), founded in 1971, was for 22 years largely the domain only of professional, white women. In 1993, for the first time, NAC elected a woman of colour, Sunera Thobani, as its leader. While the organization had finally begun to actively support women of colour, reserving spaces for members-at-large for women from marginalized groups, some powerful white women complained that they had thus lost their representation.

Showing particular rancour was Liberal member of Parliament Mary Clancy, then the Liberal Women's Issues critic. Of Thobani's victory, Clancy claimed: "They [NAC] have taken on the interests of doubly or triply disadvantaged women—and left mainstream women feeling alienated. Of course, disadvantaged women need help. But being a woman in this country is a disadvantage in itself" (quoted in Bergman 1993: 16).

Clancy, and others like her, failed to comprehend that their vision of NAC represented the interests of liberal feminists seeking formal equality before the law, career opportunities, and wage parity with men; women who lacked access to such privileges could not expect to benefit from such limited, formal gains.

Feminist organization and feminist thinking in Canada have changed a great deal since Clancy's outburst. Contemporary antiracist feminism, influenced by postcolonial and postmodern theory, provides simultaneous, critical interrogations of race, class and gender, throwing into question "the everyday world of common social relations, values, and practices of cultural and power" (Bannerji 2000: 544).

Becky Thompson (2001) reminds us of the contributions of antiracist feminists to feminism since the **second wave feminism** of the latter half of the twentieth century. She writes:

> I want young women to know the rich, complicated, contentious, and visionary history of multiracial feminism and to know the nuanced controversies with Second Wave feminism. I want them to know that Shirley Chisholm ran for president in 1972; that Celestine Ware wrote a Black radical feminist text in the 1970s which offered an inspiring conception of revolution with a deep sense of humanity; that before Mab Segrest went to work for an organization against the Klan in North Carolina, she and others published an independent lesbian journal…that included some of the most important and compelling race-conscious writing by white women and women of color to date. (p. 350)

Queer Theory Perspectives

Katherine Snider, from the University of Toronto, demonstrates in her work on multiculturalism, education, and sexuality that multicultural initiatives have been inadequate to youth populations simultaneously marginalized because of their sexuality *and* race and/or ethnicity. Taking a largely structural approach, Snider explains that the popular understanding of multiculturalism as a benign force fails to comprehend that as a policy, it operates to manage troublesome populations. Such a position does not have to interrogate its own values or systems for delivering them, thereby "avoiding the more difficult task of examining the structure of education and the curriculum, and the embedded racism on which these were built" (1996: 295). Snider directs her attention specifically to the Toronto District School Board's 1995 creation of the Triangle School, a facility set up to manage youth who risk dropping out because of their experiences of homophobia. The trouble, Snider points out, is that to enroll in the Triangle School, young people must be "out" in the *public* world, prepared to abandon the private world of family if the family cannot accept their queer sexuality. The emphasis on being "out" as a requirement for entry into the school may place in peril students who cannot divorce their sexuality from their race and/or ethnicity. Snider explains: "there is a conspicuous analytical failure

second wave feminism

Twentieth-century resurgence of feminist thought, sometimes attributed to the establishment of suffrage in Canada, to the publication of de Beauvoir's *Second Sex* in France, or to the publication of Betty Friedan's *The Feminine Mystique*.

to see gender and race (if you are male and white) as mitigating factors in the process of revealing sexual orientation....the coming out discourse categorically under-estimates the beneficial influence and support that the private sphere provides to many youth which, by coming out, they risk losing" (p. 296).

In addition to these problems, institutions like the Triangle School, while they may provide refuge, fail to enforce the multiculturalist mandate to value people's differences. Instead, they remove difference from the regular system and do not demand that homophobic students, teachers, or administrators change their behaviours.

Work like Snider's represents a new and underexplored area in Canada, but it is crucial if we are to think seriously about the specific needs, challenges, and contributions of people who experience marginalization at the place where sexuality, race, and ethnicity meet.

8.5 Prejudice and Racism

Prejudice refers to an attitude or judgment, usually negative, about an entire category of people. Prejudice may be directed toward individuals of a particular religion, sexual orientation, political affiliation, age, social class, sex, race, or ethnicity. **Racism** is a belief system, or ideology, that includes three basic ideas (Marger 2000):

1. Humans are divided naturally into different physical types.
2. The physical traits associated with each human type are innately related to the culture, personality, and intelligence of each type.
3. On the basis of their genetic inheritance, some groups are innately superior to others.

The perception that certain groups have inferior traits serves to justify subordination and mistreatment of those groups.

Aversive and Modern Racism

Compared with traditional, "old-fashioned" prejudice, which is blatant, direct, and conscious, contemporary forms of prejudice are often subtle, indirect, and unconscious. Two variants of these more subtle forms of prejudice include aversive racism and modern racism.

Aversive Racism Aversive racism represents a subtle, often unintentional form of prejudice exhibited by many well-intentioned people who possess strong egalitarian values and who view themselves as nonprejudiced. The negative feelings that aversive racists have toward minority groups are not feelings of hostility or hate, but rather feelings of discomfort, uneasiness, disgust, and sometimes fear (Gaertner and Dovidio 2000). Aversive racists may not be fully aware that they harbour these negative racial feelings; indeed, they disapprove of individuals who are prejudiced and would feel falsely accused if they were labelled as prejudiced. "Aversive racists find Blacks 'aversive,' while at the same time find any suggestion that they might be prejudiced 'aversive' as well" (Gaertner and Dovidio 2000: 14).

prejudice
An attitude or judgment, usually negative, about an entire category of people based on their group membership.

racism
The belief that certain groups of people are innately inferior to other groups of people based on their racial classification. Racism serves to justify discrimination against groups that are perceived as inferior.

aversive racism
A subtle, often unintentional form of prejudice exhibited by many individuals who possess strong egalitarian values and who view themselves as non-prejudiced.

Another aspect of aversive racism is the presence of "pro-White" attitudes—as opposed to, for example, "anti-Black" attitudes. In several studies, respondents did not indicate that Blacks were worse than Whites, only that Whites were better than Blacks (Gaertner and Dovidio 2000). For example, Blacks were not rated as being lazier than Whites, but Whites were rated as being more ambitious than Blacks. Gaertner and Dovidio (2000) explain that "aversive racists would not characterize Blacks more negatively than Whites because that response could readily be interpreted by others or oneself, to reflect racial prejudice" (p. 27). Compared with anti-Black attitudes, pro-White attitudes reflect a more subtle prejudice that, although less overtly negative, is still racial bias.

modern racism

A subtle and complex form of racism in which individuals are not explicitly racist, but tend to hold negative views of racial minorities and blame minorities for their social disadvantages.

Modern Racism Like aversive racism, **modern racism** involves the rejection of traditional racist beliefs, but a modern racist displaces negative racial feelings onto more abstract social and political issues. The modern racist believes that serious discrimination in Canada no longer exists, that any continuing racial inequality is the fault of minority group members, and that demands for employment equity for minorities are unfair and unjustified. "Modern racism tends to 'blame the victim' and place the responsibility for change and improvements on the minority groups, not on the larger society" (Healey 1997: 55). Like aversive racists, modern racists tend to be unaware of their negative racial feelings and do not view themselves as prejudiced.

Learning to Be Prejudiced: The Role of Socialization, Stereotypes, and the Media

Psychological theories of prejudice focus on forces within the individual that give rise to prejudice. For example, the **frustration-aggression theory** of prejudice (also known as the **scapegoating theory**), suggests that prejudice is a form of hostility that results from frustration. According to this theory, minority groups serve as convenient targets of displaced aggression. The **authoritarian-personality theory** of prejudice suggests that prejudice arises in people with a certain personality type. According to this theory, people with an authoritarian personality—who are highly conformist, intolerant, cynical, and preoccupied with power—are prone to being prejudiced.

frustration-aggression theory (scapegoating theory)

A psychological theory of prejudice that suggests prejudice is a form of hostility resulting from frustration. According to this theory, minority groups serve as convenient targets of displaced aggression.

Rather than focus on the individual, sociologists focus on social forces that contribute to prejudice. Earlier we explained how intergroup conflict over wealth, power, and prestige give rise to negative feelings and attitudes that serve to protect and enhance dominant group interests. In the following discussion, we explain how prejudice is learned through socialization, stereotypes, and the media.

authoritarian-personality theory

A psychological theory of prejudice that suggests prejudice arises in people with a certain personality type. According to this theory, people with an authoritarian personality, who are highly conformist, intolerant, cynical, and preoccupied with power, are prone to prejudice.

Learning Prejudice through Socialization In the socialization process, individuals adopt the values, beliefs, and perceptions of their family, peers, culture, and social groups. Prejudice is taught and learned through socialization, although it need not be taught directly and intentionally. Parents who may teach their children to not be prejudiced yet live in an all-white neighbourhood, attend an all-white church, and have only white friends may be indirectly teaching negative racial attitudes to their children. Socialization may also be direct, as in the case of a parent who uses racial slurs in the presence of her children, or forbids her children to play with children from a certain racial or ethnic background. Children may also learn prejudicial attitudes from their peers. The telling of racial and ethnic jokes among friends, for example, perpetuates stereotypes that foster negative racial and ethnic attitudes.

Stereotypes Prejudicial attitudes toward racial and ethnic groups are based on false or inadequate group images known as stereotypes. Consider, in this context, Toronto mayor Mel Lastman's "joke" about travelling to Africa: "What the hell do I want to go to a place like Mombasa?...I just see myself in a pot of boiling water with all these natives dancing around me" (Deziel and Cameron 2001/2002: 21). As noted earlier, stereotypes are exaggerations or generalizations about the characteristics and behaviour of a particular group. Shipler (1998) suggests that negative stereotyping of minorities enhances the self-esteem of majority group members. "If Blacks are less intelligent, in Whites' belief, then it follows that Whites are more intelligent. If Blacks are lazier, Whites are harder working. If Blacks would prefer to live on welfare, then Whites would prefer to be self-supporting" (p. 3).

Prejudice and the Media The media contribute to prejudice by portraying minorities in negative and stereotypical ways, or by not portraying them at all. For example, Mosher (1998) notes that the racialization of crime has a long history in Canada, with the Canadian news media displaying an increasing tendency to attribute the social problem of crime to Blacks and Asians. Research by Claxton-Oldfield and Keefe (1999) on stereotypes about the Innu of Davis Inlet, Labrador, also suggests the potency of the media in shaping public opinion about different racial and ethnic groups. In the first part of their research, a sample of 22 male and 56 female Newfoundland college students (aged 18 to 23) were asked to list the characteristics that came to mind about the Innu and to indicate where these impressions came from. At least 20 percent of the students described the Innu as being uneducated, alcoholic, poor, and isolated, and called them gas-sniffers. The two most important sources for the students' impressions of the Innu were television and newspapers. In the second phase of their investigation, the researchers examined the image of the Innu in a daily Newfoundland newspaper for one year (January to December 1996). Headline analysis revealed that conflict and deviance words (e.g., gas-sniffing, sexual abuse, protest) appeared in 44 percent of the headlines of newspaper items about the Innu. The researchers conclude that stereotypes of the Innu mirror the images portrayed of them in the media.

Consider, as well, that when the entire casts of prime-time shows in the 1999–2000 television season were considered, a majority of shows (61 percent) had more than one minority character. However, when only main characters were considered, nearly half of the shows (48 percent) had all-white casts (Children Now 2000a). Another analysis of the 1999–2000 prime-time television season revealed evidence of progress in the ways minority characters were portrayed: characters of colour were more likely than White characters to be shown as "good," competent at work, and law abiding (Children Now 2000b). However, stereotyping remained rampant. For example, stereotypes of Asians on prime-time television programs included the nerdy student, the martial arts master, the seductive "Dragon Lady," and the "clueless immigrant."

Hate on the Web

The internet provides access to a wide range of information for the over 250 million people worldwide using the World Wide Web. Among the websites are those that promote hate and intolerance toward various minority groups. In Chapter 9, for example, we refer to a website that promotes antigay sentiments: www.godhatesfags.com. Here, we focus on the use of internet technology to promote hatred toward racial and ethnic groups.

One nonprofit organization that combats hate, intolerance, and discrimination has tracked over 400 hate websites, many of which are designed to lure children and teenagers into the ideologies and organizations that promote hate (Dees 2000). According to their investigations, "the gospel of hate is being projected worldwide, more cheaply and effectively than ever before, and it is attracting a new demographic of youthful followers..." (SPLC Report 2000).

Those who live in countries where laws prohibit the wilful promotion of hatred or associated activities have embraced the internet. For example, many German neo-Nazi white supremacist groups now use U.S.-based internet servers. German intelligence officials report that 70 percent of the nearly 400 German neo-Nazi sites are on U.S. servers, and about a third of those would be illegal under German law (Kaplan and Kim 2000). One U.S.-based webpage posted in German offered a $7500 reward for the murder of a young left-wing activist, giving his home address, job, and phone number.

Although the internet is used as a vehicle for spreading messages of hate, it is also used to combat such messages. Although it is now offline, for six years the website of "HateWatch" (www.hatewatch.org) was devoted to educating the public about the proliferation of hate on the internet. In conjunction with the release of a documentary, "HATE.COM: Extremists on the Internet," which premiered on

Home Box Office in October 2000, HBO developed on its website (www.hbo.com) a special cyber-campaign, "Hate Hurts," about the impact of hate on individuals, families, and communities.

The corporate sector can also play a role in the fight against hate on the Web. In January 2001, Yahoo announced it would actively try to keep hateful material out of its auctions, classified sections, and shopping areas. This policy came shortly after a French court ordered Yahoo to pay fines of about $13 000 a day if the company did not install technology that would shield French Web users from seeing Nazi-related memorabilia in its auction site (French law prohibits the display of such material).

SOURCES: Dees, Morris. 2000 (Dec. 28). Personal correspondence. Morris Dees, co-founder of the Southern Poverty Law Center. 400 Washington Avenue, Montgomery, AL 36104; Kaplan, David E., and Lucien Kim. 2000. "Nazism's New Global Threat." *U.S. News Online*. September 25. http://www.usnews.com/usnews/issue/000925/nazi.htm; *SPLC Report*. 2000 (September). "HBO, Center Document Hate on Net." 30(3): 1. Southern Poverty Law Center. 400 Washington Ave. Montgomery, AL 36104.

Another media form that contributes to hatred of minority groups is "white power" music: music with racist lyrics and titles such as *Coon Hunt, Race Riot,* and *White Revolution*. Consider the following music lyrics from the band Berserkr:

> ...Niggers just hit this side of town, watch my property values go down. Bang, gang, watch them die, watch those niggers drop like flies...

Resistance Records, a company that sells "white power" music, sells 50 000 compact discs a year in Canada, Europe, South Africa, South America, and the United States (Intelligence Report 1998). "Skinhead" music, which contains anti-Semitic, racist, and homophobic lyrics, has become a leading recruitment tool for white supremacist groups ("Intelligence Briefs" 2000).

The internet also spreads hate messages toward minority groups through the websites of various white supremacist and hate group organizations (see this chapter's *Focus on Technology* feature).

8.6 Discrimination against Racial and Ethnic Minorities

Whereas prejudice refers to attitudes, **discrimination** refers to actions or practices that result in differential treatment of categories of individuals. Although prejudicial attitudes often accompany discriminatory behaviour or practices, one may be evident without the other.

Individual versus Institutional Discrimination

Individual discrimination occurs when individuals treat persons unfairly or unequally because of their group membership. Individual discrimination may be overt or adaptive. In **overt discrimination**, the individual discriminates because of his or her own prejudicial attitudes. For example, a White landlord may refuse to rent to a First Nations family because of her own prejudice against Aboriginal peoples.

Suppose a Vietnamese-Canadian family wants to rent an apartment in a predominantly white neighbourhood. If the landlord is prejudiced against the Vietnamese and does not allow the family to rent the apartment, that landlord has engaged in overt discrimination. However, what if the landlord is not prejudiced against the Vietnamese, but still refuses to rent to a Vietnamese family? Perhaps that landlord is engaging in **adaptive discrimination**, or discrimination that is based on the prejudice of others. In this example, the landlord may fear that if he rents to a Vietnamese-Canadian family, other renters who are prejudiced against the Vietnamese may move out of the building or neighbourhood and leave the landlord with unrented apartments. Overt and adaptive individual discrimination may coexist. For example, a landlord may not rent an apartment to a Vietnamese family because of her own prejudices *and* the fear that other tenants may move out.

Institutional discrimination occurs when normal operations and procedures of social institutions result in unequal treatment of minorities. Institutional discrimination is covert and insidious and maintains the subordinate position of minorities in society. As conflict theorists emphasize, majority group members make rules that favour their own group.

Although discrimination may have become more subtle and less overt, racial and ethnic minorities continue to experience discrimination and its effects in almost every sphere of social life (Noh and Belser 1999; Stodolska and Jackson 1998). For example, Kunz and colleagues (2000) find that

- foreign-born visible minorities experience greater discrepancies between education and occupation than other groups (less than half of those with a university education have high skill level jobs);
- even with postsecondary education, unemployment rates are higher for racial minorities, especially foreign-born visible minorities (12 percent) and Aboriginal peoples (23 percent) compared to whites (7 percent) and Canadian-born visible minorities (8 percent);
- given the same level of education, whites, whether foreign or Canadian-born, are three times as likely as Aboriginal peoples and about twice as likely as foreign-born visible minorities to be in the highest income quintile;

discrimination
Differential treatment of individuals based on their group membership.

individual discrimination
Discriminatory acts by individuals that are based on prejudicial attitudes.

overt discrimination
Discrimination that occurs because of an individual's own prejudicial attitudes.

adaptive discrimination
Discrimination that is based on the prejudice of others.

institutional discrimination
Discrimination in which the normal operations and procedures of social institutions result in unequal treatment of minorities.

- Canadian-born visible minorities are still less likely than whites (Canadian and foreign-born) to be in the top 20 percent of the income distribution (Weiner 2001).

Next, we look at the extent and brutality of hate crimes against minorities.

Hate Crime Victimization

**hate crime
(bias-motivated crime)**

An act of violence motivated by prejudice.

A **hate crime**, or **bias-motivated crime**, is an act of violence motivated by prejudice or bias against racial, ethnic, religious, and sexual-orientation groups. Examples include intimidation (e.g., threats), destruction or damage of property, physical assault, and murder. Section 718.2 of the *Criminal Code* provides that "evidence that [an offence] was motivated by bias, prejudice or hate based on race, national or ethnic origin, colour, religion, sex, age, mental or physical disability, sexual orientation or any other similar factor" is to be considered an aggravating circumstance in sentencing convicted offenders. For example, in the case of *R. v. Ingram and Grimsdale* (1977), it was held that "an assault which is racially motivated renders the offence more heinous. Such assaults, unfortunately, invite imitation and repetition by others and incite retaliation. The danger is even greater in a multicultural, pluralistic urban society." In addition, section 319 of the *Criminal Code* defines wilfully promoting hatred against any identifiable group—"any section of the public distinguished by colour, race, religion, or ethnic group"—and advocating genocide as criminal offences, punishable by up to two years' imprisonment. Perhaps the best-known prosecution under the latter section of the Code is that of James Keegstra, a former Alberta high-school teacher who was accused of fomenting hatred against the Jews in his classroom lectures. Keegstra was subsequently charged under the subsection of Canada's *Criminal Code* that prohibits hate propaganda other than in private conversations. The case was later appealed to the Supreme Court of Canada. In 1996, the Supreme Court ruled that although hate propaganda "formed part of protected freedom of expression pursuant to subsection 2(b) of the Canadian Charter of Rights and Freedoms" its prohibition was reasonable and "supported by international documents to which Canada is a party and sections 15 (equality) and 27 (multiculturalism) of the Charter" (Beaudoin 1999: 1237).

In other cases, the attempt to curtail the spread of hate propaganda has been less successful. Ernst Zundel published a brochure entitled "Did Six Million Really Die?" His brochure claimed that the Holocaust was a myth propagated by a worldwide Jewish conspiracy. He was subsequently charged under section 181 of the *Criminal Code*, which makes the wilful dissemination of false news a criminal offence. The Supreme Court of Canada ruled that this section of the Code denied Zundel the right to freedom of expression, as guaranteed under the *Canadian Charter of Rights and Freedoms*, and that section 181 was not justified in a free and democratic society.

Canada's 1999 General Social Survey produced, for the first time, estimates of self-reported hate crime victimization at the national level. It concluded that there were 272 000 crimes where the victim felt that hate was the motive, with over 4 of 10 (43 percent) believing that hatred of race or ethnicity was involved (Blackwell 2002). However, while the United States has systematically compiled statistics on hate crimes since the 1990 passage of the *Hate Crimes Statistics Act*, Canada lacks a national system for collecting hate-crime statistics. "There has been little systematic research in Canada upon the nature and incidence of hate crimes" (Roberts 1995). There is also considerable variation in Canada in the definitions of "hate crimes" employed by various Canadian police departments. Some police services, such as Montreal's, do not gather any information on hate crimes at all.

The Canadian Arab Federation, the Canadian chapter of the Council on American Islamic Relations, the Canadian Jewish Congress, and B'nai Brith Canada all report a surge in hate crimes since the September 11, 2001, terrorist attacks. For example, B'nai Brith Canada, which compiles an annual audit of anti-Semitic incidents, reports that by June 2002 there had been over 180 such offences, ranging from the burning of synagogues to bomb threats and assaults, compared to 286 in all of 2001 (Blackwell 2002). Six months after the tragedy of September 11, a report prepared by the Council on American-Islamic Relations noted 120 anti-Muslim incidents across Canada, including 10 death threats, 13 cases of physical violence, and 12 attacks on mosques and Islamic centres (Ray 2002). The 2001 annual report of the hate crimes unit of the Toronto Police Services reports 338 incidents in 2001 (up from 204 the previous year) and suggests that approximately "90 percent of the increase can be linked to the terrorist attacks...with Muslims being the group most frequently targeted" (*KW Record* 2002).

Levin and McDevitt (1995) found that the motivations for hate crimes were of three distinct types: thrill, defensive, and mission. Thrill hate crimes are committed by offenders who are looking for excitement and attack victims for the "fun of it." Defensive hate crimes involve offenders who view their attacks as necessary to protect their community, workplace, or campus from "outsiders." Perpetrators of defensive hate crimes are trying to send a message that their victims do not belong in a particular community, workplace, or campus and that anyone in the victim's group who dares to "intrude" could be the next victim. Mission hate crimes are perpetrated by offenders who have dedicated their lives to bigotry. In Levin and McDevitt's study of hate crimes in Boston, the most common type of hate crime was thrill hate crime (58 percent) followed by defensive hate crime (41 percent).

The least common, but most violent, type of hate crime is mission hate crime. Mission hate crimes are often committed by members of white supremacist organizations that endorse racist beliefs and violence against minority group members. The following message is typical of one received by calling a White Aryan Resistance phone number (Kleg 1993: 205):

> This is WAR hotline. How long, White men, are you going to sit around while these non-white mud races breed you out of existence? They have your jobs, your homes, and your country. Have you stepped outside lately and looked around while these Niggers...hep and jive to this Africanized rap music? While these Gooks and Flips are buying up the businesses around you?...This racial melting pot is more like a garbage pail. Just look at your liquor stores. Most of them are owned by Sand Niggers from Iraq, Egypt, or Iran. Most of the apartments are owned by the scum from India, or some other kind of Raghead...[Jews] are like maggots eating off a dead carcass. When you see what these Jews and their White lackeys have done, the gas chambers don't sound like such a bad idea after all. For more information write us at...

Other racist groups known to engage in hate crimes are the Aryan Nations, Heritage Front, Canadian Liberty Net, Church of the Creator, the Identity

Church Movement, neo-Nazis, and skinheads. Not all skinheads are racists, however. Many youth have adopted the skinhead "look" and lifestyle, but do not endorse racism or violence. One nonracist skinhead remarks: "Being a skinhead does not mean being a Nazi. I happen to have no hair, a black leather jacket, and army boots, and I get stopped all the time by people trying to preach nonviolence to me. I am a pacifist" (quoted in Landau 1993: 43).

8.7 Strategies for Action: Responding to Prejudice, Racism, and Discrimination

Next, we look at various strategies that address problems of prejudice, racism, and discrimination. These include multicultural education, diversity training in the workplace, and political strategies.

Multicultural Education in Schools and Communities

multicultural education

Education that includes all racial and ethnic groups in the school curriculum and promotes awareness and appreciation for cultural diversity.

In schools across the nation, **multicultural education**, which encompasses a broad range of programs and strategies, works to dispel myths, stereotypes, and ignorance about minorities, promotes tolerance and appreciation of diversity, and includes minority groups in the school curriculum (see also Chapter 12). With multicultural education, the school curriculum reflects the diversity of Canadian society and fosters an awareness and appreciation of the contributions of different racial and ethnic groups to Canadian culture. The proclaimed goals of multicultural education are not, however, effectively realized in schools. That is because they remain at the margins of a curriculum that continues to place Euro-American culture at the centre, as the benchmark against which all other things are assessed. Critical education researcher Jasmin Zine observes, for example, that schools in Canada

- Have special festival days that "reduce the wealth of your knowledge and experience to 'saris, samosa and steel bands' (and yet you know you didn't learn about Canadian history through bagpipes and meat pies)"
- Continue to be run principally by white administrators who serve as "a constant reminder of the glass ceilings that limit your chances to achieve positions of power because of your race, class and gender..."
- Have students "perform" their cultural heritage, which turns them into "a tourist spectacle, [whose] Anglo-Canadian classmates are never asked to do the same. (Cindy, could you wear a traditional costume of your British ancestors to school for Canada Day?)" (2002: 37)

Colleges and universities, perhaps because they have greater freedom to set their own curricula, have developed courses and degree programs in critical race and ethnic studies, and provide support for multicultural, student-run organizations. Evidence suggests a number of positive outcomes for both minority and majority students who take such programs, including increased racial understanding and cultural awareness, increased social interaction with students who have backgrounds different from their own, improved cognitive development, increased support for efforts to achieve educational equity, and greater satisfaction with their experience of higher education (Humphreys 1999). This chapter's *Social Problems Research Up Close* feature presents a study that identifies various factors that influence first-year students' openness to diversity.

What Influences Students' Openness to Diversity?

A study by Pascarella and colleagues (1996) sought to determine how students' openness to diversity is influenced by four different sets of factors: student background characteristics, environmental emphases of the institution attended, measures of the students' academic experience, and measures of students' social involvement.

Sample and Methods

The researchers collected data from 2290 first-year students at 18 colleges and universities. The dependent variable was a scale designed to measure openness to diversity (see scale). This scale not only assesses an individual's openness to cultural, racial, and value diversity; it also measures the extent to which an individual enjoys being challenged by different ideas, values, and perspectives.

Openness to Diversity/ Challenge Scale

(Scored on a Likert-type scale: 5 = strongly agree to 1 = strongly disagree)

1. I enjoy having discussions with people whose ideas and values are different from my own.
2. The real value of a college/ university education lies in being introduced to different values.
3. I enjoy talking with people who have values different from mine

because it helps me understand myself and my values better.

4. Learning about people from different cultures is a very important part of my university/ college education.
5. I enjoy taking courses that challenge my beliefs and values.
6. The courses I enjoy the most are those that make me think about things from a different perspective.
7. Contact with individuals whose background (e.g., race, national origin, sexual orientation) is different from my own is an essential part of my college/ university education.
8. I enjoy courses that are intellectually challenging.

Four sets of independent variables were developed, each of which consisted of numerous measures: (1) precollege/preuniversity variables (including a measure of precollege/preuniversity openness to diversity and precollege/preuniversity academic ability), (2) environmental emphasis of the college/ university (including a measure of the degree of racial discrimination at the institution), (3) student academic experiences (including number of social science courses taken and self-reported number of hours spent studying per week), and (4) student social/nonacademic experiences (including involvement in clubs and organizations and assessment of students' peer interactions and topics of conversation).

Findings

The precollege/preuniversity measure of openness to diversity/

challenge had the strongest effect on openness to diversity/challenge after the first year of attendance. Women and non-White students had higher levels of openness to diversity/challenge than men and White students.

The extent to which students perceived their institution as having a nondiscriminatory racial environment had a positive impact on openness to diversity. Hours spent studying had a small positive effect, while the number of mathematics courses taken during the first year of college had a small negative impact.

Living on campus, participating in a racial or cultural awareness workshop, and hours worked per week had positive effects on openness to diversity/challenge, while joining a fraternity or sorority had a negative effect. In addition, "the more students interact with diverse peers and the greater the extent to which such interactions focus on controversial or value-laden issues that may engender a change in perspective or opinion, the greater one's development of openness to diversity and challenge" (p. 188).

The findings of this study suggest that colleges and universities that offer racial or cultural awareness workshops can foster students' appreciation and acceptance of cultural, racial, and value diversity. Encouraging openness to diversity may also be achieved by the institution establishing policies and programs that sensitize students and personnel to racial discrimination and demonstrate that such discrimination is not acceptable. Colleges and universities may also consider interventions to counteract the

(continued)

negative influence of membership in fraternities or sororities on openness to diversity.

Finally, the fact that precollege/ preuniversity openness to diversity had the largest effect on openness to diversity among first-year students points to the need to foster openness to diversity in the elementary-school and secondary-school grades. Multicultural programs, educational approaches, and school policies that discourage and sanction prejudice and discrimination will help achieve this.

SOURCES: Based on Pascarella, Ernest T., Marcia Edison, Amaury Nora, Linda Serra Hagedorn, and Patrick T. Terenzini. 1996. "Influences on Students' Openness to Diversity and Challenge in the First Year of College." *Journal of Higher Education* 67(2): 174–93. Copyright 1996 by Ohio State University Press. All rights reserved. Used by permission.

Efforts to recruit and admit historically disadvantaged groups in institutions of higher education have also been found to foster positive relationships among diverse groups and enrich the educational experience of all students. Gurin (1999) found that students with the most exposure to diverse populations during university had the most cross-racial interactions five years after leaving university. A poll of law students at two universities also found that nearly 90 percent of the students said that diversity in the classroom provided them with a better educational experience. About 9 in 10 students also said that the contact they had with students of different racial or ethnic backgrounds influenced them to change their view on some aspect of human rights (*Race Relations Reporter* 1999).

Diversity Training in the Workplace

diversity training

Workplace training programs designed to increase employees' awareness of cultural differences in the workplace and how these differences may affect job performance.

Increasingly, corporations have begun to implement efforts to reduce prejudice and discrimination in the workplace through an educational approach known as **diversity training**. Broadly defined, diversity training involves "raising personal awareness about individual 'differences' in the workplace and how those differences inhibit or enhance the way people work together and get work done" (Wheeler 1994: 10). Diversity training may address such issues as stereotyping and cross-cultural insensitivity, as well as provide workers with specific information on cultural norms of different groups and how these norms affect work behaviour and social interactions.

In a survey of 45 organizations that provide diversity training, Wheeler (1994) found that for 85 percent of the respondents, the primary motive for offering diversity training was to enhance productivity and profits. In the words of one survey respondent, "The company's philosophy is that a diverse work force that recognizes and respects differing opinions and ideas adds to the creativity, productivity, and profitability of the company" (p. 12). Only 4 percent of respondents said they offered diversity training out of a sense of social responsibility.

Political Strategies

Various political strategies have been implemented or suggested to reduce prejudice and discrimination. However, although it is readily apparent that strategies such as employment equity (see Chapter 7) can prevent or reduce discriminatory practices, their effects are complex. For example, legal policies that prohibit discrimination can increase modern forms of prejudice, as in the case of individuals who conclude that because laws and policies prohibit discrimination, any social disadvantages of minorities must be their own fault. On the other hand, any improvements in the socio-economic status of minorities that result from legal/political policies may help to replace negative images of minorities with positive ones. For example, it has been suggested that employment equity provides minority role models. "Nonwhites in educational and professional positions where they were previously not present function as models for other, especially younger, members of their racial group who can identify with them and form realistic goals to occupy the same roles themselves" (Zack 1998: 51).

Understanding Race and Ethnicity

After considering the material presented in this chapter, what understanding about race and ethnicity are we left with? First, we have seen that racial categories are socially constructed with no scientific validity. Racial and ethnic categories are largely arbitrary, imprecise, and misleading. Although some scholars suggest that we abandon racial and ethnic labels, others advocate adding new categories—multiracial and multiethnic—to reflect the identities of a growing segment of the Canadian population.

Conflict theorists and functionalists agree that prejudice, discrimination, and racism have benefited certain groups in society. But racial and ethnic disharmony has created tensions that disrupt social equilibrium. Symbolic interactionists note that negative labelling of minority group members, which is learned through interaction with others, contributes to the subordinate position of minorities.

Prejudice, racism, and discrimination are debilitating forces in the lives of minorities. In spite of these negative forces, many minority group members succeed in living productive, meaningful, and prosperous lives; however, many others cannot overcome the social disadvantages associated with their minority status—they become victims of a cycle of poverty (see Chapter 10). Alterations in the structure of society are needed. Increasing opportunities for minorities—in education, employment and income, and political participation—is crucial to achieving racial and ethnic equality. In addition, policy-makers concerned with racial and ethnic equality must find ways to reduce the racial/ethnic wealth gap and foster wealth accumulation among minorities (Conley 1999). As noted earlier, access to wealth affects many dimensions of well-being.

Human rights activist Lani Guinier (1998) suggests that "the real challenge is to...use race as a window on issues of class, issues of gender, and issues of fundamental fairness, not just to talk about race as if it's a question of individual bigotry or individual prejudice. The issue is more than about making friends—it's about making change." But, as Shipler (1998) argues, making change requires that members of society recognize that change is necessary, that a problem that needs rectifying:

> One has to perceive the problem to embrace the solutions. If you think that racism isn't harmful unless it wears sheets or burns crosses or bars blacks from motels and restaurants, you will support only the crudest anti-discrimination laws and not the more refined methods....(p. 2)

Finally, it is important to consider the role of class in the casting of concerns related to race and ethnicity. bell hooks (2000) warns that focusing on issues of race and gender can deflect attention away from the larger issue of class division that increasingly separates the "haves" from the "have nots." Addressing class inequality must, suggests hooks, be part of any meaningful strategy to reduce inequalities suffered by minority groups.

Critical Thinking

1. At colleges and universities around North America, a number of professors are endorsing race-based theories of intelligence, Holocaust denial, and other racist ideas. For example, Professor J. Philippe Rushton of the University of Western Ontario and Professor Glayde Whitney of Florida State both describe Blacks as having smaller brains. Professor Edward M. Miller of the University of New Orleans has concluded that Blacks are "small-headed, over-equipped in genitalia, oversexed, hyper-violent and...unintelligent" ("Hate on Campus" 2000: 9). Associate Professor Arthur Butz of Northwest University publicly rejects the claim that millions of Jews were exterminated in the Holocaust ("Hate on Campus" 2000). How should institutions of higher learning respond to such claims by faculty members? What role does the right to free speech and academic freedom play?

2. Burnet (1999) has noted that government policies of multiculturalism have been attacked "as a means of buttressing Anglo-Saxon dominance, by diverting the efforts of the non-French and the non-English from political and economic affairs into cultural activities." Do you agree with this criticism? Why or why not?

3. Lieberman (1997) asked university faculty members in five disciplines from biological and anthropological sciences to indicate agreement or disagreement with the statement "There are biological races in the species Homo sapiens." In each of the disciplines, women were more likely than men to reject race as a biological reality. Why do you think women in Lieberman's study were more likely than men to reject the concept of race?

4. Some argue that multicultural policy simply places marginalized groups on display for "ethnic days" and special festivals, but does little to provide substantive antiracist social change. Think about your own schooling experiences, and reflect on Zine's (2002) critique of "multicultural" education. What do you observe?

5. Under Swedish law, giving Nazi salutes is a crime (Lofthus 1998). Do you think that the social benefits of outlawing racist expressions outweigh the impingement on free speech? Do you think such a law should be proposed in Canada? Why or why not?

"Is It True?" Quiz: Answers

1 = true; 2 = true; 3 = true; 4 = true; 5 = true

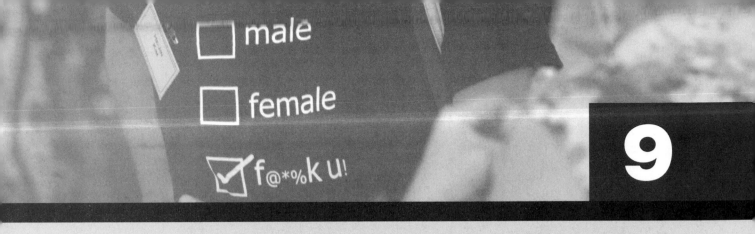

Sexualities

Outline

Is It True?

1. In some countries, same-sex activity is punishable by the death penalty.

2. People who believe that gay individuals are born that way tend to be more tolerant of gays than are people who believe that gay individuals choose their sexual orientation.

3. Most countries throughout the world have laws that protect gay individuals from discrimination because of sexual orientation.

4. Homosexuality is classified as a mental disorder.

Read more here: 1 = p. 294, 2 = p. 308, 3 = p. 294, 4 = p. 302
Answers can be found on p. 321.

© AFP/Getty Images

9.1 The Canadian Context

On November 17, 2001, 42-year-old Aaron Webster was beaten to death in a vicious attack in a parking lot in Stanley Park, Vancouver, in what is believed to have been British Columbia's first lethal incident of "gay bashing." Webster had been bludgeoned with either a baseball bat or a pool cue by a group of three to four men and left to die. At a memorial service for Webster that drew more than 1500 participants, Vancouver Police Inspector Dave Jones referred to Webster as the victim of a "hate crime, pure and simple" and promised that his department would "do everything in our power" to find the perpetrators and "bring them to justice" (Associated Press 2001; Nagle 2001).

Of the many issues raised by Aaron Webster's death, one was the adequacy of the definition of a "hate crime" under Canada's *Criminal Code* (Bush and Sainz 2001). According to the *Criminal Code* of the time, crimes committed against sexual orientation minorities were not, technically speaking, "hate crimes" (Wetzel 2001). In 1999, Justice Minister Anne McLellan had announced that she would introduce amendments to the Code to protect lesbians and gays from hate crimes, but by 2001 that had not happened (EGALE 2001).

Arising out of Aaron Webster's death, then NDP member of Parliament Svend Robinson tabled a private member's bill, C-250, in the House of Commons in 2003. The bill extended Canada's already existing hate crimes law to include as an "identifiable group" those who experience hate crimes as a result of their perceived sexual orientation—one need not *be* lesbian, transgendered, bisexual, or gay to experience a hate crime. The bill was passed by the Senate in 2004 and received royal assent in spring 2005. Thus, sexual minority groups were included in the ethnic model of multiculturalism that lay the foundations for the rationale of the initial law against hate crimes. Viewing crimes against those perceived to be sexual minorities as hate crimes instead of criminal assaults recognizes that the motivational aspect of prejudice heightens the threat to the general good of Canada's people. In principle, our hate crimes law is intended to protect not only specific groups, but also our national value system of *multiculturalism*. The law sends the message that prejudice is no excuse and that the courts and nation do not agree that some people "deserve a beating" (or worse) because of their skin colour, race, ethnicity, religion, or sexuality. At its foundation, hate crimes are specifically identified as distinct from other forms of crime because they inflict a **"disproportionate harm"** on the victims. Citing the work of Garafolo and Martin (1991), in a report for Canada's department of Justice Julian Roberts (1995) notes three distinct characteristics that separate hate crimes from other crimes. First, hate crimes attack a core feature of the victim's identity, with the implication being that there is nothing the victim can do to prevent being the target of an attack; better locks and avoiding walking alone at night do not solve the problem of prejudice. Second, hate crimes negatively impact entire communities by making other members of a vulnerable group fear for their safety and security:

> Hate crimes convey a message of fear to all members of the community to which the specific individual belongs. The seriousness of a hate crime cannot be fully understood without taking this additional element into consideration. The harm lies in the atmosphere of fear and apprehension to which all hate crimes contribute. (Roberts 1995: 3)

disproportionate harm

Exceeds harm inflicted on individuals; has as its goal to intimidate and/or injure an entire community.

Finally, research on the extent of injury in other regions that track hate crimes shows that where a crime is motivated by hate, the injuries and damage inflicted on victims are more severe than in cases of crimes not motivated by particular hatred (Roberts 1995: 4).

In 2004, on April 29, Bill C-250 was granted Royal Assent and became part of Canada's criminal legal code. Bill C-250 was introduced to the House of Commons as a private member's bill by British Columbia MP Svend Robinson. Bill C-250 was initially passed by the House of Commons on September 13, 2003, and adds "sexual orientation" to the text of subsection 318(4) so that gays and lesbians would be included in the "identifiable group" category that had previously included recognition only for colour, race, religion, and ethnic origin.

As of the writing of the current edition of this book, lobby groups and activists are hard at work to have Bill C-389 passed into law. The bill, introduced by NDP MP Bill Siksay, seeks to include both **gender identity** and **gender expression** as prohibited grounds for discrimination, and to make targeted crimes based on gender identity and/or gender expression subject to punishment under Canada's hate crimes law. The bill passed the report stage on December 8, 2010 at the House of Commons level with 143 votes in favour and 131 against (EGALE 2010).

In this chapter we examine prejudice and discrimination toward those who engage in same-sex activity whether male or female, and those who identify as lesbian, gay, transexual, or bisexual. We also address problems of homophobia and transphobia.

It is beyond the scope of this chapter, though, to explore how sexual diversity and its cultural meanings vary throughout the world. Rather, our focus is on Western conceptions of sexual diversity. Sexuality has often been thought of in terms of **"sexual orientation,"** whereby individuals are classified as heterosexual, bisexual, or homosexual, based on their emotional and sexual attractions, relationships, and self-identification. However, current scholarship and activism in the field note that the concept of orientation, while sometimes useful—as in the hate crimes law—does not allow room to think about the ways in which desires, attractions, and practices can vary over our lifetimes; furthermore, it encourages the assumption that all people in a given identity category share identical and unchanging desires and practices. Biologist Anne Fausto-Sterling (2001) has taken her own life history as an example of the shifts and complexities for which a simple use of "orientation" simply cannot account:

> This young girl didn't like dolls, kept pet snakes and frogs, and grew up first with heterosexual interests and later developed homosexual ones. How are we to interpret her life, or any life? Speculating about genes for analytic personalities or homosexuality may make for good party chitchat or provide solace for those eager to explain why someone turned out "that way." But partitioning genes from environment, nature from nurture, is a scientific dead end, a bad way of thinking about human development. Instead, I suggest we heed the words of the philosophers John Dewey and Arthur Bentley, who half a century ago "asserted the right to see together...much that is talked about conventionally as if it were composed of irreconcilable fears." (pp. 234–35)

While some advocate using the term **transgender** to include lesbians, gays, and bisexuals—those whose bodies do not fit neatly into either the

gender identity

The gender that a person feels him or herself to be. Sometimes gender identity is concordant with one's assigned sex at birth, and sometimes one's gender identity is more fluid, or can be "opposite" to one's sex of rearing.

gender expression

How we express our gender (as masculine, feminine, tomboys or androgynous, as "butch," "straight," etc.).

sexual orientation

The identification of individuals as heterosexual, bisexual, or homosexual based on their emotional and sexual attractions, relationships, self-identity, and lifestyle.

transgendered individuals

Persons who do not fit neatly into either the male or female category, or whose behaviour is not congruent with the rules and expectations for their sex in the society in which they live.

male or female category, or whose behaviour is incongruous with the roles and expectations for their sex in the society in which they live (Bornstein 1994; Bullough 2000; Gilbert 2000; Herdt 2001)—others observe that such a conceptualization risks collapsing very real political and personal experiences into one falsely homogenized image (Hines 2006; Roen 2001; Sullivan 2003). In common usage, transgender can include transexuals (individuals who have undergone hormone treatment and sex reassignment surgery to achieve a new identity as a member of the biologically opposite sex) and those who choose to assert and claim their non-adherence to standard gender roles.

There is some controversy over how people categorize transgender and transexual persons, and what distinguishes the concepts. In his critical ethnography, David Valentine (2007) seeks to map the manner in which these terms arose, what they describe, who gets to use them, and for what purposes. Valentine explains that the terms "transgender" and "transexual" are politicized categories that have largely been imposed from the outside by juridical interests, social scientists, and health workers. Very importantly, Valentine also situates the distinct conceptualization of transgender, transex/uality, and homosexual/ity as the effect of the twentieth-century medical system, which did the work of separating the previously enmeshed concepts of gender and sexuality. Valentine's account helps to explain why some people who identify as transexual have not had—and do not necessarily wish to have—surgery to effect a movement from one sex to the other; for these people the separation of gender and sexuality as imposed from the outside does not reflect their lives as they experience them. Valentine's analysis reveals that the adoption of transgender and transex has occurred mostly in circles of socio-economic privilege where people are able to use concepts in order to gain access to health benefits, or to political rights lobbying, but that many people who are gender variant find that the subtle overlapping of their experiences of sexuality, gender, class, and race cannot be captured by either term.

lesbigays

A collective term sometimes used to refer to lesbians, gays, and bisexuals.

GLBT

A term used to refer collectively to gays, lesbians, bisexuals, and transgendered individuals.

Much of the current scholarship and social activism regarding the treatment and political and social agendas of **lesbigays** also includes trans-identified persons; hence, the term **GLBT** is often used to refer collectively to gays, lesbians, bisexuals, and transgendered individuals (Craig 2002; Goldie 2001).

We begin by summarizing the legal status of lesbians and gay men around the world. Then, we review biological and environmental explanations for different sexualities, and apply sociological theories to better understand the social mechanisms that shape the way people understand and respond to various sexualities. The chapter ends with a discussion of strategies to reduce homophobia and discrimination against those who are gender variant. Because the label "homosexual" developed in the nineteenth century as a medical diagnosis of disease (Krafft-Ebing 1965), and tends to refer more to men than to women, we have chosen to use the term same-sex to refer to sexual practices and relationships that take place between persons of the same sex. This choice does not get around the problematic assumption that males and females are somehow "opposite," but it does avoid the language of pathology. We reserve the term homosexual only for historical accuracy when discussing legal and biomedical thinking on same-sex behaviour.

Because contemporary Western societies are largely heteronormative, few people who view themselves as heterosexual ever have to confront their own

■ Table 9.1 *The Heterosexual Questionnaire*

1. What do you think caused your heterosexuality?
2. When and how did you decide you were a heterosexual?
3. Is it possible that your heterosexuality is just a phase you may grow out of?
4. Is it possible that your heterosexuality stems from a neurotic fear of others of the same sex?
5. If you have never slept with a person of the same sex, is it possible that all you need is a good gay lover?
6. Do your parents know that you are straight? Do your friends and/or roommate(s) know? How did they react?
7. Why do you insist on flaunting your heterosexuality? Can't you just be who you are and keep it quiet?
8. Why do heterosexuals place so much emphasis on sex?
9. Why do heterosexuals feel compelled to seduce others into their lifestyle?
10. A disproportionate majority of child molesters are heterosexual. Do you consider it safe to expose children to heterosexual teachers?
11. Just what do men and women do in bed together? How can they truly know how to please each other, being so anatomically different?
12. With all the societal support marriage receives, the divorce rate is spiralling. Why are there so few stable relationships among heterosexuals?
13. Statistics show that lesbians have the lowest incidence of sexually transmitted diseases. Is it really safe for a woman to maintain a heterosexual lifestyle and run the risk of disease and pregnancy?
14. How can you become a whole person if you limit yourself to compulsive, exclusive heterosexuality?
15. Considering the menace of overpopulation, how could the human race survive if everyone were heterosexual?
16. Could you trust a heterosexual therapist to be objective? Don't you feel she or he might be inclined to influence you in the direction of his or her own leanings?
17. There seem to be very few happy heterosexuals. Techniques have been developed that might enable you to change if you really want to. Have you considered trying aversion therapy?
18. Would you want your child to be heterosexual, knowing the problems that she or he would face?

SOURCE: Rochlin, M. 1982. "The Heterosexual Questionnaire." *Changing Men* (Spring).

assumptions about why they are heterosexual. Instead, many heterosexuals pose questions to gay, lesbian, and bisexual people that begin with the premise that homosexuality is a problem. The "Heterosexual Questionnaire," featured as Table 9.1, first appeared in 1982 in *Changing Men*. It confronts readers with their own assumptions, forcing them to consider their ideas more carefully. Read the questionnaire for yourself. What do you think about having to provide an explanation for your own desires, whether for the same sex or the "opposite" sex? Have you ever posed these kinds of questions to people you have learned were gay, lesbian, or bisexual?

Throughout this chapter, we consider heteronormative assumptions more carefully and encourage questioning of the idea that people are "naturally" heterosexual and will remain that way unless something "goes wrong."

9.2 The Global Context: A World View of Laws Pertaining to Same-Sex Activity

Same-sex behaviour and love relationships have existed throughout human history and in most, perhaps all, human societies (Kirkpatrick 2000). Legal penalties for violating laws that prohibit same-sex sexual acts vary. In 10 countries, individuals found guilty of engaging in same-sex sexual behaviour may receive the death penalty. For example, a Somali lesbian couple were sentenced to death for "exercising unnatural behaviour" ("Jail, Death Sentences in Africa" 2001). Although executions in this region are performed by firing squads, religious tradition dictates that those convicted of homosexuality should either have a wall pushed over onto them or be thrown off a roof or other high place.

In general, countries throughout the world are moving toward increased legal protection of sexual-orientation minorities. Between 1984 and 1995, 86 countries changed their policies regarding sex between men, sex between women, or both, and nearly every change was toward increased liberalization of policies on same-sex sexual behaviour (Frank and McEneaney 1999). According to the International Gay and Lesbian Human Rights Commission (IGLHRC), 86 countries still have laws to prohibit sexual acts carried out in private between consenting adults (IGLHRC 2003). In 1996 South Africa became the first country in the world to include in its constitution a clause banning discrimination based on sexual orientation. Canada, Fiji, and Ecuador also have constitutions that ban discrimination based on sexual orientation ("Constitutional Protection" 1999). In the *Lawrence v. Texas* case, the U.S. Supreme Court settled that state laws prohibiting "homosexual sodomy" were unconstitutional and, therefore, unenforceable; it also ruled that such laws fundamentally violated the right to privacy. In Canada, meanwhile, same-sex sexual activity between consenting adults has been protected as a private matter since the passing of the 1969 Omnibus bill of Pierre Trudeau, who quipped, "The state has no business in the bedrooms of the nation." How law enforcement agencies have interpreted what counts as a private venue has still rendered the GLBT community vulnerable to persecution on occasion—with, for example, the infamous Toronto Bathhouse Raids of 1983 and the 2000 raid on a lesbian club, The Pussy Palace, in Toronto.

In Brazil, a gay, lesbian, bisexual, or transgendered individual is murdered on the average of every two days. However, the brutal gay-bashing murder of Edson Neris da Silva by a gang of about 30 people resulted in what some believe is Brazil's first trial and convictions in an antigay hate crime ("Brazilian Killers Sentenced" 2001). The first two gang members tried for this murder were sentenced to 21 years in prison.

In June 2000, Canada enacted a bill that extends to same-sex couples and unmarried heterosexual couples who have lived together for at least a year all the benefits and obligations of married couples (*LAWbriefs* 2000). (More recent changes are discussed later in this chapter.) In the same month, Brazil extended to same-sex couples the right to inherit each other's pension and social security benefits. The law represents the first time a Latin American country has legally recognized gay relationships (*LAWbriefs* 2000). Also in 2000, the Netherlands enacted a law allowing same-sex marriages. Just after

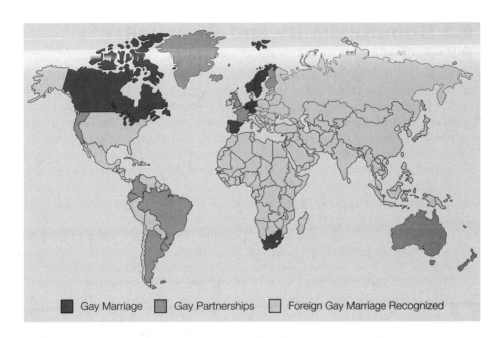

Gay Marriage   Gay Partnerships   Foreign Gay Marriage Recognized

■ **Figure 9.1** *Changing Global Attitudes toward Same-Sex Marriage and Same-Sex Partnerships*

the stroke of midnight on the day the Dutch law went into effect (April 1, 2001), the world's first fully legal same-sex civil marriages took place in Amsterdam (Drinkwater 2001).

Closer to home, a referendum on the issue of "gay marriage" was part of the 2004 federal election in the United States. All 11 states that included the question voted to ban gay marriage (NCSL 2004). Meanwhile, the Conservative minority government in Canada proposed to reopen the issue of marriages for same-sex couples in the House of Commons with a free vote; in December 2006 the issue did go to a free vote over whether to revisit the constitutionality of same-sex marriage, but was defeated with 175 nays to 123 yeas. As you will see later in this chapter, the road to equal marriage rights has been difficult to travel, with powerful groups intervening to stop the advance of civil rights to same-sex couples along the way. Figure 9.1 provides an at-a-glance view of global attitudes toward marriage and partnerships for same-sex couples.

Clearly, public legitimation of same-sex relations is occurring in the global society. Human rights treaties and transnational social movement organizations have increasingly asserted the rights of persons to engage in same-sex relations. International organizations, such as Amnesty International, which resolved in 1991 to defend those imprisoned for homosexuality, the International Lesbian and Gay Association (founded in 1978), and the International Gay and Lesbian Human Rights Commission (founded in 1990), continue to fight prejudice and discrimination against lesbians and gays. Despite the worldwide movement toward increased acceptance and protection of homosexual individuals, the status and rights of lesbians and gays in Canada continues to be one of the most divisive issues in Canadian society. Shifts in government demonstrate that rights secured through law may also be rescinded through law. In response, many queer theorists and activists question the wisdom of spending effort on legal recognition of gay marriage; they argue that it may be more practical simply to reject marriage rights.

9.3 Homosexuality and Bisexuality: Prevalence and Explanations

In their exhaustive research on sexual behaviour, Kinsey and his colleagues (1953) found that a substantial proportion of respondents reported having had same-sex sexual experiences. The data revealed that 37 percent of men and 13 percent of women had at least one homosexual experience since adolescence. Yet, very few of the individuals in Kinsey's research reported exclusive homosexual behaviour. These data led Kinsey to conclude that most people are not exclusively heterosexual or homosexual. Rather, Kinsey suggested an individual's sexuality may have both heterosexual and homosexual elements, and that exclusive heterosexuality and homosexuality represent two ends of a continuum. He felt that most individuals fall somewhere within the continuum. Kinsey's early sex research demonstrated the difficulty of classifying individuals as heterosexual, homosexual, or bisexual, demonstrating the poor grounds for creating such medicalized types.

More recent data bear out Kinsey's findings. They suggest that changes in norms, negative sanctions, and restrictions, combined with more positive sensibilities about what it means to be involved in same-sex relationships, may correlate positively with increases in the percentage of women and men reporting same-sex sexual partnering in the past five years—the percentage increased from 0.2 in 1988 to 2.8 in 1998 (Butler 2000). This research also notes the following:

> These estimates of same-gender sex partnering should not be taken as estimates of the proportion of the population that is gay or lesbian. Some people may engage in same-gender sexual activity and yet identify as heterosexual, whereas other people may identify as gay or lesbian but may not have been sexually active in recent years. (Butler 2000: 342)

Origins of Sexual-Orientation Diversity: Nature or Nurture?

One of the prevailing questions about homosexuality and bisexuality centres on origin or "cause." Because heterosexuality is considered normative and "natural," causes of heterosexuality are rarely considered. Many researchers now believe that an interaction of biological and environmental forces affects the development of one's sexual orientation (De Cecco and Parker 1995).

Environmental Explanations of Sexual Orientation According to Doell (1995), "we all probably develop, from infancy, the capacity to have heterosexual, homosexual, or bisexual relationships" (p. 352). Environmental theories propose that such factors as availability of sexual partners, early sexual experiences, and sexual reinforcement influence subsequent sexual orientation. The degree to which early sexual experiences have been negative or positive has been hypothesized as influencing sexual orientation. Having pleasurable same-sex experiences would likely increase the probability of a homosexual orientation. By the same token, it has been suggested that early traumatic sexual experiences may cause fear of heterosexual activity. However, a study that compared sexual histories of lesbian and heterosexual women found no differences in the incidence of traumatic experiences with men (Brannock and Chapman 1990).

Biological Origins of Sexual Orientation Biological explanations of sexual orientation diversity usually focus on genetic or hormonal differences between heterosexuals and homosexuals. In an overview of genetics research on homosexual and heterosexual orientations, Pillard and Bailey (1998) conclude that genes account for at least half of the variance in sexual orientation. Their review of family, twin, and adoptee studies indicates that homosexuality (and thus heterosexuality) runs in families. However, the empirical research on isolating a biological-cause basis for sexuality is less than convincing in its findings.

For example, science has yet to identify a "homosexuality" gene despite the assertion of some researchers, such as Hamer and colleagues (1993), who claim to have discovered *statistical* evidence for its existence. In their examination of 40 pairs of gay brothers, Hamer and colleagues note that a significantly higher number than expected of the pairs (33 out of 40 versus 20 out of 40) shared matching DNA in a region called Xq28 at the tip of the X chromosome, a chromosome males inherit from their biological mothers. The researchers focused on this chromosome after noting in previous research that more gay male relatives appear to be found on the mother's side of the family.

Hamer and his research team did not isolate a specific gene, or even a specific set of genes, existing within that chromosomal region; they only provided the statistics-based suggestion that such genes must be there. Nor do they specifically account for the homosexuality of those brothers who do not possess the matching DNA. Furthermore, they have not examined heterosexual brothers for the existence or nonexistence of matching DNA in the Xq28 region to determine whether heterosexual brothers are similar to or different from homosexual brothers (Peele and DeGrandpre 1995). Consider, as well, the results of a Canadian study (Rice et al. 1999) based on 62 gay male sibling pairs. When the microsatellite markers at position Xq28 were analyzed, Hamer's suggestion of an X-linked gene underlying homosexuality was not supported.

Among the serious methodological problems confronting such research is determining what counts as "homosexuality"; the definitions vary from one study to another and what subjects mean when they say they are homosexual may not be the same from one subject to the next. Is it an issue of desire? of activity? of identity? Nevertheless, researchers continue in the quest to isolate a biological cause for human sexuality. This chapter's *Social Problems Research Up Close* feature highlights one such recent effort.

Can Homosexuals Change Their Sexual Orientation? Although "homosexuality" was removed from the *Diagnostic and Statistical Manual-IV* in 1974, some conservative, often Christian organizations claim to be able to "cure" homosexuality through **reparative therapy** or conversion therapy. Some religious organizations, like the U.S.-based Exodus, sponsor ex-gay ministries, which claim to "cure" homosexuals and transform them into heterosexuals through prayer and other forms of "therapy." Critics of ex-gay ministries take a different approach:

reparative therapy
Various therapies that are aimed at changing homosexuals' sexual attraction.

Youth Speak Up about Homophobia and Transphobia

This report discusses the results of a national survey of Canadian high school students undertaken in order to identify the forms and extent of their experiences of homophobic and transphobic incidents at school and the efficacy of measures being taken by schools to combat these common forms of bullying.

Phase One of the study involved surveying almost 1700 students from across Canada through two methods: individual online participation and in-school sessions conducted in four school boards. This report analyzes the data from individual online participation.

Educators and researchers have long been aware that students experience homophobic incidents ranging from hearing "gay" used as a synonym for "stupid" or "worthless" to being insulted or assaulted because of their actual or perceived sexual or transgender identity. However, the lack of a solid Canadian evidence base has been a major impediment faced by educators who need to understand the situation of lesbian, gay, bisexual, transgender, queer, and questioning (LGBTQ) students in order to respond appropriately and to assure the school community that homophobic and transphobic bullying are neither rare nor harmless but major problems that schools need to address.

Summary of Methods for Data Gathering and Analysis

The survey itself was a 54-item questionnaire made available online and in print, and consisting mostly

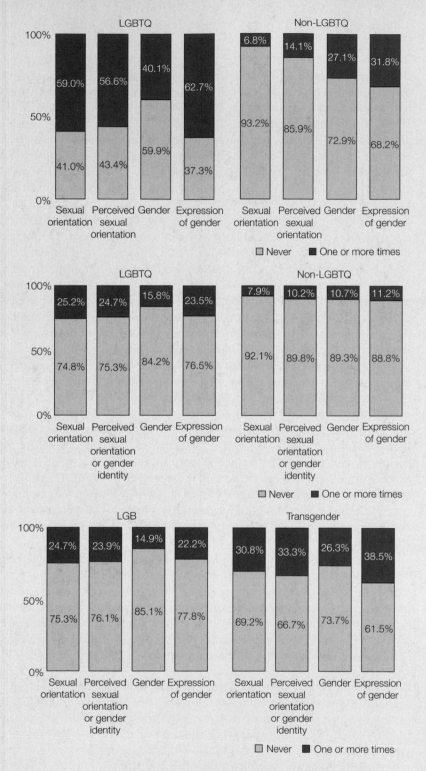

SOURCE: Taylor, Catherine, and Tracey Peter. 2009. "Youth Speak Out About Homophobia and Transphobia: The First National Climate Survey on Homophobia in Canadian Schools." EGALE Canada Human Rights Trust: Winnipeg, Ontario, p. 41. Reprinted with permission.

of multiple-choice questions of three kinds: demographic (e.g., age, province, gender identity, sexual identity), experiences (e.g., hearing the word gay used as an insult, being verbally harassed), and institutional responses (e.g., staff intervention, inclusive safe-school policies). Quantitative data were tested for statistical significance through bivariate analyses that compared the responses of various groups of students (e.g., LGBTQ and non-LGBTQ, LGB and transgender, current versus past).

Key Findings: Unsafe Spaces

Homophobic comments:

- Current students were even more likely than past students to hear expressions such as "that's so gay" in school.
- Current students were also more likely than past students to hear homophobic comments from other students every day in school.

One sign of progress:

- Current students were significantly less likely than past students to report that school staff never intervened.

Impacts

- Three-quarters of LGBTQ students and 95 percent of transgender students felt unsafe at school, compared to one-fifth of straight students.
- Over a quarter of LGBTQ students and almost half of transgender students had skipped school because they felt unsafe, compared to fewer than a tenth of non-LGBTQ.
- Many LGBTQ students would not be comfortable talking to their teachers (four in ten), their prin-

cipal (six in ten), or their coach (seven in ten) about LGBTQ issues.
- Only one in five LGBTQ students could talk to a parent very comfortably about LGBTQ issues. Three-quarters could talk to a close friend about these issues.
- Over half of LGBTQ students did not feel accepted at school, and almost half felt they could not be themselves at school, compared to one-fifth of straight students.
- Transgender students (over a third) were twice as likely as LGB students to strongly agree that they sometimes feel very depressed about their school and that they do not belong at their school, and four times as likely as straight students.

Institutional responses:

- Fewer than half of participants knew whether their school had a policy for reporting homophobic incidents.
- Of those participants who did know, only one-third believed there was such a policy.

LGBTQ students who believed their schools have anti-homophobia policies were much more likely than other LGBTQ students . . .

- to feel their school community was supportive (one-half compared to fewer than one-fifth),
- to feel comfortable talking to a counsellor (one-half compared to fewer than one-third), and to feel comfortable talking to classmates (over one-third compared to one-fifth),
- to believe their school was becoming less homophobic,
- to hear fewer homophobic comments and to say that staff intervene more often,

- to report homophobic incidents to staff and their parents, and
- to feel attached to their school.

LGBTQ students who believed their schools have anti-homophobia policies were much less likely than other LGBTQ students...

- to have had lies and rumours spread about them at school or on the internet,
- to have had property stolen or intentionally damaged,
- to feel unsafe at school, and
- to have been verbally or physically harassed.

The results were similar for students who believed that their school districts had such policies.

Conclusions and Recommendations

This survey confirms what LGBTQ students and their allies have known for some time: that despite Canada's leadership on human rights for LGBTQ people, a great deal of verbal and physical homophobic and transphobic harassment goes on in Canadian schools, that LGBTQ students are more likely to be aware of it than are other students who are not its main targets, and that the institutional response to harassment has more often than not been inadequate.

The survey also shows, however, that the situation is much improved where schools and school divisions have developed safe-schools policies and procedures that explicitly address homophobia and have informed students of their existence. In such schools, LGBTQ students are less likely to hear homophobic comments or to be targeted by verbal or physical harassment, they are more likely to report it to staff and

(continued)

parents when they are, and staff are more likely to intervene. In these schools, LGBTQ students feel safer, more accepted, and more attached to their school.

Developing inclusive safe schools policies and making them known to students is not a complete solution. However, this survey has identified significant differences between schools with and schools without inclusive policies.

Recommendations

1. That schools develop and implement anti-homophobia and anti-transphobia policies and make these policies well known to students, parents, administration, and all staff as a positive part of their commitment to making schools safe.

2. That schools strongly support the efforts of students to start Gay-Straight Alliances (GSAs).

3. That in schools where students have not come forward, administration should ask teachers to offer to work with students to start a GSA. It is not safe to assume that LGBTQ students would prefer to go through high school isolated from their peers and teachers.

4. That school divisions develop anti-homophobia and anti-transphobia policies to provide leadership for schools. Although our analysis showed that students are less likely to know about division-level policies, it would be helpful for principals to know that their school-level efforts have strong divisional endorsement in the form of official policy at that level.

5. That provincial Ministries of Education advocate the inclusion of anti-homophobia and anti-transphobia measures in safe schools policies and programs, including those of Catholic schools, along with steps for the implementation of these policies, in order to provide institutional support and motivation to divisional and school staff.

6. That individuals and organizations with expertise in anti-homophobia and anti-transphobia education be consulted in the above developments.

What students have told us in the First National Climate Survey on Homophobia in Canadian Schools is that speaking up works, and that they want the adults in their lives to do their part, too. These students are weary of seeing teachers and principals look the other way. And they are grateful to the many dedicated school staff who have worked to make schools safer for everyone in their care—not everyone but them.

SOURCE: Taylor, Catherine et al. 2009. "Executive Summary." *Youth Speak Up About Homophobia and Transphobia.* EGALE Canada: Winnipeg. Reprinted with permission.

The cure for unhappiness is not the "ex-gay" ministries—but coming out with dignity and self-respect. It is not gay men and lesbians who need to change...but negative attitudes and discrimination against gay people that need to be abolished. (Besen 2000: 7)

The Canadian Psychiatric Association, the Canadian Psychological Association, and the Canadian Medical Association agree that sexual orientation cannot be changed, and that efforts to change sexual orientation do not work and may be harmful (Human Rights Campaign 2000a). In addition, close scrutiny of reports of "successful" reparative therapy reveal that (1) many claims come from organizations with an ideological perspective on sexual orientation, rather than from unbiased researchers; (2) the treatments and their outcomes are poorly documented; and (3) the length of time that clients are followed after treatment is too short to evaluate their success or failure (Human Rights Campaign 2000a). In addition, at least 13 ministries of one reparative therapy group, Exodus, have closed because their directors reverted to homosexuality (Fone 2000).

9.4 Sociological Theories of Sexual Orientation

Sociological theories do not explain the origin or "cause" of sexual orientation, but help explain societal reactions to and contexts for sexual diversity. The sociology of sexuality can provide insight into shifting meanings in sexual identity and provide critical insight on the overlap of institutions and ideologies (like marriage, sexism, and heterosexism) and the costs of those overlaps as expressed in the form of prejudice, harm, and bias. Sociological inquiry brings a decidedly *social* understanding of the intersection of gender ideologies and sexualities.

Structural-Functionalist Perspective

Structural-functionalists, focusing on the operations fulfilled through institutions, emphasize the importance of monogamous heterosexual relationships for the reproduction, nurturance, and socialization of children. From a functionalist perspective, sexual relations are defined as "deviant" when they do not fulfill the family institution's main function of producing and rearing children. Clearly, this argument is less salient in a society in which (1) other institutions, most notably schools, have supplemented the traditional functions of the family; (2) a societal goal is to reduce population; and (3) same-sex couples can and do raise children.

Some functionalists argue that antagonisms between heterosexuals and homosexuals may disrupt social equilibrium. Durkheim, however, recognized that deviation from society's norms "may be useful as a prelude to reforms which daily become more necessary" ([1938] 1993: 66). Specifically, the gay rights movement has motivated many people to re-examine their treatment of sexual-orientation minorities; it has also produced a sense of cohesion and solidarity among members of the gay population (although bisexuals and the transgendered have often been excluded from gay and lesbian communities and organizations). Bringing benefit to society as a whole, gay activism has been instrumental in advocating for more research on HIV and AIDS, more and better health services for HIV and AIDS patients, protection of the rights of HIV-infected individuals, and HIV/AIDS public education.

Finally, the structural-functionalist focus on the interconnectedness of society fosters an understanding that urbanization has contributed to the formation of strong social networks of gays and bisexuals. Cities "acted as magnets, drawing in gay migrants who felt isolated and threatened in smaller towns and rural areas" (Button et al. 1997: 15; Goldie 2001). Given the formation of gay communities in large cities, it is not surprising that the gay rights movement first emerged in large urban centres.

Other research has demonstrated that the worldwide rise in liberalized national policies on same-sex relations and the lesbian and gay rights social movement has been influenced by three cultural changes: (1) the rise of individualism that values personal satisfaction, (2) increasing gender equality, and (3) the emergence of a global society in which nations are influenced by international pressures (Frank and McEneaney 1999). Whereas once sex was approved strictly for the purpose of family reproduction, sex increasingly serves to pleasure individualized men and women in society. Individualism "appears to loosen the tie between sex and procreation, allowing more personal modes of sexual expression" (p. 930).

Gender equality involves the breakdown of sharply differentiated sex roles, thereby supporting the varied expressions of male and female sexuality. Globalization permits the international community to influence individual nations. For example, when Zimbabwe President Robert Mugabe pursued antihomosexual policies in 1995, many international organizations and human rights associations joined to protest his actions and to ask that he halt his campaign. The pressure of international opinion led Zimbabwe's Supreme Court to rule in favour of lesbian and gay groups' right to organize.

Conflict Perspective

Conflict theorists, particularly those who do not emphasize a purely economic perspective, note that the antagonisms between "straight" and GLBT communities represent a basic division in society between those with power and those without power. When one group has control of society's institutions and resources, as in the case of heterosexuals, it has the authority to dominate other groups. Current battles over gay rights form one example of the political struggle between those with power and those without it.

A classic example of the power struggle between gays and "straights" took place in 1973. At that time, the American Psychiatric Association (APA) met to revise its classification scheme of mental disorders. Homosexual activists had been appealing to the APA for years to remove homosexuality from its list of mental illnesses, but with little success. However, in 1973, the APA's board of directors voted to remove homosexuality from its official list of mental disorders. The board's move encountered much resistance from conservative APA members. The issue was put to a referendum, which reaffirmed the board's decision (Bayer 1987).

In recent years, many organizations have recognized that implementing antidiscrimination policies that include sexual orientation is good for the bottom line. Over half (51 percent) of Fortune 500 companies and 82 percent of Fortune 1000 companies have included sexual orientation in their nondiscrimination policies, and employers are increasingly offering benefits to domestic partners of GLBT employees (Human Rights Campaign 2000b). Gay-friendly workplaces help employers maintain a competitive edge in recruiting and a talented and productive workforce.

In some settings, however, the changes have been hard won. Gay rights activists have turned to Canadian courtrooms and human rights tribunals, successfully employing the equality provision of the *Canadian Charter of Rights and Freedoms*. As a result of their activities, some Canadian workplaces have been transformed as "[g]overnments have changed legislation and policies either because courts have ordered them to do so or because of threats of court cases" (Dranoff 2001: 133).

In summary, conflict theory frames the gay rights movement and the opposition to it as a struggle over power, prestige, and economic resources. Recent trends toward increased social acceptance of homosexuality may, in part, reflect the corporate world's competition over the gay and lesbian consumer dollar.

Symbolic Interactionist Perspective

Symbolic interactionism focuses on the meanings of heterosexuality, homosexuality, and bisexuality and how these meanings are socially constructed. The meanings we associate with same-sex relations are learned from society—from family, peers, religion, and the media. Freedman and D'Emilio (1990: 485) observed: "sexual meanings are subject to the forces of culture. Human beings learn how to express themselves sexually, and the content and outcome of that learning vary widely across cultures and across time."

Historical and cross-cultural research reveals the socially constructed nature of sexuality and its meanings. Although many North Americans assume that same-sex romantic relationships have always been taboo, during the nineteenth century, "romantic friendships" between women were encouraged and regarded as preparation for a successful marriage. President Grover Cleveland's sister Rose, for example, wrote to her friend Evangeline Whipple in 1890: "It makes me heavy with emotion...all my whole being leans out to you.... I dare not think of your arms" (Goode and Wagner 1993: 49).

The symbolic interactionist perspective also points to the effects of labelling on individuals. Once individuals become identified or labelled as lesbian, gay, or bisexual, that label tends to become their **master status**. In other words, the dominant heterosexual community tends to view "gay," "lesbian," and "bisexual" as the most socially significant statuses of individuals identified as such. Esterberg (1997: 377) notes that "unlike heterosexuals, who are defined by their family structures, communities, occupations, or other aspects of their lives, lesbians, gay men, and bisexuals are often defined primarily by what they do in bed. Many lesbians, gay men, and bisexuals, however, view their identity as social and political as well as sexual."

master status

The status that is considered the most significant in a person's social identity.

Feminist Perspectives

Feminist work on sexuality is diverse, a result of highly variable concerns that arise in the attempt to understand sexuality. A foundational point, however, is the clear observation that issues related to sexuality are central to women's lives, not marginal or frivolous. Clearly, for example, women's ability to acquire education and to achieve a measure of financial independence—both very important in a capitalist context—depends on women's ability to control their reproduction, a matter tied in part to sexuality.

Feminist work has also revealed that beliefs about women's sexuality have made them extremely vulnerable to a variety of oppressive forces. Among these is the tendency to "pedestalize" some women for their ability to act appropriately as good mothers and wives, adornments for men of privileged classes; meanwhile, women from marginalized groups may be simultaneously eroticized and vilified as "excessively sexual." This oppositional pairing of women as good and bad is popularly known as the "Madonna/whore dichotomy." Feminists have pointed out that in such a symbolic and structural ordering no woman is free—a problem we take up further throughout this chapter.

It is important to remember that feminist work does not have to be done by women, though it often is. For example, Sander Gilman's historical assessment of racism and sexism in medicine revealed that nineteenth-century "experts" claimed that African women, Jewish women, and European prostitutes and lesbians all shared similarly deviant and *excessively large* genitalia (Gilman 1985).

What makes a work on sexuality feminist if it is not the body of the researcher? A central answer to that question arrives in the principle of **anti-essentialism** developed within feminist scholarship since the 1980s. Anti-essentialist work observes that nothing is guaranteed by the body, most particularly by the sex, of a person. Instead, our social and cultural contexts shape who we are. It is through this **constructionist** position that much contemporary feminist work on sexuality operates. A constructionist approach understands, for example, that "how we classify individuals according to sex [as a matter of law] is a matter of interpretation.... Moreover, what we take sex itself to be [as a biological phenomenon]...is also a question of interpretation" (Warnke 2005: 113). "Sex" then is a matter of perception and a vehicle for controlling how bodies are organized into categories. As Gayle Rubin observed in "The Traffic in Women" (1975), sex and sexuality are the central mechanisms through which societies organize their kinship systems, with those labelled as women bearing the burden of structural inequality that guarantees men the bulk of power.

Finally, feminist scholarship observes that what counts as sexuality and how sex is organized varies around the world; it is not universally identical, even though every society has a sex-based system for organizing its members.

Queer Theory Perspectives

The most prominent contributors to the sociological application of queer theory to the understanding of sexualities are Michel Foucault and Judith Butler. Their conceptual work has largely shaped the tools and approach we use to critically assess powerful and normative institutions.

Foucault's exhaustive three-volume work on sexuality (1990a, 1990b, 1990c) makes the point that bodies and sexualities came to have meaning only as a result of a variety of interventions and invasions: these label us by sex, by practice, and by general state-of-health assessments that teach us how to see ourselves and to understand our practices and desires by the tools of science, law, and medicine that Foucault labelled as a form of "gaze." A *gaze* is a view that imposes meaning rather than being simply a passive way of looking; it is, instead, a look that can pass judgment, mete out punishments, make assessments, and tell us who we are as much as demand it. For Foucault, the gaze structures the meanings of sexuality, for example, through claims to genetic foundations for predispositions, orientations, desires, and practices. The gaze can structure meanings through the admittance of some forms of marriage but not others, thereby conferring or refusing legitimacy; finally, the gaze requires that we also look back at it to confirm that we accept its conclusions as truths, for example, in popular media claims that

anti-essentialism

The refusal of simplistic biological explanations for complex social relations, motivations, behaviours, and identifications.

constructionist

The belief that social context provides the mode and meaning for both sexuality and gendered behaviours, roles, and relationships.

overstate the conclusions of biomedicine with regard to what "causes" same-sex desire.

Butler, who began writing on gender and sexuality in the late 1980s, made the powerful observation that as the symbolic basis upon which a variety of social and sexual demands are fixed, gender is not a natural expression of our sex, but a means of conveying and of securing a socially legitimated place for ourselves—a place from which we can be recognized as male or female, and out of which a variety of norms regarding sex(uality) are expressed. In her 1990 book *Gender Trouble*, Butler argued that gender was a performance, something that was unstable, and that all of us have to work at it every day, to make ourselves knowable and recognizable to others. Many people took her statement to suggest that we could simply decide on our gender and then act it out. However, Butler later argued in *Bodies That Matter* (1993) that this was a misreading: our performance could not be freely and individually willed, but was compelled by those around us; those who do not "fit in" to the performance demands are placed at grave risk in a heteronormative and homophobic society.

For the social study of sexualities, the combined observations of feminist and queer theories help us to understand that the way things are is not the way things have to be, that oppressive functions can be challenged, and that claims to "the naturalness" of one form of sexuality operate to the benefit of only a tiny minority of the population, neither providing an accurate description nor an adequate understanding of sex and sexuality. Moreover, such claims place many people, including most women and those who are in some way "queer," in highly vulnerable positions.

9.5 Heterosexism, Homophobia, and Biphobia

Heterosexism refers to "an ideological system that denies, denigrates, and stigmatizes any nonheterosexual form of behaviour, identity, relationship, or community" (Herek 1990: 316). Heterosexism is based on the belief that heterosexuality is "natural" and, therefore, "normal," that it is superior to homosexuality, and that homosexuality is what happens when something disrupts a presupposed "natural order." Heterosexism lays the foundation for prejudice and discrimination against GLBT persons. Prejudice refers to negative attitudes, whereas discrimination refers to behaviour that denies individuals or groups equality of treatment. Before reading further, you may wish to complete this chapter's *Self and Society* feature, The Homophobia Scale.

heterosexism

The belief that heterosexuality is the superior sexual orientation; it results in prejudice and discrimination against homosexuals and bisexuals.

Homophobia

The term **homophobia** is commonly used to refer to negative attitudes and emotions toward homosexuality and those who engage in it. Other terms that refer to negative attitudes and emotions toward homosexuality include *homonegativity* and *antigay bias*.

homophobia

Negative attitudes toward homosexuality.

The Homophobia Scale

Directions: Indicate the extent to which you agree or disagree with each statement by placing a check mark on the appropriate line.

	Strongly Agree	Agree	Undecided	Disagree	Strongly Disagree
1. Homosexuals contribute positively to society.	___	___	___	___	___
2. Homosexuality is disgusting.	___	___	___	___	___
3. Homosexuals are just as moral as heterosexuals are.	___	___	___	___	___
4. Homosexuals should have equal civil rights.	___	___	___	___	___
5. Homosexuals corrupt young people.	___	___	___	___	___
6. Homosexuality is a sin.	___	___	___	___	___

Scoring

Assign scores of 0, 1, 2, 3, and 4 to the five choices respectively ("strongly agree" through "strongly disagree") for items 1, 3, and 4. Assign scores of 0, 1, 2, 3, and 4 to the five choices in reverse order ("strongly disagree" through "strongly agree") for items 2, 5, and 6. All items are summed for the total score. The possible range is 0 to 28; high scores indicate greater homophobia.

Comparison Data

The Homophobia Scale was administered to 524 students enrolled in introductory psychology courses at the University of Texas. The mean score for men was 15.8; for women, it was 13.8. The difference was statistically significant.

SOURCE: Bouton, Richard A., P. E. Gallagher, P. A. Garlinghouse, T. Leal, et al. 1987. "Scales for Measuring Fear of AIDS and Homophobia." *Journal of Personality Assessment* 67(1): 609. Copyright © Francis and Taylor Group, www.informaworld.com. Used with permission.

Prevailing attitudes can, however, shift; as with most social phenomena, change is always possible. We can identify some of the features that have correlated with large shifts in popular attitudes and perception. People who are younger, more educated, never married, living in the West, living in heavily populated urban areas, and Jewish are least likely to have antigay attitudes (Klassen et al. 1989). Also, positive contact with GLBT people is associated with less homophobia (Simon 1995). The development of attitudes is, however, complex. Sociological studies reveal that issues of class, of education, of family history, of one's gender, and so forth are all influential forces in attitude development.

In a study of undergraduates (101 men, 98 women) attending a Canadian university where most students were of working-class or middle-class families of European descent, Schellenberg and colleagues (1999) found that attitudes toward gay men were more negative than toward lesbians. When compared to science or business students, students in the faculties of arts and social sciences had more positive attitudes toward gay men, and women were more positive than men were. Attitudes toward gay men improved with time spent at university, but only for male students. Although attitudes toward lesbians also improved with time at university, this trend was not associated with students' gender or faculty of enrolment. Schellenberg and colleagues conclude that university education may encourage a reduction in antihomosexual prejudice among young people, particularly among young men. In an effort to reduce homophobia and its consequences, campuses across Canada have set up "Positive Space" programs. These let people know that homophobic and hateful behaviour will not be tolerated, and that GLBT students can find a safe place to think, learn, and live on the campus.

Cultural Origins of Homophobia

Why is homosexuality viewed so negatively in North America? Antigay bias has its roots in various aspects of our culture.

1. *Religion*. Most individuals who view homosexuality as unacceptable say they object on religious grounds (Rosin and Morin 1999). Although some religious groups accept homosexuality, many religions teach that homosexuality is sinful and prohibited by God. The Roman Catholic Church rejects all homosexual expression and resists any attempt to validate or sanction the homosexual orientation. Some fundamentalist churches have endorsed the death penalty for homosexual people and teach the view that AIDS is God's punishment for engaging in homosexual sex (Nugent and Gramick 1989). In June 1999, a U.S. Baptist preacher from Topeka, Kansas, announced that he and a group of his followers would be leading a demonstration on the steps of the Supreme Court of Canada to protest its decision to extend the definition of "spouse" to same-sex couples. Mr. Phelps, who on previous occasions has picketed gay funerals, same-sex unions, and even Girl Scout meetings brandishing signs that read, "AIDS cures fags," had announced, "We're coming to spread the gospel to you sinners." Phelps referred to Canada as the "sperm bank of Satan" and vowed that he and his supporters would burn Canadian flags in protest. In the end, Mr. Phelps did not appear and his group blamed the unwillingness of Canadian police, "who are as blackhearted as the perverts," to provide him with the level of protection he sought as the reason for the group's absence (Anderssen 1999).

    Some religious groups, such as the Quakers, accept homosexuality, and other groups have made reforms toward increased acceptance of lesbians and gays. In the United States, some Episcopal priests perform "ceremonies of union" between same-sex couples; some Reform Jewish groups sponsor gay synagogues, and the United Church of Christ ordains gay men and women (Fone 2000). The United Church of Canada has ignited conflict by declaring that "all persons, regardless of their sexual orientation, are welcome to become full members of the church and are eligible for ordination as ministers" (in Dawson 1993: 323).

2. *Marital and procreative bias.* Many societies have traditionally condoned sex only when it occurs in a marital context that provides for the possibility of producing and rearing children. However, science continues to challenge the necessity of opposite-sex parents. "Under cell nuclear replacement, scientists replace the nucleus from the egg of a female donor with the nucleus from a sperm cell. The resulting 'male egg,' containing only male DNA, is then fertilized in vitro by sperm from another man" (Honore 2000). Even though already-available assisted reproductive technologies make it possible for gay individuals and couples to have children, many people believe that only heterosexual married couples should use these advances (Franklin 1993).

3. *Concern about HIV and AIDS.* Although transmission rates vary upward and downward for different groups over time and most cases of HIV and AIDS worldwide are attributed to heterosexual transmission, HIV and AIDS in Canada is more prevalent among gay and bisexual men than among other groups. Because of this, many people associate HIV and AIDS with homosexuality and bisexuality. Lesbians, incidentally, have a very low risk for sexually transmitted HIV—a lower risk than heterosexual women do.

4. *Threat to the power of the majority.* Like other minority groups, the gay minority threatens the power of the majority. Fearing loss of power, the majority group stigmatizes gays and lesbians and transgender people as a way of limiting their power.

5. *Rigid gender roles.* Antigay sentiments also stem from rigid gender roles. When Cooper Thompson (1995) was asked to give a guest presentation on male roles at a suburban high school, male students told him that the most humiliating insult was being called a "fag." The boys in this school gave Thompson the impression that they were expected to conform to rigid, narrow standards of masculinity to avoid being labelled in this way.

From a conflict perspective, heterosexual men's subordination and devaluation of gay men reinforces gender inequality. "By devaluing gay men...heterosexual men devalue the feminine and anything associated with it" (Price and Dalecki 1998: 155–56). Negative views toward lesbians also reinforce the patriarchal system of male dominance. Social disapproval of lesbians is a form of punishment for women who relinquish traditional female sexual and economic dependence on men. Not surprisingly, research findings suggest that individuals with traditional gender role attitudes tend to hold more negative views toward homosexuality (Louderback and Whitley 1997).

6. *Psychiatric labelling.* As noted earlier, before 1973 the APA (American Psychiatric Association) defined homosexuality as a mental disorder, and "treatment" included lobotomies, aversive conditioning, and, in some cases, castration. The APA definition contributed to negative reactions to gays and also created feelings of guilt, low self-esteem, anger, and depression for many gays and lesbians. The psychiatric care system is now busily treating the very conditions it, in part, created.

7. *Myths and negative stereotypes.* Prejudice toward gays and lesbians may also stem from some of the unsupported beliefs and negative stereotypes regarding same-sex sexuality. One such belief is that gays and lesbians lack

"family values," such as monogamy and commitment to relationships. While some do engage in casual sex, as do some heterosexuals, many gay and lesbian couples develop and maintain long-term committed relationships.

Another myth is that, as groups, gay men and lesbians (to a lesser extent perhaps because of the common assumption that women are less sexual than men) are child molesters. Yet, the ratio of heterosexual to gay male child molesters is approximately 11 to 1 (Moser 1992). When a father sexually assaults his daughter, the media do not report that something is wrong with heterosexuality or with traditional families, but when a homosexual is reported to have molested a child, it is viewed as confirmation of "the way homosexuals are" (Mohr 1995: 404).

Biphobia

Just as the term *homophobia* refers to negative attitudes toward gay men and lesbians, **biphobia** refers to "the parallel set of negative beliefs about and stigmatization of bisexuality and those identified as bisexual" (Paul 1996: 449). Although heterosexuals often reject both homosexual- and bisexual-identified individuals, bisexual-identified women and men also face rejection from many homosexual individuals. Thus, bisexuals experience "double discrimination."

Biphobia includes negative stereotyping of bisexuals; the exclusion of bisexuals from social and political organizations of lesbians and gay men; and fear and distrust of, as well as anger and hostility toward, people who identify themselves as bisexual (Firestein 1996). Individuals who are biphobic often believe that bisexuals are really homosexuals afraid to acknowledge their real identity or homosexuals maintaining heterosexual relationships to avoid rejection by the heterosexual mainstream. Bisexual individuals are sometimes viewed as heterosexuals who are looking for exotic sexual experiences.

Negative attitudes regarding bisexuality and people who identify as bisexual are not the exclusive domain of heterosexual homophobes. Lesbian philosopher Elizabeth Grosz suggested in a conference paper that "bisexuality was a luxury, that bisexuals want to have their cake and eat it" (Angelides 1995: 27). Steven Angelides (1995) holds out this summary of Grosz's position as a statement that exemplifies a not uncommon mistrust of bisexuals by gays and lesbians, but argues that attitudes such as Grosz's rest on ideas about identity that reinforce the notion that someone who is not oppressed based on a given trait (like race, ethnicity, or sexuality) cannot fully commit to anti-oppressive politics. Angelides argues that biphobia discounts the productive and rich political value of bisexuality and avers that our ethical commitments are built on awareness, not identity, and that our political commitments do not have to be bounded and bordered by our personal desires.

biphobia
Negative attitudes toward bisexuality and people who identify as bisexual.

Effects of Homophobia and Heterosexism on Heterosexuals

The homophobic and heterosexist social climate of our society is often viewed in terms of how it victimizes the gay population. However, heterosexuals are also victimized by homophobia and heterosexism. "Hatred, fear, and ignorance are bad for the bigot as well as the victim" (*Homophobia 101* 2000).

Due to the antigay climate, heterosexuals, especially males, are hindered in their own self-expression and intimacy in same-sex friendships. "The threat of victimization (i.e., antigay violence) probably also causes many heterosexuals to conform to gender roles and to restrict their expressions of (nonsexual) physical affection for members of their own sex" (Garnets et al. 1990: 380). Homophobic epithets frighten youth who do not conform to gender role expectations, leading some youth to avoid activities that they might otherwise enjoy and benefit from (arts for boys, athletics for girls, for example) (*Homophobia 101* 2000).

Some sexual assaults are related to homophobia and compulsory heterosexuality. For example, some men who participate in gang rape entice others into the act "by implying that those who do not participate are unmanly or homosexual" (Sanday 1995: 399). Homo-negativity also encourages early sexual activity among adolescent men. Adolescent male virgins are often teased by their peers, who say things like "You mean you don't do it with girls yet? What are you, a fag or something?" Not wanting to be labelled and stigmatized as a "fag," some adolescent boys "prove" their heterosexuality by having sex with girls.

Antigay cultural attitudes also affect family members and friends of homosexuals, who often fear that their lesbian or gay friend or family member will be victimized by antigay prejudice and discrimination. Youth with gay and lesbian family members are often taunted by their peers.

As we have already noted, extreme homophobia can lead to instances of physical violence against homosexuals. But "gay bashings" are crimes of perception because victims of antigay violence may not be homosexual, only perceived as being homosexual. Many heterosexuals have been victims of antigay physical violence because the attacker(s) perceived them to be gay. Antigay harassment has also been a factor in some cases of school violence. One study concluded, "For boys, no other type of harassment provoked as strong a reaction on average; boys in this study would be less upset about physical abuse than they would be if someone called them gay" (Dozetos 2001).

9.6 Discrimination against Sexual-Orientation Minorities

Like other minority groups in Canada, GLBT persons have experienced and continue to experience various forms of discrimination. From 1952 to 1977, immigration laws prohibited homosexuals from entering Canada and subjected homosexuals to the threat of deportation if their sexual orientation became known. From 1892 to 1969, Canadian criminal law made certain forms of sexual conduct engaged in by gay men illegal and rendered gay men vulnerable to indefinite incarceration as "dangerous sexual offenders."

Next, we look at sexual-orientation discrimination in the workplace, in family matters, and in violent expressions of hate. This chapter's *Focus on Technology* feature discusses the discriminatory effects of internet filtering and monitoring technology on sexual-orientation minorities.

The Impact of Internet Filtering and Monitoring on Sexual-Orientation Minorities

Joan Garry is the executive director of the Gay and Lesbian Alliance Against Defamation (GLAAD) and a mother of three children. When her 10-year-old daughter Sarah approached her for information about COLAGE (Children of Lesbians and Gays Everywhere), a support organization for the children of lesbian and gay parents, they signed on to America Online to look up the website. The COLAGE site was "Web Restricted": Sarah could not access the site because her computer was equipped with AOL's filtering software called Kids Only. When Joan tried to look up various family, youth, and national organization websites with lesbian and gay content, most sites came up "Web Restricted" as well (Garry 1999). For example, the Kids Only software blocked access to several youth-oriented gay and lesbian resource sites, including PFLAG (Parents, Family and Friends of Lesbians and Gays), Family Pride, !OutProud!, GLSEN (Gay, Lesbian and Straight Education Network), and *Oasis Magazine*, a gay and lesbian youth webzine (Javier 1999).

An explosion of filtering technologies to help maintain "decency" and "community standards" on the internet has occurred. Examples of filtering technologies include those that block key words or URLs. For example, the search engine Jayde.com, which marketed itself as being able to filter out pornographic material, decided to block the word "lesbian" in its search engine. The filtering software "CYBERsitter" automatically filters out such words

and phrases as "gay," "lesbian," "gay rights," and "gay community" (Javier 1999). Filtering technologies are promoted as tools to help parents, schools, libraries, and communities prevent children's access to sexually explicit and pornographic material on the internet. However, some filtering software also denies users access to several lesbian, gay, and bisexual youth resource sites.

Schneider (1999) presents the following scenario:

> Imagine a teenager seeking information about his or her sexual orientation whose attempts to go to gay-related Web sites are met with a warning that tells him or her "Bess doesn't want you to go there." In an unfiltered environment...the teen could be expected to privately retrieve all kinds of information in a discreet, nonjudgmental environment. But place a filter on that computer, and...the teen gets the message that he or she is somehow..."inappropriate." (p. 13)

Given the impact of internet filtering on the gay community, some gay rights groups oppose the use of filtering software. Instead, they advocate parental oversight, school supervision, and training of young internet users (Bowes 1999).

Another concern of sexual-orientation minorities is the use of monitoring software. This software allows parents, teachers, and other authority figures to track sites a Web surfer tries to access. The monitoring software industry markets its products by claiming that they allow for parental awareness without censorship and that parental use of monitoring software encourages open family communication. But for youth who are not ready to reveal their sexual orientation to their family, "such software could

potentially 'out' them before they are ready, leading to strained family relations and deeper isolation (Javier 1999: 8).

In addition, internet service providers may record every click of your mouse, including personal information you exchange in chat rooms, emails, and instant messages.

Say you visit a Web magazine: the time and date of your visit are recorded. You conduct a search for all articles containing the word "gay." Your inquiry is recorded. You click on an article about new AIDS drugs. Your request for that article is recorded. While reading the article, you click on an ad about online dating services, and that choice is recorded.... You decide to enter a gay-oriented chat room and see if you can make any new friends, or even get a date. You chat with a number of people, and finally connect with one special person, with whom you share instant messages, pictures, and perhaps even a virtual date. Depending on the Internet provider in question, that date could have just been recorded (Aravosis 1999: 30).

Websites also record information about your internet usage. When you visit a free news website, you may be required to "subscribe" by giving them your name and email address. After subscribing, you read a few articles. But unbeknownst to you, the news website has put a "cookie," or piece of computer code, on the hard drive of your computer. This cookie contains a unique identifier permitting the news site to recognize you when you return to that site. Cookies can do helpful things, like remember your password for accessing that site, and tailor Web pages for preset preferences. But they can also contain a

(continued)

record of what you did on that site, including what searches you made and what articles you read (Aravosis 1999). According to one study, of the 7500 busiest servers on the Web, 93 percent of the sites collect personal information from consumers, yet only 66 percent post any disclosure about their information practices (Bowes 1999).

Although some websites have strict privacy policies, others sell information about site visitors. One company boasts on its website that it is "the world's oldest and largest mailing list manager and broker for Gay, Lesbian, and HIV-related names, currently managing almost two million names, which we estimate to be about 65 percent of all those commercially available in this segment" (Aravosis 1999: 33). Databases containing the names of gay consumers are valuable because gays are perceived as a "wealthy

and wired market." A 1998 study found that the average household income of lesbians and gay men on the internet was $57 300, slightly higher than the $52 000 for the general internet population (Aravosis 1999).

The internet has been a useful tool for gays, lesbians, and bisexuals. Going online has allowed the gay community to create safe places for support and information. However, internet filtering and monitoring software that has been installed on computers in homes, schools, libraries, and workplaces represents a threat to the gay community. Filtering and monitoring technologies make it impossible or dangerous for a closeted gay or lesbian to seek out support and information about their community.

We live in an age in which the Internet has become an extremely important part of the coming out

process for many gay and lesbian youth. In many cases, it can be a lifeline to those in geographically isolated areas. To deny basic educational and support resources to lesbian and gay youth could seriously endanger their physical and emotional well being. (Appendix A 1999: 46)

SOURCES: Appendix A. 1999. "Frequently Asked Questions." In *Access Denied Version 2.0, The Continuing Threat against Internet Access and Privacy and Its Impact on the Lesbian, Gay, Bisexual and Transgender Community.* New York: Gay and Lesbian Alliance Against Defamation, pp. 45–48; Aravosis, John. 1999. "Privacy: The Impact on Lesbian, Gay, Bisexual and Transgender Community." In *Access Denied Version 2.0*, pp. 30–33; Bowes, John. 1999. "Conclusions." In *Access Denied Version 2.0*, pp. 38–44; Garry, Joan M. 1999. "Introduction: How Access and Privacy Impact the Lesbian, Gay, Bisexual and Transgender Community." In *Access Denied Version 2.0*, pp. 3–5; Javier, Loren. 1999. "The World since Access Denied." In *Access Denied 2.0*, pp. 6–9; Schneider, Karen G. 1999. "Access: The Impact on the Lesbian, Gay, Bisexual and Transgender Community." In *Access Denied Version 2.0*, pp. 10–15.

Discrimination in the Workplace

In recent years, the percentage of Canadians who express approval of equal employment rights for homosexuals has increased. Nevertheless, many Canadians still feel that homosexuals should not be entitled to the same rights and privileges as others. While support levels for gays working in a variety of different occupations increased between 1988 and 2001, certain occupations are still considered "more suitable" than others. For example, the vast majority of Canadians find it acceptable for gays to work as salespersons (94 percent vs. 72 percent in 1988), members of Parliament (86 percent vs. 62 percent in 1988), members of the Canadian Forces (82 percent vs. 60 percent in 1988), physicians (82 percent vs. 52 percent in 1988), or prison officers (75 percent vs. 44 percent in 1988). However, there is less support for gays working as junior-school teachers (67 percent vs. 45 percent in 1988) or members of the clergy (63 percent vs. 44 percent in 1988) (Bricker and Greenspon 2001: 267–68).

Only a few decades ago, there were few legal protections for gay and lesbian individuals who experienced employment discrimination. In the 1960s, hostility toward gays in the workplace led to more than 8000 gay men being investigated by the RCMP; as a result, approximately 150 gay federal civil servants resigned or were dismissed from their employment positions without just cause. It was only in 1992 that the Canadian armed forces, facing a court challenge, agreed to stop discrimination against gays. At the time of writing, discrimination on the basis of sexual orientation was prohibited everywhere in Canada except for the Northwest Territories and Nunavut. While Alberta's legislation does not state this prohibition specifically, the Supreme Court of Canada declared in the 1998 case of *Vriend v. Alberta* that Alberta's human rights legislation "would be interpreted to include sexual orientation as a prohibited ground—whether or not it is specified in the legislation.... This marked the first time the Supreme Court of Canada amended legislation on constitutional grounds by reading into law new rights that elected politicians had expressly refused to grant" (Dranoff 2001: 134).

Discrimination in Family Relationships

In addition to discrimination in the workplace, sexual-orientation minorities in Canada have also experienced discrimination in policies on marriage, child custody and visitation, and adoption.

Same-Sex Marriage In June of 1999, the Canadian House of Commons voted overwhelmingly in favour of a motion, introduced by Eric Lowther, the Reform Party critic on "Children and Families," opposing same-sex marriages. The motion, which signalled the first time same-sex marriage was the subject of a vote in the House of Commons, affirmed the exclusion of gays and lesbians from the institution of marriage; it also committed Parliament to "take all necessary steps" to preserve legal marriage as an opposite-sex institution. Although passing the motion had no immediate legal impact, it might be presumed that as an official declaration of Parliament's position on the matter, the "necessary steps" could include invoking the "notwithstanding" clause within the Constitution. This clause allows governments to opt out of the *Charter of Rights and Freedoms* and to deny equality to some of their citizens—in this case, lesbians and gay men. In total, 216 members of Parliament (MPs) from all parties voted in favour of the motion, including the overwhelming majority of the Liberal caucus (all but 11), all Reform Party MPs, and a number of those from the New Democratic Party, Bloc Québécois, and Progressive Conservative Party. Only 55 MPs voted against the motion. Although a "free vote"—with MPs able to "vote their conscience" rather than follow a party line—had been expected, in the end the Liberal government adopted a government position that supported the Reform Party (EGALE 1999). By 2005, though, the then minority Liberal government passed legislation to permit same-sex marriages.

In that year, various provincial governments also grappled with the issues presented by same-sex marriages. In May 1999, the Supreme Court of Ontario ruled that an Ontario law that excluded gays and lesbians from a definition of common-law couples was unconstitutional. Shortly after, the Ontario government passed an omnibus bill that amended 67 of its laws to include same-sex couples.

Although the Supreme Court's ruling was binding only on the Ontario government, several other provinces quickly announced plans to make similar changes. For example, in June of that year, when the Quebec National Assembly unanimously passed Bill 32, Quebec became the first Canadian province to ensure that same-sex couples would receive all the benefits and responsibilities of opposite-sex couples. Bill 32 changed the definition of "spouse" within that province and committed the Quebec government to making changes in 39 provincial laws and regulations. A month later, the British Columbia government

The *Human Side*

"It's about Love": A Canadian Couple Fighting for Recognition of Same-Sex Unions

Kevin Bourassa, 44, and Joe Varnell, 32, were one of two Canadian same-sex couples married on July 14, 2001, at Toronto's Metropolitan Community Church. When the provincial government of Ontario refused to grant them a wedding licence, Bourassa and Varnella turned to the courts. In mid-July of 2002, three Ontario Superior Court judges ruled that the federal law that prohibits same-sex couples from marrying was unconstitutional—a ruling that Ottawa is appealing. In the following extract from an interview which originally appeared in Maclean's in August 2002, Bourassa and Varnell, co-authors of Just Married: Gay Marriage and the Expansion of Human Rights, discuss their fight for the right to marry.

Were you expecting the federal government to appeal the court's decision?

Varnell: When we started, we knew there was a strong possibility that a positive decision would be appealed. But because of the overwhelmingly strong wording of the judgment, telling the government its laws were unconstitutional, we were a little surprised.

Bourassa: Various things led us to be hopeful. The polls, the provincial Conservatives saying they wouldn't appeal the ruling, the federal government floating the trial balloon about getting out of the marriage business, fueled our hope that Ottawa would honour the Charter.

What do you think of the proposal that there should be no more state-sanctioned marriages, just religious ceremonies or civil arrangements?

Varnell: It's an extremely radical step—far more radical than simply extending the definition of marriage to include gays and lesbians. But it would be a disappointing option for us because they would be saying that rather than pollute the institution of marriage with same-sex couples, they'd prefer to pick up their toys and go home.

Why is marriage so important for gay and lesbian couples?

Bourassa: First, it's about the government being allowed to treat one group that is otherwise protected by the Charter differently. It's important to send a message that gays and lesbians are not second-class citizens. But on a personal level, marriage is about love. We should be able to experience that love in the manner we choose, in a manner available to all Canadians.

Is marriage something you think other gay couples should do?

Varnell: Marriage isn't for every couple. Relationships have to be protected in law. But the formalization

introduced the "Definition of Spouse Amendment," which expanded the definition of "spouse" in that province to include "a person who has lived and cohabited with another person, for a period of at least two years immediately before the other person's death, in a 'marriage-like' relationship, including a marriage-like relationship between persons of the same gender." In that province, same-sex couples who meet this definition have the same spousal rights and responsibilities as heterosexual couples, including a right to contract into property and pensions, and to inherit from their partner as a spouse if the partner dies without a will. This chapter's *The Human Side* feature takes a personal look at the fight of Canadian couples to have their unions recognized, and to be allowed to marry.

In 2000, legislation in Nova Scotia revised the definition of "spouse" to include both opposite and same-sex couples who have lived together in a conjugal relationship for at least one year. In that year, "for the first time in the seven years it had been asking the question, less than half of Canadians [48 percent] opposed same-sex marriage" (Bricker and Greenspon 2001: 267).

Advocates of same-sex marriage maintain that as long as same-sex couples cannot be legally married, they will not be viewed as legitimate families by the larger society and will face undue stress as a result. On the other hand, opponents of same-sex marriage do not want their children to learn that

of those relationships has to be an individual choice.

How has being married affected your personal lives?

Bourassa: Over the past 12 months, I've gone from a banking career to working full time at advocacy. I couldn't do that if it wasn't for Joe. Marriage is like that—it's sharing resources and complementing one another.

And what have you personally, emotionally, got out of marriage?

Bourassa: It's brought us closer and closer together. If you can work together through stress and you can also find that you're building something together that's bigger than the two of you could do alone, that's great. And I think we're doing that.

How have people reacted when you tell them you're married?

Bourassa: Most people respond positively. It's usually not confrontational unless you're dealing with a situation such as when we were watching fireworks on a blanket, and a bunch of kids heckled us from a car. People will do it from a distance. It's much more difficult to do to your face....

Varnell: It's fine to have protection in law, but until you have acceptance in your community, the protection in law can be very cold comfort.

Update

In January of 2011, Bourassa and Varnell celebrated their tenth wedding anniversary by renewing their marriage vows. They shared their renewal along with Anne and Elaine Vatour, who had been the first lesbian couple in Canada to marry, also on January 14, 2001. In an interview that Varnell and Bourassa gave to the *Toronto Star* in 2011, looking back on their wedding day 10 years earlier, Bourassa reported that the day had come with threats against their lives and that they had required police protection for the ceremony:

> We said our goodbye to people, we told them we loved them.... We were told we were under threat. The last words the police officers said to us as we went down the aisle was, "If you hear a shot don't move, somebody will move you, just stand still." (Talaga 2011)

SOURCE: Abridged from *Maclean's*. 2002. "'It's about Love': A Pioneering Gay Couple Defends Same-Sex Unions." August 12, 2002: 46–47. Reprinted by permission of *Maclean's* magazine.

homosexuality is an accepted and acceptable life. Many of them view homosexuality as unnatural, sick, and/or immoral.

The most common argument against same-sex marriage is that it subverts the stability and integrity of the heterosexual family. Sullivan (1997), though, points out that gays and lesbians are already part of heterosexual families:

> [Homosexuals] are sons and daughters, brothers and sisters, even mothers and fathers, of heterosexuals. The distinction between "families" and "homosexuals" is, to begin with, empirically false; and the stability of existing families is closely linked to how homosexuals are treated within them. (p. 147)

According to the 2001 Canadian census, 13 percent of female same-sex couples have children living with them and 3 percent of same-sex male couples are also parenting children (Arnold 2002).

Child Custody, Visitation, and Reproductive Rights Another milestone for gay activists was attained in 2001 when, for the first time, a Canadian survey reported majority support for gay adoption (Bricker and Greenspon 2001: 267). In 1995, an Ontario provincial judge ruled that gay and lesbian couples have the right to apply to adopt a child under that province's *Child and Family Services Act*. In 1998, British Columbia passed amendments to its

Adoption Act and *Family Relations Act* that provided same-sex couples who cohabit continuously for two years with the same right to apply to adopt a child. In 1999, Alberta joined with these provinces in permitting same-sex couples to adopt.

Little was known until relatively recently about the nature of gay and lesbian family life. Many published accounts were non-empirical and saturated with a heterosexist bias that framed gay and lesbian families as "deviant" and "pathological." Even though research on gay and lesbian families expanded dramatically in the 1990s (e.g., Arnup 1995; Benkov 1994; Stone 1990; Weston 1991), generalizable information still remains sparse due to nonrandom sampling, limited sample sizes, and the diversities of these families occasioned by ethnicity, class, age of parents and offspring, and circumstances leading to family formation. However, in a review of research on family relationships of lesbians and gay men, Patterson (2001) concludes that "the greater majority of children with lesbian or gay parents grow up to identify themselves as heterosexual" and that "concerns about possible difficulties in personal development among children of lesbian and gay parents have not been sustained by the results of research" (p. 279). Patterson (2001) additionally notes that the "home environments provided by lesbian and gay parents are just as likely as those provided by heterosexual parents to enable psychosocial growth among family members" (p. 283).

At least in theory, custody and access orders in Canada are equally available to members of same-sex unions and opposite-sex unions, with decisions made in "the best interests of the child." However, while "[n]othing in Canadian law stops a homosexual parent from applying for custody, the courts will often take judicial notice of the fact that some harm might arise from living with a homosexual parent" (Yogis et al. 1996: 56). Yogis and colleagues note that Canadian case law suggests that "custody is awarded to discreet, non-militant homosexual parents who do not flaunt their sexual orientation" (p. 56).

Hate Crimes against Sexual-Orientation Minorities

In eighteenth-century North America, where laws against same-sex sexual activity often included the death penalty, violence against gays and lesbians was widespread, and included beatings, burnings, various kinds of torture, and execution (Button et al. 1997). Although such treatment of sexual-orientation minorities is no longer legally condoned, gays, lesbians, and bisexuals continue to be victimized by hate crimes. Surveys indicate that as many as one-fourth of lesbians and gay men report having been victims of physical attacks because of their sexual orientation (Herek 1989). A survey of more than 3000 high-school students found that students who reported having engaged in same-sex relations were more than three times as likely to report not going to school because they felt unsafe and more than twice as likely to report having been threatened or injured with a weapon at school (Faulkner and Cranston 1998). These students were also significantly more likely to report that their property was deliberately damaged or stolen at school.

Hate-motivated violence toward sexual-orientation minorities can be brutal. The following example is given in *Reaching Out: A Report on Lesbian, Gay, and Bisexual Youth Issues in Canada*, prepared for the United Church of Canada by

John Fisher (1999), executive director of Equality for Gays and Lesbians Everywhere (EGALE):

> When Christian Hernandez was 14 and a Grade 9 student at Notre Dame College High School in Niagara Falls, Ontario, he screwed up his courage and told his best friend that he was gay. That was his first mistake. "He told me he couldn't accept it," recalls Hernandez. "And he began to spread it around." Over the next two years, Hernandez was teased and harassed almost daily. One day, a group of boys waited for him after school. Their leader had a knife, and, says Hernandez, "He told me he didn't accept faggots, that we brought AIDS into the world." The boy then cut Hernandez on the neck, putting him in the hospital for a week. When Hernandez told his parents about the attack, his father, who has since moved back to his native El Salvador, said he would "rather have a dead son than a queer son."

Next, we highlight some of the strategies for reducing and responding to prejudice and discrimination toward sexual-orientation minorities.

9.7 Strategies for Action: Reducing Antigay Prejudice and Discrimination

Many of the efforts to change policies and attitudes regarding sexual-orientation minorities have been spearheaded by organizations. These include the above-mentioned EGALE, Canada's only national equal rights organization advocating for lesbians, gays, and bisexuals, with members in every province and territory; Parents, Family, and Friends of Lesbians and Gays (PFLAG); the Foundation for Equal Families (FFEF); Victoria Youth Pride Society; Pink Triangle Services Youth Group in Ottawa; Lesbian and Gay Health Services in Saskatoon; and the British Columbia Civil Liberties Association.

These organizations are politically active in their efforts to achieve equal rights for gays, lesbians, and bisexuals. For example, the mandate of the FFEF is to achieve equality and recognition of same-sex relationships and associated family rights through legal action and education. In January 1999, the Foundation launched an omnibus challenge of 58 federal laws affecting the rights of lesbian and gay couples. The omnibus challenge affected laws as diverse as the *Income Tax Act*, the *Canadian Pension Plan Act*, the *Criminal Code*, the *Immigration Act*, the *Evidence Act*, the *Judges' Act*, the *Old Age Security Act*, the *Veterans Allowance Act*, and the Royal Canadian Mounted Police's *Superannuation Act*. The gay rights movement is also active in promoting HIV/AIDS research, adequate health care for AIDS victims, and the rights of HIV-infected individuals.

In addition, demonstrative and cultural expressions of gay activism, such as "gay pride" celebrations, marches, demonstrations, or other cultural activities promoting gay rights, are important in organizing gay activists. However, it has been noted that

> Too many people have seen the cultural activity as a substitute for democratic political participation. In too many cases over the past decades we have left the political arena to our most dedicated opponents [of gay rights], whose letter writing, phone calling, and lobbying have easily triumphed over our marching,

demonstrating, and dancing. The most important lesson...is that politics—conventional, boring, but essential politics—will ultimately have a major impact on the extent to which we can rid our lives of prejudice. (Frank 1997: xi)

In Canada, the various political parties have shown different levels of support for gay rights issues. For example, despite its caucus dominance from 1993 to 2005, no Liberal member of Parliament identified himself or herself as gay, lesbian, or bisexual and some, such as Roseanne Stoke and Tom Wappel, consistently referred to homosexuality as "unnatural," "immoral," and a "perversion." In the New Democratic Party, an openly gay former MP, Svend Robinson, consistently demonstrated strong support for lesbian and gay equality, as has the leader of the federal NDP. In contrast, members of the federal Conservative Party and its precursor Alliance and Reform parties nearly invariably voted against bills seeking to advance GLBT rights (EGALE 2001).

Although in the late 1990s Winnipeg elected its first openly gay mayor, Glen Murray, it would seem presumptuous to suppose that the issue of a candidate's sexual orientation is not considered relevant by at least some voters. It seems undeniable that the Christian right, religious and church groups, conservative family groups, and other conservative organizations and their political allies will continue to crusade against gay rights. Nevertheless, opposition groups are up against an increasingly powerful pro–gay rights movement.

Educational Strategies: Policies and Programs in the Schools

A survey of youths' risk behaviour found that 30 percent of gay teens attempted suicide in the previous year, compared with 7 percent of their straight peers (reported in Platt 2001). Forty percent of gay youth report schoolwork being negatively affected by conflicts around sexual orientation, and over one-quarter of gay youth drop out of school (Chase 2000; *Homophobia 101* 2000). Research conducted in Calgary reports that gay and bisexual males were "almost 14 times more likely to have made a serious suicide attempt at some point in their lives than their heterosexually oriented counterparts" and that lesbian, gay, and bisexual youth of colour were dramatically overrepresented in attempted suicide statistics. According to one of the authors of this research, Pierre Tremblay, "This is the fallout of living with no guidance and no support. It's a problem every teacher knows about, but too often the attitude is, 'we would like to help, but we don't want to promote homosexuality.' It is a total abdication" (in Fisher 1999).

All of these findings suggest that if schools are to promote the health and well-being of all students, they must address the needs of gay, lesbian, and bisexual youth and promote acceptance of sexual-orientation diversity within the school setting (Flowers and Buston 2001; Murphy 2001). One strategy for promoting tolerance for diversity among students involves establishing and enforcing a school policy prohibiting antigay behaviour. Another strategy for addressing the needs of homosexual and bisexual youth is having school-based support groups. Such groups can help students increase self-esteem, overcome their sense of isolation, provide information and resources, and provide a resource for parents. In-service training for teachers and other staff is also important and may include examining the effects of antigay bias, dispelling myths about homosexuality, and brainstorming ways to create a more inclusive environment (Mathison 1998). Most public schools, though, offer little support and education regarding sexual-orientation diversity. Most schools lack support groups or special counselling services for gay and lesbian youth, and the majority of schools do not have any policies prohibiting antigay harassment (Button et al. 1997).

Nevertheless, some progress is being made. For example, in February 1997, the Calgary Board of Education approved an "Action Plan on Gay/Lesbian/ Bisexual Youth and Staff Safety" that requires guidance counsellors to provide "comprehensive information to students" when discussing sexual orientation and to "encourage students to discuss the issue with their parents." In Toronto, the Triangle Program offers gays who have been harassed at school an alternative place to study for up to 18 months and a curriculum that emphasizes the contributions of gays and lesbians in various fields, though as our chapter on education notes, this program is not without limitations. Various Canadian school boards and teaching institutes have adopted policies or initiatives that promote the equal treatment of gays and lesbians. For example, the Vancouver School Board's Statement of Mission and Beliefs states, "We believe in equitable treatment for all individuals, regardless of race, culture, gender, religion, socioeconomic status, sexual orientation or physical or mental ability." In addition, the federal government has launched a national initiative, the "Safe Spaces Project," funded by the federal Department of Health, to help produce educational materials for both heterosexual and lesbian and gay youth on lesbian, gay, and bisexual issues, and to create safe spaces for lesbian, gay, and bisexual youth.

Campus Policies Regarding Homosexuality

Student groups have been active in the gay liberation movement since the 1960s. Numerous gay student groups are organized in community colleges and universities across Canada.

D'Emilio (1990) suggests that colleges and universities have the ability and the responsibility to promote gay rights and social acceptance of homosexual people:

> For reasons that I cannot quite fathom, I still expect the academy to embrace higher standards of civility, decency, and justice than the society around it. Having been granted the extraordinary privilege of thinking critically as a way of life, we should be astute enough to recognize when a group of people is being systematically mistreated. We have the intelligence to devise solutions to problems that appear in our community. I expect us also to have the courage to lead rather than follow. (p. 18)

In addition to including sexual orientation in discrimination policies, colleges and universities have also taken more proactive measures to support the lesbigay student population. Such measures have included offering gay and lesbian studies programs, social centres, and support groups, and sponsoring events and activities that celebrate diversity. "These programs serve as both a refuge for lesbians and gay men on campus, and common ground from which to launch educational projects that foster respect for difference" (Lambda Legal Defense and Educational Fund 2000: 10).

Strategies for reducing antigay prejudice and discrimination are influenced largely by politicians, religious leaders, courts, and educators, who will continue to make decisions that either promote the well-being of sexual-orientation minorities or hinder it. Ultimately, however, each individual must decide to embrace either an inclusive or an exclusive ideology; collectively, those individual decisions will determine the future treatment of sexual-orientation minorities.

In addition, lesbigay individuals must find their own strategies for living in a homophobic and biphobic society. They may find encouragement in the following:

> If you dream of a world in which you can put your partner's picture on your desk, then put his picture on your desk...and you will live in such a world.
>
> If you dream of a world in which there are more openly gay elected officials, then run for office...and you will live in such a world.
>
> And if you dream of a world in which you can take your partner to the office party...then take her to the party. I do, and now I live in such a world.
>
> Remember, there are two things that keep us oppressed—them and us. We are half of the equation. (Baldwin 2000)

Understanding Sexualities

As both functionalists and conflict theorists note, "alternatives" to heterosexuality are threatening to traditionalists because they require new understandings and arrangements of family, childrearing, and gender roles. The conflict is expressed in economic, social, and legal discrimination by the majority. GLBT individuals are also victimized by hate crimes, and in some countries, same-sex activity is punished with sanctions ranging from fines to imprisonment and even death.

Evidence suggests that sexuality, like handedness, may have a biological component. The debate between biological and social explanations is commonly referred to as the "nature versus nurture" debate. Research indicates that both forces affect sexual orientation, although debate over which is dominant continues. Sociologists are interested in society's response to sexual-orientation diversity and how that response affects the quality of life of society's members. Because individuals' views toward sexuality are related to their beliefs about what "causes" any deviation from sexual norms, the question of the origins of sexual-orientation diversity has sociological significance.

Prejudice and discrimination toward sexual-orientation minorities are rooted in various aspects of culture, such as religious views, rigid gender roles, and negative myths and stereotypes. Hate crimes against homosexuals and bisexuals are blatant examples of the discrimination that sexual-orientation minorities continue to experience.

Attitudes toward lesbians and gays have become more accepting. One explanation for these changing attitudes is that awareness of personal contact with openly gay individuals has increased in recent years as more people come out to family and friends. "This is likely to increase support for gay and lesbian equality because contacts with openly gay individuals reduce negative stereotypes and ignorance" (Wilcox and Wolpert 2000: 414). Another explanation for changing attitudes toward homosexuality is the positive depiction of gays and lesbians in the popular media. In 1992 *Roseanne* and *Melrose Place* had gay and lesbian characters, in 1998 Ellen DeGeneres came out on her sitcom *Ellen*, and by the 2000s, central gay and lesbian characters appeared in many television shows, including

Dawson's Creek, Will & Grace, Buffy the Vampire Slayer, Friends, ER, Spin City, and *Normal, Ohio* (Deziel 2000). To these we can add the cable-television series *Six Feet Under* and *The L Word.*

But, as one scholar expressed: "the new confidence and social visibility of homosexuals...have by no means conquered homophobia. Indeed it stands as the last acceptable prejudice" (Fone 2000: 411). Although the gay rights movement has made significant gains in the last few decades, it has also suffered losses and defeat due to opposition groups and politicians. Many strategies for promoting gay rights have been successful and the Canadian public is becoming increasingly supportive of gay rights. But, as Yang (1999) points out, as the antigay minority diminishes in size, "it often becomes more dedicated and impassioned" (p. ii). For those who believe that all Canadians, regardless of sexual orientation, should be treated equally,

> Our task in the coming years is to get...[those] who support our cause to feel as passionately outraged by the injustices we face and to be as strongly motivated to act in support of our rights as our adversaries are in their opposition to our rights. (p.iii)

Critical Thinking

1. What relationship do you see between the legalization of same-sex marriages in Canada and public attitudes toward same-sex couples?

2. Sexual-orientation minorities today can readily gain access to support organizations and networks via the internet. How do you see this use of the internet influencing the gay rights movement?

3. How are GLBT populations similar to and different from other minority groups?

4. Do you think that social acceptance of homosexuality leads to the creation of laws that protect lesbians and gays? Or does the enactment of laws that protect lesbians and gays help to create more social acceptance of gays? Explain.

"Is It True?" Quiz: Answers

1 = true; 2 = false; 3 = false; 4 = false

Section 3

Problems of Inequality and Power

The 2004 Disney movie *The Incredibles* speaks to the problem of living in a world in which everyone is "special." In such a world, no differences in ability are tolerated and exceptional talents are punished. Perpetually disciplined to suppress his superhero talents in order to avoid standing out, young Dash Parr says to his former-superhero mother, "If everyone is special, doesn't that mean that no one is?" Dash's inquisitive observation hit a nerve with audiences and became a hot conversation topic at the time of the film's release.

Differences between people in and of themselves are *not* what is meant by inequality as a social problem. Few would want to live in a society where everyone was the same. Where some fear that the erasure of difference means the denial of talent, when sociologists turn attention to problems of difference we aim to remove the arbitrary barriers that prevent people from oppressing talent and from having access to a healthy and stable quality of life. Problems of inequality and power concern inequities in the quality of life—as we see with problems of poverty in Canada and around the world (Chapter 10). As we will see in Chapter 11, structural inequality affects opportunities to work and prosper, and we address the negative impact of low socio-economic status in completing higher education in Chapter 12.

The highly interrelated chapters in Section 3—"Poverty: National and International Issues," "Work and Unemployment," and "Problems in Education"—speak to the need for examining both the cultural and the structural underpinnings of the social problems described.

JOB SEEKERS ENTRANCE

Poverty: National and International Issues

Outline

10.1 The Global Context: Poverty and Economic Inequality around the World

10.2 Sociological Theories of Poverty and Economic Inequality

10.3 Wealth, Economic Inequality, and Poverty in Canada

10.4 Consequences of Poverty and Economic Inequality

10.5 Strategies for Action: Antipoverty Programs, Policies, and Proposals

Understanding Poverty: National and International Issues

Is It True?

1. Canada has the lowest poverty rate of all industrialized nations.

2. Nearly half of the world's population lives on less than $2 a day.

3. Unmarried teenagers make up most of the single-parent mothers on welfare.

4. Many single-parent mothers have many kids to boost their welfare cheques.

5. The age group with the highest poverty rate in Canada is individuals aged 65 and older.

Read more here: 1 = p. 326, 2 = p. 325, 3 = p. 360, 4 = p. 361, 5 = p. 347

Answers can be found on p. 370.

This chapter examines poverty globally and in Canada, focusing on the consequences of poverty for individuals, families, and societies. Theories of poverty and economic inequality are presented and strategies for rectifying economic inequality and poverty are considered. In this chapter we not only address the problems associated with poverty, but also provide critical insight into the systematic forms of discrimination that those living in poverty face.

10.1 The Global Context: Poverty and Economic Inequality around the World

Who are the poor? Are rates of world poverty increasing, decreasing, or remaining stable? The answers depend on how we define and measure poverty.

Defining and Measuring Poverty

Traditionally, **poverty** has been defined as the lack of resources necessary for material well-being—especially food and water, but also housing, land, and health care. This lack of resources that leads to hunger and physical deprivation is known as **absolute poverty**. **Relative poverty** refers to a deficiency in material and economic resources compared with some other population. Consider, for example, that while many Canadians are poor, they still have resources and a level of material well-being of which the millions living in absolute poverty can only dream.

Governments, researchers, and organizations use various measures of poverty. Next, we describe international and Canadian measures of poverty.

International Measures of Poverty The World Bank sets a "poverty threshold" of $1 per day to compare poverty in most of the developing world; $2 per day in Latin America; $4 per day in Eastern Europe and the Commonwealth of Independent States (CIS); and $14.40 per day in industrial countries. An estimated 2.8 billion people, nearly half of the world's population, survive on less than $2 per day, and a fifth of the world's population (1.2 billion people) live on less than $1 per day (Flavin 2001; Lozada 2003).

Another poverty measure used by the World Health Organization (WHO) is based on a household's ability to meet the minimum calorie requirements of its members. According to this poverty measure, a household is considered poor if it cannot meet 80 percent of the minimum caloric requirements (established by WHO), even when using 80 percent of its income to buy food.

In industrial countries, national poverty lines are sometimes based on the median household income of a country's population. According to this relative poverty measure, members of a household are considered poor if their household income is less than 50 percent of the median household income in that country.

Research on poverty concludes that poverty is multidimensional and includes such dimensions as food insecurity; poor housing; unemployment; psychological distress; powerlessness; hopelessness; lack of access to health care, education, and transportation; and vulnerability (Narayan 2000). To capture the multidimensional nature of poverty, the United Nations Development Programme

poverty

Lacking resources for an "adequate" standard of living.

absolute poverty

The chronic absence of the basic necessities of life, including food, clean water, and housing.

relative poverty

A deficiency in material and economic resources compared with some other population.

Human Poverty Index (HPI)

A composite measure of poverty based on three measures of deprivation: (1) deprivation of life, which is measured by the percentage of people expected to die before age 40; (2) deprivation of knowledge, which is measured by the percentage of adults who are illiterate; and (3) deprivation in living standards, which is measured as a composite of three variables—the percentage of people without access to health services, the percentage of people without access to safe water, and the percentage of malnourished children under five.

(1997) developed a composite measure of poverty: the **Human Poverty Index (HPI)**. Rather than measure poverty by income, three measures of deprivation are combined to yield the HPI: (1) deprivation of a long, healthy life, (2) deprivation of knowledge, and (3) deprivation of decent living standards. As shown in Table 10.1, the HPI for developing countries is measured differently than for industrialized countries (HPI-2). For the assessment of some OECD countries, the UN Human Development Report for 2007/2008 has added a fourth dimension, social exclusion, in HPI-2. The perspective taken by the United Nations HPI is that poverty is not a singular problem but rather one with multiple dimensions, and multiple impacts. The UN Human Development Report (2010) explains the inclusion of these four measures of deprivation, noting that "Money based measures are obviously important, but deprivations in other dimensions and their overlap need to be considered...because households facing multiple deprivations are likely to be in worse situations than income poverty measures suggest" (Klugman 2010: 94). In addition, the multidimensional approach to measuring poverty allows us to assess what kinds of community participation we can promote in impoverished areas in order to ameliorate the negative privations to which the poor are vulnerable. The Index is a useful complement to income measures of poverty and "will serve as a strong reminder that eradicating poverty will always require more than increasing the income of the poorest" (United Nations Development Programme 1997: 19).

Among the 17 industrialized countries for which the HPI-2 was calculated in 2001, Sweden had the lowest level of human poverty (6.8 percent), followed by Norway (7.5 percent) and the Netherlands (8.5 percent). By 2010, at the 20-year mark for the annual report, the Human Development Index could demonstrate some significant movement upward for some countries, especially

■ **Table 10.1** *Measures of Human Poverty in Developing and Industrialized Countries*

	Longevity	Knowledge	Decent Standard of Living	Social Exclusion (for selected OECD countries)
For developing countries	Probability at birth of not surviving to age 40	Adult illiteracy	A composite measure based on the following: Percentage of people without access to safe water Percentage of people without access to health services Percentage of children under age five who are underweight	
For industrialized countries	Probability at birth of not surviving to age 60	Adult functional illiteracy rate	Percentage of people living below the income poverty line, which is set at 50 percent of median disposable income	**Social Exclusion** Measured by the rate of long-term unemployment (greater than 12 months)

SOURCE: Adapted from United Nations Development Programme. 2000. *Human Development Report 2000*. New York: Oxford University Press; Calculating the Human Development Indices, HPI-2" Technical Note, Human Development Report 2007/2008. New York: Palgrave-Macmillan.

those that were most vulnerable in 1990, when the first data report was issued. The 2010 report explains the nuances of improvement thusly: "Someone born in The Gambia in 1970 could expect to live to age 41—some 33 years fewer than someone born in Norway. By 2010 life expectancy in The Gambia had increased by 16 years (to 57) but in Norway by only 7 years. Thus, while the gap in life expectancy between Norway and The Gambia is still huge (24 years), it has shrunk by more than a fourth" (Klugman 2010: 29). In other words, the negative impacts of global inequalities remain staggering, even when significant improvements are made in vulnerable populations. In addition, the 2010 report shows that not all movement across the HDI is markedly upward; one-quarter of all the countries surveyed had a development increase of less than one-fifth over 1990 levels, and 10 countries surveyed saw no overall improvement at all (Klugman 2010: 30).

Measures of poverty tell us how many (or what percentage of) people are living in poverty in a given year. Another way to assess poverty is to note the degree to which those who are poor stay in poverty from year to year. This assessment can be done by calculating the average annual poverty exit rate— the share of the poor in one year that have left poverty by the following year. One study followed the same families over a five-year period in six countries— Canada, Germany, Netherlands, Sweden, the United Kingdom, and the United States (reported in Mishel et al. 2001). The results indicated that, with the exception of the Netherlands, the poor in Canada were more likely than the poor elsewhere to leave poverty from one year to the next. According to this research, 44 percent of the poor in the Netherlands and 42 percent of the poor in Canada escape poverty each year, compared with 28.6 percent of the poor in the United States, 29.1 percent in the United Kingdom, 36 percent in Sweden, and 37 percent in Germany. We can extrapolate from these data that although the same proportion of people in Canada are poor every year, those who are poor are not *the same* people year after year. This observation leads in turn to another: that if the same proportion of people remains poor year after year, there must be reasons beyond individual characteristics to explain the persistence of poverty.

Canadian Measures of Poverty Statistics Canada developed the **low income cut-offs (LICOs)** as a measure of poverty in 1968. Estimating that poor families or individuals spent approximately 34.7 percent or more of their pre-tax income on such basic needs as food, shelter, and clothing, the agency then added 20 percentage points to determine the cut-off. In consequence, it was arbitrarily established as a standard that families or individuals who spent 54.7 percent of their pre-tax income on food, clothing, and shelter would be in financial difficulty. Recognizing that the minimum income level necessary to avoid financial hardship varies with changes in the cost of living, family size, and place of residence, Statistics Canada calculates different low income cut-offs for different communities and for families of varying sizes within these communities. For example, in 2004, the low income cut-off for a family of four living in an urban area with a population of half a million or more was $37 791. For a family of four living in a rural area, it was $26 015.

The Daily Bread Food Bank in Toronto has been at the fore of developing and reporting on Canadian measures of deprivation levels. The Daily Bread report from 2009 takes specific notice that not just individuals are vulnerable

low income cut-offs (LICOs)

Developed by Statistics Canada as a measure of poverty. Estimating that poor families or individuals spend approximately 34.7 percent or more of their pre-tax income on such basic needs as food, shelter, and clothing, 20 percentage points were added to this figure to determine the cut-off. This standard suggests that individuals or families who spent 54.7 percent of their pre-tax income on food, clothing, and shelter would experience financial difficulty. Different low income cut-off lines are established by Statistics Canada for different communities as well as for families of varying sizes within these communities.

to the deprivations of poverty but that entire communities are at risk, and therefore uses a "community-based poverty measure" to assess the deprivations experienced by the poor. The kinds of things that the report asked about included assessing whether people who used the food bank had the kitchens, tools, and appliances required to prepare healthy foods, whether they could keep their homes "adequately" warm, whether food bank users had a savings of $20 per month for emergencies or long-term use, and whether people had any money at all to spend on themselves (2009: 9). The results showed that for food bank users, 41 percent had no vacuum, 29 percent had no microwave oven, and 30 percent had no telephone; 21 percent could not afford to keep the home adequately warm; 68 percent were unable to save $20 a month; and 61 percent had no money to spend on themselves each week (2009: 11). The Daily Bread used this initial survey of food bank users to develop a more refined set of questions and commissioned Ipsos Reid to assess the Ontario population across income levels. The results of the Ipsos Reid poll provide a "deprivation score" for Ontario residents who live at or below the low-income measure (LIM), and are displayed in Table 10.2. Higher deprivation scores indicate the largest correspondence between the degree to which the item is out of reach for respondents, and the degree to which all respondents felt the item was necessary.

market basket measure (MBM)

An assessment of the minimum level of income required to provide for the basic needs that a given society would find it "indecent" to be without.

low-income measure (LIM)

For the purposes of assessing low income using this measure, Statistics Canada has established a figure for the needs of one adult and proceeded on the assumption that family needs increase in proportion to the size of the family, with each additional adult increasing the family needs by 40 percent of the first adult and each additional child increasing the family's needs by 30 percent.

Another way of measuring poverty is to employ the **market basket measure (MBM)**, which is based on the concept of "necessaries" as defined by the eighteenth-century economist Adam Smith: "Whatever the custom of the country renders it indecent for creditable people, even of the lowest order, to be without." While provinces use the market basket concept to set welfare rates, defining what, exactly, are "necessaries" is not easy. The concept as used by Smith implies that necessaries are broader than what is needed for mere subsistence; yet, as we discuss later, some necessary items simply do not count in the MBM.

Another way of defining low income or the "poverty line" is to employ the **low-income measure (LIM)**. Using the LIM, Statistics Canada has established a figure for the needs of one adult and proceeded on the assumption that family needs increase in proportion to family size, with each additional adult increasing the family's needs by 40 percent of the first adult and each additional child increasing the family's needs by 30 percent. To calculate how many Canadians, individuals, or family members lack sufficient income to cover their basic needs for food, clothing, shelter, and other necessities, Statistics Canada compares these income figures with the actual family and individual incomes. Table 10.3 shows gross income needed as of 2007–08 to avoid the serious depth of poverty of the low income cut-offs in Canada. The table helps us to see that the size of community in which one lives influences both the cost of living and earnings.

Clearly, estimating the numbers of Canadians who are poor is no simple task. The writings of Christopher Sarlo (1992; 1996) have repeatedly drawn attention to what he perceives to be the inadequacies of employing the LICO as a measure of poverty in Canada. For example, he notes that the LICO does not include benefits in kind, or capital gains, or, of course, unreported income. Sarlo claims that "of all households below the LICO in 1990, almost one in five owned their homes, mortgage free...97 percent had colour television...53 percent owned a car—the same rate as for those above the poverty line" (in Coyne 1997).

■ **Table 10.2** *Final List of 10 Deprivation Indicators*

Item	L = % Under LIM Who Cannot Afford	H = % Over LIM Who Cannot Afford	Under LIM Minus Over LIM A-B	P = % Who Feel Item Is Necessary	Deprivation Score = [(L-H)×P]
Dental Care	32	8	24	91	2184
Savings	43	14	29	74	0
Replace/repair broken electrical goods	35	9	26	71	1846
Replace/repair furniture	46	15	31	57	0
Small amount of money	38	12	26	65	0
Presents	25	5	20	65	1300
Clothes for job interviews	21	4	17	70	1190
Friends or family over for a meal	29	8	21	50	1050
Fresh fruits and vegetables	16	3	13	80	1040
Transportation	12	2	10	88	880
Hobby	21	7	14	55	770
Meat, fish or vegetarian equivalent	11	2	9	82	738
Pest free home	11	3	8	90	720
Prescriptions	9	3	6	88	528
Two pairs of shoes	8	2	6	84	504
Cable television	16	4	12	34	408
Warm coat	5	1	4	93	372
Vacuum cleaner	7	1	6	60	360
Personal care items	4	0	4	83	332
Warm home	5	2	3	92	276
Stereo	15	4	11	24	264
Telephone	2	0	2	89	178
Internet access at home	4	1	3	55	165
DVD player	9	2	7	23	161
Microwave	5	1	4	39	156

SOURCE: Matern, Richard, Michael Mendelson, and Michael Oliphant. 2009. "Developing a Deprivation Index: The Research Process." Daily Bread Food Bank and Caledon Institute of Social Policy.

■ **Table 10.3** *Low Income Cut-Offs (1992 base) Before Tax, 1992–2008*

| | | Community Size | | |
| | Rural areas | Urban areas | | |
Size of Family Unit		Less than 30 000[1]	30 000 to 99 999 (dollars)	100 000 to 499 999	500 000 and over
1992					
1 person	11 236	12 783	13 970	14 057	16 322
2 persons	13 988	15 913	17 391	17 499	20 320
3 persons	17 196	19 563	21 380	21 513	24 981
4 persons	20 879	23 753	25 959	26 120	30 330
5 persons	23 680	26 940	29 442	29 624	34 400
6 persons	26 708	30 384	33 206	33 412	38 797
7 or more persons	29 735	33 828	36 970	37 199	43 195
1997					
1 person	12 092	13 757	15 034	15 128	17 566
2 persons	15 054	17 125	18 716	18 832	21 868
3 persons	18 506	21 054	23 009	23 152	26 884
4 persons	22 470	25 563	27 937	28 110	32 641
5 persons	25 484	28 993	31 685	31 881	37 021
6 persons	28 743	32 699	35 736	35 958	41 753
7 or more persons	32 001	36 405	39 787	40 033	46 486
2002					
1 person	13 376	15 218	16 631	16 735	19 431
2 persons	16 652	18 944	20 704	20 832	24 190
3 persons	20 471	23 289	25 452	25 611	29 739
4 persons	24 856	28 277	30 904	31 095	36 107
5 persons	28 190	32 071	35 050	35 267	40 952
6 persons	31 795	36 171	39 531	39 776	46 187
7 or more persons	35 399	40 271	44 012	44 285	51 423
2008					
1 person	15 262	17 364	18 976	19 094	22 171
2 persons	19 000	21 615	23 623	23 769	27 601
3 persons	23 358	26 573	29 041	29 222	33 933
4 persons	28 361	32 264	35 261	35 480	41 198
5 persons	32 165	36 594	39 992	40 239	46 727
6 persons	36 278	41 272	45 105	45 385	52 699
7 or more persons	40 390	45 950	50 218	50 529	58 673

1. Includes cities with a population between 15 000 and 30 000 and small urban areas (under 15 000).

SOURCE: Adapted from Statistics Canada. "Low Income Cut-Offs for 2008 and Low Income Measures for 2007," Income Research Paper Series, Catalogue no. 75F0002M, June 2009, pp. 20–25.

According to Sarlo, "poverty, as it has been traditionally understood, has been virtually eliminated" (1992: 2). This claim, though, is based on the assumptions that nonnutritious consumables such as coffee, ketchup, and jam are unnecessary, that $245 a year is enough to provide an individual with a year's supply of clothing and footwear, and that hairdressing services can be adequately performed by family members on each other. For those who experience trouble with their vision or experience toothaches, Sarlo "assumes that dental societies will provide free dental services to low-income families and that Lions Clubs will provide free eyeglasses" (Krahn 1994: 2.8).

Ross and colleagues (1994) emphasize that in employing the LICOs "Statistics Canada does not claim to measure poverty; rather, it defines a set of income cutoffs below which people may be said to live in straitened circumstances." However, as we have noted, the way in which poverty is defined has serious practical consequences—it determines who will receive help and who will not and what types of social policies and programs are thought necessary.

The Extent of Global Poverty and Economic Inequality

The *Global Poverty Report* (2000) found that globally the proportion of people living on less than $1 per day fell from 29 percent in 1987 to 26 percent in 1998, but World Bank measures show general stagnation since then, with about one-quarter of the world population living on less than $2 a day in current dollars (World Bank 2007). Social indicators have seen some improvement over the last three decades, but the situation has not improved consistently for all populations. And, as we discuss later in this chapter in the section on poverty and racialization, the Aboriginal populations of Canada—of which those at greatest risk are Registered Indians and Inuit—remain largely excluded from the nation's general prosperity (Maxim et al. 2001). The 2005 *Report on the World Social Situation* notes that "monetary poverty has gradually worsened in many parts of the world.

Data from the *Report on the World Social Situation* show us that in terms of household wealth:

- The richest 1 percent of adults in the world own 40 percent of global household wealth; the richest 2 percent of adults own more than half of global wealth; and the richest 10 percent of adults owns 85 percent of total global wealth.
- The poorest half of the world population owns barely 1 percent of global wealth.
- Households with per adult assets of $2200 are in the top half of the world wealth distribution; assets of $61 000 per adult places a household in the top 10 percent, and assets of more than $500 000 per adult places a household in the richest 1 percent of the world population.
- Although North America has only 6 percent of the world's adult population, it accounts for 34 percent of all household wealth worldwide.

As the seriousness of the problem has grown more evident, poverty and poverty reduction strategies have become increasingly prominent in development discourse" (United Nations 2005: 54). Clearly, the strategies have not served well many of the world's poorest:

In Europe and Central Asia the total number of people living on less than US$1 a day grew by more than 14 million between 1981 and 2001. In excess worsening poverty in Eastern Europe and the commonwealth independent states (CIS) has contributed substantially to the trend towards increased poverty in Europe and Central Asia since 1993.... In Tajikistan, a 14 percent increase in the country's population was accompanied by 64 percent decline in GDP and escalating poverty levels. In Azerbaijan, sound macro economic policies have ensured economic stability andhighly real GDP growth; however, these economic successes have not been reflected in the lives of people, 49 percent of whom live in poverty. (United Nations 2005: 56)

In spite of some improvements around the globe, economic inequality remains a serious problem, with 1.4 billion of the world's population living in extreme poverty (United Nations 2008). According to economic impact studies carried out by the United Nations, reductions in global poverty have been aided by debt write-offs for the poorest nations, by improving access to clean drinking water and to basic medical care (vaccination, and maternal health care), and by improving access to primary education; however, rising costs associated with food distribution combined with the lasting impact of the 2008 economic meltdown will have a "disproportionate impact" on the world's poorest people (ibid). Consider that in 1998, the combined wealth of the world's 200 richest people was $1 trillion. In the same year, the combined income of the 582 million people living in the 43 least developed countries was $146 billion (United Nations Development Programme 2000).

As these past trends continue, global economic inequality remains a persistent problem. Pro-globalization lobbyists and economists may argue that these disparities are a feature of transition or of incomplete entry into a global economy; on the other hand, Ray Kiely argues that such claims "that the poorest countries are poor because they are 'insufficiently globalized'" deliberately obscure the hierarchical and domination-oriented structure of neo-liberal economics, blaming the poor for their poverty on a global scale (2005: 910). Moreover, developed nations have seen their wealth drastically deteriorate in the years since the onset of the 2008 economic crisis. Iceland's national wealth fell by 30 percent between 2008 and 2010 (Keating et al. 2010), and the losses for Ireland, Greece, Spain, and Portugal have been similarly devastating. Armed with this critical perspective, we can challenge the idea that the solution to global poverty is to surrender more deeply to global capitalism.

10.2 Sociological Theories of Poverty and Economic Inequality

The different theoretical perspectives have distinct ways of assessing economic inequality. For example, structural-functionalists have argued that inequalities serve a functional purpose by providing a labour force to do undesirable work, and conflict theorists have argued that inequalities benefit only those who profit from the alienation and labour of others. Feminist theorists have drawn our attention to the manner in which economic inequality is gendered and what the impact of impaired access to economic resources means for women and children around the world. In this section, we examine these and other sociological perspectives on poverty and economic inequality.

Structural-Functionalist Perspective

According to the structural functionalist perspective, social stratification serves several positive functions. Decades ago, Davis and Moore (1945) argued that because the various occupational roles in society require different levels of ability, expertise, and knowledge, an unequal economic reward system helps to ensure that the person who performs a particular role is the most qualified. As people acquire certain levels of expertise and academic accreditation, they are progressively rewarded. Such a system, argued Davis and Moore, motivates people to achieve by offering higher rewards for higher achievements. If physicians were not offered high salaries, for example, who would want to endure the arduous years of medical training and long, stressful hours at a hospital?

The structural-functionalist view of poverty suggests that a certain amount of poverty has positive functions for dominant groups. Although poor people are often viewed as a burden to society, having a pool of low-paid, impoverished workers ensures that there will be people willing to do dirty, dangerous, and difficult work that others refuse to do. Poverty also provides employment for those who work in the "poverty industry" (such as welfare workers) and supplies a market for inferior goods, such as older, dilapidated homes and automobiles (Gans 1972).

Contemporary sociologists have directed much criticism at the structural-functionalist view of poverty and economic inequality. They point out that many important occupations (such as child-care work) are poorly paid, whereas many nonessential occupations (such as professional sports and entertainment) garner astronomical sums. Functionalism also accepts poverty as unavoidable and ignores the role of inheritance in the distribution of rewards.

This chapter's *Self and Society* feature focuses on contemporary research on beliefs about poverty. The research begins with a structural view that social exclusion is a purposeful process that marginalizes some persons and groups through the implementation of formal and informal practices that include social policies, programs, institutions, and actors (Reutter et al. 2006: 2). As Reutter and her co-investigators explain,

> Framing poverty in terms of social exclusion represents a shift from viewing deprivation in terms of individual attributes to the social relations, mechanisms and institutions responsible for deprivation, thereby situating debates more explicitly within the context of power and inequality. (2006: 2)

The findings in this study are subtle, but two features emerge from the data. The first is that Canadians on the whole show a relatively high level of appreciation for the structural, rather than presumed individual reasons for poverty; the second is that greater education on poverty issues still correlated strongly with elevated understanding of structural causes for poverty (Reutter et al. 2006: 19).

Conflict Perspective

Conflict theorists, who work principally in a Marxist framework, think that economic inequality results from domination over the **proletariat** (workers) by the **bourgeoisie** (owners of the means of production). The bourgeoisie accumulate wealth as they profit from the labour of the proletariat, who earn wages

proletariat
Workers who were often exploited by the bourgeoisie.

bourgeoisie
The owners of the means of production.

Public Ideas about Poverty

Using randomly selected populations from Edmonton and Toronto, Linda Reutter from the University of Alberta, along with a group of co-investigators from Ontario and Alberta, used survey and interview methods to measure public attributions for poverty in Canada.

Within a larger set of survey questions, the investigators asked six questions on the respondents' exposure to poverty and five questions on what participants perceived to be the causes of poverty. Finding out what people think causes poverty and what kinds of perceptions they base those beliefs on is important, as Reutter and her colleagues point out. Beliefs about the causes of poverty influence ideas about who deserves help and who does not, can contribute to inclusive or exclusive behaviours—even in institutional settings, and can influence social policy (2006: 6).

Read the questions the researchers used, and answer them yourself. Then look at the results for the study. How do your beliefs compare to those of the people in the sample? How much exposure to poverty have you had? Do you think that your level of exposure provides a good basis from which to form a judgment?

Circle yes or no and compare your answers with study results.

Exposure to Poverty: Survey Items

Q1.	Have you ever received social assistance or welfare?	Yes	No
Q2.	Have you ever had close friends of family who were living on low incomes?	Yes	No
Q3.	Have you ever worked at a job where you helped people living on low incomes?	Yes	No
Q4.	Have you ever done volunteer work to help people living on low incomes?	Yes	No
Q5.	Have you read or obtained information or learned about poverty from reading newspapers, listening to the radio, or watching television?	Yes	No-
Q6.	Have you got information or learned about poverty from courses, lectures, conferences or workshops?	Yes	No

Causes of Poverty: Survey Items

1. Government policies have caused some people to be poor.	Strongly agree
	Somewhat agree
	Neutral
	Somewhat disagree
	Strongly disagree
2. Most people are poor because of unequal opportunities in our society.	Strongly agree
	Somewhat agree
	Neutral
	Somewhat disagree
	Strongly disagree
3. Most people are poor because they grew up in a poor family.	Strongly agree
	Somewhat agree
	Neutral
	Somewhat disagree
	Strongly disagree
4. Most people are poor because they are lazy.	Strongly agree
	Somewhat agree
	Neutral
	Somewhat disagree
	Strongly disagree

5. Poverty is just part of modern progress and globalization.	Strongly agree
	Somewhat agree
	Neutral
	Somewhat disagree
	Strongly disagree

Exposure to Poverty

Q1.	Yes	15.2%
	No	84.8%
Q2.	Yes	64.4%
	No	35.6%
Q3.	Yes	40.3%
	No	59.7%
Q4.	Yes	44.9%
	No	55.1%
Q5.	Yes	92.2%
	No	7.8%
Q6.	Yes	40.8%
	No	59.7%

SOURCE: Adapted from "Public Attributions for Poverty in Canada," by Linda I. Reutter et al.; as published in *The Canadian Review of Sociology and Anthropology*, (43)1, Tables 2 and 3, February 26, 2006. Reprinted with permission.

far below the earnings of the bourgeoisie. As Marx and Engels explained in *The Communist Manifesto*, the proletariat is "the class of modern wage-labourers, who, having no means of production of their own, are reduced to selling their labour power in order to live" (1967: 79). In our contemporary economy, anyone who works for an employer, even if well paid, depends on the employer to provide wages and conditions of work. If the owners decide to downsize or relocate, then even highly paid workers can find themselves in perilous conditions. However, unlike those in trades, the new professional class is more likely to be able to find new employment and to have other resources to provide stability. Skilled and unskilled workers are more vulnerable to alterations in how corporations will secure profits. They are likely to have more difficulty securing employment if their trades are moved away. In all scenarios, however, employees exchange labour for wages, and "profit" is what employers can extract above the cost of production. Marx explained that profit is "**surplus value**" and its benefits always go to the owner of the means of production rather than to the producer of the work.

Conflict theorists understand and analyze the manner in which various social institutions serve the interests of the dominant class. The educational institution furthers the ideals of capitalism by perpetuating the belief in equal opportunity and the value of the work ethic. The proletariat, dependent on the capitalistic system, learns to identify with capitalist values instead of identifying their own needs. Members continue to be exploited and to accept the belief that poverty results from personal failure rather than from a flawed economic structure.

surplus value

A concept developed by Marx; refers to the difference in the amount people will pay for a service or consumer good compared to the cost of its production—surplus value produces the profit from exploited labour.

wealthfare

Governmental policies and regulations that economically favour the wealthy.

corporate welfare

Laws and policies that favour corporations, such as low-interest government loans to failing businesses and special subsidies and tax breaks to corporations.

Conflict theorists note how laws and policies benefit the wealthy at the expense of larger societies. Laws and policies that favour the rich—sometimes referred to as **wealthfare** or **corporate welfare**—include special subsidies and tax breaks to corporations, and other laws and policies that benefit corporations and the wealthy. Between 1994 and 1999, federal handouts to businesses topped $14 billion (Canadian Centre for Policy Alternatives Monitor [CCPAM] 1999). Ed Finn (2006), a policy analyst with CCPAM, argues that corporate welfare lies behind the "broken promises by Canadian governments to eradicate poverty, notably the all-party pledge in Parliament in 1989 to eliminate child poverty by 2000." Corporate "tax breaks" or "loopholes" are the "result of an economic system that glorifies greed and bars a more equitable distribution of income" (Finn 2006: n.p.). They cost the Canadian treasury billions. "Businesses are still permitted to deduct from the money they owe in taxes 20 percent of their expenses for meals and entertainment—such as luxury boxes at the Sky-Dome and escort services—from their taxable income" (Barlow and Campbell 1995: 174–75). In addition, "generous tax subsidies to oil and gas companies for their exploration and development costs" (pp. 174–75) divert half a billion a year from Canada's treasury. Indeed,

> So many tax loopholes are available to corporations that each year tens of thousands of profitable companies pay not a penny in income taxes.... Canada has the second worst record in the industrialized world (after Australia) for taxing wealth, making it a tax haven for wealthy individuals. (pp. 175–76)

Throughout the world, "free market" economic reform policies have been hailed as a solution to poverty. Yet, while such economic reform has benefited many wealthy corporations and investors, it has also resulted in increasing levels of global poverty. As companies relocate to countries with abundant supplies of cheap labour, wages decline. Lower wages lead to decreased consumer spending, which leads to more industries closing plants, bankruptcies, and downsizing. The results include higher unemployment rates and a surplus of workers, pushing employers to lower wages even more. Chossudovsky (1998) suggests that "this new international economic order feeds on human poverty and cheap labour" (p. 299).

Symbolic Interactionist Perspective

Symbolic interactionism focuses on how meanings, labels, and definitions affect and are affected by social life. This view calls attention to ways in which wealth and poverty are defined and the consequences of being labelled as "poor." Individuals who are viewed as poor—especially those receiving public assistance, or welfare—are often stigmatized as lazy, irresponsible, and lacking in abilities, motivation, and moral values. Indeed, the phrase "poor but honest" implicitly suggests that we view honesty and low income as an unlikely combination and must single out those who are poor and honest as exceptions to the rule. Wealthy individuals, on the other hand, tend to be viewed as capable, motivated, hard working, and deserving of their wealth.

The symbolic interaction perspective also focuses on the meanings of being poor. A qualitative study of over 40 000 poor women and men in 50 countries around the world explored the meanings of poverty from the perspective of those who live in poverty (Narayan 2000). Among the study's findings is that the experience of poverty involves psychological dimensions, such as powerlessness, voicelessness, dependency, shame, and humiliation.

Meanings and definitions of wealth and poverty vary across societies and across time. For example, the Dinka are the largest ethnic group in the sub-Saharan African country of Sudan. By global standards, the Dinka are among the poorest of the poor, being among the least modernized peoples of the world. In the Dinka culture, wealth is measured in large part according to how many cattle a person owns. But to the Dinka, cattle have a social, moral, and spiritual value as well as an economic value. In Dinka culture, a man pays an average "bridewealth" of 50 cows to the family of his bride. Thus, men use cattle to obtain wives to beget children, especially sons, to ensure the continuity of their ancestral lineage and, according to Dinka religious beliefs, their linkage with God. Although modernized populations might label the Dinka as poor, the Dinka do not.

Definitions of poverty also vary within societies. For example, in Ghana men associate poverty with a lack of material assets, whereas for women, poverty is defined as food insecurity (Narayan 2000).

Lewis (1966) accounted for the persistence of poverty, arguing that, over time, the poor develop norms, values, beliefs, and self-concepts that contribute to their own plight. According to Lewis, the **culture of poverty** is characterized by female-centred households, an emphasis on gratification in the present rather than in the future, and a relative lack of participation in society's major institutions. "The people in the culture of poverty have a strong feeling of marginality, of helplessness, of dependency, of not belonging.... Along with this feeling of powerlessness is a widespread feeling of inferiority, of personal unworthiness" (Lewis 1998: 7). The culture of poverty view emphasizes that the behaviours, values, and attitudes exhibited by the chronically poor are transmitted from one generation to the next, perpetuating the cycle of poverty experienced by the **underclass**—people living in persistent poverty. Critics of the culture of poverty approach point out that behaviours, values, and attitudes of the underclass emerge from the constraints and blocked opportunities that have resulted largely from the disappearance of work (Van Kempen 1997; Wilson 1996) (see also Chapter 8).

Feminist Perspectives

Feminist perspectives on economic inequality begin with the observation that poverty is a gendered phenomenon. This is not to say that there are not poor men or that the working class is not oppressed as a group; however, when we look closely at poverty, we can see that it affects women more frequently than men. Using a **gender-based analysis**, feminist policy analysts hold gender to be a key feature for understanding vulnerability to poverty and to the differential effects of poverty on, for example, the children one would be parenting. Gender-based analysis works to understand the structures that contribute to women's poverty, seeking to understand why, for example, of those who are over age 18 and living in poverty 54 percent are women (NAPO 2006). The Canadian Research Institute for the Advancement of Women (CRIAW), however, has adopted a more complex method of assessing poverty among women, called intersectional feminist frameworks (IFFs). A framework

culture of poverty

The set of norms, values, and beliefs and self-concepts that contribute to the persistence of poverty among the underclass.

underclass

A persistently poor and socially disadvantaged group that disproportionately experiences joblessness, welfare dependency, involvement in criminal activity, dysfunctional families, and low educational attainment.

gender-based analysis

Feminist policy analysis that understands gender to be a key factor in vulnerability to poverty and the differential effects of poverty; it uses gender as a central grounding point for analysis.

involves analysis of how processes of occupation, nation building, slavery, labour migration, employment regulation, and disenfranchisement of racialised groups, among others, contribute to the depth of poverty experienced by indigenous and racialised women. (CRIAW 2006: 16)

narrative analysis

A feminist practice that combines a symbolic approach with the collection of women's life histories as legitimate sources of knowledge and information.

Feminist work on poverty also uses unique methods, such as **narrative analysis**, combining a feminist focus on women's experiences with a symbolic approach to data interpretation. For example, a group of researchers from Ontario used narrative analysis to understand how young women speak about how their experiences of poverty can intersect with negative health and housing problems. Using narrative analysis for the study revealed that poverty and homelessness are not discrete problems, but permeate all aspects of these young homeless women's lives, including experiences of violence and discrimination that contribute to lower overall health and well-being (Reid, Burman, and Forchuk 2005: 252–53).

Feminist analysis of poverty can shed light on the routes to poverty for women, making the point that disability and illness can be powerful forces that move women from being "working poor" to impoverished as they lose their jobs, their stability, perhaps their children, and their homes (Neal 2004). Work such as Neal's can also make clear what the experience of homelessness can mean when apprehended through a gender-aware lens. For example, Neal observes that "both men and women who are homeless are caught in a gender crisis. Men who are homeless are 'failed men' because they cannot support themselves [while] women who are homeless fit the gender stereotype of the feminine woman—dependent and needy" (p. 28). Normative expectations that successful men are providers and successful women are wives to successful men diminish even further those who live in poverty.

Queer Theory Perspectives

Although a tendency to treat socio-economic status as independent of concerns about sexuality exists, studies on GLBT groups reveal that sexuality is an important variable influencing economic and other measures of social well-being. Yali and Revinson (2004) note in their work on mental health and coping with crisis that people live their lives at the intersection of many different contexts: race, class, gender, ethnicity, and, of course, sexuality.

A challenge of complex intersectionality is that determining the needs of the GLBT population can be an elusive task. Carroll and Ratner (2001), in their research on GLBT social movements supported through a Vancouver community centre, point out that "pluralisation of identity and weakening of the singular collective identity have given rise to a continuing crisis. The centre's constituency is culturally and socioeconomically quite mixed, and the scope of sexuality politics is too narrow to support a broad project of moral-intellectual reform that could serve as a political basis of impunity" (p. 612). In other words, while some members of the GLBT community have moved from political vulnerability in the 1970s in Vancouver to contemporary prosperity, some still face economic challenges and social isolation that hinge partly on sexual identity. Members of the GLBT community were more able to rely on government service agencies to provide basic health care and other social support services, leaving the community centre to serve mostly as a social connection support

(p. 613). The obvious problem is that when government services separate issues of social connection from issues of economic well-being, they miss the intersections of sexuality with the experience of well-being. Meanwhile, the centre's social connection focus tends to neglect the needs of those who are less prosperous in the GLBT community.

For example, transphobia exists not only in the heterosexual world but sometimes also in gay and lesbian circles. Among the most vulnerable to poverty as a correlate of sexuality are transgender persons who, as a result of transphobia, may have a harder time finding and securing employment and housing. Lesbians, who contend with sexism as well as with homophobia, may face similarly multi-layered obstacles to socio-economic stability.

Outside Canada, work on sexual minorities around the world gives insight to the perils that sexually non-normative people may face:

> These may include men who were denied the right to love other men by the legislation left in place by the British Empire.... They may include sex workers who are routinely abused by the police, denied access to services and stayed with ties as "prostitutes," only come to the attention of development agencies when they migrate for sex work, and become the "victims" of trafficking...[and] lesbians may find it impossible to hide their sexuality in the workplace facing the prospect of losing their jobs or insuring low wages and working conditions. (Institute of Development Studies 2006: 1)

In the United States, the transgender writer and social justice activist Leslie Feinberg (1993) provides a narrative of growing up poor and transgender, suffering economically as a result of transphobia in the workplace and personal life. It is one of the few such detailed insights into the effects of discrimination on socio-economic status and well-being for transgendered persons.

10.3 Wealth, Economic Inequality, and Poverty in Canada

Canada is a nation of tremendous economic variation ranging from the very rich to the very poor. Signs of this disparity are visible everywhere, from opulent mansions to squalid rooming houses, from those who drive or are driven in luxury cars to those who cannot afford the price of a monthly bus pass.

Wealth in Canada

Wealth refers to the total assets of an individual or household, minus liabilities (mortgages, loans, and debts). Wealth includes the value of a home; investment real estate; cars; an unincorporated business; life insurance (cash value); stocks, bonds, mutual funds, and trusts; chequing and savings accounts; retirement savings plans; and valuable collectibles. A 2001 Statistics Canada study reveals that Canada is an "increasingly polarized country, with the top 20 percent of families gaining a whopping 39 percent in accumulated wealth since 1984, while the average wealth of the bottom 20 percent actually shrunk" (Centre for Social Justice 2001). As of 2005, publishing magnate Kenneth Thomson headed the richest Canadian family, with a net worth of $22.16 billion (see Table 10.4). The

wealth

The total assets of an individual or household minus liabilities.

■ **Table 10.4** *"The Rich List"*

Ranking and Individual/Family	Estimated Wealth
1. Thomson Family (Thomson Reuters)	$23.36 billion
2. Galen Weston (George Weston Ltd., Loblaw Cos. Ltd., Holt Renfrew)	$8.5 billion
3. J. K. and John Irving (Irving Oil)	$7.46 billion
4. Rogers Family (Rogers Communications)	$6.02 billion
5. James Pattison (Jim Pattison Group)	$5.53 billion
6. Paul Desmarais Sr. (Power Corp.)	$4.28 billion
7. Bernard Sherman (Apotex)	$3.94 billion
8. Jeff Skoll (eBay)	$3.56 billion
9. Saputo Family (Saputo Inc.)	$3.52 billion
10. Fred and Ron Mannix	$3.18 billion

SOURCE: Adapted from "The Rich List," *Canadian Business Magazine*. http://list.canadianbusiness.com/rankings/rich100/2010/ranking/Default.aspx?sp2=1&d1=a&sc1=0. Reprinted with permission.

holdings of those on "The Rich List" show just how great the division is between the richest and even "high income" families, as well as how marked is the concentration of wealth in very few hands in Canada.

Economic Inequality in Canada

The three decades after the end of World War II were a time of unprecedented economic prosperity in Canada. Throughout the 1950s and 1960s, unemployment and inflation were low and a steady increase in personal incomes financed the growth of the social safety net, including universal health care, the Canadian Pension Plan, unemployment insurance, and inexpensive postsecondary education. By the 1970s, however, there were increases in both consumer prices and unemployment levels, and a halt in the growth of real income. Because of economic downturns, economic inequality—the gap between the wealthy and the poor—grew significantly. Much has changed since, beginning with government introduction of various fiscally conservative tax measures and policy decisions, such as deregulation, privatization, free trade, and monetarism. These measures, which reflected a "corporate agenda," have most obviously benefited corporations and those whom economist John Kenneth Galbraith dubbed the "contented classes."

Barlow and Campbell (1995: 76) point out that income inequality in Canada not only has been growing in the past decades, "but it has been picking up speed." High-income families have reaped benefits from very high interest rates on their savings, and tax breaks, lower income tax rates, and an increase in both the numbers of those employed within professional and managerial groups and the level of executive earnings; others have fared poorly. Declines in family income and median real wages, rising unemployment, increases in part-time, temporary, and low-paying jobs, and the accelerated pace of social cuts (designed to make Canada's system of social security more "affordable" and to level the free-trade playing field) have had a huge impact on Canada's poor. According to research conducted by the Toronto Centre for Social Justice the average incomes of the top 10 percent of families with children in 1973 were 8.5 times those of the bottom 10 percent; by 1996, the ratio was to 10.2 to 1 (Yalnizyan 1998). To get a sense of just how marked the disparities are between the lowest and highest earners, it may help to use the model developed by the Dutch economist Jan Pen in *The Economist*:

> The first passers-by, the owners of loss-making businesses, are invisible: their heads are below ground. Then come the jobless and the working poor, who are midgets. After half an hour the strollers are still only waist-high, since America's median income is only half the mean. It takes nearly 45 minutes before normal-sized people appear. But then, in the final minutes, giants thunder by. With six minutes to go they are 12 feet tall. When the 400 highest earners walk by, right at the end, each is more than two miles tall. (Pen 2011)

The gap between the richest and poorest families increased after 1995, when the federal government made drastic cuts in social program spending, and the cuts have hit poorest families the hardest (Bricker and Greenspon 2001; Daub and Young 1999; National Council of Welfare 2000). While in 1989 the top quintile of families with the highest incomes received 41.9 percent of total market income, this proportion rose to 45.2 percent in 1998. In contrast, the share of the market income going to the 20 percent of families with the lowest incomes decreased from 3.8 percent to 3.1 percent over the same time period. Moreover, "[d]espite the equalizing role played by transfers and taxes, the gap between the two ends of the income scale widened slightly during the 1990s, even on an after-tax basis" (Statistics Canada 2000).

Patterns of Poverty in Canada

Poverty is not as widespread or severe in Canada as in many less developed countries, but nevertheless represents a significant social problem. According to the National Council of Welfare (2000), "[i]n 1999, there were 1 025 000 families and 1 677 000 unattached individuals living in poverty in Canada." However, poverty is not equally distributed. Poverty rates vary according to age, education, gender, family structure, disability, race/ethnicity, and labour force participation.

Age and Poverty Despite a political landscape rich in rhetoric about children, Canada has had little success in reducing child poverty (see Chapter 6). In 1989, when the House of Commons passed a unanimous resolution to eliminate child poverty in Canada by the year 2000, the child poverty rate was 15.2 percent— representing about one million poor children. While the child poverty rate in Canada peaked in 1996 (at 21.6 percent) and has declined since, the child poverty rate in 1999 was 18.7 percent (about 1.3 million children). The child poverty rate in Canada remained higher than the average poverty rate (16.2 percent). Moreover, in 1999, "most Canadian poor families with children needed, on average, more than $8000 before taxes and more than $5000 after taxes just to meet the poverty line" (National Council of Welfare 2000). During the period 1993 to 1998, children under six were the most likely of all age groups to have lived in poverty for all six years. The National Council of Welfare

(2004: 52) further notes that some measures of poverty, for instance the market basket measure (MBM), do not include costs associated with child care in their assessment of what families require to live; however, because child care is a necessity for working parents with young children, it is a basic expense. Poor families with working parents may often be living far below MBM estimates for low income.

Government programs and policies (see Chapter 6) have led to an improvement in the poverty rate among Canada's seniors. Between 1980 and 1999, the poverty rate for Canada's seniors was almost halved, from 34 percent in 1980 to 17.7 percent in 1999 (National Council of Welfare 2000). However, while the poverty rate among senior couples is low (4.7 percent in 1999), unattached seniors experience high rates of poverty. Moreover, while the poverty rate of senior unattached men decreased from 35.1 percent in 1998 to 31.9 percent in 1999, the poverty rate of unattached senior women rose from the already high rate of 47.9 percent in 1998 to an even higher rate of 48.5 percent in 1999.

Education and Poverty In general, the higher a person's level of educational attainment, the less likely that person is to be poor (see also Chapter 12). For example, in 1999, Canadian families in which the principal income earner had at least a university degree had a poverty rate of 6 percent. In contrast, single-parent mothers with less than a high school diploma had a poverty rate of 82.3 percent. However, "[a]lthough level of education and poverty rates are somewhat inversely related, education is not always a guarantee against poverty" (National Council of Welfare 2000: 7). More than half (52 percent) of the 1 667 000 poor unattached individuals in 1999 had at least a high school diploma.

feminization of poverty

The disproportionate distribution of poverty among women.

Gender and Poverty Women are more likely than men are to live below the poverty line—a phenomenon referred to as the **feminization of poverty**. As discussed in Chapter 7, women are less likely than men are to pursue advanced educational degrees in nontraditional areas of study. They also tend to be more heavily concentrated in a narrower range of jobs than men are and within lower paying jobs, such as service and clerical work (Statistics Canada 2002). Women who are minorities or who are single mothers are at increased risk of being poor. In 1999, the pre-tax poverty rates of Canadian women surpassed men's in almost all categories (National Council of Welfare 2000). Table 10.5 gives us a decade-long view of earnings stagnation for women as a proportion of average earnings of men for the same period.

Family Structure and Poverty Poverty is much more prevalent among female-headed single-parent households than among other types of family structures. The relationship between family structure and poverty helps to explain why women and children have higher poverty rates than men (see also Chapter 5). While the poverty rate for families headed by single-parent families fluctuated between 51.8 percent and 61.8 percent between 1980 and 1999, in 1999, "single-mother families were the only family type with a majority of its members still living below the poverty line" (National Council of Welfare 2000: 15). In comparison, the poverty rate in 1999 for families headed by single-parent fathers was 18 percent (down from 25.4 percent in 1980).

■ **Table 10.5** *Average Earnings by Sex and Work Patterns*

| | All earners | | |
Year	Women ($ constant 2008)	Men	Earnings ratio (%)
1999	27 000	43 000	62.6
2000	27 500	44 500	61.7
2001	27 600	44 400	62.1
2002	27 900	44 400	62.8
2003	27 600	43 800	62.9
2004	27 900	44 000	63.5
2005	28 600	44 700	64.0
2006	29 000	44 800	64.7
2007	29 900	45 500	65.7
2008	30 200	46 900	64.5

SOURCE: Statistics Canada's Summary Table, "Average Earnings by Sex and Work Pattern," July 17, 2010, http://www40.statcan.gc.ca/l01/cst01/labor01a-eng.htm.

Disability and Poverty According to data compiled by the Canadian Council on Social Development (Fawcett 1999), disability is a strong indicator of poverty. Across Canada, single persons with a disability receiving social assistance have benefits equal to only 41 to 53 percent of the LICO for their regions (National Council of Welfare 2003: 27). In 1995, 36.2 percent of women with disabilities versus 18.5 percent of Canadians without disabilities aged 15 to 64 were poor. Because of structural sexism, significant differences exist in the poverty rates between men with disabilities and women with disabilities, particularly those women who have full-time, full-year employment. However, a substantial proportion of people with disabilities do not participate in the paid labour force at all. For those whose primary source of income comes in the form of disability pension, monthly rent alone would consume between 82 and 98 percent of income in three Canadian cities sampled: Ottawa, Vancouver, and Halifax (Neal 2004: 39).

Obtaining employment and remaining employed often pose significant difficulty to persons with disabilities, regardless of gender. First, employment discontinuities are common due to the cyclical nature of some disabilities and a tendency for those with disabilities to be the "last hired and the first fired." In addition, while many income support programs, including social assistance and disability pensions, provide support for disability-related expenses (e.g., medication and transportation), such supports disappear when individuals with disabilities become employed. Accordingly, if one's employment income does not cover such expenses, one cannot "afford to work." As Fawcett (1999) points out, "persons with disabilities who look for work face a dilemma: in their attempts to convince potential employers that they are capable of working, they may disqualify themselves from the social assistance and disability supports they need in order to survive." Table 10.6 gives a sense of the consequences of poverty for those with disabilities relative to the larger population's risk.

■ **Table 10.6** *Food Insecurity among Persons with and without Disabilities, by Age and Gender*

	Age Group			
	15–34	35–49	50–64	Aged 65+
Persons with Disabilities				
Men	25.0%	20.3%	14.3%	6.4%
Women	24.4%	24.1%	19.5%	7.0%
Persons without Disabilities				
Men	10.6%	7.7%	4.1%	2.4%
Women	12.0%	8.9%	4.9%	2.5%

SOURCE: Canadian Council on Social Development. 2003. Table 4. "CCSD's Disability Information Sheet." No. 10. Used with permission of the Canadian Council on Social Development.

Compared to those without disabilities, both women and men with disabilities are more likely to be the sole providers of family income. However, the situation is particularly bleak among women with disabilities because they are more likely than other groups to live as lone parents. In 1996, almost 1 in 10 (9.7 percent) women with a disability was a lone parent (compared with 7.6 percent of women without disabilities, 2.8 percent of men with disabilities, and 1.1 percent of men without disabilities). Women with disabilities who obtain full-time, full-year employment typically earn less than either women without disabilities or men with disabilities. Figure 10.1 shows the disparity in incomes according to gender.

Race and Ethnicity and Poverty Based on the findings of the 2006 Canadian census, the negative impact of low income is high among visible minorities in Canada and especially among its Aboriginal people (Table 10.7) who live over 3.5 times more frequently in homes that require major repairs, with regionally specific disparities often being even greater. The 2006 census data also show that Canada's Aboriginal population is far more likely to live in homes with overcrowding problems. Overcrowding can exacerbate health problems and increase stress as people try to negotiate multiple, complex relationships in tight spaces.

Canada's recent immigrant population tends also to be a visible minority population, and because of the overlap of these statuses remains vulnerable to below-average employment incomes (Palameta 2005). Palameta's analysis of income data used multiple regressions to determine the influence of immigration, education, and visible minority status, and found that:

- women, unmarried persons, those with no high school diploma, and those living in a province other than Ontario were most likely to experience low income for at least one year. However, in each case, the likelihood for recent immigrants was two to three times more than for the Canadian-born
- those with university degrees [had earnings that] were about the same as non-immigrants with no high school diploma
- visible minority immigrants were significantly more likely than other immigrants to be in low income, regardless of time in Canada. (Palameta 2005: 14)

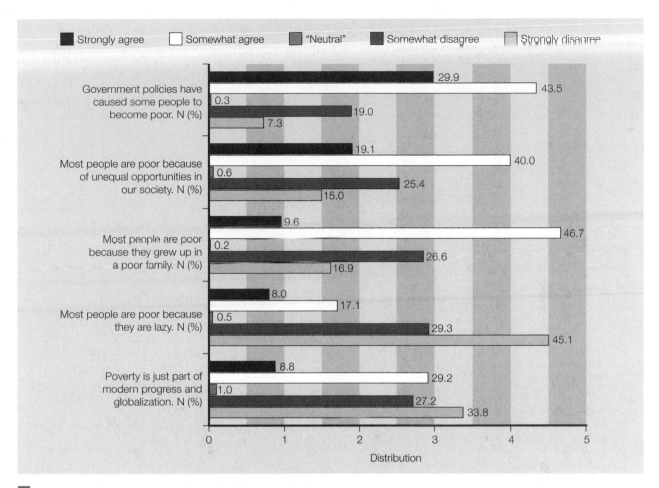

■ **Figure 10.1** *Average Earnings of Full-Year, Full-Time Earners, 2001*

SOURCE: Statistics Canada. "Canada E-Book." Catalogue No. 11-404-XIE. http://142.206.72.67/02/ 02e/02e_graph/02e_graph_008c_1e.htm.

Palameta's detailed analysis demonstrates that the longer-term patterns for income disparity between visible minority immigrants to Canada and those born in Canada remain stable (ibid). Between 1993 and 1998, approximately 42.5 percent of Canada's immigrant visible minorities lived in poverty for at least one year; that compared to 29.5 percent of the total population. In addition, "15.6 percent of immigrant visible minorities lived in poverty for all six years, compared with five percent of persons who are not visible minorities" (National Council of Welfare 2002b: 6).

Poor housing conditions are generally secondary to low earnings and low levels of relative wealth. Aboriginal people, who are vulnerable to poor housing conditions, experience heightened risk of poverty (see also Chapters 2 and 8). Excluding the Aboriginal population who lived on reserves, in Yukon, or Northwest Territories (where income is generally lower than for the Aboriginal population living off reserve), Statistics Canada found that in 1995, 44 percent of the Aboriginal population was below its low income cut-offs. Among those who identified themselves as North American Indians, almost half (48 percent) were

■ **Table 10.7** *Percentage of Population Living in Crowded Dwellings and in Dwellings in Need of Major Repairs, Canada and Selected Cities, 2006*

Selected Cities	Percentage of Population Living in Crowded Dwellings[1]		Percentage of Population Living in Dwellings in Need of Major Repairs[2]	
	Aboriginal population	Non-Aboriginal population	Aboriginal population	Non-Aboriginal population
Canada	11	3	23	7
Prince Albert	11	1	14	7
Saskatoon	9	1	12	5
Regina	9	1	14	7
Edmonton	8	2	14	5
Winnipeg	5	3	16	3
Vancouver	4	5	15	6
Toronto	3	7	12	6
Montréal	2	3	14	8
Calgary	2	2	11	5
Ottawa-Gatineau	1	2	14	5

Notes:

1. "Crowding" is defined as more than one person per room. Not counted as rooms are bathrooms, halls, vestibules, and rooms used solely for business purposes.

2. Dwelling s in need of major repairs are those that, in the judgement of the respondent, require major repairs to such things as defective plumbing or electrical wiring, and/or structural repairs to walls, floors, or ceilings, etc.

SOURCE: Statistics Canada. "Aboriginal Peoples in Canada in 2006: Inuit, Métis and First Nations, 2006 Census." *Aboriginal Peoples 2006 Census*, Catalogue No. 97-558-XIE, January 2008, p. 17.

in a low-income situation. Among the Métis (the second largest group), almost 4 in 10 (39 percent) were in a low-income situation. In that year, three out of five Aboriginal children under the age of six were in low-income families. Among those aged 6 to 14, the incidence of low income was 48 percent, or more than twice the national rate of 22 percent (Statistics Canada 1998b). Between 1993 and 1999, 49.4 percent of Aboriginal persons living off reserve lived in poverty in at least one of the six years; an estimated 12.6 percent lived in long-term poverty during this six-year period (National Council of Welfare 2002b: 6). More recent secondary analysis of the income data from 1996, 2001, and 2006 census data shows that the gains for Aboriginal populations have been so slow that "If the rate of diminishment of the income gap between 1996 and 2006 continues, it will take 63 years for the Aboriginal population to catch up to the rest of Canada" (Wilson and MacDonald 2010: 8)

An analysis of the economic performance of racialized group members and other Canadians over the period 1996–98 (Galabuzi 2001) also finds evidence of "economic apartheid," or the economic segregation and social marginalization of racialized groups, particularly in urban areas. Among Galabuzi's findings were these:

- There is a persistent and sizeable (double digit) gap between the economic performance of racialized group members and other Canadians.... In 1998 there was a 24 percent gap in average before-tax income and a 20 percent gap in after-tax income.

- A racialized labour market is an endemic feature of the Canadian economy. Characteristic of the racial and gender labour market segmentation is the overrepresentation of racialized (particularly women) members in low paid, low-end occupations and low income sectors, and also temporary work. They are especially overrepresented in low-end service sector jobs and precarious and unregulated temporary or contingent work.
- Income inequalities are a significant contributor to racialized group members' persistent above-average poverty rates across the nation, and particularly in urban areas where they are concentrated. The patterns suggest that a process of racialization of poverty is underway.

Labour Force Participation and Poverty A common image of the poor is that they are jobless and unable or unwilling to work. Although the Canadian poor are primarily children and adults not in the labour force, many poor are classified as "**working poor.**" Consider that in 1999, over 40 percent of the more than one million Canadian families who lived in poverty were headed by persons who were employed. "Single-parent mothers working full-time, full-year still had a poverty rate of 19.7 percent" (National Council of Welfare 2002b: 7).

Labour force attachment does, to be sure, offer a buffer against poverty. In 1999, the poverty rate for unattached individuals under 65 and for their families decreased as their weeks of paid employment increased. Specifically, among unattached individuals, the poverty rate for persons with no paid work was 80.1 percent versus 18.4 percent for those who worked 49 to 52 weeks. For families, the poverty rate for those with no paid work was 56 percent versus 3 percent among families with 103 or more weeks of paid work (that is, two full-year workers).

working poor
Individuals who work in the labour force, but who nevertheless live in poverty.

10.4 Consequences of Poverty and Economic Inequality

Poverty is associated with health problems, problems in education, problems in families and parenting, and housing problems. These various problems are interrelated and contribute to the perpetuation of poverty across generations, feeding a cycle of intergenerational poverty. In addition, poverty and economic inequality breed social conflict and war.

Health Problems and Poverty

In Chapter 2, we noted that poverty has been identified as the world's leading health problem. Persistent poverty is associated with higher rates of infant mortality and childhood deaths and lower life expectancies among adults. Although access to universally insured health care remains largely unrelated to income in Canada, many low-income and moderate-income Canadians have limited or no access to such health services as eye care, dentistry, mental health counselling, and prescription drugs (Health Canada 1999).

Economic inequality also affects psychological and physical health. "[P]erceptions of inequality translate into psychological feelings of lack of security, lower self-esteem, envy and unhappiness, which, either directly or through their effects on life-styles, cause illness" (Streeten 1998: 5). People who live in areas with the greatest gap between the rich and the poor are much more likely to rate their own health as poor or fair than people who live in areas where income is more equitably distributed (Kennedy et al. 1998).

Educational Problems and Poverty

Research indicates that children living in poverty are more likely to suffer academically than are children who are not poor. "Overall, poor children receive lower grades, receive lower scores on standardized tests, are less likely to finish high school, and are less likely to attend or graduate from university than are nonpoor youth" (Seccombe 2001: 323). The various health problems associated with childhood poverty contribute to poor academic performance (see Chapter 12). In addition, because poor parents have less schooling, on average, than do nonpoor parents, they may be less able to encourage and help their children succeed in school. However, research suggests that family income is a stronger predictor of ability and achievement outcomes than are measures of parental schooling or family structure (Duncan and Brooks-Gunn 1997). Poor parents have fewer resources to provide educational experiences (such as travel), private tutoring, books, and computers for their children. Not surprisingly, parental wealth strongly influences university enrollment (Conley 2001).

Poverty also presents obstacles to educational advancement among poor adults. Women and men who want to further their education in order to escape poverty may have to work while attending school or may be unable to attend school because of unaffordable child care, transportation, tuition, fees, books, or a combination of things.

Family and Parenting Problems Associated with Poverty

Family problems and poverty can aggravate each other. In some cases, family problems contribute to poverty. For example, domestic violence causes some women to flee from their homes and live in poverty without the economic support of their husbands. Poverty also contributes to family problems. The stresses associated with poverty contribute to substance abuse, domestic violence, child abuse, divorce, and questionable parenting practices. For example, poor parents unable to afford child-care expenses are more likely to leave children home without adult supervision. Poor parents are more likely than other parents are to use harsh disciplinary techniques, such as physical punishment; they are also more likely to value obedience and less likely to be supportive of their children (Mayer 1997; Seccombe 2001).

The National Longitudinal Survey of Children and Youth reports that the capacity of parents to care for children and their children's developmental outcomes are better at each step up the income ladder. Low social support, family dysfunction, and parental depression, all of which have significant negative effects on children, are all more common in low-income households. According to this study, 18 percent of children living in low-income households (versus 8 percent of children in middle-income households and 5 percent of children in higher income families) lived with parents who had many symptoms of depression (National Council of Welfare 1999c).

Another family problem associated with poverty is teenage pregnancy. Poor girls are more likely to have babies as teenagers or to become unwed single mothers. Early child-bearing is associated with numerous problems, such as increased risk of premature or low-birth-weight babies, dropping out of school, and lower future earning potential due to lack of academic achievement.

Luker (1996) notes that "the high rate of early childbearing is a measure of how bleak life is for young people who are living in poor communities and who have no obvious arenas for success" (p. 189). For poor young women, who have few employment opportunities and are disillusioned with education, "childbearing...is one of the few ways...such women feel they can make a change in their lives" (p. 182).

Housing and Homelessness

According to the National Council of Welfare (1998: 53), finding decent and affordable housing that is suitable to a family's needs "is one of the biggest financial burdens for people on welfare and for low-income people in general." The provision of housing for lower income Canadians has been an area of continuing governmental concern since the first Canadian social-housing legislation, the 1938 *National Housing Act*, made provision for the construction of low-rent housing.

The majority of low-income families and unattached individuals are renters rather than homeowners. For example, as of March 1997, 68.2 percent of all those living on welfare lived in rental housing; only a small proportion lived in their own homes (6.9 percent) or in subsidized housing (6.8 percent). Among couples with children, 71.3 percent were renters, 16.2 percent were homeowners, 8.2 percent lived in subsidized housing, and 4.2 percent lived in other forms of housing, including boarding or living with relatives. Among single-parent families, 76.6 percent were renters, 6.3 percent lived in their own homes, 11 percent lived in subsidized housing, and 6.1 percent lived in other forms of housing. In general, single parents on welfare made proportionately more use of subsidized housing and were far less likely to board or to live with relatives.

Poor individuals are more likely than their nonpoor counterparts are to have spartan accommodations in high-crime neighbourhoods (Mayer 1997); yet, even substandard housing would be a blessing to many people who live without conventional housing—the homeless.

Homelessness is a growing problem in Canada. It is estimated that as many as 200 000 Canadians are homeless, including increasing numbers of women and children, Aboriginal people, adolescents, and people with mental illnesses (Health Canada 1999). Some homeless individuals have been forced out of their houses or apartments by rising rents or the inability to pay the mortgage. The homeless population also includes runaway or "throw away" youths, and individuals who have been released from mental hospitals because of the movement to deinstitutionalize individuals with psychiatric disorders.

Intergenerational Poverty

As we have seen, problems associated with poverty, such as health and educational problems, create a cycle of poverty from one generation to the next. Poverty that is transmitted from one generation to the next is called **intergenerational poverty**.

intergenerational poverty
Poverty that is transmitted from one generation to the next.

Getting Ahead in Life: Does Your Parents' Income Count?

Parents hope their children will become successful and self-sufficient adults. But raising children is a complicated affair, and a child's fortune in life is determined not only by parenting strategies, but also by the support available in the community, the resources offered by the State, and sometimes just plain luck. That being said, a prime role in the eventual labour market outcomes of children is often attributed to money.... But...a dollar is not a dollar is not a dollar...and...the sources of a parent's income influence the employment outcomes of their adult children (see table)....

The source of the father's income is strongly associated with the adult incomes of children. Children had significantly higher market incomes as adults if their fathers had self-employment income than if they did not—almost $1200 for sons and $850 for daughters in 1994. If fathers had received Unemployment Insurance (UI) benefits, the effect was just as dramatic but in the opposite direction: sons' incomes were $1400 and daughters' $870 lower than those of children whose fathers had not received UI.

A father with asset income [net income from interest and investments, real estate, dividends from Canadian corporations, and taxable capital gains or losses] provided the most significant advantages for his children. After accounting for all other factors, sons whose fathers had some income from assets

earned over $3100 more than those whose fathers had no assets did, and daughters earned almost $2700 more. These are very substantial amounts, but what may be even more significant is that the actual dollar amount of the father's asset income seems much less important than its presence. In fact, children's adult incomes rise by only an average $28 for every $1000 increase in their father's asset income; for example, someone whose father had $10 000 in asset income would enjoy a market income that was only $252 higher ($280 − $28) than a person whose father had $1000 in asset income....

Not only do varying sources of income have different effects on an adult child's labour market success, but so too does the parent who earns it. For every $1000 increase in the father's income, the adult child's market income increased by about $91 for sons and about $47 for daughters. In contrast, sons and daughters did equally well as the mother's income rose—about $80 to $90 per $1000 increase. There are two possible explanations for this finding. The first focuses on the father's role and suggests that a high-earner father has a stronger effect on sons than on daughters by encouraging the pursuit of income. The second keys on the mother's role and suggests that mothers may be more likely to treat children of each gender equally when making spending decisions, and if women have higher incomes, they probably have greater discretion over spending....

The affluence of the neighbourhood in which children, especially

boys, spend their early teens is positively associated with their incomes as adults. For every $1000 increase in the median income of the neighbourhood, adult incomes increased by about $370 for sons, and by $72 for daughters. There are a number of reasons why high-income neighbourhoods may improve the labour market outcomes of children. They may offer a more-developed physical infrastructure—higher quality schools, recreational facilities, and social institutions—as well as the kind of network or peer group effects that are sometimes called "social capital"—that is, the set of norms or standards that exist at the community level and help to reinforce the parents' goals for their children. An alternative interpretation is that parents will select a neighbourhood with the qualities they prefer if they can afford to choose the community where they raise their children. The type of neighbourhood may thus reflect the parents' choices and priorities for their children's future, rather than being a causal factor in its own right....

Clearly, different dollars produce different effects for the "average kid." Does the same hold true for low-income children? ... In a world of equal opportunity, the labour market outcomes of adult children would not depend upon their family background. Ideally, a child with a very low-income father (bottom 10 percent of the income distribution) would have an equal chance of entering any income decile; that is, the child would be just as likely to become a very high-income earner (10 percent) as a very low-income earner (also 10 percent).

However, in fact, children of very low-income fathers were more likely to follow their father's example than to improve their own position in the income distribution. About 15 percent of sons also found themselves in the bottom decile, and another 14 percent moved up by only one decile. The figures for daughters were very similar, at 14 percent and 11 percent respectively. Only about six percent of sons and daughters of very low-income fathers managed to reach the top 10 percent of the income rankings. (In contrast, over 20 percent of sons and daughters born to fathers in the top decile also occupied the top decile, and less than 7 percent fell all the way to the bottom.) These patterns suggest that low income in one generation is associated with low income in the next, with children of very low-income families most likely to end up at the bottom of the income hierarchy.

A father's source of income had a clear effect on their adult children's incomes (see table). Children were less likely (12 to 13 percent) to remain in the bottom income decile if their father had some self-employment income than if he did not (15 to 16 percent) while children whose father received UI benefits were more likely to remain there (15 to 16 percent) than if he did not (13 to 14 percent). However, the most striking result is the improvement in income mobility if a father reported some asset income: only 12 percent of sons remained in the bottom decile, compared with over 17 percent of those whose fathers had no income from assets. For daughters, the pattern was very similar at 11 percent compared with 17 percent....

The community has as great an effect on a low-income child as on the average child. Children of very low-income fathers living in high-income neighbourhoods tended to do better. This was especially true in the case of sons; only 12 percent remained in the bottom income decile if they grew up in a high income community, compared with 16 percent if they were raised in a low-income neighbourhood. For daughters, the difference was slight, at 14 percent and 15 percent respectively....

SOURCE: Statistics Canada, "Getting Ahead in Life: Does Your Parents' Income Count?" *Canadian Social Trends*, Catalogue No. 11-008-XPE1998001, June 1998. http://www.statcan.gc.ca/bsolc/olc-cel/olc-cel?catno=11-008-XPE&lang=eng.

Children's Increase in Income Based on Parent's Sources of Income

	Market Income of Adult Child Changed by $__	
	Sons	Daughters
Father's income if father reported income from		
Self-employment	1157	850
Assets	3107	2698
Unemployment Insurance	−1442	−865
For every $1000 increase in father's income from		
Paid work	91	47
Self-employment	76	50
Assets	28	28
Unemployment Insurance	−10	−23
For every $1000 increase in		
Mother's income	90	82
Median income of neighbourhood	368	72

SOURCE: Statistics Canada, "Getting Ahead in Life: Does Your Parents' Income Count?" *Canadian Social Trends*, Catalogue No. 11-008-XPE1998001, June 1998. http://www.statcan.gc.ca/bsolc/olc-cel/olc-cel?catno=11-008-XPE&lang=eng.

Intergenerational poverty creates a persistently poor and socially disadvantaged population sometimes referred to as the underclass. The term *underclass* usually refers to impoverished individuals who have low educational attainment, have criminal records, are unmarried mothers on welfare, or are ghetto residents. Although the underclass is stereotyped as being composed of minorities living in inner-city ghetto communities, the underclass is a far more heterogeneous population than that (Alex-Assensoh 1995).

Mead (1992) argues that intergenerational poverty may be caused by welfare dependency. According to Mead, when poor adults rely on welfare, the stigma of welfare fades, and welfare recipients develop poor work ethics that are passed on to their children. William Julius Wilson attributes intergenerational poverty and the underclass to a variety of social factors, including the decline in well-paid jobs and their movement out of urban areas, the resultant decline in the availability of marriageable males able to support a family, declining marriage rates and an increase in out-of-wedlock births, the migration of the middle class to the suburbs, and the impact of deteriorating neighbourhoods on children and youth (Wilson 1987; 1996).

Using income tax information reported by a cohort of approximately 285 000 men and women aged 28 to 31 in 1994, Corak (1998) related the total market income of these young adults to the incomes of their fathers and mothers in 1982 (when his participants were 16 to 19 years of age and still living at home). Among his findings: the adult sons and daughters of very low-income fathers—those in the bottom 10 percent of income earners—were overrepresented in the lowest income decile. A detailed description of Corak's findings is contained within this chapter's *Social Problems Research Up Close*.

War and Social Conflict

Poverty is often the root cause of conflict and war within and between nations as "the desperation of the poor is never quiet for long" (Speth 1998: 281). Not only does poverty breed conflict and war, but also war contributes to poverty. For example, war contributes to homelessness as individuals and families are forced to flee from their homes. Military and weapons spending associated with war diverts resources away from economic development and social spending on health and education.

Briggs (1998) suggests that the widening economic inequalities present a threat to social order. He asks how long a country can maintain social order "when increasing numbers of persons are left out of the banquet while a few are allowed to gorge?" (p. 474). Although Karl Marx predicted that the proletariat would revolt against the capitalists, Briggs does not foresee a revival of Marxism: "the means of surveillance and the methods of suppression by the governments of industrialized states are far too great to offer any prospect of success for such endeavors" (p. 476). Instead, Briggs predicts that capitalism and its resulting economic inequalities will lead to social anarchy—a state of political disorder and weakening of political authority.

10.5 Strategies for Action: Antipoverty Programs, Policies, and Proposals

In Canada, federal, provincial, and local governments have devoted considerable attention and resources to antipoverty programs since the 1960s. In 1964, "the United States launched its 'war against poverty' and Canada began a more quiet campaign of study and legislation in an effort to understand better the causes of and remedies for poverty" (Ross and Lochhead 1999: 1881).

The 1960s and 1970s saw the introduction of several significant pieces of antipoverty legislation in Canada. Recognition that the private pension system failed to provide adequate support for retired low-income workers and their families led to the introduction of the Canada and Quebec pension plans and to the Guaranteed Income Supplement program for those elderly individuals with little or no income other than Old Age Security. In 1966, the Canada Assistance Plan (CAP) was introduced. The CAP replaced the "many piecemeal cost-shared programs that the federal and provincial governments had begun entering into as far back as 1927" with a comprehensive social-assistance program that provided a major source of funds for people with disabilities who were unemployed, offered assistance to others in low-income circumstances, and brought a wide array of social services (e.g., daycare, family counselling, homemaker and child-welfare services) under federal cost sharing (Ross and Lochhead 1999: 1888). At least in theory, the CAP was designed not only to respond to the problem of poverty, but also to prevent it. In 1968, the *Medical Care Act* (medicare) provided free access to basic health care for all Canadians. The *Unemployment Insurance Act* (1940), which ushered in Canada's first national social-insurance program, was amended in 1971 to provide greater coverage to the unemployed as well as to the sick.

In this section, we describe some national and international responses to poverty and note the role of charity and the nonprofit sector in the alleviation of poverty.

Government Public Assistance and Welfare Programs in Canada

Under the *Constitution Act*, social and welfare services are the responsibility of the provincial and territorial governments. However, the federal government is also involved in the provision of these services through its cost-sharing agreements with the provinces and territories. Before April 1996, the federal government provided financial support for social services to the provinces and territories through a 50–50 cost-sharing scheme called the Canada Assistance Plan. The CAP aimed at improving standards of provincial social-assistance programs and introduced national standards into public welfare for the first time. In place of "a confusing mix of program categories based on the poor law practice of separating the 'worthy' [e.g., people with disabilities] from the 'unworthy' poor... one program [was to be established by each province and territory in exchange for federal funding] to meet financial need—provincial social assistance" (Guest 1999a: 2203). Despite this intent, welfare remains inadequate for handling the needs of the poor in Canada. The National Council of Welfare observes that current rhetoric and policies regarding welfare remain punitive; it notes, too, that social assistance is far below poverty lines across the nation, especially for single persons whose allowable benefits may be only 20 to 44 percent of the poverty line (2003: 25, 74).

However, beginning in the 1970s and in response to rising unemployment and inflation, claims were made that Canada's economic prosperity was best assured by decreasing government expenditures, particularly for social programs.

Since that time, Moscovitch (1999: 2496) notes that both the federal and the provincial governments have used the following methods to control social expenditures: "changing eligibility and benefits, particularly under unemployment insurance and social assistance; 'privatizing' provincial social programs by contracting out responsibility for social services (particularly those relating to children and the aged); provincial attempts to raise revenues through Medicare premiums and user fees; decreasing social-program budgets relatively if not absolutely; imposing an eroding level of assistance benefits; and termination of some social programs." In an attempt to reduce expenditures on social programs, between 1984 and 1993 the federal Progressive Conservative governments further reduced old-age security benefits at middle-income levels and above, decreased the range of workers who were covered by Unemployment Insurance and the benefits available to them, and imposed spending limits on Canada's three richest provinces—Ontario, British Columbia, and Alberta—effectively forcing these provinces to absorb up to 70 percent of the costs. In its 1997 report, *Another Look at Welfare Reform*, the National Council of Welfare noted that provincial and territorial governments also implemented cuts to most welfare programs, with the most extreme example occurring in Ontario in 1995, with a 21.6 percent cut to welfare recipients. The depth of this cut, the report emphasizes, "was completely arbitrary, with no assessment of how people who depended on welfare would be able to afford adequate food, clothing and shelter, let alone the impact of these cuts on young children and their families." While those with disabilities were exempted from the cuts, families with children were not.

In February 1995, the federal budget introduced the *Canada Health and Social Transfer* (CHST) (which became effective in April 1996) and eliminated two federal transfer programs: Established Programs Financing, which provided for the consolidation of hospital, medicare, and postsecondary education funding, and the Canada Assistance Plan. The CHST combined federal transfer payments for social assistance (previously under the CAP) with those for medicare and postsecondary education into a single "block" transfer made up of cash payments and tax points. As a result, Canada's social safety net was fundamentally altered. Among the changes: "the new arrangement included a significant cut in federal support for these programs and a significant change in the way the provinces and territories account for the money they receive" (National Council of Welfare 1999b: 79).

Under the CHST, the provinces now have greater discretion in deciding how to apportion their share of the reduced federal transfer. At least theoretically, provincial and territorial governments could elect to use all of the federal money they receive for medicare and devote none to the other areas. Guest (1999a: 2203) points out that "Some have already made the decision to cut social-assistance programs to Canada's poorest families and individuals—Ontario and Alberta—while British Columbia has imposed a residence requirement of three months on all new applications for social assistance." It is also evident that not all groups affected by spending cuts are equally vocal nor are all voices equally heard. As Guest reports, "One concern by welfare advocates is that money will be siphoned from welfare to cool the anger of health and higher education supporters" (p. 2203).

Family Allowance and Child Benefits Canada's first universal welfare program, introduced in 1945, was **family allowance**, a monthly allowance paid to

family allowance

Canada's first universal welfare program, introduced in 1945, which promised a monthly allowance paid to families with children. The term *universal* here refers to the fact that the benefit flowed from the principle of entitlement and was available without reference to a recipient's income or assets.

families with children. The term *universal* here refers to the fact that such benefits flowed from the principle of entitlement and were available without reference to a recipient's income or assets. In contrast, when benefits are directed at particular groups within the population, the funds are called **demogrants**.

Following a failed attempt in 1972 to replace the universality of family allowances with selectivity related to income, the federal government introduced a new *Family Allowance Act* that made family allowances taxable. In 1978, further restructuring occurred. The government established a Refundable Child Tax Credit, which offered $200 per year for families with incomes under $18 000 and taxed away benefits entirely for those whose incomes reached $26 000. The tax credit was financed through scaling back the amount of monthly family allowance payments (from an average of $28 per month to $20) and through the reduction or elimination of other tax exemptions for children. Beginning in 1985, family benefits were further restructured with the partial indexing of family allowances and child tax credits. As well, the number of families qualifying for the tax credit was reduced when the maximum income for receipt of the credit was decreased from $26 300 to $23 500. Guest (1999b: 815) reports that by 1991, these changes "represented a spending cut in family benefits [of] $550 million…with only a token increase" in the net family benefits received by Canada's poorest families.

In 1989, the universality of family allowances disappeared, with the federal government requiring parents with upper incomes to repay all of their benefits at the time they paid their yearly taxes. In 1991, family allowances, the Refundable Child Tax Credit, and a nonrefundable child tax credit were consolidated into a new **Canada Child Tax Benefit (CCTB)**. The CCTB is a tax-free monthly payment made to eligible families to help them with the cost of raising children under the age of 18. Benefits are calculated for a 12-month period based on the number of children in a family and their ages, the applicant's province or territory of residence, the family's net income, and the applicant's (or his or her spouse's) deduction for child-care expenses. Except in Alberta, the basic benefit in 2002 was $95.91 a month for each child under age 18 plus $6.66 a month for a third or additional child, plus $19.00 for each child under 7. In Alberta, the basic monthly benefit rate was $87.91 for children under 7, $93.83 for children aged 7 to 11, $105.00 for children aged 12 to 15 and $111.25 for children aged 16 to 17 (CCRA 2002). The CCTB is based on net family income reported on the tax return of the previous year and is gradually reduced as family income reaches an "income ceiling" ($32 960 in 2002).

The federal government increased the Canada Child Tax Benefit in July of 1998 for low-income families by adding a **National Child Benefit Supplement (NCBS)**. This tax-free monthly benefit for low-income families with children under age 18 is the federal government's contribution to the **National Child Benefit (NCB)**. In 2002, the NCBS amounts were $1293 a year for a one-child family and $2380 for a two-child family. Families with three or more children receive $2380 for the first two children plus $1009 a year for the third or each additional child. The maximum NCBS is paid only to those families with a net income of under $22 397 (CCRA 2002). It is reduced by a percentage amount (which depends on the number of children within a family) when the family net income exceeds this amount. In most of Canada's provinces and territories, the NCBS is considered income and will affect the amount of social assistance that families are eligible to receive.

demogrant
A benefit directed at a particular group within the population.

Canada Child Tax Benefit (CCTB)
A tax-free monthly payment made to eligible families to help them with the cost of raising children under the age of 18. Benefits are calculated for a 12-month period based on the number of children in a family and their ages, the applicant's province or territory of residence, the family's net income, and the applicant's (or the applicant's spouse's) deduction for child care expenses.

National Child Benefit Supplement (NCBS)
A monthly benefit for low-income families with children that is the federal government's contribution to the National Child Benefit (NCB).

National Child Benefit (NCB)
Introduced in July 1998, NCB is a joint initiative of federal, provincial, and territorial governments designed to help prevent and reduce the depth of child poverty and to promote parental attachment to the workforce.

The NCB is a joint initiative of federal, provincial, and territorial governments designed to help prevent and reduce the depth of child poverty and to promote parental attachment to the workforce by improving available benefits and services. According to the *National Child Benefit Progress Report 1999,* "key to the NCB is the effort to move child benefits out of the welfare system so that when parents leave social assistance for work, these benefits go with them, helping to ensure their children's well-being during this transition" (Government of Canada 1999).

Employment Insurance Benefits In January 1997, the *Employment Insurance Act* was implemented in Canada, replacing the former Unemployment Insurance (UI) Program. Individuals may receive regular benefits if they lose a job through no fault of their own and cannot find work. Those who quit their job without just cause or who are fired for misconduct are ineligible to receive Employment Insurance (EI) benefits. Similarly, those affected by a strike, lockout, or other forms of labour dispute are ineligible unless they are not taking part in the dispute, are not giving money to support the dispute, and are not directly interested in the dispute (that is, their wages or working conditions are not affected by the dispute's outcome).

To be eligible for EI benefits, individuals must apply; have paid into the EI account; have been without work and pay for at least seven consecutive days; have worked for the required number of hours based on where they live and the unemployment rate in their area; be available for work but unable to find it; and be in Canada. The current system is based on hours of paid work and responds to variations in work situations, such as part time, extended hours, or compressed weeks. Whether a person works full time, part time, or on a seasonal basis, the hours worked for pay are accumulated toward eligibility for EI benefits. These hours include overtime (which is calculated on an hour-for-hour rate) and paid leave (which is insured for the number of hours that normally would be worked in that period).

To qualify for EI, most individuals will need to have worked between 420 and 700 hours during the last 52 weeks or since the start of their last claim, whichever is shorter. The specific number of hours of insurable employment in the past 52 weeks needed to qualify for EI depends on the unemployment rate in the region where each person lives. For example, in an area where the regional rate of unemployment is 0 percent to 6 percent, 700 hours of insurable employment are necessary; in an area with a regional unemployment rate of 9.1 percent to 10 percent, 560 hours are needed. In an area with a regional unemployment rate of 13.1 percent or higher, 420 hours are needed. In some instances, however, individuals will need a great number of insurable work hours in the past 52 weeks to qualify. For example, among those who are in the workforce for the first time, a minimum of 910 hours of insurable work in the past 52 weeks is required. Those who apply for sickness, maternity, or parental benefits will need 700 hours of insurable work. Those who have previously committed EI violations may also face increases in the number of hours they are required to possess before qualifying for EI benefits.

The length of time for which benefits can be received depends on the regional unemployment rate and how long an individual has worked in the last 52 weeks or since their last claim (whichever is shorter). Depending on the amount of insurable hours, benefits can be received from 14 to a maximum of

45 weeks. The basic benefit rate is 55 percent of average insured earnings up to a maximum payment of $413 per week. However, those who have drawn regular benefits in the past may have their benefits adjusted and reduced under the "intensity rule." Under this rule, benefit rates are reduced by 1 percent for every 20 weeks of regular benefits claimed since June 30, 1996, to a maximum of 5 percent if that person has more than 100 weeks of benefits over that five-year period.

Individuals receiving regular benefits can earn up to 25 percent of their weekly benefits or $50 (whichever is higher) without changing the weekly amount they receive. However, all earnings above this limit are deducted dollar for dollar from their weekly benefits. Other sources of money that can affect the amount of EI benefits include Canada Pension Plan or Quebec Pension Plan retirement income, self-employment earnings, or monies received in damages for wrongful dismissal. (Payments from private RRSPs, disability pensions, survivor's pensions, or dependent's pensions do not affect the calculation of EI payments.) Depending on net income and past claim history, all or some of the EI benefits received may have to be repaid at income tax time.

Families with children in a low-income situation—that is, with a family net income under $25 921 a year, and who receive the Canada Child Tax Benefit (CCTB)—automatically receive the **Family Supplement**, with a rate based on family net income and the number and ages of children in the family. If both spouses claim EI at the same time, only one can receive the Family Supplement.

Over time, the percentage of unemployed Canadians who are eligible for UI or EI benefits has fallen. Since the 1970s, the federal government has also steadily trimmed away the benefits available to unemployed workers. For example, while in the early 1970s weekly benefits were as high as 75 percent of a person's maximum weekly insurable earnings while employed, they are now, as earlier noted, 55 percent. Similarly, while in the early 1970s the maximum length available for regular benefits was 51 weeks, it is now 45 weeks. Although some of those who are unemployed are able to locate and obtain employment quickly, for others their unemployment will last far longer than the benefit coverage that EI provides.

Guest (1999a: 2203) emphasizes that we should be concerned about the separation of claimants into "normal" and "frequent user" categories. He observes that frequent users "may suffer benefit reductions and possibly be subject to an income test, and receipt of benefit might be contingent on the claimant's willingness to take part in community work projects or training programs." As a result, he argues, "This is no longer social insurance but a form of 'workfare.'"

Educational Assistance In Canada, public education is free until the end of secondary school (or "high school"). However, the costs associated with higher education have long been recognized to pose special problems to those of low income. Until 1939 and the federal government's passage of the **Dominion Provincial Student Aid Program (DSAP)**, economic assistance for low-income persons wanting to attend postsecondary institutions was limited to those high scholastic achievers who could obtain privately funded assistance from universities and colleges. The encroachment of the federal government into the area of education (which, under the *Constitution Act, 1867*, is the exclusive domain of provincial legislatures) was legitimated with reference to

Family Supplement

Those families with children in a low-income situation (i.e., having a family net income under $25 921 a year) and who receive the Canada Child Tax Benefit automatically receive the Family Supplement with a rate based on family net income and the number and ages of children in the family.

Dominion Provincial Student Aid Program (DPSAP)

An act passed by the federal government in 1939. Under DPSAP, the federal government contributed to each participating province and the province was expected to provide an equal amount of assistance to students.

economic growth, labour training, and labour mobility—areas that fell under federal jurisdiction. From this vantage point, the DSAP was simply a subset of the *Youth Training Act* or another part of national economic policy. By 1944, all of Canada's provinces had joined the plan; however, in 1954, Quebec opted out of the arrangement, "citing constitutional reasons of provincial primacy and autonomy in higher education" (Orlikow 1999: 2265). DSAP was discontinued in 1967.

Canada Student Loans Program (CSLP)

A plan that permits eligible Canadian citizens and permanent residents to finance their postsecondary education with government-sponsored loans. Full-time students, enrolled in a program that lasts for at least 12 weeks, may qualify for a loan based on the costs of their program and on the financial resources available to them.

Canada Student Financial Assistance Act (CSFA Act)

The *CSFA Act* of 1994 revised the Canada Student Loans Plan and increased the amounts of the maximum loans available for full-time and part-time students.

In 1964, the **Canada Student Loans Program (CSLP)** was established. Under this plan, the federal government guarantees loans to all full-time students demonstrating financial need to a provincial or territorial government. These loans must be repaid over a period that does not exceed 9.5 years at a rate of interest that is set annually. Students are not required to begin making payments until six months after they have ceased to be full-time students, but interest on the monies owed begins to accrue as soon as they leave full-time studies. In 1994, the *Canada Student Financial Assistance Act (CSFA Act)* revised the CSLP, increasing the amounts of the maximum loans available to full-time and part-time students; establishing a national program of grants for students with permanent disabilities, part-time students with high financial need, students with dependents, and women in doctoral programs in certain fields; and expanding interest relief for unemployed borrowers and those of low income. In 1998, the government also introduced new measures to assist students in loan repayment.

Most recently, the introduction of Registered Education Saving Plans (RESPs) represents an attempt to assist families who can afford to set monies aside for the future costs of their children's education. Family members can contribute up to $4000 a year (up to a maximum of $20 000) into RESPs on behalf of a particular beneficiary. The Canada Education Saving Grant (CESG) is added to the monies invested. The CESG is a federal government grant paid directly in a beneficiary's RESP, which provides 20 percent to the first $2000 in contributions made into an RESP per eligible beneficiary on an annual basis. RESPs grow tax free until such time as the beneficiary is ready to attend any eligible postsecondary educational institution (HRDC 2001).

Nevertheless, the rising cost of tuition (up 115 percent since 1980) will continue to make the costs of postsecondary education difficult for many and prohibitive for some (see also Chapter 12).

Maternal and Parental Benefits In Canada, maternity and parental leave is part of our federal employment insurance system. Under Canada's current EI rules, new mothers receive a maximum of 15 weeks of pregnancy benefits (the first two of which are nonpayable) *only* if they have worked at least 600 hours in the 52 weeks prior, and then they receive only 55 percent of their normal weekly pay to a maximum of $413 a week. Employment Insurance additionally provides for a maximum of 35 weeks of parental leave (to either a natural or adoptive parent) that is payable up to one year after the birth of an infant or the placement of an adopted child.

Under provincial and territorial legislation, all Canadian provinces and territories provide either 17 or 18 weeks of unpaid maternity leave. "In every jurisdiction, the laws guarantee an employee reinstatement after the leave period to at least a comparable job with the same or similar wages and benefits, without loss of seniority" (Dranoff 2001: 44). However, not all employees (e.g., domestics) are protected under most employment standards legislation.

Child Support Enforcement In February 1997, Bill C-41 received royal assent and became law in May of that year. This legislation included amendments to the *Divorce Act* to establish a framework for the use of child support guidelines; amendments to the *Family Orders and Agreements Enforcement Assistance Act* (FOAEA) that added Canada Revenue Agency to the list of federal departments whose databanks can be searched to locate persons who have breached family support orders; new provisions in the FOAEA Act to establish a federal licence denial scheme that will also authorize the suspension of passports and certain federal transport licences when a payer of child support has persistently breached support obligations; amendments to the *Garnishment, Attachment and Pension Diversion Act* to expand access to federal public service employee pension benefits to satisfy support arrears, and amendments to the *Shipping Act* to allow the wages of a person working at sea to be garnished to support a family obligation. All Canadian provinces now have their own programs to protect against the nonpayment of child support.

Under the *Divorce Act*, either spouse or former spouse may be ordered to pay child support. Child support is neither taxable for the parent who receives the support nor is it deductible for the parent who pays the support on agreements made after May 1, 1997. (Child support agreements made before this date are not affected by this ruling.) Child support is also completely protected against bankruptcy claims.

Welfare in Canada: Myths and Realities

Public attitudes toward welfare assistance and welfare recipients are generally negative. Rather than view poverty as the problem, many Canadians view welfare as the problem. What are some of the common myths about welfare that perpetuate negative images of welfare and welfare recipients?

MYTH 1 People receiving welfare are lazy and have no work ethic.

Reality First, single parents on welfare already do work—they do the work of parenting. Albelda and Tilly (1997: 111) emphasize that "raising children is work. It requires time, skills, and commitment. While we as a society do not place a monetary value on it, it is work that is invaluable—and indeed, essential to the survival of our society." Single parents and people with disabilities tend to have longer spells on welfare and those who are *able to work* tend to have shorter spells. Second, it should be evident that not all persons who would prefer to work are able to find jobs, particularly those in low-skill job categories. For example, Newfoundland has long had very high rates of unemployment, a fact that helps to explain why its welfare caseload is heavily laden with long-term welfare recipients. The National Council of Welfare (1999b: 17) notes that "Canada has seen a decline in the number of secure, full-time, well-paying jobs and an increase in the number of short-term, part-time jobs with low wages, few benefits and little or no security." As the Council emphasizes, "For those individuals with low levels of education, 'bad' jobs are often the only real possibilities of employment, yet they cannot eliminate child and family poverty, no matter how hard a parent works. When lay-offs come, parents fall still further behind." Some provinces, such as Ontario, have incorporated "workfare" into its welfare system, which requires able-bodied people to do specific jobs as a condition of welfare. However, most of the workfare jobs are menial jobs that are unlikely to lead to permanent employment.

Rather than disparage the work ethic of those on welfare, the National Council of Welfare (1998: 62) emphasizes that it might be well to recognize that "everyone is at risk of falling on welfare at some point in their lives. The numbers speak for themselves: an estimated 1 910 900 people in Canada were on welfare as of March 31, 2001" (National Council of Welfare 2002a). As the Council observes, "Losing a job, losing a spouse, and losing good health are some of the reasons that people go on welfare. The biggest myth of all would be to assume that most of us are immune to any of these personal tragedies or the many other misfortunes that can lead to reliance on welfare."

MYTH 2 Welfare benefits are granted to many people who are not eligible to receive them and welfare fraud is rampant.

Reality Although some people obtain welfare benefits through fraudulent means, it is much more common for people who are eligible to receive welfare to not receive benefits. A main reason for not receiving benefits is lack of information—people do not know they are eligible. Some people who are eligible for public assistance do not apply for it because they do not want to be stigmatized as lazy people who just want a "free ride" at the taxpayers' expense—their sense of personal pride prevents them from receiving public assistance. Others want to avoid the administrative hassles involved in obtaining it.

Nevertheless, the impression that welfare fraud is widespread is undoubtedly suggested by government statistics on welfare "fraud and misuse." For example, in December 1999, Ontario's Community and Social Service Minister John Baird boasted that $35 million in "fraud savings" had occurred because of increased government vigilance in policing welfare recipients. However, what the ministry figures show is not truly welfare "fraud" on the part of claimants at all, but rather overpayments resulting from administrative errors as well as a notable vigour in relation to the disqualification of vulnerable individuals from receiving assistance. While in 1997–98, 61 653 cases were investigated for "welfare fraud," in fewer than one in four cases (23.9 percent) did the Ministry reduce the amount of the benefit or terminate the benefit altogether; only 1.2 percent (or 1100) of the cases investigated resulted in a criminal conviction for fraud. In addition, in more than 90 percent of the 14 771 cases in which the Ministry reduced the amount of the benefit or terminated benefits altogether, such actions were the result of an administrative error, not fraud. Reductions in benefits or termination of benefits can occur in the absence of any wrongdoing on the part of welfare recipients. For example, should the Consolidated Verification Project (CVP) investigation reveal that a document is missing from a welfare recipient's file, the recipient is required to provide the necessary paperwork (whether it is two days or 20 years old) or face termination of benefits.

MYTH 3 Most welfare parents are teenagers.

Reality According to the National Council of Welfare (1998), teenage single parents accounted for only 3 percent of single parents on welfare in March 1997. Parents in their 20s to 40s accounted for 87 percent of couples with children on welfare and 91 percent of single parents on welfare.

MYTH 4 Most welfare mothers have large families with many children.

Reality Mothers receiving welfare have no more children, on average, than mothers in the general population.

MYTH 5 Unmarried women have children so they can receive benefits. If single mothers already receive benefits, they have more children to receive increased benefits.

Reality Research consistently shows that receiving welfare does not significantly increase out-of-wedlock births (Albelda and Tilly 1997).

MYTH 6 Most people on welfare also have income from part-time work or Employment Insurance or government pensions.

Reality According to the National Council of Welfare (1998), only 29 percent of welfare cases in March 1997 had outside income from work, government pensions, support payments, Employment Insurance, or other sources. Among couples with children, wages were the most common form of outside income; among single parents with children, child support or alimony was the most common source of outside income, with wages a close second. While transfer payments and wages were the main sources of outside income both for couples without children and for unattached persons, the percentage of unattached persons receiving either form of outside income was extremely low.

MYTH 7 Almost all the people on welfare are adults.

Reality According to the National Council of Welfare (1998: 31), in March 1997, dependent children accounted for nearly 1.1 million of the people on welfare in Canada.

Despite the public perception that welfare benefits are too generous, cash and other forms of assistance to the poor do not meet the basic needs for many individuals and families who receive such benefits (see this chapter's *The Human Side* feature).

Minimum Wage Increase

As noted earlier, many families that leave welfare for work are still living in poverty because of involuntary part-time work and low wages. One strategy for improving the standard of living for low-income individuals and families is to increase the minimum wage (Schenk 2001). As the National Council of Welfare (1999b: 18) has noted, "Nowhere in Canada are minimum wages high enough to allow even full-time workers to escape poverty... [and] [t]he situation is much worse when a minimum wage worker has children to support."

In Winnipeg in 1999, a single parent with one child had to work 80 hours a week simply to get to the poverty line. A two-parent family with two children in Winnipeg had to work 118 hours a week to reach the poverty line (and there are only 168 hours in a week). In Vancouver, where the minimum wage is the highest in the country, a single parent had to work 61 hours a week and a couple with two children had to work 89 hours a week to reach the poverty line. Clearly, minimum wages come nowhere near to covering the costs of living.

For this reason, the Council argues that both the federal and provincial governments must ensure that minimum wages in their jurisdictions provide adequate

The *Human Side*

Remembering Kimberly Rogers

The following is an extract of an article by Jennifer Keck that first appeared in Perception 25 (Winter/Spring 2002). The unabridged version of this article can be found on the World Wide Web at www.ccsd.ca/perception/2534/kimberly.htm.

Kimberly Rogers...died alone and eight months pregnant, in her sweltering apartment in Sudbury, Ontario, while under house arrest for welfare fraud.... Kimberly Rogers was charged with welfare fraud after collecting both social assistance and student loans to help cover the costs of attending four years of community college. She was convicted in April 2001 and the penalty was stiff: six months under house arrest (with the right to be allowed out of her hot apartment three hours per week); a requirement to repay more than $13 000 in benefits; 18 months probation and loss of the right to have part of her student loan forgiven. At the time of Rogers' conviction, Ontario Works' regulations specified that anyone convicted of welfare fraud would be automatically suspended from receiving benefits for three months. This stipulation has since been made tougher. Anyone convicted of welfare fraud in the province of Ontario will be banned for

life from ever being able to collect social assistance. In Rogers' case the three-month suspension meant that she was confined to house arrest with no source of income to cover her rent, food, or other expenses. On May 14, 2001, Kimberly Rogers became the first Ontario resident to launch a case under the Charter of Rights and Freedoms that challenged the constitutional validity of Ontario Works regulations that suspended benefits. She did this with the help of the Sudbury Community Legal Clinic. In her charter case, Rogers argued: (i) the law that allowed welfare authorities to disqualify her from receiving assistance contravened the Charter rights to life, liberty, and security of the person (she had no source of income); (ii) cutting off her assistance after she had already been severely punished constituted "cruel and unusual punishment"; and (iii) as a pregnant woman with a diagnosed disability, the automatic suspension infringed the Charter's guarantee of equality.... Judge Gloria Epstein granted a constitutional exemption to the law for Rogers while Rogers' legal team prepared her case. In making her decision, the judge pointed to Canada's human rights commitments: "In the unique circumstances of this case, if [Ms. Rogers] is exposed to the full three months suspension of her

benefits, a member of our community carrying an unborn child may well be homeless and deprived of basic sustenance. Such a situation would jeopardize the health of Ms. Rogers and the fetus, thereby adversely affecting not only mother and child but also the public—its dignity, its human rights commitments, and its health care resources. For many reasons there is overwhelming public interest in protecting a pregnant woman in our community from being destitute."... Even with Ontario Works benefits... [Rogers] was unable to support herself and her unborn child. After a deduction of 10 percent (towards repayment to Ontario Works), Rogers received $468 per month. With $450 going towards paying the rent, Rogers was left with $18 per month to cover all other necessities.... Tragically, while still under house arrest, Kimberly Rogers died just weeks after the Ontario Superior Court of Justice released its exceptional decision....

The coroner's verdict in the case of Kimberly Rogers was delivered in October 2002 and found her death to be a suicide as a result of an overdose of anti-depressant medication.

SOURCE: Keck, Jennifer. 2002. "Remembering Kimberly Rogers." *Perception* 25 (Winter/Spring). Used with permission of the Canadian Council on Social Development.

---

incomes and that these wages be indexed to rise each year with increases in the average industrial wage.

Those opposed to increasing the minimum wage argue that such an increase would result in higher unemployment and fewer benefits for low-wage workers. However, research has failed to find any systematic significant job loss associated with minimum wage increases (Economic Policy Institute 2000).

The National Council of Welfare has made these recommendations:

• The federal government must provide wage supplements to parents in the labour force to cover the additional costs of raising children.

- Governments must provide job training that prepares workers for new jobs.
- Governments must ensure that postsecondary educational opportunities are open to everyone, not just students who are lucky enough to have families able to afford to pay their tuition fees and living expenses.
- Governments must ensure that legislation governing unpaid maternity and parental leave in their jurisdictions adequately covers the time that parents are required to care for young children. Existing parental leaves cover the first months of children's lives, but parents also need time to care for sick children and take them to medical appointments when their children are much older.
- Governments must ensure that employment and pay equity laws are strengthened and enforced.

Equal Pay for Women

On paper, Canadian women have had the "right" to equal pay for equal work since the 1950s. Unfortunately, while early laws enunciated lofty goals, they failed to result in fair wages. Because of occupational sex segregation, few men and women were doing precisely the same work. Two decades later, some Canadian provinces amended their laws to require that women be paid the same as men for performing "substantially the same work." Once again, however, such laws proved ineffective. Enforcement mechanisms were meagre and employers found various ways of arguing that unequal wages did not signal discrimination on the basis of sex.

In the 1980s, researchers found women earn less than men partly because jobs in which women are concentrated are valued less than jobs in which men are concentrated. They therefore tried to establish gender-neutral standards by which they could judge the dollar value of work. These standards include such factors as the education and experience required to do a particular job and the level of responsibility, amount of stress, and working conditions associated with it. Researchers felt that, by using these criteria to compare jobs in which women and men are concentrated, they could identify pay inequities. The underpaid could then be compensated accordingly. In other words, women and men would receive equal pay for jobs of "comparable worth," even if they did different jobs. In consequence, during the mid-1980s, some governments amended the law to state that women should be paid equally for work of equal value. This amendment required employers to compare the rates of pay for women and men in dissimilar jobs that nevertheless involved the same skill, effort, responsibility, and working conditions.

In 1985, Manitoba became the first Canadian province to demand that its public sector be proactive and implement plans for "equal pay for work of equal value"—or **pay equity**, as it came to be called. With the exceptions of Alberta, Saskatchewan, and the Northwest Territories, pay equity is now official policy in 10 of 13 Canadian jurisdictions. Provisions vary widely, though. While policy on pay equity is a significant step toward achieving gender equality, inequity remains, as evidenced by both the persistence of the wage gap between working men and women and women's heightened susceptibility to poverty.

pay equity

Also known as "equal pay for work of equal value"; requires equal pay for women who perform jobs of equal value to men in the same establishment. Employers are required to compare women's and men's jobs on the basis of skill, effort, responsibility, and working conditions to determine their value.

Charity, Nonprofit Organizations, and Nongovernmental Organizations

Various types of aid to the poor are provided through individual and corporate donations to charities and nonprofit organizations. In 1996, the average charitable donation declared by tax filers was $730. Four billion dollars in donations was declared in that year. Canadians residing in the richer provinces were not more likely to donate to charities and were not the most generous donors. Rather, those residing in Manitoba and Prince Edward Island were the most likely to donate, and residents of Newfoundland, the province with the lowest total median income, made the highest median donation. Corporations also donate to charitable causes. In 1982, they contributed some $200 million; in 1995, they contributed $500 million to charities (Statistics Canada 1998a).

Charity involves giving not only money, but also time and effort in the form of volunteering. In Canada, those who reside in the Prairie provinces and the well educated are particularly likely to be volunteers. Women are slightly more likely than men are to be volunteers, and rural and small-town residents are more likely than city dwellers to serve as volunteers. Nevertheless, high rates of volunteerism are found in cities such as Saskatoon (44 percent), Calgary (38 percent), and Edmonton (Statistics Canada 1998a).

Nongovernmental organizations (NGOs) address many issues related to human rights, social justice, and environmental concerns. The number of international NGOs grew from fewer than 400 in 1900 to 26 000 in the year 2000—more than four times as many as existed just 10 years earlier (Knickerbocker 2000; Paul 2000). At the Millennium Forum meeting in 2000, representatives from more than 1000 NGOs called for a UN Global Poverty Eradication Fund to ensure that poor people have access to credit (Deen 2000). The NGOs declared that poverty is the most widespread violation of human rights and called upon governments around the world to make the alleviation of poverty a priority.

International Responses to Poverty

Alleviating worldwide poverty continues to be a major concern for developing and developed countries. Approaches to poverty reduction include promoting economic growth and investing in "human capital." Conflict resolution and the promotion of peace are also important for reducing poverty worldwide.

Promoting Economic Growth Economic growth, over the long term, generally reduces poverty (United Nations Development Programme 1997). An expanding economy creates new employment opportunities and more goods and services. In 1998, 150 million of the world's workers were unemployed (United Nations Development Programme 2000). As employment prospects improve, individuals are able to buy more goods and services. The increased demand for goods and services, in turn, stimulates economic growth. As emphasized in Chapter 14, economic development requires controlling population growth and protecting the environment and natural resources—often destroyed and depleted in the process of economic growth.

However, economic growth does not always reduce poverty; in some cases, it increases it. For example, growth resulting from technological progress may reduce demand for unskilled workers. Growth does not help poverty reduction when public spending is diverted away from meeting the needs of the poor and instead is used to pay international debt, finance military operations, and support corporations that do not pay workers fair wages. The World Bank loans about $30 billion a year to developing nations to pay primarily for roads, bridges, and industrialized agriculture that mostly benefit corporations. "Relatively little attention or money has been given to developing basic social services, building schools and clinics, and building decent public sanitation and clean water systems in some of the world's poorest countries" (Mann 2000: 2). Thus, "economic growth, though essential for poverty reduction, is not enough. Growth must be pro-poor, expanding the opportunities and life choices of poor people" (United Nations Development Programme 1997: 72–73). Because three-fourths of poor people in most developing countries depend on agriculture for their livelihoods, economic growth to reduce poverty must include raising the productivity of small-scale agriculture. Not only does improving the productivity of small-scale agriculture create employment, it also reduces food prices. The poor benefit the most because about 70 percent of their income is spent on food (United Nations Development Programme 1997). This chapter's *Focus on Technology* examines agricultural biotechnology as a strategy for alleviating global hunger.

Investing in Human Capital Promoting economic development in a society requires having a productive workforce. Yet, in many poor countries, large segments of the population are illiterate and without job skills, or are malnourished and in poor health. A key feature of poverty reduction strategies involves investing in human capital. The term **human capital** refers to the skills, knowledge, and capabilities of the individual. Investments in human capital involve programs and policies that enhance individuals' health, skills, knowledge, and capabilities. Among such programs and policies are those that provide adequate nutrition, sanitation, housing, health care (including reproductive health care and family planning), and educational and job training. Nobel Laureate Gary Becker has concluded, "the case is overwhelming that investments in human capital are one of the most effective ways to raise the poor to decent levels of income and health" (reported in Hill 1998: 279).

human capital
The skills, knowledge, and capabilities of the individual.

Poor health is both a consequence and cause of poverty; improving the health status of a population is a significant step toward breaking the cycle of poverty. Increasing the educational levels of a population better prepares individuals for paid employment and for participation in political affairs that affect poverty and other economic and political issues. Improving the educational level and overall status of women in developing countries is also associated with lower birth rates, which in turn fosters economic development.

One way to help poor countries invest in human capital and reduce poverty is to provide debt relief. If African countries were relieved of their national debts, they would have funds that would save the lives of millions of children and provide basic education to millions of girls and women. Providing debt relief to the 20 worst affected countries would cost between $5.5 billion and $7.7 billion—roughly the cost of building the Euro-Disney theme park in France (United Nations Development Programme 1997).

Global Hunger: Is Agricultural Biotechnology the Solution?

Biotechnology is any technique that uses living organisms or substances from those organisms to make or modify a product or develop micro-organisms for specific uses (see also Chapter 13). Agricultural biotechnology involves the application of biotechnology to agricultural crops and livestock; however, our discussion here focuses on crops. Various terms refer to products that have been created or modified through agricultural biotechnology, including genetically modified organisms (GMOs), genetically improved organisms (GIOs), and genetically engineered foods (GE foods).

In 1999, over 70 genetically modified varieties of crops were registered for commercial cultivation worldwide (Persley 2000). Such crops include cotton, potato, pumpkin, corn, soybean, tobacco, papaya, squash, tomato, and canola (rapeseed). An estimated 30 000 products in our supermarkets today—from ice cream to cantaloupes to corn flakes—contain genetically engineered ingredients (Environmental Defense 2000). Global areas planted with GM crops grew from 1.7 million hectares in 1996 to nearly 40 million in 1999; 72 percent of this area was in the United States, followed by Argentina (17 percent) and Canada (10 percent) (Serageldin 2000).

Scientists, academics, environmentalists, public health officials, policy-makers, corporations, farmers, and citizens throughout the world are deeply divided over the use of agricultural biotechnology. Not surprisingly, supporters of agricultural technology emphasize its potential benefits, while critics focus on the potential risks.

Ethical and other issues are also at the centre of the controversy concerning biotechnology.

Health and Environmental Benefits

- *Alleviation of Poverty, Hunger, and Malnutrition.* Worldwide, 70 percent of poor and food-insecure people live in rural areas, and most of these poor depend on agriculture for their livelihood (Pinstrup-Andersen and Cohen 2000). Any technology that improves agricultural productivity can potentially alleviate the poverty and hunger among the rural poor. Agricultural biotechnology can enable farmers to produce more food with higher nutritional value. Some GMOs are designed to have a higher yield and earlier maturation. Others are engineered to be more durable during harvest or transportation. Some crops have improved tolerance to drought and poor soil conditions. Other crops are designed to resist herbicides (chemicals used to kill weeds), insects, and diseases.

Genes that increase vitamin A production and iron have been incorporated experimentally in rice. Rice with these genes could enhance the diets of the 180 million children who suffer from vitamin A deficiency—a deficiency that causes two million deaths annually and 14 million cases of eye damage. Iron deficiency, which affects one billion people in the developing world, leads to anemia—a condition that can diminish learning capacity and contribute to illness and death (Persley 2000).

- *Reduction in Pesticide Use.* Because some GMOs are designed to repel insects, they could replace chemical (pesticide) control and reduce the excessive use of pesticides that poison field workers and contaminate land, water, and animals.

- *Less Deforestation.* As farmers have access to less land on which to plant crops, they are forced to clear forest area. As discussed in Chapter 13, deforestation contributes to environmental problems. GMOs enable farmers to reap higher yields from crops and to plant crops on soil that otherwise would not be usable in farming. Their use may reduce deforestation.

Health and Environmental Risks

"Although no clear cases of harmful effects on human health have been documented from new genetically improved food, that does not mean that risks do not exist" (Persley 2000: 12). One potential health risk is food allergens in GM foods. Other health concerns are related to possible toxicity, carcinogenicity, food intolerance, antibiotic resistance buildup, and decreased nutritional value.

A potential environmental risk is the spread of traits from GM plants to other plants, the effects of which are unknown. For example, various grasses and grain crops, such as rice, corn, and wheat, have spread from intended test fields into unintended distant regions; we do not know what effect this might have on local, native plant species or on general biodiversity. Additionally, insect populations may build up resistance to GM plants with insect-repelling traits. Another potential threat to biodiversity is posed by the widespread uniformity of GM crops.

Ethical Issues and Other Concerns

- *"Playing God."* To some, the use of agricultural biotechnology is offensive because it involves "tinkering with the natural order" and "playing God." Leisinger (2000) answers that criticism by saying, "If God created humans as intelligent creatures, it should be compatible with God's intentions that they use their intelligence to improve living conditions" (p. 175).

- *Intellectual Property Rights*. Corporations that develop biotechnologies may obtain intellectual property rights, such as patents, for their biotechnological inventions. A patent is a monopoly granted to the owner of an invention for a limited period of up to 20 years. Critics suggest that such rights result in increased prices, as other companies cannot offer the same technology at a competitive price. In response to this concern, Richer (2000) points out that intellectual property rights enable companies to recoup their investment in developing new technologies (the average cost of developing a GM plant is about $150 million).

Others are concerned that intellectual property rights give corporations ownership of life forms—an idea that is intuitively unappealing. Yet, we already accept ownership rights of plants and animals. Serageldin (2000) asks how owning a "building block of life" is different from owning the living thing itself.

Finally, critics are concerned about the "terminator gene"—the first patented technology aimed at protection of intellectual property rights regarding biotechnology. The terminator gene is designed to genetically switch off a plant's ability to germinate a second time. The terminator gene prevents farmers from planting seeds that are harvested from GMO crops and forces them to buy a fresh supply of seeds each year (if they want GMO seeds). Seeds with the terminator gene are not appropriate for small farmers in developing countries because the existing production process may not keep fertile and infertile seeds apart. If farmers accidentally planted infertile seeds, their losses could be devastating (Pinstrup-Andersen and Cohen 2000). In response to protests against terminator technology, Monsanto announced it would not market it (Shah 2001). But other approaches to property rights protection are under development. GE seeds that can be activated only through chemical treatment are being developed. Otherwise, the seed maintains its normal characteristics (without genetic modifications), but is still fertile. The farmer would have the choice to plant the seed as is, or to activate the genetically modified traits by applying the chemical (also made and sold by the same corporation that makes the seeds).

- *Corporate Greed*. Corporations that develop agricultural biotechnology do so in hopes of earning profit. However, according to Pinstrup-Andersen and Cohen (2000), corporations are not the only economic beneficiaries of GMOs. They cite a study of the distribution of the economic benefits of herbicide-tolerant soybean seed in 1997: the patent-holding company, Monsanto, received 22 percent of the economic benefits, seed companies gained 9 percent, consumers gained 21 percent, and farmers worldwide obtained 48 percent.
- *Neglect of the Needs of Developing Countries*. The development of GMOs to meet specific needs of developing countries is not likely to be profitable; consequently, relatively little biotechnology research has focused on the needs of poor farmers and consumers in developing countries. Those concerned with this neglect of the needs of developing countries call for stronger public-sector involvement in the research and development of GMOs (Pinstrup-Andersen and Cohen 2000). Globally, 80 percent of biotechnology research is done by the private sector (Persley 2000).
- *Increased Poverty and Economic Inequality*. A criticism of agricultural biotechnology is that it is too expensive and inaccessible to small farmers. Persley (2000) suggests that unless countries have policies to ensure that small farmers have access to GM crop seeds and markets, agricultural biotechnology could lead to increased inequality of income and wealth—large farmers would reap most of the benefits.
- *Scientific Apartheid*. Biotechnological knowledge and research is skewed to the potential markets of the affluent, excluding the concerns of the poor. This skewing contributes to *scientific apartheid*—the growing gap between the industrial and developing countries in the rapidly evolving knowledge frontier (Serageldin 2000). To address this concern, poor farmers and other low-income populations in developing countries must have a voice in the development of and policies concerning agricultural biotechnology.
- *Insufficient Safeguards and Regulatory Mechanisms*. In 2000, Taco Bell taco shells, made by Kraft Foods, were recalled after traces of a genetically engineered variety of corn that had not been approved for human consumption

(continued)

were found in the taco shells (Union of Concerned Scientists 2001). No one—from farmers to grain dealers to Kraft—could explain how it got mixed into corn meant for taco shells. Further, Genetically Engineered Food Alert—a coalition of biotech skeptics and foes—discovered the traces of unapproved corn.

This widely publicized incident raised disturbing questions about the regulatory oversight of GE foods. There is widespread agreement that the pursuit of agricultural biotechnology requires regulatory systems to govern food safety, assess risks, monitor compliance, and enforce regulations. But such safeguards are nonexistent in some countries and, as the Taco Bell incident suggests, even when regulatory systems are present, they are not foolproof. Some progress toward improving biotechnology safeguards was made in February 2000, though, when the landmark Biosafety Protocol was signed in Montreal by 130 nations. (Signing the protocol indicates general support for the Protocol and the intention to become legally bound by it; however, the Protocol does not become legally binding until a country ratifies the treaty by submitting a letter of acceptance to the United Nations.) The Biosafety Protocol includes the requirement that producers of a GMO must demonstrate it is safe before it is widely used. The Biosafety Protocol also allows countries to ban the import of GM crops based on suspected health, ecological, or social risks.

Concluding Remarks

Many citizens have clearly taken a stand either for or against agricultural biotechnology. However, many more are uncertain. They struggle to make sense out of the competing claims of the benefits and safety versus the potential hazards of GMOs, and the complex ethical and sociopolitical implications of using these technologies.

As we strive to make sense of these issues, is it helpful to consider that many technologies with known risks have broad social acceptance? Consider the automobile—a technology that contributes to pollution and global warming and kills thousands of people each year (Serageldin 2000). Yet, few individuals would agree to ban the automobile.

Is it helpful to consider the role of the media in shaping public views and opinions on biotechnology? Some have charged the media with biased reporting that fuels anti-biotechnology sentiments. For example, according to Leisinger (2000), when the Federal Institute of Technology in Zurich informed the world in 1999 of the possibility of genetically modifying rice to contain vitamin A and iron—a major health benefit to the 250 million poor malnourished who subsist on rice—the media had little reaction. Four months later when news broke that larvae of the monarch butterfly were damaged in a GM crop experiment, the media picked up on the story and focused on the potential harm of biotechnology to biodiversity.

Lester Brown (2001) of the World Watch Institute suggests that "perhaps the largest question hanging over the future of biotechnology is the lack of knowledge about the possible environmental and human health effects of using genetically modified crops on a large scale over the long term" (p. 52). This lack of knowledge calls for more research to answer questions about the potential risks of GM crops. But efforts to conduct such research are impeded by anti-biotechnology activists who have destroyed test sites and research offices. "Open debate about the issues involved is essential, but physical attacks on research and testing efforts contribute little to the free exchange of ideas or the formulation of policies that will advance food security" (Pinstrup-Andersen and Cohen 2000: 168).

Finally, even supporters of agricultural biotechnology remind us that such technology is not a "silver bullet" that will end poverty and hunger. Rather, "it is critical that biotechnology be viewed as one part of a comprehensive sustainable poverty alleviation strategy, not a technological 'quick-fix' for world hunger and poverty" (Persley 2000: 16).

SOURCES: Brown, Lester R. 2001. "Eradicating Hunger: A Growing Challenge." In *State of the World 2001*, eds. Lester R. Brown, Christopher Flavin, and Hilary French, pp. 43–62. New York: W. W. Norton and Co.; Environmental Defense. 2000. *2000 Annual Report*. http://www.edf.org/sites/default/files/215_ACF75.pdf; Leisinger, Klaus M. 2000. "Ethical Challenges of Agricultural Biotechnology for Developing Countries." In *Agricultural Biotechnology and the Poor*, eds. G. J. Persley and M. M. Lantin, pp. 173–80. Washington, DC: Consultative Group on International Agricultural Research, The World Bank; Persley, G. J. 2000. "Agricultural Biotechnology and the Poor: Promethean Science." In *Agricultural Biotechnology and the Poor*, pp. 3–21; Pinstrup-Andersen, Per, and Marc J. Cohen. 2000. "Modern Biotechnology for Food and Agriculture: Risks and Opportunities for the Poor." In *Agricultural Biotechnology and the Poor*, pp. 159–68; Richer, David L. 2000. "Intellectual Property Protection: Who Needs It?" In *Agricultural Biotechnology and the Poor*, pp. 159–68; Serageldin, Ismail. 2000. "The Challenge of Poverty in the 21st Century: The Role of Science." In *Agricultural Biotechnology and the Poor*, pp. 25–32; Shah, Anup. 2001. "Terminator Technology." *Genetically Engineered Food*. January 1: http://www.globalissues.org/EnvIssues/GEFood/Terminator.asp?Print5True; Union of Concerned Scientists. 2001.http://www.ucsusa.org/agriculture/0biotechnology.html.

Understanding Poverty: National and International Issues

As we have seen in this chapter, economic prosperity has not been evenly distributed: the rich have become richer, while the poor have become poorer. Meanwhile, Canada has implemented measures that essentially weaken the safety net for the most impoverished segment of the population, to a large extent, children. The decrease in assistance to the poor is a major reason poverty rates have remained high, despite the economic prosperity of the country. Many families leaving welfare report struggling to get food, shelter, medical care, child care, and transportation. The effects of poverty on children perpetuate the cycle of poverty. Larin (1998) notes that "while it always has been possible for individuals to move up the economic ladder, the odds against it are high for individuals who suffer from the ill effects of poverty during childhood" (p. 26). Given the association between poverty and poor health and low educational attainment, poor children often grow up to be poor adults who are unable to escape poverty.

Canadians commonly believe that the rich are deserving and the poor are failures. Blaming poverty on individuals rather than on structural and cultural factors implies not only that poor individuals are responsible for their plight, but also that they are responsible for improving their condition. If we hold individuals accountable for their poverty, we fail to make society accountable for making investments in human capital that are necessary to alleviate poverty. Such human capital investments include providing health care, adequate food and housing, education, child care, and job training. Economist Lewis Hill (1998) believes that "the fundamental cause of perpetual poverty is the failure of…people to invest adequately in the human capital represented by impoverished children" (p. 299). Blaming the poor for their plight also fails to recognize that there are not enough jobs for those who want to work and that many jobs fail to pay wages that enable families to escape poverty. Finally, blaming the poor for their condition diverts attention away from the recognition that the wealthy—individuals and corporations—receive far more benefits in the form of wealthfare or corporate welfare, without the stigma of welfare.

Ending or reducing poverty begins with the recognition that doing so is a worthy ideal and an attainable goal. Imagine a world where everyone had comfortable shelter, plentiful food, adequate medical care, and education. If this imaginary world were achieved, and absolute poverty were effectively eliminated, what would the effects be on such social problems as crime, drug abuse, family problems (such as domestic violence, child abuse, and divorce), health problems, prejudice and racism, and international conflict?

It would be too costly to eliminate poverty—or would it? According to one source, the cost of eradicating poverty worldwide would be only about 1 percent of global income—and no more than 2 to 3 percent of national income in all but the poorest countries (United Nations Development Programme 1997). Certainly, the costs of allowing poverty to continue are much greater than that.

Critical Thinking

1. Is it possible for a decline in Canada's "poverty rates" to be accompanied by an increase in the numbers of individuals experiencing economic hardships?

2. According to the National Council of Welfare (1999c: 8), "Many social programs support families but childcare is the backbone of them all." However, as of 2006, the federal government has refused to fund a national daycare program and favours modest disbursements to families of young children instead. Investigate this policy recommendation and assess the reasons for opposing a national child-care program.

3. The poor have low rates of voting and thus have minimal influence on elected government officials and the policies they advocate. What strategies might be effective in increasing voter participation among the poor?

4. Oscar Lewis (1998) noted that "some see the poor as virtuous, upright, serene, independent, honest, secure, kind, simple, and happy, while others see them as evil, mean, violent, sordid, and criminal" (p. 9). Which view of the poor do you tend to hold? How have various social influences, such as parents, peers, media, social class, and education, shaped your views toward the poor?

5. Think about the ways in which poverty and wealth intersect with other aspects of a person's social status. With this intersectionality in mind, what do you think about the idea that individual effort is all it takes to succeed economically?

"Is It True?" Quiz: Answers

1 = false; 2 = true; 3 = false; 4 = false; 5 = false

Work and Unemployment

Outline

Is It True?

1. Trade unionists around the world are often harassed, threatened, or assassinated—or "disappear" or commit suicide—after being threatened as a result of their labour advocacy.

2. Compared to male workers, Canadian women workers are more likely to be unionized.

3. The world's top 200 corporations control more than one-fourth of all sales in the global economy, but employ less than 1 percent of the world's workforce.

4. Women and minorities in Canada are more likely than men to lose their jobs in a weak economy.

5. There are as many people in Canada who believe they could lose their jobs in the next few years as there are those who feel secure in their jobs.

Read more here: 1 = p. 398, 2 = pp. 398–399, 3 = pp. 376–377, 4 = p. 395, 5 = p. 392

Answers can be found on p. 410.

© Bloomberg/Getty Images

In this chapter, we examine problems of work and unemployment, including child and sweatshop labour, job dissatisfaction and alienation, work–family concerns, and labour strength and representation.

Before reading further, you may want to complete the "Attitudes toward Corporations" survey in the *Self and Society* feature of this chapter. It might be interesting to retake this survey after reading this chapter and see how your attitudes may have changed.

We begin by looking at the global economy.

Self and Society

Attitudes toward Corporations

Part One

How good a job do you think corporations are doing these days? Using letter grades like those in school, give corporations an A, B, C, D, or F in:

Letter Grade

1. Paying their employees good wages   _____

2. Being loyal to employees   _____

3. Making profits   _____

4. Keeping jobs in Canada   _____

Part Two

Here are some things some large corporations are doing that some people think are serious problems, while others think they are not serious problems. For each of the following practices, indicate whether you think this is a serious problem or not.

	Serious Problem	Not a Problem	Don't Know
1. Not providing health care and pension to employees	_____	_____	_____
2. Not paying employees enough so that they and their families can keep up with the cost of living	_____	_____	_____
3. Paying CEOs 200 times what their employees make	_____	_____	_____
4. Laying off large numbers of workers even when the company is profitable	_____	_____	_____

Part Three

Which of the following statements comes closer to your view? (check one)

9A. Two major problems with the economy today are government waste and inefficiency. Excessive government spending and high taxes burden middle-class families and slow economic growth. Our government debt drives up interest rates, making it much harder for businesses to invest and create jobs.

OR

9B. A major problem with the economy today is politicians catering to the interests of powerful corporations and wealthy campaign contributors at the expense of working families. That is why politicians are not doing anything to stop large corporations from laying off large numbers of employees, denying health benefits, moving jobs overseas, and raiding pension funds.

9A. _____   9B. _____

10A. Wasteful and inefficient government is preventing the middle class from getting ahead and doing better. Excessive government spending and high taxes burden working families and slow economic growth. The budget deficit drives up interest rates and taxes, hurts consumers and business, and reduces job-creating investments. Red tape and excessive regulation are hurting business.

OR

10B. Corporate greed is preventing the middle class from getting ahead and doing better. In the past, when people did their jobs well, they could earn a decent wage and provide a better life for their children. Now, corporate Canada is squeezing their employees—cutting wages, downsizing jobs, and eliminating pensions and health benefits. Companies say they cannot afford to treat employees better, but many have growing profits, record stock prices, and huge salaries for their executives.

10A. _____   10B. _____

11A. Large corporations are laying people off, cutting benefits, and moving jobs overseas mainly because they have gotten greedy and are squeezing employees to maximize profits.

OR

11B. Large corporations are laying people off, cutting benefits, and moving jobs overseas mainly because they have to stay in business and provide jobs.

11A. _____   11B. _____

FOR COMPARISON

You may want to compare your answers to this survey with responses from a national sample of American adults. (Note: In Question 4, survey respondents were asked about keeping jobs in America. Question 10B referred to corporate America).

Part One

(Percentages do not total 100 due to individuals who responded "Don't know.")

1. 11%	2. 10%	3. 52%	4. 12%
26%	16%	26%	16%
36%	28%	9%	31%
12%	23%	3%	20%
7%	19%	2%	18%

Part Two

	Serious	Not Serious	Don't Know
5.	82%	15%	3%
6.	76%	19%	5%
7.	79%	14%	7%
8.	81%	14%	5%

Part Three

9A 33%	9B 40%	(21% answered "Both," and 6% answered "Don't know")
10A 28%	10B 46%	(22% answered "Both," and 4% answered "Don't know")
11A 70%	11B 22%	(7% answered "Don't know")

SOURCE: Adapted from "Corporate Irresponsibility: There Ought to Be Laws." 1996. EDK Poll, Washington, DC: Preamble Center for Public Policy, December 12, 1998. www.preamble.org/polledk.html. Used by permission.

11.1 The Global Context: The Economy in the Twenty-First Century

global economy

An interconnected network of economic activity that transcends national borders.

In recent decades, innovations in communication and information technology have spawned the emergence of a **global economy**—an interconnected network of economic activity that transcends national borders and spans the world. The globalization of economic activity means that, more and more, our jobs, the products and services we buy, and our nation's political policies and agendas influence and are influenced by economic activities occurring around the world. After summarizing the two main economic systems in the world—capitalism and socialism—we look at the emergence of corporate multinationalism. We then describe how industrialization and postindustrialization have changed the nature of work.

In 1999, 11 of the 15 European Union nations began making the transition from their national currency to a new common currency—the euro—that has locked them together financially. The adoption of the euro reflects the increasing globalization of economic institutions. The term **economic institution** refers to the structure and means by which a society produces, distributes, and consumes goods and services. While the first years of the euro zone brought increased power to nations that had previously had weak currencies, the interdependency of the European Union (EU) has also brought significant difficulty to the people of the EU. The recent financial crises in euro zone countries have combined with debt management problems across the EU, but where the major news media tend to report these as problems of individual state governments, sociological work on the economic problems of the EU notes that it is the financial industry's ability to offload its problems onto state governments that we need to pay attention to (Deutschmann 2011: 17–20). When states rather than industries are held accountable for financial collapse, it is the citizens who end up paying the price. Deutschmann explains that the problems of Greece, Ireland, Spain, Italy, and Belgium are related to the private financial industry crisis that emerged in the United States in 2007–08:

economic institution

The structure and means by which a society produces, distributes, and consumes goods and services.

> the American subprime crisis [was] the prelude of a global crisis, resulting from a long term over-accumulation of private financial assets, which additionally had been promoted by aggressive expansionary strategies of the international finance industry. A tremendous volume of uncovered titles had been piled up which due to its dimensions and inherent "systemic risks" could not simply be written off. Therefore the crisis became a political issue. The US- and European Governments intervened by voluminous parcels of credit, credit guarantees, subsidies and public expenditures in order to prevent a deepening of the collapse. They exchanged "bad", defaulted private assets for "good" public bonds, thus actually guaranteeing the profitability of private capital by tax money. On the one hand that helped to bring about an immediate stabilization, on the other hand, public debts exploded due to the costs of the bailout programs and to the fiscal strains resulting from the economic downturn. The increase of public debt had been even more marked in the US and in Britain than in Euroland. As a result, the financial markets became suspicious about the credit worthiness of the very agency that saved them from collapse, the national states. This means that the financial industry has managed to externalize her [sic] own problem and to transform it into a problem of the states. (2011: 17)

Deutschmann suggests that those nations most targeted as financially weak would not now be in such large-scale difficulty if they had maintained their own currencies (2011: 18), though Peter North argues in the same issue of *Economic Sociology* that the use of individual currencies for nations provides no guarantee of nation-state stability. Instead, North suggests that nations in the EU might do better with regional currencies that would operate alongside the euro (2011: 25). These smaller, regional currencies—such as the *Roland*, used in Bremen, and the *Chiemgauer*, used in Bavaria—benefit local communities for the trade of locally produced goods, food, and services. These micro-currencies exist alongside the euro but are backed by local banks and co-operatives, which allows for a high level of user adoption and robust use in regional trade operations (ibid).

The reason that people in the EU may want to adopt local currencies for use alongside the euro is that it restores local economic power to workers, merchants, and regional services, making people less vulnerable to the exploitation of a financial industry that takes big risks and then offloads its failures onto states to manage. Local currencies can help protect regions against negative consequences of national debt ratios that suddenly balloon because of fallout from financial industry crises. If local currencies prove to be helpful and viable we may see similar monetary strategies adopted outside the EU.

Capitalism and Socialism

The principal economic systems in the world are capitalism and socialism. Under **capitalism**, private individuals or groups invest capital (money, technology, machines) to produce goods and services to sell for a profit in a competitive market. Capitalism is characterized by economic motivation through profit, the determination of prices and wages primarily through supply and demand, and the absence of governmental intervention in the economy. More people are working today in a capitalist economy than ever before in history (Went 2000). Critics of capitalism argue that it creates too many social evils, including alienated workers, poor working conditions, near-poverty wages, unemployment, a polluted and depleted environment, and world conflict over resources.

Pure capitalism (known as "hands off" capitalism) exists only when market forces can operate without interference from the government. However, in Canada, many restraints to the laissez-faire model have traditionally existed. *State capitalism* is a form of capitalism in which private citizens own the means of production and pursue profits, but do so within a vast system of laws designed to protect the welfare of the population. In Canada, state capitalism also refers to public or state investment in sectors of the economy that could be private. Canada's economy was once described as "a strange mix of interventionism and free-market policies" (Hallsworth 1993: 445); however, since the 1980s, the state has begun to withdraw from the private sector by selling off public assets (e.g., Petro-Canada, Air Canada) and through an ongoing process of deregulation (e.g., the North American Free Trade Agreement, the reduction of interprovincial trade barriers, and the "open skies" agreement with the United States).

Socialism emphasizes public rather than private ownership. Theoretically, goods and services are equitably distributed according to the needs of the

capitalism
An economic system in which private individuals or groups invest capital to produce goods and services, for a profit, in a competitive market.

socialism
An economic ideology that emphasizes public rather than private ownership. Theoretically, goods and services are equitably distributed according to the needs of the citizens.

convergence hypothesis

The argument that capitalist countries will adopt elements of socialism and socialist countries will adopt elements of capitalism; that is, they will converge.

corporate multinationalism

The practice of corporations having their home base in one country and branches, or affiliates, in other countries.

citizens. Whereas capitalism emphasizes individual freedom, socialism emphasizes social equality.

Advocates for capitalism and socialism claim that the one they support results in economic well-being for society and for its members. In reality, both capitalist and socialist countries have been unable to fulfill their promises. Although the overall standard of living is higher in capitalist countries, so is economic inequality. Some theorists suggest that capitalist countries will adopt elements of socialism and socialist countries will adopt elements of capitalism. This idea, known as the **convergence hypothesis**, is reflected in the economies of Germany, France, and Sweden, which are sometimes called "integrated economies" because they have elements of both capitalism and socialism.

Corporate Multinationalism

Corporate multinationalism is the practice of corporations having a home base in one country and branches, or affiliates, in other countries. Corporate multinationalism allows businesses to avoid import tariffs and costs associated with transporting goods to another country. Access to raw materials, cheap foreign labour, and avoidance of government regulations and labour laws also drive corporate multinationalism. "By moving production plants abroad, business managers may be able to work foreign employees for long hours under dangerous conditions at low pay, pollute the environment with impunity, and pretty much have their way with local communities. Then the business may be able to ship its goods back to its home country at lower costs and bigger profits" (Caston 1998: 274–75).

Although multinationalization provides jobs for managers, secures profits for investors, and helps Canada compete in the global economy, it also has "far-reaching and detrimental consequences" (Epstein et al. 1993: 206). Corporate multinationalization must take its share of the blame for an array of social problems, such as poverty resulting from fewer jobs, urban decline resulting from factories moving away, and racial and ethnic tensions resulting from competition for jobs. In addition, as Maule (1999: 1536) points out, "[l]ess developed countries argue that they have traded political independence for economic and cultural dependence. Politically, there remains concern over the extent to which multinational corporations are used as instruments of foreign policy by the governments of countries where parent companies are located. Culturally, the concern is over the loss of national identity." Noting that the rapid increase of foreign ownership in the Canadian economy after World War I was linked to the rise of multinational corporations, economic nationalists have expressed concern over "the special problems created by this type of investment, particularly the stunted and distorted pattern of economic development" and the broader impact of multinationals on Canadian society, identity, and sovereignty (Rotstein 1999: 717). For example, Bellan (1999) points out that

> Huge and increasing amounts of money have to be remitted to U.S. owners in the form of dividends on their investment and contributions by branch plants toward head office costs of administration, research, product development and advertising.

A large proportion of these payments must be made in U.S. dollars. . . . The consequence is that a very large fraction of the U.S. dollars that Canada earns by its exports must be used to make interest and dividend payments and branch plant remittances to U.S. firms. (pp. 884–85)

Second, Bellan charges that multinational corporations have "carried on their Canadian operations to serve their own best interests, not those of Canada," with industrial research and development that are "essential to industrial innovation and growth" generally conducted in their U.S. facilities rather than at their Canadian branch plants. Third, he notes that multinationals show no particular loyalty to Canada when the demand for their products falls or a cheaper source of supplies or labour is found in another country.

Industrialization, Postindustrialization, and the Changing Nature of Work

The nature of work has been shaped by the **Industrial Revolution**, the period between the mid–eighteenth century and the early nineteenth century when the factory system was introduced in England. Industrialization dramatically altered the nature of work: machines replaced hand tools; and steam, gasoline, and electric power replaced human or animal power. Industrialization also led to the development of mass-production assembly lines and an increased division of labour. Factories contributed to the emergence of large cities, where earlier informal social interactions dominated by primary relationships were replaced by formal interactions centred on secondary groups. Instead of the family-centred economy characteristic of an agricultural society, people began to work outside the home for wages.

Postindustrialization refers to the shift from an industrial economy dominated by manufacturing jobs to an economy dominated by service-oriented, information-intensive occupations. Postindustrialization is characterized by a highly educated workforce, automated and computerized production methods, increased government involvement in economic issues, and a higher standard of living (Bell 1973). Like industrialization before it, postindustrialization has transformed the nature of work.

The three fundamental work sectors (primary, secondary, and tertiary) reflect the major economic transformation in society—the Industrial Revolution and the Postindustrial Revolution. The **primary work sector** involves the production of raw materials and food goods. In developing countries with little industrialization, about 60 percent of the labour force works in agricultural activities; in Canada less than 3 percent of the workforce is in farming (Bracey 1995; *Report on the World Social Situation* 1997; Statistics Canada 1998). The **secondary work sector** involves the production of manufactured goods from raw materials (e.g., paper from wood). The **tertiary work sector** includes professional, managerial, technical-support, and service jobs. The transition to a postindustrial society is marked by a decrease in manufacturing jobs and an increase in service and information-technology jobs in the tertiary work sector. For example, even though the high-tech sector was struggling on several fronts in 2000, the demand for computer specialists led the growth in the Canadian labour force during the 1990s, most notably in

Industrial Revolution

The period between the mid-eighteenth and the early nineteenth centuries when machines and factories became the primary means for producing goods.

postindustrialization

The shift from an industrial economy dominated by manufacturing jobs to an economy dominated by service-oriented, information-intensive occupations.

work sectors (primary, secondary, tertiary)

The division of the labour force into distinct categories (primary, secondary, and tertiary) based on the types of goods or services produced.

the latter half of the decade (Statistics Canada 2003: 8). Between 1991 and 2001, almost one-half of the growth in the Canadian labour force "occurred in highly skilled occupations that normally require university qualifications, while low skilled occupations requiring high-school or less accounted for only a quarter of the increase" (Statistics Canada 2003: 5). Consider as well that, in 2001, the "top 10 disappearing jobs" in Canada were, in order: typist; typesetter; watch/clock repairer; statistical clerk; fisher; bank teller; telephone operator; tool and die maker; farmer; and locomotive operator. In that year, the "top 10 growth careers" in Canada were, in order: in-home nurse; nurse practitioner; physician; teacher, special education; pharmacist; programmer; psychiatrist; radiology technician; registered nurse; and physiotherapist (Ash 2001: 194).

In a postindustrial society, highly skilled and technological personnel are needed, but Canada struggles to find personnel within its domestic population. Data from the 2001 census indicate that Canada has increasingly looked to immigration as a source of skills and knowledge. The 2001 census "showed a dramatic increase in the proportion of recent immigrants working in high skilled occupations—those that normally require a university education" (Statistics Canada 2003: 13). While immigrants who arrived between 1986 and 1990 accounted for 13 percent of the workforce in highly skilled occupations in 1991, in 2001, recent immigrants aged 25 to 64 who arrived during the 1990s represented almost one-quarter (24 percent) of the workforce in highly skilled occupations.

Recent immigrants have played an important role in the growth of highly skilled occupations in Canada over the 1990s, particularly in computer-related occupations and accounting. The proportion of new immigrants aged 25 to 44 who worked in information technology occupations rose from about 3 percent in 1991 to 12 percent in 2001. New immigrants were also overrepresented in engineering and natural sciences occupations. "In 2001, three percent of recent immigrants aged 25 to 44 in the labour force were in engineering compared to only one percent of the Canadian born. Similarly, 1.2 percent of recent immigrants were in natural sciences occupations compared to 0.6 percent of the Canadian born" (Statistics Canada 2003: 14). In developing countries, many individuals with the highest level of skill and education leave the country in search of work abroad, leading to the phenomenon known as the **brain drain** (see also Chapter 12). Although employers in developed countries benefit, developing countries lose valuable labour.

brain drain

The phenomenon whereby many individuals with the highest level of skill and education leave the country in search of work abroad.

The Age of Information Technology

The idea that we live in an "information age" has become popular, with news stories frequently devoting attention to the new conditions of work and ever-changing means of managing and relaying information. For example, the Waterloo-based Research In Motion (RIM) Corporation, maker of the BlackBerry, is lauded as a domestic contributor with a central position in the world market for wireless communication and data transfer.

However, popular attention is also paid to the kinds of problems that workers outfitted with BlackBerry and similar devices may face because "the gadget takes the workplace anywhere the worker goes" (NPR 2005). The resulting tendency for employees to become obsessive about answering the emails and calls that come through on their BlackBerry devices has led to the creation of the term "crackberry," referring to the inability to shut off the connection to work

Clinical psychiatrist Edward Hallowell remarks that workers with mobile devices such as the BlackBerry are increasingly burdened, to the point of collapse, under mountains of data and overwhelming employer expectations that they be perpetually "on call" (NPR 2005).

In professions defined by information relay, workers may suffer from **"technostress,"** which arises from having too many tasks to perform simultaneously, while also keeping up with perpetually changing demands to operate new and emerging technologies with ease (Clark and Kalin 1996: 30). Though written before the advent of portable communication devices for receiving wireless email and data, Clark and Kalin observed librarians at a national conference "who would never dream of having their phone calls or postal mail forwarded to the conference now feel compelled to stand in long lines to check their e-mail—even though the very people with whom they regularly communicate are likely attending that conference!" As workplaces go, postsecondary institutions have long maintained vague distinctions between workplace and home, with many professors and college instructors frequently working from home, and with some schools traditionally having faculty dons and college deans who live on campus. The world of IT (information technology) extends that tradition, bringing new problems and benefits to postsecondary education. Internet connections to libraries and use of communication technologies can move research and teaching into the home as more and more institutions offer distance education, and increase research demands on faculty. Being able to work from home may positively influence faculty life by allowing high productivity while maintaining connection to home-life and family; however, it comes with a downside, a demand for rapid responses from students accustomed to a "culture of instant information and instant response. The learner's sense of the 'rolling present' can make faculty feel pressured to spend large amounts of time interacting with . . . students who frequently perceive . . . education as 'always open' . . ." (McLean 2006). It is not unusual for faculty to report receiving several emails in a single day from a single student who, with increasing incivility, demands to know why the initial email has not yet been answered.

In addition to the problems of stress related to technology-saturated work environments, constant change in the technologies can result in three basic problems in the workplace: first, it requires workers to alter their skill sets constantly; second, the skills workers learn tend to be in the area of specific applications rather than in problem solving and decision making, so are not transferable; and third, those workers in higher level professional and managerial positions tend to receive more training and more skill upgrading than those in the lower ranks, which exaggerates the division in skill sets over time (Krahn and Lowe 2002: 297).

The use of new technologies in the production and manufacturing sector can promote the deskilling of jobs as skilled labourers are replaced with automated machines. Krahn and Lowe (2002: 296) note that automated machinery has not only replaced skilled workers in specific trades but where "[p]reviously, a group of workers with a broad range of skills relieved others, one at a time, from their various positions on the line. With the new technology every one

technostress

Stress that arises specifically from having too many tasks to perform simultaneously, while keeping up with perpetually changing demands to operate new and emerging technologies with ease.

took breaks of the same time, so that the multiskilled relief workers were no longer needed."

Finally, even those professional workers who are highly paid find that their conditions of work are extremely competitive and highly unstable, with frequent changes of both employer and career. The IT worker becomes a "free-floating individual, connected on-line to a variety of task-performing organizations, ever competing for resources and personal support, and assuming limited responsibilities towards a limited people for limited time" (Carnoy and Castells 1997: 35). Carnoy and Castells characterize such work conditions as a case of perpetual and progressive deterioration against which old methods of organizing under industrialization no longer work. To cope with this new reality, IT workers are more and more frequently turning to an older means of organizing, one that predates industrialism and trade unions: professional guilds. Although guilds have no ability to secure workers' rights through collective bargaining, Benner (2003) finds that guilds can foster a protective and developmental community in which workers compete together, rather than against one another:

> contemporary guilds have improved their members' career opportunities, through improving skill development, facilitating access to new job opportunities, and organizing advocacy efforts. Thus, given the factors that have given rise to these new occupational communities are unlikely to change, efforts to build a collective action through occupational solidarity can be an important component of broader strategies aimed at building security for workers in the information economy. (p. 182)

11.2 Sociological Theories of Work and the Economy

Numerous theories in economics, political science, and history address the nature of work and the economy. In sociology, structural-functionalism, conflict theory, and symbolic interactionism serve as theoretical lenses through which we may better understand work and economic issues and activities. In addition to the central theoretical perspectives traditionally applied to issues in work and economic systems, this edition of the text adds the increasingly important observations and critical tools provided by feminist and queer theory perspectives. Feminist and queer theory perspectives take a position focused on the unique challenges for GLBT persons and women who, as workers and economic contributors, contend with economic and work structures founded on a heterosexist division of labour.

Structural-Functionalist Perspective

The structural-functionalist perspective holds that the economic institution is one of the most important social institutions, providing fundamental necessities common to all human societies, including food, clothing, and shelter, and thus contributing to social stability. After the basic survival needs of a society are met, surplus materials and wealth may be allocated to other social uses, such as maintaining military protection from enemies, supporting political and religious leaders, providing formal education, supporting an expanding population, and providing entertainment and recreational activities. Societal development is dependent on an economic surplus in a society (Lenski and Lenski 1987).

Although the economic institution is functional for society, elements of it may be dysfunctional. For example, before industrialization, agrarian societies had a low division of labour in that few work roles were available to members of society. Limited work roles meant that society's members shared similar roles and thus developed similar norms and values (Durkheim [1893] 1966). In contrast, industrial societies are characterized by many work roles, or a high division of labour, and cohesion is based not on the similarity of people and their roles but on their interdependence. People in industrial societies need the skills and services that others provide. The lack of common norms and values in industrialized societies may result in **anomie**—a state of normlessness—which is linked to a variety of social problems, crime, drug addiction, and violence among them (see Chapters 3 and 4).

Conflict Perspective

According to Karl Marx, capitalism is responsible for the inequality and conflict within and between societies. The ruling class controls the economic system for its own benefit and exploits and oppresses the working masses. While structural-functionalism views the economic institution as benefiting society as a whole, conflict theory holds that capitalism benefits an elite class that controls not only the economy, but other aspects of society as well—the media, politics and law, education, and religion.

For example, corporate power is reflected in the policies of the International Monetary Fund (IMF) and the World Bank, which pressure developing countries to open their economies to foreign corporations, promoting export production at the expense of local consumption, encouraging the exploitation of labour as a means of attracting foreign investment, and hastening the degradation of natural resources as countries sell their forests and minerals to earn money to pay back loans (see Chapter 10). Ambrose (1998) asserts that "for some time now, the IMF has been the chief architect of the global economy, using debt leverage to force governments around the world to give big corporations and billionaires everything they want—low taxes, cheap labour, loose regulations—so they will locate in their countries" (p. 5).

Treaties such as the North American Free Trade Agreement (NAFTA) and the General Agreement on Tariffs and Trade (GATT) also benefit corporations. They provide corporations with greater access to foreign markets, many say, at the expense of workers. "These laws increasingly allow corporations to go anywhere and do anything they like, and prohibit workers and the governments that supposedly represent them from doing much about it" (Danaher 1998: 1).

According to the conflict perspective, work trends that benefit employees, such as work site health promotion programs and work–family policies (discussed later in this chapter) are not the result of altruistic or humanitarian concern for workers' well-being. Rather, corporate leaders recognize that these programs and policies result in higher job productivity and lower health-care costs. They are thus good for the bottom line.

anomie

A state of normlessness in which norms and values are weak or unclear; results from rapid social change and is linked to many social problems, including crime, drug addiction, and violence.

Symbolic Interactionist Perspective

According to symbolic interactionism, the work role is a central part of a person's identity. For example, identifying a person as a truck driver provides a different social meaning than identifying someone as a physician. The title of a person's work status also gives meaning and self-worth to the individual. A job is one of an individual's most important statuses; for many, it is the master, or the most significant, status.

In this model, distribution of economic compensation may become a primary measure of self-worth obtained through another's recognition of one's value. Heidegren (2004: 367) explains that "within a capitalist society . . . struggles for recognition mainly relate to the principle of achievement: the experience of disrespect for their achievements leads social groups to struggle for greater social esteem for raising claims to an economic redistribution in their advantage."

As symbolic interactionists note, definitions and meanings influence behaviour. Meanings and definitions of child labour (discussed later) contribute to its perpetuation. In some countries, children learn to regard working as a necessary and important responsibility and rite of passage, rather than as an abuse of human rights. Some children look forward to becoming bonded to a master "in the same way that . . . children [in our society] look forward to a communion or getting a driver's license" (Silvers 1996: 83).

Symbolic interactionism emphasizes that attitudes and behaviours are influenced by interaction with others. The applications of symbolic interactionism in the workplace are numerous—employers and managers are concerned with using interpersonal interaction techniques that achieve the attitudes and behaviours they want from their employees; union organizers are concerned with using interpersonal interaction techniques that persuade workers to unionize; and job-training programs are concerned with using interpersonal interaction techniques to motivate participants.

Feminist Perspectives

Because ideology structures the institutions of economy and family as a continuing distinction between a public and male sphere and a private and female sphere, many feminists concentrate on the challenges faced by women who operate in both worlds. Liberal feminists tend to focus on policy initiatives ensuring equal pay for equal work, family–work balance, and child-labour concerns. Though there have been some hard-won successes, the goal has been thwarted by determining what counts as "equal," by persistent devaluation of home life, and by contradictory stances on child labour (all discussed in this chapter).

Feminist work illuminates the constraints of gender-role divisions between the public and private worlds of paid employment and domestic work. Feminists observe that the distinction is very much based on classist presuppositions about what men and women are *supposed to do* in their gender roles. That is, to accept the idea that women do not work—or that they *should* not work—is to forget that some women *must* work for pay outside the home. This is not to say that we should ignore economist Marilyn Waring's (1988) detailed analysis on the significant value of domestic labour; rather, it is to acknowledge that entry into paid labour may not be a matter of choice but of necessity for women—just as much as it is for men.

Providing a sense of how we came to such a contradictory present, Jane Errington (1993) illuminates the subtle historical shifts in sensibilities about work, gender, and the needs of a changing Canada in the years around Confederation:

> the transition from pioneering communities to a stratified Victorian society was largely complete. All women were expected to remain within the private sphere of the home and those who could not were allowed to pursue only those endeavors . . . considered natural extensions of a true woman's place—teaching, nursing, and domestic service. . . . Ironically, as the ideology of dynasty city became increasingly entrenched, the industrialized nation of British North America was simultaneously encouraging the complete division of public and private spheres and forcing a growing number of unskilled women into the factories as poorly paid wage labourers. (p. 68)

Aware that gender roles constrain the lives of men as well as women, some feminists assess problems that men can face in a world that defines "proper" masculinity in contradictory terms of fatherhood and worker/economic provider. Susan Halford (2006: 385) argues that the worlds of fatherhood and work no longer have to compete and that whatever challenges new information technologies pose (discussed later in this chapter), they may also hold the promise of breaking the divide between work and home, allowing workers to maintain greater contact with their families without impairing their work productivity.

Christina Hughes (2004) reminds readers that class background, cultural capital, and ethnicity may remain as persistent causes of self-limiting behaviours, of not wanting to trespass "a step too far" (p. 539). An example is how women from marginalized groups are likely to see all the ways that they "do not belong" in a given sector or workplace. Hughes also notes, however, that women can use their recognition of their class origins to remain grounded in principles that matter to them (p. 542). Avoiding the "step too far" is about retaining honesty and integrity; it's about not "selling out."

Issues regarding employment status, class, immigration, child labour, racism, and other forms of discrimination are also important feminist concerns.

Queer Theory Perspectives

Among the many important contributions of queer theory to the understanding of work and economy is a corrective to the traditional view that the home sphere is heterosexual. Even in a current context where most families require two incomes to get by, the division of family and work, based as it is on a gendered division of labour, makes the normative assumption that women work by choice, not out of necessity, and that all women have male "breadwinners" to support them. More generally, it is now well established that GLBT persons have to maintain constant awareness, called **discrimination management**, about how safe it is to reveal their sexuality in workplaces, where it is generally assumed that everyone is heterosexual (Adams et al. 2005: 215). In short, while their co-workers can freely discuss upcoming weddings, births, breakups, and so forth, GLBT workers face worries about homophobia in the workplace that limit expression and discussion of their lives and identities.

Current scholarship on GLBT workers also reveals unique problems when class-based vulnerability intersects with homophobia at work. Elizabeth McDermott's (2006) research shows that lesbians face not only sexism, but also homophobia in

discrimination management

Individual efforts to prevent being targeted for discriminatory behaviours in the workplace.

the workplace; she notes as well that working-class lesbians tend to work in environments where "being women does not make sense [to their co-workers] except in a heterosexual relationship" so they "masquerade" as heterosexual just to survive (p. 204). McDermott finds that working-class lesbians face greater stress on their psychological well-being than other lesbians do, or than straight women do as a result of sexism (p. 205).

Queer work and activism focused on work and the economy not only is concerned with GLBT people as workers, but also argues that as a marginalized group, the queer community is uniquely placed to offer serious social justice–oriented critiques of capitalism. Canadian sociologist Alan Sears, for example, cautions against getting too excited about marketing ploys that structure the GLBT community as an affluent "niche market" in which "our real diversity is obscured by the dominance of homogeneous images [of buff, young, affluent, consumers]" (2005: 109). Instead, Sears argues that the queer community should retain and foster "the best of the liberationist politics that emerged after Stonewall: the militancy, the breadth of vision and the transformative commitments" (p. 109).

11.3 Problems of Work and Unemployment

Next, we examine unemployment and other problems associated with work. Problems of discrimination in the workplace based on gender, age, race and ethnicity, and sexual orientation appear in other chapters. Here, we discuss problems concerning child labour, health and safety hazards in the workplace, job dissatisfaction and alienation, work–family concerns, unemployment and underemployment, and labour unions and their struggles for workers' rights.

Child Labour: A Global Problem

child labour

Children performing work that is hazardous, that interferes with their education, or that harms their health or physical, mental, spiritual, or moral development.

Child labour involves children performing work that is hazardous, that interferes with a child's education, or that harms a child's health or physical, mental, spiritual, or moral development (U.S. Department of Labor 1995). In spring 2006, the B.C. legislature ruled that children could enter into paid labour at age 12, while in the rest of Canada the entry age remains set at 14. Even though virtually every country in the world has laws that limit or prohibit the extent to which children can be employed, child labour persists worldwide.

An estimated 250 million children between 5 and 14 work for a living (Human Rights Watch 2001). Child labourers work in factories, workshops, construction sites, mines, quarries, and fields, on deep-sea fishing boats, at home, and on the street. In Egypt, over one million children aged 7 to 12 work each year in cotton pest management. When they are perceived to be slowing down, they endure routine beatings with wooded switches by their supervisors. They face exposure to heat and pesticides ("Underage and Unprotected" 2001). Children typically earn the equivalent of $1 per day and work from 7:00 a.m. to 6:00 p.m. with one midday break, seven days a week.

Children as young as five or six also work in domestic service. In one Latin American country, an estimated 22 percent of all working children are employed as servants (International Labour Organization [ILO] 2000). This form of child labour is difficult to monitor because of the hidden nature of the practice.

Children additionally number among the millions of people worldwide who work in **sweatshops**—work environments characterized by less-than-minimum wage pay, excessively long hours of work (often without overtime pay), unsafe or inhumane working conditions, abusive treatment of workers by employers, and the lack of worker organizations. Sweatshop conditions occur in a wide variety of industries, including garment production, manufacturing, mining, and agriculture. The dangerous conditions of sweatshops result in high rates of illness, injury, and death. The International Labour Organization (ILO) estimates 1.4 million workers worldwide die on the job or from occupational disease each year (*Multinational Monitor* 2000). In one tragic example of death resulting from sweatshop conditions, at least 53 workers, including 10 children, were burned to death in a fire at a Sagar Chowdury garment factory in Bangladesh (Hargis 2001). The fire, caused by an electrical short circuit, engulfed the entire factory with 900 workers who were *locked inside*. Local residents and firefighters broke open the locked gates of the building and rescued survivors.

Although Canada supports the ILO's International Programme for the Elimination of Child Labour (ILO 2006: 224), Alberta and British Columbia have both lowered the minimum age of employment to include young people aged 12 to 14 in sectors previously closed to people so young. The Saskatchewan Federation of Labour (2006: 2) notes that these changes "contravene the International Labour Organization (ILO's) Minimum Age Convention, 1973 (No. 138), which states that 'The minimum age . . . shall not be less than the age of completion of compulsory schooling and, in any case, shall not be less than 15 years.'"

Bonded labour—an extreme form of child labour—refers to the repayment of a debt through labour. Typically, an employer loans money to parents, who then give the employer their children as labourers to repay the debt. Sometimes the child is taken far away from the family to work; other times the child works in the same village and continues to live at home. The children are unable to work off the debt because of high interest rates, low wages, and wage deductions for meals, lodging, and mistakes made at work (U.S. Department of Labor 1995). Bonded labour is like slavery; a bonded worker is not free to leave the workplace. Between 10 and 20 million children in the world are forced to work as bonded labourers (Parker 1998). Bonded labour is most common in India, Nepal, Bangladesh, and Pakistan. The chapter's *The Human Side* feature provides a sense of the personal toll exacted from children workers in Pakistan.

Causes of Child Labour Poverty, economic exploitation, social values, and lack of access to education are factors contributing to the persistence of child labour. One mother in Bangladesh whose 12-year-old daughter works up to 14 hours a day in a garment sweatshop explained: "Children shouldn't have to work. . . . But if she didn't, we'd go hungry" (Parker 1998: 47). The economic advantages to industries that profit from child labour perpetuate the practice. Traditional social values have also contributed to child labour. In the words of one employer in Pakistan who uses child labour, "Child labour is a tradition the West cannot understand and must not attempt to change" (Silvers 1996: 86). Finally, child labour results from failure to provide education to all children. The education system in Pakistan, for example, can accommodate about one-third of the country's school-aged children, leaving the remainder to join the child labour pool.

Child Prostitution and Trafficking One of the worst forms of child labour is child prostitution and child trafficking. Although it is impossible to identify how

sweatshops

Work environments characterized by less than minimum wage pay, excessively long hours of work often without overtime pay, unsafe or inhumane working conditions, abusive treatment of workers by employers, or the lack of worker organizations aimed at negotiating better work conditions.

bonded labour

The repayment of a debt through labour.

The *Human Side*

Child Labour in Pakistan

Like most other countries, Pakistan has laws prohibiting child labour and indentured servitude. However, these laws are largely ignored, and about 11 million children aged 4 to 14 work under brutal and squalid conditions. Children make up about a quarter of the unskilled workforce in Pakistan and can be found in virtually every factory, field, and workshop. They earn on average a third of the adult wage. The following excerpt from an Atlantic Monthly report describes child labour in Pakistan (Silvers 1996).

Soon after I arrived in Pakistan, I arranged a trip to a town whose major factories were rumored to enslave very young children. I found myself hoping during the journey there that the children I saw working in fields, on the roads, at the marketplaces, would prepare me for the worst. No amount of preparation could have lessened the shock and revulsion I felt on entering a sporting-goods factory in the town of Sialkot...where scores of children, most of them aged 5 to 10, produce soccer balls by hand for 40 rupees, or about $1.20, a day. The children work 80 hours a week in near-total darkness and total silence. According to the foreman, the darkness is both an economy and a precautionary measure; child-rights activists have difficulty taking

photographs and gathering evidence of wrongdoing if the lighting is poor. The silence is to ensure product quality: "If the children speak, they are not giving their complete attention to the product and are liable to make errors." The children are permitted one 30-minute meal break each day; they are punished if they take longer. They are also punished if they fall asleep, if their workbenches are sloppy, if they waste material or miscut a pattern, if they complain of mistreatment to their parents or speak to strangers outside the factory...Punishments are doled out in a storage closet at the rear of the factory...Children are hung upside down by their knees, starved, caned, or lashed...The punishment room is a standard feature of a Pakistani factory, as common as a lunchroom at an...assembly plant.

Here are brick kilns where five-year-olds work hip-deep in slurry pits, where adolescent girls stoke furnaces in 160-degree heat. Here are tanneries where nursing mothers mix vats of chemical dye, textile mills where eight-year-olds tend looms and breathe air thick with cotton dust...A carpet workshop... was...about the size of a subway car, and about as appealing. The long, narrow room contained a dozen upright looms. On each rough-hewn workbench between the looms squatted a carpet weaver. The room was dark and airless. Such light as there was came from a single ceiling fixture, two of its four bulbs burned out. A thermometer read 105

degrees, and the mud walls were hot to the touch....

The two youngest were brothers named Akbar and Ashraf, aged eight and nine. They had been bonded to the carpet master at age five, and now worked six days a week at the shop. A hand-knotted carpet is made by tying short lengths of fine colored thread to a lattice of heavier white threads. The process is labour-intensive and tedious: a single four-by-six-foot carpet contains well over a million knots and takes an experienced weaver four to six months to complete...Each carpet...would retail...[in North America] for about $2000—more than the boy would earn in 10 years. Abkar revealed that, "the master screams at us all the time, and sometimes he beats us...We're slapped often. I was beaten 10 days ago after I made many errors of colour in a carpet. He struck me with his fist quite hard on the face...I was fined 1000 rupees and made to correct the errors by working two days straight."...The fine was added to Akbar's debt, and would extend his "apprenticeship" by several months...

Akbar declared that "staying here longer fills me with dread. I know I must learn a trade. We'd like to play with our friends. This is not the way children should live."

SOURCE: Silver, Jonathan. 1996. From "Child Labor in Pakistan." © 1996 by Jonathan Silvers as first published in *The Atlantic Monthly*, February 1996. Reprinted by permission.

prevalent child prostitution is, research estimates suggest that the problem is widespread. For example, surveys have identified 3000 child prostitutes in Montreal, 2930 in Athens, and up to 300 000 in the United States (Dorman 2001). Child prostitution, which occurs throughout the world, is particularly prevalent in Asia and Central and South America. In poor countries, families often sell the sexual services of their children in an attempt to get money. Some children are kidnapped or lured by traffickers with promises of employment, only to end up in a brothel. An estimated one-quarter of all visitors using child prostitutes in Asia are North American businessmen or military personnel (Kennedy 1996).

Consequences of Child Labour Child labourers are at risk for a variety of health problems, such as injuries, stunted growth, and many diseases. Child carpet weavers develop gnarled fingers from the repetitive work, and their spines are curved from sitting at looms all day. Young brickworkers breathe in dust from the dry bricks and sand, causing scarring of the lungs and early death. Child farmworkers are exposed to harmful pesticides. In rural areas, more child workers in agriculture die from pesticide poisonings than from all of the most common childhood diseases put together (UNICEF 2000). Child prostitutes are often physically abused by their pimps and customers, are at high risk for acquiring HIV and other sexually transmitted infections, and suffer the emotional scars of their exploitation. Child labourers are fed inadequate diets and endure harsh punishment from their employers. One girl who was forced into prostitution in Bangkok said: "One time I refused to sleep with a man and they slapped me, hit me with a cane and bashed my head against the wall. One of my friends tried to run away but unfortunately she was caught and very badly beaten" (Parker 1998: 42).

Child labour also increases poverty by depressing already low wages. Parker (1998: 48) explains:

> For every child who works, there may be an adult who cannot find a job. Children are usually paid less than adult workers—sometimes only one-third of what adults earn. As a result, adult workers' wages stay low or go down. When parents cannot find jobs, they are more likely to send their children to work. They have more children in the hope of increasing their income. Each generation of poor, uneducated child workers becomes the next genre of poor parents who must send their kids to work. Then the cycle of poverty and illiteracy continues.

Health and Safety Hazards in the Workplace

Accidents at work and hazardous working conditions contribute to illnesses, injuries, and deaths. Globally, an estimated 1.4 million workers die on the job or from occupational diseases every year (*Multinational Monitor* 2000). Some occupational health and safety hazards are attributed to wilful disregard of information and guidelines concerning worker safety. For example, the dangers of asbestos were known as early as 1918, when insurance companies stopped selling life insurance policies to asbestos workers. Nevertheless, the asbestos industry took little action until the 1960s. Of the half-million workers exposed to "significant doses of asbestos," 100 000 will die from lung cancer, 35 000 from mesothelioma, and 35 000 from asbestosis (Coleman 1994: 79).

In 1999, the Ontario Federation of Labour (OFL) launched a campaign to push the government for stricter limits on the exposure to toxic substances in workplaces and to demand that enough inspectors be put in place to ensure those limits are adhered to in all companies. In support of these demands, the OFL produced documents, obtained by the Canadian Auto Workers union through Freedom of Information requests, that showed a blatant disregard for the health and well-being of workers. For example, even though company and government officials knew that workers at the Holmes Insulation plant in Sarnia were being poisoned and exposed to amounts of asbestos that were far beyond the allowable limits, no one did anything to stop it. The OFL has compiled a top 12 dangerous workplace materials list: asbestos, benzene, cadmium, diesel exhaust emissions, fibreglass, formaldehyde, lead, metalworking fluids (used in coolants and lubricants in cutting, drilling, and machining metal), nickel, silica, styrene, and vinyl chloride (Simone 1999). Occupations related to insulating remain classified as the seventh most dangerous in Canada because of the dangers associated with long-term exposure to asbestos (Statistics Canada 1998).

In an average year in the 1970s, approximately 11 workers for every 100 000 workers died in the course of, or because of, their employment. In the 1990s,

cumulative trauma disorders

The most common type of workplace injury; it includes muscle, tendon, vascular, and nerve injuries that result from repeated or sustained actions or exertions of different body parts. Jobs that are associated with high rates of upper body cumulative stress disorders include computer programming, manufacturing, meat packing, poultry processing, and clerical or office work.

the fatality rate fell to seven deaths for every 100 000 workers. The three most dangerous occupations in Canada are, in order, the cutting and loading of rock, general mine labouring, and operating small engines (Statistics Canada 1998).

Workplace Illnesses and Injuries Although the rate of workplace injuries that result in loss of activity and time-loss from work has been declining steadily over the last two decades, from 49 per 1000 workers in 1987 to 28 per 1000 workers in 1996, workplace injuries remain a significant hazard for Canadians. According to the most recently analyzed data on workplace injuries in Canada, approximately 630 000 Canadians were seriously injured on the job, having serious injuries that resulted in a limitation of their activities, including cognitive function (Wilkins and MacKenzie 2007: 1). In addition, an average of 465 on-the-job deaths occurred in each of the years from 2002 to 2004, with significantly greater risk for workers in the trades, workers who are male, and workers with annual income below $60 000 (ibid). According to the data gathered by Wilkins and MacKenzie, those who work as cooks and those who work as machinists are at significantly greater risk of sustaining a serious workplace injury than for any other occupation. As Table 11.1 shows, the rate of workplace injury for men is about double the rate for women whether in the white-collar or trades sectors.

The most common types of workplace illnesses that develop in white-collar workers are associated with repeated trauma, such as carpal tunnel syndrome (a wrist disorder that can cause numbness, tingling, and severe pain), tendonitis (inflammation of the tendons), lower-back injury, and noise-induced hearing loss. Such disorders—referred to by a number of terms, including **cumulative trauma disorders**,

■ **Table 11.1** *Number and Percentage Who Sustained at Least One Activity-Limiting Work Injury in Past Year, by Occupational Category and Sex, Employed Household Population Aged 18 to 75, Canada, 2003*

Occupational Category	Both Sexes		Men		Women	
	'000	%	'000	%	'000	%
Total	630	3.8	460	5.2'	170	2.2
Management	33	2.4*	27	3.0**	7ᴱ	1.4ᴱ*
Business, finance, etc.	49	1.6*	28ᴱ	2.7ᴱ*†	21	1.0*
Natural and applied sciences, etc.	28	2.4*	24	2.6*	F	F
Health	28	3.0	8ᴱ	4.4ᴱ	20	2.7
Social science, education, etc,	18	1.6*	7ᴱ	1.6ᴱ*	12ᴱ	1.5ᴱ*
Art, culture, etc.	11ᴱ	1.9ᴱ*	F	F	F	F
Sales, service	133	3.3	60	3.7*	73	3.0*
Trades, transport, etc.	201	8.5*	194	8.8**	8ᴱ	4.4ᴱ*
Primary industries	43	6.6*	37	7.0*	6ᴱ	4.9ᴱ*
Processing, manufacturing, etc.	81	7.2*	68	8.3*†	14ᴱ	4.2ᴱ*

* Significantly different from estimate for both sexes combined or from sex-specific estimate for Total (p < 0.05)

† Significantly different from corresponding estimate for women (p < 0.05)

ᴱ use with caution (coefficient of variation 16.6% to 33.3%)

F too unreliable to be published (coefficient of variation greater than 33.3%)

Note: Because of rounding, detail may not add to totals.

SOURCE: Statistics Canada. "Work Injuries." *Health Report*, vol. 18, no. 3, Catalogue no. 82-003, August 2007, p. 6.

repetitive strain disorders, and **repeated trauma disorders**—are muscle, tendon, vascular, and nerve injuries that result from repeated or sustained actions or exertions of different body parts. Cumulative trauma disorders are classified as illnesses, not as injuries, because they are not sudden, instantaneous traumatic events.

Shift work, in which workers change from one of three sets of eight-hour shifts to another on a rotating basis, holds significantly higher risk for injury than does work in which employees work a regular daytime schedule (Wilkins and MacKenzie, 2007: 10). Shift work tends to be very hard on workers' cardiovascular health, contributes to the development of obesity secondary to disrupted eating patterns, and has been associated with a greater risk of on-the-job injury due to tiredness. Overtime work also significantly increases the risk of injury to workers who are regularly asked to work beyond their regular shifts (ibid).

Job Stress and Chronic Fatigue Another work-related health hazard is job stress and chronic fatigue. To measure work stress, the 1996–97 National Population Health Survey used a scale composed of 12 questions describing working conditions that were answered on a five-point scale of agree or disagree. The minimum score on the scale was 0 and the maximum was 45; "high stress" was defined as a score of 30 or higher. Using this scale, the survey found that more women reported high work stress levels than men did in every age category, with women aged 20 to 24 almost three times as likely to report high work stress as the average Canadian worker. Notable differences in high work stress also existed among persons in different types of households. Single parents were twice as likely as Canadians in couple relationships without children to report high work stress (Health Canada 1999). Although Canadian workers report working fewer hours than 21 of the 25 countries reporting workweek information (see Figure 11.1, p. 392), many Canadian workers report feeling exhausted and emotionally drained at the end of the day.

Dissatisfaction and Alienation

If you read the classified ad section of any newspaper, you are likely to find job advertisements that entice applicants with claims such as "discover a rewarding and challenging career" and "we offer opportunities for advancement and travel." Unfortunately, most jobs do not allow workers to "be all that they can be." This chapter's *Social Problems Research Up Close* compares jobs in industries that produce knowledge-based technologies, products, and services with those in the rest of the private sector.

Factors that contribute to job satisfaction include income, prestige, a feeling of accomplishment, autonomy, a sense of being challenged by the job, opportunities to be creative, congenial co-workers, the feeling that one is making a contribution, fair rewards (pay and benefits), promotion opportunities, and job security (Bavendam 2000; Robie et al. 1998). These factors often overlap—for example, high-paying jobs tend to have more prestige, be more autonomous, provide more benefits, and permit greater creativity. However, many jobs lack these qualities, leaving workers dissatisfied. Moreover, many Canadians are worried that they may lose their jobs in the next few years. In 2001, 20 percent of Canadians told pollsters that they were concerned that someone in their household would lose a job (Bricker and Greenspon 2001: 18).

One form of job dissatisfaction is a feeling of **alienation**. A high division of labour and specialization of work roles characterize work in industrialized societies. As a result, workers' tasks are repetitive and monotonous, involving little

repetitive strain disorders (repeated trauma disorders)

The most common types of workplace illnesses include muscle, tendon, vascular, and nerve injuries that result from repeated or sustained actions or exertions of different body parts. Jobs that are associated with high rates of upper body repeated trauma disorders include computer programming, manufacturing, meat packaging, poultry processing, and clerical/office work.

shift work

The use of a 24-hour schedule to create workdays of three eight-hour shifts. Some workers have "split shifts" in which their eight hours are interrupted by unpaid periods of over an hour, effectively extending the workers' days to 10 hours or more. Split shifts are common in the hospitality sector.

alienation

The concept used by Karl Marx to describe the condition when workers feel powerlessness and meaninglessness as a result of performing repetitive, isolated work tasks. Alienation involves becoming estranged from one's work, the products one creates, other human beings, or one's self; it also refers to powerlessness and meaninglessness experienced by students in traditional, restrictive educational institutions.

Workplace and Employee Survey: Better Jobs in the New Economy?

Sample and Methods

The 1999 Workplace and Employee Survey (WES), conducted by Statistics Canada, compared jobs in industries that produce knowledge-based technologies, products, and services with those in the rest of the private sector. The WES covers the private sector (i.e., all industries with the exception of farming, fishing, hunting, trapping and public administration). Within this study, the term "knowledge-based industries" refers to "industries that spend a relatively large amount of resources on research and development and have professionals, such as scientists and engineers, as a substantial proportion of their workforce" (Statistics Canada 2002). In addition, it is limited to jobs in research and development-based firms that produce knowledge-based technologies, products, and services. Included here would be most, although not all, industries within the information and communication technology sector, including telecommunications, data processing, and computer systems design, as well as the pharmaceutical and chemical manufacturing industries.

Within this study, industries were classified into five mutually exclusive groups: (1) knowledge-based in the goods sector; (2) knowledge-based in the service sector; (3) other goods producing; (4) retail trade and consumer services; and (5) other professional and other services. The study examined job characteristics such as work hours, hourly wages, pension coverage, stock options, personal and family support programs, teamwork, performance appraisal, grievance systems, and job satisfaction.

Findings and Conclusions

Workers in knowledge-based industries receive relatively high wages, have good fringe benefits, and often profit from fitness and recreation services as well as employee assistance programs. However, many work fairly long hours, and those employed in the service sector rarely have access to a formal grievance system in their workplace . . .

1. *Workers in knowledge-based industries receive relatively high wages.* On average, employees in knowledge-based industries earned $24.09 per hour in 1999, 32 percent more than the $18.19 received by employees in other industries. The wage gap between knowledge-based

industries and other industries was 14 percent for university graduates, compared with 31 percent for other workers with some postsecondary education. Employees in knowledge-based workplaces earn relatively high wages for a number of reasons. They are generally better educated than other workers and tend to be employed in larger establishments, which generally pay higher wages. They may also receive higher wages to compensate for the relatively high costs of living in larger areas, where such workplaces tend to be located. Many of these employees are in high-paying professional occupations such as engineering and science. Lastly, some, such as university graduates, could receive higher wages as compensation for relatively long hours . . .

2. *Workers often have stock options.* Employees in knowledge-based industries were not necessarily better covered by a registered pension plan than other workers. For instance, 40 percent of employees in service-producing, knowledge-based workplaces had a pension plan in 1999, compared with 48 percent of their counterparts in professional and other services. However, 31 percent of

or no creativity. Limited to specific tasks by their work roles, workers are unable to express and utilize their full potential—intellectual, emotional, and physical. According to Marx, when workers are merely cogs in a machine they become estranged from their work, the product they create, other human beings, and themselves. Marx called this estrangement "alienation."

Alienation usually has four components: powerlessness, meaninglessness, normlessness, and self-estrangement. Powerlessness results from working in an environment in which workers have little or no control over the decisions that affect their work. Meaninglessness results when workers do not find fulfillment in their work.

employees in service-producing knowledge-based workplaces information options, five times the proportion (6 percent) in professional and other services. On average, employees in knowledge-based industries were more likely to be covered by life or disability insurance, supplemental medical insurance, and dental plans. They were also more likely to have profit-sharing plans . . .

3. *Employees often benefit from fitness services and assistance programs.* Roughly 25 percent of employees in knowledge-based industries were in workplaces that provided fitness and recreation services (on- or off-site). The corresponding numbers for other goods-producing industries, professional and other services, and retail trade and consumer services were 15 percent, 17 percent and 5 percent, respectively. In addition, 40 percent of workers in knowledge-based workplaces were offered employee assistance programs (counselling, substance abuse control, financial assistance, legal aid). Such programs were available to 35 percent, 29 percent and 8 percent of employees in professional and other services, other goods-producing industries, and retail trade and consumer services, respectively . . .

4. *University graduates in knowledge-based industries work fairly long hours.* Compared to their counterparts in the rest of the economy, university graduates employed full time in knowledge-based industries worked either longer hours or more hours of unpaid overtime. Their total workweek, including unpaid overtime, averaged 46.6 hours per week. This was at least two hours more than in professional and other services (44.3) or in retail trade and consumer services (44.4) . . .

5. *In the service sector, few have access to a formal grievance system.* In 1999, 20 percent of employees in knowledge-based industries were unionized. This compares with 13 percent in consumer services and retail trade, and 33 percent in professional and other services or in other goods-producing industries. However, there were substantial differences within the knowledge-based sector. About 14 percent of employees in service-producing workplaces were unionized, compared with 25 percent in goods-producing workplaces. As a result, only 18 percent of workers in service-producing, knowledge-based industries reported having access to a formal grievance system such as a labour-management committee or an outside arbitrator. In contrast, access to such a system was reported by 46 percent of those in goods-producing, knowledge-based industries, 41 percent in professional and other services, and 38 percent in other goods-producing industries . . .

6. *Performance appraisal is more frequent in knowledge-based industries.* At least 65 percent of employees in knowledge-based industries had their job performance evaluated through a standard process, compared with only 45 percent to 58 percent of workers in other industries. Furthermore, employees in knowledge-based industries were almost twice as likely to have their level of pay or benefits directly affected by job evaluation results. Thus, work evaluation was more systematic in the knowledge-based sector than in other industries.

SOURCE: Adapted from "Workplace and Employee Survey: Better Jobs in the New Economy?" 1999, Catalogue 11-001, July 18, 2002, http://www.statcan.gc.ca/daily-quotidien/020718/dq020718b-eng.htm.

Workers may experience normlessness if workplace norms are unclear or conflicting. For example, many companies that have family leave policies informally discourage workers from using them, or workplaces that officially promote nondiscrimination in reality practise discrimination. Finally, a feeling of self-estrangement stems from the workers' inability to realize their full human potential in their work roles and from a lack of connections to others. In general, traditional "women's work" is more alienating than "men's work" (Ross and Wright 1998). "Homemaking exposes women to routine, unfulfilling, isolated work; and part-time employment exposes them to routine, unfulfilling work, with little decision-making autonomy" (p. 343).

■ **Figure 11.1** *The Workweek: Full-Time Employees' Average Hours*

SOURCE: Adapted from "Asian Markets Tend to Work the Most, Europe the Least," 2006 Roper Reports® Worldwide, GfK Roper Consulting. Reprinted with permission.

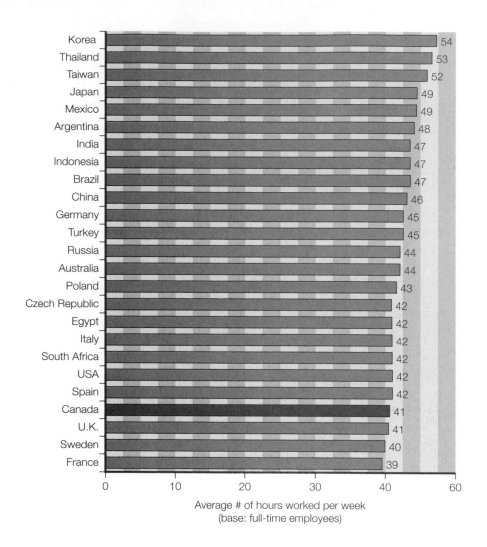

Average # of hours worked per week (base: full-time employees)

Work–Family Concerns

As a result of a combination of social forces including economic pressures, changing gender ideologies, improved contraception, increased life expectancy, and the marked trend toward smaller families, the dual-earner family has become the "new norm" in Canada (Table 11.2). Families in which there are two earners raising children have significantly higher earnings than those not raising children. There is an obvious reason for the differences in earnings between couples not raising children and those with children for whom they are financially responsible. First, the age group with dependent children tends to be at the height of their earning potential, while those without children are likely to be younger and not yet ready to have kids, or much older and finished raising children. Both the younger and older cohorts have lower average earnings, either because they are at entry stages of their careers, or have reduced their household revenues to retirement sources of income and/or part-time work. It is important to note here that families with dependent children have significantly higher costs than those who have not yet had children or have finished raising them. Moreover, the

■ **Table 11.2** *Median After-Tax Income by Selected Family Types*

	1998	1999	2000	2001	2002	2003	2004	2005	2006	2007
					2007 constant dollars					
AVERAGE										
Economic families, two persons or more	**59,300**	**61,100**	**63,000**	**65,500**	**65,600**	**65,000**	**66,600**	**67,500**	**69,100**	**71,900**
Elderly families	**43,800**	**45,700**	**45,400**	**46,900**	**47,600**	**47,300**	**48,200**	**50,200**	**51,200**	**54,200**
Married couples	42,500	44,700	44,000	45,800	46,100	46,200	47,800	48,300	49,300	52,700
Other families	48,300	49,200	50,300	51,300	53,000	51,300	50,100	57,200	57,900	59,300
Non-elderly families	**61,800**	**63,600**	**65,900**	**68,600**	**68,500**	**68,000**	**69,800**	**70,500**	**72,300**	**75,000**
Married couples	**55,100**	**59,100**	**59,900**	**64,700**	**63,900**	**62,200**	**62,900**	**65,300**	**67,200**	**70,000**
No earners	29,500	30,400	31,000	35,700	32,000	32,100	30,400	31,900	35,000	36,500
One earner	47,700	49,500	48,500	53,700	50,000	49,800	52,400	54,500	53,700	56,400
Two earners	68,500	67,500	67,800	72,300	72,800	69,900	70,000	73,100	75,300	77,500
Two-parent families with children	**66,400**	**68,600**	**71,100**	**73,700**	**74,500**	**75,000**	**77,800**	**76,100**	**78,000**	**82,000**
No earners	24,200	23,700	23,200	26,100	26,000	24,200	25,500	22,100	26,600	28,700
One earner	51,200	51,900	51,900	54,100	56,900	57,700	56,900	54,900	56,100	58,700
Two earners	68,100	69,500	72,200	74,400	74,800	75,000	77,500	76,800	77,500	81,400
Three or more earners	82,600	86,200	89,900	93,300	92,200	92,700	97,500	95,500	98,800	102,500
Married couples with other relatives	**81,400**	**86,200**	**91,300**	**90,900**	**90,000**	**90,400**	**92,600**	**96,800**	**99,800**	**101,100**
Lone-parent families	**31,500**	**32,600**	**35,200**	**36,500**	**34,900**	**35,600**	**35,700**	**40,500**	**41,100**	**41,800**
Male	43,500	43,500	47,000	45,800	46,400	49,300	47,000	53,700	55,700	52,100
Female	29,300	30,500	32,800	34,600	32,200	32,500	33,200	37,500	37,800	39,500
No earners	17,200	17,800	17,400	18,300	17,500	17,200	18,600	18,500	20,500	18,000
One earner	30,900	31,500	32,500	34,200	32,400	32,200	33,100	37,900	37,200	39,300
Two or more earners	47,800	47,900	52,200	54,600	47,700	49,700	47,900	50,300	51,400	54,200
Other non-elderly families	**55,500**	**56,700**	**57,100**	**60,200**	**61,700**	**57,400**	**60,300**	**58,800**	**60,400**	**62,500**
Unattached individuals	**24,200**	**25,400**	**25,600**	**26,800**	**27,400**	**27,700**	**27,600**	**28,100**	**29,100**	**29,800**
Elderly males	**27,000**	**26,100**	**25,100**	**27,000**	**26,900**	**27,700**	**27,400**	**28,100**	**28,500**	**31,000**
Non-earner	24,600	25,000	23,900	25,700	25,100	24,900	26,100	25,000	25,600	27,600
Earner	42,100	33,800	31,800	35,100	35,000	37,400	32,100	40,500	39,000	42,800
Elderly females	**22,100**	**22,200**	**22,500**	**23,900**	**24,400**	**23,900**	**24,800**	**24,100**	**26,100**	**25,800**
Non-earner	21,500	21,700	21,900	23,000	24,000	23,300	24,000	23,200	25,300	24,700
Earner	30,900	29,500	30,600	35,700	29,600	28,400	32,200	32,100	33,000	33,800
Non-elderly males	**26,300**	**27,600**	**28,800**	**29,700**	**30,100**	**30,700**	**30,000**	**31,200**	**32,400**	**32,700**
Non-earner	10,700	10,400	10,300	12,100	11,700	12,400	11,900	12,100	12,100	13,400
Earner	30,400	31,200	32,200	33,100	33,900	34,500	33,500	35,300	35,900	36,400
Non-elderly females	**22,000**	**24,300**	**23,400**	**24,600**	**25,800**	**25,900**	**25,900**	**26,200**	**26,600**	**27,800**
Non-earner	11,100	10,500	10,500	12,200	12,000	12,900	12,800	14,400	13,600	13,700
Earner	26,400	29,300	27,700	28,800	30,000	29,700	29,800	29,400	29,900	31,500

(continued)

■ **Table 11.2** *Median After-Tax Income by Selected Family Types* (Continued)

	1998	1999	2000	2001	2002	2003	2004	2005	2006	2007
					2007 constant dollars					
MEDIAN										
Economic families, two persons or more	**52,000**	**53,700**	**54,600**	**56,800**	**56,700**	**56,700**	**57,400**	**58,400**	**59,600**	**61,800**
Elderly families	**36,800**	**38,300**	**38,300**	**39,800**	**40,500**	**40,100**	**40,900**	**42,100**	**43,400**	**44,900**
Married couples	35,900	37,700	37,700	39,000	39,700	39,600	40,700	40,600	42,400	44,100
Other families	39,500	40,800	42,000	42,800	43,200	42,200	42,700	47,500	47,800	49,500
Non-elderly families	**55,200**	**56,700**	**57,800**	**60,400**	**50,000**	**60,300**	**61,200**	**62,200**	**63,300**	**65,500**
Married couples	**50,600**	**52,500**	**53,500**	**55,500**	**55,100**	**55,100**	**56,400**	**58,100**	**59,200**	**61,000**
No earners	27,800	27,600	29,400	30,300	28,900	29,100	28,100	29,000	31,000	33,300
One earner	40,300	44,100	42,200	44,600	44,400	44,400	46,600	49,400	47,900	48,700
Two earners	69,900	60,500	60,200	63,400	63,100	62,500	63,100	65,000	66,600	67,700
Two-parent families with children	**61,100**	**61,900**	**63,400**	**65,900**	**66,300**	**66,500**	**68,200**	**68,500**	**69,400**	**73,000**
No earners	22,400	21,100	21,600	23,300	23,700	22,000	22,300	18,800E	25,900	24,300
One earner	43,800	45,000	43,700	44,600	46,100	46,600	45,700	46,900	44,900	49,300
Two earners	63,000	63,100	64,900	67,000	67,700	67,300	69,400	69,500	69,500	73,000
Three or more earners	76,100	81,200	82,100	85,400	84,200	84.100	87,100	86.900	88.700	92,100
Married couples with other relatives	**76,600**	**80,700**	**83,000**	**84,900**	**83,500**	**83,100**	**85,500**	**88,700**	**90,700**	**93,800**
Lone-parent families	**27,000**	**29,300**	**31,200**	**32,000**	**30,500**	**30,700**	**31,700**	**34,100**	**35,700**	**36,300**
Male	37,900	39,300	40,200	40,900	41,200	41,700	42300	44.300	47.600	46,700
Female	25,300	27,300	28.900	29,700	28,200	28,700	29,300	31,600	32.400	34,600
No earners	16.300	16,500	15.900	16,400	17,000	16,200	17,000	17,700	18,700	16,700
One earner	28,500	29,500	30,700	31,700	28,800	30,200	30,200	31,900	31,700	34,400
Two or more earners	44,000	43,000	46,900	47,000	42,100	44,800	44,100	46,300	47,500	48,700
Other non-elderly families	**48,000**	**49,800**	**50,800**	**52,700**	**52,900**	**51,100**	**53,800**	**54,100**	**56,500**	**57,900**
Unattached individuals	**19,600**	**20,100**	**20,700**	**21,700**	**22,600**	**22,200**	**22,500**	**22,300**	**23,300**	**24,200**
Elderly males	**19,900**	**20,500**	**20,500**	**21,400**	**22,300**	**21,900**	**22,800**	**21,700**	**22,600**	**23,400**
Non-earner	19,100	19,700	19,600	20,200	21,100	20,300	21,300	20,800	21,200	21,000
Earner	32,800	25,000	26,900	27,500	28,700	26,700	26,800	35,800	34,400	33,300
Elderly females	**18,600**	**18,900**	**19,000**	**19,700**	**19,500**	**19,700**	**20,200**	**19,900**	**20,900**	**21,300**
Non-earner	18,300	18,600	18,800	19,400	19,200	19,300	19,800	19,400	20,500	20,700
Earner	26.000	25,900	26,700	27,700	25,900	26,500	30,100	29,000	27,600	31,200
Non-elderly males	**22,400**	**23,900**	**25,400**	**25,600**	**26,400**	**26,100**	**25,600**	**25,900**	**26,900**	**27,600**
Non-earner	10,100	10,000	10,200	10,700	9,900	10,400	10,300	10,400	10,400	10,500
Earner	27,200	28,000	28,600	29,200	29,600	29,800	29,300	29,800	30,200	31,000
Non-elderly females	**17,500**	**18,700**	**18,600**	**19,700**	**21,500**	**21,300**	**21,100**	**21,500**	**21,900**	**22,700**
Non-earner	10,300	9,900	9,800	10,700	10,600	10,400	10,400	11,100	10,700	10,800
Earner	23,800	24,300	23,900	25,400	26,200	25,800	25,500	25,500	26,100	27,100

SOURCE: Statistics Canada. 2009. "Income in Canada, 2007." Minister of Industry. June 2009. Catalogue No. 75-202-x

quality of life for dual-earner families with dependent children can be much more stressful than for childless families. Understandably, for many employed parents, balancing work and family demands is a daily challenge. When Hochschild (1997) asked a sample of employed parents, "Overall, how well do you feel you can balance the demands of your work and family?" only 9 percent said, "very well" (pp. 199–200). (Work–family concerns are also discussed in Chapters 5, 7, and 10.)

The lack of affordable, quality child care is one stressor that many Canadian parents confront. Although "[c]hild care is a fact of life for Canadian children and their families very little regulated child care even exists in Canada" (National Council of Welfare 1999b: 17). While the costs of child care in general, and for preschoolers in particular, are high and rising, the federal, provincial, and territorial governments have cut funding for social programs, cut or frozen subsidies to low-income families, and made eligibility criteria for subsidies more restrictive. In addition, parents of children with special needs and parents who work irregular hours or shift work may find it impossible to obtain child care.

Unemployment and Underemployment

The International Labour Organization (2001) reports that one-third of the world's workforce is unemployed or underemployed. Poor countries tend to suffer high rates of unemployment. For example, recent unemployment rates in South Africa and Lesotho (a southern African country) were 23 percent and 42 percent, respectively (International Labour Organization 2001).

Measures of **unemployment** consider an individual to be unemployed if he or she is currently without employment, is actively seeking employment, and is available for employment. Unemployment figures do not include "discouraged workers," who have given up on finding a job. **Underemployment** is a broader term that includes discouraged workers, and those working part time but who wish to work full time. For example, although the overall size of the Canadian labour force has grown significantly in the past three decades, much of the growth has been in part-time and self-employment, neither of which provides benefits or pensions. In 1998, about 30 percent of adult women working part-time were doing so involuntarily because they could not obtain full-time employment (Statistics Canada 1999). By 2009 the number of women in part-time work who wished to work full time had improved somewhat, dropping to 25.9 percent, but because women tend to take on higher child-care burdens and often receive less financial support from family to go to school, women still represent 70 percent of the part-time workforce, often paying significantly into their education costs (Ferrao 2010: 13).

Types and Causes of Unemployment Unemployment can be either discriminatory or structural. **Discriminatory unemployment** involves high rates of unemployment among particular social groups, such as racial and ethnic minorities and women (see Chapters 7 and 8). **Structural unemployment** exists when there are not enough jobs available for those who want them. Structural unemployment is the result of social factors rather than personal inadequacies of the unemployed or discrimination.

For example, unemployment can result from **corporate downsizing**—the corporate practice of discharging large numbers of employees. Simply put, the term *downsizing* is a euphemism for mass firing of employees (Caston 1998). Another cause of unemployment is **job exportation**, the relocation of Canadian jobs to other countries where products can be produced more cheaply. Job exportation has had a particularly profound effect on garment workers and the Canadian garment

unemployment
The unemployed are those who want and are able to work, but who have no work at present. For statistical purposes, Statistics Canada defines the unemployed in these ways: (1) as people who did not work in the labour market during the survey reference week (but may have done housework, etc.); (2) as people who were available for work and actively looked for it in the past four weeks; (3) as people laid off for 26 weeks or fewer and expecting to be recalled by their employer; or (4) as people who were waiting for new jobs to begin within four weeks.

underemployment
Employment in a job that is underpaid; is not commensurate with one's skills, experience, or education; or involves working fewer hours than desired.

discriminatory unemployment
High rates of unemployment among particular social groups, such as racial and ethnic minorities and women.

structural unemployment

Exists when there are not enough jobs available for those who want them; unemployment that results from structural variables, such as government and business downsizing, job exportation, automation, a reduction in the number of new and existing businesses, an increase in the number of people looking for jobs, and a recessionary economy where fewer goods are purchased and, therefore, fewer employees are needed.

corporate downsizing

The corporate practice of discharging large numbers of employees. Simply put, the term *downsizing* is a euphemism for mass firing of employees.

job exportation

The relocation of jobs to other countries where products can be produced more cheaply.

automation

A type of technology in which self-operated machines accomplish tasks formerly done by workers; develops as a society moves toward industrialization and becomes more concerned with the mass production of goods.

industry over the past decade (Yanz and Jeffcott 1997). **Automation**, or the replacement of human labour with machinery and equipment, is another feature of the work landscape that contributes to unemployment. For example, recorded phone trees, automated teller machines (ATMs), automatic car washes, and assembly-line robots do jobs that otherwise would be performed by workers.

Because of the changing nature of work, displaced workers may find themselves unable to obtain adequate employment. Consider, for example, that since 1989 the number of employed clerical workers in Canada has dropped from 2.2 million to 1.9 million while the number of manufacturing jobs has declined from 1.8 million to 1.7 million. Between 2004 and 2008, the manufacturing sector saw another 322 000 job losses—and, because of the recession, workers laid off from their manufacturing jobs were likely to struggle to find employment elsewhere (Bernard 2009: 1).

Effects of Unemployment and Underemployment The personal consequences of unemployment (and in some cases, underemployment) include anxiety, depression, alcohol abuse, and lowered self-esteem and confidence (Feather 1990; Liem and Liem 1990; Tremblay et al. 2002). Unemployment has consequences for families and communities as well, and has been linked to increased family violence (Reidmann et al. 2003). Unemployment may also mean losing supplemental health-care benefits for workers and their families, and underemployed individuals rarely get health-care benefits from their employers. Unemployment and underemployment result in a decline in an individual's standard of living.

11.4 Strategies for Action: Responses to Workers' Concerns

Government, private business, human rights organizations, and labour organizations play important roles in responding to the concerns of workers. Next, we look at responses to child labour, efforts to strengthen labour, workforce development and job-creation programs, responses to worker health and safety concerns, work–family policies and programs, public child care assistance for working families, the workplace and family life, and challenges to corporate power and globalization.

Responses to Child Labour

The International Programme on the Elimination of Child Labour has been working to remove child labourers from oppressive work conditions, provide them with education, and provide their parents with jobs or income. Since the program began in 1992, it has grown from six participating countries to more than 200 participating countries in 2000 (Human Rights Watch 2001).

In 1999, 174 nations adopted the Convention on the Worst Forms of Child Labour, and by September 2000, 37 countries had ratified the convention (Human Rights Watch 2001). This move represents a global consensus to end the most severe forms of child labour, and the convention requires nations to take immediate measures to abolish child slavery, trafficking, debt bondage, child prostitution and pornography, and forced labour.

Human rights organizations, such as the International Labour Organization, UNICEF, and the Child Labour Coalition, are also active in the campaign against child labour. Another organization, the Bonded Labour Liberation Front (BLLF), has led the fight against bonded and child labour in Pakistan, freeing 30 000 adults and children from brick kilns, carpet factories, and farms, and placing 11 000 children in its own primary school system (Silvers 1996). However, employers in Pakistan have threatened workers with violence if they talk with "the abolitionists" or possess "illegal communist propaganda." Human rights activists campaigning against child labour have also been victims of threats and violence.

The United Nations International Children's Emergency Fund recommends that national and international corporations adopt codes of conduct guaranteeing that neither they nor their subcontractors will employ children in conditions that violate their rights (UNICEF 1997). Some industries, including rug and clothing manufacturers, use labels and logos to indicate that child labourers do not make their products. The Fair Labour Association (FLA) involves six leading apparel and footwear companies. These companies voluntarily take part in a monitoring system to inspect their overseas factories and require them to meet minimum labour standards, such as not requiring workers to work more than 60 hours a week. However, critics point out a number of problems with the FLA, including (1) standards are too low (allows below-poverty wages and excessive overtime); (2) only 10 percent of companies' factories must be monitored yearly; (3) companies can influence which factories are inspected and who does the inspection; and (4) the FLA does not uphold workers' right to organize (Benjamin 1998). Critics charge that companies use their participation in FLA as a marketing tool. Once "certified" by FLA, companies can sew a label into their products saying they were made under fair working conditions.

Pressure from students and other opponents of child and sweatshop labour along with consumer boycotts of products made by child and sweatshop labour have resulted in some improvements. Factories that make goods for companies such as Nike and Gap have cut back on child labour, use less dangerous chemicals, and require fewer employees to work 80-hour weeks (Greenhouse 2000; Klein 2000). At many factories, supervisors have stopped hitting employees, have improved ventilation, and have stopped requiring workers to obtain permission to use the toilet. But improvements are not widespread and oppressive forms of labour continue throughout the world. According to the National Labour Committee, two areas where "progress seems to grind to a halt" are efforts to form unions and efforts to achieve wage increases (Greenhouse 2000).

Efforts to eliminate child labour cannot succeed unless the impoverished conditions that contribute to its practice are alleviated. A living minimum wage must be established for adult workers so they will not need to send their children to work. We should also keep in mind that until relatively recently in Canada, it was common for children to work to contribute to the family income. Summer "holidays" are a holdover from the need to dismiss children to work on their family farms in the growing and harvest season; prior to the mid–twentieth century many children did not attend school beyond the ninth grade because they needed to help contribute to their family income.

We need also to consider our own role in the global market's reliance on cheap goods imported from faraway places. From a conflict perspective, our own interest in getting a "bargain" is sustained from a position of power in which our own children are protected against early and dangerous labour while the children of distant countries make cheap commodities for us. Often, these commodities are toys we give to our own children. Structural-functionalists, meanwhile, may argue that child labour serves a positive purpose now in developing areas in the same way that it served a positive purpose for Canadian families from our founding to the mid–twentieth century: providing income and a better standard of living to families. In thinking about these views, we should consider whether the threat to the well-being of child labourers is adequately set off by the gains for their families (often, the answer is no), and whether we really need all those cheap goods that we would be loath to see our own children labouring to manufacture.

Efforts to Strengthen Labour

International norms established by the United Nations and the International Labour Organization declare the right of workers to organize, negotiate with management, and strike (Human Rights Watch 2000). In European countries, labour unions are generally strong (Mishel et al. 2001). However, in many less developed countries and countries undergoing economic transition, workers and labour unions struggle to have a voice. A survey of 113 countries by the International Confederation of Free Trade Unions (ICFTU) found that both corporations and governments repressed union efforts ("Global Labor Repression" 2000). Among the survey's findings are these:

- In 1999, at least 140 trade unionists around the world were assassinated, disappeared, or committed suicide after they were threatened as a result of their labour advocacy. Colombia was found to be the most dangerous country for union activists. In 1999, 76 trade unionists in Colombia were assassinated or reported missing.
- Nearly 3000 people were arrested, more than 1500 were injured, beaten, or tortured, and at least 5800 were harassed because of their trade union activities. Another 700 trade unionists received death threats.
- About 12 000 workers were unfairly dismissed or refused reinstatement, sometimes with the complicity of the government, because they were active members of a trade union. Governments, sometimes with the support of employers using strikebreakers, repressed at least 140 strikes or demonstrations; 80 of the 113 countries surveyed restrict the right to strike.

In spite of these repressive actions, labour unions have played an important role in fighting for fair wages and benefits, healthy and safe work environments, and other forms of worker advocacy. In Canada, about 3.7 million paid workers belonged to unions during the first half of 2000, with workers in Newfoundland the most likely to be union members (with just under 40 percent of all paid employees union members). In that year, the average hourly earnings of unionized workers exceeded those of nonunionized workers for both full-time and part-time workers (Statistics Canada 2002). Almost all of Canada's nurses and teachers, about one-third of Canada's white-collar workers, half of Canada's professional and managerial workers, and 4 in 10 blue-collar workers were union members (Statistics Canada 1998; Statistics Canada 2002). Although union representation of workers has remained relatively high at about one-third of all workers in Canada over the last decade, union representation is nonetheless in slow, steady decline, as we see in Figure 11.2.

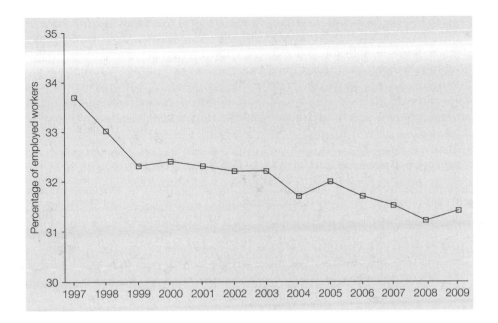

■ **Figure 11.2**

Unionization Rate, Canada, 1997–2009 (% of Employed Workers)

SOURCE: HRSDC calculations based on Statistics Canada, *Labour Force Historical Review 2009* (Table 078). Ottawa: Statistics Canada, 2010 (Cat. No. 71F0004XVB).

Although Canadian women workers are less likely than their male counterparts to be unionized, unionization among women has risen considerably over the past three decades (Figure 11.3). By 2009, just under 33 percent of women workers were unionized, while men's membership in unions is now hovering around 30 percent. In 1999, women accounted for 46 percent of all union members in Canada (Ghalam 2000: 106). The growth in unionization among women

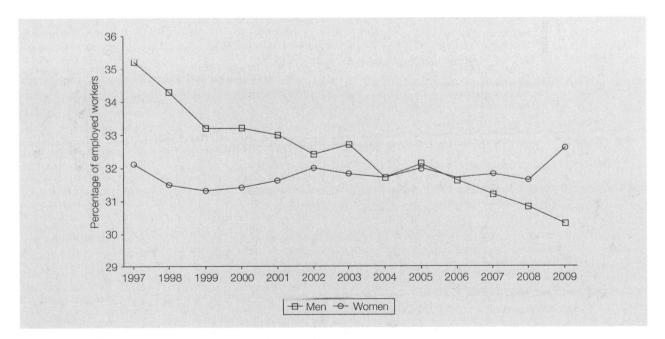

■ **Figure 11.3** *Unionization Rate by Gender, 1997–2009*

SOURCE: HRSDC calculations based on Statistics Canada, *Labour Force Historical Review 2009* (Table 078). Ottawa: Statistics Canada, 2010 (Cat. No. 71F0004XVB).

stems from several factors, including "most notably, their growing presence in the heavily unionized public sector" (Ghalam 2000: 106). Work traditionally done by men in the manufacturing sector has, by contrast, been in decline for the same time period. As more men enter into work in areas not traditionally unionized, we see their union membership numbers decline. Trades generally work through guilds that help to protect individual contractors and small business owners, and professional work outside the public sector is rarely unionized.

Workforce Development and Job-Creation Programs

The International Labour Organization estimated in 2001 that over 500 million new jobs were needed by 2010 to accommodate new entrants to the workforce and to reduce current unemployment levels by half. Developing a workforce and creating jobs involves far-reaching efforts, including those designed to improve health and health care, alleviate poverty and malnutrition, develop infrastructures, and provide universal education.

In Canada, workforce development programs have provided a variety of services, including assessment to evaluate skills and needs, career counselling, job search assistance, basic education, occupational training (classroom and on-the-job), public employment, job placement, and stipends or other support services for child care and transportation assistance (Levitan et al. 1998). Numerous studies have looked at the effectiveness of workforce development programs. In general, "evaluations indicate that employment and training programs enhance the earnings and employment of participants, although the effects vary by service population, are often modest because of brief training durations and the inherent difficulty of alleviating long-term deficiencies, and are not always cost effective" (Levitan et al. 1998: 199). However, funding for federal job training programs is insufficient to reach more than a small fraction of the workforce, and even those who complete training and retraining programs do not always find new jobs at comparable wages.

Efforts to prepare high school students for work include the establishment of technical and vocational high schools and school-to-work programs. School-to-work programs involve partnerships between business, labour, government, education, and community organizations that help prepare high school students for jobs (Leonard 1996). Although the programs vary, in general they allow high school students to explore different careers and provide job skill training and work-based learning experiences, often with pay (Bassi and Ludwig 2000). Nevertheless, for many young Canadians employment continues to be elusive, with "McJobs"—dead-end jobs in the service industry—the only option.

Regardless of the ebbs and flows in government efforts to create jobs, we must consider where the jobs are being created. The Canadian economy can be described as a **split labour market** (or dual economy) because it is made up of two labour markets. The *primary labour market* refers to jobs that are stable, economically rewarding, and associated with benefits. These jobs are usually occupied by the most educated and trained individuals (e.g., a corporate attorney, teacher, or accountant). The *secondary labour market* refers to jobs that involve low pay, no security, few benefits, and little chance for advancement. These workers often lack a union to protect them and are more

split labour market
The existence of primary and secondary labour markets. A primary labour market refers to jobs that are stable and economically rewarding and have many benefits; a secondary labour market refers to jobs that offer little pay, no security, few benefits, and little chance for advancement.

likely to be dissatisfied with their jobs than workers in the primary labour market.

Responses to Worker Health and Safety Concerns

Over the past few decades, health and safety conditions in the workplace have improved because of media attention, regulations, demands by unions for change, and more white-collar jobs. Canadian governments have expanded workplace protection through human rights laws, which prohibit discrimination in hiring, promotion, and working conditions, and workers' compensation programs, which pay partial lost wages to sick or injured workers. Although corporations may complain that there is too much interference and regulation of the workplace, the state has a long history in Canada of exercising its interest in promoting better health for its population through improved working conditions. Krahn and Lowe explain that it is to laws developed in the late nineteenth century that we owe the protection of children against dangerous labour when they are underage, but the same laws, which grouped women and children together, had the effect of removing women from paid labour in factories (2002: 311).

The *Canada Labour Code*, in 1986, established the right of workers to be told about the potential hazards of workplace materials, with this "right to know" buttressed by the national Workplace Hazardous Materials Information System. Worker health and safety committees are also a standard feature of companies in many industrialized countries and are mandatory in most of Europe. These committees are authorized to inspect workplaces and cite employers for violations of health and safety regulations. Krahn and Lowe (2002: 311) remind us that "all of these approaches to dealing with health and safety issues—standard setting and enforcement by the state, collective bargaining between unions and employers, and the no-fault compensation system—offer little room for direct involvement on the part of workers who are most directly affected by unsafe and unhealthy working conditions."

Maximizing the health and safety of workers involves more than implementing, monitoring, and enforcing regulations. Increasingly, businesses and corporations are promoting workers' health (and corporate profits) by offering work-site health programs of health education, screening, and interventions designed to achieve better health among workers. Programs range from single interventions (such as screening for high blood pressure) to comprehensive health and fitness programs, aerobic exercise and fitness, nutrition and weight control, stress management, smoking cessation, cancer-risk screening, drug and alcohol abuse prevention, accident prevention, and health information (Conrad 1999). Some workplaces have nap rooms, allowing workers to take naps (Bettelheim 1998). Many companies have employee assistance programs to help employees and their families with substance abuse, family discord, depression, and other mental health problems.

At the same time, one highly controversial health and safety strategy used by business management is behavioural-based safety programs. Instead of examining how work processes and conditions compromise health and safety on the job, **behaviour-based safety programs** direct attention to workers themselves as the problem. Behaviour-based safety programs claim that 80 to

behaviour-based safety programs

A controversial health and safety strategy used by business management in which health and safety problems in the workplace are attributed to workers' behaviour rather than to work processes and conditions.

96 percent of job injuries and illnesses are caused by workers' own carelessness and unsafe acts (Frederick and Lessin 2000).

Critics contend that behaviour-based safety programs divert attention away from employers' failures to provide safe working conditions. For example, when a worker slipped and fell on the ice in the parking lot of a tire manufacturing company,

> the official accident report . . . stated, "Worker's eyes not on path," as the cause of the injury. The report did not mention the need to have ice and snow removed from the parking lot. It did not mention that the sidewalk had not been cleared of snow and ice for several weeks, even though workers were required to use the sidewalk periodically. (Frederick and Lessin 2000)

Critics also say that the real goal of behaviour-based safety programs is to discourage workers from reporting illness and injuries. Workers whose employers have implemented behaviour-based safety programs describe an atmosphere of fear in the workplace, such that workers are reluctant to report injuries and illnesses for fear of being labelled an "unsafe worker" (Frederick and Lessin 2000).

Work–Family Policies and Programs

The influx of women into the workplace has been accompanied by an increase in government and company policies designed to help women and men balance their work and family roles. As of this writing, Canada's employment insurance program permits parents of newborns or of adoptees to take 35 weeks of paid parental leave in which either parent may take the total allowable leave, or the parents may share it. Because pregnancy and birth can be especially taxing, birth mothers may receive up to an additional 15 weeks of maternity leave and can start their claims up to 8 weeks prior to the expected birth. To make the claim for parental leave, the person receiving the benefit must have worked at least 600 hours during the previous year (HRDC 2006). These benefits provide 55 percent of their normal weekly pay to a maximum weekly gross amount of $413 (HRDC 2006). While women who claim maternity benefits are prohibited from employment, those who receive parental benefits are allowed to work part time and earn 25 percent of their wage up to a set minimum.

Results from the longitudinal Survey of Labour and Income Dynamics (SLID) indicate self-employment and the absence of maternity leave correlate with quick returns to paid work. "The odds of the mother's returning to work by the end of the first month [following a child's birth] were almost six times higher when she did *not* receive maternity leave benefits. Also, the odds of returning early were almost eight times higher for the self-employed than for employees" (Marshall 1999: 22). In general, however, mothers evidenced a strong attachment to participation in the paid labour force: only 7 percent of all Canadian women who gave birth in the early 1990s had not returned to paid work after two years. Non-returnees were more likely to have been employed in part-time work and less likely to have held, prior to giving birth, a unionized job or a professional job. In addition, non-returnees had, on average, spent less time at their last job than those who returned and earned lower median salaries ($16 700 versus $25 000).

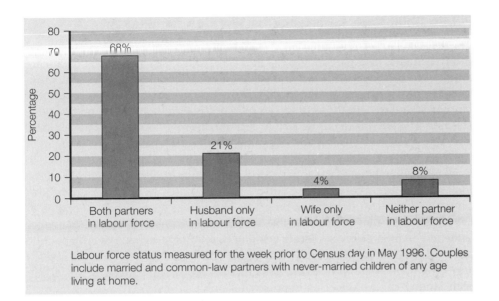

■ **Figure 11.4**
Employment of Mothers, by Age of Youngest Child and Family Status, 2004

SOURCE: "Employment of Mothers, by Age of Youngest Child and Family Status, 2004," from the Statistics Canada publication *Women in Canada: A Gender-based Statistical Report*, 2005, Catalogue No. 89-203, released March 13, 2006, page 107.

Women in Canada today are less likely to interrupt their paid work and, when interruptions do occur, return to gainful employment more quickly than women did in the past. Despite the common assumption that mothers do not work outside the home, Figures 11.4 and 11.5 show that most mothers in Canada, even those with very young children, are in paid employment. Reflecting this, the 2001 census counted more than 136 000 child-care workers—an increase of 87 percent over the past decade—with gains particularly notable in Quebec (Statistics Canada 2003: 8). Yet, not all Canadian provinces and territories have shown equal commitment to providing Canada's workers with access to safe, affordable, and accessible child care.

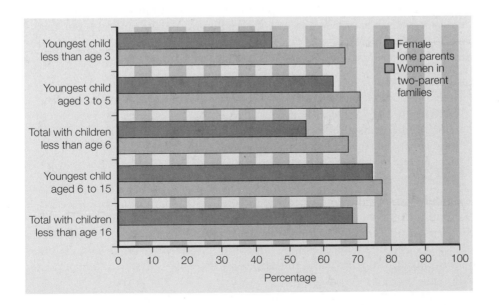

■ **Figure 11.5**
Employment of Women with Children, by Family Status, 1976–2004

SOURCE: "Employment of Female Lone Parents," from the Statistics Canada publication *Women in Canada: A Gender-based Statistical Report*, 2005, Catalogue No. 89-203, released March 13, 2006, page 106.

Public Child Care Assistance for Working Families

In 1997, Quebec introduced a comprehensive family policy aimed at integrating family benefits, paid parental level, child care, and kindergarten. Its child-care component heralded universally available, affordable child care in that province. The aim was to make every child in Quebec, by 2001, able to receive child care for $5 a day (and for as little as $2 a day for certain low-income families). This nominal fee was to entitle a child to a maximum of 10 hours a day of child care, one meal, two snacks, and use of all educational materials. In September 1997, all five-year-olds in Quebec whose families desired it became entitled to receive full-time kindergarten, with $5-a-day after-school care organized by the educational authorities; the government offered similar benefits for junior kindergarten and early intervention programs for families on welfare. In September 1998, all 3-year-olds became eligible for $5-a-day child care. In 2000, Quebec launched 10 pilot projects offering evening, weekend, and even overnight child care—all available at the same $5-a-day rate (Doherty 2001). While the costs of providing such a comprehensive system are significant, Quebec's policy has been lauded as "a pioneering approach to family supports in North America" (National Council of Welfare 1999a: 44).

In March 2000, the province of British Columbia became the second jurisdiction in North America to move toward publicly funded child care for all families "rich, poor, and the large majority in between" (Canadian Council on Social Development 2001: 6). Since January 1, 2001, families in British Columbia who seek before- and after-school care for their children became able to access licensed spaces on and off school sites at a cost to parents of $7 a day during the school year and $14 a day during school holidays.

However, elsewhere in Canada, the provision of child care remains "severely compromised on three fronts: the availability of spaces to meets the needs of children and their families, the affordability of care and the quality of services provided" (National Council of Welfare 1999b: 44). Although it is the wealthiest province in Canada, Ontario provides among the most meagre supports for working families. Under the provincial liberals in Ontario, there was no budget line for child care in the 2008 budget; by 2010, only 20 percent of children in child care were in licensed child-care spaces (Ontario Coalition for Better Childcare 2011). In Alberta, another extremely wealthy province, public funding for child care is similarly grim:

> The Alberta Family Employment Tax Credit is a non-taxable amount paid to families with a working income that have children under the age of 18. Families must be receiving the Canada Child Tax Benefit to qualify but the payments are issued separately...In 2000, families were entitled to whichever of the three amounts were the least: either $500 for the year for each child under age 18; $1,000 for the year; or eight percent of the family's working income over $6,500. The credit was reduced after a family net income of more than $25,000. (p. 69)

Under current adjustments to the Alberta policy, families would receive a maximum of $1836 in tax credits for their child-care expenses if they had four children under age 18 and a net income of $79 874 (Government of Alberta 2011). The declared mandate of the tax-credit program is to require that families be working in order to make the tax claim, because Alberta is "encouraging self-reliance and stability" (ibid). Another way of understanding the Alberta policy is that whereas provinces are dependent on the successful care and education of children, who are the next generation of human resources (i.e., future resources for the provincial GDP), the province seeks to minimize its investment in the development of that resource.

Under the Conservative government, as of July 1, 2006, all families in Canada with children under the age of six were entitled to payments of $100 per month per child under the Universal Child Care Benefit. Families that can claim the Canada Child Tax Benefit automatically receive the monthly disbursements, but others must apply and meet certain citizenship and immigration requirements to qualify (Canada Revenue Agency 2006). Like the Ontario and Alberta plans, the program claims a commitment to universal child care, but its ability to deliver universal child care is limited by meagre funding levels. Moreover, because each province and territory sets its own regulations about sources of allowable employment income for those receiving social assistance, some families will find that receipt of the child-care supplement means a partial or equal deduction in their social assistance benefits. In other words, there will be no change in parental ability to find work outside the home.

The Workplace and Family Life

Offering employees greater flexibility in their work hours could also help parents to balance their work and family demands. Flexible work arrangements, which benefit childfree workers as well as employed parents, include flextime, job sharing, a compressed workweek, and telecommuting. **Flextime** allows employees to begin and end the workday at different times, as long as 40 hours per week are maintained. With **job sharing**, two workers share the responsibility of one job. In Canada, job-sharers are most likely to be well-educated individuals. About half have a college or university education, and about 4 of 10 are professionals; nurses and teachers are most likely to participate in job sharing (Statistics Canada 1998).

A **compressed workweek** allows employees to condense their work into fewer days (e.g., four 10-hour days each week). **Telecommuting** allows employees to work part time or full time at home or at a satellite office (see this chapter's *Focus on Technology*). A study of U.S. companies found that the more women and minorities a company has in managerial positions, the more likely that company is to offer flexible work options (Galinsky and Bond 1998).

Fran Rodgers, president of Work/Family Directions, explains the need for work–family policies:

> For over 20 years we at Work/Family Directions have asked employees in all industries what it would take for them to contribute more at work. Every study found the same thing: They need aid with their dependent care, more flexibility and control over the hours and conditions of work, and a corporate culture in which they are not punished because they have families. These are fundamental needs of our society and of every worker. (Galinsky et al. 1993: 51)

flextime

An option in work scheduling that allows employees to begin and end the workday at different times as long as they perform a given number of hours of work per week.

job sharing

A work option in which two people share and are paid for one job.

compressed workweek

Workplace option in which employees work a full week, full time, but in four rather than five days.

telecommuting

A work option in which workers complete all or part of their work at home with the use of information technology.

Telework: The New Workplace of the Twenty-First Century

The ever-widening use of modern technology in the workplace, such as computers, the internet, email, fax machines, copiers, mobile phones, and personal digital assistants, makes it possible for many workers to perform their jobs at a variety of locations. The term telework (also known as "telecommuting") refers to flexible and alternative work arrangements that involve use of information technology. There are four types of telework (Pratt 2000): (1) home-based telework; (2) satellite offices where all employees telework for one employer; (3) telework centres, which are occupied by employees from more than one organization; and (4) mobile workers. Most (89 percent) teleworkers are home-based (Bowles 2000). Some people telework full-time, but a larger number telework one or two days a week. If current trends hold, the largest fraction of teleworkers will be professionals (over a third), followed by clerical and sales.

Telework holds potential benefits for employers, workers, and the environment. After presenting some of these benefits, we discuss concerns related to telework.

Benefits of Telework for Employers

Attracts and Helps Retain Employees. Companies regard telework and other flexible work arrangements as important in recruiting and maintaining good employees. Telework can also lower turnover and thus save companies expenses associated with hiring and training replacement employees. However, Bowles (2000) reports that companies are beginning to express dissatisfaction with telework "because they believe that it causes resentment among office-bound colleagues and weakens corporate loyalty" (p. 2).

Reduces Costs. Telework eliminates offices that teleworkers don't need, allows employers to consolidate others, and reduces related overhead costs (Lovelace 2000).

Increases Worker Productivity. Several studies of managers and employees at large companies conclude that telework increases worker productivity (Lovelace 2000).

Benefits of Telework for Employees

Increases Job and Life Satisfaction. Studies have shown that employee satisfaction among teleworkers is higher than for their non-teleworking counterparts (Lovelace 2000). Much of the job satisfaction among telecommuters is related to the job flexibility that enables them to balance work and family demands.

Helps Balance Work–Family Demands. Telework can provide flexibility to working parents and adults caring for aging parents, thus reducing role conflict and strengthening family life. One father of three children described his being home when his children came back from school as being "the most significant impact" of his telecommuting (Riley, Mandavilli, and Heino 2000: 5). He also took time during the day to take his children to school, to the doctor's office, and to run errands. However, a study of children whose parents work at home found that older children (grades 7 to 12) were more likely to agree that "my father does not have the energy to do things with me because of his job" and "my father has not been in a good mood with me because of his job" than the children of fathers who work in an office (Galinsky and Kim 2000). The effects of telework on parent–child relationships seem to depend then on how each parent interacts with his or her children.

Expands Work Opportunities for Canadians outside the Economic Mainstream. Telework may expand job opportunities for rural job seekers who lack local

Challenges to Corporate Power and Globalization

Challenges to corporate power have also taken root in Canada and throughout the world. Anti-globalization activists have targeted the World Trade Organization (WTO), the International Monetary Fund (IMF), and the World Bank as forces that advance corporate-led globalization at the expense of social goals such as justice, community, national sovereignty, cultural diversity, ecological sustainability, and workers' rights.

employment opportunities, and for low-income urban job seekers who lack access to suburban jobs (Kukreja and Neely 2000). Telework can also bring work opportunities to individuals with disabilities. Some of the technologies that have been developed for individuals with serious disabilities include "Eye Gaze" (a communication system that allows people to operate a computer with their eyes); "Magic Wand Keyboard" (for people with limited or no hand movement); and "Switched Adapted Mouse and Trackball" (that allows clicking the mouse with other parts of the body) (Bowles 2000).

Avoids the Commute. Telework allows individuals to reduce or eliminate daily commutes. Consider that eliminating a 50-minute daily commute allows an individual to gain almost 5 weeks per year in time (Lovelace 2000).

Environmental Benefits of Telework

Telework can reduce pollution by reducing the need for transportation to the workplace, thus reducing the pollution associated with vehicle emissions. Indeed, some maintain that "telecommuting presents a non-coercive way for corporations to help the nation achieve environmental goals and improve quality of life" (quoted in Lovelace 2000. 3).

Concerns about Telework

Blurred Boundaries between Home and Work. People who work at home may find themselves on call around the clock, responding to email, pagers, faxes, and voice mail. Without clear boundaries between home and work, teleworkers may feel that they are unable to escape the work environment and mindset (Pratt 2000). Questions about overtime pay may arise when work spills over into personal time. Having a separate office within the home and a routine work schedule may help create the psychological boundary between work and family/leisure. But for some teleworkers, learning to "log off" is a challenge.

Zoning Regulations. Teleworkers who work at home full time must contend with zoning regulations that may prohibit residents from having an "office" in their home.

Losing Benefits as a Contract Employee. Some employers attempt to convert the teleworker into a contract worker. This type of worker lacks job protections and benefits (Bowles 2000).

Social Isolation. Does telework lead to social isolation for those who live and work at home? Evidence suggests that teleworkers are able to maintain personal relationships with co-workers and are included in office networks. However, for rural and disabled individuals, telework may contribute to social isolation.

Exclusion of the Disenfranchised. Lower socio-economic groups are less likely than more affluent populations to have access to and skills in the Internet and other modern forms of information technology. Bowles (2000) suggests that "the eventual success of telework programs in the future must...account for the masses of people left behind.... All must be included in the new economy; it is not a luxury, but a must" (p. 9).

SOURCES: Bowles, Diane O. 2000. "Growth in Telework." Paper presented at the symposium *Telework and the New Workplace of the 21st Century,* Xavier University, New Orleans, October 16, 2000; Galinsky, Ellen, and Stacy S. Kim. 2000. "Navigating Work and Parenting by Working at Home: Perspectives of Workers and Children Whose Parents Work at Home." Paper presented at *Telework and the New Workplace;* Lovelace, Glenn. 2000. "The Nuts and Bolts of Telework." Paper presented at *Telework and the New Workplace;* Kukreja, Anil, and George M. Neely, Sr. 2000. "Strategies for Preventing the Digital Divide." Paper presented at *Telework and the New Workplace;* Pratt, Joanne H. 2000. "Telework and Society—Implications for Corporate and Societal Cultures." Paper presented *Telework and the New Workplace;* Riley, Patricia, Anu Mandavilli, and Rebecca Heino. 2000. "Observing the Impact of Communication and Information Technology on 'Net-Work.'" Paper presented at *Telework and the New Workplace.*

In 1999, 50 000 street protesters and Third World delegates demonstrated in opposition to the policies of the WTO that promoted corporate-led globalization. Another confrontation between pro- and anti-globalization forces occurred at the 2000 meeting of the IMF and the World Bank in Washington, and later at the 2002 meetings of the G-8 leaders in Kananaskis, Alberta. Media attention to such protests contributes to the growing worldwide awareness of the forces of corporate globalization and its social, environmental, and economic effects. However, governments that want to get business matters tended to with a minimum of interference from the people that governments putatively serve are treating resisters and demonstrators more and more aggressively. In summer 2010 the fourth meeting of the G-20 was held in Toronto, and the city was barricaded in its central core, with steel fences that restricted the movement of Toronto's residents. The CBC documentary "You Should Have Stayed at Home," presented by *The Fifth Estate*, exposed some of the most egregious violations of the civil rights of peaceful protesters and bystanders at the summit, including the violent beatings of persons "guilty" of nothing more than being within striking distance of the 10 000 police on the streets. 1150 people were arrested and detained on the weekend of the G-20 summit, held without charge. Precise numbers in publicly available reports vary, but the CBC indicated that of the roughly 1150 held only 300 were ever charged, and by mid-October 2010 charges against 159 of those had been dropped (CBC News 2010). As of the writing of this edition of the text, 18 people remain charged as "anarchist" conspirators but it could be years before they have their cases heard at trial (Krauss 2010).

Understanding **Work and Unemployment**

On December 10, 1948, the General Assembly of the United Nations adopted and proclaimed the Universal Declaration of Human Rights, some of which appears below.

> Article 23. Everyone has the right to work, to free choice of employment, to just and favourable conditions of work and to protection against unemployment.
>
> Everyone, without any discrimination, has the right to equal pay for equal work.
>
> Everyone who works has the right to just and favourable remuneration ensuring for himself [sic] and his [sic] family an existence worthy of human dignity, and supplemented, if necessary, by other means of social protection.
>
> Everyone has the right to form and to join trade unions for the protection of his [sic] interests.
>
> Article 24. Everyone has the right to rest and leisure, including reasonable limitation of working hours and periodic holidays with pay.

More than half a century later, workers around the world are still fighting for these basic rights as proclaimed in the Universal Declaration of Human Rights.

To understand social problems associated with work and unemployment, we must first recognize the power and influence of governments and corporations on the workplace. We must also be aware of the role that technological developments and postindustrialization have on what we produce, how we produce it, where we produce it, and who does the producing. Canada is moving away from producing manufactured goods toward producing services. The labour-intensive blue-collar assembly line is declining in importance, and information-intensive white-collar occupations are increasing. Because of increasing corporate multinationalization, Canadian jobs are moving to foreign countries where labour is cheap, regulations are lax, and raw materials are available. Finally, the workforce is becoming more diverse in terms of gender and racial and ethnic background and is including more contingent workers than in the past.

Decisions made by Canadian corporations about what and where to invest influence the quantity and quality of jobs available in Canada. As conflict theorists argue, such investment decisions are motivated by profit, which is part of a capitalist system. Profit is also a driving factor in deciding how and when technological devices will be used to replace workers and increase productivity, but if goods and services are produced too efficiently, workers are laid off and high unemployment results. When people lack money to buy products, sales slump, a recession ensues, and social welfare programs are needed to support the unemployed. When the government increases spending to pay for its social programs, it expands the deficit and increases the national debt. Deficit spending and a large national debt make it difficult to recover from the recession, and the cycle continues.

Those adhering to the classic view of capitalism argue for limited government intervention on the premise that business will regulate itself via an "invisible hand" or "market forces." For example, if corporations produce a desired product at a low price, people will buy it, which means workers will be hired to produce the product, and so on.

Ironically, those who support limited government intervention also sometimes advocate government intervention to bail out failed banks and troubled businesses (or hockey teams). Such government help benefits the powerful segments of our society. Yet, when economic policies hurt less powerful groups, such as minorities, there has been a collective hesitance to support or provide social welfare programs. It is also ironic that such bailout programs, which contradict the ideals of capitalism, are needed because of capitalism. For example, the profit motive leads to multinationalization, which leads to unemployment, which leads to the need for government programs. The various forces transforming our economy are interrelated—technology, globalization, capital flight through multinationalization, and the movement toward a service economy (Eitzen and Zinn 1990). For the individual worker, the concepts of work, job, and career have changed forever.

Critical Thinking

1. In 1999, 10 years after Canada and the United States signed a free trade accord that bound their economies ever more tightly, the C. D. Howe Institute released a study that argued the merits of Canada using the same currency as the United States. If Canadian nationalists reacted to the suggestion of a common currency with predictions of Canada's imminent demise, the issue of "dollarization"—instituting the U.S. dollar for local currencies—has found considerable support in such countries as Argentina and Mexico. What would be the advantages and disadvantages of Canada establishing a currency union with the United States?

2. Foreigners (chiefly Americans) control a considerable fraction of the Canadian economy. Indeed, Bellan (1999: 884) notes that "[t]his large foreign presence in the economy [is] quite unparalleled elsewhere in the world [and] has deep historic roots." Identify some of the consequences of having a huge part of the Canadian economy controlled by U.S. interests.

3. Consider the final remarks on worker benefits in the "Conflict Perspective" section. Are policies intended to benefit "the bottom line" morally defensible if benefits to employees are secondary to benefits to corporations?

"Is It True?" Quiz: Answers

1 = true; 2 = true; 3 = false; 4 = true; 5 = false

Problems in Education

Outline

Is It True?

1. In 2001, more than half of Canada's population had less than a Grade 9 education.

2. Among the OECD (Organisation for Economic Co-operation and Development) countries, Canada ranks first in the proportion of its working-age population with a university degree.

3. Regardless of gender or place of origin, immigrants arriving to Canada over the past 20 years tend to be highly educated.

4. More than half of the people living in developing nations are illiterate.

5. IQ is the best predictor of school success.

Read more here: 1 = p. 420, 2 = p. 421, 3 = p. 416, 4 = p. 412, 5 = p. 419

Answers can be found on p. 441.

© Bloomberg/Getty Images

special education

Remedial education
designed to help children
and adults who are excep-
tional in some way,
including but not limited
to, low intelligence, visual
or auditory disabilities, and
emotional or specific
learning difficulties.

Education is often claimed as a panacea—the cure-all for poverty and prejudice,
drugs and violence, war and hatred—yet, daily, it seems, we are reminded of
problems that exist in Canada's educational system. Some have charged that our
educational system is encumbered by seniority and indifference to absolute
educational outcomes, which hamper Canada's ability to compete. Others direct
attention to the ravages of budget cuts, increasing tuition costs, and staggering
levels of student debt. Others highlight funding "reforms" that have triggered
dramatic cuts to **special education** programs and the allied services of speech
pathologists and psychologists (Schofield 1999).

Can one institution, riddled with obstacles, be a solution for other social
problems? In this chapter, we focus on this question and what is being called
one of the major sociopolitical issues of the century—the educational crisis
(Associated Press 1998). We begin with a look at education around the world.

12.1 The Global Context: Cross-Cultural Variation in Education

Looking only at the Canadian educational system might lead to the conclusion
that most societies have developed some method of formal instruction for their
members. After all, there are almost 16 000 elementary and secondary schools
in Canada, employing a full-time teaching force of almost 300 000, and about
300 colleges and universities employing an additional 60 000 full-time educators (Statistics Canada 1998). In reality, many societies have no formal mechanism for educating the masses. As a result, worldwide, over 120 million children
do not attend school—42 million in sub-Saharan Africa alone—and over 880
million adults are illiterate. In 2000, the World Education Forum met in Dakar,
Senegal, where more than 1000 leaders from 145 countries recommitted their
energies to improving basic education in developing countries (U.S. Newswire
2000).

At the other end of the continuum are societies that emphasize the importance of formal education. Public expenditures on education in developed countries are 25 times higher than in less-developed countries (Population Reference
Bureau 1999). In Japan, students attend school on Saturday and the school
calendar is 57 days longer than in Canada (243 days in comparison to 186 days).
China (with a school year of 251 days), South Korea (220 days), Israel (215
days), Germany (210 days), Russia (210 days), Switzerland (207 days), the
Netherlands (200 days), Scotland (200 days), and Thailand (200 days) also have
more mandatory school days than Canada (Ash 2001: 102).

Canada continues to operate public education according to the terms of the
British North America Act, which identified education as a provincial responsibility and gave each province the constitutional authority to develop its own
educational organization. Although education in Yukon, the Northwest Territories, and Nunavut is funded by the federal government, it is governed by
ordinances of the assemblies of these regions. In consequence, Canada has 13
unique school systems that fund and administer public, private, denominational, and linguistic schools somewhat differently. The issues of religion and
language are two of the differences that exist within our system of
education.

Consider, for example, that our Constitution, unlike that of the United States, protects denominational, or "separate," schools. However, "[a]s each province joined Confederation, it brought its own approach to religious schools and Canadians are still dealing with the legacy of this process" (Statistics Canada 1998: 146). In Canada, free public education in a nondenominational public school system is available for all Canadians. So long as denominational schools operated by the Roman Catholic Church agree to admit non–Roman Catholic students, they receive public funding in Ontario (James 2004: 45). Alberta, Saskatchewan, Yukon, and the Northwest Territories also provide public funding for Roman Catholic schools. Elsewhere, any separate schools are privately funded. Until 1997, Newfoundland had an entirely denominational system of education; however, in that year, a public vote abolished its 277-year-old system of church-run schools.

"In 1982, Canada's Charter of Rights and Freedoms gave English- and French-speaking minorities the right to educate their children in their mother tongue and the courts have consistently supported this right for these two minority groups across Canada" (Statistics Canada 1998: 146). *Minority language education* is designed to offer the minority group in a province (anglophones in Quebec, francophones outside Quebec) education in their mother tongue. *Second language education*, now referred to as "international language education," developed to provide heritage instruction, generally in urban boards where multiple ethnic groups were represented; largely white, rural areas, however, did little to meet the multicultural mandate of the 1970s and the curriculum remains largely Eurocentric throughout Canada to this day (James 2004: 44).

Although the BNA Act of 1867 made the federal government responsible for the education of Aboriginal peoples, over the past few decades, the growing demand that Aboriginal peoples be allowed to run their own schools has led to a reduction in the direct involvement of the Department of Indian Affairs. Because of agreements made between First Nations bands and the Department of Indian Affairs, the role of the federal government has steadily been reduced to that of a funding source for programs controlled by the Native community. Generally, decisions on the distribution of resources, staffing, curriculum, language of instruction, and length of school year are now made by band education authorities in most areas. The reasons for such changes are complex and vary across Canada, but the changes seek to meet two fundamental goals: first, to recognize the autonomy and specificity of the educational needs of distinct bands and regions; second, to correct the legacy of damaging educational practices that had derided Indigenous cultures, languages, and knowledge in a process of "cultural invasion." Antonia Dardur (1991: 36) explains that cultural invasion "serves the sustained social, political and economic oppression of subordinate groups" largely by teaching the subordinate groups to see their own languages and cultures as inferior.

For all of the problems in education, Canadians hold a strong belief in its importance—and with good reason. Consider that in 2001, Statistics Canada reported that while the average family headed by a high school graduate enjoyed a net worth of approximately $65 000, this figure rose to $120 000 for a family headed by a university graduate and about $320 000 for those with a professional degree in law, medicine, dentistry, and the like (Bricker and Greenspon 2001: 158). At the same time, however, Canadians are increasingly likely to raise questions about the quality of education in this country. One survey reported that "a staggering 82 percent of parents worried about the quality of education received by their children," while a second found that over one in three Canadians (37 percent) thought that education was in worse shape than 25 years earlier (Bricker and Greenspon 2001: 156, 162). Many perceive that there is considerable room—and need—for improvement.

12.2 Sociological Theories of Education

The three major sociological perspectives—structural-functionalism, conflict theory, and symbolic interactionism—are important in explaining different aspects of Canadian education. This chapter also provides critical perspectives that include feminist, queer, and antiracist interventions into the institution, practice, and purpose of education.

Structural-Functionalist Perspective

According to structural-functionalism, the educational institution accomplishes important tasks for society, including instruction, socialization, the sorting of individuals into various statuses, and the provision of custodial care. Many social problems, such as unemployment, crime and delinquency, and poverty, may be linked to the failure of the educational institution to fulfill these basic functions (see Chapters 4, 10, and 11). Structural-functionalists also examine the reciprocal influences of the educational institution and other social institutions, including the family, the political institution, and the economic institution.

Instruction A major function of education is to teach students the knowledge and skills necessary for future occupational roles, self-development, and social functioning. Although some parents teach their children basic knowledge and skills at home, most parents rely on schools to teach their children to read, spell, write, tell time, count money, and use computers. The failure of schools to instruct students in basic knowledge and skills both causes and results from many other social problems.

Socialization The socialization function of education involves teaching students to respect authority—behaviour that is essential for social organization (Merton 1968). Students learn to respond to authority by asking permission to leave the classroom, sitting quietly at their desks, and raising their hands before asking a question. Students who do not learn to respect and obey teachers may later disrespect and disobey employers, police officers, and judges.

The educational institution also socializes youth into the dominant culture. Schools attempt to instill and maintain the norms, values, traditions, and symbols of the culture in a variety of ways, such as celebrating holidays (Remembrance Day, Thanksgiving); requiring students to speak and write in English and French; displaying the Canadian flag; and discouraging violence, drug use, and cheating.

Whether schools function well in Canada may be a matter of vantage point. As the number and size of racial and ethnic minority groups have increased,

Canadian schools have had to account for practices that directly contradict official policy on multiculturalism in Canada and for practices that trivialize non-dominant cultures. For example, Canadian sociologist Jasmin Zine (2002) argues that a variety of racist and Eurocentric practices still serve dominant groups while marginalizing particular groups in schools across the country. Among the commonplace, but problematic practices that Zine draws attention to are the following:

- A narration of history that focuses almost exclusively on Europe, as with "Medieval Times" curricula that entirely neglect flourishing civilizations from the time in China, Africa and Spain.
- Calling upon ethnically and/or racially "other" students to perform their culture for their classmates while Anglo-Canadian children are not called upon to perform their British heritage.
- Having all the complexity of your heritage and culture reduced to "saris, samosa and steel bands" trotted out for school festivals, while simultaneously knowing that we don't learn Canadian history via bagpipes and meat pies. (Zine 2002: 37)

Practices such as these, which developed alongside multicultural policy in the 1970s, Zine argues, are incredibly damaging for minoritized students: they learn in unequivocal terms that their cultures don't count, that their richness does not have to be acknowledged. Instead of perpetuating Eurocentric curricula and attitudes, Zine proposes a multi-centric approach, one in which diversity operates not as an "add on," but as "a starting point for knowledge integration, in which the historical achievements of all societies are examined, validated and respected" (p. 38).

Sorting Individuals into Statuses Schools sort individuals into statuses by providing credentials for individuals who achieve various levels of education at various schools within the system. These credentials sort people into different statuses—for example, "high school graduate," "Rhodes scholar," and "Ph.D." Further, schools sort individuals into professional statuses by awarding degrees in such fields as medicine, nursing, and law. The significance of such statuses lies in their association with occupational prestige and income—in general, the higher one's education, the higher one's income (Ghalam 2000). Table 12.1 shows the correspondence between education levels and income over 25 years from 1980 to 2005.

Custodial Care The educational system also provides custodial care (Merton 1968), which is particularly valuable to single-parent and dual-earner families, and the likely reason for the increase in enrollments of 3- and 4-year-olds. The school system provides free supervision and care for children and adolescents until they complete secondary, or "high," school—almost 13 000 hours per pupil. Some school districts are experimenting with offering classes on a 12-month basis, on Saturdays, and as part of longer school days. Working parents, the hope that increased supervision will reduce delinquency rates, and higher educational standards that require more hours of study are some of the motivations behind the "more time" movement (Wilgoren 2001).

■ **Table 12.1** *Median Earnings, in 2005 Constant Dollars, of Male and Female Recent Immigrant Earners and Canadian-Born Earners Aged 25 to 54, with or without a University Degree, Canada, 1980–2005*

	Recent Immigrant Earners[1]				Canadian-Born Earners[1]				Recent Immigrant to Canadian-Born Earnings Ratio			
	With a University Degree		With no University Degree		With a University Degree		With no University Degree		With a University Degree		With no University Degree	
	Males	Females	Males	Females	Males	Females	Males	Females	Males	Females	Males	Females
Year	2005 constant dollars								ratio			
1980	48 541	24 317	36 467	18 548	63 040	41 241	43 641	21 463	0.77	0.59	0.84	0.86
1990	38 351	25 959	27 301	17 931	61 332	41 245	40 757	23 267	0.63	0.63	0.67	0.77
2000	35 816	22 511	25 951	16 794	61 505	43 637	39 902	25 622	0.58	0.52	0.65	0.66
2005	30 332	18 969	24 470	14 233	62 566	44 545	40 235	25 590	0.48	0.43	0.61	0.56

Note:

The numbers refer to all earners, whether or not they worked on a full-time basis for a full year. Individuals with self-employment income are included while those living in institutions are excluded.

SOURCE: Statistics Canada, *Earnings and Incomes of Canadians Over the Past Quarter Century, 2006 Census,* 97-563-XIE2006001, May 2008; http://www.statcan.gc.ca/bsolc/olc-cel/olc-cel?catno=97-563-XIE2006001&lang=eng#formatdisp.

Conflict Perspective

Conflict theorists emphasize that the educational institution solidifies the class positions of groups and allows the elite to control the masses. Although the official goal of education in society is to provide a universal mechanism for achievement, educational opportunities and the quality of education are not equally distributed.

Conflict theorists point out that the socialization function of education is really indoctrination into a capitalist ideology. In essence, students are socialized to value the interests of the state and to function to sustain it. Such indoctrination begins in kindergarten. Rosabeth Moss Kanter (1972) coined the term *the organization child* to refer to the child in nursery school who is most comfortable with supervision, guidance, and adult control. Teachers cultivate the organization child by providing daily routines and rewarding those who conform. In essence, teachers train future bureaucrats to be obedient to authority.

cultural imperialism

The indoctrination into the dominant culture of a society; when cultural imperialism exists, the norms, values, traditions, and languages of minorities are systematically ignored.

Further, to conflict theorists, education serves as a mechanism for **cultural imperialism**, or the indoctrination into the dominant culture of a society. When cultural imperialism exists, the norms, values, traditions, and languages of minorities are systematically ignored. For example, in his analysis of the development of the educational system in Ontario in the mid-1800s, Neil McDonald emphasized how education was seen as crucial for maintaining dominant ideologies. He notes that the chief architect of the Ontario school system, Egerton Ryerson, purposefully set out to create a system in which "young people would remain loyal to the Crown . . . never participate in the kind of rebellion which had been put down in Upper Canada in 1837, and . . . cooperate with one another, regardless of their social class backgrounds." Through education, the working class were to be persuaded that "their interests were also

Education as Cultural Genocide

The province of Canada in 1847 published a report...which formed the basis for future directions in policy for Indian Education. Clearly expressed is the perception of the superiority of the European culture, the need "to raise [aboriginal people] to the level of the whites," and the ever-increasing pressure to take control of land out of Indian hands...The general recommendations of the report were that the Indians remain under the control of the Crown rather than the provincial authority, that efforts to Christianize the Indians be continued, and finally that schools, preferably manual labour ones, be established under the guidance of missionaries...Cultural oppression was becoming written policy. Within the discussion of the recommendations is the following comment:

> Their education must consist not merely of the training of the mind, but of a weaning from the habits and feelings of their ancestors, and the acquirements of the language, arts and customs of civilized life.

What clearer statement of an effort to destroy a culture could exist?...

Following the Indian Act of 1876, a consolidation of existing legislation, the government commissioned N. F. Davin to report on industrial schools established for native people in the United States. Out of his report came the strong recommendations which resulted in the establishment of many residential schools across Canada...In the introduction to the report, Davin made references to President Grant's policy on the Indian question: "The industrial school is the principal feature of the policy known as aggressive civilization..." While positively endorsing the notion of residential schools for Indians in Canada, Davin's final comment is, "If anything is to be done with the Indian, we must catch him very young..."

By 1920 amendments to the Indian Act included compulsory school attendance of Indian children and industrial or boarding schools for Indians...[I]n 1920 the House of Commons...Deputy Superintendent General Duncan Campbell Scott stated clearly the idea that Indian cultures as such were to be eliminated:

> Our object is to continue until there is not a single Indian in Canada that has not been absorbed into the body politic and there is no Indian ques-

tion, and no Indian department, that is the whole object of the Bill.

Not until 1946 was there serious possibility for change in this attitude and in the expressed intent of Department of Indian Affairs policy...[In that year,] Andrew Paull, President of the North American Indian Brotherhood, appeared before the Special Joint Committee. He was highly critical of the committee's lack of Indian representation. He condemned the existing Act as "an imposition, the carrying out of the most bureaucratic and autocratic system that were ever imposed upon any people in this world of ours." He spoke strongly of Indian self-government, and finally he commented that what was needed was

> to lift up the morale of the Indians in Canada. That is your first duty. There is no use in passing legislation about this or that if you do not lift up the morale of the people. The only way you can lift up the morale of any people is to let the members look after themselves and look after their people.

His words fell upon deaf ears.

SOURCE: Adapted from Haig-Brown, Celia. 1993. *Resistance and Renewal: Surviving the Indian Residential School.* Vancouver: Arsenal Pulp Press.

those of the middle and upper classes and that, as a collectivity, there was a 'common' or 'public good' towards which all must work" (McDonald, as cited in Curtis and Lambert 1994: 12). As Curtis and Lambert (1994: 12) remark, "In short, Ryerson's objective was social control, and he charged the schools with the responsibility of inculcating the beliefs and attitudes of mind that would accomplish it."

Traditionally, the school curriculum has not given voice to the perspective of minority groups, including women. Moreover, the cultural genocide promoted within the residential schools for Canada's Indigenous peoples must be recognized as one of the bleakest notes in the history of Canadian education (see this chapter's *The Human Side*). As only one example, Native students who dared to speak their own language were routinely punished by having a sewing needle pushed through their tongue. This practice was known as the "needle torture."

Finally, the conflict perspective focuses on what Kozol (1991) calls the "savage inequalities" in education that perpetuate racial inequality. Change must come in classroom practices that recognize cultural variability. As sociologist Pierre Bourdieu explains, every child arrives in the classroom with his or her own very rich **cultural capital**, which includes language, artistic tastes, specific knowledge, and links to community and to resources outside the school (Brooks and Thompson 2005). However, the cultural capital of all students is not equally valued; it is not a matter of student shortcomings, but a matter of highly constraining curricula do not value what children from marginalized groups have to offer the classroom. Brooks and Thompson (2005: 49) explain:

> Focusing on the academic curriculum to the exclusion of the social curriculum constricts learning for all students. But it does the most harm to students of low socioeconomic status, who may depend on teachers to bridge the gap between their own cultural capital and the mainstream . . .

Although we are faced with increasingly tight curricula and testing measures, Brooks and Thompson argue that we can still incorporate considerations about social justice. We can invite and include student contributions on, for example, the important people and occupations in their communities, even if those positions are not accorded "high status" in the mainstream view.

Symbolic Interactionist Perspective

Whereas structural-functionalism and conflict theory focus on macro-level issues, such as institutional influences and power relations, symbolic interactionism examines education from a micro perspective. This perspective is concerned with individual and small-group issues, such as teacher–student interactions, the students' self-esteem, and the self-fulfilling prophecy.

Teacher–Student Interactions Symbolic interactionists have examined the ways in which students and teachers view and relate to one another. For example, children from economically advantaged homes may be more likely to bring social and verbal skills into the classroom that elicit approval from teachers. From the teachers' point of view, middle-class children are easy and fun to teach: they grasp the material quickly, do their homework, and are more likely to "value" the educational process. Children from economically disadvantaged homes often bring fewer social and verbal skills to those same middle-class teachers, who may, inadvertently, hold up social mirrors of disapproval. Teacher disapproval contributes to the lower self-esteem among disadvantaged youth.

Self-Fulfilling Prophecy The **self-fulfilling prophecy** occurs when people act in a manner consistent with the expectations of others. For example, a teacher who defines a student as a slow learner may be less likely to call on that student or to encourage the student to pursue difficult subjects. As a consequence of the teacher's behaviour, the student is more likely to perform at a lower level.

An early study by Rosenthal and Jacobson (1968) provided empirical evidence of the self-fulfilling prophecy in the public school system. Five

cultural capital

Refers to the symbolic and material aspects of cultural heritage and understanding. To have high cultural capital is to possess and understand elite forms of art, language use and speech, dress and comportment, architecture and other aesthetic movements. Those with low cultural capital have either less access to and understanding of elite forms, or a culture unrecognized by those in power.

self-fulfilling prophecy

A concept referring to the tendency for people to act in a manner consistent with the expectations of others.

elementary school students were selected at random and identified for their teachers as "spurters." Such a label implied that they had superior intelligence and academic ability. In reality, they were no different from the other students in their classes. At the end of the school year, however, these five students scored higher on their intelligence quotient (IQ) tests and made higher grades than their classmates who were not labelled as spurters. In addition, the teachers rated the spurters more likely to succeed than the "nonspurters." Because the teachers expected the spurters to do well, they treated the students in a way that encouraged better school performance.

Critical Theories of Education

Louis Althusser was neither simply a Marxist nor only a structuralist, but a thinker who combined both views to account for how states operate and hold power. Althusser (1919–90) observed that education belonged to a group of structures—including among others, family and religion—that served state-sponsored views, or ideologies. Althusser (1971) termed these structures "Ideological State Apparatuses" (ISAs). He applied his view to unpack the main goals of education, which he saw as twofold: children learn how to do the things the state will require of them as workers and to observe the rules of their culture.

> [Children] go varying distances in their studies, but at any rate they learn to read, to write and to add—i.e. a number of techniques, and a number of other things as well, including elements (which may be rudimentary or on the contrary thorough-going) of "scientific" or "literary culture," which are directly useful in the different jobs in production (one instruction for manual workers, another for technicians, a third for engineers, a final one for higher management, etc.). Thus they learn know-how.
>
> But besides these techniques and knowledges . . . children at school also learn the "rules" of good behaviour, i.e. the attitude that should be observed by every agent in the division of labour, according to the job he is "destined" for: rules of morality, civic and professional conscience, which actually means rules of respect for the socio-technical division of labour and ultimately the rules of the order established by class domination. They also learn to "speak proper French," to "handle" the workers correctly, i.e. actually (for the future capitalists and their servants) to "order them about" properly, i.e. (ideally) to "speak to them" in the right way, etc. (Althusser 1971: 132)

In Althusser's view, the state and the dominant class profit most from the educational institution. The state profits from teaching pupils to value that particular state over all others, and the dominant class profits most from having a reliable institution to produce generation after generation of workers to carry out its will and uphold its values.

Feminist Perspectives

In Canada, it was not until the 1880s, several decades after the 1827 establishment of the nation's first university, the University of Toronto, that women were admitted as students for university education. Further, it was not until the 1970s that women could enroll in Canada's military colleges. Today, representation of women as faculty remains inequitable across disciplines even though women now far outnumber men as undergraduates.

In the 1970s, women faculty began to organize individual courses with a focus on women's contributions and issues. They recognized that women's history, experience, thinking, and contributions to culture and to the academy were largely absent from university courses that focused almost exclusively on men's accomplishments and men's lives. There is a debate over who launched "the first" Women's Studies program in Canada, but the first courses appeared in 1970–71 as initiatives of individual professors and activist collectives (Par-L n.d.).

At the high-school level, curricula continue to reflect the values and accomplishments of the dominant groups, and this pattern extends beyond the issue of class and race to gender as well. However, in Ontario in 2005, an energetic and committed group of young women undergraduates launched the Miss G_ Project. They took their name from the 1873 medical attribution of the death of a patient identified only as "Miss G_" to the supposed overexertion of her brain in the pursuit of learning (Clarke 1873). The Miss G_ Collective seeks to promote equity in education by including gender-based content at the high-school level:

> Equity in education is a policy commitment of the Ontario Secondary School Curriculum, but without recognizing gender and its implications, the curriculum fails to meet this commitment. We go through our mandatory formal education careers without ever encountering a critical study of gender and sexuality. In high school, we never encountered a fair and appropriate introduction to the very real contributions and histories of women and feminisms. (Miss G_ Collective 2005)

Whether feminists have sought to build an education for themselves, simply by means of access, or viewed their efforts as an endeavour to share with others, the goal has been to provide the benefits of information, of increased educational attainment, and of access to a world that one can understand and interpret for oneself.

Feminist perspectives also provide a critical assessment of educational traditions. They struggle to navigate the need for the power that comes with increased education while resisting the seductions of the hierarchical structure of the institution (Humble et al. 2006).

Feminists may also critique aspects of education that can thwart the educational goals of women. For example, a critique of latent functions presents this idea: "Being perceived as (hetero)sexually attractive and having a 'high-status' boyfriend elevated a young woman's standing among her classmates, which meant that schoolwork and friendship [are] pushed to the side" (Gilmartin 2005: 610).

12.3 Who Succeeds? The Inequality of Educational Attainment

The 1996 census was the first Canadian census to record a higher number of university graduates than of people reporting less than a Grade 9 education. Among the 29 countries surveyed by the Organisation for Economic Co-operation and

■ **Table 12.2** *Proportion of the Population Aged 25 to 64 with a University or College Education for the Top 10 OECD Countries*

University or College Education	
Country	Percentage
Canada	48
Japan	40
United States of America	39
Finland	35
Denmark	34
Norway	33
Australia	32
Korea	32
Iceland	31
Belgium	31

SOURCE: Statistics Canada. March 2008. "Educational Portrait of Canada, 2006 Census," Census Year 2006, Catalogue No. 97-560-X.

Development in 2000, only three countries had higher proportions of their working-age population with a university degree—the United States (28 percent), Norway (26 percent), and the Netherlands (21 percent) (Statistics Canada 2003a: 10). However, "[i]f university and college are combined, no other OECD nation had a higher proportion than Canada" in that year (Statistics Canada 2003a: 10). By 2006, Canada still had the world's highest proportion of adults with postsecondary levels of educational attainment (university or college). When ranked for university attainment only, Canada had fallen to 7th place out of 30 OECD nations surveyed for the population from age 24–65 (Table 12.2). Some of the drop in our position has to do with improvements in other OECD nations, and some of the drop can be attributed to reductions in numbers of young people in Canada who are obtaining trades certificates at the college level (Statistics Canada 2008: 11–12).

Regardless of our admirable showing in the OECD rankings, it is important to keep in mind that not all Canadian residents enjoy equal opportunity to achieve higher levels of education. As noted earlier, conflict theory focuses on inequalities in the educational system. Educational inequality is based on social class and family background, race and ethnicity, and gender. Each of these factors influences who succeeds in school.

Comparisons in 1996 and 2001 among self-identified Aboriginal individuals aged 25 to 64 suggest that progress has occurred. According to the 2006 census, the share of Aboriginal respondents with postsecondary qualifications increased to 44 percent, and those whose education was limited to a high-school diploma had fallen to 21 percent. In consequence, the gap between the educational profile of the Aboriginal and non-Aboriginal populations has narrowed somewhat, particularly in relation to the proportions with a trade certificate (16 percent of the working-age Aboriginal population and 13 percent of the working-age non-Aboriginal population) or college qualifications (15 percent among Aboriginal people and 18 percent among non-Aboriginal people). "However, the gap in university graduates remained wide. In 1996, 6 percent of Aboriginal people aged 25 to 64 had a university education. This increased to 8 percent in 2001" (Statistics Canada 2003a: 16). By 2006, this percentage remained unchanged at 8 percent, and the share of adult Aboriginal persons without a high school diploma was 34 percent (Statistics Canada 2008: 19).

Social Class and Family Background

One of the best predictors of educational success and attainment is socio-economic status (Lam 1997). Children in middle and upper socio-economic brackets are more likely to perform better in school and to complete more years of education than children from lower socio-economic brackets. For example, Muller and Schiller (2000) report that students from higher socio-economic backgrounds are more likely to enroll in advanced mathematics course credits and to graduate from high school—two indicators of future educational and occupational success. Canadian data on educational attainment released by Statistics Canada showed that young people from high-income families were 1.5 times more likely than those from low-income families to have been enrolled in a postsecondary institution (71.0/48.8 = 1.5) and about 2.5 times more likely to have gone to university in 1998 (39.6/16.3 = 2.4). Clearly, class correlates strongly with whether one gets a postsecondary education in Canada, and it correlates even more strongly with whether one will get a university education. This strong correlation is long established and got worse rather than better over the nearly two decades from 1979 to 1997. For some income groups, in fact, the disparity in participation rates has remained roughly even as more students enroll in postsecondary education (Statistics Canada 2003b).

While noting that "[p]oor children are not always disadvantaged and disadvantaged children are not always poor" (Health Canada 1999: 73), the 1996–1997 National Longitudinal Survey of Children and Youth (NLSCY) found that household income was clearly associated with school readiness—an important indicator of developmental maturity and future success at school (Doherty 1997). Figure 12.1 shows the relationship between university participation and parents' income measured over eight years. Problems of poor health, hyperactivity, and delayed vocabulary development are higher among children in low-income families than among children from more privileged families (Ross 1998). Children who score low on school readiness are also more likely to have mothers with low levels of education and to live in neighbourhoods that their mothers characterize as unsafe or as lacking in social cohesiveness (Health Canada 1999: 79).

A report released in 2005 through Statistics Canada (Drolet 2005) confirms the importance of family income to educational attainment and entry into university:

> Although university participation rates generally rise as family incomes increase, there is little difference in participation rates among youths from modest-income (below $75,000) and low-income families. Overall, the correlation between university participation and family income changed very little between 1993 and 2001. (Drolet 2005: 26)

A subtle but important point emerges in Drolet's observation above: It is not only that entry into university is prohibitively expensive for low-income

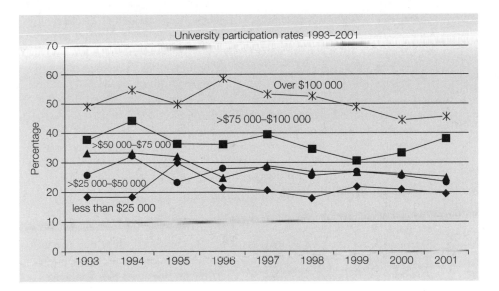

■ **Figure 12.1**

*University Participation
Rates for Youth: 1993–2001*

SOURCE: Statistics Canada.
February 2005. "Participation in
Post-Secondary Education: Has
the Role of Parental Income and
Education Changed over the 1990's?"
Analytical Studies Branch Research
Paper Series, Catalogue No.
11F0019MIE — No. 243, p. 12.

families, but also that it is beyond the reach of families with incomes that hover in the modest "middle income bracket."

In a country with widely available public education, why do we see differences in educational attainment based on income? Lower-income families have less money to buy books and computers, to hire tutors, and to provide lessons in activities such as dance and music; also, parents are less likely to take their children to museums and zoos. For example, in 1998, the majority of Canadian parents who owned a home computer reported buying it for educational purposes; 90 percent said that having a computer had positively affected their children's learning ability and 79 percent claimed that it had improved the quality of their child's homework. However, in that year, three out of four households (74 percent) in the highest income group had computers, compared with less than one in five of households (18 percent) in the lowest income group (Canadian Council on Social Development 2001).

Parents in low-income brackets are also less likely to expect their children to go to college or university, and their behaviour may lead to a self-fulfilling prophecy. "Only half of children aged 12 and 13 in families with incomes of less than $20 000 per year hoped to go to university. The figure was 71 percent for children from families with incomes over $80 000" (Canadian Council on Social Development 2001). As we have noted, a disproportionate number of children from low-income families do not go on to institutions of higher learning (Levinson 2000).

Because low-income parents often have low academic attainments, they often possess only limited language and academic skills. Children learn the limited language skills of their parents, which restricts their academic ability. Low-income parents may be unable to help their children with homework because they themselves lack the academic skills to understand the criteria. Call and colleagues (1997) report that even among impoverished youths, parental education is one of the best predictors of a child's academic success.

Although working-class parents may value education for their children, in contrast to middle- and upper-class parents they are less likely to be able to offer the parental involvement so crucial to children's academic success. They are

Special Education

Special education is designed to help children who require special educational help due to "low intelligence, visual or auditory impairment, or emotional or specific learning difficulties, disabilities or problems" (Brown 1999: 741). Special education is a critical community resource, too often absent in our schools.

Sample and Methods

In order to investigate the educational resources available for children with special needs in Canada, Angela Kierstead and Louise Hanvey (2001) conducted key informant interviews in each province with experts in the field of special education. During the summer of 2000, 17 experts from across Canada in the field of special education were interviewed. The survey was divided into three main sections: general context of special education services; assessment of how well children's needs are met; and special education resources.

Findings and Conclusions

An overwhelming majority of respondents (88 percent) reported that their educational systems have gone through major restructuring over the last five years. However, when asked if the educational system in their province was meeting the needs of children with special needs, only 19 percent said "yes." When asked if their educational system was able to identify all those children who would benefit from special education, about six in ten said, "yes."

The majority of respondents believed that there was substantial inequality in the delivery of services to children in rural and urban areas, with children in urban centres far more likely to receive a better level of service. When asked if the need for special education services had increased, decreased, or remained constant in recent years, 94 percent of respondents reported an increase. When asked to account for why the dramatic increase had occurred, respondents attributed at least part of the increase to growing parental awareness of learning disabilities. In addition, they noted that some provinces, such as Newfoundland, have systems in place to determine what the needs of a child are and whether or not the child requires supplemental special education services.

Respondents in this survey believed that children with physical disabilities were the group most likely to receive an acceptable level of service, regardless of whether they lived in an urban or rural area. Children with hearing impairments were felt to receive very different levels of service, depending on where they lived. While 71 percent of respondents believed that children with hearing impairments who lived in cities were completely or adequately served, only 28 percent felt that this group of children in rural areas received adequate levels of service. The services provided to children with attention deficit disorder (ADD) or attention deficit hyperactivity disorder (ADHD) were generally viewed as poor, regardless of where children lived: "87 percent of respondents reported that the needs of children with ADD/ADHD living in urban areas were being met only somewhat or not at all; for children…in rural areas, an overwhelming 93 percent of respondents stated that students' needs were met only somewhat or inadequately" (p. 3).

Respondents identified the lack of qualified personnel to provide such services as a key factor in explaining the inadequacy of services for ADD/ADHD children. They noted that, in many provinces, classroom teachers are not required to take courses in special education. In addition, the majority (88 percent) believed that there were not enough special education teachers available; over half (53 percent) believed that the number of special education teachers had decreased over the past five years. Finally, when asked about the level of funding for special education in their province or territory, 82 percent felt that it was inadequate. Complexities in provincial funding formulas, stringent guidelines, and an increase in the paperwork required of teachers in completing special education claims forms were all identified as factors that negatively affected the provision of services to children with special needs.

SOURCE: Kierstead, Angela, and Louise Harvey. 2001. "Special Education in Canada." *Perception* 25(2), Fall. Used with permission.

more likely to feel intimidated by their child's schools and teachers and to lack the time or job flexibility to attend teacher conferences (Lareau 1989).

Children from poor families are also more likely to have lower functioning vision, hearing, speech, mobility, dexterity, and cognition (Campaign 2000 2001). However, Canada's schools often lack special needs services to help these children (see this chapter's *Social Problems Research Up Close*). Poor children also experience a heightened likelihood of health problems and nutritional deficiencies (Campaign 2000 2001). It is obvious that children cannot learn when they are sick, in pain, hungry, or malnourished. Consider, in this context, that food bank use has risen more than 92 percent since 1989 and that the number of children relying on donated food has increased more than 85 percent. "Inadequate nutrition threatens children's overall well being as it has been linked to a variety of physical, cognitive, social and emotional problems" (Covell 2001: 25).

Early developmental programs may decrease the chances of developmental problems in children and enhance their performance within schools. For example, **Head Start** programs are based on the belief that to assist children, the entire family must be helped (Fact Sheet 2000). Evaluations of Head Start programs in Canada and the United States report such benefits as "more students completing school and with better grades; fewer young people needing mental health services; fewer parents abusing alcohol with concurrent reductions of alcohol's impact on children; a reduction in family violence; [and] fewer students with preventable disabilities and reduced demand for medical services" (Government of Canada 2001; Summary Report 2001). In Edmonton, for example, Head Start programs have existed for 25 years.

Head Start programs have been identified as particularly important in increasing the educational success of Aboriginal students. Canada introduced the Aboriginal Head Start Program in 1995 and the First Nations Head Start in 1998. In 1998, the federal government announced that it would provide permanent funding for the Aboriginal Head Start programs that already existed in Canada as well as additional funds for the establishment of new Head Start programs on reserves. It is estimated, though, that existing programs reach only about 5 percent of the Aboriginal children who could potentially benefit from their availability (George 1998). The costs of providing early childhood intervention programs are significant. Nevertheless, investments in the critical early years of a child's life benefit not only Canada's children, but our economy as well. Indeed, one Canadian study reports, "every dollar spent in early intervention can save seven dollars in future expenditures in health and social spending" (Health Canada 1999: 88).

Head Start

A U.S. project begun to help preschool children from disadvantaged families.

Racial and Ethnic Minorities

Socio-economic status interacts with race and ethnicity. Because race and ethnicity are so closely tied to socio-economic status, it appears that race or ethnicity alone can determine school success. Although race and ethnicity also have independent effects on educational achievement (Bankston and Caldas 1997; Jencks and Phillips 1998), their relationship to school success is largely due to their association with socio-economic status.

One reason why some minority students have academic difficulty is that they did not learn English as their first language. As previously noted, growing numbers of immigrant children of school age do not speak either of Canada's official languages upon arrival. Another factor that may have a negative impact upon both immigrant and minority students is the use of tests to assess academic achievement and ability that are biased against minorities. For example, questions on standardized tests often require students to have knowledge that is specific to the white middle-class majority culture, and cultural bias built into the IQ tests used in schools further privileges children from already advantaged backgrounds.

In addition, minority students may be disadvantaged by overt racism and discrimination. It has been noted, for example, that "[m]any visible minorities, such as native people and blacks, continue to have much greater school dropout rates" (Livingstone 1999: 743). Moreover, while research conducted by the Toronto Board of Education (1993) suggests that immigrant children, in general, do well at school after a period of acclimatization, a notable exception exists with respect to Afro-Canadian children. These children "experience lower rates of integration into the educational system and have lower levels of educational attainment."

An ongoing debate in Canada is whether or not students, at all levels, are better served by a faculty whose composition is less singular and reflects the diversity of our population. It has been noted that while the composition of Canada's student population is becoming increasingly multicultural, this is less true of Canada's teachers now and in the foreseeable future (Canadian Council on Social Development 1999). Moreover, as the number and size of racial and ethnic minority groups increase, some have suggested the need for more inclusive curricula to promote multicultural education. Edmonton, for example, already offers children such alternatives to French as Arabic, German, Ukrainian, and Mandarin; in 2001, the number of students enrolled in these programs (2250) exceeded the number enrolled in French immersion (1895). School boards in both Calgary and Edmonton have also launched publicly funded Spanish bilingualism programs (Bricker and Greenspon 2001: 284).

multicultural education

Education that includes all racial and ethnic groups in the school curriculum and promotes awareness and appreciation for cultural diversity.

In addition, it has been argued that **multicultural education**, education that includes all racial and ethnic groups in the school curriculum, is necessary to promote awareness and appreciation for cultural diversity (Conciatore 2000; Henry et al. 2000). Some recommend that "the experiences of women (and of First Nations people, working-class people, visible minorities and other disadvantaged groups) must be incorporated into the curriculum . . . The purpose of schooling must be to 'empower' . . . them, to give them the ability to participate fully in struggles, large and small, to gain respect, dignity and power."

Not all, however, agree. For example, Thomas Sowell (1994), a prolific African-American scholar and darling of those who oppose "affirmative action" initiatives, maintains that the limited amount of class time available makes it impossible for educators to include the experiences of non-dominant groups. He says that to try to add such experiences is foolish and unnecessary.

Canadian education specialists, such as George Dei (2001) and Jasmin Zine (2002), however, argue that positions such as Sowell's misinterpret what inclusive curricula look like. Inclusive curricula do not simply try to cover more in less time, adding more information to an already crammed curriculum; rather, inclusive and antiracist education pays critical attention to Eurocentric curricula, decentring its assumptions and its reproduction of racist attitudes about what counts as "knowledge" (Dei 2001). In other words, education should not be limited to input of facts, but of teaching different ways to consider "the facts."

Such opposing viewpoints reflect the "culture wars" that surround education today. However, as John Wilson (in Whitehead 1994: 13) has suggested, these debates may well provide educators with a unique opportunity to contemplate and reassess "the questions of what should be taught and how we ought to teach."

Gender

Worldwide, women receive less education than men. Two-thirds of the world's 920 million illiterate people are women (United Nations Population Fund 1999).

Historically, schools have discriminated against women. When Martha Humm Lewis gained entrance to a training school for teachers in New Brunswick in 1849, the principal of the school cautioned her to "enter the classroom ten minutes before the male students, sit alone at the back of the room, always wear a veil, leave the classroom five minutes before the end of the lesson and leave the building without speaking to any of the young men" (MacLellan 1972, in Schaefer et al. 1996: 282). Although Canadian schools are not typically segregated by sex any longer, a look at the elementary schools that were built prior to 1960 will likely yield a large number with the designations "Girls" and "Boys" over separate entrances, reflecting past attempts to keep the sexes apart.

Since the 1960s, the women's movement has sought to end sexism in education. For example, the 1970 Canadian Royal Commission on the Status of Women made the following recommendations: "adoption of textbooks that portray both sexes in diversified roles and occupations; provision of career information about the broad field of occupational choice for girls; improved availability of sport programs for both sexes; development of educational programs to meet the special needs of rural and immigrant women and of Indian and Inuit girls and young women; and the continuing education of women with family responsibilities" (as cited in Mackie 1991: 158). Three decades later, textbooks using gender-neutral language and images are increasingly being adopted and there has been a trend toward a more integrated curriculum in which boys and girls learn, for example, both auto mechanics and cooking.

Traditional gender roles account for many of the differences in educational achievement and attainment between women and men. As noted in Chapter 7, schools, teachers, and educational materials reinforce traditional gender roles in several ways. Some evidence suggests, for example, that teachers provide less attention and encouragement to girls than to boys and that textbooks tend to stereotype females and males in traditional roles (Evans and Davies 2000).

Most of the research on gender inequality in the school focuses on how female students are disadvantaged in the educational system. But what about male students? As discussed in Chapter 7, the argument that girls have been educationally shortchanged has recently come under attack—some academicians charge that it is boys, not girls, who have been left behind (Sommers 2000).

The problems that boys bring to school may require schools to devote more resources and attention to them. More than 70 percent of students with learning disabilities such as dyslexia are male, as are 75 percent of students identified as having serious emotional problems. Boys are also more likely than girls to have speech impairments, to be labelled as mentally retarded, to exhibit discipline problems, to drop out of school, and to feel alienated from the learning process (this chapter's *Self and Society* feature assesses student alienation) (Bushweller 1995; Goldberg 1999; Sommers 2000).

Self and Society

Student Alienation Scale

Indicate your agreement to each statement by selecting one of the responses provided:

1. It is hard to know what is right and wrong because the world is changing so fast.

    _____ Strongly agree _____ Agree _____ Disagree _____ Strongly disagree

2. I am pretty sure my life will work out the way I want it to.

    _____ Strongly agree _____ Agree _____ Disagree _____ Strongly disagree

3. I like the rules of my school because I know what to expect.

    _____ Strongly agree _____ Agree _____ Disagree _____ Strongly disagree

4. School is important in building social relationships.

    _____ Strongly agree _____ Agree _____ Disagree _____ Strongly disagree

5. School will get me a good job.

    _____ Strongly agree _____ Agree _____ Disagree _____ Strongly disagree

6. It is all right to break the law as long as you do not get caught.

    _____ Strongly agree _____ Agree _____ Disagree _____ Strongly disagree

7. I go to ball games and other sports activities at school.

    _____ Always _____ Most of the time _____ Some of the time _____ Never

8. School is teaching me what I want to learn.

    _____ Strongly agree _____ Agree _____ Disagree _____ Strongly disagree

9. I go to school parties, dances, and other school activities.

    _____ Strongly agree _____ Agree _____ Disagree _____ Strongly disagree

10. A student has the right to cheat if it will keep him or her from failing.

    _____ Strongly agree _____ Agree _____ Disagree _____ Strongly disagree

11. I feel like I do not have anyone to reach out to.

    _____ Always _____ Most of the time _____ Some of the time _____ Never

12. I feel that I am wasting my time in school.

    _____ Always _____ Most of the time _____ Some of the time _____ Never

13. I do not know anyone that I can confide in.

    _____ Strongly agree _____ Agree _____ Disagree _____ Strongly disagree

14. It is important to act and dress for the occasion.

    _____ Always _____ Most of the time _____ Some of the time _____ Never

15. It is no use to vote because one vote does not count very much.

    _____ Strongly agree _____ Agree _____ Disagree _____ Strongly disagree

16. When I am unhappy, there are people I can turn to for support.

    _____ Always _____ Most of the time _____ Some of the time _____ Never

17. School is helping me get ready for what I want to do after university.

    _____ Strongly agree _____ Agree _____ Disagree _____ Strongly disagree

18. When I am troubled, I keep things to myself.

_____ Always   _____ Most of the time   __ Some of the time   _____ Never

19. I am not interested in adjusting to Canadian society.

_____ Strongly agree   _____ Agree   _____ Disagree   _____ Strongly disagree

20. I feel close to my family.

_____ Always   _____ Most of the time   _____ Some of the time   _____ Never

21. Everything is relative and there just aren't any rules to live by.

_____ Strongly agree   _____ Agree   _____ Disagree   _____ Strongly disagree

22. The problems of life are sometimes too big for me.

_____ Always   _____ Most of the time   _____ Some of the time   _____ Never

23. I have lots of friends.

_____ Strongly agree   _____ Agree   _____ Disagree   _____ Strongly disagree

24. I belong to different social groups.

_____ Strongly agree   _____ Agree   _____ Disagree   _____ Strongly disagree

INTERPRETATION

This scale measures four aspects of alienation: powerlessness, or the sense that high goals (e.g., straight A's) are unattainable; meaninglessness, or lack of connectedness between the present (e.g., school) and the future (e.g., job); normlessness, or the feeling that socially disapproved behaviour (e.g., cheating) is necessary to achieve goals (e.g., high grades); and social estrangement, or lack of connectedness to others (e.g., being a "loner"). For items 1, 6, 10, 11, 12, 13, 15, 18, 19, 21, and 22, the response indicating the greatest degree of alienation is "strongly agree" or "always." For all other items, the response indicating the greatest degree of alienation is "strongly disagree" or "never."

SOURCE: Adapted from Mau, Rosalind Y. 1992. "The Validity and Devolution of a Concept: Student Alienation." *Adolescence* 27: 107, pp. 739–40. Used by permission of Libra Publishers, Inc., 3089 Clairemont Drive, Suite 383, San Diego, California 92117.

Some educational reformers have suggested a return to single-sex schools for both males and females. For males, the argument is that boys could benefit from the masculine environment provided by all-male academies where male teachers serve as positive role models. For females, the argument is that same-sex schools minimize the stereotyping, harassment, and discrimination that can exist in mixed-sex classrooms. However, researcher Maggie Ford concludes that the evidence indicates "that separating by sex is not the solution to gender inequity in education. When elements of good education are present, girls and boys succeed" (AAUW 1998).

12.4 Problems in the Canadian Educational System

Let us examine some of the major problems that have been identified within Canadian education today—and several potential solutions.

Low Levels of Academic Achievement

Worrisome evidence that suggested the inferiority of the Canadian school system appeared throughout the 1990s. For some social commentators, such evidence proved the inadequacy of our educational system and, in particular, the aftermath of **grade inflation** (the awarding of A's to students whose work warrants lower grades) and **social promotion** (the practice of passing students from one grade to the next even though they have not mastered the necessary grade-level skills). Canadian schools, critics charged, churned out **functional illiterates**: people who cannot "read basic signs or maps, complete simple forms, or carry on many of the tasks required of an adult" (Literacy 2000: 1).

grade inflation

Higher grades given than the work warrants; a general increase in student grades without a corresponding increase in learning.

social promotion

The passing of students from grade to grade even if they are failing.

functional illiterates

High-school graduates who have difficulty with basic reading and math skills.

In response to the disappointing performance of Canadian students on international tests, many Canadians clamoured for the administration of provincewide standardized tests for both students and teachers. Such tests, it was argued, would allow school performance to be independently and objectively assessed. Indeed, a May 2000 poll reported that more than 8 in 10 of those surveyed supported provincewide tests for students. A similar proportion believed that high school students should be required to pass both a compulsory literacy test and a standardized, provincewide knowledge test prior to graduation (Bricker and Greenspon 2001: 165–66).

However, some analysts emphasized that the results of international tests are misleading for various reasons (Barlow and Robertson 1994; Bracey 1998; Schrag 1997). First, most countries that participated in the study did not follow sampling guidelines. Specifically, many excluded those students whom educational administrators thought would perform badly on the exam. As a result, these countries artificially inflated their scores. Second, different countries have different kinds of secondary school systems. For instance, some keep students in school for 14 years, while others, like Canada, have 12-year systems. Some countries have higher dropout rates than Canada has and/or siphon off poor academic performers to trades schools and job-training programs before they complete high school. As a result, only the top performers remain by the last year of high school. In contrast, Canada attempts to ensure that as many students as possible graduate from high school since it is hoped that high rates of completion of secondary education will enhance the quality of democracy, increase social cohesion in a culturally diverse society, and improve economic performance.

Despite the limitations of international comparisons, many Canadians still felt buoyed when the results of the most recent international tests in reading, math, and science were released in 2001. Among 32 countries, Canada ranked second overall in reading and fifth in math and science. When provincial results were analyzed separately, students in Alberta, Quebec, and British Columbia ranked among the best in the world. Indeed, Alberta students obtained the highest scores in the world in reading and placed third in both science and math. Quebec came second in math with scores that rivalled those of students in Japan. Other provinces, however, most notably those in the Atlantic region, did not fare as well (Sokoloff 2001).

George Dei reminds us that measures such as these are highly politicized and sit at the centre of manufactured anxieties about global markets and Canada's ability to compete. Commenting on increased testing and restrictive curriculum changes throughout the 1990s in Ontario, Dei (1999) remarks:

The intent of these initiatives was to insert Ontario into the global marketplace, thereby ensuring that schools would be able to produce a cheap and compliant labor force. However, in order for these reforms to be pushed through without a serious public backlash, it was necessary to create a "crisis in schooling." By undermining the reputation of public education, the Conservatives manufactured a province wide concern over "the declining quality of Ontario education." . . . Within months of the Conservative accession, schools across the province found that many of the programs that had worked toward equity and social justice were either cut back severely or were terminated altogether.

School Dropouts

According to the latest available figures, Canada ranks in the middle of OECD nations with an overall dropout rate of 10.9 percent (Bowlby 2008). However, even though the stereotype of the dropout is that of a poorly motivated underachiever who prefers to live on social assistance and use drugs, a Statistics Canada report presents a different picture: "The reasons behind the decision to drop out of high school reported by 20-year-olds in the Youth in Transition Survey differed somewhat between males and females. Young men were less likely to be engaged in school than young women and were more likely to report wanting to work/earn money as a reason for dropping out of high school" (ibid). Female school leavers, by contrast, were more likely to have had children to raise, with 15.9 percent leaving due to pregnancy (ibid). The greater likelihood that young women are caring for their young children than young men are does not mean that early child-bearing is the main reason young women leave school; young mothers are a significant minority of female school leavers. In addition, the rate of young men dropping out of school—12.2 percent—is significantly greater than the rate of young women leaving school—7.2 percent (ibid).

Contrary to popular stereotypes, Sid Gilbert and Bruce Orok (1993: 3) report that many school leavers come from intact, two-parent homes, were doing well at school, and were either not working or working only moderate hours prior to leaving school. Upon leaving school, school leavers were generally employed, worked long hours, and planned to continue with further education or job training. "Among male school leavers aged 18–20, the two most important reasons for leaving were that they preferred work to school (28 percent) and boredom (19 percent) . . . . Female leavers aged 18–20 cited boredom (22 percent) and problems with schoolwork (13 percent) as the top two reasons for leaving school." Nine percent of male respondents mentioned the need to work for financial reasons, while 8 percent mentioned problems with teachers. A subtle point that should not be overlooked is that many of the respondents intended to return to school—and that is, indeed, what we find in long-term surveys of those who leave high school before completing their diplomas. Long-term surveys of youth in Canada show that by their late twenties only 6 percent of those who had left school early remained without a high school diploma or equivalent; furthermore, of those who had left school early but later returned a total of 43 percent had gone on to postsecondary education (Statistics Canada 2010). In other words, a high school diploma is not necessarily the limit in educational attainment for those who leave school early. Indeed, of the 43 percent who had gone on to postsecondary education, one-fifth did so without ever completing high school equivalency. The negative "dropout" label, which sounds so *permanent*, does not capture the full picture or long-term outcomes for school leavers, or do justice to their own educational aspirations.

Long-term improvements notwithstanding, the economic and social consequences of dropping out of school are significant. Dropouts are more likely than those who complete high school to be unemployed and to earn less when they are employed (*Digest of Educational Statistics* 2001). According to recent reports from Statistics Canada, the unemployment rate for those aged 20 to 24 without a high-school diploma or equivalent in 2004–05 was 19.4 percent, double the rate for all 20- to 24-year-olds (Bowlby 2008). There are, however, some hopeful signs:

> The substantial decline in the dropout rate over the past decade suggests that many of the programs that have been put in place to encourage young people to stay in school until they graduate are meeting with success. Programs have also been put in place to afford high school drop-outs a second chance, by offering the opportunity to return to school to complete the requirements for high school graduation. One can expect that take up of 'second-chance' programs is influenced in part by the early labour-market experiences of young drop-outs who find they face real difficulties in securing stable, long-term employment that actually pays a decent wage. (ibid)

Student Violence

On April 28, 1999, a 15-year-old boy in Taber, Alberta, gunned down one teen and wounded another in a school hallway. In February 2000, three Toronto teenagers were wounded in a gun battle in a high school parking lot; the same day, at another Toronto high school, a 13-year-old boy was charged with choking and sexually assaulting a 17-year-old girl. Concealed in his inside jacket pocket at the time was a bored-out starter's pistol, loaded with .22 calibre bullets and ready to fire (Appleby 2000). In the fall of 2006, Kimveer Gill entered Dawson College CEGEP in Montreal and shot 19 people, killing one and seriously injuring the others before killing himself with a shotgun blast to his head.

While we might prefer to think of aggression and violence in school as exceptional, evidence suggests that they are not (Table 12.3). A 1999 survey of 2000 Alberta students in Grades 7 to 12 reports that violence was highest among students in Grades 8 and 9. Approximately 16 percent of students in this survey acknowledged bringing weapons to school, with illegal knives and replica weapons the most common (Canadian Press 2000). The 2000 Project Canada Survey on teens finds that one in two Canadian teens views violence in schools as a "very serious" problem. Female teenagers were especially likely to view violence in schools in that way (59 percent of female teens versus 40 percent of males) (Bibby 2001: 81). About one in three teenagers (32 percent) reported having a close friend who had been physically attacked at school. Male teens were especially likely to report having a friend who experienced physical violence while at school (39 percent of males versus 25 percent of females) (Bibby 2001: 82). In addition, it should be noted that aggressive acts by students do not always entail physical violence. In 2002, in a landmark case that was reputedly the first to hold schoolyard bullies to account, a 16-year-old girl was found guilty of criminal harassment for her role in bullying a Grade 9 Abbotsford, B.C., student, Dawn-Marie Wesley. Wesley was so tormented that she committed suicide in November 2000 (*Maclean's* 2002).

■ **Table 12.3** *Weapons Offences, Incidents Reported in Toronto Schools during 1999*

Possession of weapon, dangerous to public	21
Carrying a concealed weapon	18
Assault with weapon, causing bodily harm	17
Dangerous use/storage of firearm	15
Robbery, mugging	8
Robbery, swarming	6
Uttering threats	5
Possession of unregulated restricted weapon etc.	4
Use of firearm in commission of offence	4
Aggravated assault	2
Assault	2
Extortion by threats, violence	2
Mischief	1
Others	2
Total offences	110

SOURCE: Appleby, Timothy. 2000. "Weapons Turn Up More Often at Schools: Police." *Globe and Mail*, February 18: A18.

Various attempts have been made to redress the problem of violence, bullying, and harassment in schools. "In what is believed to be the first measure of its kind in Canada," the city of Edmonton passed a bylaw in March 2003 that bans harassment of people under 18 (Mahoney 2003: A8). The bylaw, which took effect in May 2003, defines *bullying* as "repeated intimidation of others" including "real or threatened infliction of various types of abuse, including physical, verbal, emotional, or written," and covers bullying in public places. Those who bully can be given a $250 ticket—and it's anticipated that the use of this bylaw will be heaviest in schools. Some schools have installed security systems, hired security guards, shortened school days to eliminate free time, and expelled troublemakers.

Others schools, however, advocate a different approach to the problem of antisocial and aggressive behaviour in schools. For example, after experiencing several incidents of racially charged violence, Cole Harbour High School, in Nova Scotia, introduced a "Student of the Week" program, designed to encourage students to learn respect for the cultures of others, and implemented a system of peer mediators. Peer mediators are students who are given special training in mediation techniques under the supervision of a staff person, in order to work at the front line in conflict between small numbers of students. The Cole Harbour school mandate encourages students to develop "a sense of responsibility for the condition of their school; they feel they have control over events in the school; and the program creates an environment where a minor conflict can be handled without the principal's intervention." Alberta's Safe and Caring Schools project advocates that the problem of school violence is best dealt with through community-wide efforts to encourage responsible behaviour. According to the Safe and Caring Schools project, early intervention and prevention are needed.

Consistent with this approach, Dan Offord, former head of child psychiatry at McMaster University, has argued that attempts to reduce violent behaviour in schools must begin with screening programs directed at children in early grades who display antisocial behaviour. His argument suggests that as many as 20 percent of school-aged children and teens suffer "from some type of emotional disorder" and that "at least 12 percent" could benefit from individual attention. Moreover, he maintains that while many find a "get tough" approach appealing, "there has to be a place for everyone in schools . . . you can't just push kids out of the school system. Where do they go?" (as cited in Crane 1999: A2). Among the problems with the various "get tough" approaches and "zero tolerance" policies is that they are disproportionately targeting racially and ethnically minorized children and youth in public schools. Where these children already have their academic needs neglected, and where they are already disproportionately held out of programs that help more privileged children to stay in the academic stream, black, Muslim, and South Asian students are more frequently pushed out of the school system using a series of increasingly alienating and punitive policies (Battacharjee, 2003: 50–52).

The High Costs of Education

Canada compares favourably to many other countries in terms of various indicators of education. For example, compared to most other Western countries, we tend to spend a higher proportion of our GDP (gross domestic product) on education. Moreover, unlike the majority of countries worldwide, we encourage those who are imprisoned in Canada's penitentiaries to enroll in secondary, vocational, and postsecondary courses on site or through correspondence. At the same time, however, problems exist.

Reduced funding for public and postsecondary education and an increased reliance at the college and university level on student fees has led, in turn, to soaring increases in tuition costs for Canadian postsecondary students, demands for postsecondary institutions to accept more students (without additional funding), less academic hiring, rising student–faculty ratios, and dwindling resources. The negative consequences outlined by Johnston—shrinking numbers of lab assistants, outdated lab equipment, and the reductions to library budgets, and crumbling buildings (1999: 51)—have only gotten worse and more obvious in the decade since. Would-be and current postsecondary students and their families are increasingly forced to confront the financial burdens posed by higher education—and the costs are considerable. Figure 12.2 and Figure 12.3 provide at-a-glance views of the financial burdens that students face in the pursuit of a tertiary education.

Although the cost of postsecondary education in Canada "has always been a responsibility shared by society through tax dollars, and by parents and children through personal savings," soaring tuitions (up 115 percent since 1980) contrast sharply with the 1 percent rise in average family income (after adjusting for inflation) (Clark 1999: 24). Using data from the National Graduates Survey of 1995, Clark (1999) examined the extent of student debt and the impact of high debt on postsecondary graduates who had used government loans to finance their studies. He reports that both college and bachelor's degree graduates were most likely to finance their education through employment earnings (59 percent college, 69 percent bachelor's) and student loans (41 percent college, 42 percent

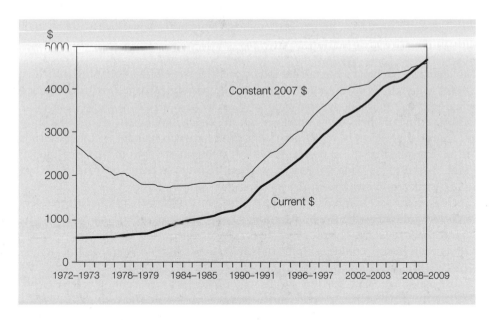

■ **Figure 12.2** *Average Tuition Fees for Full-Time Undergraduate University Students*

SOURCE: Statistics Canada, "The Financial Impact of Student Loans," *Perspectives on Labour and Income*, 75-001-XIE2010101, vol. 11 no. 1, January 2010; http://www.statcan.gc.ca/bsolc/olc-cel/olc-cel?lang=eng&catno=75-001-X.

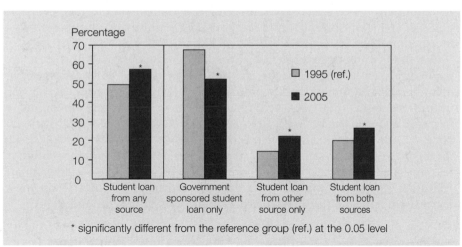

■ **Figure 12.3** *Student Loan Sources*

SOURCE: Statistics Canada, "The Financial Impact of Student Loans," *Perspectives on Labour and Income*, 75-001-XIE2010101, vol. 11 no. 1, January 2010; http://www.statcan.gc.ca/bsolc/olc-cel/olc-cel?lang=eng&catno=75-001-X.

bachelor's). While parents ranked third for those who acquired bachelor's degrees, neither college nor university students identified scholarships, fellowships, prizes, grants, or bursaries as a significant source of funding. Students from families with lower parental education (those whose fathers had not completed high school) were more likely to use student loans than those students with higher parental education. As well, students in their late 20s were more likely to borrow from government student loan programs and to borrow the most.

By the mid-2000s the patterns we see above only grew, further attenuating the already perilous position of students from middle and lower income groups:

> In constant dollars, university tuition fees in 2002 were the highest they had ever been at any time in the past century. Measured against the buying power of a middle income tradesman, university tuition fees in 2002 were more expensive than at anytime in the preceding 130 years, with the exception of the beginning of the Second World War. (Fisher et al. 2006: 58)

It is not surprising, perhaps, that those who borrowed from student loan programs often faced difficulty in paying back the monies they had received. Clark reports that "during the two years following graduation, one-sixth of 1995 college and bachelor's borrowers indicated they were already having difficulty making payments on their government student loans." Women with bachelor's degrees were more likely than men with bachelor's degrees were to have difficulty paying off their loans; however, among college graduates, there were only marginal differences in repayment difficulties between women and men. Fisher et al. explain that these problems with repayment stem from a federal policy that moved the Canada Student Loan Program into the hands of private lenders (i.e., banks) and away from the government's books (2006: 54–55). The move increased the levels and pace of repayment that students would have to undertake on graduation, and where students had previously been able to take student loans regardless of previous financial difficulties, new restrictions meant that credit history could result in students having their loan applications denied (ibid). In effect, those who had the least financial privilege as youth had the most significant cost barriers to the completion of postsecondary education. Furthermore, Fisher et al. calculated increases in tuition and note that, "When measured against after-tax family income, university tuition fees increased from 6 per cent in 1990–91 to 9 per cent in 1998–99 for families in the middle income quintile, and jumped from 14 per cent to 23 per cent for families in the lowest income quintile" (2006: 58).

For those who pursue professional degrees, the burden may be even more oppressive. Consider, for example, that since 1998, when the Ontario government deregulated tuition fees for professional and graduate programs, allowing institutions to set tuition fee levels, tuition fees have soared. Law school tuition fees rose 217 percent between 1990 and 2003 (CAUT 2005: 1). For the year 2005–06, annual tuition fess for dentistry programs in Canada averaged $12 942; for medicine programs, annual fees averaged $10 349. Finally, graduate tuition fees in Canada averaged $5699 per year compared to $4214 for undergraduate education (Statistics Canada 2005). Statistics Canada (2005) notes that these increases in fees far outstripped increases in the Consumer Price Index.

Inadequate School Facilities and Persons with Disabilities

We have previously noted that special education programs for children with learning disabilities are unavailable for many of those who could benefit from them. More broadly, however, since the early 1990s, the Canadian school system has experienced budgets cuts and the message to "do more with less." With the proclaimed intent of improving school standards, provincial governments have often removed resources from the educational system, centralized control of schools by imposing standardized testing and new curricula, and reduced the power of school boards. In theory, these measures allow provincial governments to balance their budgets, stimulate economic growth, and offer taxpayers tax cuts.

Decreasing educational resources obviously reduces the number of jobs available for principals, teachers, and support staff and increases educational inequality. With fewer teachers, a pared back curriculum, and increasing costs being shouldered by families rather than the state, the prospects of children from lower socio-economic strata may be grim. As we have seen, the Canadian educational system has generally acted to reproduce the country's stratification system. Since the early 1990s, however, it has acted to help increase the degree of social stratification in Canadian society (Johnston 2001).

According to Michael Fullan ([1982] 2001; Hammonds 2002), we must reinvest and reinvent our system of education. He argues that education must become a "meaningful learning community," a setting in which all participants engage in education because it brings them substantial moral benefits. He maintains that students learn best when engaged in achieving mastery of subjects that they deem relevant to their needs and backgrounds. Similarly, he argues that teachers teach best when they feel empowered by having the autonomy, resources, peer support, and professional development they require.

12.5 Strategies for Action: Trends and Innovations in Canadian Education

Canadians rank improving education as one of their top priorities. In 2000, when an Angus Reid Group survey asked Canadians to volunteer their "top-of-mind" priority issues, education was mentioned by 29 percent of respondents as a national priority, surpassed only by health care (Bricker and Greenspon 2001: 150). In addition, it is evident that education plays a critical role in Canadian society. Education has been referred to "as the one truly proactive public investment we make. It is not designed to address a problem, but rather to build the society we want for the future by investing in the creation of human and social capacity" (Canadian Council on Social Development 1999). Yet, at the same time, our educational system must be reactive, responsive to Canada's changing demography—changes in the age composition of our population, its ethno-racial mix, and family structures—as well as to trends in the labour market, the economy, and the development of information and communications technology.

There is no shortage of suggestions on how we can improve our educational system. Here we review but a few.

Moral and Interpersonal Education

Most school curricula neglect the human side of education—the moral and interpersonal aspects of developing as an individual and as a member of society. Proponents of character education argue that students should "be engaged in a general education that guides them in caring for self, intimate others, global others, plants, animals, the environment, objects and instruments, and ideas" (Noddings 1995: 369). For example, service learning programs are community-based initiatives in which students volunteer in the community and receive academic credit for doing so. Studies on student outcomes have linked service learning to enhanced civic responsibility and moral reasoning, increased tolerance of diversity and promotion of racial equality, and a strong commitment to volunteerism (Aberle-Grasse 2000; Waterman 1997; Zlotkowski 1996). Character education also occurs to some extent in schools that have peer mediation and conflict resolution programs. Such programs teach the values of nonviolence, collaboration, and helping others, as well as skills in interpersonal communication and conflict resolution.

Distance Learning and the New Education

Imagine never having an eight o'clock class or walking in to the lecture room late. Imagine no room-and-board bills, and not having to eat your roommate's cooking one more time. Imagine going to class when you want, even three o'clock in the morning. Imagine not worrying about parking! It's possible that the World Wide Web and other information technologies have so revolutionized education that the above scenarios are a fait accompli.

What is distance learning? Distance learning separates, by time or place, the teacher from the student. They are, however, linked by some communication technology: videoconferencing, satellite, computer, audiotape or videotape, real-time chat room, closed-circuit television, electronic mail, or the like. Examples of distance learning abound. "In 1997, New Brunswick's TeleEducation NB launched TeleCampus—one of the world's first virtual campuses—on the World Wide Web" (Statistics Canada 1998: 159), an electronic school which allows students to enroll, study, and pay for courses via the Internet. Athabasca University, in northern Alberta, is Canada's leading open university and considered a leader in developing electronic courseware. It offers students access to courses through teleconferencing-, video-conferencing, and other electronic means and offers many courses over the World Wide Web. Wasja, run by the Northern Nishnawbe Education Council, uses radio to provide educational opportunities to students in the Sioux Lookout area in Ontario. Kayas Cultural College runs the Little Red River Cree Nation in northeast Alberta and uses video-conferencing to provide academic upgrading and college courses. The University of Waterloo offers over 270 distance education courses and has approximately 10 000 registrants (Haughey 1999: 672).

Distance education has been available in Canada for over a century. It was first used in 1889 "to provide opportunities for teachers who were unable to attend McGill University in the winter months to study for their degree" (Haughey 1999: 672). However, since that time its scope and clientele has vastly expanded. At present, a minimum of half a million people in Canada study through distance education and programs. The available courses range from those at the elementary level through to university level.

> Across Canada, over 65 percent of colleges offer at least one distance education course. Over 35 universities offer distance education courses. Many government departments and over 35 percent of large companies in Canada are already using some form of distance education. Commercial suppliers as well as industrial, trade, and professional organizations are also providing distance learning courses and resources. (Haughey 1999: 672)

The benefits of distance learning are clear. Research suggests that "students of all ages learn better when they are actively engaged in a process, whether that process comes in the form of a sophisticated multimedia package or a low-tech classroom debate on current events" (Carvin 1997). Distance education also benefits those who have historically been disadvantaged in the classroom. A review of research on gender differences suggests that females outperform males in distance learning environments (Koch 1998).

But all that glitters is not gold. There is evidence that students feel more estranged from their distance learning instructors than from teachers in conventional classrooms (Freitas et al. 1998).

Additionally problematic is the proliferation of "virtual degrees." An elementary school teacher enrolled in an online university to complete a master's degree in special education. After paying $800 of a total $2000 bill, she was sent a book to summarize as part of her degree requirements. Shortly after returning her summary, she was sent not only a master's degree, but a Ph.D. and transcripts of courses she had never taken with a recorded 3.9 grade point average (GPA) (Koeppel 1998). In spite of such problems, however, distance education continues to grow, in part because it is a money-maker. Indeed, many commercial sites now offer "educational" courses while many educational sites increasingly carry advertising banners, consumer discounts, and so on.

Will distance learning solve all the problems facing education today? The answer is clearly no. While not the technological fix some are looking for, distance and virtual libraries can provide a provocative and financially lucrative alternative to traditional education providers.

SOURCES: Carvin, Andy. 1997. *EdWeb: Exploring Technology and School Reform*. http://www.ed-web. gsn.org; Freitas, Frances Anne, Scott Meyers, and Theodore Avtgis. 1998. "Student Perceptions of Instructor Immediacy in Conventional and Distributed Learning Classrooms." *Communication Education* 47(4): 366–72; Haughey, Margaret. 1999. "Distance Learning." In *The Canadian Encyclopedia: Year 2000 Edition,* edited by James H. Marsh, pp. 672–73. Toronto: McClelland and Stewart, Inc.; Koch, James V. 1998. "How Women Actually Perform in Distance Education." *Chronicle of Higher Education* 45: A60; Koeppel, David. 1998. "Easy Degrees Proliferate on the Web." *New York Times,* August 2: 17; Statistics Canada. 1998. *Canada Yearbook 1999.* Ottawa: Minister of Industry.

Computer Technology in Education

Computers in the classroom allow students to access large amounts of information (see this chapter's *Focus on Technology*). The proliferation of computers both in school and at home may mean that teachers will become facilitators and coaches rather than sole providers of information. Not only do computers enable students to access enormous amounts of information, including that from the World Wide Web, but they also allow students to progress at their own pace.

Canada was one of the first countries to link its student body to the information superhighway. By 1997, almost all Canadian schools had internet access through the SchoolNet electronic network. In that year, Industry Canada's "Computers in the Schools" program had placed more than 20 000 computers and 40 000 pieces of software in Canadian schools and libraries (Canadian Council on Social Development 1999). The attempt to make educational settings inclusive also suggests the benefits of computer technology in education. Software that reads aloud what is on the screen, large-screen monitors, voice-input software, and scanners are among the technologies used by differently abled students in Canada (Fichten et al. 1999).

Alternative School Choices

Traditionally, children have gone to school in the district where they live. However, alternative schools, home schooling, and private schools provide parents with alternative school choices for their children. **Alternative schools** began in Canada in the 1970s. According to Chernos (1998: 13), "Perhaps the one element that unifies alternative schools is their diversity. Each operates within school board and education ministry guidelines, yet maintains a unique character."

For example, in London, Ontario, Richmond Centre and Dundas Centre Schools "are intended as an interim measure for students experiencing social, emotional, psychological, behavioral or academic troubles" (Chernos 1998: 15). The London board also maintains other alternative schools for Native youth, Annishnabe and Wiingashk, both of which incorporate Native culture and traditions within a core curriculum of basic Grade 9 to 12 subjects. In Toronto, the focus of Horizon Alternative Senior School "is on creating a caring community" and on balancing "core subjects . . . with an outward world-view that emphasizes self-expression, debate, role playing dialogue and conflict resolution" (Chernos 1998: 13). In Ontario alone, there are several dozen elementary and secondary schools that bill themselves as alternative schools.

Alternative schools typically offer a variety of innovative and experimental programs. They generally have low student populations ranging from 70 to 250, with small, informal classes; they place emphasis on close interaction between students and teachers. In many alternative high schools, student representatives join teachers, parents, and, sometimes, community members on the school's board of directors. According to Levin (1999: 732), alternative schools can be distinguished by "the sense of ownership, autonomy and control that teachers, parents, and students feel towards their school even as governments and school boards move to assert and maintain stronger administrative control" upon them. Indeed, he suggests that "alternative schools may be forerunners of a more decentralized, pluralistic, community-based education system."

alternative schools

Alternative schools began in Canada in the 1970s. Each operates within school board and education ministry guidelines, but is unique in its character.

home schooling

The education of children at home instead of in a public or private school; often part of a fundamentalist movement to protect children from perceived non-Christian values in the public schools.

Some parents are choosing not to send their children to school at all but to teach them at home. For some parents, **home schooling** is part of a fundamentalist movement to protect children from perceived non-Christian values in the public schools. Other parents are concerned about the quality of their children's education and their safety.

How does being schooled at home instead of attending public school affect children? Some evidence suggests that home-schooled children perform as well as or better than their institutionally schooled counterparts (Webb 1989; Winters 2000).

Another choice parents may make is to send their children to a private school. The primary reason parents send their children to private schools is for religious instruction. The second most frequent reason is the belief that private schools are superior to public schools in terms of academic achievement. Research suggests, however, that when controlling for parents' education and income, there are few differences in private and pubic school educational outcomes (Ascher et al. 1997; Cohen 1998; Shanker 1996). Parents also choose private schools for their children in order to have greater control over school policy or to obtain a specific course of instruction, such as dance or music.

Understanding **Problems in Education**

What can we conclude about the state of the educational system in Canada? Any criticism of education must take into account that over a century ago, many children did not receive even a primary school education. Instead, they worked in factories and on farms to help support their families. Whatever education they received came from the family or the religious institution. It is evident that Canada has come a long way since that time. From humble beginnings, education in Canada has grown into a massive industry with total expenditures now exceeding $61 billion a year (Girvan 2000: 82).

At the same time, it is evident that problems exist. While public schools are supposed to provide all Canadian children with the academic and social foundations necessary to participate in society in a productive and meaningful way, some students remain marginalized and do not enjoy their benefits as much as others. As conflict theorists note, the educational institution can perpetuate a downward cycle of failure, alienation, and hopelessness. Breaking the cycle requires providing adequate funding for teachers, school buildings, equipment, and educational materials. In addition, jobs must be provided for those who successfully complete their education. Students with little hope of job success will continue to experience low motivation as long as job prospects are bleak and earnings in available jobs are low. Ray and Mickelson (1993: 14–15) explain:

> School reforms of any kind are unlikely to succeed if . . . students cannot anticipate opportunity structures that reward diligent efforts in school. Employers are not apt to find highly disciplined and motivated young employees for jobs that are unstable and low paying.

Finally, "if we are to improve the skills and attitudes of future generations of workers, we must also focus attention and resources on the quality of the lives children lead outside the school" (Murnane 1994: 290). We must provide support to families so children grow up in healthy, safe, and nurturing environments. Children are the future of our nation and of the world. Whatever resources we provide to improve the lives and education of children are sure to be wise investments in our collective future.

Critical Thinking

1. Clearly, there are both advantages and disadvantages to home schooling. After making a list of each, consider whether you would want your child to be home-schooled. Why or why not?

2. As we move into the twenty-first century, the proportion of elderly in Canada is increasing dramatically. Since the elderly are unlikely to have children in public schools, how will this demographic trend affect the allocation of funds needed for schools?

3. One response to school violence is primarily defensive; that is, expelling students, installing metal detectors, and so on. Other than such defensive tactics, what violence prevention techniques should be instituted?

4. Students who drop out of school are often blamed for their lack of motivation. How may a teenager's dropping out of high school be explained as a failure of the educational system rather than as a "motivation" problem?

"Is It True?" Quiz: Answers

1 = false; 2 = false; 3 = true; 4 = true; 5 = false

Environmental Problems

Outline

Is It True?

1. NAFTA (North American Free Trade Agreement) regulations require members to adhere to the environmental protection laws of their NAFTA trade partners.

2. According to some estimates, women have ownership of less than 2 percent of the world's available land.

3. Loss of the world's forests contributes to social instability.

4. Trade practices threaten domestic ecosystems around the world by accidentally bringing invasive species to them through international shipping.

5. Remote areas such as the Far North remain environmentally pristine.

Read more here: 1 = p. 444, 2 = p. 447, 3 = p. 452, 4 = p. 443, 5 = p. 467

Answers can be found on p. 483.

© Bloomberg/Getty Images

In this chapter we focus on problems that threaten the lives and well-being of people, plants, and animals all over the world—today and in future generations. After examining how globalization affects environmental problems, we employ the lenses of structural functionalism, conflict theory, ecofeminist theory, and symbolic interactionism to think through the issues. We then present an overview of major environmental problems, examining their social causes and exploring strategies that attempt to reduce or alleviate them.

13.1 The Global Context: Globalization and the Environment

In 1992, leaders from across the globe met at the first Earth Summit in Rio de Janeiro to forge agreements to protect the planet's environment and at the same time alleviate world poverty. When world leaders met a decade later for the second Earth Summit, held in Johannesburg, South Africa, the overall state of the environment had deteriorated and poverty had deepened. How is it that the combined efforts of leaders who met at the first Earth Summit were so ineffectual? A large part of the answer lies in the increasing globalization of the last two decades. Three aspects of globalization have affected the environment: (1) the permeability of international borders to pollution and environmental problems, (2) cultural and social integration spurred by communication and information technology, and (3) growth of free trade and transnational corporations.

Permeability of International Borders

Environmental problems such as global warming and destruction of the ozone layer (discussed later in this chapter) demonstrate that environmental problems extend far beyond their source to affect the entire planet and its inhabitants. A striking example of the permeability of international borders to pollution is the spread of toxic chemicals (such as PCBs) from the southern hemisphere into the Arctic. In as little as five days, chemicals from the tropics can evaporate from the soil, ride the winds thousands of kilometres north, condense in the cold air, and fall on the Arctic in the form of toxic snow or rain (French 2000). This phenomenon was discovered in the mid-1980s, when scientists found high levels of PCBs in the breast milk of Inuit women in the Canadian Arctic.

Another environmental problem involving permeability of borders is **bioinvasion**: the emergence of organisms in regions where they are not native. Bioinvasion is largely a product of the growth of global trade and tourism (Chafe 2005). Exotic species travel in the ballast water of ships (water taken in to stabilize empty vessels as they cross waterways), in packing material, in shipments of crops and other goods, and in many other ways. Invasive species may compete with native species for food, start an epidemic, or prey on natives, threatening not only their immediate victims but also the entire ecosystem in which the victims live.

Red fire ants are an example of a bioinvasion. In 1957, they travelled from Paraguay and Brazil on shiploads of lumber to Mobile, Alabama, and have since spread throughout the southern states, causing damage to gardens and yards, invading the food supplies (seeds, young plants, and insects) of other animals,

bioinvasion

The emergence of organisms in regions where they are not native.

and harming humans with their painful sting (Hilgenkamp 2005). You might be surprised to learn that the domestic cat is considered among the world's 100 worst invasive species. Cats, native to northeast Africa, have spread to every part of the world and are responsible for the decline and extinction of many species of birds (Global Invasive Species Database 2006).

Cultural and Social Integration

As mass media infiltrate the world, people across the globe aspire to consume the products and mimic the materially saturated lifestyles portrayed in movies, television, and advertising. As patterns of consumption in developing countries increasingly follow those in wealthier Western nations, so do the problems associated with overconsumption: depletion of natural resources, pollution, and global warming.

Conversely, the internet and other forms of mass communication have helped to integrate the efforts of diverse environmental groups, creating new opportunities for environmental groups to join forces, share information, and educate the public.

The Growth of Transnational Corporations and Free Trade Agreements

The world's economy is dominated by transnational corporations, many of which have established factories and other operations in developing countries where labour and environmental laws are lax. Transnational corporations have been implicated in environmentally destructive activities—from mining and cutting timber to dumping toxic waste.

The World Trade Organization (WTO) and free trade agreements such as NAFTA (North American Free Trade Agreement) and the FTAA (Free Trade Area of the Americas) allow transnational corporations to pursue profits, expand markets, use natural resources, and exploit cheap labour in developing countries; at the same time, the ability of governments to protect natural resources or to implement environmental legislation is weakened. Transnational corporations have influenced the world's most powerful nations to institutionalize an international system of governance that values commercialism, corporate rights, and "free" trade over the environment, human rights, worker rights, and human health (Bruno and Karliner 2002). Under NAFTA's Chapter 11 provisions, corporations can challenge local and provincial/state environmental policies; federal regulations, including those for controlled substances; and court rulings, if such regulatory measures and government actions negatively affect profits.

Any country that decides, for example, to ban the export of raw logs as a means of conserving its forests—or, as another example, to ban the use of carcinogenic pesticides—can be charged under the WTO by member states on behalf of their corporations for obstructing the free flow of trade and investment. A secret tribunal of trade officials would then decide whether these laws were "trade restrictive" under the WTO rules and should therefore be struck down. Once the secret tribunal issues its edict, no appeal is possible. The convicted country is obligated to change its laws or face the prospect of perpetual trade sanctions (Clarke 2002: 44). As of early 2005, 42 cases had been filed by corporate interests and investors, 11 of which had been finalized. Five corporations that won their claims received $35 million paid by taxpayers in Canada and Mexico. For example, in the late 1990s, Ethyl, a U.S. chemical company, used NAFTA rules to challenge Canadian environmental regulation of the toxic gasoline additive MMT. Ethyl won the suit, and Canada paid $13 million in damages and legal fees to Ethyl and reversed the ban on MMT (Public Citizen 2005). Although the United States has not, as of this writing, lost a case, it is only a matter of time before a corporation based in Mexico or Canada wins a NAFTA case against the United States (Public Citizen 2005).

13.2 Sociological Theories of Environmental Problems

Each of the three main sociological theories—structural functionalism, conflict theory, and symbolic interactionism—as well as ecofeminist theory provide insights into social causes of and responses to environmental problems.

Structural-Functionalist Perspective

Structural functionalism emphasizes the interdependence between human beings and the natural environment. From this perspective, human actions, social patterns, and cultural values affect the environment, and, in turn, the environment affects social life. Structural functionalism also helps us to understand how changes in one aspect of the social system affect other aspects of society. For example, agriculture, forestry, and fishing provide 50 percent of all jobs worldwide and 70 percent of jobs in sub-Saharan Africa, East Asia, and the Pacific (World Resources Institute 2000). As croplands become scarce or degraded, as forests shrink, and as marine life dwindles, millions of people who make their living from these natural resources must find alternative livelihoods. Globally, there are an estimated 30 million environmental refugees—individuals who have migrated because they can no longer secure a livelihood as a result of environmental problems (Margesson 2005). As individuals lose their source of income, so do nations. In one-fourth of the world's nations, crops, timber, and fish contribute more to the nation's economy than industrial goods do (World Resources Institute 2000).

The environmental impact of different regions and cultural uses of the land and its resources can be measured through an **environmental footprint**—determined by the patterns of production and consumption in that person's culture. The environmental footprint of an average person in a high-income country is about six times bigger than that of someone in a low-income country and many more times larger than in the least developed nations (United Nations Population Fund 2004).

Structural functionalism also helps us to understand and assess how changes in one aspect of the social system affect other aspects of society. For example, in the two years after the terrorist attacks of September 11, 2001, public concern about most environmental problems declined sharply, most likely as a result of increasing worry about the economy and terrorism over the same period (Saad 2002). The effect of oil prices on the economy provides another illustration of

environmental footprint

The environmental impact of building, farming, consuming, etc. The footprint is measured in terms of loss of arable land, use of water resources, fuel depletion, and carbon emissions.

how a change in one aspect of the social system affects other aspects of society. When the price of oil skyrocketed after Hurricane Katrina in 2005, businesses suffered and consumers struggled to pay higher prices for food and other goods. Because so much of our economy depends on oil, an oil shortage or price spike affects virtually every aspect of our economy.

The structural-functionalist perspective raises our awareness of latent dysfunctions—negative consequences of social actions that are unintended and not widely recognized. For example, consider the more than 840 000 dams worldwide. The dams provide water to irrigate farmlands and supply 17 percent of the world's electricity, yet dam building has had unintended negative consequences for the environment, including the loss of wetlands and wildlife habitat, the emission of methane (a gas that contributes to global warming) from rotting vegetation trapped in reservoirs, and the alteration of river flows downstream, which kills plant and animal life ("A Prescription" 2001). Dams have also displaced millions of people from their homes. As philosopher Kathleen Moore points out, "Sometimes in maximizing the benefits in one place, you create a greater harm somewhere else.... While it might sometimes seem that small acts of cruelty or destruction are justified because they create a greater good, we need to be aware of the hidden systematic costs" (Jensen 2001: 11). Being aware of latent dysfunctions means paying attention to the unintended and often hidden environmental consequences of human activities.

Conflict Perspective

The conflict perspective focuses on how wealth, power, and the pursuit of profit underlie many environmental problems. Wealth is related to consumption patterns that cause environmental problems. Wealthy nations have higher per capita consumption of petroleum, wood, metals, cement, and other commodities that deplete Earth's resources, emit pollutants, and generate large volumes of waste. The wealthiest 20 percent of the world's population is responsible for 86 percent of total private consumption (Bright 2003). Moreover, the capitalist pursuit of profit encourages making money from industry regardless of the damage done to the environment. McDaniel (2005: 22–23) notes that "our culture tolerates environmentalism only so long as it has minimal impact on big business.... In an economically centered culture, jobs come first, not the health of people or the environment." In short, wealthy nations exploit less developed nations for raw materials, labor, and as a market to sell goods to (Barbosa 2009).

planned obsolescence

The manufacturing of products that are intended to become inoperative or outdated in a fairly short time.

To maximize growth, manufacturers design products intended to become obsolete. As a result of this **planned obsolescence**, consumers continually throw away functional products and purchase replacements. Industry profits at the expense of the environment, which is subject to the constant production of goods and must absorb ever-increasing amounts of waste.

Industries also use their power and wealth to influence politicians' environmental and energy policies as well as the public's beliefs about environmental issues. ExxonMobil, the world's largest oil company, has spent millions of dollars on lobbying and has funded numerous organizations that have tried to discredit scientific findings that link fossil fuel burning to global climate change (Mooney 2005). Despite the agreement of hundreds of scientists from around the world that global warming is occurring and is largely due to "greenhouse gases" released by fossil fuel burning, the Bush administration pulled out of the Kyoto

Protocol—an international agreement to reduce greenhouse gas emissions—citing "incomplete" science as the reason.

As of this writing, the federal government in Canada, under Prime Minister Stephen Harper, has announced its commitment to the principles of the Kyoto accord (Palmer 2006); however, it has also made clear that Canada is unlikely to meet its targets for reductions in greenhouse gas emissions promised at the time the accord came into effect on February 15, 2005. That governments can claim to adhere to the spirit of the accord and simultaneously back away from keeping promises speaks to the limitations of the accord's language, couched as it is in terms of goal-setting. One can endlessly defer the goal while still claiming to be adhering to the principles of the pact.

Ecofeminist Perspective

Ecological feminism, or **ecofeminism**, began in 1974 when French feminist Françoise d'Eaubonn coined the term *ecological feminisme* to call attention to women's potential to energize an ecological revolution (Warren 2000). Ecofeminists view environmental problems as resulting from human domination of the environment and see connections between the domination of women, people of colour, children, and the poor and the domination of nature. Throughout the world and in developing countries in particular, men are dominant in deciding how natural resources are used. Men are dominant in positions of government and corporate leadership and own most of the land. By some estimates, women around the world hold title to less than 2 percent of the land that is owned (Mac-Donald and Nierenberg 2003). In contrast to a male-oriented view of natural resources as a means to an end—a means to profit and power—ecofeminists often embrace a spiritual approach to addressing environmental problems, drawing on pagan, Native, New Age, and Eastern religious traditions that emphasize the close connection between women and nature (Mother Earth) (Schaeffer 2003).

ecofeminism

A synthesis of feminism, environmentalism, and anti-militarism.

Symbolic Interactionist Perspective

The symbolic interactionist perspective focuses on how meanings, labels, and definitions learned through interaction and through the media affect environmental problems. Whether an individual recycles, drives an SUV (sport-utility vehicle), or joins an environmental activist group is influenced by the meanings and definitions of these behaviours that the individual learns through interaction with others.

Large corporations and industries commonly use marketing and public relations strategies to construct favourable meanings of their corporation or industry. The term **greenwashing** refers to the way in which environmentally and socially damaging companies portray their corporate image and products as being "environmentally friendly" or socially responsible. Greenwashing is commonly used by public relations firms that specialize in damage control for clients whose reputations and profits have been hurt by poor environmental practices. Wal-Mart, for example, has paid millions of dollars in fines and settlements for a number of environmental violations, including excessive storm runoff at construction sites, petroleum storage violations, and *Clean Air Act* violations (Wal-Mart Watch 2005). When Wal-Mart announced in 2005 that it would donate $35 million (less than 1 percent of its 2004 profits) to the National Fish

greenwashing

The corporate practice of displaying a sense of corporate responsibility for the environment. For example, many companies publicly emphasize the steps they have taken to help the environment. Another greenwashing strategy is to retool, repackage, or relabel a company's product.

and Wildlife Foundation over a 10-year period to purchase one acre of conservation land for every acre of land developed by Wal-Mart, many environmentalists accused Wal-Mart of greenwashing. Just before Earth Day (April 22) in 2005, Wal-Mart bought full-page ads in at least 20 newspapers touting its new program, Acres for America (Associated Press 2005). Such publicity suggests that Wal-Mart's Acres for America program is designed to improve Wal-Mart's public image. The comments of Eric Olson of the Sierra Club reflect the skepticism that many environmentalists have toward corporate greenwashing: "Wal-Mart thinks it can paint over its record with a nice shade of green, but that won't hide its true colors" (quoted by Associated Press 2005).

Ford Motor Company was accused of greenwashing in 2004 when it advertised its Escape Hybrid sport utility vehicle as an example of Ford's commitment to the environment when, for the fifth consecutive year, Ford's vehicles had the worst overall fuel economy of all major automakers. In fact, Ford's fleetwide fuel economy was worse in 2004 than it was in 1984! And hybrids accounted for less than 1 percent of Ford's annual sales (Johnson 2004).

Greenwashing also occurs in the political arena when political leaders attempt to portray an environmentally damaging policy or program as environmentally friendly. Consider, for example, U.S. President George Bush's Clear Skies Initiative. The initiative allows five times more mercury emissions, one and a half times more sulphur dioxide emissions, and hundreds of thousands more tonnes of smog-forming nitrogen oxide emissions than those allowed under the 1970 *Clean Air Act* (Clarren 2005). Naming it the Clear Skies Initiative is a blatant example of greenwashing.

Although greenwashing involves manipulation of public perception to maximize profits, many corporations make genuine and legitimate efforts to improve their operations, packaging, or overall sense of corporate responsibility toward the environment. For example, in 1990 McDonald's announced that it was phasing out foam packaging and switching to a new, paper-based packaging that is partially degradable. But many environmentalists are not satisfied with what they see as token environmentalism, or as Peter Dykstra of Greenpeace calls it, 5 percent of environmental virtue to mask 95 percent of environmental vice (Hager and Burton 2000).

Greenwashing can cause controversy and divisions among environmentalists. Consider Earth Day, which has brought environmentalists together to celebrate Earth and to increase public awareness of environmental issues every April 22 since 1970. In recent years, Earth Day events have been sponsored by corporations such as Office Depot, Texas Instruments, Raytheon Missile Systems, and Waste Management (a Houston-based company responsible for numerous hazardous waste sites). Some environmentalists, including Earth Day's founder, former senator Gaylord Nelson, consider the participation of corporations in Earth Day evidence of the celebration's success; other environmentalists oppose corporate sponsorship of Earth Day events, accusing corporations of using their financial support of Earth Day as a public relations greenwashing strategy. John Stauber, a critic of corporations that hide their damaging environmental practices behind green advertising and marketing, says that "Waste Management sponsoring Earth Day is similar to Enron sponsoring a seminar on corporate responsibility" (quoted by Cappiello 2003). In recent years, environmentalists have withdrawn from and protested Earth Day events in cities across the country because the events were sponsored by corporations.

13.3 Environmental Problems: An Overview

Over the past 50 years humans have altered **ecosystems**—the complex and dynamic relationships between forms of life and the environments they inhabit—more rapidly and extensively than in any other comparable period in history (Millennium Ecosystem Assessment 2005). As a result, humans have created environmental problems, including depletion of natural resources; air, land, and water pollution; global warming; environmental illness; environmental injustice; threats to biodiversity; and disappearing livelihoods. Because many of these environmental problems are related to the ways that humans produce and consume energy, we begin this section with an overview of global energy use. Before reading further, you may want to assess your attitudes toward energy and the environment in this chapter's *Self and Society* feature.

ecosystems

Complex environments that support a variety of interdependent life forms.

Energy Use Worldwide: An Overview

Being mindful of environmental problems means seeing the connections between energy use and our daily lives.

> Everything we consume or use—our homes, their contents, our cars and the roads we travel, the clothes we wear, and the food we eat—requires energy to produce and package, to distribute to shops or front doors, to operate, and then to get rid of. We rarely consider where this energy comes from or how much of it we use—or how much we truly need. (Sawin 2004: 25)

Most of the world's energy—86 percent—comes from fossil fuels, which include petroleum (or oil), coal, and natural gas (Energy Information Administration 2008) (see Figure 13.1). As you continue reading this chapter, notice that the world's major environmental problems—air, land, and water pollution, destruction of habitats, biodiversity loss, global warming, and environmental illness—are linked to the production and use of fossil fuels.

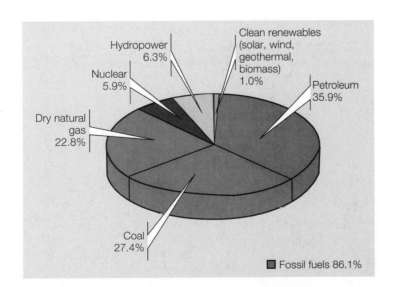

■ **Figure 13.1** *World Energy Production by Source, 2006*

SOURCE: Adapted from Energy Information Administration (2008), http://www.eia.doe.gov/iea/overview.html, April 2011.

Environmental Knowledge Survey

Directions: After answering each of the following items, check your answers for items 2 through 11 using the answer key provided. For items 2 through 11, calculate the total number of items you answered correctly.

1. In general, how much do you feel you yourself know about environmental issues and problems—would you say you know a lot, a fair amount, only a little, or practically nothing?

    a. A lot

    b. A fair amount

    c. Only a little

    d. Practically nothing

    e. Don't know

2. How is most of the electricity in Canada generated?

    a. By burning oil, coal, and wood

    b. With nuclear power

    c. Through solar energy

    d. At hydroelectric power plants

    e. Don't know

3. What is the most common cause of pollution of streams, rivers, and oceans?

    a. Dumping of garbage by cities

    b. Surface water running off yards, city streets, paved lots, and farm fields

    c. Trash washed into the ocean from beaches

    d. Waste dumped by factories

    e. Don't know

4. What do you think is the main cause of global climate change, that is, the warming of the planet Earth?

    a. A recent increase in oxygen in the atmosphere

    b. Sunlight radiating more strongly through a hole in the upper ozone layer

    c. More carbon emissions from autos, homes, and industry

    d. Increased activity from volcanoes worldwide

    e. Don't know

5. To the best of your knowledge, what percentage of the world's water is fresh and available for use?

    a. 1%

    b. 5%

    c. 10%

    d. 33%

    e. Don't know

6. The current worldwide reduction in the number of ocean fish is *primarily* the result of which of the following?

    a. Pollution in coastal waters worldwide

    b. Increased harvesting by fishing vessels

    c. Changes in ocean temperature

    d. Loss of fishing shoals and other deep sea habitats

    e. Don't know

7. What is the leading cause of childhood death worldwide?

   a. Malnutrition and starvation

   b. Asthma from dust in the air

   c. Auto and home accidents

   d. Germs in the water

   e. Don't know

8. What is the most common reason that an animal species becomes extinct?

   a. Pesticides are killing them

   b. Humans are destroying their habitats

   c. There is too much hunting

   d. Climate changes are affecting them

   e. Don't know

9. Thousands of waste disposal areas—dumps and landfills—in Canada contain toxic waste. The greatest threat posed by these waste disposal areas is

   a. Chemical air pollution

   b. Contact with farm animals and household pets

   c. Contamination of water supplies

   d. Human consumption through contaminated food

   e. Don't know

10. Many communities are concerned about running out of room in their community trash dumps and landfills. What is the greatest source of landfill material?

   a. Disposable diapers

   b. Lawn and garden clippings, trimmings, and leaves

   c. Paper products including newspapers, cardboard, and packaging

   d. Glass and plastic bottles and aluminum and steel cans

   e. Don't know

11. Some scientists have expressed concern that chemicals and certain minerals accumulate in the human body at dangerous levels. These chemicals and minerals enter the body primarily through

   a. Breathing air

   b. Living near toxic waste dumps

   c. Household cleaning products

   d. Drinking water

   e. Don't know

Answer Key for Items 2 through 11: 2d, 3b, 4c, 5a, 6b, 7d, 8b, 9c, 10c, 11d

Average Number of Correct Responses in a U.S. National Survey: 3.2 (Note: Questions 2 and 9 referred to the United States.)

SOURCE: Adapted with permission of the National Environmental Education and Training Foundation.

The next most common source of energy is hydroelectric power (6.3 percent), which involves generating electricity from moving water. As water passes through a dam into a river below, energy is produced by a turbine in the dam. Although hydroelectric power is nonpolluting and inexpensive, it is criticized for affecting natural habitats. For example, dams make certain fish unable to swim upstream to reproduce. Canada produces more hydroelectric power than any other country, followed by Brazil, China, and the United States (Energy Information Administration 2005).

Nuclear power, accounting for 5.9 percent of world energy production, is associated with a number of problems related to radioactive nuclear waste—problems that are discussed later in this chapter. Only 1 percent of the world's energy comes from clean renewable resources, which include geothermal power (from the heat of the earth), solar power, wind power, and biomass (e.g., fuel wood, crops, and animal wastes), which are primarily used by poor populations in developing countries. One-fourth of the world's population—1.6 billion people—lack access to electricity in their homes and use biomass for heating and cooking (Flavin and Aeck 2005).

Depletion of Natural Resources

Population growth, combined with consumption patterns, is depleting natural resources such as forests, water, minerals, and fossil fuels.

Water supplies around the world are dwindling while the demand for water continues to increase because of industrialization, rising living standards, and changing diets that include more food products that require larger amounts of water to produce, such as milk, eggs, chicken, and beef. Currently, 50 countries are facing moderate or severe water stress; by the year 2030, nearly half the world's population will be living in areas of high water stress (WWF 2008; World Water Assessment Program 2009). With 70 percent of freshwater use going to agriculture, water shortages threaten food production and supply.

deforestation

The destruction of Earth's rainforests.

The world's forests are also being depleted. The demand for new land, fuel, and raw materials has resulted in **deforestation**—the conversion of forestland to nonforest land (Intergovernmental Panel on Climate Change 2000). Global forest cover has been reduced by half of what it was 8000 years ago (Gardner 2005). Between the 1960s and the 1990s, one-fifth of the world's tropical forests were cut or burned (Youth 2003). The major causes of deforestation are the expansion of agricultural land, human settlements, wood harvesting, and road building. We currently lose 13 million hectares of forest every year as the trees are cut down and the land converted for human use (UNEP 2008).

Deforestation has serious negative effects. It displaces people and wild species from their habitats; soil erosion caused by deforestation can cause severe flooding; and, as we explain later in this chapter, deforestation contributes to global warming.

desertification

The expansion of deserts and the loss of usable land due to the overuse of semi-arid land on the desert margins for animal grazing and obtaining firewood.

Deforestation also contributes to **desertification**—the degradation of semi-arid land, which results in the expansion of desert land unusable for agriculture. Overgrazing by cattle and other herd animals also contributes to desertification. As more land turns into desert, populations can no longer sustain a livelihood on the land, so they migrate to urban areas or other countries, contributing to social and political instability. The problem of desertification is most severe in Africa (Reese 2001). As more land turns into desert, populations can no longer sustain a livelihood on the land, and so they migrate to urban areas or other countries, contributing to social and political instability.

The demands that humanity makes on Earth's natural resources is known as the environmental footprint. A person's environmental footprint is determined by the patterns of production and consumption in that person's culture. Environmental footprints are a measure of how much of Earth people require to provide the natural resources they consume, and are often expressed in terms of global hectares per person (1 hectare equals about 2.47 acres). Collectively, human demand on the world's natural resources exceeds Earth's capacity by nearly a third; 77 percent of us are living in ecological debt, using more natural resources than Earth can sustain. If we continue current patterns of consumption, we would need the equivalent of two planets to support us by 2030 (WWF 2008).

Air Pollution

Transportation vehicles, fuel combustion, industrial processes (such as the burning of coal and the processing of minerals from mining), and solid waste disposal have contributed to the growing levels of air pollutants, including carbon monoxide, sulphur dioxide, nitrogen dioxide, mercury, and lead. Air pollution levels are highest in areas with both heavy industry and traffic congestion, such as Los Angeles, New Delhi, Jakarta, Bangkok, Tehran, Beijing, and Mexico City. Air pollution, which is linked to heart disease, lung cancer, emphysema, chronic bronchitis, and asthma, kills about 3 million people a year (Pimentel et al. 2007). Figure 13.2 shows the per capita contributions to air pollution by region.

In Canada, the popularity among boomers of minivans, sport utility vehicles (SUVs), and other light trucks has alarmed environmentalists. These vehicles, when compared with the standard passenger car, not only guzzle one-third more gas, but also spew one-third more pollution out their tailpipes (as cited in Speirs 2000: A24). While the David Suzuki Foundation has remarked that "[t]his light truck category is a moving disaster" (Speirs 2000: A24), sales of light trucks have accounted for more than 50 percent of the passenger vehicle market in recent years. Only the high price of oil, rather than concern for the environment, is cutting into the sales of large vehicles, which suggests that if gas prices should drop again, fuel-efficient, small cars will lose their appeal.

Indoor Air Pollution When we hear the phrase *air pollution*, we typically think of industrial smokestacks and vehicle exhausts pouring grey streams of chemical

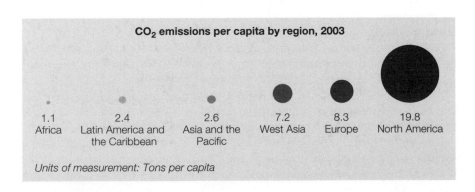

Figure 13.2 *CO_2 Emissions per Capita by Region, 2003*

SOURCE: GEO Data Portal, compiled from UNFCCC 2006 and Marland et al. 2006 as in *UNEP 2007 Year Book.*

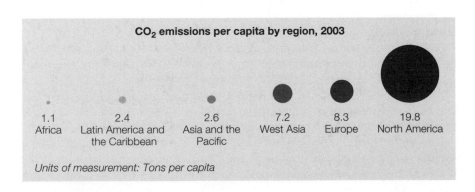

CO₂ emissions per capita by region, 2003 — Units of measurement: Tons per capita. Africa 1.1, Latin America and the Caribbean 2.4, Asia and the Pacific 2.6, West Asia 7.2, Europe 8.3, North America 19.8

matter into the air. But indoor air pollution is also a major problem, especially in poor countries.

About half the world's population and up to 90 percent of rural households in developing countries rely on wood and unprocessed biomass (dung and crop residues) for cooking and heating fuel (Bruce et al. 2000). These fuels are typically burned indoors in open fires or in poorly functioning stoves, producing hazardous emissions such as soot particles, carbon monoxide, nitrous oxides, sulphur oxides, and formaldehyde. Long-term exposure to the smoke contributes to respiratory illness, lung cancer, tuberculosis, and blindness; an estimated two million deaths in developing countries each year result from exposure to indoor air pollution. According to the World Health Organization, indoor air pollution ranks fifth as a risk factor for ill health worldwide—behind malnutrition, AIDS, tobacco use, and poor water and sanitation (Bruce et al. 2000; Mishra et al. 2002).

Even in affluent countries much air pollution, invisible to the eye, exists where we least expect it—in our homes, schools, workplaces, and public buildings. Sources of indoor air pollution include lead dust (from old lead-based paint); secondhand tobacco smoke; by-products of combustion (e.g., carbon monoxide) from stoves, furnaces, fireplaces, heaters, and dryers; and other common household, personal, and commercial products (American Lung Association 2005).

Some of the most common indoor pollutants include carpeting (which emits more than a dozen toxic chemicals); mattresses, sofas, and pillows (which emit formaldehyde and fire retardants); pressed wood found in kitchen cabinets and furniture (which emits formaldehyde); and wool blankets and dry-cleaned clothing (which emit trichloroethylene). Air fresheners, deodorizers, and disinfectants emit the pesticide paradichlorobenzene. Potentially harmful organic solvents are present in numerous office supplies, including glue, correction fluid, printing ink, carbonless paper, and felt-tip markers. Many homes today contain a cocktail of toxic chemicals: "Styrene (from plastics), benzene (from plastics and rubber), toluene and xylene, trichloroethylene, dichloromethane, trimethylbenzene, hexanes, phenols, pentanes and much more outgas from our everyday furnishings, construction materials, and appliances" (Rogers 2002).

Destruction of the Ozone Layer The ozone layer of Earth's atmosphere absorbs most of the harmful ultraviolet-B radiation from the sun and completely screens out lethal ultraviolet-C radiation. The ozone layer is thus essential to life on Earth. Yet the use of certain chemicals has weakened the ozone layer. The depletion of the ozone layer allows hazardous levels of ultraviolet rays to reach Earth's surface. It is linked to increases in skin cancer and cataracts, weakened immune systems, reduced crop yields, damage to ocean ecosystems and reduced fishing yields, and adverse effects on animals.

The ozone hole above Antarctica spanned a record 11 million square miles in 2003, exposing the southern tip of South America. The size of the hole decreased slightly in 2004, but increased in 2005 (Reuters 2005).

Consumer habits play a large part in the emission of greenhouse gases. Especially important is not only how far and how often we drive, but also how hot or cool we keep our homes in winter and summer, how often we use appliances, and whether our homes are properly insulated or not, as well as whether we purchase more local produce or more produce trucked from distant locations. Despite the impact of consumer habits, the federal Conservative government withdrew support of the "One Tonne Challenge," an initiative intended to encourage greater energy conservation by average Canadians. On why the federal government withdrew its support is only speculate, but an obvious effect of greater conservation would be a reduction in consumption, a potentially serious problem for Canada's economic growth.

Acid Rain Air pollutants, such as sulphur dioxide and nitrogen oxide, mix with precipitation to form **acid rain**. Polluted rain, snow, and fog contaminate crops, forests, lakes, and rivers. Acid rain is a particular threat in Ontario, New Brunswick, Nova Scotia, and Quebec because these provinces are directly in the path of much of the continent's SO_2 and NO_x emissions, and the nonporous granite that composes most of the Canadian Shield is less able to absorb acid rain. Roughly 40 percent of Canada's total land area (about four million square kilometres) is extremely sensitive to acid rain (Statistics Canada 1998). Moreover, because pollutants in the air are carried by the wind, industrial pollution in the midwest United States falls back to Earth as acid rain on southeast Canada and the northeast New England states. Acid rain is not just a problem in North America, though; it decimates plant and animal species around the globe. "The Parthenon, Taj Mahal, and Michelangelo's statues are dissolving under the onslaught of the acid pouring out of the skies" (Blatt 2005: 161).

acid rain
The mixture of precipitation with air pollutants, such as sulphur dioxide and nitrogen oxide.

Global Warming and Climate Change

In 2005, scientists reported that the Ilulissat glacier in Greenland, considered one of the wonders of the world, had shrunk by more than 9.6 kilometres in two or three years (Bohan 2005). In the same year, Russian researchers discovered that the world's largest frozen peat bog, located in Siberia, is melting, turning this once frozen area the size of Germany and France combined into a mass of shallow lakes (Pearce 2005). The melting of Greenland's Ilulissat glacier and Siberia's peat bog contributes to growing evidence of **global warming**.

Globally, the 1990s was the warmest decade on record since record keeping began in the late 1800s. The hottest year on record was 1998, followed by 2002 and 2003. The year 2004 rated as the fourth warmest year on record (National Oceanic and Atmospheric Administration 2005). Average global air temperature rose by 0.68 degree Celsius over the twentieth century; between 1990 and 2100, this temperature is expected to rise by as much as 5.88 degrees Celsius (Intergovernmental Panel on Climate Change 2001b).

global warming
The increasing average global air temperature, caused mainly by the accumulation of various gases that collect in the atmosphere.

Causes of Global Warming Although the cause of global warming remains a disputed topic, the prevailing scientific view is that **greenhouse gases**—primarily carbon dioxide, methane, and nitrous oxide—accumulate in the atmosphere and act like the glass in a greenhouse, holding heat from the sun close to Earth. Since 1750, atmospheric concentrations of carbon dioxide, the main greenhouse gas, have increased by 31 percent, methane by 151 percent, and nitrous oxide by 17 percent (Intergovernmental Panel on Climate Change 2001b).

The primary source of carbon dioxide emissions is fossil fuel burning. Total world carbon dioxide emissions from fossil fuels were 25.2 billion tonnes in 2003, an increase of 17.1 percent from 1993.

Deforestation also contributes to increasing levels of carbon dioxide in the atmosphere. Trees and other plant life use carbon dioxide and release oxygen

greenhouse gases
The collection of increasing amounts of chlorofluorocarbons (CFCs), carbon dioxide, methane, and other gases in the atmosphere, where they act like the glass in a greenhouse, holding heat from the sun close to the earth and preventing the heat from rising back into space.

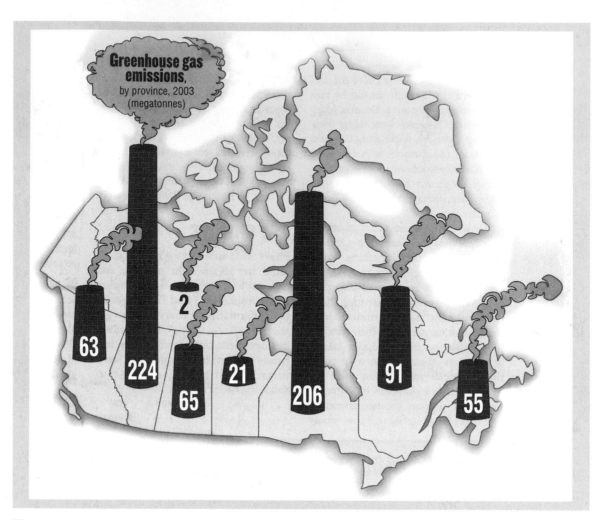

■ Figure 13.3 *Greenhouse Gas Emissions by Province, 2003*
SOURCE: "Hot Air Over Kyoto," by Jim Standford, 2006. Reprinted with permission.

into the air. As forests are cut down, fewer trees are available to absorb the carbon dioxide.

In Canada, more than a third of emissions "come directly from the energy industry, a byproduct of oil, gas, coal, and electricity production. The remaining two-thirds is released by industries and activities that subsequently use that energy. Transportation accounts for 25 percent of all emissions" (Stanford 2002: 12). Due to the heavy pollution caused by oil and gas operations, Alberta is "far and away Canada's leading greenhouse gas polluter, releasing more emissions than Ontario (which has four times the population)...[or] in per capita terms, more than three times the Canadian average" (Stanford 2002: 12) (Figure 13.3).

Effects of Global Warming and Climate Change After Hurricane Katrina devastated the U.S. Gulf Coast, increased attention was given to the role that global warming and climate change play in weather events. "While not all extreme weather events can be attributed directly to climate change, the intensity of such events is likely to increase as a result of global warming" (UNEP 2005: 2).

Global warming and climate change are projected to affect regions in different ways. As temperature increases, some areas will experience heavier rain, whereas other regions will get drier. Some regions will experience increased water availability and crop yields, but other regions, particularly tropical and subtropical regions, are expected to experience decreased water availability and a reduction in crop yields. Global warming results in shifts of plant and animal habitats and the increased risk of extinction of some species. Regions that experience increased rainfall as a result of increasing temperatures may face increases in waterborne diseases and diseases transmitted by insects. Over time, climate change may produce opposite effects on the same resource. For example, in the short term forest productivity is likely to increase in response to higher levels of carbon dioxide in the air, but over the long term forest productivity is likely to decrease because of drought, fire, insects, and disease.

As global warming melts glaciers and permafrost, the sea level will continue to rise. Global average sea levels rose 0.1 m–0.2 m during the twentieth century and are expected to rise by 0.09 m–0.88 m from 1990 to 2100. As sea levels rise, some island countries, as well as some barrier islands, are likely to disappear and low-lying coastal areas will be increasingly vulnerable to storm surges and flooding. If global warming continues, Greenland's ice cap could melt within a few hundred years, raising the level of Earth's oceans by more than 6 m and threatening the lives of the 21.2 billion people who live within 32 km of the coastline (Bohan 2005).

In urban areas, flooding can be a problem where storm drains and waste management systems are inadequate. Increased flooding associated with global warming is expected to result in increases in drownings and in diarrheal and respiratory diseases. Increases in the number of people exposed to insect- and water-related diseases, such as malaria and cholera, are also expected. Even if greenhouse gases are stabilized, global air temperature and sea level are expected to continue to rise for hundreds of years.

Another effect of global warming is that it contributes to further warming of the planet—a process known as a *positive feedback loop*. For example, the melting of Siberia's frozen peat bog—a result of global warming—could release billions of tons of methane, a potent greenhouse gas, into the atmosphere (Pearce 2005). And the melting of ice and snow—another result of global warming— exposes more land and ocean area, which absorbs more heat than ice and snow, further warming the planet.

Land Pollution

About 30 percent of the world's surface is land, which provides soil to grow the food we eat. Increasingly, humans are polluting the land with nuclear waste, solid waste, and pesticides.

Nuclear and Radioactive Waste Nuclear waste, resulting from both nuclear weapons production and nuclear reactors or power plants, contains radioactive plutonium, a substance linked to cancer and genetic defects. Radioactive plutonium has a half-life of 24 000 years, meaning that it takes 24 000 years for the radioactivity to be reduced by half (Mead 1998). Thus, nuclear waste in the environment remains potentially harmful to human and other life for thousands of years.

In Canada, radioactive waste has been produced since the early 1930s, when the first uranium mine began operating in the Northwest Territories at Port Radium (see Figure 13.4). Radium was refined for medical use and uranium was later processed at Port Hope, Ontario. In the 1940s, research and development on the application of nuclear energy to produce electricity began at the Chalk River Laboratories of Atomic Energy of Canada Limited (AECL). Currently, radioactive waste is produced from uranium mining, milling, refining and conversion; nuclear fuel fabrication; nuclear reactor operations; and nuclear research and radioisotope manufacture and use. Under Canada's Radioactive Waste Policy Framework, producers and owners of radioactive waste are responsible for the funding, organization, management, and operation of disposal and other facilities required for their waste.

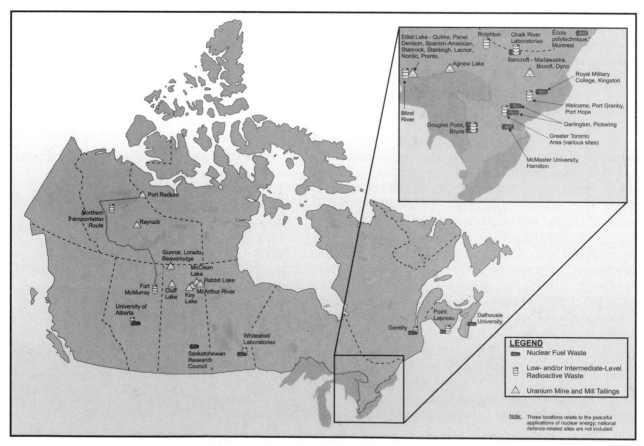

■ **Figure 13.4** *Radioactive Waste Sites in Canada as of December 31, 2010*

Note: These locations relate to the peaceful applications of nuclear energy; national defence–related sites are not included.

SOURCE: The Inventory of Radioactive Waste in Canada (Low Level Radioactive Waste Management Office). Used with permission.

Nuclear plants are home to many hazards. They have about 47 000 tonnes of radioactive spent fuel, with about 9100 tonnes of that amount sealed in casks (Vedantam 2005). Poor management of the generation and storage processes can end catastrophically. Accidents at nuclear power plants, such as the 1986 accident at Chernobyl, and the potential for nuclear reactors to be targeted by terrorists add to the actual and potential dangers of nuclear power plants.

Recognizing the hazards of nuclear power plants and their waste, Germany became the first country to order all of its 19 nuclear power plants shut down by 2020 ("Nukes Rebuked" 2000). But other countries are building or planning to build new reactors. In spring 2006, in Canada, Ontario Premier Dalton McGuinty announced a $40 billion increase for the development of nuclear power generation in his province, citing arguments that alternatives to nuclear power are "too dirty" (Howlett 2006). The decision was taken despite McGuinty's own dissatisfaction with it.

At the time of writing this chapter, the effects from the March 11, 2011 earthquake and tsunami that hit Japan, setting off a partial meltdown at the Fukushima nuclear plant, are still unfolding. The degree of meltdown and levels of radiation being released at the plant are not known in definite terms. Although the disaster is nowhere near the scale of the 1986 Chernobyl complete meltdown, these events have once again underscored the vulnerabilities of nuclear power generation. The long-term effects of the breaches in containment at Fukushima are not possible to predict at this time; however, Wade Allison (2011), a nuclear and medical physicist at Oxford, has argued that fears regarding the effects of radiation are greatly exaggerated, that acceptable limits on annual exposure to radiation are far too conservative, and that the routine use of radiation therapy to treat cancers is equal to 20 000 years worth of "acceptable levels" as stated by public policies set around the globe following the Chernobyl disaster. Allison reminds us to keep the dangers of radiation in perspective, and to be mindful of more significant dangers of climate change, chemical spills (such as the disaster in Bhopal, India), and what would happen if we had no electric power for the millions of people who rely on nuclear power generation.

Solid Waste

In Canada, the waste generated by Canadians is on the rise. Although our recycling habits are showing proportional increases, our production of unrecyclable waste is also on the rise. According to a federal report from 2005, each Canadian produces about 383 kg of solid waste per year, or about 30 green garbage bags full (Statistics Canada 2005). Of the total waste generated for the period studied, more than 9.5 million tonnes went into landfill sites or was incinerated, and about 2.5 million tonnes went into recycling (Statistics Canada 2005). Figures such as these do not include mining, agricultural, and industrial waste; demolition and construction wastes; junked autos; or obsolete equipment wastes of which more than half is taken to landfills. The availability of landfill space is limited, however. This chapter's *Focus on Technology* feature examines the hazards of disposing of computers in landfills (and other environmental and health hazards of computers).

Environmental and Health Hazards of Computer Manufacturing, Disposal, and Recycling

More than 1 billion computers worldwide have been sold, and the 2 billion mark may be reached as early as 2008 (Thibodeau 2002). In the United States alone more than 100 000 computers become obsolete each day (Silicon Valley Toxics Coalition 2005). The toxic materials used in computer manufacturing pose significant hazards for workers in the production of computers, and the toxic e-waste (waste from electronic equipment) makes the disposal and recycling of computers a human and environmental hazard.

Toxic Materials Used in Computer Manufacturing

- Lead and cadmium in computer circuit boards
- Lead oxide and barium in cathode ray tubes of computer monitors
- Mercury in switches and flat screens
- Brominated flame retardants on printed circuit boards, cables, and plastic casing
- Polychlorinated biphenyls (PCBs) present in older capacitors and transformers
- Polyvinyl chloride (PVC)-coated copper cables and plastic computer casings

Hazards of Computer Manufacturing

The manufacturing of semiconductors, printed circuit boards, disk drives, and monitors involves hazardous chemicals. Numerous reports have documented higher-than-normal rates of cancer and birth defects among computer manufacturing workers who are regularly exposed to carcinogenic and other toxic chemicals (Silicon Valley Toxics Coalition 2001).

Hazards of E-Waste Disposal

When consumers upgrade to faster and sleeker PCs with more memory and new features, what happens to their old machines? Most unwanted, obsolete computers are destined for landfills, incinerators, or hazardous waste exports; less than 10 percent of unwanted computers are recycled (Computer Take Back Campaign 2005).

Hazards of Landfill Dumping and Incinerating E-Waste

The main concern with regard to dumping e-waste in landfills is that hazardous substances in landfills can leach and contaminate the soil and groundwater. In many city landfills cathode ray tubes from computers and TVs are the largest source of lead (Motavalli 2001). Lead has toxic effects on humans as well as on plants, animals, and microorganisms. The leaching of mercury from landfilled e-waste is also a major concern. Just one-seventieth of a teaspoon of mercury can contaminate 20 acres [8 hectares] of a lake, making the fish unfit for consumption (Computer Take Back Campaign 2005).

Some computer waste is disposed of through incineration (burning). Incineration of scrap computers generates extremely toxic dioxins that are released in air emissions.

Hazards of Recycling Computers

Computers and printers can be recycled, and the plastic materials and precious metals, such as copper and gold, can be recovered. But recycling computers releases dust containing toxic polybrominated flame retardants into the air, and high concentrations of these substances have been found in the blood of workers in recycling plants (Silicon Valley Toxics Coalition 2001).

The Exportation of Hazardous E-Waste

Fifty to 80 percent of the United States' electronic waste that is collected for recycling is exported to developing countries where labor costs are cheap and worker safety and environmental regulations are lax compared with U.S. law. One pilot program that collected electronic scrap in San Jose, California, estimated that shipping computer monitors to China for recycling was 10 times cheaper than recycling them in the United States (Silicon Valley Toxics Coalition 2001).

When investigators visited a waste site in Guiyu, China, they saw men, women, and children wearing little or no protective gear smashing, picking apart, and burning computers, exposing themselves and their surroundings to toxic substances (Silicon Valley Toxics Coalition 2002). The groundwater near the site is so polluted that drinking water is trucked in from 18 miles [29 km] away. A nearby river water sample contained 190 times the pollution levels allowed by the World Health Organization.

A 1989 treaty known as the Basel Convention restricts the export of hazardous waste from rich countries to poor countries—even when the waste is destined for recycling. But the United States has not ratified this treaty and has lobbied Asian governments to establish bilateral trade agreements to allow continued exportation of hazardous waste.

Solutions to the Problem of Toxic E-Waste

Legislative Solutions. At least 26 states have considered legislation concerning the disposal of e-waste. In 2000 Massachusetts became the first state to ban dumping of video monitors (computer screens and televisions) (Massachusetts Department of Environmental Protection 2001). Maine and Minnesota also prohibit dumping cathode ray tubes (found in monitors). And in 2003, California passed the *Electronic Waste Recycling Act*, becoming the first state to pass legislation to require recycling. This act requires retailers to add a $6 to $10 fee to certain electronic products to cover the costs of collection and recycling programs and requires recycling programs to use environmentally sound methods. Electronics manufacturers favor regulating e-waste recycling through federal legislation so that all manufacturers abide by the same rules.

The European Union's WEEE Directive. In 2002 the European Union passed legislation on waste from electrical and electronic equipment (the WEEE Directive) that makes producers responsible for taking back their old products and for phasing out the use of certain toxic materials in computer manufacturing; the legislation also encourages cleaner product design and less waste generation. This strategy, known as Extended Producer Responsibility, is based on the principle that producers bear a degree of responsibility for all the environmental impacts of their products. This includes impacts arising from choice of materials and from the manufacturing process as well as the use and disposal of products. When manufacturers are financially responsible for waste management of their products, they will have a financial incentive to design those products with less hazardous and more recyclable materials.

Industry Initiatives. A number of industries have taken steps to alleviate the environmental and health hazards of computers. Some computer manufacturers, such as Dell and Gateway, lease out their products, thereby ensuring that they get them back to further upgrade and lease out again. In 1998 IBM introduced the first computer that uses 100% recycled resin in all its major plastic parts. Hewlett-Packard (HP) has developed a safe cleaning method for chips, using carbon dioxide for cleaning as a substitute for hazardous solvents. To encourage recycling of e-waste, HP's Planet Partners program allows people to have their old computers and printers picked up at their door for a fee of $17 to $31 to cover transportation and recycling costs. In exchange, they receive a $50 coupon toward the purchase of an HP product. Toshiba is working on a modular upgradable and customizable computer to reduce product obsolescence. Pressures to eliminate halogenated flame retardants and to design products for recycling have led to the use of metal shielding in computer housings, and a range of lead-free solders are now available.

As governments and industries continue to develop strategies for reducing environmental hazards associated with computer manufacturing and disposal, consumers can also make a difference by choosing manufacturers who practice "product stewardship"—making products that are less toxic, conserve natural resources, and reduce waste. A Guide to Environmentally Preferable Computer Purchasing is available from the Northwest Product Stewardship Council at www. govlink.org/nwpsc/ (Northwest Product Stewardship Council 2000).

Pesticides Pesticides are used worldwide for crops and gardens; outdoor mosquito control; the care of lawns, parks, and golf courses; and indoor pest control. Pesticides contaminate food, water, and air and can be absorbed through the skin, swallowed, or inhaled. At least 53 carcinogenic pesticides are applied to major U.S. food crops (Blatt 2005) and find their way onto Canadian dining tables every day. Many common pesticides are considered potential carcinogens and neurotoxins. In an analysis of 1260 domestic and 4252 imported food samples, pesticide residues were detected in 31.2 percent of the domestic samples and 33.4 percent of the imported samples (Food and Drug Administration 2008). Pesticides also contaminate our groundwater supplies.

Water Pollution

Around the world, water is being polluted by harmful substances, including pesticides, vehicle exhaust, acid rain, oil spills, and industrial, military, and agricultural waste.

Water pollution is most severe in developing countries, where more than one billion people lack access to clean water. In developing nations, more than 80 percent of untreated sewage is dumped directly into rivers, lakes, and seas that are also used for drinking and bathing (World Water Assessment Program 2009). Mining operations, located primarily in developing countries, are notoriously damaging to the environment. Modern gold-mining techniques use cyanide to extract gold from low-grade ore. In 2000, a dam holding cyanide-laced waste at a Romanian gold mine broke, dumping 22 million gallons of cyanide-laced waste into the Tisza River, which flowed into Hungary and Serbia. Some have called this event the worst environmental disaster since the 1986 Chernobyl nuclear explosion. In West Papua, Indonesia, a U.S.-owned gold mine still dumps 109 000 tonnes of cyanide-laced waste into local rivers every day (Ayres 2004). Most gold is used to make jewellery, hardly a necessity. About 270 000 tonnes of waste are generated for every tonne of marketable gold—which translates roughly into 3 tonnes of waste per gold wedding ring (Sampat 2003).

Canadians tend to take fresh water for granted, as they water lawns and clean their cars, take long showers, and leave the water running while they brush their teeth, but Canada's own water supply is in danger. An Environment Canada report explains:

> Although the overall extent of the problem across Canada is unknown, many individual cases of contamination have been investigated such as Ville Mercier in Quebec; the highway de-icing salt problem in Nova Scotia; industrial effluents in Elmira, Ontario; various pesticides in the Prairie provinces; industrial contamination in Vancouver, British Columbia; and so on.... Contamination problems are increasing in Canada primarily because of the large and growing number of toxic compounds used in industry and agriculture. (Environment Canada 2006)

Groundwater pollution in Canada includes—but is not limited to—flame retardants and insecticides in marine and freshwater supplies in British Columbia (Elliott et al. 2006) and in Ville Mercier, Quebec, where dumping waste into an old gravel pit rendered the water unsafe for use or consumption (Environment Canada 2006).

Chemicals, Carcinogens, and Health Problems

Although Canada's *Environmental Protection Act* sets the laws intended to protect our environment, there are serious indications that our laws are falling dangerously short of being effective. In 2005, 11 Canadians from across Canada had their blood tested for the presence of toxic chemicals and heavy metals such as lead and mercury; on average, the people tested had 44 of the 60 chemical compounds the blood tests were designed to identify, including Teflon, DDT, flame retardants, and PCBs (ENS 2005). Those who volunteered for the study were chosen from locations across the country, and although they all had what they considered to be "healthy lifestyles," all had suffered contamination as a result of day-to-day living in an industrialized nation. Similar conclusions were reached when the lead levels of Inuit women were tested and showed concentrations significantly higher than for the general population (Levesque et al. 2003). The Levesque study determined that the replacement of traditional hunting practices with the use of "modern" lead-shot shotguns presented a new danger in traditional food sources for the Inuit. Meanwhile, for Canadians everywhere, flame retardants and stain repellents are entering our bloodstreams—consumer items that fill average households pose serious hazards, as the chemicals from clothes, furniture, and cooking and storage utensils leech into our bodies through ingestion and skin contact day in and day out.

In addition to their carcinogenic (cancer-causing) potential, many chemicals found in common household, personal, and commercial products can result in temporary acute symptoms, such as drowsiness, disorientation, headache, dizziness, nausea, fatigue, shortness of breath, cramps, diarrhea, and irritation of the eyes, nose, throat, and lungs. Long-term exposure can affect the nervous system, reproductive system, liver, kidneys, heart, and blood. Fragrances, which are found in many consumer products, may produce sensory irritation, pulmonary irritation, decreases in expiratory airflow velocity, and possible neurotoxic effects (Fisher 1998). Fragrance products can cause skin sensitivity, rashes, headache, sneezing, watery eyes, sinus problems, nausea, wheezing, shortness of breath, inability to concentrate, dizziness, sore throat, cough, hyperactivity, fatigue, and drowsiness (DesJardins 1997). More and more businesses are voluntarily limiting or banning fragrances in the workplace to accommodate employees who experience ill effects from exposure to scented products. This chapter's *Social Problems Research Up Close* feature describes the *Third National Report on Human Exposure to Environmental Chemicals* (Centers for Disease Control and Prevention 2005).

Vulnerability of Children The World Health Organization estimates that 5500 children die each day from diseases linked to polluted water, air, and food (Mastny 2003). It is estimated that in the United States, 1 in 200 children suffers developmental or neurological deficits as a result of exposure to toxic substances during pregnancy or after birth (UNEP 2002). Asthma, the number one childhood illness in the United States, is linked to air pollution.

Children are more vulnerable than adults to the harmful effects of most pollutants for a number of reasons. For instance, children drink more fluids, eat more food, and inhale more air per unit of body weight than do adults; in addition, crawling and a tendency to put their hands and other things in their mouths provide more opportunities to ingest chemical or heavy metal residues.

Human Exposure to Environmental Chemicals

In 2001, the Centers for Disease Control and Prevention published a landmark study that reported measures of human exposure to 27 environmental chemicals, 24 of which had never been measured before in a nationally representative sample of the U.S. population. The Second National Report on Human Exposure to Environmental Chemicals and the Third National Report on Human Exposure to Environmental Chemicals (Centers for Disease Control and Prevention 2003, 2005) are continuations of the ongoing assessment of the U.S. population's exposure to environmental chemicals. For the Second Report, human exposure to 116 chemicals was tested. A key finding of the Second Report was that phthalates—compounds found in such products as soap, shampoo, hair spray, many types of nail polish, and flexible plastics—are absorbed by humans. For the Third Report, exposure to 148 chemicals was tested.

Methods and Sample

The Third National Report on Human Exposure to Environmental Chemicals is based on 2001-2002 data from the National Health and Nutrition Examination Survey (NHANES) conducted by the National Center for Health Statistics.

The NHANES is a series of surveys designed to collect data on the health and nutritional status of the U.S. population.

The NHANES is based on a representative sample of the noninstitutionalized, civilian U.S. population, with an oversampling of African Americans, Mexican Americans, adolescents (ages 12-19 years), older Americans (age 60 years and older), and pregnant women to produce more reliable estimates for these groups. The samples did not specifically target people who were believed to have high or unusual exposures to environmental chemicals.

Assessing research participants' exposure to environmental chemicals involved measuring the chemicals or their metabolites (breakdown products) in the participants' blood or urine-a method known as biomonitoring. Blood was obtained by venipuncture for participants one year and older, and urine specimens were collected for people six years and older.

The chemicals measured in the research participants' blood and urine were grouped into the following categories:

1. Metals (including barium, cobalt, lead, mercury, uranium, and others)
2. Cotinine (tracks human exposure to tobacco and tobacco smoke)
3. Organophosphate, organochlorine, and other pesticides

4. Phthalates (chemicals commonly used in such consumer products as soap, shampoo, hair spray, nail polish, and flexible plastics)
5. Polycyclic aromatic hydrocarbons (PAHs)
6. Dioxins, furans, and polychlorinated biphenyls (PCBs)
7. Phytoestrogens
8. Herbicides
9. Pyrethroid, carbamate, and other pesticides

How did the Centers for Disease Control and Prevention (CDC) determine which chemicals to test? In 2002, the CDC solicited nominations from the public for candidate chemicals or categories of chemicals for possible inclusion in future reports and received nominations for hundreds of chemicals. The CDC selected the chemicals to be tested on the basis of several factors, including (1) scientific data that suggested exposure in the U.S. population, (2) the seriousness of health effects known or suspected to result from exposure, (3) the need to assess public health efforts to reduce exposure to a chemical, and (4) the cost of analysis for the chemical.

The researchers conducting the study for the CDC had several objectives, including these:

- to determine which selected environmental chemicals are getting into the bodies of Americans and at what concentrations;

- for chemicals that have a known toxicity level, to determine the prevalence of people in the U.S. population with levels above those toxicity levels;

- to establish reference ranges that can be used by physicians and scientists to determine whether a person or group has an unusually high level of exposure;
- to assess the effectiveness of public health efforts to reduce the exposure of Americans to specific environmental chemicals;
- to track, over time, trends in the levels of exposure of the U.S. population to environmental chemicals; and
- to determine whether exposure levels are higher among minorities, children, women of childbearing age, or other potentially vulnerable groups.

Key Findings and Conclusions

Selected findings from the Third National Report on Human Exposure to Environmental Chemicals (Centers for Disease Control and Prevention 2005) include the following:

- *New Measures for Some Widely Used Insecticides.* The Third Report presents first-time exposure information for five commonly used pyrethroid insecticides. The findings suggest widespread exposure to pyrethroid insecticides in the U.S. population.
- *Establishment of Reference Ranges.* The levels of chemicals found in the blood and urine of the research participants provide

reference ranges (also known as background exposure levels) for all the environmental chemicals for which participants were tested. Physicians, researchers, and public health officials use the reference ranges to determine whether individuals or groups are experiencing levels of exposure that are unusually high compared to the level of exposure experienced by the rest of the population. The Third Report established reference ranges for 38 of the 148 chemicals tested (reference ranges for the remaining 110 chemicals were established in earlier reports).

- *Reduced Exposure of the U.S. Population to Environmental Tobacco Smoke.* Cotinine is a metabolite of nicotine that tracks exposure to environmental tobacco smoke (ETS) among nonsmokers; higher cotinine levels reflect more exposure to ETS. Results from the Third Report show that from 1988–1991 to 1999–2002, median levels in nonsmokers decreased by about 69 percent in children and adolescents and by about 75 percent in adults. Levels in Blacks were more than twice the levels in Mexican Americans and non-Hispanic Whites. Although efforts to reduce ETS exposure show significant progress, ETS exposure remains a major public health concern.
- *Continued Progress in Reducing Blood-Lead Levels among Children.* For the period 1999–2002, 1.6 percent of children aged 1–5 had

elevated blood-lead levels, a decrease from 4.4 percent in the early 1990s. This significant decrease reflects the success of public health efforts to lower the exposure of children to lead—this exposure could come from living in homes containing lead-based paint or lead-contaminated dust. Nevertheless, children at high risk for lead exposure remain a major public health concern.

Because the presence of an environmental chemical in a person's blood or urine does not necessarily mean that the chemical will cause disease, more studies are needed to determine which levels of these chemicals in people result in disease. Research has already documented adverse health effects of lead and environmental tobacco smoke. However, for many environmental chemicals, few studies are available, and more research is needed to assess health risks associated with different blood or urine levels of these chemicals. Future CDC reports, expected to be released every two years, will include more chemicals and will also address the following questions:

1. Are chemical exposure levels increasing or decreasing over time?

2. Are public health efforts to reduce chemical exposure effective?

3. Do certain groups of people have higher levels of chemical exposure than other groups?

multiple chemical sensitivity (MCS)

A controversial health condition in which, after one or more acute or traumatic exposures to a chemical or group of chemicals, people experience adverse effects from low levels of chemical exposure that do not produce symptoms in the general public.

Multiple Chemical Sensitivity Disorder Multiple chemical sensitivity **(MCS)**, also known as environmental illness, is a condition whereby individuals experience adverse reactions when exposed to low levels of chemicals found in everyday substances—vehicle exhaust, fresh paint, housecleaning products, perfume and other fragrances, synthetic building materials, and numerous other petrochemical-based products. Symptoms of MCS include headache, burning eyes, difficulty in breathing, stomach distress or nausea, loss of mental concentration, and dizziness. The onset of MCS is often linked to acute exposure to a high level of chemicals or to chronic long-term exposure. Sufferers of MCS often avoid public places or wear protective breathing filters to avoid inhaling the many chemical substances in the environment. Some individuals with MCS build houses made from materials that do not contain the chemicals that are typically found in building materials. Although estimates of the prevalence of chemical sensitivity vary, one study reported that in the Atlanta, Georgia, metropolitan area, 12.6 percent of a population sample reported an unusual sensitivity to common chemicals, and 3.1 percent had been diagnosed as having MCS or environmental illness (Caress et al. 2002).

Environmental Injustice

Although environmental pollution and degradation and depletion of natural resources affect us all, some groups are more affected than others. **Environmental injustice**, also referred to as **environmental racism**, refers to the tendency for socially and politically marginalized groups to bear the brunt of environmental ills.

environmental injustice

The tendency for socially and politically marginalized groups to bear the brunt of environmental ills.

environmental racism

The tendency for hazardous waste sites and polluting industries to be located in areas where the surrounding residential population is an ethnic or racial minority.

Environmental Injustice in Canada and North America Although often sold to tourists and perceived by citizens as a pristine land of wide open spaces, Canada faces worsening environmental problems related to day-to-day pollution and overconsumption and, occasionally, catastrophic crises. An ongoing and largely unacknowledged problem, urban air pollution in Southern Ontario is the attributable cause of approximately 1800 premature deaths every year in the province (Krajnc 2000: 111). Meanwhile, in the spring of 2000, on the Victoria Day weekend, the Ontario town of Walkerton was hit with a water-contamination crisis that killed 7 residents and made 2800 others sick (Snyder 2004: 270). Although many perceive the failures of the public utilities employees Stan and Frank Koebel as responsible for the water contamination, environmental disasters such as Walkerton are rarely the result of the actions of only a few people. Snyder explains that the lack of care the Koebel brothers showed to their duties was encouraged by Progressive Conservative government rhetoric of the time, which included an all-out attack on the Ministry of Environment policies developed under the previous NDP (New Democratic Party) leadership; thus, what previously had been law had become only a set of guidelines as the Harris government sought to do away with "onerous reporting requirements"— requirements that, had they been in place when flooding between May 8 and 12 caused a local farm's manure spread to contaminate town wells, would have resulted in an immediate "boil water advisory," preventing the health catastrophe that followed. Walkerton, then, was the disastrous culmination of industrial farming practices, bad weather, and abdication of responsibility at both individual and governmental levels.

But Walkerton was not the last water crisis that Ontario would see. In October 2005, nearly 500 First Nations residents from the Kashechewan reserve north of Timmins had to be evacuated because of *E. coli* contamination of their water. By the first days of November, over 850 people had been evacuated. The situation ultimately revealed to the rest of the nation that, unlike the town of Walkerton's singular crisis point, the Kashechewan reserve had faced many years of water problems, partly because the reserve had been placed in an area subject to flooding (CBC News 2005).

Other regions in Canada, largely populated by Aboriginal peoples, show the negative effects of environmental problems associated with industrial development in regions far away. Pollution in the Far North is so concentrated that the food supply is contaminated, and new mothers fear the dangers of breast-feeding their infants (Johansen 2002).

The discovery that the Inuit in Canada were suffering most from industrial pollution created many thousands of kilometres away came by accident in the mid-1980s. Bioscientist Eric Dewailly sought Inuit women as a control group for a test on PCB contamination of breast milk in Quebec women. Instead of finding that the Inuit women comprised a pristine population, however, Dewailly found that the Inuit women's milk contained levels many times higher than women in southern regions for various chemical compounds, including pesticides, PCBs, and other industrial chemicals (cited in Johansen 2002). In more recent research, Dewailly (1996) and his co-researchers found that in addition to PCBs, compounds related to the insecticide DDT were found in high concentrations in the breast milk of Inuit women. Dewailly's experiment methods were able to use the milk as a reliable predictor of the chemical compounds in the mothers' bodies; that is, not just in the milk. Based on what is already known about the effects of DDT and PCBs, Dewailly concludes that the population of Northern women is at increased risk for diseases such as breast cancer, resulting from chemical fallout from industrial practices over which the population has no control, and in which members have little if any vested interest (Dewailly 1996: 1245).

An area between New Orleans and Baton Rouge, Louisiana—known as Cancer Alley because of its high rates of cancer—has about 140 chemical plants. The people who live and work in Cancer Alley are disproportionately poor and Black. One resident of Norco, Louisiana, who lived next to a Shell Oil refinery and chemical plant, reported that nearly everyone in the community suffered from health problems caused by industry pollution (Bullard 2000). When nearly all the chemical plants in Cancer Alley were damaged by Hurricane Katrina in 2005, residents and their homes were exposed to the toxic poisons released from these plants into floodwaters.

These examples show us that race and ethnicity, as well as region, correlate with other features of socio-economic status to make some groups far more vulnerable than others to the dangers of environmental problems.

Environmental Injustice around the World Although environmental pollution and degradation and depletion of natural resources affect us all, some groups are more affected than others. Marginalized groups, including Indigenous peoples, and other vulnerable and impoverished communities, such as peasants and nomadic tribes, are often powerless to fight against government and corporate powers that maintain environmentally damaging industries. At the Second International Indigenous Youth Conference in Vancouver, a delegate from the Igorot tribal people of the Philippines explained, "Indigenous people are no longer able to plant fruits or vegetables because the...mercury poisoning, produced from massive logging and mining operations, inhibits the growth of any plant life" (Sterritt 2005: n.p.). Indigenous groups in Nigeria, such as the Urhobo, Isoko, Kalabare, and Ogoni, are facing environmental threats caused by oil production operations run by transnational corporations. Oil spills, natural gas fires, and leaks from toxic waste pits have polluted the soil, water, and air, and have compromised the health of various local tribes. "Formerly lush agricultural land is now covered by oil slicks, and much vegetation and wildlife has been destroyed. Many Ogoni suffer from respiratory diseases and cancer, and birth defects are frequent" (Renner 1996: 57). The environmental injustices experienced by the Ogoni and the Igorot represent only a very few of those that have occurred. Renner (1996) warns that "minority populations and indigenous peoples around the globe are facing massive degradation of their environments that threatens to irreversibly alter, indeed destroy, their ways of life and cultures" (p. 59).

In the United States, polluting industries, industrial and waste facilities, and transportation arteries (that generate vehicle emissions pollution) are often located in minority communities (Bullard 2000). More than half (56 percent) of people living within 3 km of a commercial hazardous waste site are people of colour (Bullard et al. 2007). Rates of poverty are also higher among households located near hazardous waste facilities. However, "racial disparities are more prevalent and extensive than socioeconomic disparities, suggesting that race has more to do with the current distribution of the nation's hazardous waste facilities than poverty" (Bullard et al. 2007: 60).

Threats to Biodiversity

About 1.9 million species of life have been identified on Earth (Baillie et al. 2004). However, there may be 10 times that number and perhaps many times more if we include microbial diversity (Chivian and Bernstein 2004). This enormous diversity of life, known as **biodiversity**, provides food, medicines, fibres, and fuel; purifies air and fresh water; pollinates crops and vegetation; and makes soils fertile.

In recent decades, we have witnessed mass extinction rates of diverse life forms. On average, one species of plant or animal life becomes extinct every 20 minutes (Levin and Levin 2002). Unlike the extinction of the dinosaurs millions of years ago, species are disappearing today due to human causes (Hunter 2001). Biologists expect that at least half of the 1.9 million species alive today will become extinct over the next few centuries as a result of habitat loss caused by deforestation and urban sprawl, overharvesting, and global warming (Cincotta and Engelman 2000). Another threat to biodiversity is overexploitation of species for their meat, hides, horns, or medicinal or entertainment value. A poacher, for example, can earn several hundred dollars for a single rhinoceros horn—equivalent to a year's salary in many African countries. That same horn, ground up and used as a medicinal product, can sell for half a million dollars in Asia (Schmidt 2004). The International Fund for Animal Welfare (2005) checked the internet for one week and found more than 9000 wild animal products and specimens and live wild animals for sale—predominantly from species protected by law—a figure that represents "only the tip of the iceberg" (p. ii).

biodiversity

The variability of living organisms on earth.

■ Table 13.1 *Threatened Species Worldwide, 2008*

Category	Number of Threatened Species
Mammals	1 101
Birds	1 213
Amphibians	1 856
Reptiles	304
Fishes	800
Invertebrates (insects, mollusks, crustaceans, etc.)	1 992
Plants	8 321
Lichens	2
Total	15 589

Threatened species include those classified as critically endangered, endangered, and vulnerable

SOURCE: Adapted from International Union for Conservation of Nature, "Changes in numbers of species in the threatened categories (CR, EN, VU) from 1996 to 2008." Used with permission.

As shown in Table 13.1, 16 928 species worldwide are threatened with extinction. Most extinctions today result from habitat loss caused by deforestation and urban sprawl, overharvesting, global warming, and bioinvasion—environmental problems caused by human activity (Cincotta and Engelman 2000; Leahy 2009).

Light Pollution

Light pollution refers to artificial lighting that is annoying, unnecessary, and/or harmful to life forms on Earth. Canada, like much of the rest of the world, has become increasingly "lit up" with artificial light. Almost all people in developed societies use artificial light, reducing the natural period of darkness at night. Yet, "darkness is as essential to our biological welfare, to our internal clockwork, as light itself" (Klinkenborg 2008: 109). Some research suggests that exposure to artificial light at night contributes to sleep disorders, depression, and other mood disorders. Other studies have found a link between exposure to artificial light at night and breast cancer (Chepesiuk 2009).

Light pollution also has adverse effects on the migration, feeding, and reproductive patterns of many animal species (Chepesiuk 2009; Klinkenborg 2008). For example, frogs have been found to inhibit their mating calls, and bats alter their feeding behaviour when they are exposed to artificial light at night. Sea turtles, which have a natural predisposition to nest on dark beaches, find fewer of them to nest on. When sea turtle eggs hatch, the babies instinctually go toward the brighter, reflective sea horizon, but are confused by artificial lighting near the beach and may wander off toward the artificially lit beach development.

Environmental Problems and Disappearing Livelihoods

Environmental problems threaten the ability of Earth to sustain its growing population. Agriculture, forestry, and fishing provide 50 percent of all jobs worldwide and 70 percent of jobs in sub-Saharan Africa, East Asia, and the Pacific (World Resources Institute 2000). As croplands become scarce or degraded, as forests shrink, and as marine life dwindles, millions of people who make their living from these natural resources must find alternative livelihoods. In Canada's Maritime provinces, collapse of the cod fishing industry in the 1990s from overfishing left 30 000 fishers dependent on government welfare payments and decimated the economies of hundreds of communities (World Resources Institute 2000).

environmental refugees

People forced to move because of environmental destruction.

Globally, there are an estimated 30 million **environmental refugees**—individuals who have migrated because they can no longer secure a livelihood as a result of deforestation, desertification, soil erosion, and other environmental problems (Margesson 2005). As individuals lose their source of income, so do nations. In one-fourth of the world's nations, crops, timber, and fish contribute more to the nation's economy than industrial goods do (World Resources Institute 2000).

13.4 Social Causes of Environmental Problems

Various structural and cultural factors have contributed to environmental problems. These include population growth, industrialization and economic development, and cultural values and attitudes, such as individualism, materialism, and militarism.

Population Growth

The world's population doubled to 6 billion in 1999 from 3 billion in 1960, and it is projected to reach more than 9 billion by 2050. Population growth places increased demands on natural resources and results in increased waste. As Hunter (2001) explains:

> Global population size is inherently connected to land, air, and water environments because each and every individual uses environmental resources and contributes to environmental pollution. While the scale of resource use and the level of wastes produced vary across individuals and across cultural contexts, the fact remains that land, water, and air are necessary for human survival. (p. 12)

However, curbing population growth is not as critical as addressing the ways in which populations produce, distribute, and consume goods and services. Wealthy, industrialized countries have the slowest rates of population growth, yet these countries consume the most natural resources and contribute most to pollution, global warming, and other environmental problems.

Industrialization and Economic Development

Many of the environmental problems confronting the world, including global warming and the depletion of the ozone layer, are associated with industrialization and economic development. Industrialized countries, for example, consume more energy and natural resources and contribute more pollution to the environment than poor countries.

The relationship between level of economic development and environmental pollution is curvilinear rather than linear. For example, industrial emissions are minimal in regions with low levels of economic development and are high in the middle-development range as developing countries move through the early stages of industrialization. At more advanced industrial stages, though, industrial emissions ease because heavy-polluting manufacturing industries decline and "cleaner" service industries increase, and because rising incomes are associated with a greater demand for environmental quality and cleaner technologies. However, a positive linear correlation has been demonstrated between per capita income and national carbon dioxide emissions (Hunter 2001).

In less developed countries, environmental problems are largely the result of poverty and the priority of economic survival over environmental concerns. Vajpeyi (1995) explains:

> Policymakers in the Third World are often in conflict with the ever-increasing demands to satisfy basic human needs—clean air, water, adequate food, shelter, education—and to safeguard the environmental quality. Given the scarce economic and technical resources at their disposal, most of these policymakers have ignored long-range environmental concerns and opted for short-range economic and political gains. (p. 24)

A major environmental concern today is the growing economy of China—the most populated country in the world. The income of China's 1.3 billion people has been growing at a rapid rate, and along with that rising income, Chinese consumers are increasingly able to spend money on cars, travel, meat, and other goods and services that use fossil fuels. If China were to increase its fuel consumption to that typical of North Americans, China would use more than the current world production of 2.5 billion tons per year. In addition, if the Chinese were to use oil at the same rate as North Americans, by 2031 China would need 99 million barrels of oil a day—more than the current world production of 79 million barrels per day (Aslam 2005).

In considering the effects of economic development on the environment, note that the ways we measure economic development and the "health" of economies also influence environmental outcomes. Two primary measures of economic development and the health of economies are gross domestic product (GDP) and consumer spending. But these measures overlook the social and environmental costs of the production and consumption of goods and services. Until definitions and measurements of "economic development" and "economic health" reflect these costs, the pursuit of economic development will continue to contribute to environmental problems.

Cultural Values and Attitudes

Cultural values and attitudes that contribute to environmental problems include individualism, materialism, and militarism.

Individualism Individualism, a way of thinking central to capitalist economies, puts individual interests over collective welfare. Although recycling may benefit the collective environment, many individuals do not recycle because of the personal inconvenience involved in washing and sorting recyclable items. Similarly, individuals often indulge in countless behaviours that provide enjoyment and convenience at the expense of the environment: taking long showers, using dishwashing machines, doing recreational boating, eating meat frequently, using air conditioning, and driving gas-powered cars to run short errands instead of walking.

Materialism Materialism, or the emphasis on worldly possessions, encourages individuals to continually purchase new items and throw away old ones. The media bombard us daily with advertisements that tell us life will be better if we purchase a particular product. After the terrorist attacks of September 11, 2001, U.S. President George Bush advised Americans that it was their patriotic duty to go to the malls and spend money. Many Canadians followed suit. Materialism contributes to pollution and environmental degradation by supporting polluting and resource-depleting industries and by contributing to waste.

Militarism The cultural value of militarism also contributes to environmental degradation. "It is generally agreed that the number one polluter in the United States is the American military. It is responsible each year for the generation of more than one-third of the nation's toxic waste...an amount greater than the five largest international chemical companies combined" (Blatt 2005: 25). Toxic substances from military vehicles, weapons materials, and munitions pollute the air, land, and groundwater in and around military bases and training areas. The Pentagon has asked Congress to loosen environmental laws for the military, so that training exercises can occur unimpeded (Janofsky 2005). In addition, the Environmental Protection Agency is forbidden to investigate or sue the military (Blatt 2005).

13.5 Strategies for Action: Responding to Environmental Problems

One strategy for alleviating environmental problems is to lower fertility rates and slow population growth. Responses to environmental problems also include environmental activism, environmental education, the use of "green" energy, modifications in consumer products and behaviour, and government regulations and legislation. Sustainable economic development and international cooperation and assistance also play important roles in alleviating environmental problems.

Environmental Activism and Industry Resistance

Environmentalist groups exert pressure on the government to initiate or intensify actions related to environmental protection. They also design and implement their own projects and disseminate information to the public about environmental issues.

In North America, environmentalist groups date back to 1892, with the establishment of the Sierra Club, followed by the Audubon Society in 1905. Other environmental groups include, but are not limited to, the Canadian Environmental Law Association, Canadian Environmental Defence Fund, Canadian Environmental Network, Great Lakes United, Common Frontiers, Greenpeace, Environmental Action, Natural Resources Defense Council, World Watch Institute, National Recycling Coalition, Campaign for Nuclear Phase-Out, and the New Brunswick Environmental Network. In Ontario, the Ontario Environment Network joins together the efforts of 187 member groups, and as a network provides affiliation to the Canadian Environmental Network. This national group encourages public participation in the development of environmental protection policy.

Industries, major contributors to environmental problems, often fight against environmental efforts that threaten their products, but not always. Some industries are joining the environmental movement for a variety of reasons, including pressure from consumers and environmental groups, the desire to improve their public image, and genuine concern for the environment. For example, in 1997, British Petroleum (BP) publicly acknowledged that global warming is a threat to human and environmental health and began working with the environmental organization Environmental Defense to develop ways to reduce its greenhouse gas emissions ("Global Corporations Join Us" 2000). This initiative led to the development of the Partnership for Climate Action—a collaboration between Environmental Defense and seven of the world's largest corporations (including companies in the petroleum, aluminum, chemical, and electric power sectors) to take action against global warming. Participating companies have committed to report their emissions publicly, and each has a firm target for emissions reductions. Environmental Defense is working with each company to devise ways to improve energy efficiency, use renewable energy sources, and improve manufacturing processes.

BP, along with several other industries, has also withdrawn from membership in the Global Climate Coalition—an industry group that denies global warming and the role that industries play in the emission of greenhouse gases. Other industries that have quit the Global Climate Coalition include Ford, Shell Oil, Dow Chemical, General Motors, and Daimler-Chrysler (Associated Press 2000).

Canadian sociologist Glenda Wall (2000) cautions, however, that when we focus on altering individual behaviours—for example with regard to consumption, recycling, and limiting family sizes—we risk being seriously distracted from the industrial practices that continue, often largely unchecked, to threaten the environment. Wall provides a critical analysis of the historical shift away from a sense of "consumerism" that in the 1970s focused on critical assessment of, and active movement to find alternatives to, capitalism. This perspective involved "thinking and talking about pollution and other environmental issues *as social issues*" [emphasis added] (p. 205). Wall argues that as we moved toward a view of consumerism as individual behaviours related to overconsumption of goods, we lost sight of the need to demand more environmentally sound industrial practices.

Ecoterrorism An extreme form of environmental activism, sometimes referred to as **ecoterrorism**, involves the use of criminal or violent actions in an effort to protect wildlife or the environment (Denson 2000). The best-known ecoterrorist groups are the Earth Liberation Front (ELF) and the Animal Liberation Front (ALF). ELF and ALF are international underground movements consisting of autonomous individuals and small groups who engage in "direct action" to (1) inflict economic damage on those profiting from the destruction and exploitation of the natural environment, (2) save animals from places of abuse (e.g., laboratories, factory farms, fur farms), and (3) reveal information and educate the public on atrocities committed against Earth and all the species that populate it. Direct actions of ELF and ALF have included setting fire to a golf club in Guelph, Ontario; setting fire to gas-guzzling Hummers and other SUVs at car

ecoterrorism
Any violent crime intended to coerce, intimidate, or change public policy on behalf of the natural world.

Our Suburban Mistake

Among the more fashionable of recently perceived (or contrived) apocalypses is "the end of suburbia," a notion popularized by a documentary of the same name, which argues coming oil scarcity will soon make modern suburbs uninhabitable.

If only it were true! For the sake of suburbanites alone, the end of suburbia would be a blessing. But that's not happening. To the extent we understand suburbia as a single place, wherever it occurs—an uncomfortably definitive mould, a collection of syndromes masquerading as a lifestyle—it is all too robust. We made our bed the past half-century, shaping increasingly homogeneous, car-dependent, over-consuming, overworked, socially exclusive suburbs, and now we must lie in it.

"There used to be different ways you could end up being suburban," notes McMaster University historian Richard Harris, author of *Creeping Conformity: How Canada Became Suburban*. Indeed it was the working class, following smokestack jobs, that led the first great wave of suburbanization after the First World War. Since then, however, suburban life has become increasingly defined by a strict "package" of factors.

"It really is a package," Prof. Harris emphasizes, and it is not found only in suburbia. In suburbia, however, that's all there is: Middle-class families with long-term mortgage debt and high-consumption lifestyles, chained for life to at least two jobs per household in order to pay for both, enslaved to their cars in absence of any other means of traversing increasingly long distances, helpless as steadily worsening congestion steals more and more of their overstructured lives.

"I just see that increasingly being the case," says the historian, whose work has documented the growing homogenization and "commodification" of the suburbs—in effect the birth of suburbia. "I don't see that changing and I don't see how that can change for a very long time."

If anything, he says, the barriers and burdens that define suburbia are intensifying in the 21st century—especially the income barrier.

"The prospect of low-income families being able to afford to move into the suburbs, and to commute and get around low-density suburban environments, is not likely," Prof. Harris says. "And the prospect that any government is going to start building low-income housing out in the suburbs is very remote."

And why would they? Such projects would only remove their occupants even further from the jobs they would need and tie them into a high-consumption lifestyle they could ill-afford.

Thus the economic apartheid of our modern cities gains strength. In Hamilton, as in Detroit, the centre has collapsed and is now occupied exclusively by the poor. In Toronto, the centre has boomed, pushing low-income families into older suburbs bordered on their outer edges by equally exclusive modern suburbia.

But life is not necessarily better for those lucky enough to earn admittance to the outer ring. In Prof. Harris's histories, suburbia begins with debt—the introduction of long-term amortization for home mortgages—and debt drives all family life in a single direction. One job becomes two, by necessity. Vehicles multiply by the same logic. Houses become bigger. Consumption becomes culture. Life choices diminish as the package takes shape... Just don't lose that job.

It may well be that suburbia "ends" in a great postoil apocalypse. Or it may be brought to crisis by some other aspect of its manifold over consumption—of land, for instance. It may be, however, that the suburbia we all love to hate is simply no longer historical, something that will change and perhaps improve in time, but anthropological: a big mistake made permanent.

SOURCE: "There's No Escaping Our Suburban Mistake," by John Barber *(The Globe and Mail)*, article dated March 14, 2006. Reprinted with permission from The Globe and Mail.

---

dealerships; vandalizing SUVs parked on streets and in driveways; setting fire to construction sites (in opposition to the development); and smashing windows at the homes of fur retailers. Because the direct actions of ELF and ALF are illegal, activists work anonymously and without any centralized organization or coordination. Although critics of ecoterrorism cite the damage done by such tactics, members and supporters of ecoterrorist groups claim that the real terrorists are corporations that plunder the Earth. While we may not condone ecoterrorism, this chapter's *The Human Side* feature draws our attention to the very real environmental destruction associated with suburban sprawl, and encourages us to rethink how we should organize our daily living habits and how we should rethink what makes a community "desirable."

The Role of Corporations in the Environmental Movement Corporations are major contributors to environmental problems and often fight against environmental efforts that threaten their profits. Some corporations, however, are joining the environmental movement for a variety of reasons, including pressure from consumers and environmental groups, the desire to improve their public image, genuine concern for the environment, and concern for maximizing current or future profits.

In 1994, out of concern for public and environmental health, Interface, with Ray Anderson as the chief executive officer, set a goal of being a sustainable company by 2020—"a company that will grow by cleaning up the world, not by polluting or degrading it" (McDaniel 2005: 33). Anderson envisioned recycling all the materials used, not releasing any toxins into the environment, and using solar energy to power all production. The company has made significant progress toward these goals.

Car manufacturers can play a role in the environmental movement by developing fuel-efficient and alternative-fuel vehicles. In collaboration with the environmental organization Environmental Defense, FedEx has developed a hybrid electric delivery truck that cuts smog-forming pollution by 65 percent, reduces soot by 96 percent, and goes 57 percent farther on a gallon of fuel (Environmental Defense 2004). In 2004, Daimler-Chrysler introduced its Smart Car in Canada; the car had already been available in Europe for several years. The Smart Car carries only two passengers and is designed for city driving, but promises far greater fuel efficiency and lower greenhouse-gas emissions than typical passenger cars. It uses just 4.2 L of diesel fuel to travel 100 km.

Environmental Education

One goal of environmental organizations and activists is to educate the public about environmental issues and the seriousness of environmental problems. Some Americans underestimate the seriousness of environmental concerns because they lack accurate information about environmental issues. In a national survey of U.S. adults, most (69 percent) rated themselves as having either "a lot" (10 percent) or "a fair amount" (59 percent) of knowledge about environmental issues and problems (National Environmental Education 1999). Yet, on 7 of 10 questions asked about emerging environmental issues, more Americans gave incorrect answers than correct ones. The average was 3.2 correct answers out of 10 questions. Even those who rated themselves as having "a lot" of environmental knowledge, as well as those with a college degree, scored only 4 of 10 items correctly. The authors of the study concluded:

> Increased knowledge is the key to changing attitudes and behaviors on issues critical to our environmental future. If Americans can answer an average of only 3 of 10 simple knowledge questions, there is a clear need to provide environmental information in a form that the American public can easily digest and act upon. (National Environmental Education 1999: 41)

For most North Americans, a main source of information about environmental issues is the media. However, because the media are owned by corporations and wealthy individuals with corporate ties, unbiased information about environmental impacts of corporate activities may not readily be found in mainstream media channels. Indeed, the public must consider the source in interpreting information about environmental issues. Propaganda by corporations sometimes comes packaged as "environmental education." Hager and Burton (2000: 107) explain: "Corporate interests realize the value of getting their spin into the classrooms of future consumers and voters." However, Canadian publications, such as *Adbusters*, continue to offer alternative news, information, and analyses independent from corporate interests or financing, and in direct opposition to values of individualist materialism.

"Green" Energy

As noted earlier, many of the environmental problems facing the world today are linked to energy use, particularly the use of fossil fuels. Increasing the use of "green" energy—energy that is renewable and nonpolluting—can help alleviate environmental problems associated with fossil fuels. Also known as clean energy, green energy sources include solar power, wind power, biofuel, and hydrogen. Although clean energy represents less than 1 percent of world energy production, it is expected to increase.

Solar Power The world's fastest developing clean energy is photovoltaic cells—a form of solar power that converts sunlight to electricity (Sawin 2005). Japan, which produces half of all photovoltaic cells, aims for photovoltaic cells to generate 10 percent of Japan's electricity by 2030. Driven by government incentive programs, Germany and other European countries are also increasing their use of solar cells to provide electricity. In the United States, California leads the nation in photovoltaic cell use.

Another form of solar power is the use of solar thermal collectors, which capture the sun's warmth to heat building space and water. China is the world's leader in solar thermal production and use, followed by Japan, Europe, and Turkey (Sawin 2005). The United States was once the world leader in solar thermal production, but has fallen far behind because of low natural gas prices and the lack of government incentives. Another form of solar power comes from "concentrating solar power plants," which use the sun's heat to make steam to turn electricity-producing turbines.

Wind Power Wind power is the world's second fastest-growing energy source, after solar power. Wind turbines, which turn wind energy into electricity, are operating in more than 65 countries, although nearly three-fourths of wind power is produced in Europe. In Germany, the leading country in wind power, wind energy meets 6.6 percent of electricity needs. As of April 2006, Canada had operational turbines sufficient to power over 280 000 homes (Natural Resources Canada 2006).

One disadvantage of wind power is that birds have been known to fly into the turbines and die. However, this problem has been mitigated in recent years through the use of painted blades, slower rotational speeds, and careful wind turbine placement.

Biofuel Biofuels are derived from agricultural crops. They burn cleaner than fossil fuels, are renewable, and can create agricultural jobs and revenues for countries while reducing dependence on imported oil.

Two types of biofuels are ethanol and biodiesel. Ethanol is an alcohol-based fuel that is produced by fermenting and distilling sugar obtained from agricultural crops such as corn, beets, sugar cane, barley, and wheat. Ethanol is blended with gasoline to create E85 (85 percent ethanol, 15 percent gasoline). Vehicles that run on E85, called flexible fuel vehicles, have been used by government and in private fleets for years. They have just recently become available to consumers. However, only a small fraction of passenger vehicles are flexible fuel vehicles, and many owners of these vehicles do not know that their vehicle can operate with E85 and/or do not have access to a gas station that sells E85 (Price 2006).

Another problem associated with ethanol fuel is that increased demand for corn, which is used to make most ethanol in the United States, has driven up the price of corn, resulting in higher food prices (many processed food items contain corn, and animal feed is largely corn). And as corn prices rise, so too do those of rice and wheat because the crops compete for land. Rising food prices threaten the survival of the world's poorest 2 billion people, who depend on grain to survive. The grain it takes to fill a 25-gallon tank with ethanol would feed one person for an entire year (Brown 2007).

Increased corn and/or sugar cane production to meet the demand for ethanol also has adverse environmental effects, including increased use and runoff of fertilizers, pesticides, and herbicides; depletion of water resources; and soil erosion. In addition, tropical forests are being clear-cut to make room for "energy crops," leaving less land for conservation and wildlife (Price 2006); biofuel refineries commonly run on coal and natural gas (which emit greenhouse gases); farm equipment and fertilizer production require fossil fuels; and the use of ethanol involves emissions of several pollutants. Finally, even if 100 percent of the U.S. corn crop were used to produce ethanol, it would only displace less than 15 percent of U.S. gasoline use (Food & Water Watch 2007).

Biodiesel fuel is a cleaner-burning diesel fuel made from vegetable oils and animal fats, including recycled cooking oil. Some individuals who make their own biodiesel fuel obtain used cooking oil from restaurants at no charge. The European Union, the leading manufacturer of biodiesel, hopes that biofuels will supply 20 percent of the fuel market in 2020 (Aeck 2005). More than 60 companies in Canada are now working to develop and improve biofuel technologies (Government of Canada 2006).

Hydrogen Power Hydrogen, the most plentiful element on Earth, is a clean-burning fuel that can be used for electricity production, heating, cooling, and transportation. Many see a movement to a hydrogen economy as a long-term solution to the environmental and political problems associated with fossil fuels. Further research is needed, however, to develop nonpolluting and cost-effective ways to extract and transport hydrogen. In the meantime, all the major auto manufacturers are developing hydrogen fuel cell technology. In 2004, California Governor Arnold Schwarzenegger issued an executive order calling for the development of a Hydrogen Highway Network Blueprint Plan to make hydrogen a viable alternative transportation fuel in his state.

Modifications in Consumer Behaviour

In industrialized countries, consumers are making "green" choices in their behaviour and in their purchases that reflect concern for the environment. In some cases, these choices cost more; for example, paying more for organically grown food or for clothing made from organic cotton. In many cases, however, consumers are motivated to make green choices in their purchasing behaviour because doing so saves money. For example, after gas prices topped $1 per litre in 2005, sales of gas-guzzling SUVs dropped, and sales of fuel-efficient cars, such as hybrids, increased. According to Dan Becker, director of the Sierra Club's global warming program, switching to fuel-efficient vehicles such as hybrids is the single biggest step to reducing dependency on foreign oil (Gartner 2005).

Consumers often consider their utility bill when they choose energy-efficient appliances and electrical equipment. To assist consumers in choosing energy-efficient products, in 1992 the U.S. Environmental Protection Agency (EPA) introduced the Energy Star label for products that meet EPA energy-efficiency standards. Globally, 37 countries use an energy-efficient labelling system for appliances and electronic equipment (Makower et al. 2005). Canada now uses the Energy Star labelling system as well.

Green energy sources, such as wind turbines and solar conversion panels, are available across Canada, but it is often up to consumers to purchase their own alternative power sources and then sell back to the utility companies any excess energy they produce. Thus, the local grid that delivers electricity combines all power—green or not. The amount of clean power available to average consumers is generated on their behalf and added to the larger pool of electricity (Vartan 2005). To check availability of green energy in their region, consumers should call their utility company and ask.

Green Building

Green building practices incorporate design elements to maximize efficient use of energy while minimizing the impact of buildings on local and global environments. The Canada Green Building Council (CGBC) has organized to ensure that buildings seeking green designation meet certain environmentally sound standards. Buildings achieve ratings on the Leadership in Energy and Environmental Design (LEED-Canada) standards scale developed to assess how environmentally friendly a given site is in the following areas: water efficiency, energy and atmospheric impact, materials and resource use, and indoor environmental quality. Ratings range through the categories certified, silver, gold, and platinum, and are derived from a points-based assessment of how well a building meets the standards.

Some outstanding examples of green architecture in Canada can be found at the Canada Green Building Council (CGBC) website. These include the Nose Creek Recreation and Library facility in Calgary, the Vancouver Port Authority head office, and the Pavillons Lassonde at l'École Polytechnique in Montreal (CGBC 2006).

Government Policies, Regulations, and Funding

Worldwide, governments spend about $1 trillion (U.S. dollars) per year in subsidies that allow the prices of fuel, timber, metals, and minerals (and products using these materials) to be much lower than they otherwise would be, encouraging greater consumption (Renner 2004). In that way, government policies can worsen environmental problems. But government policies, regulations, and funding can also play a role in protecting and restoring the environment. At the local, provincial/state, regional, and federal levels, governments have implemented policies and regulations affecting the production and use of pollutants, the preservation of natural resources and biodiversity, and the use of renewable energy.

For example, in 2003 the European Union drafted legislation known as REACH (Registration, Evaluation, and Authorization of CHemicals), which requires chemical companies to conduct safety and environmental tests to prove that the chemicals they are producing are safe. If they cannot prove that a chemical is safe, it will be banned from the market (Rifkin 2004). The European Union has become a world leader in environmental stewardship by placing the "precautionary principle" at the centre of its regulatory policy. The precautionary principle requires industry to prove that their products are safe.

Government policies and regulations also affect energy use. In 2004, more than 20 countries committed to specific targets for the renewable share of total energy use (UNEP 2005). Some environmentalists propose that governments use taxes to discourage environmentally damaging practices and products (Brown and Mitchell 1998). In the 1990s, several European governments increased taxes on environmentally harmful activities and products (such as gasoline, diesel, and motor vehicles) and decreased taxes on income and labour (Renner 2004).

Sustainable Economic Development

Achieving global cooperation on environmental issues is difficult, in part, because developed countries (primarily in the northern hemisphere) have different economic agendas than those of developing countries (primarily in the southern hemisphere). The northern agenda emphasizes preserving wealth and affluent lifestyles, whereas the southern agenda focuses on overcoming mass poverty and achieving a higher quality of life (Koenig 1995). Southern countries are concerned that northern industrialized countries—having already achieved economic wealth—will impose international environmental policies that restrict their economic growth just as they are beginning to industrialize. Global strategies to preserve the environment must address both wasteful lifestyles in some nations and the need to overcome overpopulation and widespread poverty in others.

Development encompasses more than economic growth; it involves sustainability—the long-term environmental, social, and economic health of societies. **Sustainable development** involves meeting the needs of the present world without endangering the ability of future generations to meet their own needs. "The aim here is for those alive today to meet their own needs without making it impossible for future generations to meet theirs.... This in turn calls for an economic structure within which we consume only as much as the natural environment can produce, and make only as much waste as it can absorb" (McMichael et al. 2000: 1067).

Sustainable development requires the use of clean, renewable energy. Renewable energy projects in developing countries have demonstrated that providing affordable access to green energy, such as solar, wind, and biofuels, helps to alleviate poverty. The projects provide energy for creating businesses and jobs, and provide power for refrigerating medicine, sterilizing medical

sustainable development
Societal development that meets the needs of current generations without threatening the future of subsequent generations.

equipment, and supplying freshwater and sewer services needed to reduce infectious disease and improve health (Flavin and Aeck 2005).

International Cooperation and Assistance

Global environmental concerns—global warming, destruction of the ozone layer, and loss of biodiversity among them—call for global solutions forged through international cooperation and assistance. For example, the 1987 Montreal Protocol on Substances That Deplete the Ozone Layer forged an agreement made by 70 nations to curb the production of CFCs (which contribute to ozone depletion and global warming). The 1992 Earth Summit in Rio de Janeiro brought together heads of state, delegates from more than 170 nations and nongovernmental organizations, and participants to discuss an international agenda for both economic development and the environment. The 1992 Earth Summit resulted in the Rio Declaration—"a nonbinding statement of broad principles to guide environmental policy, vaguely committing its signatories not to damage the environment of other nations by activities within their borders and to acknowledge environmental protection as an integral part of development" (Koenig 1995: 15).

In 1997, delegates from 160 nations met in Kyoto, Japan, and forged the **Kyoto Protocol**—the first international agreement to place legally binding limits on greenhouse gas emissions from developed countries. The United States, which produces one-fourth of the world's greenhouse-gas emissions, rejected Kyoto in 2001, and in 2006, Canada announced that it would be unable to meet its Kyoto targets. In 2004, the Russian Federation joined more than 120 other countries in ratifying the treaty, which came into force in early 2005.

One major criticism of the Kyoto accord is that it allows countries with high greenhouse-gas emission levels to use credit transfers to trade their levels with low producing countries, thus balancing out the emissions declared on paper. In short, industrialized nations would not have to alter their practices much, and developing nations risk being compelled by economic and political considerations to assume the burden of other countries' emissions, something that would inhibit the development of their own industrialization.

In another global environmental treaty, the Stockholm Convention, representatives from 122 countries drafted an agreement to phase out a group of dangerous chemicals known as persistent organic pollutants. More recently, Germany hosted a major intergovernmental conference, Renewables 2004. The conference resulted in the adoption of the International Action Programme on Renewables, which supports more than 200 ongoing or planned policies and projects in over 150 countries (UNEP 2005). In December 2009, the Climate Conference in Copenhagen sought to make progress where the Kyoto Accord had failed. Unfortunately, the conference failed to reach any international agreements. The failure of the conference is attributed to a variety of political and social factors, key among them that, unlike E.U. leaders, the U.S. president cannot make a decision without the approval of Congress; that the weather at the time was frigid and snowy and thus undermined people's *belief* in the seriousness of climate change; that delegates from participating countries did not have equal recognition of their concerns at the table; and that a "24-hour news culture" impaired the ability to deliver analysis and evaluation from those with

Kyoto Protocol

Developed by the United Nations Framework Convention on Climate Change, the protocol aims to have signatories make efforts to reduce greenhouse gas emissions. As of 2010, 191 countries had ratified the protocol.

the scientific ability to do so and favoured delivery of sound bites from lobbyists instead (BBC News 2009).

Some countries do not have the technical or economic resources to implement the requirements of environmental treaties. Wealthy industrialized countries can help less-developed countries address environmental concerns through economic aid. Because industrialized countries have more economic and technological resources, they bear primary responsibility for leading the nations of the world toward environmental cooperation. Jan (1995) emphasizes the importance of international environmental cooperation and the role of developed countries in this endeavor:

> Advanced countries must be willing to sacrifice their own economic well-being to help improve the environment of the poor, developing countries. Failing to do this will lead to irreparable damage to our global environment. Environmental protection is no longer the affair of any one country. It has become an urgent global issue. Environmental pollution recognizes no national boundaries. No country, especially a poor country, can solve this problem alone. (pp. 82–83)

Understanding Environmental Problems

Environmental problems are linked to a number of interrelated features of social life, including corporate globalization, rapid and dramatic population growth, expanding world industrialization, patterns of excessive consumption, and reliance on fossil fuels for energy. Growing evidence of the irreversible effects of global warming and loss of biodiversity, increased concerns about the link between global warming and extreme weather events such as Hurricane Katrina, and adverse health effects of toxic waste and other forms of pollution suggest that we cannot ignore environmental problems.

Many North Americans believe in a "technological fix" for the environment—that science and technology will solve environmental problems. Paradoxically, the same environmental problems that have been caused by technology may be solved by technological innovations designed to clean up pollution, preserve natural resources and habitats, and provide clean forms of energy. Leaders of government and industry, though, must have the will to finance, develop, and use technologies that do not pollute or deplete the environment. When asked how companies can produce products without polluting the environment, corporate attorney Robert Hinkley suggested that, first, it must become a goal to do so:

> I don't have the technological answers for how it can be done, but neither did President John F. Kennedy when he announced a national goal to land a man on the moon by the end of the 1960s. The point is that, to eliminate pollution, we first have to make it our goal. Once we've done that, we will devote the resources necessary to make it happen. We will develop technologies that we never thought possible. But if we don't make it our goal, then we will never devote the resources, never develop the technology, and never solve the problem. (quoted by Cooper 2004: 11)

But the direction of technological innovation is largely under the control of transnational corporations that place profits over environmental protection.

Unless the global community challenges the power of transnational corporations to pursue profits at the expense of environmental and human health, corporate behaviour will continue to take a heavy toll on the health of the planet and its inhabitants. Political and military conflicts centred in the Middle East are likely to continue as long as oil plays the lead role in providing the world's energy.

Global cooperation is also vital to resolving environmental concerns, but is difficult to achieve because rich and poor countries have different economic development agendas: developing poor countries struggle to survive and provide for the basic needs of their citizens; developed wealthy countries struggle to maintain their wealth and relatively high standard of living. Can both agendas be achieved without further pollution and destruction of the environment? Is sustainable economic development an attainable goal? With mounting concern about climate change, the impacts of air pollution on health, rising oil prices, and the need to ensure energy access to all, governments worldwide have strengthened their commitment to sustainable, renewable energy policies and projects (UNEP 2005).

Since September 11, 2001, world leaders, the media, and citizens in countries across the world have been preoccupied with terrorism. Lester Brown, of the Earth Policy Institute, warns against the environmental dangers of such preoccupation:

> Terrorism is certainly a matter of concern, but if it diverts us from the environmental trends that are undermining our future until it is too late to reverse them, Osama bin Laden and his followers will have achieved their goal of bringing down Western civilization in a way they could not have imagined. (Brown 2003: 5)

In 2004, the Nobel Peace Prize was given to Wangari Maathai for leading a grassroots environmental campaign to plant 30 million trees across Kenya. For the first time ever, the Nobel Peace Prize was awarded to someone for accomplishments in restoring the environment. In her acceptance speech, Maathai explained, "A degraded environment leads to a scramble for scarce resources and may culminate in poverty and even conflict" (quoted by Little 2005: 2). With ongoing conflict around the world, it is time for leaders to recognize the importance of a healthy environment for world peace and to prioritize environmental protection in their political agendas.

Critical Thinking

1. Should motives be considered in imposing penalties on individuals who are convicted of acts of ecoterrorism? For example, should a person who sets fire to a business to protest that business's environmentally destructive activities receive a lighter penalty than a person who sets fire to a business for some other reason?

2. Do you always consume the fresh produce in your fridge, or does some of it go to waste regularly? If you paid more for locally grown, organic produce—perhaps even enjoying having it delivered to your home—do you think you might eat more carefully and waste less? Investigate your local region to find out what kinds of "boxed produce" programs may be available through church groups, co-ops, and organic farms.

3. A 2005 Gallup poll (Lyons 2005) found that Americans who seldom or never attend religious services are more likely to worry about the environment than are Americans who attend church weekly (10 percent versus 28 percent). Why do you think this is so?

"Is It True?" Quiz: Answers

1 = false; 2 = true; 3 = true; 4 = true; 5 = false

Armed Conflict in Global Perspective

Is It True?

1. Canada usually spends less on defence than the estimate for any given year.

2. Canada is not at war with Afghanistan.

3. War and conflict can serve positive functions for society.

Read more here: 1 = p. 487, 2 = p. 485, 3 = p. 487

Answers can be found on p. 516.

© Bloomberg/Getty Images

Armed conflict (of which officially declared wars are only one manifestation) is one of the great paradoxes of human history. It is used to protect, but also to annihilate, and can sometimes even threaten the welfare and safety of those it aims to serve—as in the case of the use of nuclear weapons. Armed conflicts have created and defended nations but have also destroyed them. The scars of civil wars can remain for decades or centuries, even if they are resolved with the nation intact, as happened with the U.S. civil war. War, the most violent form of conflict, refers to organized armed violence aimed at a social group in pursuit of an objective. Wars have existed throughout human history and continue in the contemporary world. Whether war is just or unjust, defensive or offensive, it involves the most horrendous atrocities known to humankind. This is especially true in the twenty-first century, when nearly all wars are fought in populated areas rather than on remote battlefields. War is often conducted within the routine of daily life—and this can have deadly consequences. Thus, war is not only a social problem in and of itself; it contributes to a host of other social problems—death, disease, and disability, crime and immorality, psychological terror, loss of economic resources, and environmental devastation. In this chapter, we discuss each of these issues within the context of conflict, war, and terrorism, the most threatening of all social problems.

14.1 The Global Context: Conflict in a Changing World

Canada's Changing Role

Although Canada has a longstanding reputation as a "peacekeeper," just what that role entails remains unclear to many. The role of peacekeeper is assigned by the United Nations (UN) as part of a larger mandate that began in the Cold War era after the conclusion of World War II. UN members who were charged with peacekeeping missions were deployed specifically into regions that remained politically unstable after the end of World War II. The idea of peacekeeping was developed by Canadian Lester B. Pearson—who, six years before he became Prime Minister of Canada, was awarded the 1957 Nobel Peace Prize for his proposal that soldiers would avoid the use of force, supervise ceasefires, aid in international diplomatic efforts, and help to maintain peace in areas that had come out of a period of conflict. But in recent years, Canada's role has moved from peacekeeping in postconflict regions to active engagement in war, most particularly in Afghanistan.

Though many readers will be aware that Canada has had troops in Afghanistan since 2002, Canada's Department of National Defence currently lists 13 locations around the world where troops are actively deployed and three separate missions in Afghanistan. Figure 14.1 shows the locations of the Canadian bases in the Afghan mission. Canada's mission in Afghanistan raises the issue of why we have chosen in this chapter to talk about "armed conflict" as something distinct from "war." We may see the casualties and other damage in Afghanistan and know intuitively that it is "a war," but the language of international diplomacy splits hairs on the point. The Canadian Department of National Defence avoids the language of conflict, explaining that we "are there because the Afghan government asked for our help...to rebuild their nation as a stable, democratic, self-sufficient society"

■ **Figure 14.1** *Canadian Bases in Afghanistan*

SOURCE: Operations Map, http://www.forces.gc.ca/site/reportsrapports/budget05/back05eng.asp, National Defence. Reproduced with the permission of the Minister of Public Works and Government Services Canada, 2011.

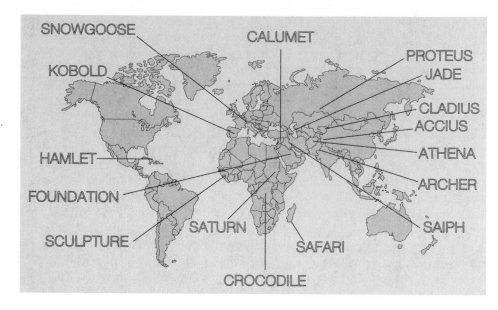

(National Defence 2010). By this account, then, the Canadian mission in Afghanistan is not an act of war, but neither is it an effort at peacekeeping: "Afghanistan is not a peacekeeping mission. There are no ceasefire arrangements to enforce or negotiated peace settlements to respect" (ibid). The National Defence explanation is certainly a narrative meant to appease a public confused about why we are there. After all, some of us remember quite clearly committing our military forces specifically to aid U.S. retaliation following the 9/11 attack by Al Qaeda in what Art Eggleton, then Minister of Defence, characterized as a "campaign against terrorism" (Eggleton 2001), but which Southam Publications labelled as the "war on terrorism" in creating the title that ran with the article. Whether we characterize the entry of the Canadian military into Afghanistan as a "campaign" or a "war" against terror, as we head into 2011 with 2830 troops—nearly three times as many as were sent in 2001—still actively deployed in three areas in Afghanistan (National Defence 2010), it is clear that ours has not been the "short-term stabilization" effort that Eggleton asserted it would be. Indeed, although *The Globe and Mail* asserted in early 2008 that the Afghan mission was winding down (Curry and LeBlanc 2008), federal spending increases in the defence budget continue, suggesting that Canada's future will include more military support work in war zones rather than peacekeeping in post-conflict territories. In 2008, David Perry, formerly a director of the Dalhousie University Centre for Foreign Policy Studies, estimated that by the time all the costs of Canada's missions in Afghanistan were tallied, including those of caring for injured and traumatized veterans, the war would cost Canada $22 billion in current dollars (Pugliese 2008). Perry's estimates were verified by retired Commodore Eric Lehre (ibid). Table 14.1 shows the difference between estimates and actual expenses in Canada's defence budget over 14 years.

War and Social Change

The very act that now threatens modern civilization—war—is largely responsible for creating the advanced civilization in which we live. Before large political states existed, people lived in small groups and villages. War broke the barriers of

■ **Table 14.1** *Canada's Defence Budget: 1993–2007*

Budget National Defence ($Billions)		
Fiscal Year	**Main Estimates**	**Actual Expenditures**
2006–07	14.80	15.70
2005–06	13.40	14.70
2004–05	13.30	13.90
2003–04	12.26	13.19
2002–03	11.83	12.42
2001–02	11.39	12.24
2000–01	11.20	11.47
1999–2000	10.30	11.52
1998–99	9.38	10.26
1997–98	9.92	10.19
1996–97	10.56	10.57
1995–96	11.08	11.37
1994–95	11.55	11.77
1993–94	11.97	12.00

SOURCE: National Defence and the Canadian Forces. http://www.forces.gc.ca/site/reportsrapports/ budget05/back05eng.asp, National Defence and the Canadian Forces, 2010. Reproduced with the permission of the Minister of Public Works and Government Services Canada, 2011.

autonomy between local groups and permitted small villages to be incorporated into larger political units known as chiefdoms. Centuries of warfare between chiefdoms culminated in the development of the state. The state is "an apparatus of power, a set of institutions—the central government, the armed forces, the regulatory and police agencies—whose most important functions involve the use of force, the control of territory, and the maintenance of internal order" (Porter 1994: 5–6). The creation of the state in turn led to other profound social and cultural changes:

> And once the state emerged, the gates were flung open to enormous cultural advances, advances undreamed of during—and impossible under—a regimen of small autonomous villages. . . . Only in large political units, far removed in structure from the small autonomous communities from which they sprang, was it possible for great advances to be made in the arts and sciences, in economics and technology, and indeed in every field of culture central to the great industrial civilizations of the world. (Carneiro 1994: 14–15)

Industrialization and technology could not have developed in the small social groups that existed before military action consolidated them into larger states. Thus, war contributed indirectly to the industrialization and technological sophistication that characterize the modern world. Industrialization, in turn, has had two major influences on war. Cohen (1986) calculated the number of wars fought per decade in industrial and preindustrial nations and concluded that "as societies become more industrialized, their proneness to warfare decreases" (p. 265). Thus, for example, in 2008 there were 16 major armed conflicts, the majority of which were in less developed countries in Africa and Asia (SIPRI 2009a).

Although industrialization may decrease a society's propensity to war, it also increases the potential destruction of war. With industrialization, military technology became more sophisticated and more lethal. Rifles and cannons replaced the clubs, arrows, and swords used in more primitive warfare and, in turn, were replaced by tanks, bombers, and nuclear warheads. Today, the use of new technologies such as high-performance sensors, information processors, directed energy technologies, precision-guided munitions, and computer worms and viruses have changed the very nature of conflict, war, and terrorism. For example, according to one defence analyst, "the U.S. military alone fields 7,000 unmanned drones in the air, like the Predators that fire missiles into Pakistan—and roughly another 12,000 on the ground, like the Packbots that hunt for roadside bombs in Iraq" (Singer 2009: 1).

In the postindustrial information age, computer technology not only has revolutionized the nature of warfare but also has made societies more vulnerable to external attacks. For example, in 2009, North Korea attacked computer systems in the United States and in South Korea, resulting in brief disruptions to government and major commercial networks (Sang-Hun and Markoff 2009). Information technologies are also forcing governments to become more accountable with regard to foreign policy, intelligence gathering and dissemination, and diplomatic relations. The highly controversial website WikiLeaks, for example, has prompted excoriating criticism from world leaders and analysts who have characterized the leaks as irresponsible and purposeless—or even as dangerous to the safety of deployed troops around the world (ABC News 2010). In response to these characterizations, WikiLeaks founder Julian Assange has defended the right of the public to know the horrors, both intended and collateral, of the armed conflict in regions such as Iraq. WikiLeaks' July 2010 release of more than 90 000 documents related to the Afghan war revealed, for example, that "all these people [were] killed in the small events that we haven't heard about which numerically eclipse the big events.... It's the boy killed by a shell that missed the target. It's villagers that have gone to hospital as a result of a missed air strike" (Assange, quoted in ABC News 2010). It is not clear yet to what degree new public awareness of the costs of war will influence the pursuit of new means of creating positive social change, but the hope of those who defend the release of the information seek at the very least not to achieve social change on the backs of vulnerable citizens.

14.2 Sociological Theories of Armed Conflict and War

Sociological perspectives can help us understand various aspects of armed conflict, especially as it manifests in the formality of "war." In this section, we describe how structural functionalism, conflict theory, symbolic interactionism, and feminist thought can be applied to the study of war.

Structural-Functionalist Perspective

Structural functionalism focuses on the functions that war serves and suggests that war would not exist unless it had positive outcomes for society. We have already noted that war has served to consolidate small autonomous social groups into larger political states. An estimated 600 000 autonomous political units existed in the world at about 1000 B.C. Today, that number has dwindled to fewer than 200.

Another major function of war is that it produces social cohesion and unity among societal members by giving them both a "common cause" and a common enemy. Unless a war is extremely unpopular, military conflict also promotes economic and political cooperation. Internal domestic conflicts between political parties, minority groups, and special interest groups often dissolve as they unite to fight the common enemy. During World War II, Canadian and British troops consolidated under British military organizational structures to defeat Germany and the Axis Powers (Italy, Japan, Hungary, Bulgaria, and Romania). More recently, in the years since the American invasion into Afghanistan, Canada has demonstrated its social support for the United States by supplying troops to "police" the Kandahar. However, under the Chretien government Canada refused to enter the war against Iraq and urged instead that the Bush government continue to exert pressure on Iraq through United Nations channels. Although Canada's refusal to enter the war has been vindicated in the long run by the absence of evidence for the development of "weapons of mass destruction" (WMD), at the time American Ambassador Paul Cellucci asserted that Canada's refusal undermined our claims of support for the U.S. people (Barry 2005: abstract). Just because the demonstration of allegiance can serve claims for social cohesion and solidarity does not mean that war is always perceived as an appropriate cost of that cohesion.

In the short term, war may also increase employment and stimulate the economy. The increased production needed to fight World War II helped pull Canada, Britain, and the United States out of the Great Depression. The investments in the manufacturing sector during World War II also had a long-term impact on the U.S. economy. Hooks and Bloomquist (1992) studied the effect of the war on the U.S. economy between 1947 and 1972, and concluded that the U.S. government "directed, and in large measure, paid for a 65 percent expansion of the total investment in plant and equipment" (p. 304). War can also have the opposite effect, however. In a 2005 restructuring of the military, the Pentagon, seeking a "meaner, leaner fighting machine," recommended shutting down or reconfiguring nearly 180 military installations, "ranging from tiny Army reserve centers to sprawling Air Force bases that have been the economic anchors of their communities for generations" (Schmitt 2005), at a cost of thousands of civilian jobs.

Wars also function to inspire scientific and technological developments that are useful to civilians. For example, innovations in battlefield surgery during World War II and the Korean War resulted in instruments and procedures that later became common practice in civilian hospital emergency wards (Zoroya 2006). Research on laser-based defence systems led to laser surgery; research in nuclear fission and fusion facilitated the development of nuclear power; and the internet was created by the Pentagon for military purposes. In the U.S. airline industry, which owes much of its technology to the development of air power by the Department of Defense, the distinction between military and civilian technology is important because different government agencies regulate its export. The Department of Commerce regulates the export of parts produced for use on commercial airlines, whereas the Department of State imposes stricter controls on parts produced for military aircraft to prevent sales to countries at odds with U.S. foreign policy objectives (Millman 2008). Other **dual-use technologies**, a term referring to defence-funded innovations that have commercial and civilian applications, include SLICE, a high-speed twin-hull water vessel originally made for the Office of Naval Research. SLICE has a variety of commercial applications,

dual-use technologies

Defence-funded innovations that have commercial and civilian applications.

"including its use as a tour or sport fishing boat, oceanographic research vessel, oil spill response ship, and high-speed ferry" (State of Hawaii 2000).

War also serves to encourage social reform. After a major war, members of society have a sense of shared sacrifice and a desire to heal wounds and rebuild normal patterns of life. They put political pressure on the state to care for war victims, improve social and political conditions, and reward those who have sacrificed lives, family members, and property in battle. As Porter (1994) explained, "Since...the lower economic strata usually contribute more of their blood in battle than the wealthier classes, war often gives impetus to social welfare reforms" (p. 19).

Finally, the U.S. military has historically provided an alternative for the advancement of poor or disadvantaged groups who otherwise face discrimination or limited opportunities in the formal economy. The military's specialized training, tuition assistance programs for a college education, and preferential hiring practices improve the prospects of veterans to find a decent job or career after their service (Military 2007).

Conflict Perspective

Conflict theorists emphasize that the roots of war are often antagonisms that emerge whenever two or more ethnic groups (e.g., Bosnians and Serbs), countries (United States and Vietnam), or regions within countries (the U.S. North and South) struggle for control of resources or have different political, economic, or religious ideologies. In addition, conflict theory suggests that war benefits the corporate, military, and political elites. Corporate elites benefit because war often results in the victor taking control of the raw materials of the losing nations, thereby creating a bigger supply of raw materials for its own industries. Indeed, many corporations profit from defence spending. Under the Pentagon's bid-and-proposal program, for example, corporations can charge the cost of preparing proposals for new weapons as overhead on their Department of Defense contracts. Also, Pentagon contracts often guarantee a profit to the developing corporations. Even if the project's cost exceeds initial estimates, called a cost overrun, the corporation still receives the agreed-on profit. In the late 1950s, President Dwight D. Eisenhower referred to this close association between the military and the defence industry as the **military-industrial complex**.

military-industrial complex

The close association between the military and the defence industry.

Contemporary examples of the military-industrial complex include the Bush administration's direct link to defence spending. Even as the U.S. government was deciding on the war in Iraq, "many former Republican officials and political associates of the Bush administration [were] associated with the Carlyle Group, an equity investment firm with billions of dollars in military and aerospace assets" (Knickerbocker 2002: 2). Further, news media have come to rely heavily on retired military professionals with ties to the defence establishment and military contractors for interpretation of the Iraq and Afghanistan wars. This close "intersection of network news and wartime commerce" blurs the line between security policy and private commercial interests (Barstow 2008: 1).

The military elite benefit because war and the preparations for it provide prestige and employment for military officials. For example, Military Professional Resources Inc. (MPRI), an organization staffed by former military, defence, law enforcement, and other professionals, serves "the national security needs of the U.S. government, selected foreign governments, international organizations, and the private sector" and lists capabilities such as war gaming, force development and management, and democracy transition assistance (Military Professional Resources Inc. 2009). MPRI is one of four U.S. firms that are under a $300 million contract from the Department of Defense to produce public service announcements, news, and entertainment for the Iraqi media. The three-year project (2009 to 2011) supports Iraqi and U.S. political goals such as promoting reconciliation and nonsectarian nationalism, as well as pro-military, pro-police, and pro-U.S. attitudes (DeYoung and Pincus 2009).

According to some estimates, private contractors such as MPRI and many others contributed more than 180 000 civilians to the occupation of Iraq, about 20 000 more than the U.S. military and government employees deployed in country (Miller 2007). Private security companies—for-profit organizations contracted by the U.S. government to perform security functions that the military formerly provided—account for a significant portion of the U.S. forces. According to estimates from Congressional Research Service, 50 private security companies employ more than 30 000 personnel in Iraq. Twenty of these companies and at least 10 000 of their employees are under contract with the U.S. government, costing between $3 billion and $6 billion from 2003 to 2007 (CRS 2008).

War also benefits the political elite by giving government officials more power. Porter (1994) observed that "throughout modern history, war has been the level by which…governments have imposed increasingly larger tax burdens on increasingly broader segments of society, thus enabling ever-higher levels of spending to be sustained, even in peacetime" (p. 14). Political leaders who lead their country to a military victory also benefit from the prestige and hero status conferred on them.

Feminist Perspectives

Feminists and many other analysts often note the overwhelming association between war and gender. By and large, men have historically carried out active combat. Nature-based arguments about gender—that is, that men are innately aggressive or violent and women inherently peaceful—are not generally supported by social science research and do not adequately explain why men are more likely to kill than women. Feminists emphasize the social construction of aggressive masculine identities and their manipulation by elites as important reasons for the association between masculinity and militarized violence (Alexander and Hawkesworth 2008). In this section we discuss the controversy regarding gendered participation in armed conflict, and also address the historical participation of Canadian women in military service. In this chapter's *Social Problems Research Up Close* feature we discuss the negative effect of war on young women and girls in Northern Uganda.

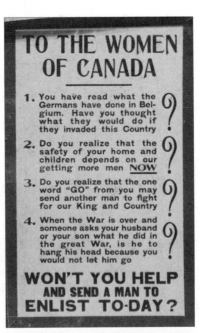

SOURCE: Queen's University Archives. World War I poster collection, V043. Used with permission.

The Effect of War on Young Women and Girls in Northern Uganda

In January 2006, Olara Otunnu, a former United Nations advocate for child victims of war, described Uganda as "the worst place in the world to be a child" (Large 2006). For 20 years, starting in 1986, northern Uganda has experienced a guerrilla war that has displaced nearly two million people and caused widespread poverty. For much of the war, the two main combatants were the government of Uganda and the Lord's Resistance Army (LRA), a rebel group led by Joseph Kony, a ruthless and unstable commander who fought to restore his ethnic group to power. Tens of thousands of Ugandan children were forcibly conscripted into the government's army or abducted by the LRA where they were sexually abused and forced into combat. Many thousands more were killed or wounded.

When the fighting subsided in 2006, more than 800 000 Ugandans were living in government-run camps (Large 2006). In view of the dependence on international aid groups such as the United Nations World Food Programme, UNICEF, and Médecins Sans Frontières for food and medical care, other international groups intervened in the most war-torn areas to develop additional support projects. Among the most important of these projects were those designed to reintegrate child soldiers into the local communities.

Annan et al. (2008), in conducting the Survey of War Affected Youth (SWAY), wanted to provide information to the United Nations and other international agencies to help them develop and improve youth-related social services. Focusing, in part, on the impact of the war on young women and girls, SWAY provides reliable data about this population through a systematic random sample of households in the most affected areas.

Sample and Methods

Between October 2006 and August 2007, the SWAY team employed two methods of data collection. First, they administered a large-scale quantitative survey to young women and girls in two districts of Uganda. Relying on lists used by the World Food Programme for food distribution, 1100 households were randomly selected. Household members were interviewed and asked to identify all youth living in the household in 1996. From this retrospective sample, Annan and colleagues identified 857 female youth between the ages of 14 and 35 in 2006 (who were between the ages of 4 and 25 in 1996, as the worst violence of the war began). The researchers then identified, located, and interviewed 619 respondents from this sample. Second, Annan et al. (2008) drew a nonrandom subsample of 30 girls from these respondents and conducted in-depth, qualitative interviews with them.

The data the researchers collected focused on the women's and girls' experiences during and after the war including their experiences with abduction, as "forced wives" assigned to LRA commanders, and with their families, communities, and nongovernmental organizations (NGO) upon returning home. In addition, the SWAY team collected data about the well-being of women and girls in the study, including their recent economic activity, education, physical and mental health, and community participation, among many other variables.

Findings and Conclusions

The data that SWAY researchers collected detailed the extent of violence and identified some important and surprising results. Because Annan and her colleagues had randomly sampled the population, they could use their data to estimate the total amount of violence that young women and girls experienced. They concluded that about 66 000 (20 percent) of all women and girls between the ages of 14 and 30 in 2006 had been abducted by the LRA during the previous 10 years. The researchers report that, "The average age for females at first abduction is approximately 16 years of age, with the majority of females experiencing abduction between the ages of 10 to 18 years of age" (p. 46). Forty percent of abductees were held in captivity for less than 14 days, 25 percent between two weeks and one year, and 19 percent for over a year. Five percent never returned home and are presumed dead. Twenty-five percent were given to LRA members as "forced wives," and of that number, half gave birth to at least one child as a result of their captivity.

Many of the abducted young women and girls witnessed horrendous acts of violence during their captivity, at rates well above what non-abductees experienced. They witnessed (1) the beating and torture of others (83 percent); (2) the violent death of a family member or friend (53 percent); (3) occupied houses being set on fire (42 percent); (4) multiple, simultaneous killings (38 percent); and (5) injuries from combat or a land mine (24 percent).

The abductees were also forced to commit a variety of brutal acts. Seventeen percent said they were forced to kill an opposing soldier; 21 percent were forced to kill an unknown civilian; and 5 percent were forced to kill a family member or friend. In addition, 21 percent were forced to beat or cut a civilian, and 25 percent were made to step on or otherwise abuse a corpse. In each of these categories, less than 1 percent of non-abducted girls and youth committed such acts.

The LRA commanders distributed the young women and girls as "forced wives," partly on the basis of seniority. Half of the senior commanders took five or more wives, whereas low-ranking commanders took, on the average, two wives. When many young women and girls were abducted at the same time, they were distributed randomly among the rebels, as this account from a woman forcibly married after her abduction at 17 illustrates:

> After reaching the LRA camp, I was grouped with other females who were recently abducted. [The commander] gave the orders to his escorts to distribute the wives. Clothes were placed in bags and put into a pile. The men who wanted wives stood nearby and watched as girls were told to pick a bag of clothing. Whoever owned the clothing then became the man to that girl. The clothes I picked belonged to a 35-year-old fighter. (p. 40)

Other forced wives reported that commanders chose wives on the basis of their appearance and their educational level. As one abductee remembered: "The prettiest, more educated girls were the first to be chosen and commanders always chose before fighters.... [Commanders] preferred girls with education because they needed them to write down numbers when radio codes were coming in" (p. 43).

Most of the young women and girls (68 percent) who were held for more than two weeks escaped on their own. Of the remainder, the LRA captors released 27 percent and the Ugandan Army rescued 5 percent. Forced wives were more carefully guarded by their captors than other detainees—83 percent escaped, 10 percent were rescued by the Ugandan military, and only seven percent were released by the LRA.

Surprisingly, only a small percentage of female abductees reported severe psychological distress. Forced wives exhibited a slightly higher rate of distress than other abductees. Problems were most pronounced when the captives returned home to their families, but generally lessened over time. In fact, 83 percent of abductees reported positive relationships with their families and communities. According to Annan et al. (2008), "resilience and acceptance rather than rejection or trauma" was the norm in most families. Despite the violence they were forced to commit in captivity, former abductees were no more likely to commit violence, engage in fights, or report hostility after their release than non-abductees.

The SWAY team used this and other data they created to help aid agencies identify sub-groups within the population of abductees who were especially in need of assistance as they returned home. One of these groups was forced wives who gave birth during their abduction: "Girls who return from captivity with children are three times less likely to return to school than those who do not conceive children in captivity and 10 times less likely to return to school than girls who were never abducted" (p. 43). Also, because about one-third of female abductees returned home at the age of 18 or older, the researchers advised that age-based social service programs that targeted children under 18 were missing a significant percentage of the population in need.

Finally, NGO and government aid programs used categories like "abducted" and "forced wives" to determine categories of people requiring the most assistance. Based on the data, the research team concluded that these were "crude and poor predictors of vulnerability" among young women and girls affected by the war. In fact, regardless of whether they had been abducted or not, female youth who came from poor households, were unemployed, estranged from their families, suffered injuries or illness, and exhibited the highest levels of stress were ironically the least likely to receive assistance. By using rigorous methods of sampling and data collection, the Survey of War Affected Youth helped support groups revise their category-based approach in targeting the population to one based on "real needs" among those who suffered most from the devastation brought on by the war.

SOURCE: Annan, J. & Blattman, C. (2008). "The Reintegration of Child and Youth Combatants in Northern Uganda: Myth and Reality." In Muggah, R. (Ed.). *Securing Protection: Dealing with Fighters in the Aftermath of War.* New York, NY: Routledge Press.

Canadian Women's Roles in the Armed Forces Often, people assume that women have participated very little in war efforts until quite recently; however, the inability to enlist for active duty did not mean that women did not participate in the larger "war effort" in each of the World Wars, both of which had Canadian soldiers subsumed into the larger British armed forces. The Queen's University Archives on Canadian Women's participation in World War I, for example, note that

> Over 2000 women enlisted as nursing sisters in the Canadian Expeditionary Force during WWI. The role of women at the front was very limited because of army rules and social constraints. The women of Canada started an organization called, "The Canadian Women's Hospital Ship Fund". They raised money by organizing concerts, tag days, teas, card parties, lectures, and bazaars. Women also raised money for the Red Cross, Belgian Relief, and Canadian Patriotic Fund. (Queen's University 2010)

In the midst of World War II, following several years of effort to incorporate women into military service, Carolyn Gossage (2001) notes that the Canadian Women's Army Corps (CWAC) was established. Although the service stopped short of permitting women to enter into combat roles, many women were eager for such inclusion. The years of persistent arguments made by women that they had more to offer to the war effort than just to work in mess halls and clerical positions finally resulted in CWAC members performing more active roles, including driving transport vehicles, running messages, and operating phones; the rationale was that adding these kinds of jobs to those already done by women during World War II would relieve male soldiers for combat service (Gossage 2001: 41–42). Other historical accounts give a sense of just how many women ended up serving following the 1941 creation of the CWAC: "In 1941, the Canadian government recruited over 45,000 women volunteers for fulltime military service other than nursing. Women worked as mechanics, parachute riggers and heavy mobile equipment drivers" (CBC News 2006). Canadian women's contributions to military service have been expanding ever since, and women have served in active combat roles since 1989 (ibid).

Women's participation in these and other "war efforts" has been encouraged with a variety of patriotic messages that invoke women's unique duty, but the reasons for women's participation is more complex than simply responding to the call for patriotism. Women's participation in military service has been, in part, an effort for women not to be indebted to men for their freedom and inclusion as citizens.

Although some feminists view women's participation in the military as a matter of equal rights, others object because they see war as an extension of patriarchy and the subordination of women in male-dominated societies. Ironically, because protection of women is perceived as a feature of masculine identity, feminists also point out that war and other conflicts are often justified using "the language of feminism" (Viner 2002). For example, President Bush used respect for women's rights and protection of women subjugated under the Taliban as a partial justification for the attack on Afghanistan in 2001 (Viner 2002). As we discuss below, there has been considerable feminist resistance to this justification tactic, and other similar ones.

To a large extent, says Mariane Eide, "if rights were won for women through war work, then combat eligibility, while an ambivalent privilege, must have more than symbolic meaning for women's full citizenship" (Eide 2008: 49). In other words, many of the day-to-day privileges of citizenship that women enjoy are the result of wars waged to create the nations that are capable of conferring citizenship and granting the rights and protections that go along with citizenship. However, the historical fact of the creation of nations and citizens, argues Eide, can be used in dangerous ways to mobilize support for wars that we suspect may not be just. For example, military strategists and journalists seized on the idea that the current war in Afghanistan was a just war rather than an unjust invasion because

> occupation and regime change would...provide the occasion for the transformation of an extreme patriarchal culture imposed by the Taliban in which women were forced to live in conditions akin to slavery. Feminist discourse and its cosmopolitan allegiances were conscripted in this war effort.... When Allied forces entered Kabul in 2001, Western journalists fed the need for activist intervention in Afghani women's plight; they "gathered with the specific intent of broadcasting images of women abandoning their burqas." (p. 57)

What Eide's essay and the critical work of other feminist scholars interested in these justifications for war argue is that the "liberation" of Afghani women leaves them in a similar predicament of having their citizenship rely on a war in which they have no say, and, moreover, which has done away with the religious traditions that they have understood as part of their spiritual and physical "home."

Danielle Poe's work uses the idea of an ethical position based in women's sexual difference from men to question the very concept of justifiable war—such as one that, it is claimed, will liberate the vulnerable and transform an oppressive regime into a free society. Thus, Poe goes further than critiquing claims such as those that Eide brings to our attention, and makes the point that "of the many flaws with just war theorizing, perhaps the most damning is that just war doctrine tends to justify wars...at a time when we ought to be thinking about ways to eliminate wars" (Poe 2008: 33). Poe's argument favours a view of human connectedness as a horizontal rather than hierarchical set of relations grounded in the values of kindness, compassion, and hospitality (p. 40). According to this view, one does not have to take an absolute stand against all wars, but should act in ways that preserve and protect the interests and safety of others—as Poe argues is exemplified in the actions of Carlos Mejia, who "was deployed to Iraq in April 2003, and after a two week leave, filed to be a conscientious objector; he refused to return to Iraq to participate in an unjust war. His application was denied, and he served a one-year jail sentence for desertion.... Mejia does not support abolition of war; he maintains that the Iraq war is unjust and he has a moral obligation not to participate" (p. 43).

Symbolic Interactionist Perspective

The symbolic interactionist perspective focuses on how meanings and definitions influence attitudes and behaviours regarding conflict and war. The development of attitudes and behaviours that support war begins in childhood. Movies romanticize war, children play war games with toy weapons, and various video and computer games glorify heroes conquering villains.

Symbolic interactionism helps to explain how military recruits and civilians develop a mindset for war by defining war and its consequences as acceptable

A World War II RAF Soldier's View

The images in this feature show the disjuncture between Canadian World War II recruiting propaganda and the experiences of an RAF pilot, Nicholas Cowan—the uncle of one of your textbook's authors—who joined the Air Force at age 17 and was killed in 1944 at age 19 in World War II.

Beyond the subversion of efforts to create a peaceful objection to war, popular culture mechanisms may simply ignore resistance altogether. Douglas Kellner argues that in terms of popular messages, Hollywood cinema has maintained a tradition of "following the trajectory of U.S. foreign policy at least since the end of the Second World War" (1995: 83). For a current generation of students, Hollywood separates the world into "good guys" and "bad guys," and casts soldiers on "our side" as heroes who have no doubts about the clarity of their missions. Indeed, films that came out around the 9/11 attacks—such as *Rules of Engagement*—chastise viewers who think that the Arab population could be anything other than evil. Indeed, a military leader who visited the Wilfrid Laurier University campus in the fall of 2002 underscored the very same message about Arab people, stating at a campus lecture that "It's impossible for us as rational human beings to figure out their irrational minds. They're not really of this world" (Stogran 2002). Stogran's comments were intended to recruit students into considering a military career without any moral conundrum—because, after all, the "enemy" really *is* evil. But if young people succumb to recruiting posters like the one in Image 1, or to films and lectures, this does not mean that they remain forever sin-

SOURCE: http://digital.library.mcgill.ca/warposters/search/searchdetail.php?ID=8736&version=e

gularly committed to the romanticized patriotism that drew them into military service in the first place.

The sketches in Image 2 and Image 3 appear in their original

SOURCE: Personal archive of M. Morgan Holmes; artist: Nicholas E. Cowan, circa 1944.

SOURCE: Personal archive of M. Morgan Holmes; artist: Nicholas E. Cowan, circa 1944.

format on a single sheet of double-sided paper; they were messages sent home in 1942 by an 18-year-old enlistee, Nicholas Cowan, who had gone to war hoping to become the kind of hero he envisions in Image 2, but who recognized that his actual experiences in the war were destroying him (and those around him), as he shows in the unflattering self-portrait in Image 3.

The final, simple facts of his narrative, which included thousands of drawings sent home over two years in the service, are these: Nicholas Cowan and his crew went missing in action on or about the night of June 28, 1944. On this particular night, RAF Six Group out of Tholthorpe lost 22 crews, each with five boys, its largest losses to that point in the war. At the time that the crews were lost there were more than 230 bombers in the air, making it very likely that the lost crews were hit by their own flak. When he was killed, Nicky, as he was known to his family, had just turned 19 and had been promoted to Pilot Officer, though the papers delivering that information arrived to his mother, unopened, along with his other personal effects; Nicky never knew of his promotion. His mother, Kay Cowan, was compensated for her loss with the silver cross, a pendant awarded to mothers and widows of soldiers killed in service. Unlike the mother in Image 1, Kay never got to see her eldest son, a gifted classics student, return from the war. Like the mothers of 22 456 airmen and women whose bodies were never recovered, the best Kay could do to remember her child would be to visit the Air Forces Memorial in Surrey, England (Image 5). For the rest of her life, Kay regretted having signed the permission forms required for her son to enlist in the armed forces while he was still only 17 years old.

SOURCE: © Chrislofoto/Shutterstock

As with any other official record, Nicky's enlistment records indicate his date of enlistment, height, eye colour, rank, general health, level of education, and religion. All the vital statistics are noted, but the record provides very little that is useful for developing an understanding of what is lost in a war.

It is partly because the official records are so spare that a symbolic interactionist approach can be so helpful for enhancing our understandings. The drawings that Nicky sent home during the war were deeply conflicted. Image 2 and Image 3, as exemplars of a larger collection, present two opposing self-images. On the one hand we see a projected self, well decorated for various and wildly spectacular feats—including 900 sorties, whereas the highest number of missions actually completed by any single RAF soldier in the Second World War was 222. The image is clearly a fantasy with an audience of civilians and soldiers looking on with rapt attention while Nicky appears confident almost to the point of being arrogant. His hands are thrust in his pockets and a cigarette dangles nonchalantly from his lips, evoking highly recognizable versions of masculinity drawn from Hollywood cinema at the time.

That masculine trope of the conquering hero is not simply an artifact of the distant past. In the fall of 2002, When Lt. Col Pat Stogran was giving his public lecture at Wilfrid Laurier University, he stepped up to the microphone to speak and took up a posture similar to the stance we see in Image 2. Lt. Col. Stogran opened his address by saying, "In my next lifetime I could hope for nothing better than to come back and tell war stories all day long" (Stogran 2002). Obviously, the hero telling tales of adventure is a persistent trope that, knowingly or not, works with other forms of propaganda feeding heroic dreams. However, that young people, men especially, are seduced by such narratives does not mean that they never develop other, more critical views. In Image 3 we see a less glamorous depiction of life at Tholthorpe. In this single frame, Nicky rejects the British notion of the commando as a member of the military elite and shows himself as hung-over, possibly ill, and definitely unfit for battle—perhaps because few soldiers actually have the stomach to do what they were recruited to do. The drawings that Nicky sent home, with the exception of ones like Image 3, were

(continued)

always about life on the ground, on leave, in the barracks. He never sent home letters or drawings about his missions. What is speakable in the collection is a variety of ways of being young and male (from dashing and heroic to slovenly and hungover, from invincible to irascible). What is unspeakable is the actual act of war.

As an illustrative case, the meanings that one young boy/man gives to himself illuminate the particular areas of vulnerability that young men can inhabit and experience. Sometimes the experiences register in a manner that seems fully self-aware, and sometimes with little or no critical reflection at all. What is clear for us as readers is that

recruiting propaganda is extremely effective in making its appeals, and that awareness that armed conflicts are horrific rather than heroic comes too late for soldiers on all sides of a conflict.

and necessary. Through its use in various phrases, the word "war" has achieved a positive connotation of actively working to combat a given problem, as in the examples of the war on drugs, the war on poverty, and the war on crime. Positive labels and favourable definitions of military personnel facilitate military recruitment and public support of armed forces.

McGill University in Montreal houses an extensive collection of war posters that were used from World War I onward to rally support for the wars, to encourage the enlistment of young men into the armed forces, and to enlist the support of women who were expected willingly to deliver their sons into combat. *The Human Side* feature in this chapter discusses the belief that one young RAF soldier in World War II had when he enlisted, and the difference he found in combat compared to the romanticization of the war effort in enlistment propaganda.

Governments may use propaganda and appeals to patriotism to generate support for war efforts and to motivate individuals to join armed forces. Salladay (2003), for example, notes that those in favour of the war on Iraq have commandeered the language of patriotism, making it difficult but necessary for peace activists to use the same symbols or phrases. In their study of the U.S. peace movement, Woehrle et al. (2008) observed that the government and supporters of U.S. wars often framed the issue as "supporting our boys" or "supporting the troops." This made public discussion about whether a particular war is effective or justifiable appear to be a betrayal of soldiers. A similar framework and imperative operate in Canada, where it is not at all unusual to encounter bumper stickers that command us to "support the troops." By analyzing public statements from leading peace movement groups that opposed the first Gulf War (1991) and the Iraq war, the researchers documented how opponents of these wars developed a counternarrative that "peace is patriotic" and reframed the issue around how war itself endangered the troops, how government policies failed to provide for the welfare of troops, and how the well-being of civilians was negatively affected by war.

To legitimize war, the act of killing in war is not regarded as "murder." Deaths that result from war are referred to as casualties. Bombing military and civilian targets appears more acceptable when nuclear missiles are "peacekeepers" that are equipped with multiple "peace heads." Killing the enemy is more acceptable when derogatory, racist, and dehumanizing labels convey the attitude that the enemy is less than human.

Such labels are socially constructed as images, often through the media, and are presented to the public. Social constructionists, like symbolic interactionists in general, emphasize the social aspects of "knowing." Thus, Li and Izard (2003) used content analysis to analyze newspaper and television coverage of the World Trade Center and Pentagon attacks on September 11. The researchers examined the first eight hours of coverage of the attacks presented on CNN, ABC, CBS, NBC, and Fox, as well as in eight major U.S. newspapers (including the *Los Angeles Times*, the *New York Times*, and the *Washington Post*). Results of the analysis indicated that newspaper articles tended to have a "human interest" emphasis, whereas television coverage was more often "guiding and consoling." Other results suggested that both media relied most heavily on government sources, that newspapers and the networks were equally factual, and that networks were more homogeneous in their presentation than newspapers. One indication of the importance of the media lies in former President George W. Bush's creation of the Office of Global Communications—"a huge production company, issuing daily scripts on the Iraq war to U.S. spokesmen around the world, auditioning generals to give media briefings, and booking administration stars on foreign news shows" (Kemper 2003: 1).

14.3 Roots of Armed Conflict

The causes of war and armed conflict are numerous and complex. Most armed conflicts involve more than one cause. The immediate cause of a war may be a border dispute, for example, but religious tensions that have existed between the two combatant countries for decades may also contribute to the war. The following section reviews various causes of war.

Conflict Over Land and Other Natural Resources

Nations often go to war in an attempt to acquire or maintain control over natural resources, such as land, water, and oil. Michael Klare, author of *Resource Wars: The New Landscape of Global Conflict* (2001), predicted that wars will increasingly be fought over resources as supplies of the most needed resources diminish. Disputed borders have been common motives for war. Conflicts are most likely to arise when borders are physically easy to cross and are not clearly delineated by natural boundaries such as major rivers, oceans, or mountain ranges.

Water is another valuable resource that has led to wars. Unlike other resources, water is universally required for survival. At various times, the empires of Egypt, Mesopotamia, India, and China all went to war over irrigation rights. In 1998, five years after Eritrea gained independence from Ethiopia, forces clashed over control of the port city Assab and, with it, access to the Red Sea.

Not only do the oil-rich countries in the Middle East present a tempting target in themselves, but war in the region can also threaten other nations that are dependent on Middle Eastern oil. Thus, when Iraq seized Kuwait and threatened the supply of oil from the Persian Gulf, the United States and many other nations reacted militarily in the Gulf War. In a document prepared for the Center for Strategic and International Studies, Starr and Stoll (1989) warned that soon water, not oil, will be the dominant resource issue of the Middle East. According to World Watch Institute, "despite modern technology and feats of engineering, a secure water future for much of the world remains elusive." The prognosis for Egypt, Jordan, Israel, the West Bank, the Gaza Strip, Syria, and Iraq is especially alarming. If present consumption patterns continue, emerging water shortages, combined with a deterioration in water quality, will lead to more competition and conflict (p. 1).

Despite such predictions, tensions in the Middle East have erupted into fighting repeatedly in recent years—but not over water. In July 2006, Israel and Lebanon fought a border war that killed a thousand people and displaced a million Lebanese. Civil war erupted in the Palestinian territories between rival parties when Hamas seized control of the Gaza Strip in response to Fatah's refusal to hand over the government after Hamas won legislative elections (BBC 2007a). Further, in the summer of 2007, hundreds were killed when Lebanese security forces attacked Palestinian militants based in Lebanon's refugee camps (BBC 2007b). In December 2008, the Israeli military launched air strikes against Gaza to prepare the way for its January 2009 ground invasion that lasted 22 days. Israeli authorities claimed the campaign was intended to stop Hamas's rocket attacks against civilians in southern Israel (BBC 2009a)

Conflict Over Values and Ideologies

Many countries initiate war not over resources but over beliefs. World War II was largely a war over differing political ideologies: democracy versus fascism. The Cold War involved the clash of opposing economic ideologies: capitalism versus communism.

Conflicts over values or ideologies are not easily resolved. They are less likely to end in compromise or negotiation because they are fuelled by people's convictions. For example, when a representative sample of American Jews were asked, "Do you agree or disagree with the following statement? 'The goal of Arabs is not the return of occupied territories but rather the destruction of Israel,'" 81 percent agreed, 13 percent disagreed, and 6 percent were unsure (American Jewish Committee 2007).

If ideological differences can contribute to war, do ideological similarities discourage war? The answer seems to be yes; in general, countries with similar ideologies are less likely to engage in war with each other than countries with differing ideological values (Dixon 1994). Democratic nations are particularly disinclined to wage war against one another (Brown et al. 1996; Rasler and Thompson 2005).

Racial, Ethnic, and Religious Hostilities

Racial, ethnic, and religious groups vary in their cultural beliefs, values, and traditions. Thus, conflicts between racial, ethnic, and religious groups often stem from conflicting values and ideologies. Such hostilities are also fuelled by competition over land and other scarce natural and economic resources. Gioseffi (1993) noted that "experts agree that the depleted world economy, wasted on war efforts, is in great measure the reason for renewed ethnic and religious strife. 'Haves' fight with 'have-nots' for the smaller piece of the pie that must go around" (p. xviii). Racial, ethnic, and religious hostilities are sometimes perpetuated by a wealthy minority to divert attention away from their exploitations, and to maintain their own position of power. Such **constructivist explanations** of ethnic conflict—those that emphasize the role of leaders of ethnic groups in stirring up inter-communal hostility—differ sharply from primordial explanations, or those that emphasize the existence of "ancient hatreds" rooted in deep psychological or cultural differences between ethnic groups.

As described by Paul (1998), sociologist Daniel Chirot argued that the recent worldwide increase in ethnic hostilities is a consequence of "re-tribalization"—that

constructivist explanations

Emphasize the role of leaders of ethnic groups in stirring up inter-communal hostility.

is, the tendency for groups, lost in a globalized culture, to seek solace in the "extended family of an ethnic group" (p. 56). Chirot identified five levels of ethnic conflict: (1) multiethnic societies without serious conflict (e.g., Switzerland), (2) multiethnic societies with controlled conflict (e.g., United States and Canada), (3) societies with ethnic conflict that has been resolved (e.g., South Africa), (4) societies with serious ethnic conflict leading to warfare (e.g., Sri Lanka), and (5) societies with genocidal ethnic conflict, including "ethnic cleansing" (e.g., Darfur).

Religious differences as a source of conflict have recently come to the fore-front. An Islamic jihad, or holy war, has been blamed for the September 11 attacks on the World Trade Center and Pentagon as well as for bombings in Kashmir, Sudan, the Philippines, Indonesia, Kenya, Tanzania, Saudi Arabia, Spain, and Great Britain. Some claim that Islamic beliefs in and of themselves have led to recent conflicts (Feder 2003). Others contend that religious fanatics, not the religion itself, are responsible for violent confrontations.

Defence against Hostile Attacks

The threat or fear of being attacked may cause the leaders of a country to declare war on the nation that poses the threat. This is an example of what experts in international relations refer to as the security dilemma: "actions to increase one's security may only decrease the security of others and lead them to respond in ways that decrease one's own security" (Levy 2001: 7). Such situations may lead to war inadvertently. The threat may come from a foreign country or from a group within the country. After Germany invaded Poland in 1939, Britain and France declared war on Germany out of fear that they would be Germany's next victims. Germany attacked Russia in World War I, in part out of fear that Russia had entered the arms race and would use its weapons against Germany. Japan bombed Pearl Harbor hoping to avoid a later confron-tation with the U.S. Pacific fleet, which posed a threat to the Japanese military. In 2001, a United States-led coalition bombed Afghanistan in response to the September 11 terrorist attacks. Moreover, in March 2003, the United States, Great Britain, and a loosely coupled "coalition of the willing" invaded Iraq in response to perceived threats of weapons of mass destruction and the reported failure of Saddam Hussein to cooperate with United Nations weapons inspec-tors. Yet, in 2005, a presidential commission concluded that the attack on Iraq was based on faulty intelligence and that, in fact, "America's spy agencies were 'dead wrong' in most of their judgments about Iraq's weapons of mass destruc-tion" (Shrader 2005: 1). As a result, by 2007, many Americans—more than 60 percent—favoured a partial or complete withdrawal from Iraq (CNN/Opinion Research Corporation Poll 2007). Many believe that the public's desire for withdrawal from Iraq was a key factor in the outcome of the 2008 U.S. presi-dential election.

Revolutions and Civil Wars

Revolutions and civil wars involve citizens warring against their own govern-ment and often result in significant political, economic, and social change. The difference between a revolution and a civil war is not always easy to determine. Scholars generally agree that revolutions involve sweeping changes that fundamentally alter the distribution of power in society (Skocpol 1994). The

American Revolution resulted from colonists revolting against British control. Eventually, they succeeded and established a republic where none existed before. The Russian Revolution involved a revolt against a corrupt, autocratic, and out-of-touch ruler, Czar Nicholas II. Among other changes, the revolution led to wide-scale seizure of land by peasants who formerly were economically dependent on large landowners.

Civil wars may result in a different government or a new set of leaders but do not necessarily lead to such large-scale social change. Because the distinction between a revolution and a civil war depends upon the outcome of the struggle, it may take many years after the fighting before observers agree on how to classify it. Revolutions and civil wars are more likely to occur when a government is weak or divided, when it is not responsive to the concerns and demands of its citizens, and when strong leaders are willing to mount opposition to the government (Barkan and Snowden 2001; Renner 2000).

One of the world's longest running civil wars came to an end in May 2009. Since 1983, the government of Sri Lanka fought an insurgency led by the Liberation Tigers of Tamil Eelam (LTTE). Also known as the Tamil Tigers, the LTTE were separatist militants who sought to carve an independent state out of the northern and eastern portions of this island country. The war resulted in more than 68 000 deaths (Gardner 2007). The Sri Lankan Army defeated the last remnants of the LTTE and killed their leader in May 2009 (Buncombe 2009). Like many civil wars, the war in Sri Lanka was also a struggle between a majority community (in this case, Sinhalese Buddhists) and a relatively poor and disadvantaged minority community (Hindu Tamils). Despite the end of the war, a political settlement with the minority community has not been achieved. Civil wars have also erupted in newly independent republics created by the collapse of communism in eastern Europe, as well as in Rwanda, Sierra Leone, Chile, Uganda, Liberia, and Sudan.

14.4 Social Problems Associated with Armed Conflict

Social problems associated with armed conflict include death and disability; rape, forced prostitution, and displacement of women and children; social-psychological costs; diversion of economic resources; and environmental destruction.

Death and Disability

Many Canadian lives have been lost in wars, including 64 944 in World War I and 42 042 in World War II (Common Wealth War Graves Commission). Since entering Afghanistan in 2001, 154 Canadian soldiers have been killed (Brewster and Rennie 2010). The CBC maintains a Web-based archive of in-depth coverage of the Afghanistan conflict, and includes photographs, rank and unit information, the province of residence, and date of death for each soldier killed. Many civilians and enemy combatants also die or are injured in war. For example, based on a survey by the World Health Organization, an estimated 151 000 Iraqi civilians and insurgents died from war-related injuries between

March 2003 and June 2006 (Wilson 2008). Despite thousands of Iraqi deaths, many North Americans are unaware of this tremendous loss of life. In a program the Pentagon developed, American reporters were "embedded" into U.S. military units to provide "journalists with a detailed understanding of military culture and life on the frontlines" (Lindner 2009: 21). One of the byproducts of this program, however, was that 90 percent of the stories by embedded journalists were written from the perspective of the American soldier, focusing "on the horrors facing the troops, rather than upon the thousands of Iraqis who died" (p. 45). With so much U.S.-based broadcast news being available to Canadians, and with the reliance on agencies such as A.P. Reuters, the impact of bias in U.S. news reporting on the perceptions of Canadian news consumers should not be underestimated.

The impact of war and terrorism extends far beyond those who are killed. Many of those who survive war incur disabling injuries or contract diseases. For example, one million people worldwide have been killed or disabled by land mines—a continuing problem in the aftermath of the 2003 war with Iraq (Renner 2005). In 1997, the Mine Ban Treaty, which requires that governments destroy stockpiles within four years and clear land mine fields within 10 years, became international law. To date, 156 countries have signed the agreement; 39 countries remain, including China, India, Israel, Russia, and the United States (ICBL 2009). War-related deaths and disabilities also deplete the labour force, create orphans and single-parent families, and burden taxpayers who must pay for the care of orphans and disabled war veterans (see Chapter 2 for a discussion of military health care).

The killing of unarmed civilians is also likely to undermine the credibility of armed forces and make their goals more difficult to defend. In Iraq, for example, the events in Haditha, a city in western Iraq, became international news, outraged Iraqis, and led to intense condemnation of the U.S. mission. In November 2005, after a roadside bomb killed one Marine and wounded two others, "Marines shot five Iraqis standing by a car and went house to house looking for insurgents, using grenades and machine guns to clear houses" (Watkins 2007: 1). Twenty-four Iraqis were killed, many of them women and children, "shot in the chest and head from close range" (McGirk 2006: 3). After *Time* magazine broke the story in March 2006 (McGirk 2006), the military investigated and reversed its claim that the civilians died as a result of the roadside bomb. Eight marines were accused of wrongdoing during the incident; charges against six of them were dismissed, one was cleared of all charges, and one awaits court martial proceedings (Puckett and Faraj 2009; Reuters 2008).

Rape, Forced Prostitution, and Displacement of Women and Children

Half a century ago, the Geneva Convention prohibited rape and forced prostitution in war. Nevertheless, both continue to occur in modern conflicts.

Before and during World War II, the Japanese military forced 100 000 to 200 000 women and teenage girls into prostitution as military "comfort women." These women were forced to have sex with dozens of soldiers every day in "comfort stations." Many of the women died as a result of untreated sexually transmitted diseases, harsh punishment, or indiscriminate acts of torture.

Since 1998, Congolese government forces have fought Ugandan and Rwandan rebels. Women have paid a high price for this civil war, in which gang rape is "so violent, so systematic, so common . . . that thousands of women are suffering from vaginal fistula, leaving them unable to control bodily functions and enduring ostracism and the threat of debilitating health problems" (Wax 2003: 1). Though much less common than violence against women, aid workers also see increasing incidents of rape and sexual violence against men as "yet another way for armed groups to humiliate and demoralize Congolese communities into submission" (Gettleman 2009: 1). United Nations officials call the situation in Congo "the worst sexual violence in the world" (Gettleman 2008: 1).

Feminist analyses of wartime rape emphasize that the practice reflects not only a military strategy but also ethnic and gender dominance. For example, Refugees International, a humanitarian aid group, reports that rape is "a systematic weapon of ethnic cleansing" against Darfuris and is "linked to the destruction of their communities" (Boustany 2007: 9). Under Darfur's traditional law, prosecution of rapists is nearly impossible: Four male witnesses are required to accuse a rapist in court and single women risk severe corporal punishment for having sex outside of marriage.

War and terrorism also force women and children to flee to other countries or other regions of their homeland. For example, since 1990, at least 17 million children have been forced to leave their homeland because of armed conflict (Save the Children 2005). Refugee women and female children are particularly vulnerable to sexual abuse and exploitation by locals, members of security forces, border guards, or other refugees. In refugee camps, women and children may also be subjected to sexual violation. A 2003 report by Save the Children examined the treatment of women and children in 40 conflict zones. The use of child soldiers was reported in 70 percent of the zones, and trafficking of women and girls was reported in 85 percent of the zones. Wars are particularly dangerous for the very young—"Nine out of ten countries with the highest under-5 mortality rates are experiencing, or emerging from, armed conflict." These include Sierra Leone, Angola, Afghanistan, Niger, Liberia, Somalia, Mali, Chad, and the Democratic Republic of the Congo (Save the Children 2007: 13). Save the Children also estimated that, worldwide, 40 million children of primary school age—nearly one in three of all children in war zones—are prevented from attending school because of armed conflict (Save the Children 2009).

Social-Psychological Costs

Living with or under the threat of war disrupts social-psychological well-being and family functioning. For example, Myers-Brown et al. (2000) report that Yugoslavian children suffer from depression, anxiety, and fear as a response to conflicts in that region, emotional responses not unlike those Americans experienced after the events of 9/11 (NASP 2003). More recently, as a result of the war, there is evidence that many Iraqi children suffer from everything from "nightmares and bedwetting to withdrawal, muteness, panic attacks and violence towards other children, sometimes even to their own parents" (Howard 2007: 1). Further, a study of children in postwar Sierra Leone found that over 70 percent of boys and girls whose parents had been killed were at "serious risk" of suicide (Morgan and Behrendt 2009).

Guerrilla warfare is particularly costly in terms of its psychological toll on soldiers. In Iraq, soldiers were repeatedly traumatized as "guerrilla insurgents attack[ed] with impunity," and death was as likely to come from "hand grenades thrown by children, [as] earth-rattling bombs in suicide trucks, or snipers hid hidden in bombed out buildings (Waters 2005: 1).

Military personnel who engage in combat and civilians who are victimized by war may experience a form of psychological distress known as **posttraumatic stress disorder (PTSD)**, a clinical term referring to a set of symptoms that can result from any traumatic experience, including crime victimization, rape, or war. Symptoms of PTSD include sleep disturbances, recurring nightmares, flashbacks, and poor concentration (NCPSD 2007). For example, Canadian Lieutenant General Romeo Dallaire, head of the United Nations peacekeeping mission in Rwanda, witnessed horrific acts of genocide. Four years after his return, he continued to have images of "being in a valley at sunset, waist deep in bodies, covered in blood" (quoted in Rosenberg 2000: 14). PTSD is also associated with other personal problems, such as alcoholism, family violence, divorce, and suicide. Estimates of PTSD vary widely, although are consistently higher among combat versus noncombat veterans. In a telephone study of 1965 military personnel who had been deployed to Iraq and Afghanistan, 14 percent reported current symptoms of PTSD, 14 percent reported current symptoms of major depression, and 9 percent reported symptoms consistent with both conditions (Tanielian et al. 2008). If these estimates are correct, the researchers calculate that, as of April 2008, 303 000 Iraq and Afghanistan veterans were suffering from PTSD or major depression. However, the rate of PTSD among soldiers is difficult to measure for several reasons. First, there is a lag, often of several years, between the time of exposure to trauma and the manifestation of symptoms. Second, soldiers are generally reluctant to report symptoms or to seek help (Wein 2009).

posttraumatic stress disorder (PTSD)

A clinical term referring to a set of symptoms that can result from any traumatic experience, including crime victimization, rape, or war.

Diversion of Economic Resources

As discussed earlier, maintaining the military and engaging in warfare require enormous financial capital and human support. In 2008, worldwide military expenditures totalled more than $1.46 trillion (SIPRI 2009b). This amount exceeds the combined government research expenditures on developing new energy technologies, improving human health, raising agricultural productivity, and controlling pollution.

Money that is spent for military purposes could be allocated to social programs. In Canada, however, even as social programs including health, education, environmental protection, and social assistance are subject to continual budget reductions, our military spending has risen to levels that exceed those of the Cold War era, surpassing that amount by 2.3 percent annually in adjusted dollars (Staples and Robinson 2007). Yet the popular perception is that we do not spend *enough* on our military. Bill Robinson (2009) explains that politicians and pundits like to promote the idea that Canada is a miserly spender when it comes to military expenses, and yet:

> According to the latest budget estimates, Canada will spend $21.185 billion on its military forces in fiscal year (FY) 2009–101, 9.6% more than it did last year (FY 2008–09) and about 15% more than it did in its peak spending year during the Cold War (FY 1952–53). Our military spending will be 22% higher than it was in the year

the Berlin Wall came down, FY 1989–90, and 56% higher than it was in FY 1998–99, the year Canadian spending reached its post–Cold War minimum (all figures adjusted for inflation). It is twenty times the size of federal Environment Department spending ($1.064 billion). (n.p.)

Writing for the *Edmonton Journal*, Elinor Sloan, a Carleton University professor of international relations, demonstrates the verity of Robinson's assertions in her claim that "Some 58 per cent [of Canadians] think we should spend what the military needs to sustain the Canadian Forces' ability to fight terrorism in places like Afghanistan, support humanitarian missions, such as what we saw in Haiti, and defend Canada's homeland, for example in the North" (2010: A16). These attitudes likely developed in an era of military budget cutbacks in the late twentieth century, after the end of the Cold War—when, in the 1990s, Canada cut military spending by $29 billion over the previous decade (Feiler 2003). The cuts "led to calls for increased spending by a diverse group of critics, including increasingly vocal Canadian defense-oriented think tanks, veterans organizations, Liberal members of Parliament and, from Washington, President Bush" (ibid).

Environmental Destruction

The environmental damage that occurs during war devastates human populations long after war ends. As the casings for land mines erode, poisonous substances—often carcinogenic—leak into the ground (United Nations Association of the United States of America 2003). In 1991, during the Gulf War, Iraqi troops set 650 oil wells on fire, releasing oil, which covers the surface of the Kuwaiti desert and continues to seep into the ground, threatening underground water supplies. The smoke from the fires that hung over the Gulf region for eight months contained soot, sulphur dioxide, and nitrogen oxides—the major components of acid rain—and a variety of toxic and potentially carcinogenic chemicals and heavy metals. The U.S. Environmental Protection Agency estimates that, in March 1991, about 10 times as much air pollution was being emitted in Kuwait as by all U.S. industrial and power-generating plants combined (Environmental Media Services 2002; Funke 1994; Renner 1993).

Combatants often intentionally exploit natural resources to fuel their efforts. The local elephant population was heavily depleted during the civil war in southern Angola. The rebel group UNITA killed the animals to trade ivory for money to buy weapons. In addition, many were killed or fatally crippled by land mines planted by the guerrillas, though scientists report

Oil smoke from the 650 burning oil wells left in the wake of the Gulf War contains soot, sulphur dioxide, and nitrogen oxides, the major components of acid rain, along with a variety of toxic and potentially carcinogenic chemicals and heavy metals.

© Michel Lipschitz/AP/Wide World Photo

that, remarkably, the animals seemed to have learned to avoid mined areas (Marshall 2007). Between 1992 and 1997, UNITA also earned $3.7 billion to support its fighting from the sale of "conflict" or "blood" diamonds (GreenKarat 2007). Depending upon the location of diamonds, mining can be highly destructive to riverbed ecosystems or to areas surrounding open-pit mines.

The ultimate environmental catastrophe facing the planet is a massive exchange thermonuclear war. Aside from the immediate human casualties, poisoned air, poisoned crops, and radioactive rain, many scientists agree that the dust storms and concentrations of particles would block vital sunlight and lower temperatures in the northern hemisphere, creating a nuclear winter. In the event of large-scale nuclear war, most living things on Earth would die. For example, a nuclear blast and the resulting blast wave create overpressure—the amount of pressure in excess of ordinary atmospheric levels as measured by pounds per inch (psi). As described in a report sponsored by the U.S. Air Force:

- At 20 of overpressure, even reinforced-concrete buildings are destroyed
- Most factories and commercial buildings, as well as wood-frame and brick houses
- Most houses and lightly constructed commercial and industrial structures
- Suffices to blow away the walls of steel-frame buildings
- Even 1 will produce flying glass and debris sufficient to injure large numbers of people. (Ochmanek and Schwartz 2008: 6)

The fear of nuclear war has greatly contributed to the military and arms buildup, which, ironically, also causes environmental destruction even in times of peace. For example, in practising military maneuvers, the armed forces demolish natural vegetation, disturb wildlife habitats, erode soil, silt up streams, and cause flooding. Bombs exploded during peacetime leak radiation into the atmosphere and groundwater. From 1945 to 1990, 1908 bombs were tested—that is, exploded—at more than 35 sites around the world. Although underground testing has reduced radiation, some radioactive material still escapes into the atmosphere and is suspected of seeping into groundwater.

Finally, although arms control and disarmament treaties of the last decade have called for the disposal of huge stockpiles of weapons, no completely safe means of disposing of weapons and ammunition exist. Many activist groups have called for placing weapons in storage until safe disposal methods are found. Unfortunately, the longer the weapons are stored, the more they deteriorate, increasing the likelihood of dangerous leakage. In 2003, a federal judge gave permission, despite objections by environmentalists, to incinerate 2000 tons of nerve agents and mustard gas left from the Cold War era. Although the army says that it is safe to dispose of the weapons, they have issued protective gear in case of an "accident" to the nearly 20 000 residents who live nearby (CNN 2003).

14.5 Strategies for Action: In Search of Global Peace

Various strategies and policies are aimed at creating and maintaining global peace. These include the redistribution of economic resources, peacekeeping activities of the United Nations, mediation and arbitration, and arms control and disarmament.

Redistribution of Economic Resources

Inequality in economic resources contributes to conflict and war because the increasing disparity in wealth and resources between rich and poor nations fuels hostilities and resentment. Therefore, any measures that result in a more equal distribution of economic resources are likely to prevent conflict. John J. Shanahan (1995), retired U.S. Navy vice admiral and former director of the Center for Defense Information, suggested that wealthy nations can help reduce the social and economic roots of conflict by providing economic assistance to poorer countries. Nevertheless, U.S. military expenditures for national defence far outweigh U.S. economic assistance to foreign countries. For instance, the Obama administration's 2010 budget request for foreign affairs (including all nonmilitary foreign aid, the U.S. Department of State, the Peace Corps, and scholarly exchange programs) was $51.7 billion, or about 4 percent of the entire federal budget and 7.7 percent of the total request for the Department of Defense, the wars in Afghanistan and Iraq, and the global war on terrorism (Office of Management and Budget 2009a).

Strategies that reduce population growth are likely to result in higher levels of economic well-being. Funke (1994) explained that "rapidly increasing populations in poorer countries will lead to environmental overload and resource depletion in the next century, which will most likely result in political upheaval and violence as well as mass starvation" (p. 326). Although achieving worldwide economic well-being is important for minimizing global conflict, it is important that economic development does not occur at the expense of the environment.

Finally, former United Nations Secretary General Kofi Annan, in an address to the United Nations, observed that it is not poverty per se that leads to conflict but rather the "inequality among domestic social groups" (Deen 2000). Referencing a research report completed by the Tokyo-based United Nations University, Annan argued that "inequality...based on ethnicity, religion, national identity, or economic class...tends to be reflected in unequal access to political power that too often forecloses paths to peaceful change" (Deen 2000).

Peacekeeping Activities of the United Nations

Founded in 1945 after the devastation of World War II, the United Nations (UN) today includes 192 member states and is the principal organ of world governance. In its early years, the UN's main mission was the elimination of war from society.

In fact, the UN charter begins, "We the people of the United Nations—Determined to save succeeding generations from the scourge of war." During the past 65 years, the UN has developed major institutions and initiatives in support of international law, economic development, human rights, education, health, and other forms of social progress. The Security Council is the most powerful branch of the United Nations. Comprised of 15 member states, it has the power to impose economic sanctions against states that violate international law. It can also use force, when necessary, to restore international peace and security.

The United Nations has engaged in more than 60 peacekeeping operations since 1948 (United Nations 2009). United Nations peacekeepers—military personnel in their distinctive blue helmets or blue berets, civilian police, and a range of other civilians—help implement peace agreements, monitor ceasefires, create buffer zones, or support complex military and civilian functions essential to maintain peace and begin reconstruction and institution building in societies devastated by war (United Nations 2003: 1). Recently, the UN has been involved in overseeing multinational peacekeeping forces in Bosnia, East Timor, Sudan, Burundi, Haiti, Liberia, and Ethiopia (United Nations 2009).

In the last few years, the UN has come under heavy criticism. First, in recent missions, developing nations have supplied more than 75 percent of the troops while developed countries—United States, Japan, and Europe—have contributed 85 percent of the finances. As one UN official commented, "You can't have a situation where some nations contribute blood and others only money" (quoted by Vesely 2001: 8). Second, a review of UN peacekeeping operations noted several failed missions, including an intervention in Somalia in which 44 U.S. marines were killed (Lamont 2001). Third, as typified by the debate over the disarming of Iraq, the UN cannot take sides but must wait for a consensus of its members that, if not forthcoming, undermines the strength of the organization (Goure 2003). The consequences of delays can be staggering. For example, under the Genocide Convention of 1948, the UN is obligated to prevent instances of genocide, defined as "acts committed with the intent to destroy, in whole or in part, a national, racial, ethnical or religious group" (United Nations 1948). In 2000, the UN Security Council formally acknowledged its failure to prevent the 1994 genocide in Rwanda (BBC 2000). After the death of 10 Belgian soldiers in the days leading up to the genocide, and without a consensus for action among the members, the Security Council ignored warnings from the mission's commander about impending disaster and withdrew its 2500 peacekeepers.

Finally, the concept of the UN is that its members represent individual nations, not a region or the world. And because nations tend to act in their own best economic and security interests, UN actions performed in the name of world peace may be motivated by nations acting in their own interests.

As a result of such criticisms, outgoing UN Secretary General Kofi Annan called on the 191 members of the UN to approve the most far-reaching changes in the 60-year history of the organization (Lederer 2005). One of the most controversial recommendations concerns the composition of the Security Council, the most important decision-making body of the organization. Annan's recommendation that the 15 members of the Security Council—a body dominated by the United States, Great Britain, France, Russia, and China—be changed to include a more representative number of nations could, if approved, shift the global balance of power. Ban Ki-moon, former foreign minister of South Korea, was elected as the eighth Secretary General in October 2006 (MacAskill et al. 2006), after campaigning for the position on a platform that included support for the UN reforms. So far, the United Nations has not been able to reach agreement about whether and how to expand the membership of the Security Council.

Mediation and Arbitration

Most conflicts are resolved through nonviolent means (Worldwatch Institute 2003). Mediation and arbitration are just two of the nonviolent strategies used to resolve conflicts and to stop or prevent war. In **mediation**, a neutral third party intervenes and facilitates negotiation between representatives or leaders

mediation

A nonviolent strategy used to resolve conflicts and to stop or prevent war where a neutral third party intervenes and facilitates negotiation between representatives or leaders of conflicting groups.

of conflicting groups. Good mediators do not impose solutions but rather help disputing parties generate options for resolving the conflict (Conflict Research Consortium 2003). Ideally, a mediated resolution to a conflict meets at least some of the concerns and interests of each party to the conflict. In other words, mediation attempts to find "win-win" solutions in which each side is satisfied with the solution.

Although mediation is used to resolve conflict between individuals, it is also a valuable tool for resolving international conflicts. For example, former U.S. Senator George Mitchell successfully mediated talks between parties to the conflict in Northern Ireland in 1998. The resulting political agreement continues to hold today. President Obama appointed Senator Mitchell as special envoy to the Middle East in order to pursue a negotiated political settlement. Also, in May 2008, the government of Qatar mediated talks between Lebanon's political parties that resulted in an agreement that averted civil war after an 18-month political crisis. Using mediation as a means of resolving international conflict is often difficult, given the complexity of the issues. However, research by Bercovitch (2003) shows that there are more mediators available and more instances of mediation in international affairs than ever before. For example, Bercovitch identified more than 250 separate mediation attempts during the Balkan wars of the early and mid-1990s.

arbitration

A nonviolent strategy used to resolve conflicts and to stop or prevent war where a neutral third party in arbitration arrives at a decision that the two conflicting parties agree in advance to accept.

Arbitration also involves a neutral third party who listens to evidence and arguments presented by conflicting groups. Unlike mediation, however, the neutral third party in arbitration arrives at a decision that the two conflicting parties agree in advance to accept. For instance, the Permanent Court of Arbitration—an intergovernmental organization based in The Hague since 1899—arbitrates disputes about territory, treaty compliance, human rights, commerce, and investment among any of its 107 member states who signed and ratified either of its two founding legal conventions. Recent cases include a dispute between France, Britain, and Northern Ireland about the Eurotunnel, a boundary dispute between Eritrea and Ethiopia, and a boundary dispute between the government of Sudan and the Sudan People's Liberation Army (Permanent Court of Arbitration 2009).

Arms Control and Disarmament

In the 1960s, the United States and the Soviet Union led the world in a nuclear arms race, with each competing to build a larger and more destructive arsenal of nuclear weapons than its adversary. If either superpower were to initiate a full-scale war, the retaliatory powers of the other nation would result in the destruction of both nations as well as much of the planet. Thus, the principle of mutually assured destruction (MAD) that developed from nuclear weapons capabilities transformed war from a win-lose proposition to a lose-lose scenario. If both sides would lose in a war, the theory suggested, neither side would initiate war. At its peak year in 1966, the U.S. stockpile of nuclear weapons included more than 32 000 warheads and bombs (see this chapter's *Self and Society* feature).

As their arsenals continued to grow at an astronomical cost, both sides recognized the necessity for nuclear arms control including the reduction of defence spending, weapons production and deployment, and armed forces. Throughout the Cold War and even today, much of the behaviour of the United

The Nuclear Numbers Game

Carefully read each of the following questions and select the correct answer. When you are finished, compare your answers to those provided and rank your performance using the scale at the end of this box.

1. How many nuclear weapons has the United States built since starting production in 1951?

   a. About 67 500

   b. About 100 000

   c. Nearly 25 000

   d. The number is classified

2. If you knew where to look, you could find 2000 nuclear weapons in the state of Georgia.

   a. True

   b. False

3. How many nuclear weapons did the United States detonate in tests between 1945 and 1992 (the last year it detonated a nuclear weapon)?

   a. 13

   b. 130

   c. 1030

   d. 10 300

4. What is the total volume (in cubic metres) of radioactive waste resulting from weapons activities?

   a. 650 000

   b. 104 000 000

   c. 426 000 000

   d. 1.2 billion

5. How many nuclear bombs has the United States lost (and not recovered) in accidents?

   a. 0

   b. 1

   c. 6

   d. 11

6. How many nuclear warheads and bombs does the United States currently possess in its stockpile?

   a. 3416

   b. 7982

   c. 10 600

   d. 32 750

7. With the end of the Cold War and the fall of the Soviet Union, most U.S. nuclear weapons are no longer targeted at specific sites around the world.

   a. True: Only about 100 weapons are targeted against other nuclear powers.

   b. False: The U.S. arsenal targets 2500 sites for nuclear destruction around the world.

8. On U.S. soil, the government restricted its nuclear tests only to the Southwest desert because of the remote terrain and relatively low risks to human populations.

   a. True: There have been no nuclear tests on U.S. soil except those in Nevada and New Mexico.

   b. False: Nuclear weapons have been detonated in Alaska, Colorado, and Mississippi.

(continued)

9. Which arm of the U.S. government supervises its nuclear weapons stockpile?

    a.   Department of Defense

    b.   Department of Energy

    c.   National Security Council

    d.   Department of State

10. Which was the last year that the United States detonated a nuclear bomb?

    a.   1945

    b.   1962

    c.   1992

    d.   1999

Answers: 1: a; 2: a; 3: c; 4: b; 5: d; 6: c; 7: b; 8: b; 9: b; 10: c.

Rank Your Performance:
Number Correct 9 or 10: Excellent
7or 8: Good
5 or 6: Average
3 or 4: Fair
2 or less: Poor

*Since 1998, the time of this study, the United States has not detonated nuclear weapons for tests and has not added new nuclear weapons to its arsenal (Federation of American Scientists 2007).

SOURCE: Adapted from U.S. Nuclear Weapons Cost Study Project, 1998.

States and the Soviet Union has been governed by major arms control initiatives. These initiatives include:

- The Limited Test Ban Treaty that prohibited testing of nuclear weapons in the atmosphere, underwater, and in outer space
- The Strategic Arms Limitation Treaties (SALT I and II) that limited the development of nuclear missiles and defensive antiballistic missiles
- The Strategic Arms Reduction Treaties (START I and II) that significantly reduced the number of nuclear missiles, warheads, and bombers
- The Strategic Offensive Reduction Treaty (SORT) that requires that the United States and the Russian Federation (i.e., the remaining countries of the former Soviet Union) each reduce their number of strategic nuclear warheads to between 1,700 and 2,200 by 2012. (Atomic Archive 2009)

In 2009, the United States and the Russian Federation announced plans to negotiate further cuts in their nuclear stockpiles, reducing them to between 1500 and 1675 strategic nuclear warheads each (Baker and Cooper 2009).

With the end of the Cold War came the growing realization that, even as Russia and the United States greatly reduced their arsenals, other countries were poised to acquire nuclear weapons or expand their existing arsenals. Thus, the focus on arms control shifted toward the issue of nuclear proliferation—that is, the spread of nuclear technology to nonnuclear states.

Nuclear Nonproliferation Treaty The Nuclear Nonproliferation Treaty (NPT) was signed in 1970, and was the first treaty governing the spread of nuclear weapons technology from the original nuclear weapons states (i.e., the United

States, the Soviet Union, the United Kingdom, France, and China) to nonnuclear countries. The NPT was renewed in 2000, and adopted by 187 countries. The NPT holds that countries without nuclear weapons will not try to get them; in exchange, the countries with nuclear weapons agree that they will not provide nuclear weapons to countries that do not have them. Signatory states without nuclear weapons also agree to allow the International Atomic Energy Agency to verify compliance with the treaty through on-site inspections (Atomic Archive 2009). Only India, Israel, and Pakistan have not signed the agreement, although each of these states is known to possess a nuclear arsenal. Further, many experts suspect that Iran and Syria—both signatories to the NPT—are developing nuclear weapons programs. Both countries claim that their nuclear reactors are for peaceful purposes (e.g., domestic power consumption), not to develop a nuclear weapons arsenal. However, a recent report by the International Atomic Energy Agency tentatively concluded that Iran has "sufficient information to be able to design and produce a workable" atomic bomb (Broad and Sanger 2009: 1).

In January 2003, North Korea, under suspicion of secretly producing nuclear weapons, announced that it was withdrawing from the treaty, effective immediately (Arms Control Association 2003). In July 2005, after "more than a year of stalemate, North Korea agreed…to return to disarmament talks…and pledged to discuss eliminating its nuclear-weapons program" (Brinkley and Sanger 2005: 1). However, in May 2009, shortly after testing a long-range missile over Japan, North Korea detonated a nuclear device underground, heightening fears that it would launch a nuclear attack against South Korea, China, or Japan (NTI 2009).

Even if military superpowers honour agreements to limit arms, the availability of black-market nuclear weapons and materials presents a threat to global security. One of the most successful nuclear weapons brokers was Pakistan's Abdul Qadeer Khan. Khan, the "father" of Pakistan's nuclear weapons program, sold the technology and equipment required to make nuclear weapons to rogue states such as Iran and North Korea. He is also suspected of selling nuclear weapons to Al Qaeda (Powell and McGirk 2005).

In 2003, the United States accused Iran of operating a covert nuclear weapons program. Although Iranian officials responded that their nuclear program was solely for the purpose of generating electricity, concerns escalated with Iran's successful test of a 1200-mile-range missile in 2009 (Dareini 2009). Hostile public statements about Israel by Iran's president Mahmoud Ahmadinejad deepen already grave concerns about Iran's possible acquisition of nuclear weapons. Analysts fear the development of nuclear weapons by Iran would spur a nuclear competition with Israel, the only other state in the Middle East to possess nuclear weapons, and provoke other states in the region to acquire them (Salem 2007). Nonetheless, analysts disagree about whether there is evidence that Iran, despite the capability, is designing a nuclear warhead (Broad et al. 2009).

Many observers consider South Asia the world's most dangerous nuclear rivalry. India and Pakistan are the only two nuclear powers that share a border and have repeatedly fired upon each other's armies while in possession of nuclear weapons (Stimson Center 2007). India first detonated nuclear weapons in 1974. Pakistan detonated six weapons in 1998, a few weeks after India's second round of nuclear tests. Although precise figures are hard to come by, experts estimate that India has about 50 nuclear bombs, and Pakistan has between 40 and 70 nuclear bombs (Center for Defense Information 2007). Pakistan, however, is aggressively expanding its nuclear weapons program (Shanker and Sanger 2009).

Many fear that a conventional military confrontation between these two countries may some day escalate to an exchange of nuclear weapons. In addition, widespread social unrest in Pakistan coupled with clashes in 2009 between Taliban forces and Pakistan's army 60 miles from the capital, Islamabad, have heightened fears about the security of Pakistan's nuclear arsenal and its vulnerability to seizure by extremist forces (Kerr and Nikitin 2009).

As states that want to obtain nuclear weapons are quick to point out, nuclear states that advocate for nonproliferation possess well over 25 000 weapons, a huge reduction in the world's arsenal from Cold War days but still a massive potential threat to Earth. "Do as I say not as I do" is a weak bargaining position. Recognizing this situation, and with concern about the possibility of new arms races, many high-level experts have begun to advocate a more comprehensive approach to banning nuclear weapons—with the United States leading the nuclear powers toward complete nuclear disarmament. In January 2007, three former U.S. Secretaries of State (George Schultz, William Perry, and Henry Kissinger) and former chairman of the Senate Armed Services Committee Sam Nunn published an editorial in the *Wall Street Journal* advocating that the United States "take the world to the next stage" of disarmament to "a world free of nuclear weapons" (Schultz et al. 2007). As a start, their proposal advocated the elimination of all short-range nuclear missiles, a complete halt in the production of weapons-grade uranium, and continued reduction of nuclear forces. President Barack Obama visited Russia in July 2009 to sign an agreement that reduced the strategic nuclear arsenals of the United States and the Russian Federation by about 25 percent. This was reportedly "a first step in a broader effort intended to reduce the threat of such weapons drastically and to prevent their further spread to unstable regions" (Levy and Baker 2009).

The Problem of Small Arms Although the devastation caused by even one nuclear war could affect millions, the availability of conventional weapons fuels many active wars around the world. Small arms and light weapons include handguns, submachine guns and automatic weapons, grenades, mortars, land mines, and light missiles. The Small Arms Survey estimated that, in 2006, 639 million firearms were in circulation, with about 59 percent of them being owned legally (Geneva Graduate Institute for International Studies 2006). Civilians purchased 80 percent of these weapons and were the victims of 90 percent of the casualties caused by them. Half a million people die each year as a result of small arms use, 200 000 in homicides and suicides and the rest during wars and other armed conflicts.

Unlike control of weapons of mass destruction such as chemical and biological weapons, controlling the flow of small arms is not easy because they have many legitimate uses by the military, by law enforcement officials, and for recreational or sporting activities (Schroeder 2007). Small arms are easy to afford, to use, to conceal, and to transport illegally. The small arms trade is also lucrative. Between 2000 and 2006, the top five exporters of military small arms were the United States ($228.5 million), Belgium ($27.1 million), France ($22.6 million), Germany ($16.2 million), and the United Kingdom ($13.6 million). The United States accounted for 54 percent of small arms exports during this time period (Small Arms Survey 2009).

The U.S. State Department's Office of Weapons Removal and Abatement (WRA) administers a program that has supported the destruction of 1.3 million weapons and 50 000 tons of ammunition in 33 countries since its founding in 2001 (Office of Weapons Removal and Abatement 2009). The availability of these weapons fuels terrorist groups and undermines efforts to promote peace after wars have formally concluded. "If not expeditiously destroyed or secured, stocks of arms and ammunition left over after the cessation of hostilities frequently recirculate into neighboring regions, exacerbating conflict and crime" (U.S. Department of State 2007: 1). Operating on a budget of $16.1 million in 2007, the Bush administration increased the WRA budget to $44.3 million in 2008 (Office of Weapons Removal and Abatement 2009).

Understanding Armed Conflict and War

Each of the theoretical positions discussed in this chapter reflects the realities of global conflict. As structural functionalists argue, war offers societal benefits—social cohesion, economic prosperity, scientific and technological developments, and social change. Furthermore, as conflict theorists contend, wars often occur for economic reasons because corporate elites and political leaders benefit from the spoils of war—land and water resources and raw materials. The symbolic interactionist perspective emphasizes the role that meanings, labels, and definitions play in creating conflict and contributing to acts of war. Feminist approaches use gender-based analyses to consider the impact of armed conflict and political instability on women and children, but also offer corrective history of women's participation in various war efforts.

The September 11 attacks on the World Trade Center and the Pentagon and the aftermath—the battle against terrorism, the bombing of Afghanistan, and the war with Iraq—changed the world we live in. For some theorists, these events were inevitable. Political scientist Samuel P. Huntington argued that such conflict represents a clash of civilizations. In *The Clash of Civilizations and the Remaking of World Order* (1996), Huntington argued that in the new world order

> the most pervasive, important and dangerous conflicts will not be between social
> classes, rich and poor, or economically defined groups, but between people
> belonging to different cultural entities … the most dangerous cultural conflicts are
> those along the fault lines between civilizations … the line separating peoples of
> Western Christianity, on the one hand, from Muslim and Orthodox peoples on the
> other. (p. 28)

Although not without critics, the clash-of-civilizations hypothesis has some support. In an interview of almost 10 000 people from nine Muslim states representing half of all Muslims worldwide, only 22 percent had favourable opinions toward the United States (CNN 2003). Even more significantly, 67 percent saw the September 11 attacks as "morally justified," and the majority of respondents found the United States to be overly materialistic and secular and having a corrupting influence on other nations. Moreover, according to a poll of world public opinion taken every year since 2002, positive attitudes about the United States are consistently lowest in predominantly Muslim countries (Pew Research Center 2009). Although favourable views of the United States increased dramatically in a small number of Muslim countries after the election of President Obama, the 2009 poll found that only small minorities continued to see the United States favourably in most predominantly Muslim counties (for example, 14 percent in Turkey, 15 percent in Palestinian territories, 16 percent in Pakistan, 25 percent in Jordan, and 27 percent in Egypt).

Ultimately, we are all members of one community—Earth—and have a vested interest in staying alive and protecting the resources of our environment for our own and future generations. But, as we have seen, conflict between groups is a feature of social life, and human existence, that is not likely to disappear. What is at stake—human lives and the ability of our planet to sustain life—merits serious attention. World leaders have traditionally followed the advice of philosopher Karl von Clausewitz: "If you want peace, prepare for war." Thus, nations have sought to protect themselves by maintaining large military forces and massive weapons systems. These strategies are associated with serious costs, particularly in hard economic times. In diverting resources away from other social concerns, defence spending undermines a society's ability to improve the overall security and well-being of its citizens. Conversely, defence-spending cutbacks, although unlikely in the present climate, could potentially free up resources for other social agendas, including lowering taxes, reducing the national debt, addressing environmental concerns, eradicating hunger and poverty, improving health care, upgrading educational services, and improving housing and transportation. Therein lies the promise of a "peace dividend." The hope is that future dialogue on the problems of war and terrorism will redefine national and international security to encompass social, economic, and environmental well-being.

Critical Thinking

1. Using a symbolic interactionist approach, provide a reading of three to five recruiting images currently in use by the Canadian military. What emotions and values do those recruiting images appeal to, and what assumptions do the images make about the value of entering the military? What information is excluded? What promises are implied? Why do you think they still aim most recruitment efforts at young people?

2. Feminist arguments about women's roles in armed conflict may value the contributions of women to military service even while deploring the impact of war. What do you think about the social location of girls and women in various conflict zones? Does your opinion change based on the particular situation? Why? Why not?

3. The military-industrial complex is a central component of most world economies. Use a conflict theory perspective to assess the financial investment of the world's most powerful groups in the continuation of armed conflict.

4. From a functionalist perspective, wars and armed conflicts can serve positive social functions. How would you propose that we serve these positive social functions while still reducing our involvement in armed conflict with other groups?

5. Do you think it is better for Canada to insist on its claims of being committed to peacekeeping, or is it time to publicly redefine the objective of our military? Using a symbolic approach, explain your reasoning.

"Is It True?" Quiz: Answers

1 = false; 2 = contextual; 3 = true

References

Preface

Safransky, Sy. 1990. *Sunbeams: A Book of Quotations*. Berkeley, CA: North Atlantic Books.

Chapter 1

Benoit, Cecilia, Dena Carroll, and Munaza Chaudry. 2003. "In Search of a Healing Place: Aboriginal Women in Vancouver's Eastside." *Social Science and Medicine* 56: 821–33.

Bibby, Reginald W. 1995. *The Bibby Report: Social Trends Canadian Style*. Toronto: Stoddart.

—————. 2001. *Canada's Teens: Today, Yesterday, and Tomorrow*. Toronto: Stoddart.

Bibby, Reginald W., and Donald C. Posterski. 1992. *Teen Trends: A Nation in Motion*. Toronto: Stoddart.

Blumer, Herbert. 1971. "Social Problems as Collective Behavior." *Social Problems* 8(3): 298–306.

Bruckert, Chris. 2002. *Taking It Off, Putting It On*. Toronto: Women's Press.

Chafetz, Janet S. 1997. "Feminist Theory and Sociology: Underutilized Contributions to Mainstream Theory." *Annual Review of Sociology* 23: 97–120.

Dordick, Gwendolyn A. 1997. *Something Left to Lose: Personal Relations and Survival among New York's Homeless*. Philadelphia: Temple University Press.

Eitzen, Stanley, and Maxine Baca Zinn. 2000. *Social Problems*. Boston: Allyn and Bacon.

Globe and Mail. n.d. "Globe Poll." *The Globe and Mail*, Web version only; http://www.globeandmail.com.

Goldie, Terry. 2001. "Queer Nation?" In Terry Goldie (ed.), *In a Queer Country: Gay and Lesbian Studies in the Canadian Context*, pp. 7–26. Vancouver: Arsenal Pulp Press.

Hewlett, Sylvia Ann. 1992. *When the Bough Breaks: The Cost of Neglecting Our Children*. New York: Harper Perennial.

Hills, Stuart L. (ed.). 1987. *Corporate Violence: Injury and Death for Profit*. Lanham, MN: Rowman and Littlefield.

Inglis, David, and John Hughson. 2003. *Confronting Culture: Sociological Vistas*. Oxford: Polity Press.

Jagose, Annamarie. 1996. *Queer Theory: An Introduction*. New York: NYU Press.

Jekielek, Susan M. 1998. "Parental Conflict, Marital Disruption and Children's Emotional Well-Being." *Social Forces* 76: 905–35.

Krahn, Harvey. 2004. "Choose Your Parents Carefully." In Edward Grabb, James Curtis, and Neil Guppy (eds.), *Social Inequality in Canada*, 4th ed., pp. 187–203. Toronto: Prentice Hall.

Krahn, Harvey, and Graham S. Lowe. 2002. *Work, Industry, and Canadian Society*, 4th ed. Scarborough, ON: Thomson Nelson.

Leach, Belinda. 2005. "Agency and the Gendered Imagination: Women's Actions and Local Culture in Steelworker Families." *Identities: Global Studies in Culture and Power* 12(1): 1–22.

Marshall, Joan, and Natalie Foster. 2002. "'Between Belonging': Habitus and the Migration Experience." *The Canadian Geographer* 46: 63–83.

May, Richard. 2000. "Human Development Report." *Journal of American Planning Association* 66: 219.

Merton, Robert K. 1968. *Social Theory and Social Structure*. New York: Free Press.

Miki, Roy. 2000. "Altered States: Global Currents, the Spectral Nation, and the Production of 'Asian Canadian.'" *Canadian Studies* 33(3): 43–72.

Mills, C. Wright. 1959. *The Sociological Imagination*. London: Oxford University Press.

Mouw, Ted, and Yu Xie. 1999. "Bilingualism and Academic Achievement of Asian Immigrants." *American Sociological Review* 64: 232–52.

Nader, Ralph, Nadia Milleron, and Duff Conacher. 1993. *Canada Firsts*. Toronto: McClelland & Stewart Inc.

Romer, D., R. Hornik, B. Stanton, M. Black, X. Li, I. Ricardo, and S. Feigelman. 1997. "'Talking Computers': A Reliable and Private Method to Conduct Interviews on Sensitive Topics with Children." *Journal of Sex Research* 34: 3–9.

Schwalbe, Michael. 1998. *The Sociologically Examined Life: Pieces of the Conversation*. Mountain View, CA: Mayfield Publishing Company.

Spector, Malcolm, and John I. Kitsuse. 2001. *Constructing Social Problems*. New Brunswick, NJ: Transaction Publishers.

Stackhouse, John. 1999. "My Life without a Home." *The Globe and Mail* (December 18): A17.

Thomas, W. I. [1931] 1966. "The Relation of Research to the Social Process." In Morris Janowitz (ed.), *W. I. Thomas on Social Organization and Social Personality*, pp. 289–305. Chicago: University of Chicago Press.

Wilson, John. 1983. *Social Theory*. Englewood Cliffs, NJ: Prentice-Hall.

Chapter 2

Adetunji, Jacob. 2000. "Trends in under-5 Mortality Rates and the

HIV/AIDS Epidemic." *Bulletin of the World Health Organization* 78(10): 1200–06.

American Psychiatric Association. 2000. *Diagnostic and Statistical Manual of Mental Disorders*, 4th ed., Text Revision DSM–TR. Washington, DC: American Psychiatric Association.

Antezana, Fernando S., Claire M. Chollat-Traquet, and Derik Yach. 1998. "Health for All in the 21st Century." *World Health Statistics Quarterly* 51: 3–6.

Armstrong, Pat, Hugh Armstrong, and Claudia Fegan. 1998. *Universal Health Care: What the United States Can Learn from the Canadian Experience*. New York: The New Press.

Arnold, Tom. 2001. "Drugs Account for 15.5% of Health Care Spending." *National Post* (March 15): A11.

Ash, Russell. 2001. *The Top 10 of Everything: Canadian Edition 2002*. Toronto: Dorling Kindersley Limited.

Baer, Nicole. 1997. "Canada's Organ Shortage Is Severe and Getting Worse." *Canadian Medical Association Journal* 157: 179–82.

Barlow, Maude, and Elizabeth May. 2000. *Frederick Street: Life and Death on Canada's Love Canal*. Toronto: HarperCollins.

Bibby, Reginald W. 2001. *Canada's Teens: Today, Yesterday, and Tomorrow*. Toronto: Stoddart.

Bricker, Darrell, and Edward Greenspon. 2001. *Searching for Certainty: Inside the New Canadian Mindset*. Toronto: Doubleday Canada.

Brundtland, Gro Harlem. 2000. "Mental Health in the 21st Century." *Bulletin of the World Health Organization* 78(4): 411.

Canadian Aboriginal News. 2001. "Innu, Health Officials Settle Differences over Treatment for Gas Sniffers." http://www.canadianaboriginal. com/health/health26b.htm.

Canadian Centre on Substance Abuse. 1999. *Canadian Profile, 1999: Alcohol, Tobacco, and Other Drugs*. Ottawa: Canadian Centre on Substance Abuse and Centre for Addiction and Mental Health.

CBC News. 2010. "Misdiagnosed: Anatomy of Newfoundland's Cancer Testing Scandal." http://www.cbc.ca/news/background/cancer/misdiagnosed.html.

CMA (Canadian Medical Association). 1999. *Access to Health Care in Canada Report*. http://www.cma.ca/advocacy/access/index.asp.

————. 2001. "Canadians Give a B Grade to the Health Care System" (news release). August 13. http://www.cma.ca/cma/common/displayPage.do?pageID=/staticContent/HTML/N012/adovcacy/news/2001/08-13.htm.

Canadian Psychiatric Association. 2002. "Anxiety, Depression and Manic Depression." http://www.cpa-apc.org/MIAW/pamphlets/Anxiety.arp.

Cockerham, William C. 1998. *Medical Sociology*, 7th ed. Upper Saddle River, NJ: Prentice Hall.

Diamond, Catherine, and Susan Buskin. 2000. "Continued Risky Behavior in HIV-Infected Youth." *American Journal of Public Health* 90(1): 115–18.

Dias, Lisa V. 2009. "Burdening Women with Responsibility for Containment: A Discourse Analysis of Public Health Initiatives and Pharmaceutical Advertising for Gardasil, 'The HPV Vaccine.'" Major Research Paper, Master of Arts. Wilfrid Laurier University: Waterloo.

Everett, Sherry A., Rae L. Schnuth, and Joanne L. Tribble. 1998. "Tobacco and Alcohol Use in Top-Grossing American Films." *Journal of Community Health* 23: 317–24.

Family Care International. 1999. "Safe Motherhood." http://www.safemotherhood.org/init_facts.htm.

————. 2007. "Safe Motherhood: A Review." http://www.familycareintl.org/UserFiles/File/SM%20A%20Review_%20Full_Report_FINAL.pdf

Feachem, Richard G. A. 2000. "Poverty and Inequality: A Proper Focus for the New Century." *The International Journal of Public Health* (Bulletin of the World Health Organization) 78: 1–2.

Garfinkel, P. E., and D. Goldbloom. 2000. "Mental Health—Getting

Beyond Stigma and Categories." *Bulletin of the World Health Organization* 78(4): 503–5.

Gergen, Kenneth J. 1994. *Realities and Relationships: Soundings in Social Construction*. Cambridge, MA: Harvard University Press.

"Global Summary of the HIV/AIDS Epidemic, 2007." http://www.unaids.org.

Goldstein, Michael S. 1999. "The Origins of the Health Movement." In Kathy Charmaz and Debora A. Paterniti (eds.), *Health, Illness, and Healing: Society, Social Context, and Self*, pp. 31–41. Los Angeles: Roxbury Publishing Co.

Gottlieb, Scott. 2000. "Oral AIDS Vaccine to Be Tested in the Republic of Uganda." *Bulletin of the World Health Organization* 78(7): 946–56.

Graham, Mel. 1999. "Budget 2000 and People with Disabilities." *Abilities: Canadian Lifestyle Magazine for People with Disabilities* 41 (Winter): 48.

Grann, Victor, et al. 2005. "Regional and Racial Disparities in Breast Cancer–Specific Mortality." *Social Science and Medicine* 62: 337–47.

Grant, Karen R. 1993. "Health and Health Care." In Peter S. Li and B. Singh Bolaria (eds.), *Contemporary Sociology: Critical Perspectives*, pp. 394–409. Toronto: Copp-Clark Pitman.

Gray, Gary. 2009. "The Responsibilization Strategy of Health and Safety." *British Journal of Criminology* 49: 326–42.

Groce, N. E., M. Chamie, and A. Me. 2000. "Measuring the Quality of Life: Rethinking the World Bank's Disability Adjusted Life Years." *Disability World* 3 (June-July). http://www.disabilityworld.org/June-July2000/International/DALY.html.

Health Canada. 1999a. *Toward a Healthy Future: Second Report on the Health of Canadians*. Prepared by the Federal, Provincial, and Territorial Advisory Committee on Population Health for the Meeting of Ministers of Health, Charlottetown, PEI, September.

————. 1999b. *Statistical Report on the Health of Canadians*. December 25.

http://www.hc-sc.gc.ca/hppb/phdd/report/state/eng/over.html.

————. 2002a. "HIV and AIDS among Women in Canada." *HIV/AIDS Epi Update*, April. http://www.hc-sc.gc.ca/pphb-dgspsp/publicat/epiu-aepi/hiv-vih/women_e.html.

————. 2002b. "A Report on Mental Illness in Canada." Catalogue no. 0-6623817-5.

————. 2004. "HIV and AIDS among Youth in Canada." *HIV/AIDS Epi Update*, May.

————. 2005a. *HIV/AIDS in Canada: Surveillance Report to December 31, 2004*. Ottawa: Public Health Agency of Canada.

————. 2005b. *HIV/AIDS Epi Updates*. Ottawa: Public Health Agency of Canada.

————. 2007. "HIV/AIDS Epi Updates." Ottawa: Public Health Agency of Canada.

Higgins, Michael. 2002. "Twelve in Manitoba Being Tested for West Nile." *National Post* (July 29): A1.

Inciardi, James A., and Lana D. Harrison. 1997. "HIV, AIDS, and Drug Abuse in the International Sector." *Journal of Drug Issues* 27: 1–8.

Joint United Nations Programme on HIV/AIDS. 2000a. "AIDS: Men Make a Difference: World AIDS Campaign." http://www.unaids.org.

————. 2000b. "HIV/AIDS and Development." http://www.unaids.org.

————. 2000c. "Innovative Approaches to HIV Prevention." http://www.unaids.org.

Joralemon, Donald, and Kim Fujinaga. 1996. "Studying Quality of Life after Organ Transplantation: Research Problems and Solutions." *Social Science and Medicine* 44(9): 1259–69.

Kennedy, Mark. 1999. "Doctors Warn Ottawa to Heed Physician Shortages Right Away." *National Post* (August 3): A6.

————. 2001. "Health Costs Rocket Past $100B." *National Post* (December 19): A1, A6.

Kerzner, Lana, and David Baker. 1999. *A Canadians with Disability Act?* May 14. http://www.hc-sc.gc.ca.

Kessler, Ronald C., Katherine A. McGonagle, Shanyang Zhao, Christopher B. Nelson, Michael Hughes, Suzann Eshleman, Hans-Ulrich Wittchen, and Kenneth D. Kendler. 1994. "Lifetime and 12-Month Prevalence of DSM-III-R Psychiatric Disorders in the United States." *Archives of General Psychiatry* 51: 8–19.

Kolata, Gina. "Panel Urges Mammograms at 50, Not 40." *New York Times*, Nov. 17, 2009.

Labonte, Ronald. 1992. "Heart Health Inequalities in Canada: Models, Theory and Planning." *Health Promotion International* 72(2): 119–28.

Lamptey, Peter. 2002. "Reducing Heterosexual Transmission of HIV in Poor Countries." *British Medical Journal* 342 (January): 207–11.

Lantz, Paula M., James S. House, James M. Lepkowski, David R. Williams, Richard P. Mero, and Jieming Chen. 1998. "Socioeconomic Factors, Health Behaviors, and Mortality: Results from a Nationally Representative Prospective Study of U.S. Adults." *Journal of the American Medical Association* 279: 1703–8.

LaPorte, Ronald E. 1997. "Improving Public Health via the Information Superhighway." June 8, 1998. http://www.the-scientist.library.upenn.edu/yr1997/august/opin_97018.html.

Lerer, Leonard B., Alan D. Lopez, Tord Kjellstrom, and Derek Yach. 1998. "Health for All: Analyzing Health Status and Determinants." *World Health Statistics Quarterly* 51: 7–20.

Markovic, Milica, Vesna Kesic, Lidija Topic, and Bojana Matejic. 2005. "Barriers to Cervical Cancer Screening: A Qualitative Study with Women in Serbia." *Social Science and Medicine* 61: 2528–35.

Marshall, Katherine. 2001. "Working with Computers." *Perspectives on Labour and Income* 13(2): 5–11.

Miller, K., and A. Rosenfield. 1996. "Population and Women's Reproductive Health: An International Perspective." *Annual Review of Public Health* 17: 359–82.

Milne, Celia. 2002. "Condition Critical." *Maclean's* (June 3): 40–41.

Mitchell, Alana. 1995. "Down's Transplant Bid Poses Dilemma." *The Globe and Mail* (April 28): A1, A10.

Moise, Minna. 1998. "The Killer Mosquitoes." *Utne Reader* (May-June): 14–15.

Murray, C., and A. Lopez (eds.). 1996. *The Global Burden of Disease*. Boston: Harvard University Press.

National AIDS Trust. 2005. *Fact Sheet 3: Global Impact*. London: National AIDS Trust.

National Council of Welfare. 2001. "Welfare Rates." http://www.ncwcnbes.net/htmdocument.htm.

Nelson, Heidi. 2009. "Screening for Breast Cancer: An Update for the U.S. Preventive Services Task Force." *Annals of Internal Medicine* 151(100): 727–37.

Ostrof, Paul. 1998. "Readers Write: My Chair." *The Sun* (August): 33–40.

Parsons, Talcott. 1951. *The Social System*. New York: The Free Press.

Pate, Russell R., Michael Pratt, Steven N. Blair, William L. Haskell, Caroline A. Macera, Claude Bouchard, David Buchner, Walter Ettiger, Gregory W. Health, Abby C. King, Andrea Kriska, Arthur L. Leon, Bess H. Marcus, Jeremy Morris, Ralph S. Paffenbarger, Kevin Patrick, Michael L. Pollock, James M. Rippe, James Sallis, and Jack H. Wilmore. 1995. "Physical Activity and Public Health: A Recommendation from the Centers for Disease Control and Prevention and the American College of Sports Medicine." *Journal of the American Medical Association* 273(5): 402–6.

Picard, André. 2009. "Base Breast-Screening on Reason, Not Passion." *The Globe and Mail*, Nov. 19, 2009.

"Poverty Threatens Crisis." 1998. *Popline* 20 (May-June): 3.

Reid, Robert. 1998. Canadian Cardiovascular Society 1998: Consensus Conference on the Prevention of Cardiovascular Diseases: The Role of the Cardiovascular Specialist.

Rice, Amy L., Lisa Sacco, Adnan Hyder, and Robert E. Black. 2000. "Malnutrition as an Underlying Cause of Childhood Deaths Associated with Infectious Diseases in Developing Countries." *Bulletin* of the World Health Organization 78(10): 1207–21.

Roterman, Michelle. 2005. "Sex, Condoms, and STDs among Young People." *Health Reports* 16: 39–42.

Royal Commission on Aboriginal Peoples. 1996. *Looking Forward, Looking Back: Report of the Royal Commission on Aboriginal Peoples*, Vol. 1. Ottawa: Supply and Services Canada.

Rustein, Shea O. 2000. "Factors Associated with Trends in Infant and Child Mortality in Developing Countries During the 1990s." *Bulletin of the World Health Organization* 78(10): 1256–70.

Safe Motherhood Initiative. 1998. "Fact and Figures." September 24. http://www.safemotherhood.org/init_facts.htm.

Save the Children Foundation. 2004. *State of the World's Mothers 2004: Children Having Children*. Washington, DC: Save the Children Foundation. Available at http://www.savethechildren.org/publications/.

Scott, K. 1997. "Indigenous Canadians." In D. McKenzie, R. William, and E. Single (eds.), *Canadian Profile, 1997: Alcohol, Tobacco and Other Drugs*. Ottawa: Canadian Centre on Substance Abuse.

Shkilnyk, Anastasia. 1985. *A Poison Stronger Than Love*. New Haven, CT: Yale University Press.

Simmie, Scott, and Julie Nunes. 2001. *The Last Taboo: A Survival Guide to Mental Health Care in Canada*. Toronto: McClelland & Stewart Inc.

Statistics Canada. 1998a. *Canada Yearbook 1999*. Ottawa: Ministry of Industry.

———. 1998b. *The Daily*, October 29. http://www.statcan.ca/Daily/English/981029/d981029.htm.

———. 1998c. "Health Reports: Multiple-Risk Behaviour in Teenagers and Young Adults 1994/95." *The Daily*, October 29. http://www.statcan.ca/english/ads/82-003-X1B/10-98.htm.

———. 2002. "Deaths, 1999." *The Daily*, May 7. http://www.statcan.ca/Daily/English/020507/d020507b.htm.

———. 2005. "Divorce and the Mental Health of Children." *The Daily*, December 13.

Stine, Gerald J. 1998. *Acquired Immune Deficiency Syndrome: Biological, Medical, Social, and Legal Issues*. Upper Saddle River, NJ: Prentice Hall.

Szasz, Thomas. [1961] 1970. *The Myth of Mental Illness: Foundations of a Theory of Personal Conduct*. New York: Harper and Row.

Thomas et al. 2002. "Randomized Trial of Breast Self-Examination in Shanghai: Final Results." *Journal of the National Cancer Institute* 94(19): 1445–1457.

UNICEF (United Nations International Children's Emergency Fund). 2003. *The State of the World's Children, 2003*. New York: UNICEF. http://www.unicef.org/sowc03/contents/pdf/SOWC03-eng.pdf

United Nations. 2008. "Report on the Global AIDS Epidemic, 2008." Joint United Nations Programme on HIV/AIDS (UNAIDS), 2008.

United Nations Population Fund. 2000. *The State of World Population Report 2000*. http://www.unfpa.org/SWP/2000/english/index.

U.S. Department of Health and Human Services. 1999. *Mental Health: A Report of the Surgeon General: Executive Summary*. Rockville, MD: U.S. Government Printing Office.

USPSTF. 2009. "Screening for Breast Cancer: U.S. Preventive Services Task Force Recommendation Statement." *Annals of Internal Medicine* 151(100): 716–26.

Verbrugge, Lois M. 1999. "Pathways of Health and Death." In Kathy Charmaz and Debora A. Paterniti (eds.), *Health, Illness, and Healing: Society, Social Context, and Self*, pp. 377–94. Los Angeles: Roxbury Publishing Co.

Visschedijk, Jan, and Silvere Simeant. 1998. "Targets for Health for All in the Twenty-First Century." *World Health Statistics Quarterly* 51: 56–67.

Ward, Darrell E. 1999. *The AmFAR AIDS Handbook*. New York: W. W. Norton & Company.

Weitz, Rose. 2001. *The Sociology of Health, Illness, and Health Care: A Critical Approach*, 2nd ed. Belmont, CA: Wadsworth Publishing Co.

Wente, Margaret. 2009. "Does Cancer Screening Do Harm?" *The Globe and Mail*, Nov. 17, 2009.

Wente, Margaret. 2010. "Prostate Cancer Dilemma." *The Globe and Mail*, Feb. 8, 2010.

Williams, David R., and Chiquita Collins. 1999. "U.S. Socioeconomic and Racial Differences in Health: Patterns, and Explanations." In Kathy Charmaz and Debora A. Paterniti (eds.), *Health, Illness, and Healing: Society, Social Context, and Self*, pp. 349–76. Los Angeles: Roxbury Publishing Co.

World Health Organization (WHO). 1946. "Constitution of the World Health Organization." New York: World Health Organization Interim Commission.

———. 1997. "Fact Sheet No. 178: Reducing Mortality from Major Childhood Killer Diseases." July 28, 1998. http://www.cdc.gov/ogh/frames.htm.

———. 1998. "Fifty Facts from the World Health Report 1998." August 8. http://www.who.int/whr/1998/factse/htm.

———. 2000. *The World Health Report 2000*. http://www.who.int.

———. 2001. *The World Health Report 2001*. http://www.who.int.

———. 2004. Summary of Probable SARS Cases with Onset of Illness from 1 November 2002 to 31 July 2003.

Chapter 3

Alcohol Alert. 2000. "Mechanisms of Addiction." *National Institute on Alcohol Abuse and Alcoholism* 46 (April): 2.

Aldridge, Judith. 2008. "Decline But No Fall? New Millennium Trends in Young People's Use of Illegal and Illicit Drugs in Britain." *Health Education* 108(3): 189–206.

AP (Associated Press). 1999. "Alcoholism Touches Millions." December 30. http://abcnews.go.com.

Auditor General (of Canada). 2001. *2001 Report of the Auditor General of Canada*. http://www.oag-bvg.gc.ca/domino/reports.nsf/html/0111xe06.html.

AAP (Australian Associated Press). 1998. "Genetics of Alcoholism." *Institute of Alcohol Studies Update.* London: IAS Publications.

Becker, H. S. 1966. *Outsiders: Studies in the Sociology of Deviance.* New York: Free Press.

Bibby, Reginald W. 2001. *Canada's Teens: Today, Yesterday, and Tomorrow.* Toronto: Stoddart.

Bureau of Justice Statistics. 1992. "Drugs, Crime, and the Justice System: A National Report from the Bureau of Justice Statistics." U.S. Department of Justice, Office of Justice Programs. Washington, DC: U.S. Government Printing Office, Superintendent of Documents.

CCSA (Canadian Centre on Substance Abuse). 1999. *Canadian Profile, 1999: Alcohol, Tobacco, and Other Drugs.* Ottawa: Canadian Centre on Substance Abuse and Centre for Addiction and Mental Health.

————. 2007. "Substance Abuse in Canada: Youth in Focus." http://www.ccsa.ca/Eng/KnowledgeCentre/OurPublications/Pages/SubstanceAbuseinCanada.aspx.

————. 2009. "Clearing the Smoke on Cannabis: Cannabis Use and Driving." CCSA: Ottawa. http://www.ccsa.ca/2009 CCSA Documents/ccsa-11789-2009.pdf.

Canadian Press Service. 2005. "Officials Say Safe Injection Site a Success." CTV.ca "Health." December 30, 2005. http://www.ctv.ca/servlet/ArticleNews/story/CTVNews/1126834518603_80/?hub=Health.

City of Vancouver. 2003. "Supervised Injection Sites: Frequently Asked Questions." Pamphlet. Vancouver: City of Vancouver.

Cloud, John. 2000. "The Lure of Ecstasy." *Time* (June 5): 63–72.

Cooper, M., R. Corrado, A. M. Karlberg, and L. P. Adams. 1992. "Aboriginal Suicide in British Columbia: An Overview." *Canada's Mental Health* (September): 19–23.

DEA (Drug Enforcement Administration). 2000. "An Overview of Club Drugs." *Drug Intelligence Brief*, February. 1–10.

Washington, DC: U.S. Department of Justice.

Dembo, Richard, Linda Williams, Jeffrey Fagan, and James Schmeidler. 1994. "Development and Assessment of a Classification of High Risk Youths." *Journal of Drug Issues* 24: 25–53.

Department of Finance Canada. 2002. "Government Announces Tobacco Tax Increases to Discourage Smoking." June 17. http://www.fin.gc.ca/news/02/02-052e.html.

Duke, Steven, and Albert C. Gross. 1994. *America's Longest War: Rethinking Our Tragic Crusade against Drugs.* New York: G. P. Putnam and Sons.

Duster, Troy. 1995. "The New Crisis of Legitimacy in Controls, Prisons, and Legal Structures." *American Sociologist* 26: 20–29.

Easley, Margaret, and Norman Epstein. 1991. "Coping with Stress in a Family with an Alcoholic Parent." *Family Relations* 40: 218–24.

Economist. 2003. "The Americas: Needling the Neighbours; Canadian Drug Policy." (September 20): 68.

Feagin, Joe R., and C. B. Feagin. 1994. *Social Problems.* Englewood Cliffs, NJ: Prentice-Hall.

Fife, R. 1999. "Police Chiefs Get through to the Top." *National Post*, April 22.

Gans, Herbert J. 1971. "The Uses of Poverty: The Poor Pay All." *Social Policy* July/August: 20–24.

Gentry, Cynthia. 1995. "Crime Control through Drug Control." In Joseph F. Sheley (ed.), *Criminology*, 2nd ed., pp. 477–93. Belmont, CA: Wadsworth.

Gfellner, B. M., and J. D. Hundelby. 1995. "Patterns of Drug Use among Native and White Adolescents: 1990–1993." *Canadian Journal of Public Health* 86: 95–97.

Giffen, P. J., S. Endicott, and S. Lambert. 1991. *Panic and Indifference: The Politics of Canada's Drug Laws.* Ottawa: Canadian Centre on Substance Abuse.

Green, Melvyn. 1986. "The History of Canadian Narcotics Control: The Formative Years." In Neil Boyd (ed.), *The Social Dimensions of Law*, pp. 24–40. Scarborough, ON: Prentice Hall.

Gusfield, Joseph. 1963. *Contested Meanings: The Construction of Alcohol Problems.* Madison: University of Wisconsin Press.

Hackler, James C. 2000. *Canadian Criminology: Strategies and Perspectives*, 2nd ed. Scarborough, ON: Prentice Hall Allyn and Bacon Canada.

Health Canada. 1999. *Statistical Report on the Health of Canadians.* December 25. http://www.hc-sc.gc.ca/hppb/phdd/report/stat/eng/over.html.

————. 2001. "Research Results for First Half of 2001—February to June 2001." http://www.hc-sc.gc.ca/hl-vs/tobac-tabac/research-recherche/stat/ctums-esutc/2001/rfh-rppma-2001_e.html.

————. 2002. *The Scoop on Smoking—Health Canada for Youth.* http://www.hc-sc.gc.ca/hecs-sesc/tobacco/youth/scoop.html.

————. 2005. *HIV and AIDS in Canada: Surveillance Report to December 31, 2004.* Ottawa: Public Health Agency of Canada.

HHS (U.S. Department of Health and Human Services). 1998. "Tobacco Use Continues to Rise among High School Students in the U.S." *Substance Abuse and Mental Health Service Administration.* Press release, April 2. Washington, DC.

Janhevich, Derey, et al. 2004. "Impaired Driving and Other Traffic Offenses, 2002." *Juristat* 23(9).

Jarvik, M. 1990. "The Drug Dilemma: Manipulating the Demand." *Science* 250: 387–92.

Järvinen, Margaretha. 2001. "Accounting for Trouble: Identity Negotiations in Qualitative Interviews with Alcoholics." *Symbolic Interaction* 24(3): 263–284.

Johnson, Holly. 1996. *Dangerous Domains: Violence against Women in Canada.* Scarborough, ON: Nelson.

Join Together. 1998 (July 11). "Inhalant Abuse." *Hot Issues.* http://www.jointogether.org/sa/issues/hot_issues/inhalants/default.html.

Klutt, Edward C. 2000. "Pathology of Drug Abuse." http://www.medlib-utah.edu/WebPath.

Leinwand, Donna. 2000. "20% Say They Used Drugs with Their Mom or Dad..." *USA Today* (August 24): 1A.

Leonard, K. E., and H. T. Blane. 1992. "Alcohol and Marital Aggression in a National Sample of Young Men." *Journal of Interpersonal Violence* 7: 19–30.

Lipton, Douglas S. 1994. "The Correctional Opportunity: Pathways to Drug Treatment for Offenders." *Journal of Drug Issues* 24: 331–48.

Mayell, Hillary. 1999. "Tobacco on Course to Become World's Leading Cause of Death." *National Geographic News.* http://ngnews/news/1999/121499.

McCaffrey, Barry. 1998. "Remarks by Barry McCaffrey, Director, Office of National Drug Control Policy, to the United Nations General Assembly: Special Session on Drugs." Office of National Drug Control Policy. http://www.whitehousedrugpolicy.gov/news/speeches.

McLellan, Anne. 2002. "Medical Marijuana." *National Post* (August 29): A19.

Mercer, B., and M. Marshall. 2005. *The Magnitude of the Alcohol/Drug-Related Crash Problem in Canada Overview.* Oakville, ON: MADD (Mothers Against Drunk Driving).

Morgan, Patricia A. 1978. "The Legislation of Drug Law: Economic Crisis and Social Control." *Journal of Drug Issues* 8: 53–62.

Murphy, Judge Emily. 1922. *The Black Candle.* Toronto: Thomas Allen.

NIAAA (National Institute on Alcohol Abuse and Alcoholism). 2000. "Tenth Special Report on Alcohol and Health to the U.S. Congress." Washington, DC.

NIDA (National Institute on Drug Abuse). 1999. "Principles of Effective Treatment." NIDA. National Institute of Health. Publication No. 99-4180. Washington, DC.

———. 2000a. "Researcher Announces Latest Study on Drug Dependence and Abuse." News Releases. http://www.nida.nih.gov.

———. 2000b."Club Drugs." Community Alert Bulletin. http://www.nida.nih.gov/ClubAlert/Clubdrugalert.html.

ONDCP (Office of National Drug Control Policy). 2000. "The Link between Drugs and Crime." Chapter II. *The National Drug Control Strategy 2000 Annual Report.* http://whitehousedrugpolicy.gov.

Rehm, J. et. al. 2006. "The Costs of Substance Abuse in Canada 2002." Figure 2. Canadian Centre on Substance Abuse. www.ccsa.ca.

Rorabaugh, W. J. 1979. *The Alcoholic Republic: An American Tradition.* New York: Oxford University Press.

Rychtarik, Robert G., Gerald J. Connors, Kurt H. Dermen, and Paul Stasiewicz. 2000. "Alcoholics Anonymous and the Use of Medications to Prevent Relapse." *Journal of Studies on Alcohol* 61: 134–41.

Sheldon, Tony. 2000. "Cannabis Use among Dutch Youth." *British Medical Journal* 321: 655.

Silverstein, Martin. 2006. "Justice in Genderland: Through a Parole Looking Glass." *Symbolic Interaction* 29(3): 393–410.

Simoni-Wastila, Linda, et al. 2004. "Gender and Other Factors Associated with the Non-Medical Use of Abusable Prescription Drugs." *Substance Use and Misuse* 39(1): 1–23.

Solomon, Robert. 1999. "Alcohol and Drug Law." In Canadian Centre on Substance Abuse, *Canadian Profile, 1999: Alcohol, Tobacco and Other Drugs*, pp. 295–315. Ottawa: Canadian Centre on Substance Abuse and Centre for Addiction and Mental Health.

Statistics Canada. 2001. "Impact of Smoking on Life Expectancy and Disability." *The Daily*, June 22. http://www.statcan.ca/Daily/English/010622/d010622a.htm.

———. 2002a. "Control and Sale of Alcoholic Beverages." *The Daily*, July 12. http://www.statcan.ca/Daily/English/020712/d020712b.htm.

———. 2002b. "Crime Statistics, 2001." *The Daily*, July 17. http://www.statcan.ca/Daily/English/020717/d020717b.htm.

Sullivan, Thomas, and Kenrick S. Thompson. 1994. *Social Problems.* New York: Macmillan.

Thomson, Hilary. 2003. "Vancouver Ready for Safe Injection Sites, Say UBC Experts." *UBC Reports* 49(1).

Tubman, J. 1993. "Family Risk Factors, Parental Alcohol Use, and Problem Behaviors among School-Aged Children." *Family Relations* 42: 81–86.

United Nations. 2009. *World Drug Report.* United Nations Office on Drugs and Crime. http://www.unodc.org/unodc/en/data-and-analysis/WDR-2009.html.

Van Dyck, C., and R. Byck. 1982. "Cocaine." *Scientific American* 246: 128–41.

Van Kammen, Welmoet B., and Rolf Loeber. 1994. "Are Fluctuations in Delinquent Activities Related to the Onset and Offset in Juvenile Illegal Drug Use and Drug Dealing?" *Journal of Drug Issues* 24: 9–24.

VCH. 2010. "Supervised Injection: Legal Status." http://supervisedinjection.vch.ca/legal_status/.

White, Helene Raskin, and Erich W. Labouvie. 1994. "Generality versus Specificity of Problem Behavior: Psychological and Functional Differences." *Journal of Drug Issues* 24: 55–74.

Witters, Weldon, Peter Venturelli, and Glen Hanson. 1992. *Drugs and Society*, 3rd ed. Boston: Jones and Bartlett.

World Drug Report. 1997. "Report Highlights." United Nations International Drug Control Program. New York: United Nations.

Wysong, Earl, Richard Aniskiewicz, and David Wright. 1994. "Truth and Dare: Tracking Drug Education to Graduation and as Symbolic Politics." *Social Problems* 41: 448–68.

Zivi, Karen. 2000. "Who Is the Guilty Party? Rights, Motherhood, and the Problem of Prenatal Drug Exposure." *Law and Society Review* 34(1): 237–58.

Chapter 4

Anderson, Elijah. 1994. "The Code of the Streets: Sociology of Urban Violence." *Atlantic* 273(5): 80–91.

Ash, Russell. 2001. *The Top 10 of Everything: Canadian Edition 2002.*

Toronto: Dorling Kindersley Limited.

AuCoin, Kathy. 2005. "Children and Youth as Victims of Violent Crime." *Juristat* 25(1). Catalogue no. 85-002-XIE. Ottawa.

Becker, Howard S. 1963. *Outsiders: Studies in the Sociology of Deviance.* New York: Free Press.

Belknap, Joanne, and Kristi Holsinger. 2006. "The Gendered Nature of Risk Factors for Delinquency." *Feminist Criminology* 1(1): 48–71.

Besserer, Sandra. 2002. "Criminal Victimization: An International Perspective: Results of the 2000 International Crime Victimization Survey." Ottawa: Canadian Centre for Justice Statistics. 17 pages. Issued as *Juristat* 22(4). Catalogue no. 85-002-XPE.

Bibby, Reginald W. 1995. *The Bibby Report: Social Trends Canadian Style.* Toronto: Stoddart.

————. 2001. *Canada's Teens: Today, Yesterday, and Tomorrow.* Toronto: Stoddart.

Bourrie, Mark. 1999. "Compensating the Innocent." *Canadian Lawyer* (November/December): 29–32.

Brantingham, Paul J., Shihong Mu, and Arvind Verma. 1995. "Patterns in Canadian Crime." In Margaret A. Jackson and Curt T. Griffiths (eds.), *Canadian Criminology: Perspectives on Crime and Criminality,* 2nd ed., pp. 187–246. Toronto: Harcourt Brace and Company.

Bryant, Marian E. 1999. "Sentencing Aboriginal Offenders." *Law Now* (October/November): 20–21.

Business Network on Crime Prevention. 2001. "The Cost of Crime." http://www.crime-prevention.org/english/publications/economic/invest/cost_e.html.

Canadian Mental Health Association. 2003. "Women's Mental Health." *Special Populations.* January 14, 2006. http://www.ontario.cmha.ca/content/about_mental_illness/women.asp?cID=3974.

CATW (Coalition Against Trafficking in Women). 1997. "Promoting Sex Work in the Netherlands." *Coalition Report* 4(1). http://www.uri.edu/artsci/wms/hughes/catw.

Chesney-Lind, Meda. 2006. "Patriarchy, Crime, and Justice." *Feminist Criminology* 1(1): 6–26.

Chesney-Lind, Meda, and R. G. Sheldon. 1992. *Girls, Delinquency and Juvenile Justice.* Belmont, CA: Wadsworth.

Chwialkowska, Luiza. 2001. "Anti-Terrorism Bill Becomes Law." *National Post* (December 19): A6.

Conklin, John E. 1998. *Criminology,* 6th ed. Boston: Allyn and Bacon.

COPS. 1998. "About the Office of Community Oriented Policing Services (COPS)." http://communitypolicing.org/copspage.html.

Correctional Service Canada. 2005. "Basic Facts about the Correctional Service of Canada." Catalogue no. HS 82-17/2005 (p. 9).

Daly, K. 1992. "Women's Pathways to Felony Court." *Review of Law and Women's Studies* 2: 11–52.

D'Augelli, A. R., and L. J. Dark. 1994. "Lesbian, Gay, and Bisexual Youths." In L. D. Enron et al. (eds.), *Reason to Hope: A Psychological Perspective on Violence and Youth,* pp. 177–96. Washington, DC: American Psychological Association.

Demerson, Velma. 2004. *Incorrigible.* Waterloo, ON: Wilfrid Laurier University Press.

Department of Justice (Canada). 2002a. "Highlights of Anti-Terrorism Act." http://www.canada.justice.gc.ca/en/news/nr/2001/doc_27787.html.

————. 2002b. "Canada's Youth Criminal Justice Act: A New Law—A New Approach." http://www.canada.justice.gc.ca/en/dept/pub/ycja/youth_html.

————. 2002c. "Organized Crime Legislation Comes into Force." http://www.canada.justice.gc.ca/en/news/nr/2002/doc_29525.html.

————. 2005. "The National Strategy on Community Safety and Crime Prevention." Department of Justice.

Deveau, Scott. 2006. "Crime Bill Sets Mandatory Minimum Sentences." *The Globe and Mail Update,* national ed., May 4. http://www.theglobeandmail.com/servlet/story/RTGAM.20060504.wcrime0505/PPVStory/?DENIED=1.

DiIulio, John. 1999. "Federal Crime Policy: Time for a Moratorium," *Brookings Review* 17(1): 17.

Doyle, Roger. 2000. "The Roots of Homicide." *Scientific American* (October). http://www.sciam.com/2000.

Economist, The. 2000. "Dead Man Walking Out." (June 10): 21–23.

Erikson, Kai T. 1966. *Wayward Puritans.* New York: John Wiley and Sons.

Evans, John, and Alexander Himelfarb. 2000. "Counting Crime." In Rick Linden (ed.), *Criminology: A Canadian Perspective,* 4th ed., pp. 60–93. Toronto: Harcourt Brace and Company.

Faith, K. 1993. *Unruly Women: The Politics of Confinement and Resistance.* Vancouver: Press Gang.

Fattah, Ezzat A. 1991. *Understanding Criminal Victimization: An Introduction to Theoretical Victimology.* Scarborough, ON: Prentice Hall.

Fedorowycz, Orest. 1999. "Homicide in Canada, 1998." *Juristat* 19 (October). Catalogue no. 85-002-XIE.

Felson, Marcus. 1998. *Crime and Everyday Life,* 2nd ed. Thousand Oaks, CA: Pine Forge Press.

Felson, Marcus, and Rachel Boba. 2010. *Crime and Everyday Life.* Thousand Oaks, CA: Sage.

Gannon, Marie. 2001. "Crime Comparisons between Canada and the United States." *Juristat* 21 (December). Catalogue no. 85-002-XPE.

Garey, M. 1985. "The Cost of Taking a Life: Dollars and Sense of the Death Penalty." *U.C. Davis Law Review* 18: 1221–73.

Gest, Ted, and Dorian Friedman. 1994. "The New Crime Wave." *U.S. News and World Report* (August 29): 26–28.

Hackler, James C. 2005. *Canadian Criminology: Strategies and Perspectives,* 2nd ed. Scarborough, ON: Prentice Hall Allyn and Bacon Canada.

Hagan, John. 2000. "White-Collar and Corporate Crime." In Rick Linden (ed.), *Criminology: A Canadian Perspective,* 4th ed., pp. 459–82. Toronto: Harcourt Brace and Company.

Hartnagel, Timothy F. 2000. "Correlates of Criminal Behaviour."

In Rick Linden (ed.), *Criminology: A Canadian Perspective*, 4th ed., pp. 94–136. Toronto: Harcourt Brace and Company.

Hirschi, Travis. 1969. *Causes of Delinquency*. Berkeley: University of California Press.

Hochstetler, Andrew, and Neal Shover. 1997. "Street Crime, Labor Surplus, and Criminal Punishment, 1980–1990." *Social Problems* 44(3): 358–67.

Hogeveen, Brian R. 2005. "If We Are Tough on Crime, If We Punish Crime, Then People Get the Message." *Punishment and Society* 7(1): 73–89.

Human Rights Watch. 2000. *Human Rights Watch World Report 2000. United States*. http://www.hrw.org/wr2k/us.html.

Jacobs, David. 1988. "Corporate Economic Power and the State: A Longitudinal Assessment of Two Explanations." *American Journal of Sociology* 93: 852–81.

Janoff-Bulman, Ronnie, C. Timko, and L. Carli. 1985. "Cognitive Biases in Blaming the Victim." *Journal of Experimental Social Psychology* 23: 161–77.

John Howard Society. 1999. *Check & Balance: The Facts about Facts*. Toronto: The John Howard Society of Ontario.

Koenig, Daniel J. 2000. "Conventional or 'Street' Crime." In Rick Linden (ed.), *Criminology: A Canadian Perspective*, 4th ed., pp. 396–429. Toronto: Harcourt Brace and Company.

Kong, Deborah, and Jon Swartz. 2000. "Experts See Rash of Hack Attacks Coming..." *USA Today* (September 27): 1B.

Kong, Rebecca. 1999. "Canadian Crime Statistics, 1997." In Canadian Centre for Justice Statistics, *The Juristat Reader: A Statistical Overview of the Canadian Justice System*, pp. 117–37. Toronto: Thompson Educational Publishing, Inc.

Kong, Rebecca, and Kathy AuCoin. 2008. "Female Offenders in Canada." *Juristat* 28(1). Catalogue no. 85-002-XIE.

Laub, John, Daniel S. Nagan, and Robert Sampson. 1998.

"Trajectories of Change in Criminal Offending: Good Marriages and the Desistance Process." *American Sociological Review* 63 (April): 225–38.

Lehrur, Eli. 1999. "Communities and Cops Join Forces." *Insight on the News* 15 (January 25): 16.

Li, Geoffrey. 2007. "Homicide in Canada: 2006." *Juristat*. Catalogue no. 85-002-XPE, Ottawa.

Liebman, James S., Jeffery Fagan, and Valerie West. 2000. "A Broken System: Error Rates in Capital Cases, 1973–1995." http://justice.policy.net/jpreport.

Lipsey, M. W. and D. B. Wilson. 1998. "Effective Intervention for Serious Juvenile Offenders: A Synthesis of Research." In R. Loeber and David Farrington (eds.), *Serious and Violent Offenders*. Thousand Oaks, CA: Sage Publications.

Logan, Ron. 2001. "Crime Statistics in Canada, 2000." *Juristat* 21 (July). Catalogue no. 85-002-XPE.

Lonmo, Charlene. 2001. "Adult Correctional Services in Canada, 1999–2000." *Juristat* 21 (July). Catalogue no. 85-002-XPE.

MacIntyre, John. 1999. "...and Counting." *Canadian Lawyer* (November/December): 6.

Madriz, Esther. 2000. "Nothing Bad Happens to Good Girls." In Frances Moulder (ed.), *Social Problems of the Modern World*, pp. 293–97. Belmont, CA: Wadsworth.

Manzo, John F., and Monetta M. Bailey. 2005. "On the Assimilation of Racial Stereotypes and Black Canadian Young Offenders." *Canadian Review of Sociology and Anthropology* 42(3): 283–300.

Merton, Robert. 1957. "Social Structure and Anomie." In *Social Theory and Social Structure*. Glencoe, IL: Free Press.

Moore, Elizabeth, and Michael Mills. 1990. "The Neglected Victims and Unexamined Costs of White Collar Crime." *Crime and Delinquency* 36: 408–18.

Murray, Mary E., Nancy Guerra, and Kirk Williams. 1997. "Violence Prevention for the Twenty-First Century." In Roger P. Weissberg, Thomas Gullota, Robert L. Hampton, Bruce Ryan, and Gerald

Adams (eds.), *Enhancing Children's Awareness*, pp. 105–28. Thousand Oaks, CA: Sage Publications.

National Research Council. 1994. *Violence in Urban America: Mobilizing a Response*. Washington, DC: National Academy Press.

Olmsted, A. D. 1988. "Morally Controversial Leisure." *Symbolic Interaction* 11: 277–87.

Paterson, Stephanie. 2010. "'Resistors,' 'Helpless Victims,' and 'Willing Participants': The Construction of Women's Resistance in Canadian Anti-Violence Policy." *Social Policy* 17(2): 159–184.

Pertossi, Mayra. 2000. "ANALYSIS—Argentine Crime Rate Soars." September 27. http://news.excite.com.

Public Safety Canada. 2010. "Corrections and Conditional Release in Canada: A General Primer 2010." Catalogue no. PS4-64/2010E-PDF. http://www.publicsafety.gc.ca/res/cor/rep/2010-03-nt-bkgr-eng.aspx.

Roberts, Julian, and Thomas Gabor. 1990. "Race and Crime: A Critique." *Canadian Journal of Criminology* 92 (April): 291–313.

Sanday, P. R. 1981. "The Sociocultural Context of Rape: A Cross-Cultural Study." *Journal of Social Issues* 37: 5–27.

Seagrave, J. 1997. *Introduction to Policing in Canada*. Scarborough, ON: Prentice Hall.

Sherrill, Robert. 2000. "A Year in Corporate Crime." In Frances Moulder (ed.), *Social Problems in the Modern World*, pp. 302–8. Belmont, CA: Wadsworth.

Siegel, Larry. 2000. *Criminology*. Belmont, CA: Wadsworth.

Snider, Laureen. 2000. "The Sociology of Corporate Crime: An Obituary (Or: Whose Knowledge Claims Have Legs?)." *Theoretical Criminology* 4(2): 169–206.

Solicitor General. 1999. "Organized Crime." http://www.sgc.gc.ca/EFact/eorgcrime.htm.

———. 2002. "Factsheets." http://www.sgc.ca/Efact/emyths.htm.

Stamler, Rodney T. 2000. "Organized Crime." In Rick Linden (ed.), *Criminology: A Canadian Perspective,*

4th ed., pp. 429–58. Toronto: Harcourt Brace and Company.

Statistics Canada. 1998. *Canada Yearbook 2000.* Ottawa: Ministry of Industry.

————. 2002. "Crime Statistics, 2001." *The Daily,* July 17. http://www.statcan.ca/Daily/English/020717/d020717b.htm.

————. 2009. "Measuring Crime in Canada: Introducing the Crime Severity Index and Improvements to the Uniform Crime Reporting Survey." Canadian Centre for Justice Statistics.

Steffensmeier, Darrell, and Emilie Allan. 1995. "Criminal Behavior: Gender and Age." In Joseph F. Sheley (ed.), *Criminology: A Contemporary Handbook,* 2nd ed., pp. 83–113. Belmont, CA: Wadsworth.

Sutherland, Edwin H. 1939. *Criminology.* Philadelphia: Lippincott.

Swartz, Joel. 1978. "Silent Killers at Work." In M. David Ermann and Richard Lundman (eds.), *Corporate and Governmental Deviance,* pp. 114–28. New York: Oxford University Press.

The Sentencing Project. 2005. *New Incarceration Figures: Growth Continues.* Washington, DC: The Sentencing Project.

Thomas, Jennifer. 2008. "Youth Court Statistics, 2003/04." *Juristat* 25(4). Catalogue no. 85-002-XPE.

Thomas, Mikhail. 2004. "Adult Criminal Court Statistics 2003/04." *Juristat* 24(12). Catalogue no. 85-002-XPE.

Tufts, Jennifer. 2000. "Public Attitudes toward the Criminal Justice System." *Juristat* 20(12). Catalogue no. 85-002-XPE.

Wallace, Marnie. 2004. "Crime Statistics in Canada." *Juristat* 24(6). Catalogue no. 85-002-IXE.

————. 2009. "Police-Reported Crime Statistics in Canada, 2008." *Juristat* 29(3). Catalogue no. 85-002-X.

Warner, Barbara, and Pamela Wilcox Rountree. 1997. "Local Social Ties in a Community and Crime Model." *Social Problems* 4(4): 520–36.

White, Michael. 1999. "GM Ordered to Pay Accident Victims $49 B." *National Post* (July 10): A1.

Williams, Linda. 1984. "The Classic Rape: When Do Victims Report?" *Social Problems* 31: 459–67.

Worden, Amy. 2000. "More Whites Than Blacks Evade Death Penalty." http://www.apbnews.com/newscenter/breakingnews/2000/07/24deathpleas0/24_01.html.

Chapter 5

Amato, Paul R. 2001. "The Consequences of Divorce for Adults and Children." In Robert M. Milardo (ed.), *Understanding Families into the New Millennium: A Decade in Review,* pp. 488–506. Minneapolis: National Council on Family Relations.

Ambert, Anne-Marie. 1998. "Divorce: Facts, Figures and Consequences." Vanier Institute of the Family. http://www.vifamily.ca/cft/divorce/divorce.htm.

Anderson, Kristin L. 1997. "Gender, Status, and Domestic Violence: An Integration of Feminist and Family Violence Approaches." *Journal of Marriage and the Family* 59: 655–59.

Arnold, Tom. 2002. "Common-law Families on the Rise." *National Post* (October 23): A9.

AuCoin, Kathy. 2005. "Talking— Criminal Harassment." *Family Violence in Canada: A Statistical Profile 2005.* Statistics Canada. Catalogue no. 85-224-XIE: 33–37.

Beattie, Karen. 2005. *Spousal Homicides.* Ottawa: Statistics Canada, Canadian Centre for Justice Statistics.

Beitchman, J. H., K. J. Zuker, J. E. Hood, G. A. daCosta, D. Akman, and E. Cassavia. 1992. "A Review of the Long-Term Effects of Child Sexual Abuse." *Child Abuse and Neglect* 16: 101–19.

Bibby, Reginald W. 2001. *Canada's Teens: Today, Yesterday, and Tomorrow.* Toronto: Stoddart.

Browning, Christopher R., and Edward O. Laumann. 1997. "Sexual Contact between Children and Adults: A Life Course Perspective." *American Sociological Review* 62: 540–60.

Bunge, Valerie Pottie. 2000. "Spousal Violence." In Statistics Canada, *Family Violence in Canada: A Statistical Profile 2000,* pp. 11–21. Catalogue no. 85-224-XIE. Ottawa: Minister of Industry.

Butler, Judith. 2004. *Undoing Gender.* London and New York: Routledge.

Coontz, Stephanie. 2000. "Marriage: Then and Now." *Phi Kappa Phi Journal* 80: 10–15.

Crawford, Trish. 1997. "Sexual Health Programs Are at Risk." *Toronto Star* (August 23): M1.

Crompton, Susan. 2005. "Always a Bridesmaid." *Canadian Social Trends* 77 (Summer): 2–8.

Dauvergne, Mia. 2005a. "Spousal Homicide Rate in Canada, 2004." *Juristat* 25(6). Catalogue no. 85-002-XPE.

————. 2005b. "Homicide in Canada, 2004." *Juristat* 26(6). Catalogue no. 85-002-XPE.

Demo, David H. 1992. "Parent-Child Relations: Assessing Recent Changes." *Journal of Marriage and the Family* 54: 104–17.

————, Mark A. Fine, and Lawrence H. Ganong. 2000. "Divorce as a Family Stressor." In P. C. McKenry and S. J. Price (eds.), *Families & Change: Coping with Stressful Events and Transitions,* 2nd ed., pp. 279–302. Thousand Oaks, CA: Sage Publications.

DiLillo, D., G. C. Tremblay, and L. Peterson. 2000. "Linking Childhood Sexual Abuse and Abusive Parenting: The Mediating Role of Maternal Anger." *Child Abuse and Neglect* 24: 767–79.

"Domestic Violence and Homelessness." 1998. *NCH Fact Sheet No. 8.* National Coalition for the Homeless.

Dranoff, Linda Silver. 2001. *Everyone's Guide to the Law.* Toronto: HarperCollins Publishers Ltd.

Drummond, Tammerlin. 2000. "Mom on Her Own." *Time* (August 28): 54–55.

Edgerton, Robert B. 1992. *Sick Societies: Challenging the Myth of Primitive Harmony.* New York: The Free Press.

Edin, Kathryn. 2000. "What Do Low-Income Single Mothers Say about Marriage?" *Social Problems* 47(1): 112–33.

Edwards, Tamala M. 2000. "Flying Solo." *Time* (August 28): 49–53.

EGALE. 2005. "We Won!" *Info-Egale* 2(5).

Elliott, D. M., and J. Briere. 1992. "The Sexually Abused Boy: Problems in Manhood." *Medical Aspects of Human Sexuality* 26: 68–71.

Eltahawy, Mona. 2000. "Giving Wives a Way Out." *U.S. News & World Report* 128 (March 6): 35.

Emery, Robert E. 1999. "Postdivorce Family Life for Children: An Overview of Research and Some Implications for Policy." In R. A. Thompson and P. R. Amato (eds.), *The Postdivorce Family: Children, Parenting, and Society*, pp. 3–27. Thousand Oaks, CA: Sage Publications.

Family Court Reform Council of America. 2000. "Parental Alienation Syndrome." 31441 Santa Margarita Parkway, Suite A184. Rancho Santa Margarita, CA 92688.

Fathalla, Mahmoud F. 2005. "Comment: When Home Is No Longer Safe: Intimate-Partner Violence." *Lancet* 366: 1909–10.

Gardner, Richard A. 1998. *The Parental Alienation Syndrome*, 2nd ed. Cresskill, NJ: Creative Therapeutics, Inc.

Gearing, Robin, Niloo Zand, and Geordie Colvin. 2001. "Engaging Fathers: A Point of Entry in Promoting a Culture of Peace." *Journal of the Association for Research on Mothering* 3(2): 57–73.

Gelles, Richard J. 1993. "Family Violence." In Robert L. Hampton, Thomas P. Gullotta, Gerald R. Adams, Earl H. Potter III, and Roger P. Weissberg (eds.), *Family Violence: Prevention and Treatment*, pp. 1–24. Newbury Park, CA: Sage Publications.

————. 2000. "Violence, Abuse, and Neglect in Families." In P. C. McKenry and S. J. Price (eds.), *Families & Change: Coping with Stressful Events and Transitions*, 2nd ed., pp. 183–207. Thousand Oaks, CA: Sage Publications.

Gelles, Richard J., and Jon R. Conte. 1991. "Domestic Violence and Sexual Abuse of Children: A Review of Research in the Eighties." In Alan Booth (ed.), *Contemporary Families:*

Looking Forward, Looking Back, pp. 327–40. Minneapolis: National Council on Family Relations.

Geronimus, Arline. 1997. "Teenage Childbearing and Personal Responsibility: An Alternative View." *Political Science Quarterly* 112(3): 405–30.

————. 2003. "Damned If You Do: Culture, Identity, Privilege, and Childbearing in the United States." *Social Science and Medicine* 57: 881–93.

Global Study of Family Values. 1998. The Gallup Organization. April 13. http://198.175.140.8/Special_ Reports/family.htm.

Halpern, Carolyn Tucker, et al. 2004. "Prevalence of Partner Violence in Same-Sex Romantic and Sexual Relationships in a National Sample of Adolescents." *Journal of Adolescent Health* 35: 124–31.

Harrington, Donna, and Howard Dubowitz. 1993. "What Can Be Done to Prevent Child Maltreatment?" In Robert L. Hampton, Thomas P. Gullotta, Gerald R. Adams, Earl H. Potter III, and Roger P. Weissberg (eds.), *Family Violence: Prevention and Treatment*, pp. 258–80. Newbury Park, CA: Sage Publications.

Health Canada. 1999. *Statistical Report on the Health of Canadians*. December 25. http://www.hc-sc. gc.ca/hppb/phdd/report/ state/eng/ over.html.

Henry, Ronald K. 1999. "Child Support at a Crossroads: When the Real World Intrudes upon Academics and Advocates." *Family Law Quarterly* 33 (Spring): 235–64.

Hewlett, Sylvia Ann, and Cornel West. 1998. *The War against Parents: What We Can Do for Beleaguered Moms and Dads*. Boston: Houghton Mifflin Company.

Hochschild, Arlie Russell. 1989. *The Second Shift: Working Parents and the Revolution at Home*. New York: Viking/Penguin.

Hogan, D. P., R. Sun, and G. T. Cornwell. 2000. "Sexual and Fertility Behaviors of American Females Aged 15–19 Years: 1985, 1990, and 1995. *American Journal of Public Health* 90: 1421–25.

Jacobs, C. D., and E. M. Wolf. 1995. "School Sexuality Education and Adolescent Risk-Taking Behavior." *Journal of School Health* 65: 91–5.

Jasinski, J. L., L. M. Williams, and J. Siegel. 2000. "Childhood Physical and Sexual Abuse as Risk Factors for Heavy Drinking among African-American Women: A Prospective Study." *Child Abuse and Neglect* 24: 1061–71.

Jekielek, Susan M. 1998. "Parental Conflict, Marital Disruption and Children's Emotional Well-Being." *Social Forces* 76: 905–35.

Johnson, Holly, and Tina Hotton. 2001. "Spousal Violence." In Statistics Canada, *Family Violence in Canada: A Statistical Profile 2001*, pp. 26–41. July. Catalogue no. 85-224-XIE. Ottawa: Minister of Industry.

Johnson, Michael P., and Kathleen Ferraro. 2001. "Research on Domestic Violence in the 1990s: Making Distinctions." In Robert M. Milardo (ed.), *Understanding Families Into the New Millennium: A Decade in Review*, pp. 167–182. Minneapolis: National Council on Family Relations.

Jorgensen, Stephen R. 2000. "Adolescent Pregnancy Prevention: Prospects for 2000 and Beyond." Presidential Address at the National Council on Family Relations 62nd Annual Conference, November 11. Minneapolis, MN.

Kaufman, Joan, and Edward Zigler. 1992. "The Prevention of Child Maltreatment: Programming, Research, and Policy." In Diane J. Willis, E. Wayne Holden, and Mindy Rosenberg (eds.), *Prevention of Child Maltreatment: Developmental and Ecological Perspectives*, pp. 269–95. New York: John Wiley & Sons.

Kephart, William. 1963. "Experimental Family Organization: An Historico-Cultural Report on the Oneida Community." *Marriage and Family Living* 25(3): 261–71.

Knox, David (with Kermit Leggett). 1998. *The Divorced Dad's Survival Book: How to Stay Connected with Your Kids*. New York: Insight Books.

Kong, R. 1997. "Criminal Harassment in Canada." *Canadian Social Trends* 45 (Autumn): 29–33.

Krug, Ronald S. 1989. "Adult Male Report of Childhood Sexual Abuse by Mothers: Case Description, Motivations, and Long-Term Consequences." *Child Abuse and Neglect* 13: 111–19.

Lanz, Jean B. 1995. "Psychological, Behavioral, and Social Characteristics Associated with Early Forced Sexual Intercourse among Pregnant Adolescents." *Journal of Interpersonal Violence* 10: 188–200.

Le Bourdais, Celine, Neill Ghislaine, and Pierre Turcotte. 2001. "The Changing Face of Conjugal Relationships." *Canadian School Trends* (Spring). 14–17.

Leite, Randy W., and Patrick C. McKenry. 2000. "Aspects of Father Status and Post-Divorce Father Involvement with Children." Poster session at the National Council on Family Relations 62nd Annual Conference, November 10–13. Minneapolis, MN.

Lewin, Tamar. 2000. "Fears for Children's Well-Being Complicates a Debate over Marriage." *The New York Times on the Web*, November 4. http://www.nytimes.com/2000/11/04/arts/04MARR.html.

Lloyd, Sally A. 2000. "Intimate Violence: Paradoxes of Romance, Conflict, and Control." *National Forum* 80(4): 19–22.

Lloyd, S. A., and B. C. Emery. 1993. "Abuse in the Family: An Ecological, Life-Cycle Perspective." In T. H. Brubaker (ed.), *Family Relations: Challenges for the Future*, pp. 129–52. Newbury Park, CA: Sage Publications.

———. 2000. *The Dark Side of Courtship: Physical and Sexual Aggression*. Thousand Oaks, CA: Sage Publications.

Locke, Daisy, Sara Beattie, and Sean Miller. 2001. "Homicide of Children and Youth." In Statistics Canada, *Family Violence in Canada: A Statistical Profile 2001*, pp. 15–18. July. Catalogue no. 85-224-XIE. Ottawa: Minister of Industry.

Luxton, Meg. 1996. "Conceptualizing 'Families': Theoretical Frameworks and Family Research." In Maureen Baker (ed.), *Families: Changing Trends in Canada*, 3rd ed. Toronto: McGraw-Hill Ryerson.

Mahapatra, Dhananjay. 2008 (Feb.). "Customary Payments, Gifts Not Dowry: SC." *The Times of India*. http:timesofindia.indiatimes.com.

Marlow, L., and S. R. Sauber. 1990. *The Handbook of Divorce Mediation*. New York: Plenum.

Milan, Ann, Mireille Vézina, and Carrie Wells. 2007. "Family Portrait: Continuity and Change in Canadian Families and Households in 2006: 2006 Census." Statistics Canada. Catalogue no. 97-553-X.

Monson, C. M., G. R. Byrd, and J. Langhinrichsen-Rohling. 1996. "To Have and to Hold: Perceptions of Marital Rape." *Journal of Interpersonal Violence* 11: 410–24.

Morrison, N. 1987. "Separation and Divorce." In M. J. Dymond (ed.), *The Canadian Woman's Legal Guide*, pp. 125–43. Toronto: Doubleday.

Morton, M. 1990. "Controversies within Family Law." In M. Baker (ed.), *Families: Changing Trends in Canada*, pp. 211–40. Toronto: McGraw-Hill Ryerson.

National Center for Injury Prevention and Control. 2000. "Intimate Partner Violence Fact Sheet." Atlanta, GA: National Center for Injury Prevention and Control.

National Coalition for the Homeless. 1999. NCH Fact Sheet #1. "Why Are People Homeless?" http://www.nationalhomeless.org/causes.html.

National Council of Welfare. 1999. *Children First: A Pre-Budget Report by the National Council of Welfare*. Autumn. http://www.ncwcnbes.net.htmdocument/reportchildfirst.htm.

Nelson, B. S., and K. S. Wampler. 2000. "Systemic Effects of Trauma in Clinic Couples: An Exploratory Study of Secondary Trauma Resulting from Childhood Abuse." *Journal of Marriage and Family Counseling* 26: 171–84.

Nielsen, L. 1999. "College Aged Students with Divorced Parents: Facts and Fiction." *College Student Journal* 33: 543–72.

Nock, Steven L. 1995. "Commitment and Dependency in Marriage." *Journal of Marriage and the Family* 57: 503–14.

Novac, S., J. Brown, and C. Bourbonnais. 1996. *No Room of Her Own: A Literature Review on Women and Homelessness*. Canadian Mortgage and Housing Corporation. May 1, 2000. http://www.cmhc-schl.gc.ca/cmhc.html.

Ogrodnick, Lucie. 2007. "Family Violence in Canada: A Statistical Profile: 2007." Statistics Canada. Catalogue no. 85-224-XIE.

Parker, Marcie, R. Edward Bergmark, Mark Attridge, and Jude Miller-Burke. 2000. "Domestic Violence and Its Effect on Children." *National Council on Family Relations Report* 45(4): F6–F7.

Pasley, Kay, and Carmelle Minton. 2001. "Generative Fathering after Divorce and Remarriage: Beyond the 'Disappearing Dad.'" In T. F. Cohen (ed.), *Men and Masculinity: A Text Reader*, pp. 239–48. Belmont, CA: Wadsworth.

Peterson, Richard R. 1996. "A Re-evaluation of the Economic Consequences of Divorce." *American Sociological Review* 61: 528–36.

Popenoe, David. 1993. "Point of View: Scholars Should Worry about the Disintegration of the American Family." *Chronicle of Higher Education* (April 14): A48.

Resnick, Michael, Peter S. Bearman, Robert W. Blum, Karl E. Bauman, Kathleen M. Harris, Jo Jones, Joyce Tabor, Trish Beubring, Renee E. Sieving, Marcia Shew, Marjore Ireland, Linda H. Berringer, and J. Richard Udry. 1997. "Protecting Adolescents from Harm." *Journal of the American Medical Association* 278 (September 10): 823–32.

Reidmann, Agnes, Mary Ann Lamanna, and Adie Nelson. 2003. *Marriages and Families: Making Choices in a Diverse Society*, 1st Canadian ed. Toronto: Thomson Nelson.

Russell, D. E. 1990. *Rape in Marriage*. Bloomington: Indiana University Press.

Schacht, Thomas E. 2000. "Protection Strategies to Protect Professionals and Families Involved in High-Conflict Divorce." *UALR Law Review* 22(3): 565–92.

Scott, K. L., and D. A. Wolfe. 2000. "Change among Batterers: Examining Men's Success Stories." *Journal of Interpersonal Violence* 15: 827–42.

Shapiro, Joseph P., and Joannie M. Schrof. 1995. "Honor Thy Children." *U.S. News and World Report* (February 27): 39–49.

Singh, Susheela, and Jacqueline E. Darroch. 2000. "Adolescent Pregnancy and Childbearing: Levels and Trends in Developed Countries." *Family Planning Perspectives* 32(1): 14–23.

Spiegel, D. 2000. "Suffer the Children: Long-Term Effects of Sexual Abuse." *Society* 37: 18–20.

Statistics Canada. 2000. "Women in Canada 2000." *The Daily*, September 14. http://www.statcan.ca/Daily/English/000914/d000914c.htm.

—————. 2001. *Family Violence in Canada: A Statistical Profile 2001.* Catalogue no. 85-224-XIE. Ottawa: Ministry of Industry.

—————. 2004. "Divorces." *The Daily,* May 4.

—————. 2005a. "Family Violence in Canada: A Statistical Profile." *The Daily,* July 14.

—————. 2005b. "Divorces." *The Daily,* March 9.

Stock, J. L., M. A. Bell, D. K. Boyer, and F. A. Connell. 1997. "Adolescent Pregnancy and Sexual Risk-Taking among Sexually Abused Girls." *Family Planning Perspectives* 29: 200–203.

Straus, Murray. 2000. "Corporal Punishment and Primary Prevention of Physical Abuse." *Child Abuse and Neglect* 24: 1109–14.

Thakkar, R. R., P. M. Gutierrez, C. L. Kuczen, and T. R. McCanne. 2000. "History of Physical and/or Sexual Abuse, and Current Suicidality in College Women." *Child Abuse and Neglect* 24: 1345–54.

Thompson, Ross A., and Paul R. Amato. 1999. "The Postdivorce Family: An Introduction to the Issues." In R. A. Thompson and P. R. Amato (eds.), *The Postdivorce Family: Children, Parenting, and Society*, pp. xi–xxiii. Thousand Oaks, CA: Sage Publications.

Thompson, Ross A., Paul R. Amato, and Jennifer M. Wyatt. 1999.

"Values, Policy, and Research on Divorce." In R. A. Thompson and P. R. Amato (eds.), *The Postdivorce Family: Children, Parenting, and Society*, pp. 191–232. Thousand Oaks, CA: Sage Publications.

Trocmé, Nico, and David Wolfe. 2001. "The Canadian Incidence Study of Reported Child Abuse and Neglect." In Statistics Canada, *Family Violence in Canada: A Statistical Profile 2001*, pp. 4–14. July. Catalogue no. 85-224-XIE. Ottawa: Minister of Industry.

Trocmé, Nico, et al. 2001. *Canadian Incidence Study of Reported Child Abuse and Neglect: Final Report.* Health Canada. Catalogue no. H49-151/2000E. Ottawa: Minister of Public Works and Government Services.

Turcotte, Pierre. 2003. "Update on Families." *Canadian Social Trends.* pp. 11–15. Catalogue no. 11-008.

Turell, Susan. 2000. "A Descriptive Analysis of Same-Sex Relationship Violence for a Diverse Sample." *Journal of Family Violence* 15(3): 281–93.

UNIFEM (United Nations Development Fund for Women). 2007. http://www.unifem.org/campaigns/trust_fund_10th_anniversary/facts_figures.php?page=4.

United Nations Development Programme. 2000. *Human Development Report 2000.* Cary, NC: Oxford University Press.

Vanier Institute of the Family. 2000. *Profiling Canada's Families II.* Nepean, ON: Vanier Institute of the Family.

Venkatesan, J. 2009 (June 2). "Supreme Court Anguish over Dowry Deaths." *The Hindu.* http://www.hindu.com/2009/06/02/stories/2009060260980100.htm.

Ventura, Stephanie J., Sally C. Curtain, and T. J. Matthews. 2000. "Variations in Teenage Birth Rates, 1991–1998." *National Vital Statistics Reports* 48 (April 24).

Viano, C. Emilio. 1992. "Violence among Intimates: Major Issues and Approaches." In C. E. Viano (ed.), *Intimate Violence: Interdisciplinary Perspectives*, pp. 3–12. Washington, DC: Hemisphere.

Walker, Alexis J. 2001. "Refracted Knowledge: Viewing Families through the Prism of Social Science." In Robert M. Milardo (ed.), *Understanding Families into the New Millennium: A Decade in Review,* pp. 52–65. Minneapolis: National Council on Family Relations.

Wall, Glenda. 2001. "Moral Constructions of Motherhood in Breastfeeding Discourse." *Gender and Society* 15(4): 592–610.

Wherry, Aaron. 2002. "Shelternet.ca aims to reach women across the country." *The Globe and Mail* (August 13): A18.

Whiffen, V. E., J. M. Thompson, and J. A. Aube. 2000. "Mediators of the Link between Childhood Sexual Abuse and Adult Depressive Symptoms." *Journal of Interpersonal Violence* 15: 1100–20.

WHO (World Health Organization). 2009 (Nov.). Fact Sheet No. 239.

Willis, Diane J., E. Wayne Holden, and Mindy Rosenberg. 1992. "Child Maltreatment Prevention: Introduction and Historical Overview." In Diane J. Willis, E. Wayne Holden, and Mindy Rosenberg (eds.), *Prevention of Child Maltreatment: Developmental and Ecological Perspectives*, pp. 1–14. New York: John Wiley and Sons.

Chapter 6

Adler, Jerry. 1994. "Kids Growing Up Scared." *Newsweek* (January 10): 43–50.

Anetzberger, Georgia J., Jill E. Korbin, and Craig Austin. 1994. "Alcoholism and Elder Abuse." *Journal of Interpersonal Violence* 9: 184–93.

Arluke, Arnold, and Jack Levin. 1990. "'Second Childhood': Old Age in Popular Culture." In W. Feigelman (ed.), *Readings on Social Problems*, pp. 261–65. Fort Worth, TX: Holt, Rinehart and Winston.

Arnold, Tom. 1999. "Older Heart-Attack Patients Less Likely to Get Vital Drugs." *National Post* (November 30): A5.

Begley, Sharon. 2000. "The Stereotype Trap." *Newsweek* (November 6): 66–68.

Biggs, Simon. 2003. "Age, Gender, Narratives and Masquerades." *Journal of Aging Studies* 18: 45–58.

Blackburn, Mollie. 2005. "Agency in Borderland Discourses: Examining Language Use in a Community Center with Black Queer Youth." *Teachers College Record* 107(1): 89–103.

Boudreau, François A. 1993. "Elder Abuse." In R. L. Hampton, T. P. Gullota, G. R. Adams, E. H. Potter III, and R. P. Weissberg (eds.), *Family Violence: Prevention and Treatment*, pp. 142–58. Newbury Park, CA: Sage Publications.

Brazzini, D. G., W. D. McIntosh, S. M. Smith, S. Cook, and C. Harris. 1997. "The Aging Woman in Popular Film: Underrepresented, Unattractive, Unfriendly, and Unintelligent." *Sex Roles* 36: 531–43.

Brooks-Gunn, Jeanne, and Greg Duncan. 1997. "The Effects of Poverty on Children." *Future of Children* 7(2): 55–70.

Calasanti, Toni. 2004. "Feminist Gerontology and Old Men." *Journal of Gerontology* 59(6): 305–14.

————, and Neal King. 2005. "Firming the Floppy Penis: Age, Class and Gender Relations in the Lives of Old Men." *Men and Masculinities* 8(1): 3–23.

Canada Council on Social Development. 2006a. "Economic Security." *The Progress of Canada's Children and Youth, 2006:* 16–22.

————. 2006b. "Labour Force Profile of Youth." *The Progress of Canada's Children and Youth, 2006:* 77–83.

Canadian Red Cross. "The Prevalence of Abuse, Harassment and Assault in Young Lives." Accessed June 10, 2006. http://www.redcross.ca/article.asp?id=011147&tid=001.

CARP (Canadian Association of Retired Persons). 2002. http://www.fifty-plus.net.

Covell, Katherine. 2001. *Canada's Non-Governmental Organizations Report.* Submitted for the United Nations General Assembly Special Session September 19–21, 2001 (on behalf of the Canadian Coalition for the Rights of Children), February 2001.

Cowgill, Donald, and Lowell Holmes. 1972. *Aging and Modernization.* New York: Appleton-Century-Crofts.

Cummings, Elaine, and William Henry. 1961. *Growing Old: The Process of Disengagement.* New York: Basic Books.

DeAngelis, Tori. 1997. "Elderly May Be Less Depressed Than the Young." *APA Monitor* (October). http://www.apa.org/monitor/oct97/elderly.html.

DHHS (Department of Health and Human Services). 1998. "Statement of Jeanette Takamura." U.S. Department of Health and Human Services, Administration on Aging. June 8. http://www.aoa.dhhs.gov/pr/graying.html.

Dranoff, Linda Silver. 2001. *Everyone's Guide to the Law.* Toronto: HarperCollins Publishers Ltd.

Dube, Francine. 2002. "25% of Households Have Only One Person." *National Post* (October 23): A9.

Duncan, Greg, W. Jean Yeung, Jeanne Brooks-Gunn, and Judith Smith. 1998. "How Much Does Childhood Poverty Affect the Life Chance of Children?" *American Sociological Review* 63: 402–23.

Eisler, Lauren, and Bernard Schissel. 2004. "Privation and Vulnerability to Victimization for Canadian Youth." *Youth Violence and Juvenile Justice* 2(4): 359–73.

Fields, Jason, and Kristin Smith. 1998. "Poverty, Family Structure, and Child Well-Being." Population Division. Washington, DC: U.S. Bureau of the Census.

GLARP (Gay and Lesbian Association of Retiring Persons). 2000. http://www.gaylesbianretiring.org/about.htm.

Goldberg, Beverly. 2000. *Age Works.* New York: Free Press.

Harris, Kathleen, and Jeremy Marmer. 1996. "Poverty, Paternal Involvement and Adolescent Well-Being." *Journal of Family Issues* 17(5): 614–40.

Health Canada. 1999. *Statistical Report on the Health of Canadians.* December 25. http://www.hc-sc.gc.ca/hppb/phdd/report/state/eng/over.html.

Heaphy, Brian, Andrew Yip, and Debbie Thompson. 2004. "Ageing in a Non-Heterosexual Context." *Ageing & Society* 24(6): 881–902.

Kehoe, M. 1989. *Lesbians over 60 Speak for Themselves.* New York: Haworth Press.

Kinsella, K., and C. M. Taeuber. 1993. *An Aging World.* Washington, DC: U.S. Bureau of the Census.

Knoke, David, and Arne L. Kalleberg. 1994. "Job Training in U.S. Organizations." *American Sociological Review* 59: 537–46.

Krahn, H. K., and G. S. Lowe. 1993. *Work, Industry, and Canadian Society,* 2nd ed. Scarborough, ON: Nelson.

Liao, L. M., et al. 2005. "Experience of Early Pubertal Development: A Preliminary Analysis." *Journal of Reproductive and Infant Psychology* 23(3): 219–33.

Lindsay, Colin. 2000. "Income." In *Women in Canada: A Gender-Based Statistical Report*, pp. 135–54. Catalogue No. 89-503-XPE. Ottawa: Statistics Canada.

Livni, Ephrat. 2000 (September 21). "Exercise, the Anti-Drug." http://abcnews.go.com/sections/living/Daily/News/depression_elderly000921.htm.

Long, Ron. 2001. "Becoming the Men We're Ceasing to Be: A Gay Agenda for Aging in a Youth Culture." *Theology and Sexuality* 15: 94–113.

Lynott, Patricia, and Barbara Logue. 1993. "The 'Hurried Child': The Myth of Lost Childhood in Contemporary American Society." *Sociological Forum* 8(3): 471–91.

Massoulay, Karim. 2010. "Participation in Private Retirement Savings Plans, 1997 to 2008." Statistics Canada. Catalogue no. 13F0026M, no. 1.

Matras, Judah. 1990. *Dependency, Obligations, and Entitlements: A New Sociology of Aging, the Life Course, and the Elderly.* Englewood Cliffs, NJ: Prentice-Hall.

Miner, Sonia, John Logan, and Glenna Spitze. 1993. "Predicting Frequency of Senior Center Attendance." *Gerontologist* 33: 650–57.

Mouton, Charles, et al. 2001. "Abuse and Neglect in Older Men." *Clinical Gerontologist* 24(3/4): 15–26.

National Council of Welfare. 1998. *Profiles of Welfare: Myths and Realities:*

A Report by the National Council of Welfare. Spring. http://www. ncwcnbes.net/htmdocument/ reportprowelfare.repprowelfare. htm.

Nelson, Adie, and Barrie W. Robinson. 2002. *Gender in Canada,* 2nd ed. Toronto: Prentice Hall.

NIH (National Institute of Health). 2000. "Nation's Children Gain Many Areas." NIH news release, July 13. http://www.nih.gov/news/ pr/jul2000.

Novak, Mark. 1997. *Aging and Society: A Canadian Perspective,* 3rd ed. Scarborough, ON: Nelson.

Peterson, Peter. 2000. "Gray Dawn." In Frances Moulder (ed.), *Social Problems of the Modern World,* pp. 126–133. Belmont, CA: Wadsworth.

PHAC. 2005. "Seniors on the Margins: Aging in Poverty in Canada." Minister of Public Works and Government Services Canada. Catalogue no. H88-5/3-2005.

Pillemer, Karl, and Beth Hudson. 1993. "A Model Abuse Prevention Program for Nursing Assistants." *Gerontologist* 33(1): 128–31.

Reidmann, Agnes, Mary Ann Lamanna, and Adie Nelson. 2003. *Marriages and Families.* Toronto: Thomson Nelson.

Riley, Matilda W., and John W. Riley. 1992. "The Lives of Older People and Changing Social Roles." In Hugh Lena, William Helmreich, and William McCord (eds.), *Issues in Society,* pp. 220–31. New York: McGraw-Hill.

Schieber, Sylvester. 2000. "The Global Aging Crisis." *Electric Perspectives* 25: 18–28.

Seeman, Teresa E., and Nancy Adler. 1998. "Older Americans: Who Will They Be?" *National Forum* (Spring): 22–5.

Simon-Rusinowitz, Lori, Constance Krach, Lori Marks, Diane Piktialis, and Laura Wilson. 1996. "Grandparents in the Workplace: the Effects of Economic and Labor Trends." *Generations* 20(1): 41–44.

Statistics Canada. 1998. *Canada Yearbook.* Ottawa: Ministry of Industry.

————. 2002. "2001 Census: Canada." http://www12.statcan.ca/ english/census01/products/ analytic/companion/age/canada. cfm.

————. 2004. "Study: Duration of Non-Standard Employment." *The Daily,* December 15.

————. 2005. "Projections of the Aboriginal populations, Canada, Provinces and Territories 2001 to 2017." Catalogue no. 91-547-XIE. Ottawa.

————. 2006. "A Portrait of Seniors in Canada." Catalogue no. 89-519-XIE: 46.

————. 2007. "Portrait of the Canadian Population in 2006, by Age and Sex, 2006 Census." Catalogue no. 97-551-XIE. Ottawa.

————. 2008. "Canadian Demographics at a Glance." Catalogue no. 91-003-X: 25.

Straka, Sylvia, and Lise Montminy. 2006. "Responding to the Needs of Older Women Experiencing Domestic Violence." *Violence against Women* 12(3): 251–67.

Thurow, Lester C. 1996. "The Birth of a Revolutionary Class." *New York Times Magazine* (May 19): 46–47.

Townson, Monica. 1995. *Financial Futures: Mid-Life Prospects for a Secure Retirement.* Ottawa: Canadian Advisory Council on the Status of Women.

————. 2005. "Poverty Issues for Canadian Women." *Gender Equality Consultation.* http://www.swc-cfc. gc.ca/resources/consultations/ ges09-2005/poverty_e.html#_ ednref17.

UNICEF (United Nations International Children's Emergency Fund). 1998. "The First Nearly Universally Ratified Human Rights Treaty in History." *Status.* Washington, DC: UNICEF. http://www. unicef.org/ crc/status.html.

————. 2005. *Canada: Children Still Waiting.* Florence: Innocenti Research Centre.

Vanier Institute of the Family. 2000. *Profiling Canada's Families II.* Nepean, ON: Vanier Institute of the Family.

Weissberg, Roger P., and Carol Kuster. 1997. "Introduction and Overview: Let's Make Healthy Children 2010 a National Priority." In Roger Weissberg, Thomas Gullotta, Robert Hampton, Bruce Ryan, and Gerald Adams (eds.), *Enhancing Children's Well-Being,* pp. 1–16. Thousand Oaks, CA: Sage Publications.

Wittaker, Terri. 1996. "Violence, Gender and Elder Abuse." In Brid Featherstone (ed.), *Violence and Gender Relations: Theories and Interventions,* pp. 147–60. Thousand Oaks, CA: Sage Publications Inc.

Chapter 7

Adamson, N., L. Briskin, and M. McPhail. 1988. *Feminists Organizing for Change: The Contemporary Women's Movement in Canada.* Don Mills, ON: Oxford University Press.

Anderson, John, and Molly Moore. 1998. "The Burden of Womanhood." In Robert Jackson (ed.), *Global Issues 98/99,* pp. 170–75. Guilford, CT: Dushkin/McGraw-Hill.

Anderson, Margaret. 2005. "Thinking about Women." *Gender and Society* 19(4): 437–55.

Atcheson, E., M. Eberts, E. Symes, and J. Stoddart. 1984. *Women and Legal Action.* Ottawa: Canadian Advisory Council on the Status of Women.

Austin, Jonathan D. 2000. "U.N. Report: Women's Unequal Treatment Hurts Economies." CNN. com, September 20. http://www. cnn.com/2000/world/ europe/09/20.un.population.report.

Bacchi, C. L. 1983. *Liberation Deferred? The Ideas of the English-Canadian Suffragists,* 1877–1918. Toronto: University of Toronto Press.

Baker, Robin, Gary Kriger, and Pamela Riley. 1996. "Time, Dirt and Money: The Effects of Gender, Gender Ideology, and Type of Earner Marriage on Time, Household Task, and Economic Satisfaction Among Couples with Children." *Journal of Social Behavior and Personality* 11: 161–77.

Bannon, Lisa. 2000. "Why Girls and Boys Get Different Toys." *The Wall Street Journal,* February 14: B1.

Basow, Susan A. 1992. *Gender: Stereotypes and Roles,* 3rd ed. Pacific Grove, CA: Brooks/Cole.

Begley, Sharon. 2000. "The Stereotype Trap." *Newsweek* (November 6): 66–68.

Bianchi, Susanne M., Melissa A. Milkie, Liana C. Sayer, and John Robinson. 2000. "Is Anyone Doing the Housework? Trends in the Gender Division of Household Labor." *Social Forces* 79: 191–228.

Bittman, Michael and Judy Wajcman. 2000. "The Rush Hour: The Character of Leisure Time and Gender Equity." *Social Forces* 79: 165–89.

Burger, Jerry M., and Cecilia H. Solano. 1994. "Changes in Desire for Control over Time: Gender Differences in a Ten-Year Longitudinal Study." *Sex Roles* 31: 465–72.

Burke, R.J. 1994. "Canadian Business Students' Attitudes towards Women as Managers." *Psychological Reports* 75: 1123–29.

Butler, Judith. 1990. *Gender Trouble.* New York: Routledge.

———. 1993. *Bodies That Matter: On the Discursive Limits of Sex.* New York: Routledge.

Cassidy, B., R. Lord, and N. Mandell. 1998. "Silenced and Forgotten Women: Race, Poverty, and Disability." In N. Mandell (ed.), *Feminist Issues: Race, Class and Sexuality,* 2nd ed., pp. 26–54. Scarborough, ON: Prentice Hall Allyn and Bacon Canada.

CAUT (Canadian Association of University Teachers). 2006. "CAUT Survey Shows P.S.E. Gender Inequity Widespread." *Bulletin.* http://www.caut.ca/en/bulletin/issues/2006_apr/news_pse_gender.asp.

Cejka, Mary Ann, and Alice Eagley. 1999. "Gender Stereotypic Images of Occupations Correspond to the Sex Segregation of Employment." *Personality and Social Psychology Bulletin* 25: 413–23.

Cianni, Mary, and Beverly Romberger. 1997. "Life in the Corporation: A Multi-Method Study of the Experiences of Male and Female Asian, Black, Hispanic and White Employees." *Gender, Work and Organization* 4: 116–29.

Cohen, Theodore. 2001. *Men and Masculinity.* Belmont, CA: Wadsworth.

Cornish, M. 2008. "Please Act to End Ontario's Violation of United Nations Human Rights Standards." Open Letter to Premier Dalton McGuinty. Toronto: Equal Pay Coalition. 3.

De Walque, Damien. 2006. *Who Gets AIDS and How?* World Bank Report.

Dranoff, Linda Silver. 2001. *Everyone's Guide to the Law.* Toronto: HarperCollins Publishers Ltd.

Driedger, D. 1993. "Discovering Disabled Women's History." In L. Carty (ed.), *And Still We Rise*, pp. 173–88. Toronto: Women's Press.

England, Paula, and Su Li. 2006. "Desegregation Stalled: The Changing Gender Composition of College Majors, 1971–2002." *Gender & Society* 20: 657–677.

Errington, J. 1993. "Pioneers and Suffragists." In S. Burt, L. Code, and L. Dorney (eds.), *Changing Patterns: Women in Canada*, 2nd ed., pp. 59–91. Toronto: McClelland & Stewart Inc.

Evans, Lorraine, and Kimberly Davies. 2000. "No Sissy Boys Here." *Sex Roles* (February): 255–71.

Fausto-Sterling, Anne. 2000. *Sexing the Body.* New York: Basic Books.

Fitzgerald, Louise F., and Sandra L. Shullman. 1993. "Sexual Harassment: A Research Analysis and Agenda for the '90s." *Journal of Vocational Behavior* 40: 5–27.

Fitzpatrick, Catherine. 2000. "Modern Image of Masculinity Changes with Rise of New Celebrities." *Detroit News*, June 24. http://detnews.com/2000/religion/0006/24.

Frank, J. 1994. "Voting and Contributing: Political Participation in Canada." In *Canadian Social Trends: A Canadian Studies Reader* 2, pp. 333–57. Toronto: Thompson Educational Publishing.

Goldberg, Stephanie. 1997. "Making Room for Daddy." *American Bar Association Journal* 83: 48–52.

Gruenbaum, Ellan. 2005. "Socio-Cultural Dynamics of Female Genital Cutting: Research Findings, Gaps and Directions." *Culture, Health and Sexuality* 7(5): 429–41.

Guy M. E., and M. A. Newman. 2004. "Women's Jobs, Men's Jobs: Sex Segregation and Emotional Labor." *Public Administration Review* 64(3): 289–298.

Henslin, J., and A. Nelson. 1997. *Essentials of Sociology.* Scarborough, ON: Allyn and Bacon.

Hochschild, Arlie. 1989. *The Second Shift: Working Patterns and the Revolution at Home.* New York: Viking Penguin.

Hunter, A., and M. Denton. 1984. "Do Female Candidates 'Lose' Votes?" *Canadian Review of Sociology and Anthropology* 2: 395–406.

IWRP (International Women's Right's Project). 2000. "The First CEDAW Impact Study." http://www.yorku.ca/iwrp/cedawReport.

Kalb, Claudia. 2000. "What Boys Really Want." *Newsweek*, July 2. http://www.msnbc.com/news/428301.asp.

Kenworthy, Lane, and Melissa Malami. 1999. "Gender Inequality in Political Representation: A Worldwide Comparative Analysis." *Social Forces* 78: 235–69.

Kessler, Suzanne, and Wendy McKenna. 1978. *Gender: An Ethnomethodological Approach.* Chicago: University of Chicago Press.

Kilbourne, Barbara S., George Farkas, Kurt Beron, Dorothea Weir, and Paula England. 1994. "Returns to Skill, Compensating Differentials, and Gender Bias: Effects of Occupational Characteristics on the Wages of White Women and Men." *American Journal of Sociology* 100: 689–719.

Klein, Matthew. 1997. "Blue Jeans." *American Demographics* (August): 23.

———. 1998. "Women's Trip to the Top." *American Demographics* (February): 22.

Leeman, Sue. 2000 (September 20). "The More Things Change..." ABC News.

Leo, John. 1997. "Fairness? Promises, Promises." *U.S. News and World Report* 123(4): 18.

Long, J. Scott, Paul D. Allison, and Robert McGinnis. 1993. "Rank Advancement in Academic Careers: Sex Differences and the Effects of Productivity." *American Sociological Review* 58: 703–22.

Lorber, Judith. 1998. "Night to His Day." In Amanda Konradi and Martha Schmidt (eds.), *Reading between the Lines*, pp. 213–20.

Mountain View, CA: Mayfield Publishing.

Macklin, A. 1992. *"Symes v. M.N.R.:* Where Sex Meets Class." *Canadian Journal of Women and the Law* 5:498.

Mandell, N. 1995. "Introduction." *Feminist Issues: Race, Class and Sexuality*, pp. vii-xxi. Scarborough, ON: Prentice Hall Allyn and Bacon Canada.

Marini, Margaret Mooney, and Pi-Ling Fan. 1997. "The Gender Gap in Earnings at Career Entry. *American Sociological Review* 62: 588–604.

Martin, Patricia Yancey. 1992. "Gender, Interaction, and Inequality in Organizations." In Cecilia Ridgeway (ed.), *Gender, Interaction, and Inequality*, pp. 208–31. New York: Springer-Verlag.

Mensh, Barbara, and Cynthia Lloyd. 1997. "Gender Differences in the Schooling of Adolescents in Low-Income Countries: The Case of Kenya." *Policy Research Working Paper no. 95.* New York: Population Council.

Mossman, Mary Jane. 1997. *Readings on Law, Gender, Equality.* Materials prepared for the study use of students at Osgoode Hall School of Law of York University.

————. 1998. "The Paradox of Feminist Engagement with Law." In N. Mandell (ed.), *Feminist Issues: Race, Class, and Sexuality*, pp. 180–207. Scarborough, ON: Prentice Hall Allyn and Bacon Canada.

National Post. 1999. "Job Ad Seeking Only Women Draws Criticism." (August 6): A4.

NCFM (National Coalition of Free Men). 1998. "Historical." Manhasset, NY: NCFM. http:// ncfm.org.

Nelson, Adie, and Barrie W. Robinson. 2002. *Gender in Canada,* 2nd ed. Toronto: Pearson Education Canada Inc.

Olson, Josephine E., Irene H. Frieze, and Ellen G. Detlefsen. 1990. "Having It All? Combining Work and Family in a Male and a Female Profession." *Sex Roles* 23: 515–34.

Padavic, Irene, and Barbara Reskin. 2002. *Women and Men at Work,* 2nd ed. Thousand Oaks, CA: Pine Forge Press.

Pollock, William. 2000a. *Real Boys' Voices.* New York: Random House.

————. 2000b. "The Columbine Syndrome." *National Forum* 80: 39–42.

Population Reference Bureau. 1999. "World Population: More Than Just Numbers." Washington, DC. http:// www.prb.org.

Purcell, Piper, and Lara Stewart. 1990. "Dick and Jane in 1989." *Sex Roles* 22: 177–85.

Rabin, Sarah. 2000. "Feminists Take CEDAW into Our Own Hands." National Organization for Women. http://63111.42.146/cgs/gs_article. asp?ArticleD=1863.

Reid, Pamela T., and Lillian Comas-Diaz. 1990. "Gender and Ethnicity: Perspectives on Dual Status." *Sex Roles* 22: 397–408.

Robinson, John P., and Suzanne Bianchi. 1997. "The Children's Hours." *American Demographics* (December): 1–6.

Rosenberg, Janet, Harry Perlstadt, and William Phillips. 1997. "Now That We Are Here: Discrimination, Disparagement, and Harassment at Work and the Experience of Women Lawyers." In Dana Dunn (ed.), *Workplace/Women's Place,* pp. 247–59. Los Angeles: Roxbury.

Rubenstein, Carin. 1990. "A Brave New World." *New Woman* 20(10): 158–64.

Sadker, Myra, and David Sadker. 1990. "Confronting Sexism in the College Classroom." In S. L. Gabriel and I. Smithson (eds.), *Gender in the Classroom: Power and Pedagogy,* pp. 176–87. Chicago: University of Illinois Press.

Sapiro, Virginia. 1994. *Women in American Society.* Mountain View, CA: Mayfield.

Schneider, Margaret, and Susan Phillips. 1997. "A Qualitative Study of Sexual Harassment of Female Doctors by Patients." *Social Science and Medicine* 45: 669–76.

Schroeder, K. A., L. L. Blood, and D. Maluso. 1993. "Gender Differences and Similarities between Male and Female Undergraduate Students Regarding Expectations for Career and Family Roles." *College Student Journal* 27: 237–49.

Schwalbe, Michael. 1996. *Unlocking the Iron Cage: The Men's Movement, Gender Politics, and American Culture.* New York: Oxford University Press.

Sheehan, Molly. 2000. "Women Slowly Gain Ground in Politics." In Linda Starke (ed.), *Vital Signs: The Environmental Trends That Are Shaping Our Future,* pp. 152–53. New York: W. W. Norton Company.

Signorielli, Nancy. 1998. "Reflections of Girls in the Media: a Content Analysis across Six Media." *Overview.* http://childrennow.org/ media/mc97/ReflectSummary.html.

Smolken, Rachael. 2000. "Girls SAT Scores Still Lag Boys." *Post Gazette.* http://www.post-gazette.com/ headlines/20000830sat2.asp.

Sommers, Christina Hoff. 2000. *The War against Boys: How Misguided Feminism Is Harming Young Men.* New York: Simon and Schuster.

Stark, R. 1992. *Sociology,* 4th ed. Belmont, CA: Wadsworth.

Statistics Canada. 1998. "1996 Census: Labour Force Activity, Occupation and Industry, Place of Work, Mode of Transportation to Work, Unpaid Work." *The Daily,* March 17. http:// www.statcan.ca/Daily/ English/980317/d980317.htm.

————. 1999. *The Daily,* April 14. http://www.statcan.ca/Daily/ English/990417/d990417.htm.

————. 2001. "Impact of Smoking on Life Expectancy and Disability." *The Daily,* June 22. http://www. statcan.ca/Daily/English/010622/ d010622a.htm.

————. 2003a. "The Changing Profile of Canada's Labour Force." *2001 Census: Analysis Series.* Catalogue no. 96F0030XIE2001009 (released February 11, 2003), p. 36.

————. 2003b. "Earnings of Canadians: Making a Living in New Economy." Catalogue no. 96F0030XIE2001013. http:// www12.statcan.ca/english/census01/ Products/Analytic/companion/earn/ charts/menwom.cfm.

————. 2006. *Women in Canada, 5th Edition: A Gender-Based Statistical Report.* Catalogue no. 0010589-503-XIE.

————. 2011. "Education Indicators in Canada: Doctoral Students and University Teaching Staff." Catalogue no. 81-599-X (006). 4.

Tannen, Deborah. 1990. *You Just Don't Understand: Women and Men in Conversation.* New York: Ballantine Books.

Tepperman, Lorne, and Jim Curtis. 2004. *Social Problems: A Canadian Perspective.* Toronto: Oxford.

Tomaskovic-Devey, Donald. 1993. "The Gender and Race Composition of Jobs and the Male/Female, White/Black Pay Gap." *Social Forces* 72(1): 45–76.

United Nations. 2000a. "Convention on the Elimination of All Forms of Discrimination against Women." http://un.org/womenwatch/daw/cedaw.

————. 2000b. "Strengthening Women's Economic Capacity." United Nations Development Fund for Women. http://www.unifem.undp.org/economic.htm.

————. 2000c. *The World's Women 2000: Trends and Statistics.* New York: United Nations Statistics Division.

————. 2005a. *Human Development Report, 2005.* New York: UN Development Programme.

————. 2005b. *Progress towards the Millennium Development Goals.* New York: UN Development Programme.

Van Willigen, Marieke, and Patricia Drentea. 1997. "Benefits of Equitable Relationships: The Impact of Sense of Failure, Household Division of Labor, and Decision-Making Power on Social Support." Presented at the Meeting of the American Sociological Association, Toronto, Ontario, August.

Whitla, W. 1995. "A Chronology of Women in Canada." In N. Mandell (ed.), *Feminist Issues: Race, Class and Sexuality,* pp. 315–53. Scarborough, ON: Prentice Hall Canada.

Wilkins, K. 1996. "Causes of Death: How the Sexes Differ." *Canadian Social Trends* 41: 11–17.

Williams, John E., and Deborah L. Best. 1990. *Measuring Sex Stereotypes: A Multination Study.* London: Sage Publications.

Wilmot, Alyssa. 1999. "First National Love Your Body Day a Big Success." Press release. *National Organization for Women Newsletter* (Winter). http://www.now.org.

Wine, J. D., and J. L. Ristock (eds.). 1991. "Introduction: Feminist Activism in Canada." In *Women and Social Change: Feminist Activism in Canada,* pp. 1–18. Toronto: James Lorimer.

WIN (Women's International Network) News. 2000. "Reports from around the World." (Autumn): 50–58.

Witt, S. D. 1996. "Traditional or Androgynous: An Analysis to Determine Gender Role Orientation of Basal Readers." *Child Study Journal* 26: 303–18.

Wittig, Monique. 1992. *The Straight Mind.* New York: Beacon Press.

World Bank. 2001. "Engendering Development." *World Bank Policy Research Report.* http://www.worldbank.org/gender/pur/newsummary.htm.

Yamaguchi, Mari. 2000. "Female Government Workers Face Harassment." http://news.excite.com/news/ap/001227/05/int. Japan.

Yumiko, Ehara. 2000. "Feminism's Growing Pains." *Japan Quarterly* 47: 41–48.

Zimmerman, Marc A., Laurel Copeland, Jean Shope, and T. E. Dielman. 1997. "A Longitudinal Study of Self-Esteem: Implications for Adolescent Development." *Journal of Youth and Adolescence* 26(2): 117–41.

Chapter 8

Abella, Irving. 1999. "Anti-Semitism." In James H. Marsh (ed.), *The Canadian Encyclopedia: Year 2000 Edition,* p. 90. Toronto: McClelland & Stewart Inc.

————, and H. Troper. 1998. *None Is Too Many: Canada and the Jews of Europe, 1933–1948.* Toronto: Lester Publishing.

Balthazar, Louis. 1997. "Quebec and the Idea of Federalism." An Occasional Paper. Montreal: McGill Institute for the Study of Canada, pp. 1–8.

Bannerji, Himani. 2000. "The Paradox of Diversity: The Construction of a Multicultural Canada and 'Women of Colour.'" *Women's Studies International Forum* 23(5): 537–60.

Beaudoin, Gerald A. 1999. "Keegstra Case." In James H. Marsh (ed.), *The Canadian Encyclopedia: Year 2000 Edition,* pp. 1237. Toronto: McClelland & Stewart Inc.

Behiels, M. D. 1999. "Francophone–Anglophone Relations." In James H. Marsh (ed.), *The Canadian Encyclopedia: Year 2000 Edition,* pp. 909–13. Toronto: McClelland & Stewart Inc.

Bergman, Brian. 1993. "A Break with Custom." *Maclean's* 106(34): 16.

Bibby, Reginald W. 2001. *Canada's Teens: Today, Yesterday, and Tomorrow.* Toronto: Stoddart.

Blackwell, Tom. 2002. "Racial Tension Peaked after Sept. 11 Attacks." *National Post* (July 16): A7.

Boyd, Monica. 2000. "Canada's Refugees Flows: Gender Inequality." *Canadian Social Trends* 3: 84–87. Toronto: Thompson Educational Publishing.

Breton, R. 1988. "French–English Relations." In J. E. Curtis and L. Tepperman (eds.), *Understanding Canadian Society,* pp. 557–85. Toronto: McGraw-Hill Ryerson Limited.

Bricker, Darrell, and Edward Greenspon. 2001. *Searching for Certainty: Inside the New Canadian Mindset.* Toronto: Doubleday Canada.

Burnet, Jean. 1999. "Multiculturalism." In James H. Marsh (ed.), *The Canadian Encyclopedia: Year 2000 Edition,* p. 1535. Toronto: McClelland & Stewart Inc.

Children Now. 2000a. Fall Colors I: How Diverse Is the 1999–2000 Prime-Time Season? http://www.childrennow.org.

————. 2000b. Fall Colors II: Exploring the Quality of Diverse Portrayals on Prime-Time Television. http://www.childrennow.org.

Chui, T., Kelly Tran, and Hélène Maheux. 2007. "Immigration in Canada: A Portrait of the Foreign-Born Population: 2006 Census."

Statistics Canada. Catalogue no. 97-557-X: 37.

Claxton-Oldfield, Stephen, and Sheila M. Keefe. 1999. "Assessing Stereotypes about the Innu of Davis Inlet, Labrador." *Canadian Journal of Behavioural Sciences* 31(2): 86–91.

Cohen, Mark Nathan. 1998. "Culture, Not Race, Explains Human Diversity." *Chronicle of Higher Education* 44(32): B4–B5.

Collins, F. S. 2004. "What We Do and Don't Know about 'Race,' 'Ethnicity,' Genetics and Health at the Dawn of the Genome Era." *Nature Genetics Supplement* 36(11): s13–s15.

Columbo, J. R. 1986. *1001 Questions about Canada*. Toronto: Doubleday.

Conley, Dalton. 1999. *Being Black, Living in the Red: Race, Wealth, and Social Policy in America*. Berkeley: University of California Press.

Crauford-Lewis, M. 1999. "Nunavut." In James H. Marsh (ed.), *The Canadian Encyclopedia: Year 2000 Edition*, p. 1686. Toronto: McClelland & Stewart, Inc.

Day, R. 1998. "Constructing the Official Canadian: A Genealogy of the Mosaic Metaphor in State Policy Discourse." *Topia* 2: 42–66.

Deziel, Shanda, and Amy Cameron. 2001/2002. "Overbites." *Maclean's* (December 31–January 7): 11.

Doerr, A. 1999. "Royal Commission on Aboriginal Peoples." In James H. Marsh (ed.), *The Canadian Encyclopedia: Year 2000 Edition*, pp. 3–4. Toronto: McClelland & Stewart, Inc.

Donakowski, D. W., and V. M. Esses. 1996. "Native Canadians, First Nations, or Aboriginals: The Effects of Labels on Attitudes toward Native Peoples." *Canadian Journal of Behavioural Science* 28: 86–91.

Driedger, L. 1999. "Prejudice and Discrimination." In James H. Marsh (ed.), *The Canadian Encyclopedia: Year 2000 Edition*, pp. 1888–92. Toronto: McClelland & Stewart Inc.

Esses, Victoria, et al. 2002. "Public Attitudes toward Immigration in the United States and Canada in Response to the September 11, 2001 'Attack of America.'" *Analyses of Social Issues and Public Policy* 2(1): 69–85.

Etzioni, Amitai. 1997. "New Issues: Rethinking Race." *Public Perspective* (June–July): 39–40. May 11, 1998. http://www.ropercenter.unconn. edu/pubper/pdf/!84b.htm.

Fitzhugh, T. V. 1991. *The Dictionary of Genealogy*, 3rd ed. London: A. and C. Black.

Frideres, J. S. 1993. "Health Promotion and Indian Communities: Social Support or Social Disorganization." In B. Singh Bolaria and R. Bolaria (eds.), *Racial Minorities, Medicine and Health*, pp. 269–95. Halifax, NS: Fernwood.

Gaertner, Samuel L., and John F. Dovidio. 2000. *Reducing Intergroup Bias: The Common Ingroup Identity Model*. Philadelphia: Taylor & Francis Group.

Goonewardena, Kanishka, and Stefan Kipfer. 2005. "Spaces of Difference: Reflections from Toronto on Multiculturalism, Bourgeois Urbanism and the Possibility of a Radical Urban Politics." *International Journal of Urban and Regional Research* 29(3): 670–78.

Granastein, Ron. 2002. "Al-Qaida's Here." *Toronto Sun* (September 6): 4.

Guillebeau, Christopher. 1999. "Affirmative Action in a Global Perspective: The Cases of South Africa and Brazil." *Sociological Spectrum* 19(4): 443–65.

Guinier, Lani. 1998. Interview with Paula Zahn. *CBS Evening News*, July 18.

Gurin, Patricia. 1999. "New Research on the Benefits of Diversity in College and Beyond: An Empirical Analysis." *Diversity Digest* (Spring): 5–15.

"Hate on Campus." 2000. *Intelligence Report* 98 (Spring): 6–15.

Healey, Joseph F. 1997. *Race, Ethnicity, and Gender in the United States: Inequality, Group Conflict, and Power*. Thousand Oaks, CA: Pine Forge Press.

Health Canada. 1999. *Toward a Healthy Future: Second Report on the Health of Canadians*. Prepared by the Federal, Provincial, and Territorial Advisory Committee of Population Health for the Meeting of Ministers of Health, Charlottetown, PEI, September.

Henry, Frances, and Carol Tator. 1985. "Racism in Canada: Social Myths and Strategies for Change." In Rita M. Bienvenue and Jay E. Goldstein (eds.), *Ethnicity and Ethnic Relations in Canada*, 2nd ed., pp. 321–35. Toronto: Butterworths.

Henry, Frances, Carol Tator, Winston Mattis, and Tim Rees. 1995. *The Colour of Democracy*. Toronto: Harcourt Brace.

hooks, bell. 2000. *Where We Stand: Class Matters*. New York: Routledge.

Horwood, Harold. 1969. *Newfoundland*. Toronto: Macmillan.

Humphreys, Debra. 1999. "Diversity and the College Curriculum: How Colleges & Universities Are Preparing Students for a Changing World." *DiversityWeb*. http://www. inform.umd.edu/EdRes/Topic/Di... Leadersguide/CT/curriculum_ briefing.html.

"Intelligence Briefs." 2000. *SPLC Report* 30 (September): 3.

Intelligence Report. 1998. *Teaching Tolerance* 89 (Winter). Montgomery, AL: Southern Poverty Law Center.

Janigan, Mary. 2002. "Immigrants." *Maclean's* (December 16): 10–25.

Jedwab, Jack. 2002. "The Impact of September 11th on Immigration." Toronto: Environics Canada.

Jensen, Derrick. 2001. "Saving the Indigenous Soul: An Interview with Martin Prechtel." *The Sun* 304 (April): 4–15.

Keita, S. O. Y., and Rick A. Kittles. 1997. "The Persistence of Racial Thinking and the Myth of Racial Divergence." *American Anthropologist* 99(3): 534–44.

Kilgour, David. 1988. *Uneasy Patriots: Western Canadians in Confederation*. Edmonton: Lone Pine Press.

Kleg, Milton. 1993. *Hate, Prejudice, and Racism*. Albany: State University of New York Press.

Kunz, Jean Lock, Anne Milan, and Sylvain Schetagne. 2000. *Unequal Access: A Canadian Profile of Racial Differences in Education, Employment & Income*. Toronto: Canadian Race Relations Foundation. http://www. crr.ca.

Kitchener-Waterloo Record. 2002. "Feeling the Backlash." *Kitchener-Waterloo Record* (September 3): C11.

Landau, Elaine. 1993. *The White Power Movement: America's Racist Hate Groups*. Brookfield, CT: Millbrook Press.

Leggon, Cheryl B. 1999. "Introduction: Race and Ethnicity—A Global Perspective." *Sociological Spectrum* 19(4): 381–85.

Levin, Jack, and Jack McDevitt. 1995. "Landmark Study Reveals Hate Crimes Vary Significantly by Offender Motivation." *Klanwatch Intelligence Report* (August): 7–9.

Lieberman, Leonard. 1997. "Gender and the Deconstruction of the Race Concept." *American Anthropologist* 99(3): 545–58.

Lofthus, Kai R. 1998. "Swedish Biz Decries Racist Music." *Billboard* (January 24): 71, 73.

Maclean's. 1999. "What Makes a Canadian?" (December 20): 45–48.

Maclean's. 2001/2002. "Since Sept. 11: The Responses Show How Terrorism and War Have Left Their Mark." (December 31–January 7): 38–39.

Marger, Martin N. 2000. *Race and Ethnic Relations: American and Global Perspectives*, 5th ed. Belmont, CA: Wadsworth.

Milan, A., Hélène Maheux, and Tina Chui. 2010 (April 20). "A Portrait of Couples in Mixed Unions." Statistics Canada. Ottawa. *Canadian Social Trends*: 70–80.

Molnar, Stephen. 1983. *Human Variation: Races, Types, and Ethnic Groups*, 2nd ed. Englewood Cliffs, NJ: Prentice-Hall.

Mosher, Clayton J. 1998. *Discrimination and Denial: Systemic Racism in Ontario's Legal and Criminal Justice System, 1892–1961*. Toronto: University of Toronto Press.

Nash, Manning. 1962. "Race and the Ideology of Race." *Current Anthropology* 3: 258–88.

National Post. 1999a. "StatsCan Debates: How Canadian Are We?" (November 30): A1.

————. 1999b. "Conditions Curtail Quebec's Right to Self-Determination." (December 11): A11.

————. 1999c. "Clarity Act Fails to Arouse Separatist Sentiments." (December 15): A7.

Niemonen, Jack. 1999. "Deconstructing Cultural Pluralism." *Sociological Spectrum* 19(4): 401–19.

Noh, S., and M. Belser. 1999. "Perceived Racial Discrimination, Depression, and Coping: A Study of Southeast Asian Refugees in Canada." *Journal of Health and Social Behavior* 40(3): 193–207.

Race Relations Reporter. 1999. Volume VII (8), October 15. New York: CH II Publishers, Inc. 200 West 57th St., New York, NY 10019.

Ray, Peter. 2002. "Arabs, Muslims Still Live in Fear of Attacks." *Toronto Star* (March 23): A20.

Roberts, J. 1995. "Disproportionate Harm: Hate Crime in Canada." http://ftp.nizkor.org/hweb/orgs/Canadian/canada/justice/disproportionate-harm.

Rowe, Frederick W. 1977. *Extinction: The Beothuks of Newfoundland*. Toronto: McGraw-Hill Ryerson.

Schaefer, Richard T. 1998. *Racial and Ethnic Groups*, 7th ed. New York: HarperCollins.

Sher, J. 1983. *White Hoods: Canada's Ku Klux Klan*. Vancouver: New Star Books.

Shipler, David K. 1998. "Subtle vs. Overt Racism." *Washington Spectator* 24 (March 15): 1–3.

Snider, Katherine. 1996. "Race and Sexual Orientation: The (Im)Possibility of These Intersections on Educational Policy." *Harvard Educational Review* 66(2): 294–302.

Statistics Canada. 1998. "1996 Census: Ethnic Origin, Visible Minorities." *The Daily*, February 17. http://www.statcan.ca/Daily/English/980217/d980217/d980217.htm.

————. 2003a. "Canada's Ethnocultural Portrait: The Changing Mosaic." 2001 Census: Analysis Series. Catalogue no. 96F0030XIE2001008.

————. 2003b. "Census of a Population: Immigration, Birthplace, Birthplace of Parents, Citizenship, Ethnic Origin, Visible Minorities and Aboriginal Peoples." *The Daily*, January 21. http://www.statcan.ca/Daily/English/030121/d030121.htm.

————. 2003c. "Earnings of Canadians: Making a Living in the New Economy." Catalogue 96F0030XIE2001013. http://www12.statcan.ca/english/census01/Products/Analytic/companion/earn/charts/menwom.cfm.

————. 2008a. "2006 Census: Ethnic Origin, Visible Minorities, Place of Work and Mode of Transportation." *The Daily*, April 2. http://www.statcan.gc.ca/daily-quotidien/080402/dq080402a-eng.htm.

————. 2008b. "Aboriginals Peoples in Canada in 2006: Inuit, Metis, and First Nations: 2006 Census." Ottawa, Minister of Industry. Catalogue no. 97-558-XIE.

————. 2008c. "Canada's Ethnocultural Mosaic: 2006 Census," Census Year 2006. Ottawa. Catalogue no. 97-562-X.

————. 2009. "Earnings and Incomes of Canadians over the Past Quarter Century: 2006 Census: Earnings." Ottawa. Catalogue 97-563-X.

Stodolska, M., and E. L. Jackson. 1998. "Discrimination in Leisure and Work Experience by a White Ethnic Minority Group." *Journal of Leisure Research* 30(1): 23–41.

Such, P. 1978. *The Vanished People: The Beothuk People of Newfoundland*. Toronto: NC Press.

Thompson, Becky. 2001. *A Promise and a Way of Life: White Antiracist Activism*. Minneapolis: University of Minnesota Press.

Weiner, Nan. 2001. "Employment Barriers Still Block Aboriginals & Visible Minorities." *CAUT Bulletin* (April): A9, A10.

Wheeler, Michael L. 1994. *Diversity Training: A Research Report*. New York: The Conference Board.

Williams, Eddie N., and Milton D. Morris. 1993. "Racism and Our Future." In Herbert Hill and James E. Jones Jr. (eds.), *Race in America: The Struggle for Equality*, pp. 417–24. Madison: University of Wisconsin Press.

Winks, Robin W. 1999. "Slavery." In James H. Marsh (ed.), *The Canadian Encyclopedia Year 2000 Edition*, p. 2174. Toronto: McClelland Stewart, Inc.

Wood, Patricia, and Liette Gilbert. 2005. "Multiculturalism in Canada: Accidental Discourse, Alternative Vision, Urban Practice." *International Journal of Urban and Regional Research* 29(3): 679–91.

Zack, Naomi. 1998. *Thinking about Race.* Belmont, CA: Wadsworth Publishing Co.

Zine, Jasmin. 2002. "Inclusive Schooling in a Plural Society: Removing the Margins." *Education Canada* 42(3): 36–39.

Chapter 9

Anderssen, Erin. 1999. "Gay-Bashing Preacher Calls Off Protest." *The Globe and Mail,* June 29. http://www.egale.ca/archives/press/9906299gm.htm.

Angelides, S. 1995. "Rethinking the Political: Poststructuralism and the Economy of (Hetero)Sexuality." *Critical Inqueeries* 1(1): 27–46.

Arnold, Tom. 2002. "Common-Law Families on the Rise." *National Post* (October 23): A9.

Arnup, Katherine (ed.). 1995. *Lesbian Parenting: Living with Pride and Prejudice.* Charlottetown, PEI: gynergy books.

Associated Press. 2001. "Vancouver Gay Man Beaten to Death: Police Suspect Hate Crime." http://www.planetqnews.com/0812/11.shtml.

Baldwin, Tammy. 2000. "Never Doubt." Speech delivered at Millennium March, Washington, DC, April 2000.

Bayer, Ronald. 1987. *Homosexuality and American Psychiatry: The Politics of Diagnosis,* 2nd ed. Princeton, NJ: Princeton University Press.

Benkov, Laura. 1994. *Reinventing the Family: The Emerging Story of Gay and Lesbian Parents.* New York: Crown Publishers.

Besen, Wayne. 2000. "Introduction." In Human Rights Campaign, *Feeling Free: Personal Stories: How Love and Self-Acceptance Saved Us from "Ex-Gay" Ministries,* p. 7. Washington, DC: Human Rights Campaign Foundation.

Bornstein, Kate. 1994. *Gender Outlaw: On Men, Women, and the Rest of Us.* New York: Routledge.

Brannock, J. C., and B. E. Chapman. 1990. "Negative Sexual Experiences with Men among Heterosexual Women and Lesbians." *Journal of Homosexuality* 19: 105–10.

"Brazilian Killers Sentenced." 2001. PlanetOut.com, February 15. http://www.planetout.com/news/article-print.html?2001/02/15/1.

Bricker, Darrell, and Edward Greenspon. 2001. *Searching for Certainty: Inside the New Canadian Mindset.* Toronto: Doubleday Canada.

Bullough, Vern L. 2000. "Transgenderism and the Concept of Gender." *International Journal of Transgenderism.* Special issue 4 (July-September).

Bush, Irene R., and Anthony Sainz. 2001. "Competencies at the Intersection of Difference, Tolerance, and Prevention of Hate Crimes." In Mary E. Swigonski and Robin S. Mama (eds.), *From Hate Crimes to Human Rights: A Tribute to Matthew Shepard,* pp. 205–24. New York: Haworth Press.

Butler, Amy C. 2000. "Trends in Same-Gender Sexual Partnering, 1988–1998." *The Journal of Sex Research* 37(4): 333–43.

Butler, Judith. 1990. *Gender Trouble.* New York: Routledge.

————. 1993. *Bodies That Matter: On the Discursive Limits of 'Sex.'* New York: Routledge.

Button, James W., Barbara A. Rienzo, and Kenneth D. Wald. 1997. *Private Lives, Public Conflicts: Battles over Gay Rights in American Communities.* Washington, DC: CQ Press.

Chase, Bob. 2000. "NEA President Bob Chase's Historic Speech from 2000 GLSEN Conference." http://www.glsen.org/templates/resources/record.html?section=14&record=255.

"Constitutional Protection." 1999. GayLawNet, February 14. http://www.nexus.net.au/~dba/news.html#top.

Craig, Kellina M. 2002. "Examining Hate-Motivated Aggression: A Review of the Social Psychological Literature on Hate Crimes as a Distinct Form of Aggression."

Aggression & Violent Behavior 7 (January-February): 85–101.

Dawson, Lorne. 1993. "Religion and Legitimacy." In Peter S. Li and B. Singh Bolaria (eds.), *Contemporary Sociology: Critical Perspectives*, pp. 311–27. Toronto: Copp Clark Pitman.

De Cecco, John P., and D. A. Parker. 1995. "The Biology of Homosexuality: Sexual Orientation or Sexual Preference?" *Journal of Homosexuality* 28: 1–28.

D'Emilio, John. 1990. "The Campus Environment for Gay and Lesbian Life." *Academe* 76(1): 16–9.

Deziel, Shanda. 2000. "Gaily Prime Time." *Maclean's* (October 30): 54.

Doell, R.G. 1995. "Sexuality in the Brain." *Journal of Homosexuality* 28: 345–56.

Dozetos, Barbara. 2001. "School Shooter Taunted as 'Gay.'" PlanetOut.com, March 7. http://www.planetout.com/news/article-print.html?2001/03/07/1.

Dranoff, Linda Silver. 2001. *Everyone's Guide to the Law.* Toronto: HarperCollins Publishers Ltd.

Drinkwater, Gregg. 2001. "Netherlands to Celebrate First Gay Marriages." PlanetOut.com, March 30. http://www.planetout.com/news/article-print.html?2001/03/2.

Durkheim, Emile. 1993. "The Normal and the Pathological." Originally published in *The Rules of Sociological Method, 1938.* In Henry N. Pontell (ed.), *Social Deviance*, pp. 33–63. Englewood Cliffs, NJ: Prentice-Hall.

EGALE. 1999. "Press Release." June 7. http://www.egale.ca/politics.motion.htm.

————. 2001. "Svend Robinson Introduces Bill, EGALE Renews Call for Hate Crimes Protection in Wake of Murder of Gay Man in Vancouver." Press release, November 22. http://www.egale.ca/pressrel/011122.htm.

————. 2010. "Update on Bill C-389." http://trans.egale.ca/2010/12/update-on-bill-c-389/.

Esterberg, K. 1997. *Lesbian and Bisexual Identities: Constructing Communities, Constructing Selves.* Philadelphia: Temple University Press.

Faulkner, Anne H., and Kevin Cranston. 1998. "Correlates of Same-Sex Sexual Behavior in a Random Sample of Massachusetts High School Students." *Journal of Public Health* 88 (February): 262–66.

Fausto-Sterling, Anne. 2001. *Sexing the Body.* New York: Basic Books.

Firestein, B. A. 1996. "Bisexuality as Paradigm Shift: Transforming Our Disciplines." In B. A. Firestein (ed.), *Bisexuality: The Psychology and Politics of an Invisible Minority,* pp. 263–91. Thousand Oaks, CA: Sage.

Fisher, John. 1999. *A Report on Lesbian, Gay and Bisexual Youth Issues in Canada.* Ottawa: EGALE.

Flowers, Paul, and Katie Buston. 2001. "'I Was Terrified of Being Different': Exploring Gay Men's Accounts of Growing-Up in a Heterosexist Society." *Journal of Adolescence.* Special Issue: Gay, Lesbian, and Bisexual Youth 24 (February): 51–65.

Fone, Byrne. 2000. *Homophobia: A History.* New York: Henry Holt and Company.

Foucault, Michel. 1990a. *The History of Sexuality, Volume One: An Introduction.* Trans. Robert Hurley. New York: Vintage.

———. 1990b. *The History of Sexuality, Volume Two: The Use of Pleasure.* Trans. Robert Hurley. New York: Vintage.

———. 1990c. *The History of Sexuality, Volume Three: The Care of the Self.* Trans. Robert Hurley. New York: Vintage.

Frank, Barney. 1997. Foreword. In J. W. Button, B. A. Rienzo, and K. D. Wald, *Private Lives, Public Conflicts: Battles over Gay Rights in American Communities.* Washington, DC: CQ Press.

Frank, David John, and Elizabeth H. McEneaney. 1999. "The Individualization of Society and the Liberalization of State Policies on Same-Sex Relations, 1984–1995." *Social Forces* 77(3): 911–44.

Franklin, Sarah. 1993. "Essentialism, Which Essentialism? Some Implications of Reproductive and Genetic Techno-Science." *Journal of Homophobia* 24: 27–39.

Freedman, Estelle B., and John D'Emilio. 1990. "Problems Encountered in Writing the History of Sexuality: Sources, Theory, and Interpretation." *Journal of Sex Research* 27: 481–95.

Garnets, L., G. M. Herek, and B. Levy. 1990. "Violence and Victimization of Lesbians and Gay Men: Mental Health Consequences." *Journal of Interpersonal Violence* 5: 366–83.

Gilbert, Michael. 2000. "The Transgendered Philosopher." *International Journal of Transgenderism.* Special issue 4 (July-September).

Gilman, Sander. 1985. *Difference and Pathology: Stereotypes of Sexuality, Race and Madness.* Ithaca: Cornell University Press.

Goldie, Terry. 2001. *In a Queer Country: Gay & Lesbian Studies in the Canadian Context.* Vancouver: Arsenal Pulp Press.

Goode, Erica E., and Betsy Wagner. 1993. "Intimate Friendships." *U.S. News and World Report* (July 5): 49–52.

Hamer, D., P. F. Copeland, S. Hu, V. L. Magnuson, N. Hu, and A. M. L. Pattatucci. 1993. "A Linkage between DNA Markers on the X Chromosome and Male Sexual Orientation." *Science* 261: 321–27.

Herdt, Gilbert. 2001. "Social Change, Sexual Diversity, and Tolerance for Bisexuality in the United States." In Anthony R. D'Augelli and Charlotte J. Patterson (eds.), *Lesbian, Gay, and Bisexual Identities and Youth: Psychological Perspectives,* pp. 267–83. New York: Oxford University Press.

Herek, Gregory M. 1989. "Hate Crimes against Lesbians and Gay Men." *American Psychologist* 44: 948–55.

———. 1990. "The Context of Anti-Gay Violence: Notes on Cultural and Psychological Heterosexism." *Journal of Interpersonal Violence* 5: 316–33.

Hines, S. 2006. "Intimate Transitions: Transgender Practices of Partnering and Parenting." *Sociology* 40(2): 353–71.

Homophobia 101: Teaching Respect for All. 2000. The Gay, Lesbian, and Straight Education Network. http://www.glsen.org.

Honore, Carl. 2000. "'Male Egg' Could Enable Two Men to Conceive a Child." *National Post* (September 26): A1, A12.

Human Rights Campaign. 2000a. *Feeling Free: Personal Stories: How Love and Self-Acceptance Saved Us from "Ex-Gay" Ministries.* Washington, DC: Human Rights Campaign.

———. 2000b. *The State of the Workplace for Lesbian, Gay, Bisexual and Transgendered Americans, 2000.* Washington, DC: Human Rights Campaign Foundation.

International Gay and Lesbian Human Rights Commission (IGLHRC). 2003. "Where Having Sex Is a Crime: Criminalization and Decriminalization of Homosexual Acts." www.iglhrc.org/site/iglhrc/content.php?type=1&id=77.

"Jail, Death Sentences in Africa." 2001. PlanetOut.com, February 21. http://www.planetout.com/news/articleprint.html?2001/02/21/2.

Kinsey, A. C., W. B. Pomeroy, C. E. Martin, and P. H. Gebhard. 1953. *Sexual Behavior in the Human Female.* Philadelphia: W. B. Saunders.

Kirkpatrick, R. C. 2000. "The Evolution of Human Sexual Behavior." *Current Anthropology* 41(3): 385.

Klassen, Albert D., Colin J. Williams, and Eugene E. Levitt. 1989. *Sex and Morality in the United States.* Middletown, CT: Wesleyan University Press.

Krafft-Ebing, Richard von. 1965. *Psychopathia Sexualis.* Introd. by Franklin S. Klaf. London: Staples Press.

Lambda Legal Defense and Education Fund. 2000. *Student Advocacy for University Anti-Bias Policies That Include Sexual Orientation.* Publications, July 6. http://www.lambdalegal.org.

LAWbriefs. 2000. "Recent Developments in Sexual Orientation and Gender Identity Law." *LAWbriefs* 3 (Fall).

Louderback, L. A., and B. E. Whitley. 1997. "Perceived Erotic Value of Homosexuality and Sex-Role Attitudes as Mediators of Sex Differences in Heterosexual College Students' Attitudes toward

Lesbians and Gay Men." *Journal of Sex Research* 34: 175–82.

Mathison, Carla. 1998. "The Invisible Minority: Preparing Teachers to Meet the Needs of Gay and Lesbian Youth." *Journal of Teacher Education* 49: 151–55.

Mohr, Richard D. 1995. "Anti-Gay Stereotypes." In P. S. Rothenberg (ed.), *Race, Class, and Gender in the United States*, 3rd ed., pp. 402–8. New York: St. Martin's Press.

Moser, Charles. 1992. "Lust, Lack of Desire, and Paraphilias: Some Thoughts and Possible Connections." *Journal of Sex and Marital Therapy* 18: 65–69.

Murphy, Timothy F. 2001. "Commentary: Lesbian, Gay, Bisexual, and Transgender Medical Students and Their Ethical Conflicts." *Journal of the Gay & Lesbian Medical Association.* Special issue 5 (March): 31–35.

National Conference of State Legislatures. 2004. "Voters Decide High-Profile Issues on State Ballots Same Sex Marriage Bans Pass, Mixed Results for Tort Reform." http://www.ncsl.org/programs/legman/statevote/ir2004.htm.

Nagle, Matt. 2001. "Gay Man Murdered in Vancouver's Stanley Park." *Seattle Gay News*, November 23. http://www.sgn.org/2001/11/23.

Nugent, Robert, and Jeannine Gramick. 1989. "Homosexuality: Protestant, Catholic, and Jewish Issues: A Fishbone Tale." *Journal of Homosexuality* 18: 7–46.

Patterson, Charlotte J. 2001. "Family Relationships of Lesbians and Gay Men." In Robert M. Milardo (ed.), *Understanding Families into the New Millennium: A Decade in Review*, pp. 271–88. Minneapolis, MN: National Council on Family Relations.

Paul, J. P. 1996. "Bisexuality: Exploring/Exploding the Boundaries." In R. Savin-Williams and K. M. Cohen (eds.), *The Lives of Lesbians, Gays, and Bisexuals: Children to Adults*, pp. 436–61. Fort Worth, TX: Harcourt Brace.

Peele, S., and R. DeGrandpre. 1995. "My Genes Made Me Do It." *Psychology Today* 28 (July/August): 50–53.

Pillard, Richard C., and J. Michael Bailey. 1998. "Human Sexuality Has a Heritable Component." *Human Biology* 70 (April): 347–65.

Platt, Leah. 2001. "Not Your Father's High School Club." *The American Prospect* 12(1): A37–A39.

Price, Jammie, and Michael G. Dalecki. 1998. "The Social Basis of Homophobia: An Empirical Illustration." *Sociological Spectrum* 18: 143–59.

Rice, G., C. Anderson, N. Risch, and G. Ebers. 1999. "Male Homosexuality: Absence of Linkage to Micro-satellite Markets at Xq28." *Science* 284 (April 23): 665–67.

Roberts, J. V. (1995). "Disproportionate Harm: Hate Crime in Canada." Ottawa, Department of Justice Canada. WD1995-11e.

Roen, Katrina. 2001. "Transgender Theory and Embodiment: The Risk of Racial Marginalisation." *Journal of Gender Studies* 10(3): 253–63.

Rosin, Hanna, and Richard Morin. 1999. "In One Area, Americans Still Draw a Line on Acceptability." *Washington Post*, national weekly edition, 16 (January 11): 8.

Rubin, Gayle. 1975. "The Traffic in Women: Notes on the Political Economy of Sex." In Rayna R. Reiter (ed.), *Toward an Anthropology of Women*, pp. 157–210. New York: Monthly Review Press.

Sanday, Peggy R. 1995. "Pulling Train." In P. S. Rothenberg (ed.), *Race, Class, and Gender in the United States*, 3rd ed., pp. 396–402. New York: St. Martin's Press.

Schellenberg, E. Glenn, Jessie Hirt, and Alan Sears. 1999. "Attitudes toward Homosexuals Among Students at a Canadian University." *Sex Roles* 40(1/2): 139–52.

Simon, A. 1995. "Some Correlates of Individuals' Attitudes toward Lesbians." *Journal of Homosexuality* 29: 89–103.

Stone, Sharon D. (ed.). 1990. "Lesbian Mothers: Organizing." In *Lesbians in Canada*, pp. 191–205. Toronto: Between the Lines.

Sullivan, A. 1997. "The Conservative Case." In A. Sullivan (ed.), *Same-Sex Marriage: Pro and Con*, pp. 146–54. New York: Vintage Books.

Sullivan, Nikki. 2003. *A Critical Introduction to Queer Theory.* New York: New York University Press.

Talaga, T. 2011. "Ten Years On, Same-Sex Couples Renew Their Vows." *The Toronto Star.* http://www.thestar.com/news/canada/article/920947--ten-years-on-same-sex-couples-renew-their-vows.

Taylor, C. 2009. *Youth Speak Up About Homophobia and Transphobia: The First National Climate Survey on Homophobia in Canadian Schools.* Winnipeg: EGALE Canada Human Rights Trust: 96.

Thompson, Cooper. 1995. "A New Vision of Masculinity." In P. S. Rothenberg (ed.), *Race, Class, and Gender in the United States*, 3rd ed., pp. 475–81. New York: St. Martin's Press.

Valentine, D. 2007. *Imagining Transgender.* Durham and London: Duke University Press.

Warnke, Georgia. 2005. "Race, Gender, and Antiessentialist Politics" *Signs* 31(1): 93–116.

Weston, Kath. 1991. *Families We Choose: Lesbians, Gays, Kinship.* New York: Columbia University Press.

Wetzel, Janice Wood. 2001. "Human Rights in the 20th Century: Weren't Gays and Lesbians Human?" In Mary E. Swigonski and Robin S. Mama (eds.), *From Hate Crimes to Human Rights: A Tribute to Matthew Shepard*, pp. 15–31. New York: Haworth Press.

Wilcox, Clyde, and Robin Wolpert. 2000. "Gay Rights in the Public Sphere: Public Opinion on Gay and Lesbian Equality." In Craig A. Rimmerman, Kenneth D. Wald, and Clyde Wilcox (eds.), *The Politics of Gay Rights*, pp. 409–32. Chicago: University of Chicago Press.

Yang, Alan. 1999. *From Wrongs to Rights 1973 to 1999: Public Opinion on Gay and Lesbian Americans Moves toward Equality.* New York: The Policy Institute of the National Gay and Lesbian Task Force.

Yogis, J. A., R. R. Duplak, and J. R. Trainor. 1996. *Sexual Orientation and Canadian Law: An Assessment of the Law Affecting Lesbian and Gay Persons.* Toronto: Emond Montgomery Publications Limited.

Chapter 10

Albelda, Randy, and Chris Tilly. 1997. *Glass Ceilings and Bottomless Pits: Women's Work, Women's Poverty*. Boston, MA: South End Press.

Alex-Assensoh, Yvette. 1995. "Myths about Race and the Underclass." *Urban Affairs Review* 31: 3–19.

Barlow, Maude, and Bruce Campbell. 1995. *Straight through the Heart*. Toronto: HarperCollins Publishers Ltd.

Bricker, Darrell, and Edward Greenspon. 2001. *Searching for Certainty: Inside the New Canadian Mindset*. Toronto: Doubleday Canada.

Briggs, Vernon M. Jr. 1998. "American-Style Capitalism and Income Disparity: The Challenge of Social Anarchy." *Journal of Economic Issues* 32(2): 473–81.

Canada Customs and Revenue Agency. 2002. "About the Canada Child Tax Benefit (CCTB)." http://www.ccra-adrc.gc.ca/benefits/faq_about-e.html.

Canadian Centre for Policy Alternatives Monitor. 1999. September. http://www.policyalternatives.ca.

Canadian Research Institute for the Advancement of Women (CRIAW). 2006. "Intersectional Feminist Frameworks: An Emerging Vision." Ottawa: CRIAW.

Carroll, William, and R. S. Ratner. 2001. "Sustaining Oppositional Cultures in 'Post-Socialist' Times: A Comparative Study of Three Social Movement Organisations." *Sociology* 35(3): 605–29.

Centre for Social Justice. 2001. "Wealth of the Top 20% of Families Surges 39% since 1984, while the Bottom Sinks." March 15. http://www.socialjustice.org/media/releas/wealthgap.html.

Chossudovsky, Michel. 1998. "Global Poverty in the Late Twentieth Century." *Journal of International Affairs* 52(1): 293–303.

Conley, Dalton. 2001. "Capital for College: Parental Assets and Postsecondary Schooling." *Sociology of Education* 74 (January): 59–72.

Corak, Miles. 1998. "Getting Ahead in Life: Does Your Parents' Income Count?" *Canadian Social Trends* 49 (Summer): 6–15.

Coyne, Andrew. 1997. "Poverty Study Data a 'Monumental Absurdity.'" *Waterloo Record* (July 17): A7.

Daub, Shannon, and Margaret Young. 1999. "Families Need More Than Tax Fairness." http://www.policyalternatives.ca.

Davis, Kingsley, and Wilbert Moore. 1945. "Some Principles of Stratification." *American Sociological Review* 10: 242–49.

Deen, Thalif. 2000. "NGOs Call for UN Poverty Eradication Fund." Global Policy Forum. http://www.globalpolicy.org/msummit/millenni/millfor3.htm.

Dranoff, Linda Silver. 2001. *Everyone's Guide to the Law*. Toronto: HarperCollins Publishers Ltd.

Duncan, Greg J., and Jeanne Brooks-Gunn. 1997. "Income Effects across the Life Span: Integration and Interpretation." In Greg J. Duncan and Jeanne Brooks-Gunn (eds.), *Consequences of Growing Up Poor*, pp. 596–610. New York: Russell Sage Foundation.

Economic Policy Institute. 2000. "Issue Guide to the Minimum Wage." http://www.epinet.org/Issuesguides/minwage/minwagefaq.html.

Fawcett, Gail. 1999. "Disability in the Labour Market: Barriers and Solutions." *Perception* 23 (December). Canadian Council on Social Development. http://www.ccsd.ca/perception/233/disab.htm.

Feinberg, Leslie. 1993. *Stone Butch Blues*. New York: Firebrand Books.

Finn, Ed. 2006. "December 2005: The 'Big Business Bang' Theory: Social, Economic, Environmental Ills All Have the Same Cause." Ottawa: Canadian Centre for Policy Alternatives. June 10. http://www.policyalternatives.ca/MonitorIssues/2005/12/MonitorIssue1274/index.cfm?pa=DDC3F905.

Flavin, Christopher. 2001. "Rich Planet, Poor Planet." In Lester R. Brown, Christopher Flavin, and Hilary French (eds.), *State of the World 2001*. Worldwatch Institute. New York: W.W. Norton & Co.

Galabuzi, Grace Edward. 2001. *Canada's Creeping Economic Apartheid: The Economic Segregation and Social Marginalisation of Racialised Groups*, 2nd ed. Toronto: CSJ Foundation for Research and Education.

Gans, Herbert J. 1972. "The Positive Functions of Poverty." *American Journal of Sociology* 78 (September): 275–388.

Global Poverty Report. 2000. G8 Okinawa Summit, July 2000.

Government of Canada. 1999. *National Child Benefit Progress Report 1999*. http://www.socialunion.gc.ca/NCB-99/html.

Guest, Dennis. 1999a. "Social Security." In James H. Marsh (ed.), *The Canadian Encyclopedia: Year 2000 Edition*, pp. 2200–2204. Toronto: McClelland & Stewart Inc.

Guest, Dennis. 1999b. "Family Allowance." In James H. Marsh (ed.), *The Canadian Encyclopedia: Year 2000 Edition*, pp. 1815–16. Toronto: McClelland & Stewart, Inc.

Health Canada. 1999. *Toward a Healthy Future: Second Report on the Health of Canadians*. Prepared by the Federal, Provincial, and Territorial Advisory Committee on Population Health for the Meeting of Ministers of Health, Charlottetown, PEI, September 1999.

Hill, Lewis E. 1998. "The Institutional Economics of Poverty: An Inquiry into the Causes and Effects of Poverty." *Journal of Economic Issues* 32(2): 279–86.

Human Resources Development Canada. 2001. "What is the CESG?" http://www.hrdc-drhc.gc.ca/brib/learnlit/cesg/013/001_e.shtml.

Institute of Development Studies. 2006. *Realising Sexual Rights*. U.K.: Institute of Development Studies.

Keating, G., Michael O'Sullivan, Anthony Shorrocks, James B. Davies, Rodrigo Lluberas. 2010 *Global Wealth Report*. Zurich: Credit Suisse.

Kennedy, Bruce P., Ichiro Kawachi, Roberta Glass, and Deborah Prothrow-Stith. 1998. "Income

Distribution, Socioeconomic Status, and Self-Rated Health in the U.S.: Multilevel Analysis." *British Medical Journal* 317(7163): 917–22.

Kiely, Ray. 2005. "Globalization and Poverty, and the Poverty of Globalization Theory." *Current Sociology* 53(6): 895–914.

Klugman, J. 2010. *Human Development Report 2010: The Real Wealth of Nations—Pathways to Human Development.* New York: United Nations Development Programme.

Knickerbocker, Brad. 2000. "Nongovernmental Organizations Are Fighting and Winning Social, Political Battles." Global Policy Forum. http://www.globalpolicy. org/ngos/00role.htm.

Krahn, Harvey. 1994. "Social Stratification." In Robert Brym (ed.), *New Society Brief Edition: Sociology for the Twenty-First Century,* pp. 2.1–2.31. Toronto: Harcourt Brace Jovanovich.

Larin, Kathryn. 1998. "Should We Be Worried about the Widening Gap between the Rich and the Poor?" *Insight on the News* 14(5): 24–28.

Lewis, Oscar. 1966. "The Culture of Poverty." *Scientific American* 2(5): 19–25.

—————. 1998. "The Culture of Poverty: Resolving Common Social Problems." *Society* 35(2): 7–10.

Lozada, Carlos. 2003. "Measuring Poverty: Harder Than It Looks." *Commonweal,* November 7.

Luker, Kristin. 1996. *Dubious Conceptions: The Politics of Teenage Pregnancy.* Cambridge, MA: Harvard University Press.

Mann, Judy. 2000. "Demonstrators at the Barricades Aren't Very Subtle, but They Sometimes Win." *The Washington Spectator* 26 (May 15): 1–3.

Marx, Karl, and Friedrich Engels. 1965[1888]. *The Communist Manifesto.* New York: Penguin.

Maxim, Paul, et al. 2001. "Dispersion and Polarization of Income among Aboriginal and non-Aboriginal Canadians." *Canadian Review of Sociology and Anthropology* 38(4): 465–76.

Mayer, Susan E. 1997. *What Money Can't Buy: Family Income and Children's Life Chances.* Cambridge, MA: Harvard University Press.

Mead, L. 1992. *The New Politics of Poverty: The Non-Working Poor in America.* New York: Basic Books.

Mishel, Lawrence, Jared Bernstein, and John Schmitt. 2001. *The State of Working America 2000/2001.* Ithaca, NY: Cornell University Press.

Moscovitch, Allan. 1999. "Welfare State." In James H. Marsh (ed.), *The Canadian Encyclopedia: Year 2000 Edition,* pp. 2493–96. Toronto: McClelland & Stewart, Inc.

Narayan, Deepa. 2000. *Voices of the Poor: Can Anyone Hear Us?* New York: Oxford University Press.

National Council of Welfare. 1997. "Canada Welfare Incomes." http:// csf.colorado.edu/lists/psn/ dec97/0071.html.

—————. 1998. *Profiles of Welfare: Myths and Realities: A Report by the National Council of Welfare.* Spring. http://www.ncwcnbes.net/ htmdocument/reportprowelfare. repprowelfare.htm.

—————. 1999a. *Children First: A Pre-Budget Report by the National Council of Welfare.* Autumn. http:// www.ncwcnbes.net/htmdocument/ reportchildfirst/repchildfirst.htm.

—————. 1999b. "No Such Thing as a 'Typical' Welfare Case, Says National Council of Welfare Report." http://www.ncwcnbes.net/ htmdocument/reportprowelfare/ PRESSPROWELFARE.htm.

—————. 1999c. *Preschool Children: Promises to Keep.* Spring. http:// www.ncwcnbes.net/htmdocument/ reportpromise/firstpag.htm.

—————. 2000. *Poverty Profile 1998.* Ottawa: Ministry of Public Works.

—————. 2002a. "Fact Sheet: Welfare Recipients." http://www. ncwcnbes.net/htmdocument/ principales/numberwelfare.htm.

—————. 2002b. *Poverty Profile 1999.* http://www.ncwcnbes.net/ htmdocument/reportpovertypro000/ Introduction.html.

—————. 2003. *Welfare Incomes 2003.* Ottawa: National Council of Welfare.

—————. 2004. *Income for Living?* Ottawa: National Council of Welfare.

National Anti-Poverty Organization. 2006. "The Face of Poverty in Canada: An Overview." Ottawa: National Anti-Poverty Association.

Neal, Rusty. 2004. *Voices: Women, Poverty and Homelessness in Canada.* Ottawa: National Anti-Poverty Association.

Orlikow, Lionel. 1999. "Students, Financial Aid." In James H. Marsh (ed.), *The Canadian Encyclopedia: Year 2000 Edition,* pp. 2264–65. Toronto: McClelland & Stewart Inc.

Palameta, B. 2005. "Low Income among Immigrants and Visible Minorities: Perspectives." Statistics Canada. Catalogue no. 75-001-XIE. Ottawa.

Paul, James A. 2000. "NGOs and Global Policy-Making." Global Policy Forum. http://www. globalpolicy.org/ngos/analysis/ anal00htm.

Pen, Jan. 2011 (Jan. 20). "The Rise and Fall of the Cognitive Elite." *The Economist.* London: The Economist Newspaper Limited.

Reid, Shyanne, Helen Burman, and Cheryl Forchuk. 2005. "Living on the Streets in Canada: A Feminist Narrative Study of Girls and Young Women." *Issues in Comprehensive Pediatric Nursing* 28: 237–56.

Reutter, Linda, et al. 2006. "Public Attributions for Poverty in Canada." *Canadian Review of Sociology and Anthropology* 43(1): 1–22.

Ross, David P., and Clarence Lochhead. 1999. "Poverty." In James H. Marsh (ed.), *The Canadian Encyclopedia: Year 2000 Edition,* pp. 1880–82. Toronto: McClelland & Stewart, Inc.

Ross, David P., E. Richard Shillington, and Clarence Lochhead. 1994. *The Canadian Fact Book on Poverty.* Ottawa: Canadian Council on Social Development.

Sarlo, Christopher. 1992. *Poverty in Canada.* Vancouver: The Fraser Institute.

—————. 1996. *Poverty in Canada.* Vancouver: The Fraser Institute.

Schenk, Christopher. 2001. *From Poverty Wages to a Living Wage.* Toronto: CJS Foundation for Research and Education.

Seccombe, Karen. 2001. "Families in Poverty in the 1990s: Trends, Causes, Consequences, and Lessons Learned." In Robert M. Milardo (ed.), *Understanding Families into the*

New Millennium: A Decade in Review, pp. 313–32. Minneapolis, MN: National Council on Family Relations.

Speth, James Gustave. 1998. "Poverty: A Denial of Human Rights." *Journal of International Affairs* 52(1): 277–86.

Statistics Canada. 1998a. *Canada Yearbook 1999*. Ottawa: Minister of Industry.

————. 1998b. *The Daily*, May 12. http://www.statscan.ca:80/Daily/English/980512/d980512.htm.

————. 2000. "Family Income 1998." *The Daily*, June 12. http://www.statcan.ca/Daily/English/000612/d000612a.htm.

————. 2002. "Gender Pay Differentials: Impact of the Workplace." *The Daily*, June 19. http://www.statcan.ca/Daily/English/020619/d0201619b.htm.

Streeten, Paul. 1998. "Beyond the Six Veils: Conceptualizing and Measuring Poverty." *Journal of International Affairs* 52(1): 1–8.

United Nations. 2005. "Reports on the World Social Situation, 2005." New York: United Nations.

————. 2008. "More People Living in Extreme Poverty Than Previously Thought—World Bank." http://www.un.org/apps/news/story.asp?NewsID=27842&Cr=poverty&Cr1=world%20bank.

————. 2010. Press Release. "MDG Report 2008: End Poverty 2015." New York.

United Nations Development Programme. 1997. *Human Development Report 1997*. New York: Oxford University Press.

————. 2000. *Human Development Report 2000*. New York: Oxford University Press.

Van Kempen, Eva T. 1997. "Poverty Pockets and Life Chances: On the Role of Place in Shaping Social Inequality." *American Behavioural Scientist* 41(3): 430–50.

Wilson, D., and David MacDonald. 2010. *The Income Gap between Aboriginal Peoples and the Rest of Canada*. Ottawa: Canadian Centre for Policy Alternatives.

Wilson, William J. 1987. *The Truly Disadvantaged: The Inner City, the Underclass, and Public Policy*.

Chicago: University of Chicago Press.

————. 1996. *When Work Disappears: The World of the New Urban Poor*. New York: Knopf.

World Bank. 2007. "Understanding Poverty." www.worldbank.org.

Yali, Ann Marie, and Tracey Revinson. 2004. "How Changes in Population Demographics Will Impact Health Psychology: Incorporating a Broader Notion of Cultural Competence into the Field." *Health Psychology* 23(2): 147–55.

Yalnizyan, A. 1998. *The Growing Gap*. Toronto: Centre for Social Justice.

Chapter 11

Adams, Eve, Betsy Cahill, and Stacy Ackerland. 2005. "A Qualitative Study of Latino Lesbian and Gay Youths' Experiences with Discrimination and the Career Development Process." *Journal of Vocational Behaviour* 66:199–218.

Ambrose, Soren. 1998. "The Case against the IMF." Campaign for Human Rights Newsletter 12, December 8. http://www.summersault.co...wsletter/news12.html.

Ash, Russell. 2001. *The Top 10 of Everything: Canadian Edition 2002*. Toronto: Dorling Kindersley Limited.

Bassi, Laurie J., and Jens Ludwig. 2000. "School-to-Work Programs in the United States: A Multi-Firm Case Study of Training, Benefits, and Costs." *Industrial and Labor Relations Review* 53 (January): 219.

Bavendam, James. 2000. "Managing Job Satisfaction." Special Reports 6: 1–2. Bavendam Research Incorporated. http://www.bavendam.com.

Bell, Daniel. 1973. *The Coming of Post-Industrial Society*. New York: Basic Books.

Bellan, Ruben C. 1999. "Foreign Investment." In James H. Marsh (ed.), *The Canadian Encyclopedia: Year 2000 Edition*, pp. 884–85. Toronto: McClelland & Stewart Inc.

Benjamin, Medea. 1998. "What's Fair about Fair Labor Association (FLA)?" Sweatshop Watch. http://www.sweatshopwatch.org/swatch/

headlines/1998/org/swatch/headlines/1998/gex_fla.html.

Benner, Chris. 2003. "'Computers in the Wild': Guilds, and Next-Generation Union Is Center in the Information Revolution." *IRSH* 48: 181–204.

Bernard, A. 2009. "Job Stability and Unemployment Duration in Manufacturing." Ottawa: Statistics Canada. Catalogue no. 75-001-X.

Bettelheim, Adriel. 1998. "Sleep Deprivation." *CQ Researcher* 8(24): 553–76.

Bracey, Gerald W. 1995. "The Fifth Bracey Report on the Condition of Public Education." *Phi Delta Kappan* (October): 149–62.

Bricker, Darrell, and Edward Greenspon. 2001. *Searching for Certainty: Inside the New Canadian Mindset*. Toronto: Doubleday Canada.

Canada Revenue Agency. 2006. "Universal Child Care Benefit." http://www.cra-arc.gc.ca/benefits/uccb/faq-e.html#q2.

Canadian Council on Social Development. 2001. The Progress of Canada's Children 2001—Highlights. March. http://www.ccsd.ca/pubs/2001/pcc2001.hl.htm.

Carnoy, Martin, and Manuel Castells. 1997. *Sustainable Flexibility: A Prospective Study on Work, Family and Society in the Information Age*. Paris: Organization for Economic Development.

Caston, Richard J. 1998. *Life in a Business-Oriented Society: A Sociological Perspective*. Boston: Allyn and Bacon.

CBC News. 2010. (Oct. 14). "Dozens of G20 Accused Have Charges Dropped." http://www.cbc.ca/news/canada/toronto/story/2010/10/14/g20-charges-dropped685.html.

CBC News (Gillian Findlay). 2011. "You Should Have Stayed at Home." *The Fifth Estate*. T. Weinstein. Canada, CBC: 45 min.

Clark, Katie, and Sally Kalin. 1996. "Technostressed Out? How to Cope in the Digital Age." *Library Journal* (August): 30–32.

Coleman, James. 1994. *The Criminal Elite: The Sociology of White Collar Crime*, 3rd ed. New York: St. Martin's Press.

Conrad, Peter. 1999. "Wellness in the Work Place: Potentials and Pitfalls of Work-Site Health Promotion." In K. Charmaz and D. A. Paterniti (eds.), *Health, Illness, and Healing: Society, Social Context, and Self*, pp. 263–75. Los Angeles: Roxbury Publishing Company.

Danaher, Kevin. 1998. "Are Workers Waking Up?" Global Exchange: Education for Action. December 17. http://www.globalexchange. org/education/economy/laborday. html.

Deutschmann, C. 2011. "The Euro Trouble and the Global Financial Crisis." *Economic Sociology: The European Electronic Newsletter* 12: 17–21.

Doherty, Gillian. 2001. "Moving towards Achieving Quality Child Care." In Gordon Cleveland and Michael Krashinsky (eds.), *Our Children's Future: Child Care Policy in Canada*, pp. 126–41. Toronto: University of Toronto Press.

Dorman, Peter. 2001. "Child Labour in the Developed Economies." Geneva: International Labour Office.

Durkheim, Emile. [1893] 1966. *On the Division of Labor in Society*, trans. G. Simpson. New York: Free Press.

Eitzen, Stanley, and Maxine Baca Zinn (eds.). 1990. *The Reshaping of America: Social Consequences of the Changing Economy*. Englewood Cliffs, NJ: Prentice-Hall.

Epstein, Gerald, Julie Graham, and Jessica Nembhard (eds.). 1993. "Third World Socialism and the Demise of COMECON." In Creating a New World Economy: Forces of Change and Plans of Action, pp. 405–20. Philadelphia: Temple University Press.

Errington, Jane. 1993. "Pioneers and Suffragists." In Lorraine Code, Lindsay Dorney, and Sandra Burt (eds.), *Changing Patterns: Women in Canada*, 2nd ed., pp. 59–91. Toronto: McClelland & Stewart Inc.

Feather, Norman T. 1990. *The Psychological Impact of Unemployment*. New York: Springer-Verlag.

Ferrao, Vincent. 2010. "'Paid Work' Series: Women in Canada: A Gender-Based Statistical Report."

Statistics Canada. Catalogue no. 89-503-X.

Frederick, James and Nancy Lessin. 2000. "Blame the Worker: The Rise of Behavioral-Based Safety Programs." *Multinational Monitor* 21 (November). http://www.essential. org/monitor/ mm2000/00november/toc.html.

Galinsky, Ellen, and James T. Bond. 1998. *The 1998 Business Work-Life Study*. New York: Families and Work Institute.

Ghalam, Nancy Zukewich. 2000. "Paid and Unpaid Work." In Statistics Canada, *Women in Canada 2000: A Gender-Based Statistical Report*, pp. 97–134. Ottawa: Statistics Canada.

"Global Labor Repression." 2000. Behind the Lines. *Multinational Monitor* 21 (November). http:// www.essential.org/monitor/ mm2000/00november/toc.html.

Government of Alberta. 2011. "Alberta Family Employment Tax Credit." http://www.finance. alberta.ca/business/tax_rebates/ alberta_family_employment_ taxcredit.html.

Greenhouse, Steven. 2000. "Anti-Sweatshop Movement Is Achieving Gains Overseas." *The New York Times on the Web*. http://nytimes. com.

Halford, Susan. 2006. "Collapsing the Boundaries? Fatherhood, Organization and Home-Working." *Gender, Work and Organization* 13(4): 383–402.

Hallsworth, Alan. 1993. "The External Trade of Canada." In *The U.S.A. and Canada*, pp. 432–39. London: Europa Publications.

Hargis, Michael J. 2001. "Bangladesh: Garment Workers Burned to Death." *Industrial Worker* #1630, 98 (January/February). http://parsons. ww.org/~iw/jan2001/stories/intl. html.

Health Canada. 1999. Statistical Report on the Health of Canadians. December 25. http://www.hc-sc. gc.ca/hppb/phdd/report/state/eng/ over.html.

Heidegren, Carl-Goran. 2004. "Recognition and Social Theory." *Acta Sociologica* 47(4): 365–73.

Hochschild, Arlie Russell. 1997. *The Time Bind: When Work Becomes Home*

and Home Becomes Work. New York: Henry Holt and Company.

Hughes, Christina. 2004. "Class and Other Identifications in Managerial Careers: The Case of the Lemon Dress." *Work and Organization* 11(5): 526–43.

Human Resources and Development Canada (HRDC). 2006. "Employment Insurance (EI) and Maternity, Parental and Sickness Benefits." Ottawa: HRDC. Accessed June 10, 2006. http:// www.hrsdc.gc.ca/asp/gateway. asp?hr=en/ei/types/special. shtml&hs=aed#Who.

Human Rights Watch. 2000. "Unfair Advantage: Workers' Freedom of Association in the United States under International Human Rights Standards." http://www.hrw.org/ reports/2000/uslabor.

————. 2001. World Report 2001. http://www.hrw.org.

International Labour Organization. 2000. "Statistics: Revealing a Hidden Tragedy." http://www.ilo. org/public/...ish/standards/idec/ simpoc/stats/4stt.htm.

————. 2001. World Employment Report 2001: Life at Work in the Information Economy. Geneva: International Labour Organization.

————. 2006. Review of Annual Reports under the Follow-up to the International Labour Organization Declaration of Fundamental Principles and Rights at Work. Geneva: International Labour Organization.

Kennedy, Joseph II. 1996. "Keynote Address." In *Forced Labor: The Prostitution of Children*, pp. 1–6. Washington, DC: U.S. Department of Labor, Bureau of International Labor Affairs.

Klein, Naomi. 2000. *No Logo: Taking Aim at the Brand Name Bullies*. Toronto: Vintage Canada.

Krahn, Harvey, and Graham Lowe. 2002. *Work, Industry and Canadian Society*. Toronto: Thomson Nelson.

Krauss, K. 2010. "G8/G20 Communique: G20 News and Legal Fall Out." Rabble.ca: News for the Rest of Us. http://www.rabble.ca/ blogs/bloggers/statica/2010/09/ g8g20-communiqu%C3%A9-g20-news-and-legal-fall-out.

Lenski, Gerard, and J. Lenski. 1987. *Human Societies: An Introduction to Macrosociology*, 5th ed. New York: McGraw-Hill.

Leonard, Bill. 1996. "From School to Work: Partnerships Smooth the Transition." *HR Magazine* (Society for Human Resource Management). December 8, 1998. http://www.shrm.org/hrmag... articles/0796cov.htm.

Levitan, Sar A., Garth L. Mangum, and Stephen L. Mangum. 1998. *Programs in Aid of the Poor*, 7th ed. Baltimore: Johns Hopkins University Press.

Liem, Joan H., and G. Ramsey Liem. 1990. "Understanding the Individual and Family Effects of Unemployment." In J. Eckenrode and S. Gore (eds.), *Stress between Work and Family*, pp. 175–204. New York: Plenum Press.

Marshall, Katherine. 1999. "Employment after Childbirth." *Perspectives on Labour and Income* (Autumn): 15–25. Catalogue no. 75-001-XPE.

Maule, C.J. 1999. "Multinational Corporation." In James H. Marsh (ed.), *The Canadian Encyclopedia: Year 2000 Edition*, pp. 1536. Toronto: McClelland & Stewart Inc.

McDermott, Elizabeth. 2006. "Surviving in Dangerous Places: Lesbian Identity Performances in the Workplace." *Feminism and Psychology* 16: 193–211.

McLean, Jennifer. 2006. "Forgotten Faculty: Stress and Job Satisfaction among Distance Educators." *Online Journal of Distance Learning and Education* 9(2). http://www.westga.edu/~distance/ojdla/summer92/mclean92.html.

Mishel, Lawrence, Jared Bernstein, and John Schmitt. 2001. *The State of Working America, 2000–2001*. Economic Policy Institute Series. Ithaca, NY: Cornell University Press.

Multinational Monitor. 2000. "Editorial: What Is Society Willing to Spend on Human Beings?" *Multinational Monitor* 21 (November). http://www.essential.org/monitor/mm2000/00november/.

National Council of Welfare. 1999a. Children First: A Pre-Budget Report by the National Council of Welfare. http://www.ncwcnbes.net/htmdocument/reportchildrenfirst.htm.

———. 1999b. Preschool Children: Promises to Keep. http://www.ncwcnbes.net/htmdocument/reportpromise/firstpag.html.

National Public Radio (NPR). 2005. "Blackberry or Crackberry?" The Morning Edition, originally broadcast January 12, 2005. Available at http://www.npr.org/templates/story/story.php?storyId=4279486.

North, P. 2011. "Should Crisis-Hit Countries Leave the Eurozone?" *Economic Sociology: The European Electronic Newsletter* 12: 21–26.

Ontario Coalition for Better Childcare. 2011. "Child Care: Ontario Can't Work Without It." http://www.childcareontario.org/?p=4205.

Parker, David L. (with Lee Engfer and Robert Conrow). 1998. *Stolen Dreams: Portraits of Working Children*. Minneapolis: Lerner Publications Company.

Reidmann, Agnes, Mary Ann Lamanna, and Adie Nelson. 2003. *Marriages and Families*. Toronto: Thomson Nelson.

Report on the World Social Situation. 1997. New York: United Nations.

Robie, Chet, Ann Marie Ryan, Robert A. Schmieder, Luis Fernando Parra, and Patricia C. Smith. 1998. "The Relation between Job Level and Job Satisfaction." *Group and Organizational Management* 23(4): 470–86.

Ross, Catherine E., and Marylyn P. Wright. 1998. "Women's Work, Men's Work, and the Sense of Control." *Work and Occupations* 25(3): 333–55.

Rotstein, Abraham. 1999. "Economic Nationalism." In James H. Marsh (ed.), *The Canadian Encyclopedia, Year 2000 Edition*, pp. 716–17. Toronto: McClelland & Stewart Inc.

Saskatchewan Federation of Labour. 2006. Brief to the Saskatchewan Minimum Wage Board on Minimum Age of Employment and Employer-Provided Transportation Home.

Sears, Alan. 2005. "Queer Anti-Capitalism: What's Left of Lesbian and Gay Liberation." *Science and Society* 69(1): 92–112.

Silvers, Jonathan. 1996. "Child Labor in Pakistan." *Atlantic Monthly* 277(2): 79–92.

Simone, Rose. 1999. "Couple Speak Out about Dangers of Toxic Substances in Workplace." Kitchener-Waterloo Record (November 10): B7.

Statistics Canada. 1998. Canadian Profile 2000. Ottawa: Ministry of Industry.

———. 1999. "Labour Force Update: An Overview of the Labour Market." *The Daily*, January 27.

———. 2002. "Unionization." *The Daily*, August 24. http://www.statcan.ca/Daily/English/000824/d000824d.htm.

———. 2003. "Earnings of Canadians: Making a Living in the New Economy." *The Daily*, March 11. http://www12.statcan.ca/english/census01/Products/Analytic/companion/earn/contents.cfm.

Tremblay, Stephane, Nancy A. Ross, and Jean-Marie Berthelot. 2002. "Regional Socio-Economic Context and Health." Supplement to Health Reports 13. Catalogue no. 92-003. Ottawa: Statistics Canada.

U.S. Department of Labor. 1995. "By the Sweat and Toil of Children." The Use of Child Labor in U.S. Agricultural Imports and Forced and Bonded Child Labor, Vol. 2. Washington, DC: U.S. Department of Labor, Bureau of International Labor Affairs.

"Underage and Unprotected: Child Labor in Egypt's Cotton Fields." 2001. Human Rights Watch 13 (January).

UNICEF (United Nations International Children's Emergency Fund). 1997. State of the World's Children, 1997. New York: United Nations.

———. 2000. The Progress of Nations 2000. New York: United Nations.

Waring, Marilyn. 1988. *If Women Counted*. Toronto: Macmillan.

Went, Robert. 2000. *Globalization: Neoliberal Challenge, Radical Responses*. Sterling, VA: Pluto Press.

Wilkins, K., and S. G. Mackenzie. 2007. "Work Injuries." *Health*

Reports. Statistics Canada. Catalogue no. 82-003: 18.

Yanz, Lynda, and Bob Jeffcott. 1997. "Fighting Sweatshops/Building Solidarity: Exposing the Gap." *Canadian Dimensions* 31 (October): 25–29.

Chapter 12

AAUW (American Association of University Women). 1998. "Report Finds Separating by Sex Not the Solution to Gender Inequity in School." Press release (2300). http://aauw.org.

Althusser, Louis. 1971. "Ideology and Ideological State Apparatuses." Trans. Ben Brewster. *Lenin and Philosophy and Other Essays.* New York: Monthly Review Press. Pages 127–86.

Aberle-Grasse, Melissa. 2000. "The Washington Study Service-Learning Year of Eastern Mennonity University: Reflections on 23 Years of Service Learning." *American Behavioral Scientist* 43: 848–57.

Appleby, Timothy. 2000. "Weapons Turn Up More Often at Schools: Police." *The Globe and Mail* (February 18): A18.

Ascher, Carol, Norm Fruchter, and Robert Berne. 1997. *Hard Lessons: Public Schools and Privatization.* New York: Twentieth Century Fund.

Ash, Russell. 2001. *The Top 10 of Everything: Canadian Edition 2002.* Toronto: Dorling Kindersley Limited.

Associated Press. 1998. "Education Becomes Major Political Issue as Candidates Listen to Voters." *New York Times* (September 20): A5.

Bankston, Carl, and Stephen Caldas. 1997. "The American School Dilemma: Race and Scholastic Performance." *Sociological Quarterly* 38(3): 423–29.

Barlow, Maude, and Heather-Jane Robertson. 1994. *Class Warfare: The Assault on Canada's Schools.* Toronto: Key Porter Books.

Bhattacharjee, K. 2003. *The Ontario Safe Schools Act: School Discipline and Discrimination.* Toronto: Ontario Human Rights Commission. http://www.ohrc.

on.ca/en/resources/discussion_consultation/SafeSchoolsConsult RepENG?page=SafeSchoolsConsult RepENG-V_.html.

Bibby, Reginald W. 2001. *Canada's Teens: Today, Yesterday, and Tomorrow.* Toronto: Stoddart.

Bowlby, G. 2008. "Provincial Drop-Out Rates." *Labour Force Survey.* Ottawa: Statistics Canada. http://www.statcan.gc.ca/pub/81-004-x/2005004/8984-eng.htm.

Bracey, Gerald W. 1998. "Are U.S. Students Behind?" *The American Prospect* 37 (March-April): 54–70. http://www.prospect.org/archives/37/37bracfs.html.

Bricker, Darrell, and Edward Greenspon. 2001. *Searching for Certainty: Inside the New Canadian Mindset.* Toronto: Doubleday Canada.

Brooks, Jacqueline, and E. G. Thompson. 2005. "Social Justice in the Classroom." *Educational Leadership* 63(1): 48–52.

Bushweller, Kevin. 1995. "Turning Our Backs on Boys." *Education Digest* (January): 9–12.

Call, Kathleen, Lorie Grabowski, Jeylan Mortimer, Katherine Nash, and Chaimun Lee. 1997. "Impoverished Youth and the Attainment Process." Presented at the annual meeting of the American Sociological Association, Toronto, Canada, August.

Campaign 2000. 2001. "Child Poverty in Canada: Report Card 2000." Toronto Campaign 2000.

Canadian Council on Social Development. 1999. *Thinking Ahead: Trends Affecting Public Education in the Future.* Ottawa: Canadian Council on Social Development.

———. 2001. *The Progress of Canada's Children 2001—Highlights.* http://www.ccsd.ca/pubs/2-1/pcc2001.hl.htm.

CAUT. 2005. "University Tuition Fees in Canada, 2003." *Education Review* 5(1): 1–4.

Canadian Press. 2000. "School Violence: Read All about It." *The Globe and Mail* (May 6): A15.

Chernos, Saul. 1998. "Alternative Route." *Education Today* 10 (Winter): 12–15.

Clark, Warren. 1999. "Paying off Student Loans." *Canadian Social Trends* 51 (Winter): 24–28.

Clarke, Edward H. 1873. *Sex in Education; or, a Fair Chance for the Girls.* Boston: J. R. Osgood and Co.

Cohen, Warren. 1998. "Vouchers for Good and Ill." *U.S. News and World Report* (April 27): 46.

Conciatore, Jacqueline. 2000. "Study Shows That More than Half of American Colleges Now Have Diversity Requirements." *Black Issues in Higher Education* 17: 22.

Covell, Katherine. 2001. *Canada's Non-Governmental Organizations Report.* Submitted for the United Nations General Assembly Special Session, September 19–21 (on behalf of the Canadian Coalition for the Rights of Children), February 2001.

Crane, Jennifer. 1999. "Help Troublemakers, Schools Told: Expelling Kids Breeds Violence, Psychiatrist Says." *Toronto Star* (May 24): A2.

Curtis, James E., and Ronald D. Lambert. 1994. "Ideology and Social Change." In Lorne Tepperman, James E. Curtis, and R. Jack Richardson (eds.), *The Social World,* 3rd ed., pp. 710–58. Toronto: McGraw-Hill.

Dardur, Antonia. 1991. *Culture and Power in the Classroom: A Critical Foundation for Bicultural Education.* New York: Bergin and Garvey.

Dei, George. 1999. "School Reforms in Ontario: The Marketization of Education and the Resulting Silence on Equity." *Alberta Journal of Educational Research* 45(2): 111.

———. 2001. "Rescuing the Theory: Anti-Racism and Inclusive Education." *Race, Gender and Class* 8(1): 139.

Digest of Educational Statistics. 2001. Chapters 1–6. National Center for Educational Statistics. http://nces.ed.gov/pubs2001/digest.

Doherty, G. 1997. *Zero to Six: The Basis for School Readiness.* Ottawa: Applied Research Branch, Human Resources Development Canada (#R-97-8E).

Drolet, M. 2005. "Participation in Post-secondary Education in Canada: Has the Role of Parental Income and Education Changed over the 1990s?" Ottawa: Statistics Canada. 11F0019MIE No. 243.

Evans, Lorraine, and Kimberly Davies. 2000. "No Sissy Boys Here." *Sex Roles* (February): 255–71.

Fact Sheet. 2000. "2000 Head Start Fact Sheet." Research and Statistics. Washington, DC: Department of Health and Human Services.

Fichten, Catherine S., Maria Barile, and Evelyn Reid. 1999. "Computer Technologies and Women with Disabilities: Is There Common Ground?" *1999 SWC Supplement*, pp. 5, 10. Ottawa: CAUT.

Fisher, Donald, et al. 2006. *Canadian Federal Policy and Postsecondary Education*. University of British Columbia: The Centre for Policy Studies in Higher Education and Training: Faculty of Education. www.chet.educ.ubc.ca.

Fullan, Michael. [1982] 2001. *The New Meaning of Educational Change*, 3rd ed. New York: Teachers College Press.

George, Jane. 1998. "Kuujjuaq Daycare Thrives on Federal Head Start Program." *Nunatsiaq News*, October 29.

Ghalam, Nancy Z. 2000. "Paid and Unpaid Work." In *Women in Canada 2000: A Gender-Based Report*, pp. 97–134. Ottawa: Statistics Canada.

Gilbert, Sid, and Bruce Orok. 1993. "School Leavers." *Canadian Social Trends* (Winter): 2–7.

Gilmartin, Shannon. 2005. "The Centrality and Costs of Heterosexual Romantic Love among First-Year College Women." *The Journal of Higher Education* 76(6): 609–33.

Girvan, Susan (ed.). 2000. *Canadian Global Almanac*. Toronto: Macmillan Canada.

Goldberg, Carey. 1999. "After Girls Get Attention, Focus is on Boys' Woes." In *Themes of the Times: New York Times*, p. 6. Upper Saddle River, NJ: Prentice-Hall.

Government of Canada. 2001. "Early Intervention Programs." http://www.hrdc-drhc.gc.ca.

Hammonds, Bruce. 2002. "The Latest Ideas on School Reform by Michael Fullan." *Leading and Learning for the 21st Century* (June 29): 1, 3. http://www.leading-learning.co.nz/newsletters/vol101-no03-2002.html.

Health Canada. 1999. *Statistical Report on the Health of Canadians*. December 25. http://www.hc-sc.gc.ca/hppb/phdd/report/state/eng/over.html.

Henry, Frances, Carol Tator, Winston Mattis, and Tim Rees. 2000. *The Colour of Democracy: Racism in Canadian Society*, 2nd ed. Toronto: Harcourt Brace Canada.

Humble, Aine, Catherine Richards Solomon, Katherine Allen, Karen Blaisure, and Michael Johnson. 2006. "Feminism and Mentoring of Graduate Students." *Family Relations* 55: 2–15.

James, Carl. 2004. "Assimilation to Accommodation: Immigrants and Changing Patterns of Schooling." *Education Canada* 44(4): 43–45.

Jencks, Christopher, and Meredith Phillips. 1998. "America's Next Achievement Test: Closing the Black–White Test Score Gap." *The American Prospect* (September/October): 44–53.

Johnston, Ann Dowsett. 1999. *Maclean's* (November 15): 31.

———. 2001. "Survival of the Fittest." *Maclean's* (April 23). http://www.macleans.ca.

Kanter, Rosabeth Moss. 1972. "The Organization Child: Experience Management in a Nursery School." *Sociology of Education* 45: 186–211.

Kozol, Jonathan. 1991. *Savage Inequalities: Children in America's Schools*. New York: Crown Publishers.

Lam, Julia. 1997. "The Employment Activity of Chinese-American High-School Students and Its Relationship to Academic Achievement." Presented at the Annual Meeting of the American Sociological Association, Toronto, ON, August.

Lareau, Annette. 1989. *Home Advantage: Social Class and Parental Intervention in Elementary Education*. Philadelphia: Falmer Press.

Levin, Malcolm. 1999. "Alternative Education." In James H. Marsh (ed.), *The Canadian Encyclopedia: Year 2000 Edition*, p. 732. Toronto: McClelland & Stewart Inc.

Levinson, Arlene. 2000. "Study Evaluates Higher Education." Excite.News. http://www.excite.com/news/ap/00130/08/grading.

Literacy. 2000. "Basic Literacy." Literacy Volunteers of America. http://www.literacyvolunteers.org/about/basic.

Livingstone, D. N. 1999. "Educational Opportunity." In James H. Marsh (ed.), *The Canadian Encyclopedia: Year 2000 Edition*, pp. 743–44. Toronto: McClelland & Stewart, Inc.

Mackie, Marlene. 1991. *Gender Explorations in Canada: Further Explorations*. Toronto: Butterworths.

Maclean's. 2002. "Ruling against Bullying." (April 8): 14.

Mahoney, Jill. 2003. "New Edmonton Bylaw Aims to Fight Bullying." *The Globe and Mail* (March 12): A8.

Miss G– Collective. 2005. "The Miss G– Project." Accessed July 1, 2006. http://www.themissgproject.org/.

Merton, Robert K. 1968. *Social Theory and Social Structure*. New York: Free Press.

Muller, Chandra, and Katherine Schiller. 2000. "Leveling the Playing Field?" *Sociology of Education* 73: 196–218.

Murnane, Richard J. 1994. "Education and the Well-Being of the Next Generation." In Sheldon H. Danziger, Gary D. Sandefur, and Daniel H. Weinberg (eds.), *Confronting Poverty: Prescriptions for Change*, pp. 289–307. New York: Russell Sage Foundation.

Noddings, Nel. 1995. "A Morally Defensible Mission for Schools in the Twenty-first Century." *Phi Delta Kappan* (January): 365–68.

Parl-L. n.d. "A Chronology of the Development of Women's Studies in Canada: The 1970's." Accessed June 27, 2006. http://www.unb.ca/PAR-L/chronology1.htm.

Population Reference Bureau. 1999. "World Population: More Than Just Numbers." http://www.prb.org.

Ray, Carol A., and Roslyn A Mickelson. 1993. "Restructuring Students for Restructured Work: The Economy, School Reform, and Non-College-Bound Youths." *Sociology of Education* 66: 1–20.

Rosenthal, Robert, and Lenore Jacobson. 1968. *Pygmalion in the Classroom: Teacher Expectations and Pupils' Intellectual Development*. New York: Holt, Rinehart and Winston.

Ross, David. 1998. "Rethinking Child Poverty." *Insight, Perception* 22(1): 9–11.

Schaefer, Richard T., Robert P. Lamm, Penny Biles, and Susannah J. Wilson. 1996. *Sociology: An Introduction*. Toronto: McGraw-Hill Ryerson.

Schofield, John. 1999. "Learning on the Front Lines." *Maclean's* (January 15): 90–94.

Schrag, Peter. 1997. "The New-Myth of Our Failing Schools." *The Atlantic Monthly* (October). http://www.theatlantic.com/issues/97oct/fail.htm.

Shanker, Albert. 1996. "Mythical Choice and Real Standards." In Michael Darby (ed.), *Reducing Poverty in America*, pp. 154–72. Thousand Oaks, CA: Sage.

Sokoloff, Heather. 2001. "OECD Shows Alberta No. 1 in Reading Skills." *National Post* (December 5): A1, A17.

Sommers, Christina Hoff. 2000. *The War against Boys: How Misguided Feminism Is Harming Young Men*. New York: Simon and Schuster.

Sowell, Thomas. 1994. "Multicultural Education Is Harmful." In David Bender and Bruno Leone (eds.), *Culture Wars: Opposing Viewpoints*, pp. 104–8. San Diego, CA: Greenhaven Press, Inc.

Statistics Canada. 1998. *Canada Yearbook 1999*. Ottawa: Minister of Industry.

————. 2001. "Building Their Futures." http://www2.acf.dhhs.gov/programs/hsb/EHS.

————. 2003a. "Education in Canada: Raising the Standard." Catalogue no. 96F0030XIE2001012. http://www12.statcan.ca/english/census01/products/Analytic/companion/educ/contents.cfm.

————. 2003b. "Family Income and Participation in Postsecondary Education." Catalogue no. 11F0019MIE No. 210.

————. 2005. "University Tuition Fees." *The Daily*, September 1.

————. 2008. "Educational Portrait of Canada, 2006 Census." Ottawa: Minister of Industry. Catalogue no. 97-560-X.

————. 2010. "Education Indicators in Canada: Interrupting High School and Returning to Education." Catalogue no. 81-599-X (005).

Toronto Board of Education. 1993. *The 1991 Every Secondary Student Survey, Part II: Detailed Profiles of Toronto's Secondary School Students*. Toronto: Toronto Board of Education Research Services.

U.S. Newswire. 2000. "Fact Sheet: Building a Stronger Global Partnership." http://www.usnewswire.com/topnews/current_releases.

United Nations Population Fund. 1999. "Campaign Issues: Facing the Facts." Face to Face. http://www.facecampaign.org.

Waterman, Alan. S. (ed.). 1997. *Service-Learning: Applications from the Research*. Mahwah, NJ: Lawrence Erlbaum Associates Publishers.

Webb, Julie. 1989. "The Outcomes of Home-Based Education: Employment and Other Issues." *Educational Review* 41: 121–33.

Whitehead, Fred (ed.). 1994. *Culture Wars: Opposing Viewpoints*. San Diego, CA: Greenhaven Press, Inc.

Wilgoren, Jodi. 2001. "Calls for Change in the Scheduling of the School Day." *The New York Times on the Web*, January 10. http://www.nytimes.com/2001/01/10/nyregion/10scho.html.

Winters, Rebecca. 2000. "From Home to Harvard." *Time*, September 11. http://www.time.com/time/magazine/articles.

Zine, Jasmin. 2002. "Inclusive Schooling in a Plural Society: Removing the Margins." *Education Canada* 42(3): 36–39.

Zlotkowski, E. 1996. "Opportunity for All: Linking Service-Learning and Business Education." *Journal of Business Ethics* 1: 5–19.

Chapter 13

Aeck, Molly. 2005. "Biofuel Use Growing Rapidly." In Linda Starke (ed.), *Vital Signs 2005*, pp. 38–39. New York: W. W. Norton.

Allison, W. 2011. "Viewpoint: We Should Stop Running Away from Radiation." BBC News: World Edition. http://www.bbc.co.uk/news/world-12860842.

American Lung Association. 2005. *Lung Disease Data in Culturally Diverse Communities: 2005*. Available at http://www.lungusa.org.

Aslam, Abid. 2005 (October 9). "Planet Faces Nightmare Forecasts as Chinese Consumption Grows and Grows." Common Dreams News Center. Available at http://www.commondreams.org.

Associated Press. 2000 (January 7). "DaimlerChrysler Corporation Quits Global Climate Coalition." *Environmental News Network*. http://www.enn.com/news/.

Associated Press. 2005 (April 13). "Wal-Mart Pledges $35 Million for Wildlife." MSNBC.com. Available at http://www.msnbc.msn.com.

Ayres, Ed. 2004. "The Hidden Shame of the Global Industrial Economy." *World Watch Magazine* (January-February):18–29.

Baillie, J. E. M., C. Hilton-Taylor, and S. N. Stuart (eds.). 2004. *2004 IUCN Red List of Threatened Species: A Global Species Assessment*. Cambridge, England: International Union for Conservation of Nature and Natural Resources.

Barbosa, L. C. 2009. "Change by Necessity: Ecological Limits to Capitalism, Climate Change, and Obstacles to Transition to an Environmentally Sustainable Economy." SSRN. http://ssrn.com/abstract=1458114.

BBC News. 2009. "Why Did Copenhagen Fail to Deliver a Climate Deal?" http://news.bbc.co.uk/2/hi/8426835.stm.

Blatt, Harvey. 2005. *America's Environmental Report Card: Are We Making the Grade?* Cambridge, MA: MIT Press.

Bohan, Caren. 2005 (August 23). "The Illulissat Glacier, a Wonder of the World Melting Away." Common Dreams News Center. Available at http://www.commondreams.org.

Bright, Chris. 2003. "A History of Our Future." In Linda Starke (ed.), *State of the World 2003*, pp. 3–13. New York: W. W. Norton.

Brown, L. 2007 (Jan. 4). "Distillery Demand for Grain to Fuel Cars Vastly Understated: World May Be Facing Highest Grain Prices in History." *Earth Policy News.* http://www.earthpolicy.org.

Brown, Lester R. 2003. *Plan B: Rescuing a Planet under Stress and a Civilization in Trouble.* New York: W. W. Norton.

Brown, Lester R., and Jennifer Mitchell. 1998. "Building a New Economy." In Lester R. Brown, Christopher Flavin, and Hilary French (eds.), *State of the World 1998,* pp. 168–87. New York: W. W. Norton.

Bruce, Nigel, Rogelio Perez-Padilla, and Rachel Albalak. 2000. "Indoor Air Pollution in Developing Countries: A Major Environmental and Public Health Challenge." *Bulletin of the World Health Organization* 78(9): 1078–92.

Bruno, Kenny, and Joshua Karliner. 2002. *Earthsummit.biz: The Corporate Takeover of Sustainable Development.* CorpWatch and Food First Books. Available at http://www.corpwatch.org.

Bullard, Robert D. 2000. *Dumping in Dixie: Race, Class, and Environmental Quality,* 3rd ed. Boulder, CO: Westview Press.

—————, et al. 2007. *Toxic Wastes and Race at Twenty 1987–2007.* Cleveland: United Church of Christ.

CGBC (Canada Green Building Council). 2006. "Leed Certified Buildings." http://www.cagbc.org/green_building_projects/leed_certified_buildings.php.

Cappiello, Dina. 2003. "Corporations Co-opt Earth Day." *Houston Chronicle,* April 22. Available at http://www.houstonchronicle.com.

Caress, Stanley, Anne C. Steinemann, and Caitlin Waddick. 2002. "Symptomatology and Etiology of Multiple Chemical Sensitivities in the Southeastern United States." *Archives of Environmental Health* 57(5): 429–436.

CBC News. 2005 (October 30). "McGuinty Visits Kashechewan Evacuees." CBC News Online. http://www.cbc.ca/story/canada/national/2005/10/30/kashechewan051030.html.

Centers for Disease Control and Prevention, National Center for Environmental Health. 2003. *Second National Report on Human Exposure to Environmental Chemicals.* Atlanta, GA: Centers for Disease Control and Prevention.

—————. 2005. *Third National Report on Human Exposure to Environmental Chemicals.* Atlanta, GA: Centers for Disease Control and Prevention.

Chafe, Zoe. 2005. "Bioinvasions." In Linda Starke (ed.), *State of the World 2005,* pp. 60–61. New York: W. W. Norton.

Chepesiuk, R. 2009. "Missing the Dark: Health Effects of Light Pollution." *Environmental Health Perspectives* 117: A20–A27.

Chivian, Eric, and Aaron S. Bernstein. 2004. "Embedded in Nature: Human Health and Biodiversity." *Environmental Health Perspectives* 112(1). Available at http://ehp.niehs.nih.gov.

Cincotta, Richard P., and Robert Engelman. 2000. *Human Population and the Future of Biological Diversity.* Washington, DC: Population Action International.

Clarke, Tony. 2002. "Twilight of the Corporation." In Kurt Finster-Busch (ed.), *Social Problems, Annual Editions 02/03,* 30th ed., pp. 41–45. Guilford, CT: McGraw-Hill/Dushkin.

Clarren, Rebecca. 2005. "Dirty Politics, Foul Air." *The Nation* (March 14): 6, 8.

Cooper, Arnie. 2004. "Twenty-eight Words That Could Change the World: Robert Hinkley's Plan to Tame Corporate Power." *The Sun* 345 (September): 4–11.

Denson, Bryan. 2000. "Shadowy Saboteurs." *The IRE Journal* (Investigative Reports and Editors, Inc.) 23 (May/June): 12–14.

DesJardins, Andrea. 1997. "Sweet Poison: What Your Nose Can't Tell You about the Dangers of Perfume." January 20, 1999. http://members.aol.com/enviroknow/perfume/sweet_poison.htm.

Dewailly, Eric, et al. 1996. "Polychlorinated Biphenyl (Pcb) and Dichlorodiphenyl Dichloroethylene (Dde) Concentration in the Breast Milk of Women in Quebec." *American Journal of Public Health* 86(9): 1241–46.

Elliott, John E., et al. 2006. "Brominated Flame Retardants and Halogenated Phenolic Compounds in North American West Coast Bald Eaglet." *Environmental Science and Technology* 40(20): 6275–81.

Energy Information Administration. 2005. *International Energy Annual 2003.* U.S. Department of Energy. Available at http://www.eia.doe.gov.

—————. 2008. *World Energy Overview: 1996–2006.* Washington DC: Energy Information Administration.

ENS (Environmental News Service). 2005 (November 15). "Lab Tests Find 60 Toxic Chemicals in Canadians' Blood." http://www.ens-newswire.com/ens/nov2005/2005-11-15.asp.

Environmental Defense. 2004. *2004 Annual Report.* Available at http://www.environmentaldefense.org.

Environment Canada. 2006. "Clean Energy Canada." http://www.cleanenergy.gc.ca/canada/companies_e.asp?item=179.

Fisher, Brandy E. 1998. "Scents and Sensitivity." *Environmental Health Perspectives* 106(12). February 1, 1999. http://ehpnet1.niehs.nih.gov/docs/1998/106-12/focus-abs.html.

Flavin, Chris, and Molly Hull Aeck. 2005 (September 15). "Cleaner, Greener, and Richer." *Tom.Paine.com.* Available at http://wu.oneworld.net.

Food and Drug Administration. 2005 (May). *Pesticide Program Residue Monitoring 2003.* Available at http://www.cfsan.fda.gov.

—————. 2008. "Pesticide Residue Monitoring Program Results and Discussion FY 2006." http://www.fda.gov/Food/FoodSafety/FoodContaminantsAdulteration/Pesticides/ResidueMonitoringReports/ucm125187.htm.

Food and Water Watch and Network for New Energy Choices. 2007. *The Rush to Ethanol: Not All Biofuels Are Created Equal.* http:www.newenergychoices.org.

French, Hilary. 2000. "Environmental Treaties Gain Ground." In Lester R. Brown, Michael Renner, and Brian Halwell (eds.), *Vital Signs 2000*, pp. 134–35. New York: W. W. Norton & Co.

Gardner, Gary. 2005. "Forest Loss Continues." In Linda Starke (ed.), *Vital Signs 2005*, pp. 92–93. New York: W. W. Norton.

Gartner, John. 2005 (September 13). "Sierra Club Gets Behind the Wheel." *Wired News*. Available at http://www.wired.com/news.

"Global Corporations Join Us to Reduce Greenhouse Gas Emissions." 2000. *Environmental Defense* 31 (November): 5.

Global Invasive Species Database. 2006. *100 of the World's Worst Invasive Alien Species*. Auckland, NZ: Invasive Species Specialist Group, University of Auckland.

Government of Canada. 2006. "Innovation Roadmap on Bio-based Feedstocks, Fuels and Industrial Products." *Technology Roadmaps*, June 6. http://strategis.ic.gc.ca/epic/internet/intrm-crt.nsf/en/rm00115e.html.

Hager, Nicky and Bob Burton. 2000. *Secrets and Lies: The Anatomy of an Anti-Environmental PR Campaign*. Monroe, ME: Common Courage Press.

Hilgenkamp, K. 2005. *Environmental Health: Ecological Perspectives*. London and Mississauga: Jones and Bartlett.

Howlett, Karen. 2006. "I Don't Like Nuclear Energy." *Globe and Mail* (June 26): A5.

Hunter, Lori M. 2001. *The Environmental Implications of Population Dynamics*. Santa Monica, CA: Rand Corporation.

Intergovernmental Panel on Climate Change. 2001a. *Climate Change 2001: The Scientific Basis*. United Nations Environmental Programme and the World Meteorological Organization. http://www.ipcc.ch.

————. 2001b. *Climate Change 2001: Impacts, Adaptation, and Vulnerability*. United Nations Environmental Programme and the World Meteorological Organization. http://www.ipcc.ch.

International Fund for Animal Welfare. 2005. *Caught in the Web: Wildlife Trade on the Internet*. Available at http://www.ifaw.org.

IUCN. 2008. "2008 IUCN Red List of Threatened Species." http://www.iucnredlist.org.

Jan, George P. 1995. "Environmental Protection in China." In O. P. Dwivedi and Dhirendra K. Vajpeyi (eds.), *Environmental Policies in the Third World: A Comparative Analysis*, pp. 71–84. Westport, CT: Greenwood Press.

Janofsky, Michael. 2005. "Pentagon Is Asking Congress to Loosen Environmental Laws." *New York Times*, May 11. Available at http://www.nytimes.com.

Jensen, Derrick. 2001. "A Weakened World Cannot Forgive Us: An Interview with Kathleen Dean Moore." *The Sun* 303 (March): 4–13.

Johansen, Bruce E. 2002. "The Inuit's Struggle with Dioxins and Other Organic Pollutants." *American Indian Quarterly* 26(3): 479–90.

Johnson, Geoffrey. 2004 (April). *Don't Be Fooled: America's Ten Worst Greenwashers*. The Green Life. Available at http://www.thegreenlife.org.

Klinkenborg, V. 2008. "Our Vanishing Night." *National Geographic* 214(5).

Koenig, Dieter. 1995. "Sustainable Development: Linking Global Environmental Change to Technology Cooperation." In O. P. Dwivedi, and Dhirendra K. Vajpeyi (eds.), *Environmental Policies in the Third World: A Comparative Analysis*, pp. 1–21. Westport, CT: Greenwood Press.

Krajnc, Anita. 2000. "Whither Ontario's Environment? Neo-Conservatism and the Decline of the Environment Ministry." *Canadian Public Policy* 26(1): 111–27.

Leahy, S. 2009. *Tight Controls Could Save Global Fisheries*. Inter Press Service. http://ipsnews.net/news.asp?idnews=47912.

Levesque, B., et al. 2003. "Monitoring of Umbilical Cord Blood Lead Levels and Sources Assessment among the Inuit." *Occupational and Environmental Medicine* 60: 693–95.

Levin, Phillip S., and Donald A. Levin. 2002. "The Real Biodiversity Crisis." *American Scientist* 90(1): 6.

Little, Amanda Griscom. 2005. "Maathai on the Prize: An Interview with Nobel Peace Prize Winner Wangari Maathai." *Grist Magazine*, February 15. Available at http://www.grist.org.

Lyons, Linda. 2005 (April 19). *Daily Concerns Overshadow Environment Worries*. Gallup Organization. Available at http://www.gallup.com.

MacDonald, Mia, and Danielle Nierenberg. 2003. "Linking Population, Women, and Biodiversity." In Linda Starke (ed.), *State of the World 2003*, pp. 38–61. New York: W. W. Norton.

Makower, Joel, Ron Pernick, and Clint Wilder. 2005. *Clean Energy Trends 2005*. Clean Edge. Available at http://www.cleanedge.com.

Margesson, Rhoda. 2005. "Environmental Refugees." In Linda Starke (ed.), *State of the World 2005*, pp. 40–41. New York: W. W. Norton.

Mastny, Lisa. 2003. "State of the World: A Year in Review." In Linda Starke (ed.), *State of the World 2003*, pp. xix-xxiii. New York: W. W. Norton.

McDaniel, Carl N. 2005. *Wisdom for a Livable Planet*. San Antonio: Trinity University Press.

McMichael, Anthony J., Kirk R. Smith, and Carlos F. Corvalan. 2000. "The Sustainability Transition: A New Challenge." *Bulletin of the World Health Organization* 78(9): 1067.

Mead, Leila. 1998. "Radioactive Wastelands." *The Green Guide* 53 (April 14):1–3.

Millennium Ecosystem Assessment. 2005. *Ecosystems and Human Well-Being: Synthesis*. Washington, DC: Island Press.

Mishra, Vinod, Robert D. Retherford, and Kirk R. Smith. 2002. "Indoor Air Pollution: The Quiet Killer." *Asia Pacific Issues* 63: 1–8.

Mooney, Chris. 2005. "Some Like It Hot." *Mother Jones* (May-June). Available at http://www.MotherJones.com.

National Environmental Education and Training Foundation, and Roper Starch Worldwide. 1999. *1999 NEETF/Roper Report Card.* Washington, DC: National Environmental Education and Training Foundation.

National Oceanic and Atmospheric Administration. 2005 (January 13). *Climate of 2004 Annual Review.* Available at http://www.ncdc.noaa.gov.

Natural Resources Canada. 2006. "About Wind Energy." www.canren.gc.ca/tech_appl/index.asp?CaId=6&PgId=232.

Northwest Product Stewardship Council (Computer Subcommittee). 2000 (October). *A Guide to Environmentally Preferable Computer Purchasing.* Available at http://www.govlink.org/nwpsc.

"Nukes Rebuked." 2000 (July 1). *Washington Spectator* 26(13): 4.

Palmer, Randall. 2006 (July 14). "Canada Stresses Commitment to Kyoto Climate Pact." Reuters Canada. http://ca.today.reuters.com/news/newsArticle.aspx?type=domesticNews&storyID=2006-07-14T154612Z_01_L14904845_RTRIDST_0_CANADA-GROUP-BRITAIN-CANADA-COL.XML.

Pearce, Fred. 2005. "Climate Warming as Siberia Melts." *New Scientist,* August 11. Available at http://www.NewScientist.com.

Pimental, D. S. 2007. "Ecology of Increasing Diseases: Population Growth and Environmental Degradation." *Human Ecology* 35(6): 653–668.

"A Prescription for Reducing the Damage Caused by Dams." 2001. *Environmental Defense* 32 (March).

Price, T. 2006. "The New Environmentalism." *QC Researcher* 16(42): 987–1007.

Public Citizen. 2005 (February). *NAFTA Chapter 11 Investor-State Cases: Lessons for the Central America Free Trade Agreement.* Public Citizens Global Trade Watch Publication E9014. Available at http://www.citizen.org.

Reese, April. 2001 (February). *Africa's Struggle with Desertification.* Population Reference Bureau. Available at http://www.prb.org/regions/africa/africadesertification.html.

Renner, Michael. 1996. *Fighting for Survival: Environmental Decline, Social Conflict, and the New Age of Insecurity.* New York: W. W. Norton.

———. 2004. "Moving toward a Less Consumptive Economy." In Linda Starke (ed.), *State of the World 2004,* pp. 96–119. New York: W. W. Norton.

Reuters. 2005 (August 23). *Antarctic Ozone Hole Grows from Last Year: WMO.* Available at http://today.reuters.com.

Rifkin, Jeremy. 2004. *The European Dream: How Europe's Vision of the Future Is Quietly Eclipsing the American Dream.* New York: Tarcher/Penguin.

Rogers, Sherry A. 2002. *Detoxify or Die.* Sarasota, FL: Sand Key.

Saad, Lydia. 2002. *Americans Sharply Divided on Seriousness of Global Warming.* Gallup News Service. Available at http://www.gallup.org.

Sampat, Payal. 2003. "Scrapping Mining Dependence." In Linda Starke (ed.), *State of the World 2003,* pp. 110–129. New York: W. W. Norton.

Sawin, Janet L. 2004. "Making Better Energy Choices." In Linda Starke (ed.), *State of the World 2004,* pp. 24–43. New York: W. W. Norton.

———. 2005. "Solar Energy Markets Booming." In Linda Starke (ed.), *Vital Signs 2005,* pp. 36–37. New York: W. W. Norton.

Schaeffer, Robert K. 2003. *Understanding Globalization: The Social Consequences of Political, Economic, and Environmental Change,* 2nd ed. Lanham, MD: Rowman & Littlefield.

Schmidt, Charles W. 2004. "Environmental Crimes: Prompting at the Earth's Expense." *Environmental Health Perspectives* 112(2): A96–A103.

Silicon Valley Toxics Coalition. 2001. *Just Say No to E-Waste: Background Document on Hazards and Waste from Computers.* Available at http://www.svtc.org.

———. 2002. *Exporting Harm: The High-Tech Trashing of Asia.* Available at http://www.svtc.org.

———. 2005 (March 7). *Toxic Sentence: E-Waste, Prisons, and Environmental Justice.* Available at http://www.svtc.org.

Snider, Laureen. 2004. "Resisting Neo-Liberalism: The Poisoned Water Disaster in Walkerton, Ontario." *Social and Legal Studies* 13(2): 265–89.

Speirs, Rosemary. 2000. "For Boomers, Minivans Are Still a Big Gas." *Toronto Star* (March 11): A24.

Stanford, Jim. 2002. "Hot Air over Kyoto." *THIS* magazine (July/August): 12–13.

Statistics Canada. 1998. *Canada Year Book 2000.* Ottawa: Ministry of Industry.

———. 2005. "Human Activity and the Environment: Solid Waste." *The Daily,* December 2.

Sterritt, Angela. 2005. "Indigenous Youth Challenge Corporate Mining." *Cultural Survival, Weekly Indigenous News,* July 15. Available at http://www.cs.org/publications/win/win-article.cfm?id=2699&highlight=Angela%20Sterritt.

Thibodeau, Patrick. 2002. "Handling E-Waste." *Computerworld* 36(47):46.

UNEP (United Nations Environment Programme). 2002. *North America's Environment: A Thirty-Year State of the Environment and Policy Retrospectives.* Available at http://www.na.unep.net.

———. 2005. *GEO Yearbook 2004/5.* Available at http://www.unep.org.

———. 2007. *GEO Yearbook 2007: An Overview of Our Changing Environment.* http://www.unep.org.

———. 2008. *Yearbook 2007: An Overview of Our Changing Environment.* http://www.unep.org.

United Nations Population Fund. 2004. *The State of World Population 2004.* New York: United Nations.

Vajpeyi, Dhirendra K. 1995. "External Factors Influencing Environmental Policy-making: Role of Multilateral Development Aid Agencies." In O. P. Dwivedi and Dhirendra K. Vajpeyi (eds.), *Environmental Policies in the Third World: A Comparative Analysis,* pp. 24–45. Westport, CT: Greenwood Press.

Vartan, Starre. 2005. "Money Matters: Buying Cleaner Energy." *E Magazine* 16(5). Available at http://www.emagazine.com.

Vedantam, Shankar. 2005. "Storage Plan Approved for Nuclear Waste." *Washington Post*, September 10. Available at http://www.washingtonpost.com.

Wall, Glenda. 2000. "Recent Representations in Popular Environmental Discourse: Individualism, Wastefulness and the Global Economy." *Canadian Review of Sociology and Anthropology* 37(3): 249–65.

Wal-Mart Watch. 2005. *Wal-Mart Watch*. Press release, April 6. Available at http://walmartwatch.com.

Warren, Karen J. 2000. *Ecofeminist Philosophy: A Western Perspective on What It Is and Why It Matters*. Lanham, MD: Rowman & Littlefield.

World Resources Institute. 2000. "Why Care about Ecosystems?" In *World Resources 2000–2001: People and Ecosystems—The Fraying Web of Life*. Washington, DC: World Resources Institute.

World Water Assessment Program. 2009. "Water in a Changing World." United Nations World Water Development Report 3, UNESCO.

WWF. 2008. "Infrastructure Problems: River Navigation Schemes." www.panda.org/about_wwf/what_we_do/freshwater/problems/infrastructure/river_navigation/index.cfm.

Youth, Howard. 2003. "Watching Birds Disappear." In Linda Starke (ed.), *State of the World 2003*, pp. 85–109. New York: W. W. Norton.

Chapter 14

ABC News. 2010 (Oct. 26). "Defence Says Most WikiLeaks Material Already Public." ABC News Australia. http://www.abc.net.au/news/stories/2010/10/26/3048922.htm.

Alexander, Karen, and Mary E. Hawkesworth, eds. 2008. *War and Terror: Feminist Perspectives*. Chicago: University of Chicago Press.

American Jewish Committee. 2007. *2006 Annual Survey of American Jewish Opinion*. Available at http://www.ajc.org

Annan, Jeannie, Christopher Blattman, Khristopher Carlson, and Dyan Mazurana. 2008. "Findings from the Survey of War-Affected Youth (SWAY) Phase II." Available at https://wikis.uit.tufts.edu/confluence/display

Arms Control Association. 2003 (May). *The Nuclear Proliferation Treaty at a Glance*. Available at http://www.armscontrol.org/factsheets

Atomic Archive. 2009. *Arms Control Treaties*. Available at http://www.atomicarchive.com

Baker, Peter, and Helene Cooper. 2009. "U.S. and Russia to Consider Reductions of Nuclear Arsenals in Talks for New Treaty." *New York Times*, March 31. Available at http://www.nytimes.com

Barkan, Steven, and Lynne Snowden. 2001. *Collective Violence*. Boston: Allyn and Bacon.

Barry, Donald. 2005. "Chretien, Bush and the War in Iraq." *American Review of Canadian Studies* 35(2): 215–246.

Barstow, David. 2008. "One Man's Military-Industrial-Media Complex." *New York Times*, November 29. Available at http://www.nytimes.com

BBC. 2000. "UN Admits Rwanda Genocide Failure." BBC News, April 15. Available at http://news.bbc.co.uk

—————. 2007a. "Hamas Takes Full Control of Gaza." BBC News, June 15. Available at http://news.bbc.co.uk

—————. 2007b. "Fresh Clashes Engulf Lebanon Camp." BBC News, June 1. Available at http://news.bbc.co.uk

—————. 2009a. "Gaza Crisis: Key Maps & Timelines." BBC News, January 18. Available at http://news.bbc.co.uk

Bercovitch, Jacob, ed. 2003. *Studies in International Mediation: Advances in Foreign Policy Analysis*. New York: Palgrave Macmillan.

Boustany, Nora. 2007. "Janjaweed Using Rape as 'Integral' Weapon in Darfur, Aid Group Says." *Washington Post*, July 3. Available at http://www.washingtonpost.com

Brewster, Murray, and Steve Rennie. 2010. "Canadian Soldier Killed in Roadside Bomb." *The Globe and Mail*. Accessed December 20, 2010. http://www.theglobeandmail.com/news/world/asia-pacific/canadian-soldier-killed-in-a-roadside-bomb-in-afghanistan/article1843714/.

Brinkley, Joel, and David E. Sanger. 2005. "North Koreans Agree to Resume Nuclear Talks." *New York Times*, July 10. Available at http://www.nytimes.com

Broad, William J., Mark Mazzetti, and David E. Sanger. 2009. "A Nuclear Debate: Is Iran Designing Warheads?" *The New York Times*, September 28. Available at http://www.nytimes.com

Broad, William J., and David E. Sanger. 2009 (October 3). "Report Says Iran Has Data to Make a Nuclear Bomb." Available at http://www.nytimes.com

Brown, Michael E., Sean M. Lynn-Jones, and Steven E. Miller, eds. 1996. *Debating the Democratic Peace*. Cambridge, MA: MIT Press.

Buncombe, Andrew. 2009. "End of Sri Lanka's Civil War Brings Back Tourists." *The Independent*, August 16. Available at http://www.independent.co.uk

Carneiro, Robert L. 1994. "War and Peace: Alternating Realities in Human History." In *Studying War: Anthropological Perspectives*, S. P. Reyna and R. E. Downs, eds. (pp. 3–27). Langhorne, PA: Gordon & Breach.

CBC News. 2006 (May 30). "Canada's Military Women in the Canadian Military." Accessed December 14, 2010. http://www.cbc.ca/news/background/cdnmilitary/women-cdnmilitary.html.

—————. 2010 (Nov. 29). "WikiLeaks Reveals Undiplomatic U.S. Critiques." http://www.cbc.ca/world/story/2010/11/28/wikileaks-release.html.

—————. 2011. "CBC News in Depth: Afghanistan." Accessed January 4, 2011. http://www.cbc.ca/news/background/afghanistan/casualties/list.html.

Center for Defense Information. 2007 (April 30). *The World's Nuclear Arsenals.* Available at http://www.cdi.org

CNN. 2003 (February 26). *Poll: Muslims Call U.S. Ruthless, Arrogant.* Available at http:// www.cnn.com

CNN/Opinion Research Corporation Poll. 2007 (June 22–24). *Iraq.* Available at http:// www. pollingreport.com/iraq3.htm

Cohen, Ronald. 1986. "War and Peace Proneness in Pre- and Post-industrial States." In *Peace and War: Cross-Cultural Perspectives*, M. L. Foster and R. A. Rubinstein, eds. (pp. 253–267). New Brunswick, NJ: Transaction Books.

Conflict Research Consortium. 2003. *Mediation.* Available at http://www .colorado.edu/confl ict/peace

CRS (Congressional Research Service). 2008 (August 25). *Private Security Contractors in Iraq: Background, Legal Status, and Other Issues.* Available at http://www.opencrs. com

Curry, Bill, and Daniel LeBlanc. 2008 (Feb. 23). "Defence Priorities Subject to Tough Budget Decisions." *The Globe and Mail.*

Dareini, Ali Akbar. 2009. "Iran Missile Test: Ahmadinejad Says It's Within Israel's Range." *Huffington Post*, May 20. Available at http://www.huffi ngtonpost.com

Deen, Thalif. 2000 (September 9). *Inequality Primary Cause of Wars, Says Annan.* Available at http://www. hartford-hwp.com/ archives

DeYoung, Karen, and Walter Pincus. 2009 (October 3). *Iraq: U.S. to Fund Pro-American Publicity in Iraqi Media.* Available at http://www.corpwatch.org

Dixon, William J. 1994. "Democracy and the Peaceful Settlement of International Conflict." *American Political Science Review* 88(1):14–32.

Eggleton, Art. 2001 (Nov. 30). "Canada a Full Partner in War on Terrorism, Insists Eggleton." *Edmonton Journal*: A17.

Eide, Mariane. 2008. "'The Stigma of Nation': Feminist Just War, Privilege and Responsibility." *Hypatia* 23(2): 48–60.

Environmental Media Services. 2002 (October 7). *Environmental Impacts of War.* Available at http://www. ems.org

Feder, Don. 2003. "Islamic Beliefs Led to the Attack on America." In *The Terrorist Attack on America*, Mary E. Williams, ed. (pp. 20–23). Farmington Hills, MA: Greenhaven Press.

Feiler, Jeremy. 2003 (Aug. 7). "Canada Prepares for Major Defense Review with Transformation in Mind." *Inside the Pentagon.* Reprinted: http://www.forces.gc.ca/site/focus/ canada-us-canada-eu/ pentagon1-eng.asp.

Funke, Odelia. 1994. "National Security and the Environment." In *Environmental Policy in the 1990s: Toward a New Agenda*, 2nd ed., Norman J. Vig and Michael E. Kraft, eds. (pp. 323–345). Washington, DC: Congressional Quarterly.

Gardner, Simon. 2007 (February 22). *Sri Lanka Says Sinks Rebel Boats on Truce Anniversary.* Available at http://www. reuters.com

Gettleman, Jeffrey. 2009. "Symbol of Unhealed Congo—Male Rape Victims." *New York Times*, August 4. Available at http://www. nytimes. com.

———. 2008. "Rape Victims' Words Help Jolt Congo into Change." *New York Times*, October 18. Available at http:// www. nytimes.com.

Geneva Graduate Institute for International Studies. 2006. *Small Arms Survey, 2006.* New York: Oxford University Press.

Gioseffi, Daniela. 1993. "Introduction." In *On Prejudice: A Global Perspective*, Daniela Gioseffi, ed. (pp. xi–l). New York: Anchor Books, Doubleday.

Gossage, Carolyn. 2001. *Greatcoats and Glamour Boots.* Revised ed. Toronto: Dundurn Press.

Goure, Don. 2003. *First Casualties? NATO, the U.N.* MSNBC News, March 20. Available at http://www. msnbc.com/news

GreenKarat. 2007. *Mining for Gems.* Available at http://www. greenkarat.com

Hooks, Gregory, and Leonard E. Bloomquist. 1992. "The Legacy of World War II for Regional Growth and Decline: The Effects of Wartime Investments on U.S.

Manufacturing, 1947–72." *Social Forces* 71(2):303–337.

Howard, Michael. 2007. "Children of War: The Generation Traumatised by Violence in Iraq." *The Guardian*, February 6. Available at http:// www.guardian.co.uk.

Huntington, Samuel. 1996. *The Clash of Civilizations and the Remaking of World Order.* New York: Simon and Schuster.

ICBL (International Campaign to Ban Landmines). 2009. *Making the Treaties Universal.* Available at http://www.icbl.org.

Kellner, Douglas. 1995. *Media Culture.* New York and London: Routledge.

Kemper, Bob. 2003. "Agency Wages Media Battle." *Chicago Tribune*, April 7. Available at http://www. chicagotribune.com.

Kerr, Paul K., and Mary Beth Nikitin. 2009. *Pakistan's Nuclear Weapons: Proliferation and Security Issues.* Congressional Research Service, June 12. Available at http://www. opencrs.com

Klare, Michael. 2001. *Resource Wars: The New Landscape of Global Conflict.* New York: Metropolitan Books

Knickerbocker, Brad. 2002. "Return of the Military-Industrial Complex?" *Christian Science Monitor*, February 13. Available at http://www. csmonitor.com

Knight, Andy. 2006 (April 12). "Canada Abandons Its Role as UN Peacekeeper." *Edmonton Journal.* http://www2.canada.com/ edmontonjournal/news/ideas/story. html?id=ce49cf0d-4aa4-48b7- 9843-feb4d9066cd0.

Lamont, Beth. 2001. "The New Mandate for UN Peacekeeping." *The Humanist* 61:39–41.

Large, Tim. 2006. *Crisis Profile: What's Going on in Northern Uganda?* Thomas Reuters Foundation. Available at http://www. alertnet.org

Lederer, Edith. 2005 (May 20). "Annan Lays out Sweeping Changes to U.N." Associated Press. Available at http://www.apnews. com

Levy, Jack S. 2001. "Theories of Interstate and Intrastate War: A Levels of Analysis Approach." In *Turbulent Peace: The Challenges of Managing International Conflict*,

Chester A. Crocker, Fen Osler Hampson, and Pamela Aall, eds. (pp. 3–27). Washington, DC: U.S. Institute of Peace.

Levy, Clifford J., and Peter Baker. 2009. "U.S.Russian Nuclear Agreement Is First Step in Broad Effort." *The Washington Post,* July 6. Available at http://www. washingtonpost.com

Li, Xigen, and Ralph Izard. 2003. "Media in a Crisis Situation Involving National Interest: A Content Analysis of Major U.S. Newspapers' and TV Networks' Coverage of the 9/11 Tragedy." *Newspaper Research Journal* 24:1–16.

Lindner, Andrew M. 2009. "Among the Troops: Seeing the Iraq War Through Three Journalistic Vantage Points." *Social Problems* 56 (1): 21–48.

MacAskill, Ewen, Ed Pilkington, and Jon Watts. 2006. "Despair at UN over Selection of 'Faceless' Ban Ki-moon as General Secretary." *The Guardian*, October 7. Available at http://www.guardian.co.uk

Marshall, Leon. 2007 (July 16). *Elephants "Learn" to Avoid Land Mines in War-Torn Angola.* National Geographic News. Available at http://www.nationalgeographic. com

McGirk, Tim. 2006. "Collateral Damage or Civilian Massacre in Haditha?" *Time*, March 19. Available at http://www.time.com

Military. 2007. *Tuition Assistance (TA) Program Overview.* Available at http:// education.military.com

Military Professional Resources Inc. 2007. *About MPRI.* Available at http://www.mpri. com

Miller, T. Christian. 2007. "Private Contractors Outnumber U.S. Troops in Iraq." *Los Angeles Times*, July 4. Available at http:// www. latimes.com

Millman, Jason. 2008. "Industry Applauds New Dual-Use Rule." *Hartford Business Journal,* September 29. Available at http:// www. hartfordbusiness.com

Morgan, Jenny, and Alice Behrendt. 2009. *Silent Suffering: The Psychological Impact of War, HIV, and Other High-Risk Situations on Girls and Boys in West and Central Africa.*

Woking: Plan. Available at http:// plan-international.org

Myers-Brown, Karen, Kathleen Walker, and Judith A. Myers-Walls. 2000. "Children's Reactions to International Conflict: A Cross-Cultural Analysis." Paper presented at the National Council of Family Relations, Minneapolis, November 20.

NASP (National Association of School Psychologists). 2003. *Children and Fear of War and Terrorism.* Available at http:// www.nasponline.org

National Defence. 2010 (April 27). "Canadian Expeditiary Force Command." Accessed December 12, 2010. http://www.cefcom.forces. gc.ca/pa-ap/ops/fs-fr/afg-eng.asp.

NCPSD (National Center for Posttraumatic Stress Disorder). 2007. *What Is Post Traumatic Stress Disorder?* Available at http://www. ncptsd.va.gov.

NTI (Nuclear Threat Initiative). 2009. *North Korea Profi le.* Available at http://www.nti .org

Office of Management and Budget. 2009a. Table S-7: Funding Levels for Appropriated ("Discretionary") Programs by Agency. Available at http://www.whitehouse.gov

Office of Weapons Removal and Abatement. 2009. To Walk the Earth in Safety: The United States' Commitment to Humanitarian Mine Action and Conventional Weapons Destruction. Available at http://www.state.gov

Ochmanek, David and Lowell H. Schwartz. 2008. "The Challenge of Nuclear- Armed Regional Adversaries." Rand Project Air Force. Available at http://www.rand.org

Paul, Annie Murphy. 1998. "Psychology's Own Peace Corps." *Psychology Today* 31:56–60.

Permanent Court of Arbitration. 2009. *About Us* and *Cases.* Available at http://www. pca-cpa.org

Pew Research Center. 2009 (July 23). *Confidence in Obama Lifts U.S. Image Around the World: Most Muslim Publics Not So Easily Moved.* Pew Global Attitudes Project. Available at http://www.pewglobal.org

Poe, Danielle. 2008. "Replacing Just War Theory with an Ethics of Sexual Difference." *Hypatia* 23(2): 33–47.

Porter, Bruce D. 1994. *War and the Rise of the State: The Military Foundations of Modern Politics.* New York: Free Press.

Powell, Bill, and Tim McGirk. 2005. "The Man Who Sold the Bomb." *Time*, February 14, pp. 22–31.

Puckett, Neal, and Haytham Faraj. 2009 (June 25). *Navy-Marine Corps Court Hears Appeal in Wuterich v. U.S.* Available at http://www. puckettfaraj.com

Pugliese, David. 2008 (Sept. 18). "Afghan War Costs $22b, So Far." *Ottawa Citizen*: A18.

Queen's University. 2010. "An Archival Look at World War I: Women and the War." http:// archives.queensu.ca/Exhibits/ archres/wwi-intro/women.html.

Rasler, Karen, and William R. Thompson. 2005. *Puzzles of the Democratic Peace: Theory, Geopolitics, and the Transformation of World Politics.* New York: Palgrave Macmillan.

Renner, Michael. 2005. "Disarming Postwar Societies." In *State of the World: 2005*, Linda Starke, ed. (pp. 122–123). New York: W. W. Norton.

Renner, Michael. 2000. "Number of Wars on Upswing." In *Vital Signs: The Environmental Trends That Are Shaping Our Future*, Linda Starke, ed. (pp. 110–111). New York: W. W. Norton.

Renner, Michael. 1993. "Environmental Dimensions of Disarmament and Conversion." In *Real Security: Converting the Defense Economy and Building Peace*, Karl Cassady and Gregory A. Bischak, eds. (pp. 88–132). Albany: State University of New York Press.

Reuters. 2008. "Case Dropped Against Officer Accused in Iraq Killings." *New York Times*, June 18. Available at http://www.nytimes.com

Robinson, Bill. 2009. "Canadian Military Spending 2009." Canadian Centre for Policy Alternatives. http://www.policyalternatives.ca. remote.libproxy.wlu.ca/sites/ default/files/uploads/publications/ reports/docs/Canadian%20 Military%20Spending%202009.pdf.

Rosenberg, Tina. 2000. "The Unbearable Memories of a U.N. Peacekeeper." *New York Times*, October 8, pp. 4, 14.

Salem, Paul. 2007. "Dealing with Iran's Rapid Rise in Regional Influence." *The Japan Times,* February 22. Available at http://www.carnegieendowment.org.

Salladay, Robert. 2003 (April 7). Anti-War Patriots Find They Need to Reclaim Words, Symbols, Even U.S. Flag from Conservatives. Available at http://www .commondreams.org.

Sang-Hun, Choe, and John Markoff. 2009. "Cyberattacks Jam Government and Commercial Web Sites in U.S. and South Korea." *The New York Times,* July 8. Available at http://www.nytimes.com.

Save the Children. 2009. *Last in Line, Last in School 2009.* Available at http://www. savethechildren.org.

————. 2007. *State of the World's Mothers: Saving the Lives of Children Under Five.* Available at http://www .savethechildren.org.

————. 2005. One World, One Wish: The Campaign to Help Children and Women Affected by War. Available at http:// www. savethechildren.org.

Schmitt, Eric. 2005. "Pentagon Seeks to Shut Down Bases Across Nation." *New York Times,* May 14. Available at http://www .nytimes.com.

Schroeder, Matt. 2007. "The Illicit Arms Trade." Washington, DC: Federation of American Scientists. Available at http:// www.fas.org.

Schultz, George P., William J. Perry, Henry A. Kissinger, and Sam Nunn. 2007. "A World Free of Nuclear Weapons." *Wall Street Journal,* January 4 Available at http://www.wsj.com.

Shanahan, John J. 1995. "Director's Letter." *Defense Monitor* 24(6):8.

Shanker, Thom, and David E. Sanger. 2009. "Pakistan Is Rapidly Adding Nuclear Arms, U.S. Says." *New York Times,* May 17. Available at http://www.nytimes.com

Shrader, Katherine. 2005. "WMD Commission Releases Scathing Report." *Washington Post,* March 31. Available at http://www . washingtonpost.com

Singer, Peter W. 2009. "Attack of the Military Drones." *The National,* June 29. Available at http://www. brookings.edu

SIPRI (Stockholm International Peace Research Institute). 2009a. *SIPRI Yearbook 2009: Armaments, Disarmament, and International Security.* Oxford, UK: Oxford University Press.

————. 2009b. *Recent Trends in Military Expenditure.* Available at http://www.sipri .org

Skocpol, Theda. 1994. *Social Revolutions in the Modern World.* Cambridge, UK: Cambridge University Press.

Sloan, Elinor. 2010 (Mar. 11). "Government Missing Mark in Plan to Cut Back Military Spending: Poll Shows Canadians Like Idea of Strong, Well-Equipped Armed Forces." *Edmonton Journal*: A16.

Small Arms Survey. 2009. *Shadows of War.* Available at http://www. smallarmssurvey .org

Staples, Steven, and Bill Robinson. 2007. "More Than the Cold War: Canada's Military Spending 2007–2008." Canadian Centre for Policy Alternatives: http://www. policyalternatives.ca.remote. libproxy.wlu.ca/documents/ National_Office_Pubs/2007/More_ Than_the_Cold_War.pdf.

Starr, J. R., and D. C. Stoll. 1989. *U.S. Foreign Policy on Water Resources in the Middle East.* Washington, DC: Center for Strategic and International Studies.

State of Hawaii. 2000. *Dual-Use Technologies.* Available at http:// www.state.hi.us.

Stimson Center. 2007. *Reducing Nuclear Dangers in South Asia.* Available at http:// www.stimson.org.

Stogran, P. 2002 (Nov. 29). Public Lecture at Wilfrid Laurier University, Waterloo, ON.

Tanielian, Terri, Lisa H. Jaycox, Terry L. Schell, Grant N. Marshall, Audrey Burnam, Christine Eibner, Benjamin R. Karney, Lisa S. Meredith, Jeanne S. Ringe, Mary E. Vaiana, and the Invisible Wounds Study Team. 2008. "Invisible Wounds of War: Summary and Recommendations for Addressing Psychological and Cognitive Injuries." Available at http://www.rand.org.

United Nations. 1948. Convention on the Prevention and Punishment of the Crime of Genocide. Available at http://www.un.org

————. 2003. *Some Questions and Answers.* Available at http://www. unicef.org

————. 2009. *United Nations Peacekeeping Operations.* Available at http:// www.un.org/Depts/dpko/ dpko/bnote.htm

United Nations Association of the United States of America. 2003. *The Problem: Impact of Landmines.* Available at http://www.landmines. org.

U.S. Department of State. 2007. *Small Arms/ Light Weapons Destruction.* Available at http://www.state.gov

U.S. Nuclear Weapons Cost Study Project. 1998. *50 Facts About U.S. Nuclear Weapons.* Available at http:// www. brookings.edu

Vesely, Milan. 2001. "UN Peacekeepers: Warriors or Victims?" *African Business* 261:8–10.

Viner, Katharine. 2002. "Feminism as Imperialism." *The Guardian,* September 21. Available at http:// www/guardian.co.uk.

Waters, Rob. 2005. "The Psychic Costs of War." *Psychotherapy Networker,* March– April, pp. 1–3.

Watkins, Thomas. 2007. *Haditha Hearings Enter Fourth Day.* Time, May 11. Available at http://www. time.com.

Wax, Emily. 2003. "War Horror: Rape Ruining Women's Health." *Miami Herald,* November 3. Available at http://www.miami.com.

Wein, Lawrence. 2009. "Counting the Walking Wounded." *New York Times,* January 25. Available at http://www.nytimes.com.

Wilson, Brenda. 2008. "WHO Estimates Iraqi Death Toll at 151,000," January 9. Available at http://www.npr.org.

Woehrle, Lynne M., Patrick G. Coy, and Gregory M. Maney. 2008. *Contesting Patriotism: Culture, Power, and Strategy in the Peace Movement.* Lanham, Md.: Rowman & Littlefield Publishers, Inc.

Worldwatch Institute. 2003. *Vital Signs: The Trends That Are Shaping Our Future.* New York: W. W. Norton.

Zoroya, Gregg. 2006. "Lifesaving Knowledge, Innovation Emerge In War Clinic." *USA Today,* March 27. Available at http://www. usatoday.com.

Name Index

Subject Index